HENRY VIII

Alison Weir lives and works in Surrey. Her books include *Britain's Royal Families*, *The Princes in the Tower*, *Children of England*, *Eleanor of Aquitaine*, *The Six Wives of Henry VIII*, *Mary, Queen of Scots* and most recently, *Katherine Swynford*.

ALSO BY ALISON WEIR

Britain's Royal Families
Lancaster and York
The Princes in the Tower
Children of England
Eleanor of Aquitaine
Mary, Queen of Scots
The Six Wives of Henry VIII
Isabella
Katherine Swynford

ALISON WEIR

Henry VIII

King and Court

VINTAGE BOOKS
London

First published in Great Britain by Jonathan Cape 2001
Pimlico edition 2002

Vintage
Random House, 20 Vauxhall Bridge Road,
London SW1V 2SA

www.vintage-books.co.uk

Addresses for companies within The Random House Group Limited
can be found at: www.randomhouse.co.uk/offices.htm

The Random House Group Limited Reg. No. 954009

A CIP catalogue record for this book
is available from the British Library

ISBN 9780099532422

The Random House Group Limited supports The Forest
Stewardship Council (FSC), the leading international forest
certification organisation. All our titles that are printed on
Greenpeace approved FSC certified paper carry the FSC logo.
Our paper procurement policy can be found at:
www.rbooks.co.uk/environment

Mixed Sources
Product group from well-managed
forests and other controlled sources
www.fsc.org Cert no. TT-COC-2139
© 1996 Forest Stewardship Council
FSC

Printed in the UK by CPI Bookmarque, Croydon, CR0 4TD

This book is dedicated to
David and Catherine
to mark the occasion of their marriage

Contents

Illustrations

Anne of Cleves by Hans Holbein the Younger (V&A Picture Library).

Portrait of a Lady called Katherine Howard by Hans Holbein the Younger (The Royal Collection © 2001, Her Majesty Queen Elizabeth II).

Katherine Parr by Lucas Horenbout (Christie's Images).

Thomas Boleyn, Earl of Wiltshire (?) by Hans Holbein the Younger (The Royal Collection © 2001, Her Majesty Queen Elizabeth II).

Mary Boleyn (?), artist unknown (Hever Castle/Bridgeman).

Sir Thomas Wyatt by Hans Holbein the Younger (The Royal Collection © 2001, Her Majesty Queen Elizabeth II).

Thomas Howard, third Duke of Norfolk by Hans Holbein the Younger (The Royal Collection © 2001, Her Majesty Queen Elizabeth II).

Thomas Cranmer, Archbishop of Canterbury by Gerlach Flicke (National Portrait Gallery, London).

Edward Seymour, Earl of Hertford, artist unknown (Hulton Collection).

Thomas Cromwell, first Earl of Essex after Hans Holbein the Younger (National Portrait Gallery, London).

Henry Fitzroy, Duke of Richmond by Lucas Horenbout (The Royal Collection © 2001, Her Majesty Queen Elizabeth II).

Design for a gold cup for Jane Seymour by Hans Holbein the Younger (Ashmolean Museum, Oxford/Bridgeman).

Fragments of a leather mâché frieze from Hampton Court (© Crown Copyright: Historic Royal Palaces).

Whitehall Palace by Anthony van Wyngaerde (Ashmolean Museum, Oxford/Bridgeman).

Henry VII, Elizabeth of York, Henry VIII and Jane Seymour, copy of Hans Holbein's lost Whitehall mural by Remigius van Leemput (The Royal Collection © 2001, Her Majesty Queen Elizabeth II).

Detail from *Hampton Court Palace, the South Front* by Hendrick Danckerts (The Royal Collection © 2001, Her Majesty Queen Elizabeth II).

The great hall, Hampton Court Palace (© Crown Copyright: Historic Royal Palaces).

The chapel royal, Hampton Court Palace (© Crown Copyright: Historic Royal Palaces).

Henry VIII dining in the privy chamber, artist unknown (British Museum).

Sir William Butts by Hans Holbein the Younger (Isabella Stewart Gardner Museum, Boston/Bridgeman).

Detail from *View of Nonsuch Palace in the Time of King James I*, Flemish School (Fitzwilliam Museum, Cambridge/Bridgeman).

Henry VIII, Jane Seymour, Prince Edward, the Lady Mary and the Lady Elizabeth: The Whitehall Family Group, artist unknown (The Royal Collection © 2001, Her Majesty Queen Elizabeth II).

William Paget, first Baron Paget, attributed to Master of the Statthalterin Madonna (National Portrait Gallery, London).

Henry Howard, Earl of Surrey, attributed to Guillim Scrots (National Portrait Gallery, London).

Henry VIII reading in his bedchamber, Royal MSS. 2 A XVI f.3 (British Library/Bridgeman).

Endpapers: *The Great Tournament Roll of Westminster*, showing Henry VIII jousting before Katherine of Aragon, 1511, artist unknown (The College of Arms).

Acknowledgements

Of the hundreds of source books that I have used, I wish to acknowledge my particular indebtedness to the following: Simon Thurley's *The Royal Palaces of Tudor England*, David Loades' *The Tudor Court*, Neville Williams' *Henry VIII and His Court*, David Starkey's *The Reign of Henry VIII*, *Henry VIII: A European Court in England* and *Rivals in Power*, Carolly Erickson's *Great Harry*, Lacey Baldwin Smith's *Henry VIII: The Mask of Royalty* and Peter Brears' *All the King's Cooks*. I owe a great debt of gratitude to Dr Simon Thurley and Dr David Starkey, whose excellent books have made available to historians a wealth of unpublished contemporary sources. I must stress, however, that the conclusions in this book are entirely my own.

I wish to thank my editors, Will Sulkin and Anthony Whittome in the UK and Joanne Wyckoff in the USA, and my agent, Julian Alexander, for their unfailing support and kindness. I should also like to thank my mother, Doreen Cullen, for selflessly giving up so many hours to act as my secretary, general amanuensis and counsellor; likewise – as ever – my husband Rankin, my children John and Kate, my stepfather Jim Cullen and my cousin Christine Armour for rallying round and assisting me so readily, to help me meet my deadline. My grateful thanks also go to Lily Richards, for her hard work and diligence in obtaining the illustrations.

I owe a further debt of gratitude to all the other kind and generous people who have given support and encouragement in various ways whilst this book was in preparation: Catherine Agnew, Moore and Jill Armstrong, Beverley Arthur, Angela Bender, Carol Bingham, Tracy Borman, Neil Bradford, Richard and Yvonne Burnett, Terrence Cahill, Lucinda Cook, Paul and Paula Danholm, Suzanne Dean, Julian L. Dexter Williams, David Driver, Paul Eaglen, Deborah Emberson, Kate Gordon, Lewis Hales, Julie Handley, Eileen Hannah, Jörg Hensgen,

Bruce Heydt, Katherine Howe, Max Hull, Stephanie Hunt, Fraser Jansen, Roger Katz, Margaret Kirk, Louise Lawton, T. Anna Leese, Arnold and Edna Mann, John and Pauline Marston, Lyn Mathew, Janet McL. Mackay, Loukia Michael, Mary Moore, Syd Moore, Brad Mortensen, Sue Phillpott, Peter Razzell, Anne and Michael Richards, Margaret Samborn, Karin Scherer, Patrick Smith, Sue Stephens, Jerry Sullivan, Inga Walton, Kenneth and Elizabeth Weir, Margaret Weir, Ronald and Alison Weir, Martha Whittome and Jon Woolcott.

To you all, may I say again, thank you from the heart.

Introduction

In 1517, the papal nuncio, Francesco Chieregato, arrived at the court of Henry VIII and was stunned by its magnificence. 'The wealth and civilisation of the world are here,' he marvelled, 'and those who call the English barbarians appear to me to render themselves such. I here perceive very elegant manners, extreme decorum and great politeness, and amongst other things there is this invincible King, whose acquirements and qualities are so many and excellent, that I consider him to excel all who ever wore a crown.'

Coming from a Venetian imbued with the culture of the Italian Renaissance, this was praise indeed, and a reminder of what Henry VIII achieved during the first decade of his reign. Today, we need such a reminder, because the splendours of Henry's court are long vanished, and it requires a great leap of the imagination to reconstruct the reality from what few remains there are.

Henry VIII succeeded to the throne in 1509, to great acclaim. He had all the virtues expected of a Renaissance prince. Yet by the time he died in 1547, he had acquired the reputation of a tyrant whose hands were soaked in the blood of the many he had executed – among them two of his six wives. Because he married so many times, he has gone down in history as a veritable Bluebeard. Over the centuries, the truth about the King has become blurred by his legend, which culminated in Charles Laughton's caricature of him in the 1930s film, *The Private Life of Henry VIII*. Thanks to this, Henry still lives in the popular imagination as a man who thought of nothing but chasing the ladies, and who threw chicken bones over his shoulder as he presided over court feasts in the great hall.

The reality, of course, was strikingly different. As a rule, Henry did not dine in the great halls of his palaces, and his table manners were highly refined, as was the code of etiquette followed at his court. He was in fact a most fastidious man, and – for his time – unusually obsessed with hygiene. As for his pursuit of the ladies, there is plenty of evidence, but most of it fragmentary, for Henry was also far more discreet and prudish than we have been led to believe. These are just superficial examples of how the truth about historical figures can become distorted.

Fortunately, scholars during the last few decades have undertaken a vast amount of research on Henry VIII and his court, and it is now clear that many of our earlier perceptions of both must be revised. Henry was a complex personality of many talents, and there is so much surviving source material for his reign that we know even the most intimate details of his personal life. Furthermore, this man of exquisite taste and a grand sense of majesty established the most magnificent court ever seen in England. No English sovereign ever owned as many houses as Henry VIII, or spent so lavishly on a lifestyle deliberately calculated to enhance his own prestige. Few monarchs have been surrounded by so many talented and charismatic personalities as Henry was. And few have ever been so controversial.

My aim in this book has been to draw together a multitude of strands of research in order to develop a picture of the real Henry VIII, his personal life throughout his reign, the court he created and the people who influenced and served him. Hitherto, studies of the Henrician court have concentrated on household organisation, art and culture or courtier factions. I aim to paint a far broader canvas, which incorporates all these themes and much more, and sets the life and reign of the King, for the first time ever, against a realistic portrayal of his court.

In an age of personal monarchy the court was at the hub of royal government, but this is not a political history of the reign: my brief has been to record the events that help build up a picture of the life and ethos of the King and the court. Henry VIII's wives naturally played a large part in the life of that court, but, having already written a book about them, I have taken care to avoid too much repetition: where events were dealt with in detail in that former book, they are touched upon briefly here, and only where relevant. I have also taken the opportunity to revise some of my conclusions in *The Six Wives of Henry VIII* in the light of recent research.

Although this book is presented in a largely chronological format, the first third is largely devoted to setting the scene and describing the court and the royal palaces. This is a necessary prologue to the account of the King's life and reign that follows, for without it much of the context of events would be blurred. However, the book is not just a descriptive account of Henry's court and reign, but is packed with anecdotal evidence intended to illuminate this most colourful period of English history and the larger-than-life character who dominated it.

I have also attempted to describe and analyse the cultural and social development of the English court, and to this end have included every aspect of court life: the ceremonial and pageantry, state occasions, entertainments, sports, poetry and drama, art, music, religious observances, sexual and political intrigues, banquets and feasts, dress, transport, household organisation and administration, finance, hygiene and even pets!

The Tudor court, however, was primarily the place where a host of persons, great and lowly, gathered about the King; therefore one of my chief aims has been to weave the lives of queens, princes, princesses, lords, ladies, privy councillors, knights, gentlemen, artists, craftsmen and servants into the rich tapestry of court life, intrigue and vicious faction fights.

In the notes and references at the end of the book, I have given details of the surviving buildings and artefacts connected with Henry VIII and his court. Where monetary values are quoted in the text, the modern equivalent (which is approximately three hundred times the sum quoted) is given in brackets – with some surprising results. We should contrast the vast sums spent on clothes and royal meals, for example, with the meagre salaries paid to artists such as Hans Holbein.

Finally, a note about capital letters, which I have used for titles of household departments and officers but usually not for the names of rooms within the royal palaces. Thus, the department that provided for the King's personal needs is referred to as the Privy Chamber, while the lodgings he occupied are called the privy chamber. Similarly, the Chapel Royal was the religious establishment of the court, whereas the chapel royal was a place of worship.

I hope that this book will convey to those who read it the same pleasure and sense of affinity with its subject that it afforded me whilst I was researching and writing it, and that they will be able to make that great leap of imagination across the centuries and arrive at a very lively understanding of the subject, and that, for them, Henry VIII and his court will come to life.

Alison Weir,
Carshalton, Surrey,
13 March–17 September,
2000

I

'A Most Accomplished Prince'

On 21 April 1509, the corpse of King Henry VII, ravaged by tuberculosis, was laid in state in the chapel at Richmond Palace, whence it would shortly be taken to Westminster Abbey for burial. Few mourned that King's passing, for although he had brought peace and firm government to England and established the usurping Tudor dynasty firmly on the throne, he had been regarded as a miser and an extortionist.

The contrast between the dead King and his son and heir could not have been greater. The seventeen-year-old Henry VIII was proclaimed King on 24 April,[1] which – most apt for a prince who embodied all the knightly virtues – was also the day after St George's Day. The rejoicings that greeted Henry's accession were ecstatic and unprecedented, for it was believed that he would usher in 'a golden world'.[2]

William Blount, Lord Mountjoy, a courtier, expressed the national mood in a letter to his fellow humanist, the renowned Desiderius Erasmus:

> I have no fear but when you heard that our prince, now Henry the Eighth, whom we may well call our Octavius, had succeeded to his father's throne, all your melancholy left you at once. What may you not promise yourself from a prince with whose extraordinary and almost divine character you are acquainted? When you know what a hero he now shows himself, how wisely he behaves, what a lover he is of justice and goodness, what affection he bears to the learned, I will venture to swear you will need no wings to make you fly to behold this new and auspicious star!
>
> If you could see how here all the world is rejoicing in the possession of so great a prince, how his life is all their desire, you could not contain your tears for sheer joy. The heavens laugh, the

earth exults . . . Avarice is expelled from the country, extortion is
put down, liberality scatters riches with a bountiful hand. Yet our
King does not desire gold, gems or precious metals, but virtue,
glory, immortality![3]

To his contemporaries, Henry VIII was the embodiment of kingship.
Thomas More's coronation eulogy states that 'among a thousand noble
companions, the King stands out the tallest, and his strength fits his
majestic body. There is fiery power in his eyes, beauty in his face, and
the colour of twin roses in his cheeks.'[4] Other evidence proves that this
was not just mere flattery. Henry's skeleton, discovered in 1813, was six
feet two inches in length. He was certainly of strong and muscular build:
the Spanish ambassador reported in 1507 that 'his limbs are of a gigantic
size'.[5] In youth, he was slim and broad-shouldered: his armour of 1512
has a waist measurement of thirty-two inches, while that of 1514
measures thirty-five, with a forty-two-inch chest.

Several sources testify to Henry's fair skin, among them the poet John
Skelton, who called him 'Adonis, of fresh colour'. His hair, strands of
which still adhered to his skull in 1813, was auburn, and he wore it
combed short and straight in the French fashion. For many years he
remained clean-shaven. In visage, the young King resembled his
handsome grandfather, Edward IV,[6] with his broad face, small, close-set,
penetrating eyes and small, sensual mouth; Henry, however, had a high-
bridged nose. He was, wrote a Venetian envoy in 1516, 'the handsomest
prince ever seen',[7] an opinion in which most contemporaries concurred.

The young Henry enjoyed robust good health, and was a man of great
energy and drive. He had a low boredom threshold and was 'never still
or quiet'.[8] His physician, Dr John Chamber, described him as 'cheerful
and gamesome',[9] for he was quick to laugh and enjoyed a jest. One
Venetian called him 'prudent, sage and free from every vice',[10] and
indeed it seemed so in 1509, for Henry was idealistic, open-handed,
liberal and genial. Complacency, self-indulgence and vanity appeared to
be his worst sins – he was an unabashed show-off and shamelessly
solicited the flattery of others. He was also highly strung, emotional and
suggestible. Only as he grew older did the suspicious and crafty streaks
in his nature become more pronounced; nor were his wilfulness,
arrogance, ruthlessness, selfishness and brutality yet apparent, for they
were masked by an irresistible charm and affable manner.

Kings were expected to be masterful, proud, self-confident and
courageous – and Henry had all these qualities in abundance, along with
a massive ego and a passionate zest for life. He combined the
Renaissance ideal of the man of many talents with the qualities of the
mediaeval chivalric heroes whom he so much admired. He was 'simple

and candid by nature',[11] and used no worse oath than 'By St George!' A man of impulsive enthusiasms, he could be often naive.

Decision-making did not come easily to Henry – it was his habit 'to sleep and dream upon the matter and give an answer in the morning'[12] – but once his mind was made up he always judged himself, as the Lord's Anointed, to be in the right. Then, 'if an angel was to descend from Heaven, he would not be able to persuade him to the contrary'.[13] Cardinal Wolsey was later to warn, 'Be well advised what ye put in his head, for ye shall never pull it out again.'[14]

Few could resist Henry's charisma. 'The King has a way of making every man feel that he is enjoying his special favour,' wrote Thomas More.[15] Erasmus called Henry 'the man most full of heart'.[16] He would often put his arm around a man's shoulder to put him at his ease, although he 'could not abide to have any man stare in his face when he talked with them'.[17] There are many examples of his kindness to others, as will be seen. Yet the King also had a spectacular and unpredictable temper, and in a rage could be terrifying indeed. He was also very jealous of his honour, both as King and as a knight, and had the tenderest yet most flexible of consciences. His contemporaries thought him extraordinarily virtuous, a lover of goodness, truth and justice – just as he was always to see himself.

Because the young King was not quite eighteen, his father's mother, the venerable Lady Margaret Beaufort, Countess of Richmond and Derby, acted as regent during the first ten weeks of the reign. Lady Margaret had exercised considerable influence over the upbringing of her grandson, since it had been she, and not Henry's mother, Elizabeth of York, who had been in charge of the domestic arrangements in Henry VII's household. And it was she who had been entrusted with perfecting Edward IV's series of ordinances for the regulation of the royal household;[18] the procedures she established would continue to be enforced throughout Henry VIII's reign and beyond, and they covered, amongst other things, the rules to be observed in the royal nurseries.

The Lady Margaret was now a frail, nun-like widow of sixty-six, renowned for her piety, learning and charitable works, yet her influence was formidable. She had been an inveterate intriguer during the Wars of the Roses, and had outlived four husbands. After the King, she held more lands than anyone else in the kingdom. Henry VII, born when she was only thirteen, was her only child, and she had been utterly devoted to him. That devotion extended to her grandchildren, whose education she probably supervised. For this she was admirably qualified, being a generous benefactor of scholarship and the foundress of Christ's College and St John's College at Cambridge. A patron of William Caxton, she was both a lover of books and a true intellectual. She was also an ascetic, wearing a severe widow's barbe up to her chin and a hair shirt beneath her black robes, and her rigorous religious regime represented the harsher aspects of mediaeval piety. From her, the Prince inherited his undoubted intellectual abilities and a conventional approach to religious observance.

Henry had been born on 28 June 1491, and was created Duke of York at the age of three. His seventeenth-century biographer, Lord Herbert of Cherbury, who had access to sources lost to us, claimed that Henry VII intended this second son to enter the Church, and had him educated accordingly; certainly Henry was pious and very well grounded in theology. Yet on the death of his elder brother, Arthur, in 1502, he became Prince of Wales and heir to the throne. The death of his mother, Elizabeth of York, in 1503, seems to have affected him deeply: in 1507, having learned of the death of Duke Philip of Burgundy, he confided to Erasmus that 'never, since the death of my dearest mother, hath there come to me more hateful intelligence . . . It seemed to tear open again the wound to which time had brought insensibility'.[19]

Henry was very well educated in the classical, humanist fashion; Thomas More later asked, 'What may we not expect from a king who has been nourished on philosophy and the Nine Muses?' The poet John Skelton was the Prince's tutor for a time, as was William Hone, of whom little is known.

Skelton may have owed his appointment to Margaret Beaufort, for he was a Cambridge man, a Latin classicist in holy orders. He had been appointed poet laureate by the universities of Cambridge, Oxford and Louvain, and was described by Erasmus as 'that incomparable light and ornament of British letters'. He had probably been Henry's first teacher, for he claimed

> The honour of England I learned to spell,
> In dignity royal at that doth excel . . .
> I gave him drink of the sugared well
> Of Helicon's waters crystalline,
> Acquainting him with the Muses nine.

He probably also taught Henry to read, and to write in a rounded, Italianate hand. Skelton was a colourful and eccentric character, an indifferent poet who wrote scurrilous, vitriolic satires such as 'The Bouche of Court', which targeted the corrupt courtiers in Henry VII's household. Unlike most court versifiers, Skelton wrote in English, not the customary French or Latin. He was conceited, quarrelsome and often ribald – he took a cruel pleasure in exposing ladies of the court as whores, and was obsessed with young girls – yet at the same time he set himself up as a champion of morality. Not surprisingly, he made many enemies.

Skelton may have been in post by the time Henry was three, for, in a poem he composed to mark the boy's creation as Duke of York, he referred to him as 'a brilliant pupil'. Around 1501, Skelton wrote a rather pessimistic Latin treatise, *Speculum Principis* – 'The Mirror of a Prince', for the edification of his charge; he urged him never to relinquish power to his inferiors, and to 'choose a wife for yourself, prize her always and uniquely'. In 1502, Skelton spent a short spell in prison for a minor misdemeanour, which effectively terminated his royal duties; upon his release he was appointed rector of Diss in Norfolk, but around 1511 he was dismissed for living with a concubine. Thereafter he lived at Westminster, where he would write his most vituperative and famous poems.

Along with Skelton, Prince Arthur's former tutor, the poet Bernard André, may have taught Henry Latin, and Giles d'Ewes was perhaps his French master. The Prince showed a flair for languages at an early age. By the time he became King he was fluent in 'French, English and Latin, and understands Italian well';[20] in 1515, Venetian envoys conversed with Henry VIII 'in good Latin and French, which he speaks very well indeed'.[21] Henry customarily used Latin when speaking to ambassadors. He later acquired some Spanish, probably from his first wife, Katherine of Aragon. In 1519, he began studying Greek with the humanist Richard Croke, but soon gave it up, possibly for lack of time.

Henry showed early on that he had inherited the family aptitude for music, and in 1498 his father bought him a lute, although no details of his tuition survive. He was also given instruction in 'all such convenient sports and exercises as behoveth his estate to have experience in',[22] and that included the gentlemanly skills of riding, jousting, tennis, archery and hunting.

In 1499, when Henry was eight, Thomas More took Erasmus to visit the royal children at Eltham Palace, which resulted in the Prince corresponding in Latin with Erasmus. The Dutch humanist suspected that Henry's tutors were helping him with the letters, and was later amazed to discover from Lord Mountjoy that they were all his own work. He later flattered himself that Henry's style emulated his own because he had read Erasmus' books when young.[23]

Erasmus, who was by no means a sycophant, was to call Henry VIII 'a universal genius. He has never neglected his studies'. As King, he would continue those studies, taking Cardinal Wolsey's advice to read the works of Duns Scotus, Thomas Aquinas and the Church Fathers. He saw himself as a scholar and humanist, and desired to be recognised as such by learned men. His interest was genuine, and is attested to by the numerous annotations in his own hand in the margins of his surviving books. For Henry, learning was a great source of enjoyment, a journey of discovery for a mind avid for new information. He was extraordinarily well read for a layman, and had wide interests. He also had some ability as a writer – his letters to the Vatican were exhibited as some of the most elegantly written ever received there – and as a speaker, his eloquence was 'worthy of a great orator rather than a king'.[24]

Henry had a sharp eye for detail and an encyclopaedic memory. 'There was no necessary kind of knowledge from a king's degree to a carter's, but he had an honest sight of it.'[25] He had a quick mind, superb organisational skills and a formidable intellect. He possessed, wrote Erasmus, 'a lively mentality which reached for the stars, and he was able beyond measure to bring to perfection whichever task he undertook'.[26] 'The King's Majesty has more learning than any English monarch possessed before him,'[27] Thomas More claimed, with some truth. 'He is in every respect a most accomplished prince,' commented one Venetian,[28] while another declared him to be 'so gifted and adorned with mental accomplishments of every sort that we believe him to have few equals in the world'.[29] Princes were routinely eulogised by commentators and ambassadors at this period, but the unanimous praises heaped on Henry VIII – sometimes expressed in private letters – undoubtedly contain a high degree of sincerity.

Beyond his academic interests, Henry was creative and inventive, loved novelties, and enjoyed experimenting with mechanics and technology. He designed weapons and fortifications, and took an active interest in building plans. He also had 'a remarkable docility for mathematics'[30] and was 'learned in all sciences';[31] the cupboards in his privy lodgings contained various scientific instruments.[32]

Henry had a passion for astronomy. The reformer Philip Melanchthon called him 'most learned, especially in the study of the movement of the heavens'.[33] Henry's astrolabe, bearing his crowned coat of arms and made by a Norman, Sébastien le Senay, is in the British Museum. As king, he would appoint as his chaplain the Oxford astronomer and mathematician, John Robyns, who dedicated his treatise on comets to his master. The two men enjoyed many a discussion on astronomy. In 1540, Peter Apianus, a professor of mathematics from Ingolstadt, presented to Henry VIII his treatise *Astronicum Caesareum* on astronomy and navigation.[34]

Henry's interest in maps is well documented, and it prepared the ground for the eventual mapping of England in the late sixteenth century. The King owned many maps, most of them rolled up in cupboards and drawers in his chambers and libraries, as well as map-making tools, 'a globe of paper' and 'a map made like a screen',[35] indicating that he himself was something of a cartographer. Elaborate maps hung on the walls of the royal palaces and were used in court entertainments or for political strategy. In 1527, a Venetian map-maker, Girolamo Verrazano, presented the King with a world map which was later hung in his gallery at Whitehall, along with thirty-four other maps, and there were maps of England, Scotland, Wales and Normandy in the gallery at Hampton Court.[36]

Later in the reign the defence of the realm was a major preoccupation, and the King commissioned a plan of Dover from Sir Richard Lee, surveyor of Calais,[37] as well as a map of the English coastline from the Dieppe mariner John Rotz, who was appointed royal hydrographer in 1542. The atlas he produced, *The Book of Idrography*, was dedicated to Henry. Henry also employed a French cosmographer, Jean Mallard, who produced a book containing one of the first circular maps of the world.[38]

Henry emerged from his education as 'a prodigy of precocious scholarship'.[39] But by 1508, for reasons that are not clear, the autocratic Henry VII was keeping his son under such strict supervision that he might have been a young girl.[40] Unlike his late brother, the Prince was given no royal responsibilities, nor, it seems, much training in the arts and duties of kingship, apart from some sound schooling in history from the King himself.[41] He was not permitted to leave the palace unless it was by a private door into the park, and then only in the company of specially appointed persons. No one dared approach him or speak to him. He spent most of his time in a room that led off the King's bedchamber, and appeared 'so subjected that he does not speak a word except in response to what the King asks him'.[42]

It may be that, having lost his three other sons, Henry VII was overly concerned for the health and safety of his surviving heir. Another theory is that he was well aware of the Prince's capabilities, and did not trust him; he is said to have been 'beset by the fear that his son might during his lifetime obtain too much power'.[43] The Prince's cousin, Reginald Pole, later claimed that Henry VII hated his son, 'having no affection or fancy unto him'.[44] Once, in 1508, the King quarrelled so violently with young Henry that it appeared 'as if he sought to kill him'.[45]

Perhaps Henry VII was all too aware of the boy's weaknesses, for he ensured that 'all the talk in his presence was of virtue, honour, cunning, wisdom and deeds of worship, of nothing that shall move him to vice'.[46] Nor did the Prince have any opportunity of indulging in licentious behaviour: the chances are that he retained his virginity until he married.

Henry's tutelage did not last much longer. In 1509, the King died, and this untried youth came into his own.

2

'The Triumphal Coronation'

A king's first duty was to marry for political advantage and produce a son and heir. Henry VIII chose to marry his brother's widow, Katherine of Aragon, to whom he had been betrothed since 1503. Six years his senior, she was the daughter of Ferdinand of Aragon and Isabella of Castile, sovereigns of a united Spain, yet Henry VII had treated her most shabbily during her widowhood, keeping her in penury and refusing to allow her marriage to Prince Henry to take place.

There were two reasons for this: the death of Queen Isabella in 1504 had relegated Katherine to the status of a mere princess of Aragon, and Henry felt that other, more advantageous marriage alliances might be found; more importantly, although the Pope had granted a dispensation for the match with Prince Henry, canon law forbade a man to marry his brother's widow. In this case, however, Katherine had sworn that her union with Prince Arthur had never been consummated. Nevertheless, Henry VII had not been satisfied that the marriage would be lawful. His son, however, chose to ignore his reservations.

Like Henry, Katherine had received a classical education from humanist tutors, among them Peter Martyr. She was as familiar with the works of ancient Rome as with those of St Augustine and St Jerome. Erasmus called her 'a rare and fine advocate' of humanist learning, and recorded that she 'loved good literature, which she had studied with success since childhood'; Henry VIII would often read with her, and allowed her the freedom of his libraries. Katherine was especially well read in the Scriptures: Erasmus told the King, 'Your wife spends that time in reading the sacred volume that other princesses occupy in cards and dice.' Her missal, dated 1527, may still be seen in the chapel at Leeds Castle, Kent.

An expert Latinist – her letters to Prince Arthur were described as worthy of Cicero himself – Katherine also spoke fluent French and had no trouble learning English, although she never lost her Spanish accent, as is apparent from the phonetic spelling in her letters, where Hampton Court becomes 'Antoncurt' and Greenwich 'Granuche'.

Erasmus thought Katherine 'miraculously learned for a woman'.[1] She was highly intelligent and a perfect intellectual match for Henry VIII; in fact, Erasmus considered her a better scholar than Henry. He was therefore very upset when, in 1516, she censured his Greek New Testament, translated from the Latin Vulgate of St Jerome.

'Why does Erasmus correct Jerome? Is he wiser than Jerome?' she asked.[2] She was much more impressed by his book *The Institution of Marriage* (1526), which she commissioned. 'Her Majesty the Queen correctly regards it as being of supreme importance,' commented Thomas More.

Katherine was small of stature and plump; her bearing was regal and dignified. Unlike most Spaniards, she had a fair and 'very beautiful'[3] complexion, grey eyes and auburn hair 'of a very great length, beautiful and goodly to behold'.[4] In her youth she was described as 'the most beautiful creature in the world',[5] with 'a pretty and most healthy colour in her face'.[6] A portrait of a demure, round-faced girl by Miguel Sittow, dating from 1505 and now in the Kunsthistorisches Museum, Vienna, is almost certainly of Katherine: the sitter's collar links the initial K with her pomegranate badge.

Katherine had learned patience and discretion during her troubled youth. Henry VIII was to call her 'a woman of most gentleness, of most humility and buxomness [amiability]',[7] whilst a Flemish envoy thought her 'a lady of lively, kind and gracious disposition';[8] she 'always had a smile on her countenance',[9] even in adversity. Of a more serene and serious cast of mind than Henry, she was a woman of firm moral convictions, 'as religious and virtuous as words can express',[10] yet at the same time stubborn and uncompromising. Her outward submissiveness and graciousness concealed a resolute will and single-minded tenacity. Her great integrity, kindness and shrewdness inspired devoted friendship and loyalty in many. She was, as Erasmus declared, 'a brilliant example of her sex'.

Katherine's piety was deep-seated and orthodox, and probably had a considerable influence on the religious life of the court during the first half of Henry's reign. She spent hours at her devotions, kneeling without a cushion[11] in her oratory before a Spanish crucifix and statues of St Catherine with her wheel and St Margaret with a crown and cross.[12] The Queen studied the Office of the Blessed Virgin daily, and after dinner it was her custom to read aloud from pious works to her ladies. She rose at midnight to say Matins and again at dawn to hear Mass, and fasted every Friday and Saturday, on the vigils of saints' days and during Lent. Luis Caroz, King Ferdinand's ambassador during the early years of Henry's reign, claimed that all this fasting led to Katherine suffering from irregular periods,[13] and it almost certainly had an effect on her obstetric history.

The Queen confessed her sins every week, and received the Eucharist on Sundays. Over the years, she made several pilgrimages to Our Lady of Walsingham, Our Lady of Caversham and other shrines,[14] and had a special devotion to the Franciscans. In later years, she wore the rough serge habit of the Third (Lay) Order of St Francis under her royal robes.[15] For the present, however, she was a young woman delighted with the sudden change in her fortunes and happily anticipating the future.

In June 1509, the young King brought Katherine to Greenwich Palace, where they were to be married. Royal connections with Greenwich went back to the eleventh century, but the Thames-side palace, five miles down the river from London, had been built after 1433 by Humphrey, Duke of Gloucester, brother of Henry V, who had named it Bella Court; he also built a tower in Greenwich Park, on the site of the present Royal Observatory. Bella Court had been remodelled and luxuriously refurbished after 1447 for Henry VI's queen, Margaret of Anjou, who renamed it Placentia or Pleasaunce, and stocked the surrounding park with deer.

Between 1498 and 1504,[16] Henry VII, probably inspired by reports of the palaces of the Dukes of Burgundy at Princenhof and Ghent, virtually rebuilt Placentia around three great courtyards.[17] He had the river frontage with its bay windows refaced in Burgundian-style red brick,[18] and changed the palace's name once more, to Greenwich. It was thereafter one of the chief and most splendid residences of the Tudor dynasty, and the scene of many important historical events. Excavations have shown that the palace stood on the site of the present Royal Naval College, and that the royal apartments overlooked the river. All around were beautiful gardens with fountains, lawns, flowers and orchards.[19]

The design of Greenwich Palace was revolutionary. It had no moat, and although the royal apartments were stacked one above the other in a five-storey donjon or keep, in the traditional castellar manner, there were no fortifications. This, like the Burgundian palaces, was first and foremost a domestic residence, and its design was to be repeated in many great houses of the early Tudor period.[20]

The donjon was situated between a chapel to the east and the privy kitchen to the west. Although there are several external views of the palace, notably those executed by Anthony van Wyngaerde in the 1550s, we know very little about what the interior looked like. The complex included a great hall, with its roof timbers painted yellow ochre, a great chamber and a range of domestic offices.[21] Henry's closet overlooking the Thames had murals depicting the life of St John.[22]

Henry VIII loved Greenwich; it was his birthplace, and during the first half of his reign he spent more time there than at any other palace. Here he could hunt and hawk in the two-hundred-acre park, or watch his ships being built at the dockyards he established at nearby Woolwich and Deptford in 1513. London was easily accessible by barge. The King spent lavishly on improving the palace, and in the 1530s the antiquarian John Leland wrote

> Lo! with what lustre shines this wished-for place,
> Which, star-like, might the heavenly mansions grace.
> What painted roofs! What windows charm the eye!
> What turrets, rivals of the starry sky![23]

In 1478, Edward IV had established at Greenwich a community of the Observant Friars of St Francis; Henry VII later built a similar friary beside his palace at Richmond. Henry VIII, like Katherine of Aragon, was deeply attached to the Observants 'for their strict adherence to poverty, their sincerity, charity and devotion'.[24] During the first half of the reign, the Order would benefit from royal patronage and provide several chaplains for the King and Queen, and their conventual church at Greenwich, built after 1482 and linked to the royal lodgings by a gallery,[25] was a favourite place of prayer for Katherine, who wished one day to be buried there.

It was at Greenwich, in the Queen's closet, that Henry and Katherine were quietly married on 11 June 1509, with William Warham, Archbishop of Canterbury, officiating. There were no public celebrations, nor does the traditional ceremony of putting the bride and groom to bed seem to have been observed. When Katherine had married Prince Arthur in 1501, the ceremonial laid down by Margaret Beaufort was followed: the bed was prepared and sprinkled with holy water before the bride was led away from the wedding feast by her ladies, undressed, veiled, and 'reverently' laid in bed. Her young husband, 'in his shirt, with a gown cast about him',[26] had then been escorted by his gentlemen and a host of merry courtiers into the bedchamber, to the sound of shawms, viols and tabors. Then the music ceased, to allow the bishops to bless the bed and pray that the marriage might be fruitful, and only then were the young couple left alone, with some wine and spices to fortify them.[27] This is the only recorded instance of an English royal couple being publicly bedded together in the sixteenth century.

The Queen Consort's duties were to produce heirs to the throne, engage in charitable works, and act as a helpmeet to her husband and as a civilising influence over his court. She was not expected to play a political role, although most of Henry VIII's wives did, even if it was merely to secure the advancement of their families and supporters.

Until 1514, Katherine acted as an unofficial ambassador for King Ferdinand, and Henry respected her political judgement; but then her father tricked him, as we shall see, and he never again valued her advice as highly. Her influence was always greatest in the domestic sphere, overseeing the management of the royal household, administering her estates, presiding over the councils held by her chief officers, and attending to the charitable works that won her the love of the English people. Nor was she above sewing her husband's shirts, living up to her motto, 'Humble and loyal'.

Katherine's badges, the pomegranate of Granada and the arrow-sheaf of Aragon, were soon seen everywhere in the royal palaces, entwined with Tudor roses, crowns and portcullises. A queen was expected to dress the part, and Katherine always appeared sumptuously attired, often with her hair falling loose over her shoulders – a fashion permitted only to unmarried girls and queens – or adorned with a Venetian cap. It was she who introduced into England the Spanish farthingale, a petticoat of linen or canvas stiffened with ever-increasing hoops of cane, whalebone or steel into a bell shape. This was worn under the gown and kirtle, and remained fashionable throughout the sixteenth century.

Katherine's badges also adorned many items in her vast collection of jewellery, which included the official jewels handed down from one English queen consort to the next. Like many people, she believed that some jewels had supernatural powers: one of her rings was said to cure fits. She owned a pomander with a dial in it – probably an early watch – as well as very costly ropes of pearls with jewelled crucifixes and pendants of St George, and exquisite brooches with pendant pearls for her corsage.

Katherine shared Henry's enthusiasm for hunting and elaborate court entertainments, as well as his intellectual interests. She loved music, dancing, engaging in stimulating conversation and watching tournaments; the King always sported her favours when he jousted. In true courtly tradition, he wrote poems and songs for her:

> As the holly groweth green
> And never changeth hue,
> So I am, e'er hath been
> Unto my lady true.[28]

Henry was fond of telling people that 'he loved true where he did marry'.[29] He wrote to Katherine's father, 'If I were still free, I would choose her for wife before all others.'[30] In Elizabeth of York's missal, which he gave to his wife, he inscribed the words, 'I am yours, Henry R., for ever.' After the midday meal he was usually to be found in the Queen's apartments, discussing politics, theology or books, receiving visitors, or just 'taking his pleasure as usual with the Queen'.[31] Often he took his supper there, and he always joined Katherine for Vespers. His chief desire was to please her.

Katherine adored him. She referred to him variously as 'Your Grace', 'my husband' or even 'my Henry'. Soon after her marriage, her confessor described her as being in 'the greatest gaiety and contentment that ever there was'.[32] All that was needed to complete the royal couple's happiness and secure the succession was a son.

Henry VIII inherited a great fortune from his careful father, which has been estimated at £1,250,000 (£375 million). His kingdom, 'this fertile and plentiful realm of England, at that time flourished in all abundance of wealth and riches, and grace and plenty reigned within this realm',[33] which, under Tudor rule, had come to enjoy the benefits of peace after thirty years of dynastic struggles.

Plans were soon in hand for the new King's coronation, which was to be the first of the many displays of magnificent pageantry that would characterise Henry's reign. Stocks of the scarlet, white and green fabrics required for kitting out the entire court ran out, and the Keeper of the Great Wardrobe had to send to Flanders for further supplies. Tailors, embroiderers and goldsmiths could hardly keep pace with the demand.[34]

On 21 June 1509 King and court moved to the Tower of London, where sovereigns traditionally stayed before being crowned. The Tower proper, or central keep – it became known as the White Tower in 1234, when it was whitewashed – had been built to defend London by William the Conqueror around 1080. The royal apartments had then occupied the upper floors of the keep. Successive kings had built further towers and a ring of outer fortifications, and in the thirteenth and fourteenth centuries every monarch from Henry III to Richard II had helped to create a lavishly appointed palace.

Henry III built a great hall and chambers on the east side of the inner ward between the White Tower and the Wakefield and Lanthorn Towers. The great hall had a steeply pitched timber roof, tall windows and stone pillars (it was crumbling into ruin by the late sixteenth century). Edward I had constructed the original royal watergate beneath St Thomas's Tower, which has been called Traitors' Gate since the sixteenth century. By then, the court was using the gate built by Edward

III near the Cradle Tower. The Wardrobe Tower was used from mediaeval times to store royal robes and hangings.

The Tower had been a favourite residence of Edward IV, who divided Henry III's great chamber into an audience chamber, privy chamber and bedchamber. Henry VII added a gallery to the Cradle Tower, and converted the Lanthorn Tower into a royal lodging with a bedchamber and a privy closet; Henry VIII would have a Renaissance-style altar in here, 'wrought round about the edges with antique'.[35] These rooms were later hung with tapestries depicting Antiochus, King of Syria, which are said to have been the work of Katherine of Aragon, Katherine Parr and Mary I. Henry VII also built a tower to house a library next to the King's Tower, in which was the bedchamber used by Henry VIII and from which projected a gallery traversing the garden below.[36]

For centuries the Tower had housed a royal menagerie – in the sixteenth century lions were actually kept in the Lion Tower – the royal armouries, the royal mint and the royal treasure. Until 1661, the crown jewels were housed at Westminster Abbey, not at the Tower.

Although it had not yet acquired a sinister reputation, the Tower held unhappy associations for Henry. His mother had died in childbirth there, and her brothers, the Princes in the Tower, were widely reputed to have been murdered in the fortress by Richard III. Henry would rarely visit the Tower, although he carried out works there – it was he who added the decorative caps on the White Tower and who first had ordnance placed along the Tower wharf. As a royal residence, the Tower was old-fashioned, cold, damp and malodorous: its moat was now a squalid refuse dump. Nevertheless, Henry had had the royal lodgings refurbished for his coronation, and they were now gaily hung with cloths of red, green and white – the last two being the Tudor colours.

On 22 June, the King, in a ceremony instituted by Henry IV at his coronation in 1399, dubbed twenty-six new Knights of the Bath,[37] many of whom were his closest friends and attended upon him in his privy chamber. All had been purified in the requisite ritual baths, served the King at dinner, and kept vigil throughout the night in the Norman Chapel of St John in the White Tower, the earliest-surviving royal chapel. Prior to the Reformation, it boasted brilliant wall-paintings, stained-glass windows and a colourful rood screen; all had disappeared by 1550.

The next day, 23 June, saw London rejoicing as the King and Queen went in a glittering procession through Cheapside, Temple Bar and the Strand to Westminster Palace. London was still a walled, mediaeval city, although its suburbs were rapidly sprawling out beyond the walls: along the Strand, for example, were to be found the great houses of the nobility, with gardens leading down to the river. The city's skyline was dominated by the spires of the Gothic cathedral of St Paul and eighty other churches. London was prosperous, lively and very congested, due to its narrow streets and crammed-in, jettied buildings; most citizens, therefore, used the Thames as the main thoroughfare.

In honour of the coronation, buildings along the processional route were hung with tapestries, and free wine flowed from the conduits. Henry rode beneath a canopy borne by the barons of the Cinque Ports, with his heralds going before him; he was resplendent in a doublet of gold embroidered with precious stones beneath a robe of crimson velvet furred with ermine; across his shoulder was slung a baldrick of rubies. Katherine, in embroidered white satin and ermine, followed in a litter hung with white silk and golden ribbons. Her ladies, in blue velvet, rode behind on matching palfreys.[38] Henry's grandmother, Margaret Beaufort, watching from a window in Cheapside, wept for joy, over-come by the occasion.

In the late afternoon, the King and Queen arrived at the Palace of Westminster, which had been the seat of royal government and the monarch's chief London residence since the eleventh century. The palace was a sprawling complex of mediaeval stone and timber buildings that covered six acres; much of it had been rebuilt in the thirteenth century by Henry III, although the magnificent Westminster Hall had been erected by William Rufus in 1097–9; its impressive hammerbeam roof was installed by Richard II in 1394. The law courts of King's Bench, Chancery and Common Pleas sat here during the legal term, while the House of Lords met in the great hall – called the White Hall or Chamber – of the palace itself. There was therefore limited space for large-scale court ceremonials.

The royal apartments, which had been refurbished by Edward IV and Henry VII, still bore signs of the faded splendour of a bygone age. Like his father, Henry VIII used as his bedchamber Henry III's vast Painted Chamber, which measured eighty-six by twenty-six feet. Above the King's bed was a thirteenth-century mural in red, blue, silver and gold portraying the coronation of St Edward the Confessor, and on the adjacent walls were vivid depictions of Old Testament battles. Being so close to the river, the palace was damp and difficult to heat; tapestry hung over the doors to keep out the draughts. Beggars thronged the rubbish-strewn forecourt with its clock tower and fountain. Yet Henry spent much time here in the first years of his reign.

Throughout the night before their coronation, the King and Queen kept vigil in the Chapel of St Stephen, founded by King Stephen in the twelfth century; Edward III had remodelled it in the fourteenth century and commissioned murals of himself and his large family.

On Midsummer's Day, Sunday 24 June, Henry and Katherine, wearing royal robes of crimson and preceded by the nobility in furred gowns of scarlet, walked to Westminster Abbey along a carpet of striped cloth strewn with herbs and flowers.[39] As soon as the King disappeared into the Abbey, the crowds ripped the carpet to pieces for souvenirs.[40]

'This day consecrates a young man who is the everlasting glory of our age,' exulted Thomas More. 'This day is the end of our slavery, the fount of our liberty, the beginning of joy. Now the people, liberated, run before their king with bright faces'.[41]

After being acclaimed by the peers, Henry swore his coronation oath and was anointed with holy oil. He was then consecrated by Archbishop Warham with the crown of St Edward the Confessor.[42] The choir burst into *Te Deum Laudamus* as the newly consecrated monarch was led by thirty-eight bishops to his throne to receive the homage of his chief subjects.

Chief among the choristers that day was Dr Robert Fairfax, who was to become renowned as 'the prime musician of the nation'.[43] A Cambridge graduate, he was the first man to take a degree in music at Oxford. Henry had heard of his fame as organist and choirmaster of St Albans Abbey, and had already persuaded him to become a Gentleman of the Chapel Royal. Fairfax was to write grand polyphonic masses and motets for the Chapel, as well as delightful secular ballads for the court. The King paid him only £9.2s.6d. (£2,737) a year, less than a royal gardener would earn, but he was handsomely rewarded each New Year's Day for composing anthems and copying out music.

In a much shorter ceremony, the Queen was crowned with a heavy gold diadem set with sapphires, rubies and pearls.[44] When the royal couple emerged from the Abbey, the King was wearing his lighter 'imperial' or arched crown and a purple velvet robe lined with ermine; as the crowds cheered, the organ and trumpets were sounding, drums thundering and bells pealing to signify that Henry VIII 'had been gloriously crowned to the comfort of all the land'.[45]

After the coronation, the King and Queen led the great procession back to Westminster Hall for the coronation banquet, which was to be 'greater than any Caesar had known'.[46] When all were seated a fanfare sounded, and the Duke of Buckingham and the Earl of Shrewsbury rode into the hall on horseback to herald the arrival of the 'sumptuous, fine and delicate meats [in] plentiful abundance'.[47] When the second course was finished, the King's Champion, Sir Robert Dymmocke, paraded up and down the hall on his courser before throwing down his gauntlet with the customary challenge to anyone who dared contest the King's title. Henry rewarded him with a gold cup. After the banquet, 'a tournament was held which lasted until midnight'.[48]

The celebrations continued for several days.

> To further enhance the triumphal coronation, jousts and tourneys were held in the grounds of the palace of Westminster. For the comfort of the royal spectators, a pavilion was constructed, covered with tapestries and hung with rich Arras cloth. And nearby there was a curious fountain over which was built a sort of castle with an imperial crown on top and battlements of roses and gilded pomegranates. Its walls were painted white [with] green lozenges, each containing a rose, a pomegranate, a quiver of arrows or the letters H and K, all gilded.
>
> The shields of arms of the jousters also appeared on the walls, and on certain days red, white and claret wine ran from the mouths of the castle's gargoyles. The organisers of these jousts were Lord Thomas Howard, heir to the Earl of Surrey, Admiral Sir Edward Howard, his brother, Lord Richard Grey, Sir Edmund Howard, Sir Thomas Knyvet and Charles Brandon esquire. The trumpets sounded and the fresh young gallants and noblemen took the field. All the participants were magnificently attired.[49]

The challengers, wearing plumed gold helmets and calling themselves the Knights of Diana, included Edward Neville, Edward Guildford and John Pechy, while the defenders were the Knights of Pallas. Charles Brandon distinguished himself at barriers against a huge German challenger, 'when he so pummelled the German about the head' that his nose bled and he was led away defeated.[50] On the next day, in honour of Diana, the goddess of the hunt, deer were hunted and slaughtered in a miniature park and castle which had been created in the tiltyard, and their bloody carcasses, hung on poles, presented to the Queen and the ladies.[51]

The festivities were brought to an end by the death of Margaret Beaufort on 29 June, the day after the King attained his majority; at the last, she urged him to take as his mentor the austere and devout John Fisher, Bishop of Rochester – her confessor, fellow humanist and associate in her educational projects. Fisher, who had enjoyed a distinguished academic career and had a reputation for being 'the most holy and learned prelate in Christendom',[52] was a man of firm principle and deep sincerity, who wore a hair shirt beneath his clerical robes, slept on hard straw matting, scourged himself regularly and ate mainly bread and pottage. His patroness felt he was the right man to guide a young and inexperienced king, being no flatterer as bishops often were; but there is no evidence that Henry paid much attention to him.

The King ordered the church bells to toll for six days to mark the Lady Margaret's passing. Bishop Fisher paid tribute to her virtues in an oration preached at her funeral at Westminster Abbey, and Erasmus, a friend of Fisher, wrote her epitaph.

Having attained his majority, Henry VIII now began ruling his kingdom.

3

'A Prince of Splendour and Generosity'

In 1509, with remarkable prescience, a Venetian wrote of Henry VIII: 'for the future, the whole world will talk of him'.[1] In an age when monarchs ruled as well as reigned, a king's personality could have a profound effect upon the land he governed, and few sovereigns have left such an indelible imprint on national institutions and the national consciousness as Henry. He inspired in his contemporaries 'a pleasant and terrible reverence'.[2]

Sovereigns in the sixteenth century were perceived as semi-divine beings; the King was not just a normal man but also the Lord's Anointed, His deputy on earth, and called 'by divine right' to hold dominion over his subjects. Since mediaeval times, the King had been seen as two bodies in one: a mortal entity and 'the King's person', representing unending royal authority; monarchs therefore referred to themselves in the plural form as 'we'. A king was thus set apart from his people,[3] and invested with an insight into the subtle mysteries of state denied mere mortals. 'Kings of England,' Henry told his judges, 'never had any superior but God.'[4]

So sacrosanct was the institution of monarchy that it was seen as near sacrilege for a subject to question or criticise the acts of his sovereign. 'Princes ought to be obeyed by the commandment of God; yea, and to be obeyed without question,' wrote Stephen Gardiner, Bishop of Winchester.[5] A king was entitled to expect the same devotion and obedience from his people as he himself rendered to God, for there was a presumption that the King's law was God's law.[6] The royal prerogative was the will of God working through the will of the King, and the King could do no wrong. This explains why treason was regarded as the most serious of crimes, and why it was punished so harshly.

The normal penalty for treason was hanging, disembowelling and quartering, although the King usually commuted the sentence to beheading for peers of the realm. Traitors, as Henry declared, had to be punished severely 'for the example and terror of others'.[7] In 1541, the King angrily censured his Councillors for not committing to the Tower some felons who had robbed Windsor Castle, 'as though you made no difference between the enterprise of robbing His Majesty and the attempting of the same towards any mean subject'.[8] The thieves were forthwith sent to the Tower.

Since he governed 'by the grace of God', the King bore a weighty moral responsibility towards his subjects, of which Henry VIII was well aware, 'being in the room that I am in'.[9] Henry saw God as his ally; early on, he told a Venetian ambassador that no one kept faith in the world save him, 'and therefore God Almighty, who knows this, prospers my affairs'.[10] Kings were guaranteed a special place in Heaven, and were therefore expected to set a good example. The King's chief duties, enshrined in his coronation oath, were to defend his realm, uphold the Church and administer justice fairly. He was also the fount of honour, and, in times of war, the military leader of his armies.

Although they were not strictly speaking absolute monarchs, the Tudor sovereigns bore the entire responsibility for the government of the kingdom. Parliament, the Privy Council, the officers of state, judges, sheriffs and mayors all exercised authority in the King's name. Royal power was therefore the unifying force within the realm.

The Tudors elevated the English monarchy to unprecedented heights while extending the royal authority. Their prestige was enhanced by the increasingly elaborate ceremonial that attended every aspect of their highly public lives, as well as by pageantry and symbolism, calculated to enhance the royal image. The development of royal palaces and progresses constituted just two aspects of this policy: a king needed to be visible, and to be in touch with his subjects, and also to impress them and foreigners with a display of magnificence. Henry VIII was the first English king to adopt the style 'Your Majesty', rather than the traditional 'Your Grace' or 'Your Highness'; foreign ambassadors were addressing him as such before 1520. Like other European sovereigns, Henry was influenced by humanist teachings on sovereignty, which emphasised strong, centralised rule, dynastic continuity and the consolidation of royal power. 'The Prince is the life, the head and the authority of all things that be done in England,' wrote Sir Thomas Smith.[11] More than a century before Louis XIV, the King was seen as the embodiment of the state.[12]

At the foundation of the Tudor monarchy was the concept of princely magnificence. The outward show of power and status, displayed by both King and court, was extremely important in an age of widespread illiteracy, and also in a culture that valued the trappings of rank; and it had the advantages of impressing foreigners and attracting talented and able men to the royal service. Magnificence, or *majestas*, was calculated to dazzle the beholder; it could create an illusion of wealth and power that might belie the reality, and was therefore very effective as a propaganda tool.

Mediaeval monarchs had certainly understood the value of outward display, but it was not until the reign of Edward IV (1461–83) that the promotion of princely magnificence became official policy and the focus of Edward's household ordinances. Edward IV had 'the most splendid court that could be found in all Christendom'.[13]

Edward and his successors were merely emulating the fifteenth-century Valois Dukes of Burgundy, who had created the cult of magnificence and set standards in taste, ceremonial and culture for the rest of Europe. The Burgundian Dukes impressed the service of architects, artists, musicians and scholars, and in so doing enhanced their own prestige. By Henry VIII's reign, the court of Burgundy was no more,[14] but its influence was everywhere to be seen. The Italian writer, Baldassare Castiglione, in his book *The Courtier*, stated that the perfect ruler 'should be a prince of splendour and generosity, giving freely to everyone. He should hold magnificent banquets, festivals, games and public shows'.

Henry VIII exemplified this ideal. His court was the most magnificent in English history. Henry was rich enough to lavish extravagant sums of money on his palaces, clothes, entertainments and lifestyle, and on the open-handed hospitality that was expected of a great prince. He was determined from the first to outshine his European rivals, the King of France and the Emperor, each of whom had at least four times the resources he did. By clever bluffing, he managed to achieve this aim. And Henry himself embodied the virtues of magnificence. This big, impressive man had a natural authority and assurance. He looked and acted like a king.

Henry made the most of his opportunities. He had a genius for choosing talented men to serve him, notably Cardinal Wolsey and Thomas Cromwell. But whilst Henry delegated much of his power to these ministers and left them to work out the details of his policies, he remained very much in control, and kept his own counsel. 'If my cap knew my counsel, I would throw it in the fire,' he once said.[15] It was indisputably he who directed the course of his reign. If any dared cross him, he threatened, 'there was no head in his kingdom so noble but he would make it fly'.[16] Court factions might seek to influence the King, for he was not averse to intrigue, but he was not so suggestible as to let them utterly usurp his prerogative. He never forgot that his was the ultimate authority.

Many historians have claimed that Henry grew more ruthless and bloodthirsty only as he got older, yet in 1510 he coolly executed his father's hated ministers, Richard Empson and Edmund Dudley, in the interests of political expediency, and similarly eliminated the Earl of Suffolk in 1513. The Elizabethan antiquarian John Stow claimed that during his reign he executed seventy thousand people, although this is certainly a gross exaggeration. It proves, however, that Henry had gained a reputation for cruelty by the end of his life, and it is true that he did not scruple to remove, often by savage means, those who opposed him.

Henry had an eye for detail. 'He wants to have his feet in a thousand shoes,' commented a Milanese envoy.[17] Little escaped his scrutiny. His encyclopaedic knowledge was an advantage when it came to briefing ambassadors or intervening in disputes, and since knowledge gave a king an advantage, he made sure he was kept up-to-date on events. When told by French envoys that ten thousand Swiss troops had been killed at the Battle of Marignano in 1515, the King replied that that was remarkable, since only ten thousand soldiers had fought in the battle.[18]

Henry had international ambitions, and was determined to play a prominent role in Europe. He was 'rich, ferocious and greedy for glory',[19] desiring nothing more than to display his knightly skills at the head of an army and win honour and renown for himself by reopening the Hundred Years War and winning back the lands his predecessors had lost in France, which Henry believed to be his by right. 'The new King is magnificent, liberal, and a great enemy of the French,' commented a Venetian ambassador in 1509.[20] At this time, Ferdinand of Aragon was Henry's ally, but time would prove Ferdinand untrustworthy.

Henry's hatred of the French festered. In 1510, learning that his Councillors had written in his name to Louis XII offering friendship and peace, he shouted, 'Who wrote this letter? I ask peace of the King of France, who dare not look me in the face, still less make war on me?' Then he stormed out of the room and proceeded to insult the French ambassador by inviting him to watch a tournament but making sure he had nowhere to sit. Eventually a cushion was provided, and the envoy had to watch the King displaying his martial prowess.[21]

Henry was a focus for the growing nationalism of his people, and he enjoyed an instinctive rapport with many of his subjects. 'Love for the King is universal with all who see him, as His Highness does not seem a person of this world but one descended from Heaven,' observed a Venetian.[22] In 1513, another Italian wrote, 'He is very popular with his own people, and indeed with all, for his qualities.'[23] Henry's hearty charm and affability won him golden opinions, although he was never referred to as Bluff King Hal in his lifetime. Erasmus found him to be 'more of a companion than a king'.

Henry revelled in his popularity; he was a consummate showman who understood the value of being accessible to his subjects, and who made sure, in his early years, that he had a highly visible profile. The public were allowed into his palaces to watch tournaments, processions or the great court entertainments, and it was not unheard of for Henry to go into London in disguise to mingle among them. And of course a large number of his subjects saw him when he went on progress.

Many of those subjects brought the King gifts in the expectation of a reward; indeed, such largesse, or tipping, was expected of a monarch. Lots of the offerings were humble, such as herbs, green peas or live foxes, and many were foodstuffs such as orange pies, fruit, pheasants, salmon or baked lampreys, which were known to be one of his favourite foods. The King gave 6d. to a gardener who gave him a drink of water, £1 (£300) to a priest who preached before him, a total of £4.17s.4d. (£1,230) to divers poor people who brought him 'capons, hens, books of wax and other trifles', and £2 (£600) to a man who won a wager by eating a whole buck at one sitting.[24] Wherever he went, the poor waited for his charity, and he would patiently listen to their tales of woe: one William Kebet had lost his job and was 'fallen in poverty and decay' – Henry succoured him with £5 (£1,500) on one occasion and £4 (£1,200) on another. He donated £5 to another man 'like to be lost', £3.6s. (£990) to a needy father of thirteen, and a further sum of money so that a poor woman could redeem her husband from debtors' prison. He also gave funds to his jester 'for his surgery when sick in London', and to his Groom, Thomas, 'to relieve him in his sickness'.[25]

Henry VIII's popularity did not wane with time, and it survived his reforms and his cruelties: his subjects generally revered him as a great king who had England's interests at heart.

4

'This Magnificent, Excellent and Triumphant Court'

The court was not just the palace where the King resided but also the people and the household that surrounded him. It was at the centre of affairs, and revolved around the man who was the fount of all power, honours and patronage.

The fifteenth century had witnessed a steady decline in the court's prestige; the weak Henry VI had failed to maintain 'a worshipful and great household',[1] and there was consequently less honour and status in being attached to the royal service.

Henry's successor, Edward IV, had visited the court of Burgundy, with which England enjoyed good trading and political links, and from about 1471 he modelled his court along Burgundian lines, as did other Western European rulers. The unprecedented splendour of the great banquets and tournaments at the English court reflected the practice in Burgundy, where the cult of chivalry had enjoyed a revival. It was in imitation of the Toison d'Or, or Golden Fleece, an order of knighthood founded by Duke Philip the Good in 1430, that Edward IV and his successors revived the Order of the Garter, with its chivalric association with St George, England's patron saint. Entertainments, sports and etiquette at the English court all began to follow the highly refined Burgundian pattern, and the King became a lavish patron of the arts. All was designed to emphasise the authority and magnificence of the sovereign, and it brought about a resurgence of the importance of the court itself.

This new perception of the court and of the royal status heralded changes in the constitution of the royal household, which would be designed not just for the display of magnificence but also for the needs of monarchs who had an increasing desire for privacy.

Although Henry VII had a reputation for parsimony, he understood the value of display: like Edward IV, he built fine palaces and spent vast sums on dazzling occasions and entertainments, and although he was no great patron of the arts like Edward IV or Henry VIII, his court was never dull. 'He knew well how to maintain his royal majesty and all that appertains to kingship,' wrote the Italian historian Polydore Vergil.

Henry VIII's court was the most 'magnificent, excellent and triumphant'[2] in English history. First and foremost the King's house, it also became the political and cultural hub of the nation, a seat of government, a sophisticated arts centre and a meeting place of scholars, all in a setting of unprecedented splendour. As the focus of society at large, the court set the fashion in every aspect of English life. It was also a military academy for the noble elite, who could be called upon to defend the realm at any time, and many of its pleasures had a martial content.

At first, Burgundian influence prevailed at Henry's court. Henry VII had owned examples of Italian art and sculpture, but only in the field of scholarship, in which the rediscovery and study of the classical literature of ancient Greece and Rome was known as the 'New Learning', had the Italian Renaissance made any impact in England. But during the first decade of Henry VIII's reign, Renaissance influence began to appear in architecture, decoration, art and other fields. It was Henry who first realised how valuable the sophisticated culture of Italy could be to a king who wanted to be at the forefront of European affairs, and how useful it could be in enhancing his majestas.

The court was the place to be for those who desired royal favour and high office. It was the natural habitat of the nobles, whose ancient right it was to attend upon the King, and it also attracted 'new men', who had made it to the top through wealth or mere ability. In fact, anyone who was smartly dressed, appeared to have some legitimate business or had cash for bribes could gain entry to the court. There were consequently many hangers-on and people who had no right to be there.

These 'strangers' were a constant problem; many courtiers brought with them more servants, relatives and friends than was permitted, and there were also constant edicts against 'rascal boys', who hung about in the hope of receiving tips for errands and messages, and who seem to have posed a particular problem. In addition, 'vagabonds and vile persons' could be aggressive in their demands for work, robbing and intimidating household servants, and trying to pass on stolen goods.[3] When the court moved on, these delinquents would squat in the empty palaces and generally make a nuisance of themselves.

In 1526, the Eltham Ordinances specifically forbade anyone to 'bring to court any boy or rascal';[4] in 1533, 'all vagabonds and other idle persons which follow the court' were given a day to get out,[5] while in 1543, orders were given that no one was to keep any page or boy contrary to the King's ordinances.[6] Strangers were not only a security risk, but they also appropriated food and lodgings to which they were not entitled, thus placing a further strain on overstretched household resources. But it proved impossible to control the problem, because the Serjeant Porter, who manned the palace gates, had a staff of only five Yeomen and two Grooms.[7]

Most people who visited the court came in search of employment, preferment, land, privileges or the patronage of some influential personage. The status and prestige of courtiers depended largely upon nearness to the King. Those close to Henry were therefore in a position to advance the fortunes of less fortunate petitioners, and so extend what was termed 'good lordship' to them. Petitioners could themselves become patrons of those even further from the throne, and thus was formed a complicated web of clientage. Such patronage could be a highly lucrative business, for every favour had its price.

Sometimes, petitioners might be fortunate enough to present their pleas to the King himself at his 'coming forth' from his apartments, or when he was about to go hunting, when he was said to be especially receptive to requests. Although Henry knew that those who came to court were 'desirous both of spoil and glory',[8] he could be prodigiously open-handed, and successive ministers had a tough job curbing his impulsive generosity.

For Henry VIII, the ideal courtier was one who, whatever his rank, offered good service and congenial companionship. Both frequently led to preferment and honours. Personal service and usefulness to the monarch were the chief requirements of a Renaissance courtier and could confer great power and influence, since such courtiers had the King's ear and controlled access to him. Such personal service was often combined with political responsibility, since those who helped the King govern were often among his intimates. However, it was not Henry's policy to delegate responsibility to a courtier who lacked the ability to bear it, however good a friend he might be.

As a result of his constantly changing enthusiasms and shifts of policy, Henry's court was often divided by fluctuating courtier factions dedicated to promoting themselves and their ideas. Unable to confront or oppose the King directly, they used the politics of persuasion to achieve their aims. Charles de Marillac, the French ambassador, wrote in 1540: 'The subjects take example from the Prince, and the ministers seek only to undo each other to gain credit; and under colour of their master's good, each attends his own. For all the fine words of which they are full, they will act only as necessity and interest compel them.'[9]

Henry's successive marriages brought to prominence families of a particular political or religious persuasion, such as the Boleyns, the

Seymours, the Howards and the Parrs. Generally, courtiers in favour could attract parties of supporters. These factions, however, were rarely stable, shifting in composition and opinions, and their existence depended on the current situation or on whoever was chief minister. Nevertheless, they were an essential part of the political process in Tudor times.

In 1528, Baldassare Castiglione's *The Courtier* was published in Italy, enshrining the virtues and qualities of the ideal courtier. Modelled upon Cicero's orator, he would be eloquent, learned, well informed and thus able to influence and manipulate his ruler. He also had to be the embodiment of chivalry and courtesy, a lover of the arts, and expert in martial exercises and sports. The book was based on the ideals of antiquity, and it enjoyed huge popularity, even in remote England, where its influence upon the court was felt almost immediately.

But the ideal was much removed from the realities of courtier life. Sir Thomas More believed that a courtier had no choice but to compromise his moral principles and his honesty in order to survive, a view echoed by the poet Sir Thomas Wyatt, who, while he recognised why people were attracted to the court, cynically wrote of men greedy for gold, buying friends and selling women, betraying friendships for profit and pretending to be virtuous.[10]

At court, wrote Sir Francis Bryan, there was 'overplus malice and displeasures',[11] while Marillac loathed 'the tainted air of the court'.[12] 'Every man,' warned John Husee, Lady Lisle's agent, should 'beware the flattering of the court'; Queen Jane Seymour would ask him to deter his mistress from sending her daughters to a place that was 'full of pride, envy, indignation, mocking, scorning and derision'.[13] The superficial life of outward courtesy, frivolity, luxury and idle pastimes masked deep-seated frustrations, resentment, vicious intrigue, treachery and backbiting. Most courtiers were motivated by greed, which led to intense competition and rivalry.

Life at court could also be routine and boring. There was much waiting and hanging about, and every distraction was welcome. A large number of young men of a military bent unable to find an outlet for their energy and aggression could have caused problems, but Henry ensured that they were provided with many opportunities for sport and feats of arms and a succession of entertaining diversions.

There was great formality at Henry's court, but it was also chaotic, wasteful and hugely expensive to maintain. Continual efforts were made to improve the efficiency of the royal household, with only varying success, yet given the numbers of people present at court at any one time, its administrators managed rather well. In winter it was not unheard of for between a thousand and fifteen hundred persons to be in residence, of whom only about a hundred had access to the King; up to a thousand might be in service in the royal household. Numbers fluctuated depending on the season or the occasion. In the summer, when many courtiers were away at their estates, the court numbered perhaps eight hundred people.

There were probably less than one hundred women at court. Many were the wives and daughters of courtiers, and waited on the Queen. Others visited with their husbands, often for ceremonial occasions. Women enjoyed no formal political role at court, although several did involve themselves in politics and intrigues, as will be seen.

Upon marriage, Henry had assigned to Katherine a household of 160 persons, many of whom were female. She had eight ladies in waiting. Two, Elizabeth, Lady Fitzwalter, and Anne, Lady Hastings, were the sisters of England's premier peer, the Duke of Buckingham. They served alongside the Countesses of Suffolk, Oxford, Surrey, Shrewsbury, Essex and Derby. By 1517, some of these ladies had been replaced by the Countess of Salisbury, Lady Guildford, Lady Maud Parr and Lady Elizabeth Howard, wife of Sir Thomas Boleyn.[14] Sir Thomas' brother, Sir Edward, and his wife Anne, would also join the Queen's household in the 1520s.

Katherine was also attended by thirty maids of honour, among them the Ladies Dacre, Scrope, Percy, Ferrers and Bergavenny (who was Buckingham's daughter, Mary Stafford) – their names a roll-call of the mediaeval peerage. Most of their husbands served in the King's household, creating an intricate network of family ties amongst the chief courtiers.

The other maids of honour included Gertrude Blount, daughter of Lord Mountjoy, and Maria de Salinas, who had come with Katherine from Spain. The daughter of a Castilian nobleman and a former maid of honour to Katherine's mother Queen Isabella, Maria selflessly had shared the tribulations of Katherine's penurious widowhood, shelving her hopes of making a good marriage, and was the lady closest to her, 'whom she loves more than any other mortal'.[15] Maria had also earned the esteem of Henry VIII, who named one of his ships in her honour. Her sister Iñez, who was married to a Spaniard then resident in England, may also have been one of Katherine's attendants. Jane Popincourt, a Frenchwoman, was another maid of honour, who had once served Elizabeth of York and, since 1500, had attended upon Henry's sister Mary. Anne Luke, the King's former nurse, was one of Katherine's chamberwomen.

The Spanish ambassador Luis Caroz dismissed the ladies of the Queen's household as 'rather simple',[16] but her damsels were 'handsome, and make a sumptuous appearance'.[17] Katherine set high standards for her household, but she was a kind mistress and her servants invariably became devoted to her.

The chief officers of the Queen's household were naturally men. At its head was her Chamberlain, the ageing Thomas Butler, Earl of Ormonde, a veteran of the Wars of the Roses. His post was a virtual sinecure, since most of his duties were carried out by Sir Robert Poyntz, who was later appointed the Queen's Chancellor.[18] Sir Thomas Bryan, the Vice-Chamberlain, would later be replaced by Sir Edward Baynton, who would hold this office under all the King's subsequent wives. Katherine had her own Steward and Keeper of her Privy Purse; Griffin Richards, her Clerk of the Signet, had formerly worked for Margaret Beaufort.[19]

There were only eight Spaniards in the Queen's household, among them her secretary, John de Scutea, her apothecary and her physicians, the humanist Ferdinand de Vittoria and Miguel de la Sá. Most of her original Spanish servants had now returned to Spain.

Two devout Englishmen, Father William Forrest and the Observant John Forest, were among Katherine's chaplains. Her confessor (since 1508) was a Castilian Franciscan, Fray Diego Fernandez. By virtue of his position and his mesmeric, forceful personality, he was said to wield more influence over the Queen than anyone else. Because he was also insufferably proud and a manipulative intriguer, he was much vilified by those who feared his hold over his mistress, notably successive Spanish ambassadors, who even expressed fears – before her marriage – that he was her lover. What they really resented was the friar's advice to the Queen to 'forget Spain and gain the love of the English'.[20] But there was no denying the fact that the friar was a notorious womaniser who behaved 'scandalously, in an extreme manner'.[21] Even Henry VII had warned Katherine against him, using 'strong words',[22] but she refused to believe anything bad of Fray Diego. That she was never his lover is borne out by her sworn oath in 1529 that she had come to the King 'a true maid, without touch of man'.[23] Nor would Henry VIII have allowed her to retain the friar if he had believed the gossip. Yet Fray Diego would continue to cause trouble for some years to come.

Many of those at court had to be housed and fed. It was the Lord Chamberlain's responsibility to decide who was entitled to lodgings, meals and 'bouche of court' – a daily allowance of bread, wine, beer, candles and firewood. The rations were allocated according to rank and the season of the year. This privilege was generally extended to the courtiers closest to the King, the great nobles, the chief officers of the household and important servants. Those who were not entitled to it received just their wages or fees.

Numbers at court were swelled by the servants whom the courtiers were allowed to bring with them, in recognition of their status. Each was allowed a number appropriate to his rank: a duke or archbishop might have twelve servants, the Lord Chamberlain ten, and a Gentleman of the Privy Chamber four, while Serjeants and Clerks were permitted just one each. The Serjeant Porter was ordered to forbid entry to any surplus servants,[24] although there is ample evidence that the rules were bent.

The royal palaces were designed to accommodate large numbers of courtiers and servants, and whole ranges were given over to courtier lodgings, as in the Base Court at Hampton Court, which could house forty courtiers,[25] and the Green Court at Knole. Servants usually slept in rooms above their departments. The entitlements to lodgings were laid down in the Household Ordinances, and were the responsibility of the Lord Steward, but in smaller houses it was often a case of first come, first served. Only about a hundred courtiers were entitled to permanent rooms at court, most of them Councillors, peers and the chief officers – in short, all those on whom the King relied for advice and efficient service; the Duke of Norfolk, for example, had lodgings in nine of the King's palaces. When he was not at court, no one else could use them.

The gentlemen attendant upon the King were also entitled to lodgings at court, although when on duty they would sleep in the privy chamber, on call should their master need them.[26] Some important courtiers and officers were given houses within or near the palace precincts, while Cardinal Wolsey was even allowed to stay at Eltham Palace and Thomas Cromwell sometimes had the use of St James's Palace.[27] Other courtiers had homes near the palaces: at Greenwich, several courtiers owned houses in the town,[28] and many nobles had mansions in the Strand, near to Westminster and Whitehall.

Courtier lodgings were of two types: double lodgings had two rooms, each with a fireplace and a garderobe, while single lodgings had just one room with a fireplace. Their occupants were obliged to use the public latrines. All lodgings were meant to accommodate a courtier and his or her servants, so space was very limited. The most desirable lodgings, however small, were those nearest the King's apartments.[29]

While the Office of the King's Works would take care of repairs and maintenance, each courtier was responsible for furnishing his lodging and keeping it clean. Occasionally, the King would help: Henry provided his cousin the Marquess of Exeter with a pallet from the Royal Wardrobe of the Beds and ordered the Office of Works to make him two stools.[30] When, in 1534, Lord Rochford wanted mullioned windows in his lodgings, the King paid to have them installed.[31]

Aspiring courtiers who had not been allocated lodgings had to ask the

King's permission to come to court. The giving or withholding of such permission was a fair indicator of whether or not the supplicant was in favour. The termination of a courtier's right to lodgings was usually an ominous sign; if he was allowed to remain in attendance upon the King, he could face the ruinous cost of paying for accommodation near the court. Banishment from the King's presence was calamitous in the extreme, and meant utter social disgrace: Sir Ralph Sadler told Thomas Cromwell that compulsory absence from court would mar a man's fortunes for ever.[32]

The Comptroller of the Household allocated stabling for courtiers' horses and beds for their retainers: twenty-four horses and nine beds were allowed for a duke or archbishop, three horses and two beds for a chaplain.[33]

To begin with, courtiers were allowed to bring dogs with them, but they caused such a nuisance that in 1526 the Eltham Ordinances banned all dogs except ladies' lap-dogs from the precincts of the court; if courtiers did obtain the King's permission to bring their pets with them, they had to keep them in the kennels provided so that the palace 'may be sweet, wholesome, clean and well-furnished, as to a prince's house and state doth appertain'.[34] Ladies were also allowed singing birds. Other animals, too, were kept as pets: Cardinal Wolsey had a cat, while in 1539 the King was offered 'two musk cats, two little monkeys and a marmoset'.[35] Katherine of Aragon owned a pet monkey, and appears with it in a miniature by Lucas Horenbout.

Henry VIII kept canaries and nightingales in ornamental birdcages hanging in the windows at Hampton Court; he also kept ferrets, although he forbade other courtiers to do so.[36] His favourite pets were his dogs, especially beagles, spaniels and greyhounds; the latter were considered a particularly noble breed.[37] Over the years the King sent hundreds of such dogs, all 'garnished with a good iron collar', as gifts to the Emperor and the King of France.[38] Henry's own dogs wore decorative collars of velvet – only permitted to royal dogs – and kid, with or without torettes (spikes) of silver and gold; some were adorned with pearls or the King's arms and his portcullis and rose badges; his dogs' coats were of white silk,[39] and they had their fur regularly rubbed down with 'hair cloth'.[40] Sixty-five dog leashes were found in Henry's closets after his death.[41] Pet dogs were fed bread, not meat, to discourage them from developing hunting instincts. Two of Henry's dogs, Cut and Ball, were prone to getting lost, and he paid out the huge sum of nearly 15s. (about £225 today) in rewards to those who brought them back.[42]

Henry VIII's court was never as licentious as the court of Francis I of France. By comparison with his French rival, Henry appeared a paragon of virtue, although he was simply far more discreet and, unlike Francis, he sometimes married his mistresses. The fact that Nicholas Wotton, Henry's ambassador in Paris, was so shocked by the behaviour at the French court is proof that much higher standards prevailed at the English court.

The English were not squeamish about sexual matters – in fact, they were frank, outspoken and 'somewhat licentious in their disposition'.[43] Erasmus commented on the fact that the women always kissed a man on the lips when they greeted him, a custom he found delightful. In a court where women were very much in the minority, and most of the men were away from home, some sexual dalliance was inevitable. Yet the King would not permit any open display of wanton behaviour; he commanded his Knight Harbinger to banish lewd women from his household,[44] and foreigners were often impressed by the relative circumspection and dignity of his courtiers. Drunkenness, however, was common.

A double standard certainly prevailed. While fornication and adultery could never tarnish a man's honour – and many noblemen had complicated private lives – women were expected to be above reproach. Some considered the ladies of the English court to be of easy virtue. In 1536, Eustache Chapuys, the imperial ambassador, was sceptical about Jane Seymour's much vaunted chastity: 'You may imagine whether, being an Englishwoman and having been long at court, she would not hold it a sin to be still a maid.'[45] That same year, when the King's niece, the Lady Margaret Douglas, was caught in an illicit love affair with Lord Thomas Howard, an observer commented that it would not have been surprising if she had slept with him, 'seeing the number of domestic examples she has seen and sees daily'.[46]

Foreigners did not rate the court ladies highly: the French Admiral Bonnivet, preparing for an embassy to England, told his gentlemen to 'warm up those cold ladies of England'.[47] In 1520, a Mantuan ambassador wrote disparagingly of the looks and attire of the ladies of Henry's court, and asserted that they drank too much.

The twin cults of chivalry and courtly love, which underpinned court life at this time, often acted as a brake on the passions that could flourish in the hothouse atmosphere of the court. The preferred reading matter of the nobility was works of chivalry and romance, which had proliferated since the invention of printing, and the code enshrined in them governed all forms of social behaviour and infiltrated every aspect of court life, from pageants to the decoration of palaces. Technological advances in warfare meant that the cult of chivalry was in its last flowering, but that was not apparent in 1509.

Henry VIII himself, although a typical Renaissance prince, was passionately committed to the principles of the mediaeval knightly code, and expected his courtiers to be so too. He was fascinated by the legends of King Arthur and the Knights of the Round Table, although it was not until the Reformation that he impressed his imagined descent from Arthur into the service of justifying his definition of England as an empire.

Henry's view of himself as a knight errant had a profound effect upon his treatment of women. Since the twelfth century, the art of courtly love had governed social interaction between aristocratic men and women, and it had enjoyed a revival at the court of Burgundy. A knight was permitted to pay his addresses to a lady who was usually above him in rank and perhaps married – in theory, unattainable. In the elaborate courtship dance that followed, she would be the mistress – not usually in the physical sense – and he the unswervingly devoted servant. He would wear her favour in the tournament, compose verses in her honour, ply her with gifts imbued with symbolic meaning, or engage in conversations rich with witty innuendo. Word-play between lovers was very popular at the Tudor court, with each adopting ciphers comprised of initial letters. When Henry VIII wrote to Anne Boleyn, he often ended his letters with a cipher, enclosing her initials within a heart. Jewellery in the form of ciphers was common.

Simple courtly games such as Blind Man's Buff, Post and Pillar, Prisoner's Base, shuttlecock and fortune-telling had a hidden code of their own in the game of courtly love, while love itself was a common theme in court entertainments, poetry and songs; every St Valentine's Eve, each lady of the court would hold a lottery to choose a partner for the next day, and he was supposed to buy her a gift. Being in love was the fashion, but it was a world away from the realities of the marriage market.

Real affection was not always involved in courtly love, for it was sometimes the lady's favour and kindness, expressed through profitable patronage, that the knight sought to attain. Although physical fulfilment was not its prime object, courtly love was often the occasion for adultery. Henry VIII's courtships were conducted according to its rules, but the King was a man like any other and governed by sexual imperatives.

Katherine of Aragon exerted a civilising influence upon the social life of the court. Her presence pre-empted any vulgar behaviour. She expected her ladies to behave as decorously as she did, forbade any vain amusements in her household,[48] and admitted to her circle members of the older nobility, who provided a counterbalance to the high-spirited young men of the King's entourage. Together with the King, she worked hard to create the semblance, if not the reality, of a virtuous environment.

5

'A Perfect Builder of Pleasant Palaces'

The setting for magnificence was the royal palaces, which were often built on a large scale and deliberately designed or refurbished with a view to emphasising the majesty and power of the sovereign, since any house where the King took up residence became, for the duration of his visit, the seat of government. The royal palaces also provided a suitable backdrop for court ceremonials and space for entertaining and lodging large numbers of people.[1]

Henry VIII was to own more houses than any other English monarch. Most were in London and the Home Counties, while the most important palaces were situated on the banks of the River Thames so as to facilitate easy access by barge to London and Westminster. Many of the other houses were located near the royal parks or chases.

Unfortunately, little remains today to testify to the sheer splendour of these Tudor palaces. The most extensive remains are at Hampton Court, where some of Henry VIII's state rooms and service quarters survive, but even these have been remodelled over the centuries. During the last few years, however, detailed archaeological surveys of some of the palaces have been made, along with several comprehensive studies of the King's building accounts, with the result that far more is known than hitherto about these vanished residences.

In the sixteenth century, there were two kinds of royal house: the 'greater houses', which were the most magnificent and where 'hall was kept', meaning that the whole court could be accommodated, and its servants fed in the great hall; and the 'lesser houses', with smaller capacity, which were often used as progress houses or hunting lodges. Sometimes the King would set up court in one of the greater houses and then retreat with a few companions and servants to a nearby lesser house in search of greater privacy.

From his predecessors, Henry inherited seven greater houses:

Westminster Palace, the Tower of London, Greenwich Palace, Richmond Palace, Eltham Palace, Woodstock Palace and Windsor Castle.

He also inherited seventeen lesser houses. The only one in London was Baynard's Castle. In Oxfordshire there were four houses: two hunting lodges, Beckley Manor at Otmoor, and Langley Manor at Shipton-under-Wychwood, once owned by Warwick the Kingmaker, which Henry VII had rebuilt and often visited;[2] Minster Lovell Hall, confiscated from the Lovell family in 1485, but never used by Henry VIII;[3] and Ewelme, which had been the property of the de la Pole Dukes of Suffolk prior to the last Duke's attainder. In Surrey were Woking Palace and the manors of Wimbledon[4] and Byfleet, the latter once part of the duchy of Cornwall. Collyweston, Northamptonshire, had been a favourite residence of Margaret Beaufort, while Ditton, Buckinghamshire, was to become a nursery palace for Henry's daughter Mary. In Windsor Great Park was Windsor Manor,[5] and in Windsor Forest was Easthampstead Park, a house favoured by Katherine of Aragon and often used by Henry as a hunting lodge.[6] Hanworth in Middlesex was later greatly embellished and assigned in turn to Anne Boleyn and Katherine Parr. In Essex, on the border of Epping Forest, was a small hunting lodge at Wanstead, which Henry renovated before 1515;[7] and not far away was Havering, a dower house of the queens of England, now assigned to Queen Katherine. The King's House at Lyndhurst, Hampshire, was not used by any of the Tudor monarchs, but designated the headquarters of the Warden of the New Forest. Lastly, Tickenhill Manor at Bewdley, Worcestershire, was where Prince Arthur and Katherine of Aragon had spent much of their short married life.

Henry VIII's inheritance also included fourteen mediaeval castles. Berkhamsted Castle in Buckinghamshire had not been used since the death in 1495 of Henry's great-grandmother, Cecily Neville, Duchess of York, and was falling into ruin.[8] Rochester Castle in Kent dated from Norman times, but when the King stayed in the city en route for Dover, he preferred to stay at nearby Rochester Priory. Also in Kent was Leeds Castle, another dower house of the queens of England, and Dover Castle, fortified and refurbished by Edward IV, and boasting luxurious royal apartments decorated with painted royal leopards and fleurs-de-lys; Henry VIII stayed here several times. Higham Ferrers Castle, Northamptonshire, had been owned by the Dukes of Lancaster, but Henry VIII pulled it down in 1533 and used its stones to embellish Kimbolton, whither Katherine of Aragon had been banished. Also in Northamptonshire was Fotheringhay Castle, a former stronghold of the House of York, but now decaying. At Hertford was a Norman castle which Henry VIII would renovate as a residence for his children, believing that the air there was healthy – something he was very fussy about.[9] Warwick Castle, built in the thirteenth century, was – and still is – a massive fortress;[10] Henry never stayed there, but he had the fortifications strengthened. Four miles to the north was Kenilworth Castle, extensively rebuilt in the fourteenth century by John of Gaunt, Duke of Lancaster; Henry V had built there a 'pretty banqueting house of timber' in a moated garden,[11] which Henry VIII demolished, replacing it with a timber 'pleasaunce' in the Base Court.[12] Nothing remains of this today. Ludgershall Castle in Wiltshire dated from the twelfth century, but the King maintained only a small hunting lodge there. The towering fortress of Ludlow in Shropshire served as the administrative centre for the government of Wales; Prince Arthur had died there in 1502. Likewise, fourteenth-century Sheriff Hutton Castle in Yorkshire was the administrative centre for the North of England.[13] Also in Yorkshire was Pontefract Castle, dating from the twelfth century, where Richard II had been murdered in 1400.[14] Much of Sudeley Castle, Gloucestershire, dated from the fifteenth century, when it had been embellished by Richard III.[15]

Henry VIII showed little interest in most of these castles; they were old-fashioned, inconvenient, and largely redundant. He preferred his newer, unfortified residences, with their emphasis on comfort and style.

Henry also owned the remains of the old palace of the Plantagenets at Clarendon, Wiltshire, which was never used by any of the Tudors and was in ruins by the reign of Elizabeth. Another mediaeval palace was that of the Black Prince at Kennington, two miles south of London Bridge. Katherine of Aragon had briefly stayed there in 1501, but the palace was demolished in 1531, and its stones used to build Whitehall. Finally, there were the ruins of the Savoy Palace on the Strand, once a fabulous residence owned by John of Gaunt, Duke of Lancaster, but burned down by the mob in the Peasants' Revolt of 1381 and never rebuilt. Henry VII had left funds for the building of a hospital on the site, but his plans were never carried out. The Savoy Chapel, like Westminster Abbey a royal peculiar, was completed in 1517, but has since been rebuilt.

Henry VIII was 'a perfect builder of pleasant palaces',[16] 'the only phoenix of his time for fine and curious masonry'.[17] Such palaces 'as he erected (for he was nothing inferior in this trade to Hadrian the Emperor and Justinian the Lawgiver) excell all the rest that he found standing in this realm; they are a perpetual precedent unto those that come after. Certes, masonry did never better flourish in England than in his time'.[18]

Henry was very interested in architecture and open to new ideas. There were no architects as such in those days, and most property owners designed their own houses with help from surveyors, master masons and 'masters of the works'.[19] Henry appointed an Italian, John of Padua, to be deviser of his buildings at a wage of 2s. (£30) a day, but it is clear that he was just one of many experts who had a hand in designing the palaces. The names of several other master craftsmen employed by the King are recorded; they were provided with drawing offices at all the main royal building sites, notably Greenwich, Whitehall and Hampton Court.[20] Henry could draw up his own very competent building plans, keeping such plans as well as drawing instruments – scissors, compasses, drawing irons and a steel pen – in his closet at Greenwich,[21] and he would often ask for plans or reports while a house was being built.[22] Sometimes he would visit a site to inspect work in progress, and he was active in managing the workforce. Any workman, be he carpenter, mason, plumber or labourer, could be impressed to work for the King at any time, even if he was engaged upon another project.

The King was a demanding employer. He was impatient to see his houses finished, and often insisted that the men worked through the night by candle-light in order to keep to the punishing schedule he set. He had canvas tents erected over the scaffolding so that work could continue during bad weather.[23] Once, at midnight, he provided beer, bread and cheese to labourers standing deep in mud, digging foundations in wet weather.[24]

During the second half of his reign Henry was to embark on an extravagant programme of building and acquiring property: some of his houses came via Acts of Attainder (which confiscated a traitor's property), exchange or the Dissolution of the Monasteries, while most he purchased. When he died he owned over seventy residences, on which he had spent over £170,000 (£51 million).[25] A huge share of this money had paid for repairs and maintenance.[26]

Henry's houses were built essentially in the English late Perpendicular style with Burgundian-influenced embellishments, such as the use of brick or terracotta. Before long, the impact of the Italian Renaissance would manifest itself in 'antique' ornamental motifs. The chief distinguishing features of the Tudor palace were the multi-storeyed gatehouse with crenellated turrets, bay windows with stone mullions, and tall chimney-pots. Most were constructed on a courtyard, or multi-court, plan, like the Burgundian palaces. Glass was still mainly to be seen only in well-to-do homes and in churches: the proliferation of windows with decorated and stained glass in the King's houses proclaimed his wealth and exalted status.

Every palace was lavishly adorned with the royal arms, heraldic badges, initials, mottoes and other emblems, executed in stone, terracotta, glass and paint in the manner of the period: on the exterior these were to be seen above doorways, on walls and weather-vanes, and in windows. This was the great age of decorated glass; hardly any survives from Henry's palaces, but the evidence suggests that figural glass was restricted to the chapels and that heraldic glass was used for the other rooms.

These motifs were a recurrent theme in interior decoration also, and appeared on jewellery, plate, furniture, fabrics and servants' liveries. Heraldry was an international code, fully understood by the upper classes – Henry VIII was an expert in this field – and in an age when many people could not read, such powerful symbolism proclaimed triumphantly to the world the identity of a house's owner; in the case of the King, it served as architectural propaganda emphasising his ancient lineage and reinforcing the royal image and authority in the minds of his subjects. During this period, it became fashionable for the upper classes to proclaim their loyalty to the monarch by decorating their own houses with the royal arms and emblems, often in anticipation or com- memoration of a royal visit. However, given Henry VIII's frequent marriages, these decorations often had to be changed.

The masons who built the Tudor palaces were English, but many of the craftsmen who adorned them were Flemings – or 'Doche' (Dutch), as they were known – who usually worked as glaziers, and Italians, who were responsible chiefly for sculptural decoration. Foreign craftsmen were greatly resented; they were not allowed to join the English craft guilds, and three Acts were passed in Henry's reign limiting their activities. Members of the royal House were specifically exempted from observing these restrictions, so the King was free to employ whom he liked.

The royal palaces were built to a set plan that changed during the course of Henry VIII's reign in order to meet the King's increasing desire for privacy and his conviction that familiarity bred contempt. Until the fourteenth century, kings had lived, eaten and slept in the great hall and chamber; life had been communal with little concept of privacy. Throughout the fifteenth century, however, these arrangements had gradually changed, as had the design of royal palaces in order to accommodate the changes, and it was now the custom for the King to act out his public role in a series of increasingly elaborate state rooms yet be able to retreat into smaller, more intimate rooms to eat and sleep or enjoy some privacy in the company of his wife or his favoured gentle- men. Even here, however, he was never alone, and his most intimate functions were attended to by his gentlemen. For other courtiers, and to a greater extent for household servants, privacy was an elusive luxury or non-existent.

The King and Queen had separate sets of apartments, often a mirror image of each other, which were known as the King's Side and the Queen's Side. Each included a presence (or audience) chamber, a privy chamber, a bedchamber, and usually further private chambers. Early in the reign, following the Burgundian precedent copied by Edward IV and Henry VII, these lodgings were stacked one above the other in a central donjon. The King's apartments were often built on the south side of the palace, which enjoyed more sunshine.

The King's state apartments consisted of a sequence of three rooms: two outward chambers – the great watching chamber or guard room, and the presence chamber – and one inward chamber, the privy chamber. The outward chambers were public, the inner private. To begin with, these state rooms were accessed from the great hall, and/or approached by a processional or ceremonial stair, and entry to them depended on how much in favour a courtier was with the King. Only the most favoured ever got as far as the privy chamber.

The great hall, although built to impress and sometimes used for large-scale entertainments, served first and foremost as a dining room for the household servants, who ate at trestle tables which were taken down after use. Only during the early years of his reign did the King feast here, at the great festivals of the year. By Tudor times, thanks to the increasing desire of monarchs and nobles for privacy, the great hall was declining rapidly in importance; Henry VIII's magnificent hall at Hampton Court was the last one built in England.

The great watching chamber, or guard room, often led off the great hall. In this room, hung with tapestries and furnished with buffets laden with gold plate, the Yeomen of the Guard stood on duty. Any courtier or servant was allowed to frequent this room, which also functioned as a venue for court entertainments or ceremonies, as a dining room for the nobility, Councillors, ambassadors and chief officers of the household,[27] and as an antechamber for those awaiting an audience with the monarch. There was often a pages' chamber attached to the great watching chamber, where courtiers could put on robes of estate before proceeding to the presence chamber to be ennobled by the King. At night, pages and Esquires of the Chamber slept on the floor of the watching chamber on straw pallets.

A door led from the great watching chamber into the presence chamber, or what we would now call the throne room. It was dominated by a great chair of estate on a dais, surmounted by a rich canopy of estate, which faced the door; no one 'of whatsoever degree' might 'come nigh the King's chair nor stand under the cloth of estate'.[28] This was the room where the sovereign held court, received ambassadors and dined in state. When he was not present, courtiers might frequent the room, but had to doff their caps and bow to the empty throne as they passed. The presence chamber was often the most richly furnished and decorated room in the palace, and certainly the most formal and ceremonial of the state rooms. As Henry's reign progressed, more and more people were permitted access to it, and it consequently declined in importance. As a result, its functions would in time shift to the privy chamber.

The privy chamber, the King's inner sanctum, was separated by a short passage from the presence chamber. Here he conducted his private life, usually took his meals, worked on state business, or relaxed. Access to this room and those behind it was strictly controlled: only the members of the Privy Chamber department and the King's Councillors had right of entry. Others had to wait for an invitation.

The privy chamber was usually a medium-sized room lavishly furnished with vivid tapestries, floor carpets and a chair of estate. In the privy chamber at Greenwich there were also

> a breakfast table of walnut tree, a round table covered with black velvet, a square table, a cupboard of wainscot, three joined forms with three stools, a table and a pair of trestles, a clock, a painted table,[29] a standing glass of steel, a branch of flowers wrought upon wire, three comb cases of bone, four little coffers for jewels, a chair of joined work, one pair of regals[30] with a case, one pair of tables of bone and wood[31] in a case of leather, a pair of gridirons, a fire shovel and a fire fork.[32]

The Privy Chamber was one of the two power centres of the court (the other being the Privy Council). Its staff were the King's intimates; they were his chosen companions and performed every personal service for him, so they were in a strong position to influence political affairs and act as Henry's chief advisers.

Beyond the privy chamber was usually a small complex of inner chambers or privy lodgings which varied in size and number, depending on the dimensions of the palace. Often lined with timber linenfold panelling and therefore somewhat dark, they included at least one bedchamber, a garderobe or 'stool chamber', a 'withdrawing room', a 'raying' or robing chamber, a closet or oratory, and perhaps a study, library or bathroom. These rooms later became known as the 'secret lodgings',[33] and they were usually linked by a privy stair or gallery to the Queen's apartments. The only courtier officially allowed entry to the privy lodgings was the Groom of the Stool, who was head of the Privy Chamber department.

Henry VIII's formal bedchamber contained his massive bed of estate, but he normally slept in a second bedchamber beyond it. At Greenwich and Hampton Court he had a third bedchamber, on the Queen's Side. Each of his bedchambers had a garderobe leading off it, and some also had a study next door. Comparatively little is known about Henry's bedchambers because of the high degree of privacy he achieved.

Most privy lodgings had at least one closet. Closets were used either for storage or for business, or they were fitted out as oratories where the King could perform his private devotions; such a closet at Hampton Court had a painted altarpiece,[34] while the King's 'privy closet' there was used as a study and furnished with cupboards, tables, boxes, chests and a clock.[35] In other closets, curios and objets d'art were displayed in glass cabinets. At Greenwich, one closet had coffers and chests crammed with such items.[36] Closets might also serve as libraries in the lesser houses.

Henry took a keen interest in planning the gardens around his palaces and stocking them with rare and beautiful plants.[37] There were fewer varieties of flowers in England then; roses were naturally a particular favourite, and the damask rose is said to have been introduced into the country by Thomas Linacre, Henry's physician.[38] Among other flowers to be found were lilies, violets, primroses, gilliflowers, columbines, lavender and daffodils, as well as a large variety of herbs which were used in cooking and for medicines. None of the Tudor royal gardens survive, but we know they were formal in design and initially mediaeval in style. The King's privy gardens were usually accessible from his privy lodgings by a private stair, and they were screened by high walls and locked to all but members of the Privy Chamber.[39]

Some gardens had lawns, others symmetrically placed flowerbeds edged with low railings or trellises and divided by a network of paths. Situated at intervals were striped poles bearing sculptures of the King's heraldic beasts; there might be a sundial[40] or trees shaped by topiary. Such a garden may be seen in the background of the portrait of Henry VIII and his family, now at Hampton Court; the setting is Whitehall Palace. One feature of the period was the 'knot garden', with square beds edged with tiles, bricks or box and containing shrubs and flowers shaped into interwoven geometrical patterns, or 'knots'. Henry VII had built such a garden at Richmond with 'royal knots, alleyed and herbed',[41] and thus set a fashion.

In many of his gardens Henry VIII built banqueting houses, as well as fountains, and arbours of brick, stone, branches or trellis, set against the wall. During his reign French Renaissance influence began to manifest itself in the royal gardens, since the King had imported most of his gardeners from France. Soon, Renaissance features such as statues, columns, spheres and urns would be introduced;[42] Renaissance gardens were designed to please the senses and tease the intellect, so many of their decorative features had symbolic meanings. One of Henry's chief pleasures was to walk in his gardens, and in the summer he often transacted business there with favoured ministers.

Many of Henry's palaces were sketched by Anthony van Wyngaerde in the 1540s and 1550s; some were later the subjects of paintings by various artists. Although some of these pictures are now known not to be entirely accurate, they contain a wealth of detail and provide a unique visual record of these long-vanished buildings.

6

'The King's House'

Inside his palaces, Henry VIII lived in unprecedented splendour. The Tudor age was one in which outward show counted for a great deal: if you had wealth, you flaunted it. The interior decor of the period was rich, vivid, even gaudy: the walls, ceilings, tapestries and furnishings of the King's apartments gleamed with gold and bright colours; everything that could be gilded, or shot through with gold thread, was so adorned. Next in importance came silver, then baser metals. The decoration of a room was determined by its status. Everything in the King's inward and outward chambers was carefully co-ordinated to delight the eye and create a magnificent setting.

Henry VIII was determined to be at the forefront of fashion, and as the reign progressed and Renaissance influence grew stronger, the interior decoration of the palaces became increasingly European in style. After January 1516, when the term is first mentioned,[1] 'antique' decoration began to proliferate.[2] 'Antique work' was supposed to derive from the classical art and sculpture of ancient Greece and Rome, but it had a sixteenth-century quality all of its own, and it has been suggested that the word 'antique' (or 'antick', as it was often spelt) should read 'antic', because the style was whimsical and sometimes mischievous in concept.[3]

Henry VIII decorated his palaces and banqueting houses with antique ornament and motifs; such decoration was perhaps out of place in mediaeval buildings, where it sat side by side with heraldic emblems and mottoes, yet it lent Henrician interiors a Renaissance patina and rendered them unique.

One of the most popular types of antique work was 'grotesque' decoration. It derived from first-century paintings discovered in the 1490s in the grottoes (Italian, *grottesco*) on the sites of the Golden House of Nero and the baths of Titus in Rome. Grotesque decoration was highly mannerist, extravagant and often absurd: it took the form of painted or carved borders, friezes, panels and pilasters featuring human figures, flora and fauna, weapons, masks and plates, arranged in a formal yet fantastic composition around a spinal candelabrum.[4] Such work often featured elaborate gilding. The craze for grotesque decoration reached France before 1510, but it was not until the 1520s and 1530s that it became common in Henry VIII's palaces.

The ceilings in Henry's palaces were normally flat and featured moulded fretwork with pendants; some were lavishly gilded and embellished with battens and bosses bearing colourful badges and heraldic devices. Sometimes the ground between the battens was painted or filled in with painted leather-mâché panels, as in the so-called Wolsey Closet at Hampton Court. The Whitehall family group painting mentioned in the last chapter features a battened ceiling in the antique style. Ceilings in large rooms such as halls and kitchens sometimes had exposed timbers.[5]

The walls inside the palaces were mainly of plastered brick; in utilitarian rooms they were painted, while those in important chambers were often clad with the linenfold panelling so characteristic of the age, although it is clear that more elaborate and ornate panelling, often embellished with grotesque motifs, adorned the royal apartments, as may be seen in the Whitehall family group painting. A few rooms had murals or painted grotesque work at the centre of their decorative schemes. Grotesque work also ornamented the pillars flanking the thrones in some of Henry's presence chambers.[6] Many rooms had moulded friezes and cornices. At Hampton Court there was a frieze of putti in the King's Long Gallery; some fragments are still extant.[7]

Most important rooms were hung with tapestry or fabrics, the richest being reserved for the royal apartments. Henry's sets of Italian silk hangings were amongst his most priceless possessions, while at Hampton Court he had hangings of cloth of gold and velvet embroidered with royal emblems.[8] Some hangings were fringed, some lined: they were either hung taut or in folds.

Henry VIII owned over two thousand tapestries,[9] of which about four hundred had been inherited from his father; some were extremely valuable. The display of tapestries denoted great wealth, since they were made of costly silk and wool thread dipped in expensive dyes, and each one took a team of skilled weavers three years to complete. In 1528, the King paid £1,500 (about £450,000 today) for one ten-panel set of tapestries depicting *The Life of King David*.

Twenty-eight of Henry's tapestries survive at Hampton Court. They include the ten-panel set portraying *The Story of Abraham*, which was commissioned by Henry in the 1530s or 40s for the great hall – where it still hangs today; this set, the most expensive in his collection and woven entirely of silk and silver-gilt thread, came from Brussels and is thought to have been based on paintings or designs by the Flemish master, Bernard van Orley. Other sets, including the three panels of the *Seven Deadly Sins* and the four panels of *The Triumph of Petrarch*, had been originally owned by Cardinal Wolsey. Henry VIII also owned four sets of tapestries portraying the story of Esther, and others entitled *The Story of Youth* and *The Seven Ages*, as well as several showing hunting scenes.[10] Armorial tapestries were popular: a Flemish tapestry bearing the arms of Henry VIII is at Hever Castle.

Many early-sixteenth-century tapestries were Flemish; they were usually fashioned by master weavers and combined new classical trends with traditional chivalric themes. In 1515, however, the Italian artist Raphael set a new trend when he designed a set of tapestries, *The Acts of the Apostles*, for Pope Leo X. What was novel about them was the minute detail in Raphael's cartoons, which left no scope for improvisation by the master weavers. Unfortunately, enthusiastic patrons, anxious to follow this new method, often commissioned artists of a lesser calibre than Raphael, with the result that tapestry design deteriorated during the sixteenth century. Henry VIII managed to acquire a set of tapestries copied from Raphael's designs for the Pope, which he probably hung at Windsor Castle.[11]

Before 1542, the King commissioned for his new lodgings at Whitehall Palace another set of outstanding Brussels tapestries on a classical theme, *The Triumph of the Gods*; only two panels survive of the original seven – *The Labours of Hercules*, and *The Triumph of Bacchus*, which may be seen in William III's presence chamber at Hampton Court. Such tapestries, with their Italian mannerist designs, complemented the antique decor in the palace rooms.

Tapestries were frequently changed around, the best being displayed on state occasions; when not in use, they were stored in huge presses: one at Greenwich was fifty-five feet long.[12] The Master of the King's Great Wardrobe was responsible for their maintenance and repair. Tapestries were rubbed clean with bread, then the crumbs brushed away. They were usually hung from hooks and eyes, or nailed to battens attached to the walls.

Painted cloths, which were much cheaper than tapestries, were sometimes hung on the walls of rooms of lesser status.

Window frames and mullions were usually whitewashed, and the window bars painted red or black, as at Hampton Court.[13] Mottoes or heraldic decorations were sometimes carved or painted on the sills or in a border around the window. The windows of the King's inward chambers were hung with curtains or blinds, often both,[14] and some-times with tapestries or carpets. His curtains were chiefly of satin or silk stiffened with buckram; one pair was 'of purple, white and black satin paned together'.[15] The curtains were hung from gilded rings over fixed rods, while tall poles were used for drawing curtains at high windows.[16]

Miniatures in Henry VIII's Psalter,[17] which dates from around 1540, show Italian Renaissance interiors with marbled walls, columns and arched doorways and gaily tiled floors. One picture features a classically styled bed with a blue and gold tester, or canopy, and drapes. It has been suggested that these rooms are the invention of a fanciful artist, but many items – the bed itself, the floor tiles and the X-framed chair – are typical of the period, so it is possible that these rooms did exist, perhaps at Nonsuch Palace, Henry's long-vanished novelty house. The King and his family were depicted in similar classically inspired surroundings by Hans Holbein in his lost Whitehall mural.

The floors in Henry's palaces were either of oak, which might be plastered or painted to look like marble, or tiled. Those on the ground floor were often paved with brick or flagstones. Many rooms were still strewn with 'grise', rushes scented with sweet-smelling herbs such as saffron, in the mediaeval manner. These collected dirt and dust, and sweetened the air, but after a while they stank of the 'leakages of men, cats and dogs';[18] the King ordered the rushes to be renewed 'every eight to ten days',[19] and daily in the presence and privy chambers, but this did not always eliminate the smell, so the house had to be vacated for cleaning. During Henry's reign, it became customary for rush matting to be used instead of loose rushes;[20] the matting was sewn together in four-inch strips and fitted to cover the whole floor. In 1539, Master John Craddock was granted a monopoly for life to provide rush matting for all the royal houses near London.[21] A fragment of such matting was found recently under the floorboards of a former courtier lodging at Hampton Court.[22]

Carpets, usually made of wool or velvet (although the word was also used to describe any strong, durable furnishing fabric), were to be seen on the floors of the royal apartments only; they were also used to cover tables, windows, cupboards and walls. Henry VIII owned over eight hundred carpets, most of them from Turkey;[23] one or two are to be seen in full-length portraits of him. The King also had a large number of oriental rugs, or 'foot cloths', which were often placed in front of chairs of estate.[24] Carpets, like tapestries, were very costly, and therefore potent status symbols.

The royal apartments were heated by 'fire pans', movable charcoal braziers on wheels, or by hearth fires, fuelled by faggots or large logs called 'talshides', which were issued to all those entitled to bouche of court. At Whitehall and at Greenwich there were ceramic wood-burning stoves, which had been used in Europe since the thirteenth century; green glazed earthenware tiles unearthed during excavations at Whitehall in 1939 came from one such stove; they bear the monogram 'HR', which suggests that the stoves were built for the King's use, as does the fact that the expensive sea coal that was burned in them was reserved exclusively for the royal family. The household department responsible for the purchase and supply of coal and charcoal was the Coal House.

Most rooms in the palaces had fireplaces; these were normally flush with the wall and featured a four-centred Perpendicular arch, often decorated, but those in the royal apartments could be grandiosely elaborate. Henry is known to have had Renaissance-style chimney-pieces at Whitehall, Greenwich and Hampton Court. A pair of cast-iron and polished steel gridirons, or firedogs, bearing the badges and initials of Henry VIII and Anne Boleyn were once at Hever Castle, and can now be seen in the great hall at Knole in Kent. Made by Henry Romains, the King's locksmith, they would have been placed on the hearth to support burning logs. In the summer, screens were set in front of the fireplaces; Henry had a screen carved with his arms, with feet fashioned as lions, dragons and greyhounds.[25]

The palace courtyards and stairways were lit by lanterns; torches, or links, were set in iron wall-brackets or on iron cressets on poles[26] in the state apartments,[27] while candles illuminated smaller rooms. Candles were of beeswax, and expensive: those in the royal apartments alone cost £400 (£120,000) a year;[28] they were usually fixed on pricket-type or socketed candlesticks or candelabra, the latter being cross-beamed or wheel-shaped. Some candelabra were suspended from the ceiling, others were free-standing. Candlesticks were made of silver-gilt, iron, brass or latten, and those used by the King might be fashioned in the antique style.

Henry VIII's rooms were lit by quarriers, square blocks of fine beeswax with a wick,[29] while 'salad' oil was used by the King to fuel small oil lamps.[30] Cheaper candles, called 'white lights', or rush lights were used in the palace's lesser rooms and the service quarters. Each morning before nine, the servants would collect all lanterns, unfinished candle stubs and torches in the interests of preventing waste. Candles, wax and tallow were made and stored in the Chandlery, under the supervision of the Serjeant of the Chandlery, assisted by three Yeomen and a Page. Because of the high cost of heating and lighting, the court went to bed earlier in the winter than in the summer.

There was relatively little furniture in Henry VIII's palaces; space had to be made for the hordes of people who came to court, so most furniture was strictly utilitarian. It was generally solid, but roughly fashioned, usually by the Office of Works, and the chief material was oak. Items designated for the royal apartments might be decorated with panels carved with crude mediaeval designs; only after c1540 did Renaissance-style carvings begin to replace them. The Royal Wardrobe was the department responsible for providing furniture for the King's houses.

The finest furniture was naturally to be found in the royal chambers. The most important pieces comprised the furniture of estate used by the King – his chairs of estate, his beds and his buffets. His furniture was sacrosanct: no one else was allowed to sit on the throne, 'nor to lean upon the King's bed, nor to approach the cupboard where the King's cushion is laid, nor to stand upon his carpet'.[31]

Hardly any of Henry's furniture survives, but contemporary sources give some idea of what it was like. His many chairs of estate were made in the typical X-frame design of the period,[32] upholstered in velvet or cloth of gold with gilt nails,[33] and provided with a braided and tasselled cushion and perhaps a footstool. The chair of estate was set on a dais beneath a sparver, or canopy of estate, made of cloth of gold, damask or velvet, with a canopy comprising a tester and ceiler, perhaps trimmed and tasselled with Venice gold;[34] its dorsal, the section hanging down the wall, might be embroidered with the royal arms or cipher and Tudor roses. The King's cushion was carried before him in processions, and any seat it was placed on became a chair of estate – the seat of royal authority.[35] Henry VIII's first Great Seal shows him on a mediaeval throne, but by 1542, when his third Great Seal was made, it was common for his chairs of estate to be embellished with intricate antique carvings in the Renaissance style.[36]

The Queen would sit on a smaller chair, equally lavishly appointed, with a lower canopy.[37] Chairs of any other sort were scarce, and along with a few settles were reserved for those of higher rank. Everyone else sat on stools, in the inward chambers, or on benches, in the outward chambers. No one apart from the Queen sat in the presence of the King, except by invitation.

A person's wealth was often measured by the number of beds he owned: because of their carved decoration and sets of rich hangings, beds were usually the most valuable pieces of furniture anyone could own, and were frequently bequeathed in wills. Henry VIII possessed many rich beds. One at Windsor was eleven feet square and had a gold and silver canopy with silken hangings;[38] a similar bed had belonged to Henry VII. Another was a 'great rich bedstead' inherited from Wolsey: it had gilt posts, four boules bearing cardinals' hats, a tester of red satin embroidered with roses, garters and portcullises, and a valance of white and green. Henry's bed at Hampton Court was eight feet long, and had a ceiler and tester of cloth of gold and silver edged with silk fringes and purple velvet ribbon, as well as purple and white taffeta curtains bordered with gold ribbon.[39]

The King's wives also slept in lavish splendour. Anne Boleyn had a 'great bed' decorated with fringes of Venice gold and tassells of Florence gold,[40] while Jane Seymour slept in 'a great rich bed' with hangings she embroidered herself.[41]

Early in the reign, most of the King's beds were tester beds, with a heavy wooden frame and wooden boards or, after c1525, rope mesh, to support the mattress or feather bed. The tester would have been suspended from the ceiling by cords. During the day, the hangings, which were suspended from rails attached to the wall, would be drawn back and knotted. Sometimes heavy hangings were used in winter, and lighter ones in summer. Later in Henry's reign, the first four-poster beds appeared, and headboards grew taller and more intricately carved and painted; designs included heraldic emblems, ciphers, foliage, figures and medallions. An oak headboard with the painted initials of Henry VIII and Anne of Cleves and grotesque carvings, dated 1539, is in the Burrell Collection in Glasgow, while a carved headboard at Hever Castle bears the royal arms of England and is said to have belonged to Anne Boleyn; these are the only two pieces of furniture surviving from Henry VIII's collection.

Henry's bed coverings were made of the finest materials: his counter-points, or coverlets, were of silk, velvet or even fur. His sheets were of best lawn, and he had woollen fustians, or blankets, and feather bolsters and pillows. He slept on no fewer than eight mattresses, each stuffed with thirteen pounds of carded wool. A wheeled trestle (or truckle) bed was kept under the royal bed. Each evening, it was pulled out for the Gentleman of the Privy Chamber whose turn it was to attend the King during the night.

The King did not sleep in his beds of estate, but used them for the daily ceremonies of rising and retiring. As mentioned earlier, his nights were spent in smaller, less elaborate beds in his privy bedchambers.

Important visitors to court were assigned chambers containing splendid beds; Henry ordered ten such 'rich beds' for Whitehall in 1532.[42] Household officers and servants slept in simple beds or on pallets on the floor.

Buffets for displaying plate, cupboards and sideboard tables were everywhere to be seen in the royal apartments. They were frequently covered with carpets or sumptuous cloths of velvet or tissue.[43] In accordance with Burgundian practice, buffets were usually built in tiers or steps: the taller the display of plate, the grander the owner. Henry

VIII had buffets of up to twelve tiers for use on state occasions, which were guarded by his buffetiers (perhaps the origin of the word 'Beefeaters'). Buffets were used also as sideboards for serving food and drink.

Gold and silver plate – cups, dishes, goblets, chargers (large plates), ewers and salt-cellars, or 'salts' – was one of the most important status symbols of the age. A man's rank and affluence were gauged by his being able to host a dinner without using any of the plate on display. Henry owned 2,028 items of plate,[44] but most of it was later melted down, and only three items from his collection survive: the silver-gilt Royal Clock Salt – a combined clock and salt-cellar – an exquisite example of Gothic-Renaissance craftsmanship, which was a gift from Francis I in c1535;[45] the Royal Gold Cup,[46] once owned by the Dukes of Burgundy; and a gold and enamel crystal bowl.[47] Some of the King's plate was stored in his privy chamber in 'great trussing coffers' covered in leather and lined with 'Bristol red' cloth.[48]

Katherine of Aragon is said to have been bequeathed the Howard Grace Cup, a jewelled ivory and silver-gilt basin; in 1520, she and the King owned gilt goblets with their names engraved around the borders, a gold salt-cellar engraved with H and K and enamelled with red roses, and a gold basin enamelled with red and white roses, which had been 'given to the King by the Queen'.[49] Anne Boleyn's falcon perches atop the antique-style Boleyn Cup which bears the London hallmark of 1535–6.[50]

Of all his plate, Henry particularly prized his clocks, which were luxury items available only to the very affluent. His inventory lists seventeen standing clocks with chimes and 'alarums', which 'strike the quarter and half of an hour'; two were 'fashioned like books' – Katherine of Aragon also owned a clock set in a gold enamelled book – while another was set in crystal and adorned with rubies and diamonds.[51] He also had 'a hanging clock closed in glass with plummets [weights] of lead and metal', clocks that charted 'how the sea doth ebb and flow' or showed 'all the days of the year with the planets, with three moving dials', clocks of antique work or adorned with roses or pomegranates, and a striking clock 'like a heart'. One clock stood on a carved pillar in the privy chamber at Hampton Court,[52] others on cupboards, buffets or wall-mounted brackets. The King paid a specialist clock technician 40s. (£600) a year to maintain all these clocks. Only one survives, a Renaissance-style, gilt-metal bracket clock in the Royal Library at Windsor, which has weights engraved with the initials and mottoes of Henry VIII and Anne Boleyn – 'Dieu et mon droit' and Anne's motto, 'The most happy' – surrounded by lovers' knots. This clock may have been a wedding gift from Henry to Anne. A facsimile is at Hever Castle.

Other items in the royal chambers were not nearly as valuable or as interesting. Early Tudor tables were often basic in design. Sometimes, the table on the hall dais was handsomely carved and a permanent fixture, as at The More,[53] a house Henry later acquired from Wolsey; some were over twenty feet long. Most tables, however, were simply boards set on trestles, which could be taken down after a meal. Heavy fringed tablecloths covered tables in both the royal apartments and the household offices.[54]

Henry VIII's beautifully fashioned portable writing desk survives.[55] It is of stained walnut and gilded leather painted by Lucas Horenbout with the arms of the King and Katherine of Aragon supported by putti with trumpets, figures of Venus and Mars, Renaissance medallions and antique motifs. Lined with velvet, it has a pull-down flap at the front, which is released when the lid is lifted, revealing three drawers; handles are at the sides.

Many items, notably clothes and linen, were stored in oak chests, which were sometimes carved with linenfold panels, foliage or figures. Painted and gilded chests were imported by the wealthy from Flanders or Italy. Master Green, the King's 'coffer-maker', regularly supplied him with chests with drawers, covered with fabric or leather and provided with leather travelling cases.[56]

A vain man, Henry was well provided with 'glasses to look in', which were of polished steel: glass mirrors were unknown. One had 'purple velvet and a passement [braid] of Venice gold set square about the same'.[57] Another, ordered in 1530, was full length.[58] The King's mirrors were hung on the walls alongside his paintings and maps: four were displayed in the Long Gallery at Hampton Court, and fourteen at Whitehall.[59]

Also on display were three rare 'pots of earth, painted, called porcelain',[60] which must have come from Venice, where porcelain had been manufactured since c1470. Thirty-eight items of glass were on show in the King's lower study at Greenwich alone.[61]

Henry's was an itinerant court, as royal courts had been throughout the Middle Ages. The King removed on average around thirty times annually, less in his later years. In the winter he stayed nearer London; at other times he might go further afield or on progress. His moves from house to house, and the length of his stay at each one – which could be measured in days or weeks – depended on several factors: first and foremost were political considerations, followed closely by the King's desire to hunt in his various chases. A house would need cleaning and sweetening after being occupied for a time, or water supplies or locally available provisions might prove insufficient for a longer stay. On many

occasions, the King moved house to escape the plague. Often, he
followed a planned itinerary known as a 'giest', but this could be
disrupted.

The sheer amount of work involved in moving the court from place
to place was staggering. Not only did hundreds of courtiers and servants
have to relocate, but most furniture was taken too; this was arranged by
the Royal Wardrobe. Beds had to be dismantled, tapestries taken down,
clothing and linen packed, valuables safely stored away or transported.
The new house was made ready by the Grooms of the Chamber and
Privy Chamber, who had to have everything in place by the time of the
King's arrival.[62] The house just vacated was left an empty shell, with just
a skeleton staff under the supervision of the Keeper, usually a favoured
courtier who was allowed to reside in the house, or was provided with
accommodation nearby.[63] The official responsible for the smooth
completion of each move was the Knight Harbinger, and he had the
final say as to where everyone was to be accommodated. His success
depended on his acquiring a wide knowledge of the layout and of
previous arrangements at each house.

Most household items were transported on carts, wagons, mules or
sumpter horses, or by boat.[64] Everything was packed in chests or
wrapped in canvas, and watched over whilst in transit by specialised
sumptermen; boar hides were sometimes spread over the baggage to
keep it dry. Other things were left in storage until they were needed:
every house had its 'removing wardrobe', and the greater houses had
Wardrobes of the Beds, Wardrobes of the Robes and Jewel Houses.[65]

The King, like most people, travelled on horseback. Sixteenth-
century roads were generally poor, because it was left to local land-
owners to keep them in repair and many defaulted. Some roads were
mere dirt tracks with potholes, which could be treacherous or impassable in bad weather, and there were so few signposts that in remote areas
(notably the far North) travellers had to employ local guides; even
Henry VII had once got lost between Bristol and Bath. The chief roads
were those built by the Romans, but even these were poorly maintained. An added hazard was the threat posed to travellers by beggars and
robbers. Early in his reign, Henry VIII ordered the building of several
new roads and the repair of important older ones, which led to an
increase in the use of wheeled vehicles. The best roads were those
reserved especially for the sovereign's use, such as the King's Road,
which now runs through Chelsea in London and was once part of a
private road linking Whitehall and Hampton Court. There were half a
dozen of these roads, which provided connections between most of the
greater houses.

The Queen and the ladies of the court would either ride on palfreys or travel in a chair (or chariot) or litter. 'Chairs' were unsprung carriages like gaily painted covered wagons, drawn by horses, and with the coach suspended on leather straps. Such carriages were probably first used in England in the fourteenth century – an illustration of an early example may be seen in the Luttrell Psalter.[66] Katherine of Aragon's ladies rode in one at her coronation.

A litter was a long, box-like structure fixed above two poles, which could be carried by men or horses. An aristocratic mode of transport since the twelfth century, particularly for ladies, it was convenient for use on roads that could not take wheeled vehicles. Litters normally had hooped roofs, or bails, with horizontal pommels, or rods; they were hung with rich curtains or blinds. Litters were frequently used in ceremonial processions. In 1514, Henry's sister Mary owned 'a beautiful litter covered with cloth of gold embroidered with fleurs-de-lys, and carried by two large horses equipped with both saddles and harness, all covered with similar cloth. Inside the litter there are four large cushions covered with cloth of gold, and on the outside this litter is covered with scarlet English cloth'.[67]

Because of the problems encountered in travelling by road – especially through London, where the streets were narrow and congested – the King preferred to travel by barge along the Thames, the capital's principal highway, beside which many of his palaces were located. Henry owned several state barges, which were looked after by the Master of the King's Barge, the King's Barge being a department staffed by a team of Royal Watermen. Henry's barges were magnificent, lavishly embellished vessels: in 1530, the court painter Vincenzo Volpe was paid £15 (£4,500 now) for decorating a new one. Royal barges were large: Katherine of Aragon's had twenty-four oars. Henry's chief barge was called *The Lyon*. Docks and boathouses were reserved for the King's use at most riverside palaces; one was built at Whitehall in 1540,[68] while stone heraldic beasts lined the privy steps at Greenwich.

Members of the nobility with town houses would also maintain barges and watermen; others had to hire barges or pay the London boatmen to row them across or along the busy river.[69] Fares started at 1d. (£1.25 now), but it cost 12d. (£15.20) to get from Greenwich to the City.[70] Henry VIII enjoyed pleasure rides along the river, which was then the habitat of thousands of swans; one such trip took place in 1539, when he took his barge to Whitehall and Lambeth, with his drums and fifes playing, and sailed up and down the Thames for an hour after Evensong.

Because he hated unnecessary disruption, the King would often secretly remove to another house for a short time, taking only a few friends and servants. This small retinue was known as his 'riding household', as opposed to his 'abiding household'.[71] One such visit took place in 1518, when he arranged to meet Cardinal Wolsey privately at Greenwich. Richard Pace, the King's Secretary, informed Wolsey that the King 'desireth Your Grace to command provision to be made there for his supper and yours, for he will depart hence secretly with a small number of his Chamber, without any such persons as should make provision for him'.[72]

Henry VIII was a fastidious man, and obsessed with cleanliness. He waged a constant battle against the dirt, dust and smells that were unavoidable when so many people lived in one establishment. Erasmus was shocked by the filthy conditions in English houses, and there is evidence that many of those who came to court had disgusting habits. Men commonly relieved themselves against walls and in fireplaces; there were frequent official strictures about dirty dishes, tankards and leftover food lying around the palaces and courtyards; and visitors to the royal apartments had to be constantly reminded not to 'wipe or rub their hands upon none arras of the King's whereby they might be hurted' or place dirty dishes 'upon the King's bed, for fear of hurting the King's rich counterpoints'.[73]

Henry and his contemporaries knew of and feared the connection between dirt and disease, although no one was aware of the existence of germs. Infection was thought to be transmitted through bad air or foul smells. Cleanliness was seen as a virtue, but it was very difficult to achieve or impose. Henry VIII issued numerous ordinances enforcing the observance of strict hygiene in the royal residences, but they were not always obeyed, probably because his courtiers and servants did not share his sensibilities.

The Grooms of the Chamber were commanded to keep the royal apartments free 'of all manner of filthiness', and were not allowed to delegate their duties to 'mean persons';[74] they had to rise at six o'clock in order to clean and tidy the King's rooms before he got up at eight. The pages who slept in the guard chamber were expected to rise at seven to help with the finishing touches.[75]

Houses were only cleaned properly when empty; once the court had left, the remaining servants, under the supervision of the Keeper and the Office of Works, would sweep out the rooms, carry away the dirty rushes, and 'dust out all the lodgings within the manor'.[76] They also dusted and washed the panelling and even the ceilings.[77] In the 1540s, Henry employed three permanent staff to keep the vast palace of Whitehall clean during his absence.[78]

Some courtiers clearly had little respect for the King's houses and property, since the Office of Works was constantly repairing or renewing windows, hearths, roofs, floorings, paintwork and locks.

Hygiene in the royal kitchens was the subject of many regulations. After Cardinal Wolsey discovered that scullions were going about their duties 'naked, or in garments of such vileness as they now do', the Clerk of the Kitchen was provided with money to buy 'honest and whole garments' for his staff 'for the better avoiding of corruption and all uncleanness out of the King's house, which doth engender danger of infection and is very noisome and displeasant'.[79] Pissing in the cooking hearths was expressly forbidden at the same time.[80]

Each morning and afternoon, the scullions had to 'sweep and make clean the courts, outward galleries and other places of the court, so there remain no filth or uncleanness in the same', and the Serjeant of the Hall would check that this was done properly.[81] Used washing-up water was to be poured down the drains that led directly into the sewers. Dumping rubbish in the moat was prohibited, as was the feeding of waste food to dogs, for fear of encouraging them; such leftovers were to be set aside for beggars.[82] If the rules were not obeyed, the transgressor would receive an oral warning; upon a second offence, his perquisites would be withdrawn, and on a third he would lose for good his lodgings, entitlement to bouche of court, and even his job.[83]

Conditions in the kitchens were not conducive to hygiene. The overpowering heat from the great ovens and fires and the press of people resulted in sweaty scullions turning the spits, 'interlarding their own grease to help the drippings'.[84] Furthermore, the kitchens and dining areas were continually infested with dogs, cats and rats, who resisted all attempts to scare them away with whips and bells.

Cleanliness was dependent on an efficient water supply, and that was not always available in Tudor palaces. In the Middle Ages, monastic builders had pioneered the supply of running water to buildings. Water had first been piped into a royal palace in 1234, when conduits had been built at Westminster. In the late fourteenth century, Richard II had had running water in his bathroom at Sheen Palace, Richmond, only but this was rare, and even in Henry VIII's reign some royal houses, including Ashridge and Rochester,[85] were served only by wells.

In the greater houses, changes had to be made to accommodate a larger court and meet the King's desire for longer sojourns. Cardinal Wolsey, and later Henry VIII, built such an efficient system of pipes and drains at Hampton Court that it remained in use until 1871.[86] By means of a stunning feat of engineering, the water was piped from natural springs three miles away at Coombe Hill, while the conduits were embedded in the river bed under the Thames. The three Tudor conduit houses at Coombe Hill may still be seen. The supply served the whole palace, and many household offices and even courtier lodgings were supplied with a tap, while the King and Queen had water piped into their bathrooms. The overflow from the cisterns was used to supply fountains, moats and fishponds. Efficient conduit systems were also installed or in place at Eltham, Woodstock, Beaulieu, Greenwich, Whitehall and St James's Palace, and at Nonsuch, Hatfield, Enfield and Otford Palaces.[87] Some of these systems were not very efficient, and were constantly being serviced or upgraded.

In 1533, the King took on a man whose job it was to clean out all the sinks and drains in the royal palaces. Other men were employed to regularly cleanse the moats, which were usually supplied with fresh water and might contain fish for household consumption.[88]

Given the frequent purchases of scents and herbs to sweeten the air that appear in the royal accounts,[89] personal hygiene seems to have been found generally wanting. There were no deodorants, and only the rich could afford perfumes, which came mainly from Italy and consisted chiefly of little balls of ambergris, musk and civet. These were known as 'pomanders', which was also the name given to the filigreed gold balls in which they were carried, which hung from a lady's girdle and could be held to the nose to ward off bad smells.

Soap was expensive, even though it was manufactured in London and Bristol; it was made from wood-ash, tallow or olive oil. Many large households made their own. The best, and dearest, soaps were imported from Venice and Spain. The wealthy classes also used aromatic oils and scented salts in their baths. But most fine garments were made from unwashable fabrics, and must have smelt very stale after several wearings, particularly if the weather was hot. Body linen, however, was regularly laundered, along with chapel and table linen and towels. This was done by the Laundry, a department of the Wardrobe, which was staffed by the Yeoman Launderer and his team of five men.[90] All whites were boiled, then hung by braziers to dry. The laundry at Eltham, with its enormous fireplaces, survives.

The provision of a water supply proves that people did wash, but how often and how extensively is not known. Thorough washing was recommended by many authorities, but taking a bath could be a complicated business, since the wooden bathtubs had to be filled with water, lined with sheets, and emptied afterwards. Fleas, bedbugs and head lice were certainly a problem. To ward off fleas, people put bunches of mulberry twigs beneath their beds at night. Henry VIII always wore a small piece of fur next to his skin to attract all the parasites that pestered him.[91]

Toothpicks were used for cleaning teeth, which were then polished with a linen cloth. A person suffering from bad breath was advised to sleep with his mouth open and wear a nightcap with a hole in it, 'through which the vapour will go out'.[92]

Sanitary facilities at Henry VIII's court of necessity had to be efficient, given the large numbers of people present. Garderobes were provided next to all the major rooms and in the larger courtier lodgings; they were always well ventilated and some could be flushed with water from a cistern,[93] but they invariably began to stink after regular use, and it was at this stage that a house was usually vacated, so that they could be scoured. Garderobes, which had wooden seats, usually emptied into stone cesspits, which had to be 'feyed', or cleaned out, every so often; the poor unfortunate who had to do this was called a 'gong fermour', gong meaning 'latrine'.[94]

In the 1530s, in the wing to the right of the gatehouse at Hampton Court, Henry VIII built his Great House of Easement, a two-storey communal public lavatory with fourteen seats. The waste emptied into the palace's main drain, bypassing the moat over which the building projected, and was flushed away by tidal water from the river.[95] Similar facilities were provided at all the greater houses and at some of the lesser ones.

The physician Andrew Boorde urged that 'piss pots' be avoided because they were malodorous,[96] but stone or lead urinals were installed around the palace courtyards for the convenience of those who might otherwise have used the walls.[97] The painting of red crosses on those same walls was also meant to act as a deterrent, in the hope that no man would desecrate such a holy symbol.[98]

The fact that, eight months after Henry's death, it was felt necessary to issue a proclamation forbidding any person to 'make water or cast any nuisance within the precinct of the court'[99] suggests that standards had rapidly slipped, and that the old King had succeeded to a degree in enforcing certain standards of hygiene.

7

'The Worship and Welfare of the Whole Household'

Since the reign of Edward IV, the royal household had been divided into two separate departments: the Chamber, or the 'domus regis magnificencie' (the King's House of Magnificence), which comprised the 'above-stairs' apartments where the King lived; and the Household (which was different from the 'household', which meant the whole court), formerly the Hall – this was the 'domus providencie' (the House of Providence), the 'downstairs' kitchens and offices that serviced the Chamber and facilitated the display of royal magnificence.[1] The nominal head of the entire royal household was the Lord Great Chamberlain, an office held by successive Earls of Oxford until 1540.

At the head of the Chamber was the Lord Chamberlain. From 1526, his department officially comprised two sections:[2] the Privy Chamber, with a staff of gentlemen, grooms, esquires, ushers and pages, who all looked after the King's personal needs; and the Great Chamber, with a similar staff, which comprised the outward chambers and the Privy Wardrobes.

The Lord Chamberlain was also responsible for all those who worked in the Chamber, such as the royal chaplains, physicians, cupbearers, sewers (who waited at table), carvers, craftsmen, musicians, entertainers, watermen and guards. The Lord Chamberlain could have as many as four hundred people under his jurisdiction; by 1547, about half of them were in posts 'worth a gentleman's having'.[3] Henry VIII's first Lord Chamberlain was his cousin, Charles Somerset, Lord Herbert, an illegitimate scion of the Beaufort family.

The Lord Chamberlain was always an experienced nobleman and Councillor; his role was both administrative and political, for he often advised the King or spoke for him in the Council or Parliament. He was also responsible for arranging court ceremonies. Somerset was assisted in his duties by his deputy, the Vice-Chamberlain; this was Sir Henry

Marney, a Privy Councillor who in 1497 had helped suppress the Cornish rebellion against Henry VII, and had been rewarded with the Order of the Bath at Henry VIII's coronation.

The Queen's Side had a similar organisation, under the authority of her Chamberlain, although it was smaller than the King's and many of its members were women.

The Household was headed by the Lord Steward, who was always a senior nobleman and whose office dated from Saxon times. His legal jurisdiction extended throughout the Verge of the Court – the area, or liberty, within a ten- or twelve-mile radius of wherever the King was staying. Much of his work was delegated to his subordinates – the Treasurer, Vice-Treasurer and Comptroller – on the Board of the Greencloth, the controlling body of the Household, although his post was no sinecure, and he took an active role and interest in the running of his department. George Talbot, Earl of Shrewsbury, whose motto was 'Ready to accomplish' and whose family had a long tradition of service to the Crown, had been Lord Steward since 1502, and would remain in post until his death in 1538.

The Lord Steward was in charge of twenty-five service departments, five hundred staff and vast financial expenditure. He was responsible for the provision of food, heating, lighting and cleaning services for the whole court.

Outside the jurisdiction of the Lord Chamberlain and Lord Steward were other household departments, including the Office of the Revels, the Jewel House, the Office of the Tents, the Office of Works, the King's Barge, the Royal Mews and Kennels, the Royal Ordnance, the Stables and the Chapel Royal.

Given the numbers at court, the prevalent chaos, and the need to reconcile strict limits on expenditure with the outward show of royal magnificence, the household administration was generally managed skilfully and efficiently. It was given two major overhauls in Henry's reign, by Cardinal Wolsey in 1526 and by Thomas Cromwell in 1539, and although frequent ordinances had to be issued against waste, disorder and infringements of the rules, it remained a stable, strongly bureaucratic institution.

The Lord Chamberlain, the Lord Steward and the Master of the Horse were the three 'Great Officers of the Household'; next in importance came the Vice-Chamberlain, the Treasurer and the Comptroller. These six officers all carried white wands of office signifying that they held their authority direct from the King, and were therefore known as the 'White Sticks'. The Treasurer and Comptroller were subordinates of the Lord Steward, and ranked immediately below him. The Lord Steward and his officers occupied good lodgings in the service quarters, where it was customary for servants to sleep and eat communally in or above their various departments.[4]

The office of Treasurer, held from 1502 to 1522 by Sir Thomas Lovell, was first instituted in the reign of Edward III. The Treasurer, 'cherishing the good officer and punishing the evil-doer',[5] was responsible for the purchasing of provisions for the household and for the efficiency of his staff. The office of Comptroller dated from the time of Edward IV; he kept detailed accounts, sanctioned payments, audited returns and managed the Treasurer's finances. Sir Edward Poynings, who had served the Crown in Calais and Ireland, was Henry VIII's first Comptroller.

Each Household department had a Serjeant, Keeper or Master in charge, and under him a staff of yeomen, grooms and pages. Much of the administrative work was done by clerks. Nearly all Household servants were male; the younger ones usually lodged in the palace, and the older ones lived outside with their families whenever possible, since there were few married quarters. The same names occur frequently in the records (Weldon is one), which suggests that a certain nepotism was at play. Nevertheless, all servants were expected to be 'personages of good honesty, gesture, behaviour and conversation'.[6]

Only six women were employed indoors in the Household. Five of them worked in the Laundry. One, Anne Harris (of whom more will be said later), dealt only with the King's linen, while the rest worked for his successive queens.[7] The other female employee was 'the wife who makes the King's puddings',[8] who worked in the Confectionary; her name was Mrs Cornwallis, and the King was so enamoured of her cooking that he rewarded her with a fine house in Aldgate.[9] She was lucky, because female servants were paid less than their male counterparts.

The Household also employed many part-time and casual servants, as well as artists, craftsmen, tailors, embroiderers, silkwomen, masons, labourers, bricklayers, carpenters, plumbers and plasterers. Numbers of gardeners were on the payroll, as well as women who worked as 'weeders in the King's garden'.[10] Master Walsh, a gardener at Greenwich, earned £3.10s. (£1,050) a year; he probably worked on a part-time or seasonal basis. Jasper, a gardener at Beaulieu, earned the same amount quarterly, and supplemented his income with frequent rewards of 6s.8d. (£100) from the King for bringing fresh herbs wherever Henry was staying.[11]

Despite the strict social hierarchy that existed in the royal household, relationships that would have been unthinkable in later centuries flourished. The King took an interest in the members of his Household, and was on good terms with many of them. Between 1527 and 1539,

Richard Hill, the Serjeant of the Cellar, often played cards and dice with his sovereign; the Clerks of the Greencloth repeatedly petitioned the King on behalf of their friends; and when Henry went to war, he took many of his Household servants with him.

Competition for places in the Chamber and Household was often fierce, not only because it was a high honour to be employed by royalty, but also because the conditions of service were excellent compared with elsewhere. Jobs were relatively secure, and a certain status attached to them; there was no official retirement age, and servants could continue to work as long as they were able. It was rare for anyone to be dismissed for misconduct, and although the Lord Steward was commanded by the King to lay off staff who were 'impotent, sickly, unable and unmeet' for work,[12] those affected could make a profit from the sale of their posts (a practice condoned by the White Sticks, even though it was illegal), and would usually receive a pension from the monarch. Most redundancies occurred when a queen consort died, and then those dismissed would receive a quarter's pay. When staff were temporarily off sick, they could receive good 'board wages' in lieu of lodgings and allowances.[13]

Salaries, wages and allowances were determined by the White Sticks, and were listed in a detailed ledger. The King was a generous employer who paid his Chamber staff twice what a noble such as the Earl of Northumberland would have done, and they also received tips on a graduated scale for specific tasks. Household servants' pay was somewhat lower, but could be supplemented by perquisites. Salaries varied surprisingly: the Cofferer earned £50 a year, about the same as the Master of the Minstrels, while a Page of the Chamber got double that 'during pleasure'.[14] There is evidence that salaries rose gradually during Henry's reign. Household servants were paid by the Cofferer, Chamber servants by the Exchequer or the Treasurer of the Chamber. In 1539, the Cofferer was made responsible for paying everyone; in the first year he outlaid £33,000 (£9,900,000).[15]

Most servants had an established right to certain perquisites, which were basically the unwanted by-products or rejects of their departments. Perquisites included candle ends, unbroken meats (that is, untouched food left on the table), discarded saddles and bridles, deerskins, wine casks, lambs' and calves' heads, feathers and giblets from poultry, and dripping from roast meat. These items could be kept for personal use or sold for high profits. There was usually a ready market for them: for example, courtiers not entitled to eat at the King's expense were always eager to buy food.[16]

Servants trained on the job and, provided they proved competent and flexible, had good opportunities for promotion. Promotion was at the discretion of the Lord Chamberlain or the Lord Steward and the Board of the Greencloth, and was usually awarded on the recommendation of a Serjeant or Clerk of the appropriate department. The career prospects were so good that a high-ranking gentleman such as Sir John Gage, who served as Vice-Chamberlain (1528–36) and Comptroller (1540–7), was delighted to secure for his son James the humble post of Groom. James rose quickly through the ranks, and later became a Master of the Household.[17] A scullion might be trained as a cook, and so be set up in a career for life. There is evidence that servants also transferred from department to department,[18] often to their profit. Versatility served one well in the Household.

Servants were required to wear liveries in red or the Tudor colours of green and white, and were provided with two sets a year, for winter and summer. In 1534, Hans Holbein painted a miniature of an unknown man in royal livery, with the initials 'HR' embroidered with a flourish on his red doublet.[19] Privy Chamber servants were distinguished by a livery embroidered with the King's arms and Tudor roses.

Good work practices and conduct were constantly reinforced. Both the King and his Household officers demanded a high standard of service. Servants were to be unobtrusive when in attendance on the monarch, and under no circumstances were they to scratch themselves, pick their noses, blow those noses on their sleeves, spit, belch, 'claw their cods' or breathe stinking breath over their master.[20] Discretion was mandatory: upon taking up a post, every member of the household, of whatever rank, had to take an oath swearing loyalty to the King and promising not to work for anyone else and to carry out his or her duties faithfully and diligently.[21]

Henry himself, with his eagle eye for detail, was a stickler for punctuality. If he gave a courtier leave of absence, he expected him back by a set time, and woe betide anyone who was late. The Clerks Comptroller of the Board of the Greencloth maintained 'establishment lists' of servants and their duties on rolls of parchment, and they would check every day to see that no one was absent and that each person was where he should be; a servant could take leave only with the prior permission of one of the White Sticks. Wages were docked for unauthorised absences. The same lists were used to check whether unauthorised persons were working in the Household. If any were found, the Serjeant at the head of that department would be penalised with the loss of two days' wages if he did not immediately expel the interloper.[22] The Board also prepared an 'ordinary', listing those persons entitled to bouche of court.[23]

Early in the reign, the Scots poet, the black monk Alexander Barclay, author of the satirical *The Ship of Fools*, visited court and came to the conclusion that Henry's servants were under-occupied and lazy:

> They have no labour, yet are they well beseen,
> Bearded and guarded in pleasant white and green.

Some were also careless, quarrelsome, dishonest, dirty and surly.[24] Barclay evidently spent a night in one of the common sleeping chambers, and was appalled by the behaviour of the occupants:

> It is great sorrow for to abide their shout,
> Some fart, some flingeth, and other snort and rout;
> Some buck and some babble, some cometh drunk to bed,
> Some brawl and some jangle, when they be beastly fed;
> Some laugh and some cry, each man will have his will,
> Some spew and some piss, not one of them is still.
> Never be they still till middle of the night,
> And then some brawleth, and for their beds fight.

The Household Ordinances make it clear that stealing was rife, yet few offenders were ever caught. Those serving at table were not allowed to wear cloaks in case they smuggled out food beneath them.[25] The Eltham Ordinances of 1526 forbade courtiers and servants to 'despoil commodities in gentlemen's houses' when the court was on progress, 'because it is often daily seen that, as well in the King's own houses, as in the places of other noblemen and gentlemen, locks, tables, forms, cupboards, trestles and other household implements be purloined and taken away, to the King's great dishonour'.[26] Even the nobly born, it appears, were no respecters of property.

The Board of the Greencloth, which was to be found in the Counting House, was the chief governing body of the Household. It was so called because its officers sat around a table (or board) covered with a green baize tablecloth. Since the reign of Edward IV, the Board had maintained 'the worship and welfare of the whole household',[27] and it had its own coat of arms depicting a key and a white rod on a green background. At Hampton Court, the Counting House was housed in the room directly above the entrance to the service complex, which is to the left as one faces the main gatehouse; its windows afforded a good view of the comings and goings in the court below. Similar arrangements were in place at other palaces.

The Board of the Greencloth was responsible for administration, finance, personnel, discipline and provisioning.[28] At least one of the White Sticks had to be present at the Board's daily meetings, with two or three Clerks of the Greencloth to assist him.[29]

Much of the work was done by the Cofferer – under Henry VIII, this office was first held by John Shurley – who received money allocated to the Household, issued advances to purveyors, settled their accounts and paid out wages. He had to keep weekly records of expenditure, based on daily figures supplied by the Serjeants of the various departments, and make quarterly returns. It was the job of the Clerks to visit the larders and kitchens daily and check the stores.

Henry had to dig deep into the wealth left by his father in order to finance his court and household and maintain the degree of magnificence appropriate to his position as King. Before long, his inheritance was spent. The annual revenues of the Crown remained stable, thanks to fixed rents and dues, at about £100,000 (£30 million) throughout the reign. Consequently, rampant inflation and rising prices caused by Henry's wars and the demands of a growing population made inroads into the royal finances. Out of their income, Tudor monarchs had to fund all the expenses of government and administration, yet throughout the period the cost of maintaining the court was enormous, amounting to about one third of the royal income. That there was no criticism of this underlines the unquestioning acceptance of the majestas of the sovereign.

The King sought to solve his financial problems by twice devaluing the coinage, in 1526 and 1539, by borrowing, and by purchasing property in order to increase his income from rents. Both Wolsey and Cromwell brought in measures to reduce wastefulness in the royal household, but to little avail. Henry was to die in debt.

The Chamber had two financial departments. The Treasury of the Chamber had originally been a chest containing money for the King's private use, but by Henry VIII's time it had become an important financial department receiving the bulk of the royal revenues and funding many of the King's wide-ranging interests and commitments, such as state affairs, tournaments, wages, tips, gambling debts and offerings at shrines. The Treasurer of the Chamber, initially Sir John Heron, was in charge of these funds.[30] The King's Privy Purse, which was equally, if not more, important, was the responsibility of the Groom of the Stool, who was head of the Privy Chamber; its funds were used for royal enterprises such as maintaining palaces or purchasing plate, jewels and tapestries.[31]

The third financial department of the court was the Great Wardrobe, which had been its chief treasury since the fourteenth century. In 1445, it had been established at Baynard's Castle in London, where were stored furnishings, fabrics, clothing, liveries and the finery needed for ceremonial occasions. The Keeper of the Wardrobe was responsible for purchasing these items, keeping them in repair, and issuing them to the court when needed. The Offices of the Revels and the Tents came under his jurisdiction.

Security was somewhat lax at court. The King was an exalted being, but he remained very accessible to his subjects. Renaissance monarchs were supposed to be highly visible, and this often precluded taking strict security measures. Yet certain precautions were in place.

Entry to the court was controlled by the Serjeant Porter, who kept watch at the service gate for unauthorised persons or servants attempting to smuggle out stolen goods or provisions. He and his staff searched the palace three or four times a day to make sure that no 'vagabonds, rascals or boys' had slipped in unnoticed.[32] The Porter carried a staff of office, signifying his authority, and was provided with a small pair of stocks in which to restrain offenders.[33] He himself could be fined or lose wages if he was lax in his duties.

The Yeomen of the Guard, armed with fearsome gilt halberds, swords and silver breastplates, would be lined up along the walls of the great watching chamber, guarding the entrance to the royal apartments around the clock. Founded in 1485 by Henry VII, the Yeomen of the Guard were the sovereign's permanent personal bodyguard, under the command of their Captain (who was the Vice-Chamberlain, Sir Henry Marney), and responsible for keeping the King safe at all times. They were of yeoman birth, and had to be 'good archers, hardy, strong and of agility'.[34] Most were chosen for their size and strength: 'They were all very handsome, and by God, they were like giants!' exclaimed a Venetian envoy in 1515.[35] Wherever the King went, they lined the way. During the Field of Cloth of Gold, when he approached, they cleared the crowds 'by force. Drawn up in broad ranks on this side and that, the glittering guard of King Henry makes a wide path, 200 halberd-bearers in all, gleaming with gold'.[36]

In time of war, the Yeomen of the Guard were divided into two sections, archers and mounted halberdiers. Their numbers fluctuated: Henry VIII increased the Guard from three hundred to six hundred for his French campaign of 1513; in 1526 their numbers, which had fallen to about two hundred, were reduced to a hundred. By 1547, there were 150 of them.[37] Twelve members of the Yeomen of the Guard were permanently stationed at the Tower of London, and were called Tower Warders (the name Beefeaters does not occur until the seventeenth century).

The earliest picture of a Yeoman of the Guard appears on an Anglo-French treaty of 1527:[38] he wears the original green and white striped velvet tunic[39] embroidered back and front with the crowned Tudor rose, 'with spangles of silver and gilt' and goldsmiths' work.[40] Each guard had three changes of livery: one for state occasions (just described), a similar everyday livery made of cheaper cloth, and a 'russet' livery, which may have been worn for the night watches. The famous scarlet livery was first introduced in 1514, and replaced the green and white tunics around 1530.[41]

In 1509, Henry VIII instituted another troop of royal guards, the Band of Gentlemen Pensioners or 'Gentlemen of the Spears', a mounted bodyguard armed with spears and lances, whose duty it was to look to his safety on the field of battle, at court and on ceremonial occasions. The King seems to have copied this idea from Louis XI of France, who in 1474 had founded the 'Gentilhommes de l'Hôtel du Roy ou Pensionnaires'.[42] Unlike the Yeomen of the Guard, who were cheaper to maintain but not so prestigious, the fifty Gentlemen Pensioners were of aristocratic birth; they were highly paid,[43] better armed, with swords, halberds, battleaxes and poleaxes, and had to provide three servants each. They wore the fine clothes of gentlemen; the chronicler Edward Hall once saw them dressed in cloth of gold and mounted on horses caparisoned with the same. Full training was given to recruits as yet 'unexercised in the feat of arms'.[44] Their first Captain was Henry Bourchier, Earl of Essex, and their first Lieutenant Sir John Pechy.

Every door in the King's apartments was fitted with a lock made by the royal locksmith, Henry Romains.[45] The King himself held one master key, and an appointed officer another. The Groom of the Stool, as head of the Privy Chamber, held a full set. There were two locks on the door of the wine cellar, and on the door of the room at Hampton Court where the King stored his paintings.[46] The Queen held her own privy keys. Occasionally, Romains was ordered to change all the royal locks.[47] When Henry went on progress, he took with him a portable lock for his bedchamber door, and Romains went too, to fit it. One such lock survives; originally at Beddington Park, it bears the royal arms and a Tudor rose and is now in the Victoria and Albert Museum; a facsimile is at Hever Castle.

Every gentleman considered it his right to carry a sword, and honour demanded that insults or 'proud and opprobrious words'[48] be met with a challenge. Although there is little evidence of duelling, violence did break out at court from time to time, and occasionally the King himself intervened, declaring 'he would have no grudge among his gentlemen'.[49] Below stairs, there were frequent fights.

Because violence occurring in such close proximity to the King constituted a serious threat to his safety, Parliament imposed ruthless penalties. A man who struck another and drew blood within the Verge of the Court could be sentenced to a fine, imprisonment and the loss of his right hand. In 1542, one Collins, a gentleman, was hanged for committing manslaughter within the Verge of the Court,[50] and on another occasion three servants found guilty of murder were hanged in their royal livery, as a deterrent to others. Young men indulging in unwise excesses of high spirits might find themselves under house arrest or in prison for a time. Prostitutes working near the royal palaces did a roaring trade; one courtier, who acted as a pimp, jokingly suggested that the King reward him for his services with a patent.

It was the duty of the Knight Marshal and his team of Provost Marshals to expel 'all such common women as follow the court' and to patrol the palace and deal with troublemakers. They were dealt with by the Lord Steward's court and either fined or sent to prison. Swearing, drunkenness, 'haunting bad houses', fighting and drawing graffiti – huge penises were a favourite – on the palace walls were all punishable by warnings, loss of wages, one month's imprisonment or dismissal.[51]

The King's valuables – jewellery, plate and money – were stored either in the palace's Jewel House or in the privy coffers in his lodgings.[52] The Master of the Jewel House was responsible to the King for the security of the treasures deposited with him, which were locked in strongboxes called 'standards'[53] behind barred windows. Yet not all Jewel Houses were very secure: that at Hampton Court was by the service gate. The King therefore stored only lesser articles there, and kept his more precious belongings in his coffers.[54]

8

'Such Plenty of Costly Provision'

Feeding the court resembled a major military operation. This was catering on a vast scale, for everyone who lodged at court was entitled not only to bouche of court but also to three cooked meals each day. The court consequently consumed gargantuan quantities of food. In a single day in 1532, when the King and just his travelling household were en route to Calais, they polished off 6 oxen, 8 calves, 40 sheep, 12 pigs, 132 capons, 7 swans, 20 storks, 34 pheasants, 192 partridges, 192 cocks, 56 herons, 84 pullets, 720 larks, 240 pigeons, 24 peacocks and 192 plovers and teals.[1] Not surprisingly, it cost the equivalent of over £6 million a year to feed the whole court.[2]

Each of the royal palaces had its kitchen complex: that at Hampton Court, which was typical of the period, occupied one third of the palace area,[3] and much of it survives today.[4] The policy of magnificence required bigger and more sophisticated facilities than hitherto. Henry VIII's great kitchens had vast ovens, roaring fires and several charcoal stoves; they were hot, smoky and noisy, and when operating at full stretch resembled 'veritable hells'.[5] The Great Kitchen comprised the 'hall place' kitchen, which prepared food for the Household, and the Lord's Side kitchen, which supplied finer dishes for Household officers and courtiers; the separate King's and Queen's privy kitchens served the choicest food of all. The larders supplying raw food were at one end of the Great Kitchen, and finished dishes were brought to the 'bars' or stone hatches at the other, where they were checked by the Clerk of the Kitchen and garnished for the table, then passed to the servitors queuing in the 'Great Space' beyond.[6]

Dirty dishes were washed in the Scullery in great pans set on iron trivets or brick boilers; lye made from wood-ash was added to the water, and every item was supposed to be scoured with a cloth,[7] but Andrew Barclay believed that the cups for the hall were scrubbed clean only once a year, for they were 'old, black and rusty', with such foul slime coating the bottom that it was conceivable they had been used as pisspots. It is worth mentioning, however, that there is no evidence of any large-scale outbreaks of food poisoning at the Tudor court.

The Scullery also supplied and maintained all kitchen utensils and equipment; replacing or repairing broken items could cost over £66 (nearly £20,000) a year.[8]

The Clerk of the Kitchen, who was in charge of all the kitchens, had to be an expert manager of staff and resources, and capable of working under tremendous pressure. He held the keys to the stores, distributed food as it was needed, and made out accounts for the Board of the Greencloth. He also had to ensure that 'the King's dish be of the best and sweetest stuff that can be got, and in like wise for every estate, according to their degrees'.[9] In return, he was permitted to eat the same food as was served to senior courtiers.[10]

The Clerk was assisted in his duties by three Master Cooks, who were important personages in the Household hierarchy and lorded it over the Great Kitchen and the King's and Queen's privy kitchens. They planned menus, giving due regard to the different diets for each rank and the requirements of feast and fast days, and each had a staff of perhaps twelve assistant cooks and twelve 'galapines', or scullions, to help prepare the food; the Master Cooks only did the more fancy cooking. Henry VIII also had a French cook, Pero Doux, working in his privy kitchen as 'the Yeoman Cook for the King's Mouth', earning £23.16s.8d. (£7,150) a year. He worked alongside the King's Master Cook, John Bricket, who was responsible for all the royal kitchens and received several valuable grants from his master.[11] The King's cooks wore white linen aprons, and were respected professionals capable of serving excellent cuisine of the highest order.

There were three teams of kitchen staff: one for the Great Kitchen and its subsidiaries, and one each for the privy kitchens. There could be between 180[12] and 350[13] people working in the kitchen complex at any one time, including 33 young boys[14] and various specialist craftsmen. Fifty people worked in the Great Kitchen, the largest service department. Most of them took their meals there, and slept there at night, on straw pallets.[15]

The service complex was built around a number of courts, off which were found the various Household departments. There were sixteen subsidiary kitchen offices, each under a Serjeant, who might supervise up to twenty-one members of staff, including a clerk and purveyor. These offices comprised the Bakehouse, Cellar, Acatery, Pastry, Scullery,[16] Larder, Pantry, Spicery, Saucery, Buttery, Wafery, Confectionary, Boiling House, Scalding House, Poultry, Ewery or Napery, and Pitcher House.

The Bakehouse provided bread for the whole court. In an age before potatoes, rice or vegetables were served as accompaniments to meat, bread was a staple of every meal. High-quality wheat came from the royal estates, or by purchase, and was cleaned and sieved in the King's granaries. The wheatmeal was delivered to the Bakehouse for making two hundred 'cheat' loaves each day; this was the bread most commonly used by the court. Some of the wheatmeal was finely sieved for making seven hundred white 'manchet' loaves daily for the upper courtiers; these loaves resembled small rolls. John Wynkell, the Yeoman Baker for the King's Mouth, who worked in the privy bakehouse, made the finest manchet loaves of all for his royal master.[17]

Even though fresh spring water was piped into the palaces, it was not thought safe for human consumption,[18] so most people drank ale, beer or wine; the Cellar outlaid a massive £3,000 (£900,000) each year on alcoholic beverages. The Serjeant of the Cellar, William Abbott,[19] was in charge of three departments – the Cellar, the Buttery and the Pitcher House. At Hampton Court, the great cellar, which supplied the court, was underneath the great watching chamber; next door was the vaulted privy cellar, built in 1536 and used for storing the King's own wine.[20] The barrel racks are still there today.

Ale was the staple drink, and the 600,000 gallons drunk each year by the court came from the royal breweries, but during Henry's reign beer, initially imported from Flanders, gained in popularity despite the King's efforts to ban it. But the hops his brewer was forbidden to use preserved beer for longer, whereas ale rapidly deteriorated. Neither drink was very potent. At court, ale was served in leather jugs at the Buttery hatches.

Wines were imported from all over Europe, especially Anjou, Gascony and Burgundy; over 120 varieties were known. Wine was a gentleman's drink, bought by the barrel, not bottled; a barrel might contain 105 or 205 gallons. The King spent a fortune on wines: £700 (£210,000) on claret alone in 1526, and £844 (£253,000) on Bordeaux wines in 1528,[21] while the court consumed three hundred barrels of wine a year. Many sixteenth-century wines did not keep well; those that did often had a higher alcohol content than today (up to 17 per cent). Wine was very much a status symbol, an essential adjunct to polite society. Sweet, strong wines, such as Osney from Alsace were very popular, as was hippocras, a warm, richly spiced, sugared red wine which was served at the end of banquets.[22]

Under strict security, wine was drawn off from the barrels, then taken in leather jugs up from the Cellar to the Buttery (French, *boutellerie*), which was usually at the lower end of the hall.[23] Here, the Butler and his staff would decant it into pitchers supplied by the Pitcher House. The Pitcher House also distributed silver plate, goblets and other vessels.[24] Each day, the Yeomen of the Pitcher House had to collect the jugs and goblets left in the chambers of those who had taken drinks to bed.[25] Next to the Buttery was the Pantry (from *panis*, Latin for bread), where bread from the Bakehouse was stored in wooden chests called 'arks', along with table linen and candles. The Pantler's duty was to lay the tables in the hall and slice the loaves.

All food eaten in Tudor times was organic, but much of it was available only on a seasonal basis. Refrigeration was unknown, so perishable stuffs had to be supplied on a daily basis. Food was stored in the Larders, mainly in barrels. The greater houses had wet larders, dry larders and flesh larders; at Hampton Court, they all led off Fish Court. It was understood that raw and cooked foods should be kept separate. The wet larders were used for storing the numerous varieties of fish, and had their own cisterns. The court's chief contractor for fresh sea fish was Thomas Hewyt of Hythe, Kent,[26] while at several palaces there were moats and fishponds containing freshwater fish such as carp and bream; the three fishponds at Hampton Court occupied the site of the present Pond Gardens, whose walls date from 1536.

A wide range of raw game was hung in the well ventilated flesh larders, and the amount required for the next day was cut every evening for issue to the kitchens after 5 a.m. Venison, which came from the royal deer parks, was hung for up to six weeks before it was eaten;[27] it was a high-status meat, reserved for royalty and their guests. General provisions were kept in the dry larders. The Serjeant of the Larder would inspect all food as it arrived.[28]

The purchase and storage of perishable goods such as meat, cheese, vegetables and eggs, which were known as 'achates', was the responsibility of the Acatery (from which derives the word 'cater'). Vegetables were mostly imported from Flanders, and the King employed a Flemish gardener to grow his salad vegetables, which were often eaten cooked, with sugar, oil and vinegar. During Henry's reign vegetables gained in popularity, after having been regarded as a poor man's food for a century.[29] The King was especially fond of artichokes, which were grown in his gardens.[30]

The Poultry, which was usually some distance from the palace, supplied poultry, lamb and mutton. At Hampton Court, there was also a pheasant yard. The birds were slaughtered by the staff of the nearby Scalding House, who then plunged the carcasses into huge vats of boiling water preparatory to plucking them.

Meat made up the bulk of the daily diet. Most meat for the court was boiled, or roasted on spits. Seven boys were employed to turn the spits, and were given extra rations of ale to help keep them cool. Each kitchen had an adjacent Boiling House with a huge copper cauldron, set over a furnace, for cooking beef[31] for pies or stews and making stock for pottage; the cauldron at Hampton Court held eighty gallons, enough for eight hundred meals.[32] Sometimes meat or fish was fried in skillets or broiled on gridirons.

Several kitchen offices were staffed by specialists. The Pastry, which had four great ovens – at Hampton Court, the largest was twelve feet in diameter – made hundreds of raised pie crusts, or 'coffins', and tart cases. Most were of wholemeal or wheatmeal flour, but the King's pastry was concocted from the best unbleached white flour. The Pastry also made him enormous pasties containing whole sides of venison.[33]

The Serjeant of the Pastry was also in charge of the Saucery, which made mustard and a variety of garnishes and sauces. Many sauces were flavoured with herbs, vinegar – which was made by the Cellar from 'feeble or dull wines'[34] – or verjuice, the juice from sour crab apples,[35] which was the main product of the few English vineyards remaining in the sixteenth century.

Spices were used in both cookery and medicines, but most came from the Mediterranean and were very expensive, so their use was restricted to the upper ranks. They would be ground by the Yeoman of the Spicery using a pestle and mortar, and distributed where needed in the kitchens. The Spicery also bought and stored loaves and cones of sugar – another costly commodity – and fruit from the royal orchards,[36] two of which were at Hampton Court.

There is plenty of evidence that Henry VIII loved fruit. His orchards supplied a rich yield of pears, apples, plums, damsons, cherries and strawberries – the last two were particular favourites of the King and Anne Boleyn[37] – and in 1533 the royal gardener, Richard Harris, established a market garden at Tenham Manor, Kent, which supplied fruit to the court. Citrus fruits were costly and rare, as they had to be imported from Spain; Katherine of Aragon was instrumental in popularising oranges in England. Henry loved them, especially in pies and preserves; in 1534, he bought an orange strainer. Peaches were grown at Richmond, and it was Henry who late in his reign introduced apricots into England, in the gardens of Nonsuch. People often brought him gifts of fruit – pomegranates, apples, pears, grapes, dates, even an orange pie and a melon.[38] Raw fruit was believed to cause fevers, so it was usually served cooked in tarts, or dried, or made into preserves. Fruit might to served to important courtiers only at the beginning and end of meals, or as a dressing for meat or fish, or simply eaten as a snack.[39]

The Chief Clerk of the Spicery also supervised the Confectionary, Wafery, Ewery, Chandlery and Laundry. Sweet dishes and comfits such as marchpane,[40] gingerbread and Henry's favourite quince marmalade, a preserve so thick it could be sliced, were prepared in the

Confectionary,[41] where the cooks had to have artistic as well as culinary skills. In 1517, when the Papal Nuncio was entertained by the King, he was impressed by the 'jellies of some twenty sorts made in the shape of castles and animals' by the Confectionary.[42] The King was particularly fond of jelly made with hippocras. Sugar could cost up to 1od. (£12.50) per pound, so most confections were luxury items produced for the royal table or for banquets. Sweet wafer biscuits stamped with the royal arms were made exclusively for the King and senior courtiers by the Wafery.[43] These wafers were usually served with hippocras at the end of a banquet.

Tablecloths, napkins, fingerbowls and ewers were bought, stored and issued daily by the Ewery, a department sometimes referred to as the Napery. The basins and ewers were normally of silver gilt, whilst the royal napery would be of the finest linen damask, often embroidered with silver or gold thread. Tablecloths were changed at least twice a week, or sooner if they became grubby.[44]

The ancient royal right of purveyance, or 'prise', meant that the King was allowed to buy food on demand at prices fixed at a lower rate than normal. His purveyors not only seized upon the choicest goods at markets, farms and ports, but also commandeered horses and wagons to transport the goods. They did not pay in cash, but issued receipts, which could only be redeemed by the hapless vendor in person at the Board of the Greencloth, often putting him to considerable inconvenience and expense. The royal purveyors were consequently very unpopular, especially in the south-east where the court was usually based, and the system was open to abuses and corruption. Thomas Cromwell tried to improve it in 1539, insisting that vendors be paid in cash and making each county responsible for supplying its quota of goods at the 'King's price', or for paying taxes to make up for any shortfall, but it was a long time before the new arrangements came fully into force, and there were still many complaints.[45]

In the greater houses, about six hundred lesser members of the household ate in the great hall, which at Hampton Court could hold as many as three hundred at a sitting; in the lesser houses, there were outer guard chambers which served as dining rooms. About 230 officers and servants took meals in their own departments.

The senior officers of the household, the nobility and the Gentlemen of the Privy Chamber ate in some style off silver dishes at tables set up in the great watching chamber. Privy Councillors had the right to dine in the council chamber. All were served by Gentlemen Ushers, Sewers, Grooms and Pages of the Chamber, who ate what was left after their betters had departed.[46]

By the sixteenth century, people of high rank preferred to dine in privacy and comfort, rather than presiding over their household. The King normally took his meals in the privy chamber, or, if he was entertaining guests, in greater state in the presence chamber. There were frequent, obviously unsuccessful injunctions against courtiers eating their meals in their lodgings or 'in corners and secret places',[47] or entertaining guests at the King's expense, which caused endless problems for the kitchens. The Clerk of the Kitchen kept detailed records of where and what each person should be eating, and made regular checks that everyone was where he was supposed to be. Only the Lord Chamberlain, the Vice-Chamberlain, the Captain of the Guard and the Lord Steward were allowed to take meals in their own lodgings.

Breakfast, comprising bread, meat and ale, was served around 7 a.m.; dinner, the main meal of the day, was between 10 a.m. and 1 p.m., and supper between 4 and 7 p.m. An evening snack, called 'all night', was distributed around 8 to 9 p.m.[48] Dinner and supper consisted of two courses with a prescribed number of dishes at each.

What a man ate was an outward manifestation of his rank. The number of dishes and type of food served to each person differed according to degree, being determined by sumptuary laws and the dietaries laid down in the Household Ordinances: the Lord Chamberlain got sixteen dishes at dinner and eleven at supper, whilst Household servants received four at each.[49] The Gentlemen of the Privy Chamber enjoyed a rich daily diet consisting of beef, mutton, veal, capons, conies, pheasants and either lamb, pigeon or chicken, followed by tart, butter and fruit.[50] Smaller, cheaper portions of meat were served to servants, as well as bowls of that Tudor staple, pottage, which was meat stock thickened with oatmeal or barley and seasoned with salt, vegetables and herbs.[51]

The poet Alexander Barclay complained bitterly about the food served to the lower ranks; while he and his companions 'gnawed' on brown bread and cheese, 'as hounds ravenous', they had to watch 'dainteous dishes' destined for their superiors' tables being carried past them:

> To see such dishes and smell the sweet odour,
> And nothing to taste, is utter displeasure.

Occasionally, as a sign of favour, lords would send down choice morsels to their servants, which Barclay says caused 'great anguish and torment' to those not so favoured. Even if one was lucky, such 'scraps' did not

> . . . allay thy hunger and desire,
> But, by their sweetness, set thee more on fire.

Rank and precedence also dictated where a person sat at meals. Tables were usually arranged in a U-shape, with the top table being set on the dais. This was where the most important people sat, 'above the salt', with the persons of highest estate occupying chairs; the ceremonial salt-cellar, or nef, was always placed to the right of the most important person present. Those on the lower tables were seated according to their degree, with the lowliest at the far end.

If important guests were present at meals, the menu would be more lavish in their honour, and appropriate to their rank, not to that of the host. The Dukes of Burgundy had elevated the art of dining into a powerful status symbol, and much of what was produced by the royal kitchens was beautifully presented and designed to impress visitors. Food might be gilded with gold or silver leaf, or painted with edible natural dyes; taste was not a priority. Some food was even scented with musk or ambergris, and rosewater was a common ingredient.

At every mealtime, trestle tables were set up and spread with cloths, which were then strewn with herbs and flowers to purify the air. In the Chamber, each diner's place was set with a silver or perhaps pewter[52] trencher, a spoon, goblet and sauce bowl, manchet loaves wrapped in a napkin, and a flagon of wine. Every person brought his own eating knife, which he kept in a sheath attached to his belt, but the King owned sets of eating knives – one set was garnished with 'emeralds, pearls, rubies and amethysts, with knives having diamonds at the end of them'[53] – which were placed at the convenience of guests. Some had matching forks, an Italian invention, but forks were used only to serve meat or sticky foods, not for eating. It was customary to eat with a knife and one's fingers, having due regard for the sensibilities of others: one used the left hand to take food from communal dishes, and the thumb and first two fingers of the right hand to eat with. The knife was for serving and cutting meat, and helping oneself from the salt bowls. Spoons were used to eat liquid food, and were rubbed clean with bread several times during a meal.[54] Henry VIII owned sixty-nine gold spoons and twelve silver spoons 'with columns at the ends'.[55]

Similar place settings to those in the Chamber were laid in the great hall, but the utensils were of wood, the bread was cheat, and ale, not wine, was served in a leather jug. In both Chamber and hall, food was served in 'messes' in large dishes, each mess being sufficient for four persons. A cooked mess of beef weighed 700g, so each person received about 175g of meat.[56]

Meals were served with great ceremony; the company was summoned by minstrels blowing trumpets, shawms or pipes.[57] A fanfare sounded as the high table was seated, then a Latin grace was said by the Chaplain. The company stood, the men bareheaded, as dishes were carried in procession into the dining chamber, where the diners were served in order of rank and numerous servants stood by to attend to their needs. Good table manners, a sign of good breeding, were expected of everyone. People washed their hands before dinner and between courses. Napkins were not spread on laps but laid across the left shoulder. Elbows or fists were not to rest on the table, and picking one's nose or scratching one's head was unthinkable, although diners might spit discreetly and wipe runny noses on their sleeves.[58] It was the mark of a gentleman to be familiar with the intricate rules for carving the many cuts of meat that were served.

In the hall, however, the courtesies were not always strictly observed. It was so crowded and chaotic that there were frequent spillages and breakages. And the company, as Alexander Barclay observed, was far too hungry to observe niceties:

> If the dish is pleasant, either flesh or fish,
> Ten hands at once swarm in the dish;
> And if it be flesh, ten knives shalt thou see
> Mangling the flesh, and in the platter flee.
> To put there thy hands is peril without fail
> Without a gauntlet, or else a glove of mail . . .
> Slow be the servers in serving alway,
> But swift be they after taking meat away.

This last was because those serving would eat whatever was left after the sitting had ended.

It was considered uncharitable to finish all one's food. Leftover food, known as 'manners', was placed on a dish called a 'voider' and passed down to those of lesser rank, or collected by the Almoner and given to the beggars who crowded outside the palace gates.[59]

9

'Elegant Manners, Extreme Decorum, and Very Great Politeness'

The King's magnificence was expressed through elaborate rituals and spectacular ceremonial. The propaganda value of colourful and sumptuous display, in which Henry delighted, was well understood, and the pageantry of his court incorporated dynastic, heraldic and allegorical themes. John Skelton had told his pupil, 'Be bountiful, liberal and lavish.'[1] The King never forgot his advice, and his extravagant lifestyle, set against the splendid backdrop of his residences, was designed to emphasise to others the dignity of his elevated calling and place England firmly in the eye of Europe.

A rigid code of etiquette was observed at court, especially in the King's presence. Entertainments and festivals were organised with the maximum ceremony, and during the reign there were six great occasions of state: two coronations, one near-legendary summit meeting, two royal visits and a reception for a future queen.[2] Then there were public processions and the solemnities attendant upon royal births, betrothals, marriages and deaths, receptions of ambassadors and the rituals observed on the creation of peers. Court ceremonies and functions were usually organised by the Lord Chamberlain and/or Garter King of Arms, assisted by the Vice-Chamberlain.[3]

The court was at its most splendid on the feast days that marked the major festivals: Christmas, New Year, the Feast of the Epiphany (or Twelfth Night), Easter, Ascension Day, the Feast of the Assumption and the Feast of St John the Baptist on Midsummer's Day. These days were marked by pious observances as well as feasting and merrymaking. At Candlemas, the Feast of the Purification of the Virgin Mary on 2 February, the King walked in a candle-lit procession to chapel, his candle borne by a nobleman on his right.[4] On festival days, the court ate exceptionally well, and the King would feast in public; his subjects – provided they were respectably dressed – could come to watch.

There were times when food was not so plentiful. The court fasted on fish and dairy foods – 'white meats' – on Fridays and Saturdays, and observed an even stricter regime during Lent, when dairy foods were not allowed.[5] The King relaxed this rule in 1541.

Tudor feasts were extravaganzas of excess. The King's hospitality was boundless, and cost the equivalent of around £4 million a year. Up to seven hundred guests might be invited, and 240 different dishes served on gold or silver-gilt plates. When Henry entertained thirty people at Windsor, there were 14 varieties of meat, 800 eggs, 90 dishes of butter, 80 loaves of chestnut bread, 300 wafers, gingerbread coated in gold leaf, and sufficient fruit and drink for each diner to have ten oranges and twenty alcoholic beverages.[6] Guests were always seated in order of rank, and served with impressive ceremony. The cup-bearers and food-tasters attending royalty would remain kneeling throughout the proceedings. The choicest food was reserved for the top table, but might be passed down to lesser mortals as a mark of favour. Along the walls stood buffets groaning with plate; candles were often placed in front of this plate, to reflect more light.

The centrepiece of a feast would be a 'prodigy dish', such as a roasted peacock re-dressed in its plumage[7] or pies baked in the shape of St Paul's Cathedral. But the *pièce de résistance* was the 'subtlety', an artistic confection brought in at the end of every course and offered to the high table. Subtleties, which originated in Burgundy, were the *magnum opus* of the Confectioner's artistry: they were made entirely of sugar and almond paste, which was moulded into fantastic sculptures up to two or three feet high, then painted and gilded. Subtleties, which were unsurprisingly 'an assault for valiant teeth',[8] might be made in the form of scenes from romances, myths, battles, or religious works; some represented coats of arms, others ships, castles, churches – Wolsey served a subtlety of St Paul's Cathedral[9] – or even the guest of honour. Many had some political significance, and most bore mottoes. At Garter feasts, 'a George on horseback' had been customary since 1400.[10]

Feasts could last for several hours. Once, when the King got bored, he amused himself by throwing sugar plums at his guests;[11] on a few other occasions, he himself served those guests. Such feasting could stretch the resources of the kitchens beyond their limits, as at Greenwich on Twelfth Night, 1533.[12]

After a court entertainment or feast, the King might hold a banquet for the most honoured guests. A banquet might be a grand meal, but it was usually a dessert of sweet dishes and confectionery, known as the 'void', and it was usually held in the intimacy of the King or Queen's privy chamber or in one of the banqueting houses in the palace gardens. A banquet was a gourmet's delight, with only the best and rarest foods and wines being served in the richest of settings.

Banquets were served buffet-style, with the guests helping themselves after the servants had been dismissed. Amongst the delicacies were suckets, or pieces of fruit in syrup, which were eaten with fork-like sucket spoons,[13] marchpane, jellies, biscuits, 'kissing comfits' of sugar fondant, and mounds of syllabub called 'Spanish paps'.[14] Much of this food and wine was intended to act as an aphrodisiac. Later, comfits such as apples with caraway seeds and sugared spices were passed round on ornate spice plates: Henry had one of silver gilt set upon four antique heads with an elaborate cover of silver, agate, porcelain and emerald chased with roses and fleurs-de-lys.[15] At the end of the evening, the King and Queen were ceremonially presented with their gold cups, and hippocras and wafers were served.[16] Then the company departed, many, presumably, to amorous adventures.

The King's daily life was governed by ritual.[17] As already noted, even when he was not on show to the world he was rarely alone, even in his privy lodgings or stool chamber. His Gentlemen, Grooms, Ushers or Pages would usually be in attendance. Four knights acting as Esquires of the Body waited upon the King day and night, two each to a shift.

At 7 a.m. every day, the morning watch of the Yeomen of the Guard would relieve the night watch in the presence chamber, and the Ushers would take their places at the door of the privy chamber, ready to challenge all who wished to enter. The King rose around eight. By then, the Grooms and Pages had lit the fire, ensured it was not smoking, cleaned and tidied the royal apartments, and tried – not always success-fully – to awaken the Esquires of the Body, who slept in the 'pallet chamber' next door to the royal bedchamber.[18] Sometimes the King complained that they were still snoring when he was up and dressed.

Each morning, a Yeoman of the Wardrobe would bring the freshly brushed clothes chosen by the King to the door of the privy chamber, and there pass them to a Groom or Page, who would hand them to the King's Gentlemen who were waiting to attend him. Meanwhile, the Esquires of the Body would have entered Henry's bedchamber 'to array him and dress him in his [under]clothes'.[19] Clean body linen, strewn with fresh herbs provided by Mrs Harris, the King's Laundress, was kept in one of two chests in the bedchamber; the other chest held the dirty linen awaiting collection by Mrs Harris, who, out of her wages (which gradually rose to £20 (£6,000) a year), had to pay for the two chests and the herbs as well as for sweet powder and soap, and wood for her fire.[20] Every week, she washed the King's clothes and all his other linen, including 14 breakfast cloths, 8 hand towels and 36 napkins.[21]

Any other garments needed by the Esquires were handed to them at the bedchamber door by a Groom. Then, 'loosely dressed', Henry would emerge into the privy chamber, where his Gentlemen had the privilege of completing his robing. No Groom was allowed 'to lay hands upon the royal person, or intermeddle with dressing, except it be to warm clothes and hand these to the Gentlemen; both Grooms and Ushers must keep a convenient distance from the King's person, not too homely or bold advancing themselves'.[22]

When the King was dressed, he seated himself on a chair with a footstool, and a kerchief was laid around his shoulders. Then Penny, his barber, came to shave him, bringing a basin of water scented with cloves, plus cloths, knives, combs of ivory, bone or horn,[23] and scissors in case the royal hair or beard needed trimming. Since Penny came into such close contact with his sovereign, he was required to keep himself 'pure and clean' and to avoid 'vile persons' and 'misguided women'.[24]

Nowhere in the Household Ordinances is there any reference to the King bathing. Although he had bathrooms at most of his houses, and wooden tubs at others, we do not know how often he used them. He certainly took herbal baths for medicinal purposes in winter, and, for fear of catching evil humours, avoided bathing during plague epidemics[25] – which suggests he was taking baths at other times; as noted earlier, he was a fastidious man, and would surely not have gone to the trouble of installing so many sophisticated bathrooms if he did not intend to use them.

The King's bathroom, or 'bain' (French for 'bath'), in the Bayne Tower at Hampton Court, built in 1529, had a ceiling laced with gilded battens, and window seats. The bath was attached to the wall, and there were two taps for hot and cold water, the hot water being heated by a stove in the next room. There were comparable facilities at the Tower, Windsor, Beaulieu, Bridewell and even in some lesser houses; all were on the first floor near the royal bedchamber.[26] During the latter part of his reign, the King built himself huge sunken baths on the ground floor, like those of Francis I of France at Fontainebleau; the one at Woodstock had water piped from a spring called Rosamund's Well, and was cold in summer and warm in winter.[27] There was a similar bath at Hampton Court, and another was excavated at Whitehall in the 1930s. The latter is known to have been equipped with thirty-five towels of Holland linen, washing cloths, bathrobes, pails, and sheets and sponges for lining the bath.[28] At Beaulieu and Greenwich, the bathrooms contained folding beds complete with curtains:[29] it was customary for a bather to retire to bed for a time after a bath to ensure that he did not take a chill.

There was a garderobe adjacent to each of the King's bedchambers, and sometimes a stool chamber; those at Greenwich and Hampton Court had pictures and bookshelves.[30] A 'close stool' was a pewter chamber pot set in an elaborate boxed seat; one of the King's close stools was upholstered in black velvet, silk fringing and two thousand gilt nails, and had 'elbows and side pieces'.[31] It is often claimed that the King did not use close stools until the end of his reign, but his sister Mary took one to France with her in 1514,[32] so they must have been in use much earlier. Five of Henry's were recorded at Hampton Court in 1547: one was covered in green velvet and silk, 'embroidered with the King's arms and badges'.[33] Two of his close stools at Ampthill had backs, and some even had their own cisterns for flushing.[34]

The title of Groom of the Stool derived from that gentleman's privilege of attending his sovereign whenever he used the close stool; his duties were to provide him with a flannel 'to wipe his nether end',[35] and summon a Yeoman of the Chamber to empty and clean the pot. Sir Thomas Heneage, Groom of the Stool from 1536 to 1546, was witness to the King's chronic constipation and his efforts to relieve it, and was present when, one night in 1539, the King took a laxative: 'he slept until two of the clock in the morning, and then rose to go to the stool, which by working of the pills had a very fair siege'.[36]

Once he was ready to face the world, the King 'came forth' from his privy chamber, and was immediately crowded by the hordes of courtiers and petitioners waiting outside.[37] When he had fought his way past them, having graciously dealt with some of their requests, he went in procession to Matins in the chapel royal; then, whenever possible, he spent the morning hunting before returning for a late dinner. Alternatively he might read or work in his library, visit the stables to see his horses, or spend time mixing the medicinal remedies that he was fond of devising. Often, he was to be found relaxing in the privy chamber in the company of his gentlemen, and might not 'come forth' at all that day.[38]

The King's schedule meant that he did not always eat his meals at the same time as the rest of the court.[39] Since the thirteenth century English monarchs had enjoyed the advantages of having their own privy kitchens: mealtimes could be flexible, the King could be served the choicest menus, and there was less risk of his food being poisoned, accidentally or deliberately. At Hampton Court, the privy kitchen was directly below the King's apartments, connected by a spiral stair, so meals arrived hot,[40] which was not always the case elsewhere. There were similar arrangements in other royal residences, and on the Queen's Side.[41] The royal menus were always decided by the Master Cook in consultation with the King's physicians and the Sewer, and the Gentlemen Ushers let the privy kitchen know when and where Henry wished his meals to be served and how many guests would be present. The Ushers were also responsible for ensuring that the table was set properly and that everyone was seated in the right place. The King always sat in the middle of the high table, 'a little above the salt, his face being to the whole view of the chamber'.[42]

Even when he ate in the privacy of his privy chamber, Henry's meals were always conducted with great ceremony and formality. After arriving with the Lord Chamberlain to the sound of trumpets, he sat alone at a table set up before the chair under his canopy of estate, and his Gentlemen and Grooms served him bareheaded and on bended knee, while favoured courtiers, Councillors, clergy and men of letters would stand behind and to the side, conversing with their master.[43] The two Esquires of the Body sat at Henry's feet throughout the meal.[44]

The King's damask tablecloth might be embroidered with flowers, knots, crowns or fleurs-de-lys, while the water in the royal fingerbowl would have been heated in a chafing dish.[45] On the table, in front of the King, would be the splendid gold nef, a prestige item of plate fashioned like a ship, which held his knife, spoon, napkin and salt. His manchet bread would be wrapped in a 'coverpain' of embroidered linen or silk,[46] and his meat placed by the Carver on his plate, which might be of silver gilt or marble, with a depression for salt at one edge.[47] Thirteen dishes in two courses were served to the King at each meal, at a cost equivalent to a staggering £1,285.[48] His favourite dishes included venison, game pies stuffed with oranges, haggis, eels, baked lampreys, salmon, sturgeon, ling and an early version of beef olives.[49] For the void, he preferred custards, fritters, tarts, jelly and cream of almonds. He was always eager to try any new and rare foods, such as porpoise, which became a Tudor delicacy – and even, probably, coconuts, or what were described as 'nuts of India, greater than a man's fist'.[50] All the food prepared for the King would be assayed for poison by the Master Cook and the Lord Steward before it was presented at table.

When Henry had finished eating, the Carver scraped the cloth free of crumbs with a knife, and the King stood while a kneeling Usher brushed the crumbs from his clothes. He remained standing while the table was cleared and removed, again with meticulous ceremony, then washed his hands in a basin brought by a nobleman.

A pen-and-ink drawing, in the British Museum, of Henry VIII dining in solitary state in his privy chamber shows officers of the Chamber, holding their staves of office and standing to one side, while on the other is a buffet displaying plate.[51]

If the King was entertaining guests in his presence chamber, a fanfare would herald the arrival of a procession led by the Lord Steward and officers of the Greencloth, followed by the Master Cook, the Carver, the Sewer – the latter two were always of noble or gentle birth, and wore towels of office over their shoulders – and Grooms bearing the food on heavy silver-gilt chargers.[52] The King's Cupbearer would assay his drink from a few drops poured into the lid of the royal cup, which might be of precious metal, mother of pearl, alabaster, porcelain or colourful ornamented glass imported from Venice.[53] When the King had placed his cup on the table, drinks might then be served to the rest of the company. The King's leftovers were always given to the poor.[54]

It was not unknown for Henry to take his meals in his secret lodgings, where there was less formality. In 1528, for example, he 'supped apart' in 'a chamber within a tower' at Hunsdon.[55]

In the afternoon, the King might exercise his horses or receive ambassadors, often summoning them at very short notice. After supper, he sometimes attended to state business, but his Councillors complained that he often put it off until late at night.[56]

It was rare for the King and Queen to dine together, but Henry often took supper in his wife's apartments, usually as a prelude to sleeping with her. Sometimes, without warning, and often at a late hour, he brought guests to join them at table. Alternatively, he spent the evenings watching some entertainment, making music, or gambling with his courtiers. When it was dark, he might go up to the palace roof to study the stars, using 'speculative glasses'.[57] Sometimes, late at night, he would order a snack such as a bowl of aleberry[58] – a kind of bread pudding flavoured with ale – and a host of servants would have to bestir themselves.

In the evening, the King's bed – which had been stripped and left airing all day – was 'arrayed' to a prescribed ritual laid down in the Household Ordinances. It took ten men to accomplish this. A Groom was sent to collect clean linen, pillows and blankets from the Wardrobe of the Beds; then he would stand at the end of the bed holding a torch while eight Yeomen of the Chamber and Wardrobe lined up, four at each side of the bed. A Gentleman Usher was in charge of the proceedings, which began with a Yeoman thrusting a dagger into the straw of the bottom mattress to rout out any hidden assassin. The Usher saw that the King's sword was hung within reach of the bed, and that a poleaxe was to hand in the bedchamber, in case Henry was attacked during the night.

A canvas cover was placed on the mattress and 'a bed of down' was shaken and beaten and laid on top. A Yeoman had to 'roll up and down' it to make sure that no harmful object was hidden inside. Then the bed was made up with a bolster and pillows, fine linen sheets, blankets and a rich counterpoint lined with ermine, which were all smoothed and tucked in with great precision. Finally, each Yeoman made the sign of the Cross over the bed, kissed the places where he had touched it, and – until 1526, when the rules were changed – sprinkled them with holy water. Then the curtains were drawn, and a mantle of crimson velvet lined with ermine was laid out for the King to wear when he arose from bed. When the Usher and Yeomen withdrew to refresh themselves with bread and wine, the Groom had to remain, kneeling, to guard the bed until the King arrived. Before then, a Yeoman of the Wardrobe would place a 'nightstool and urinal' in the bedchamber. The Queen's bed was made by her ladies, following a similar ritual.[59]

The King rarely retired before midnight, 'which is our accustomed hour at court to go to bed'.[60] His Gentlemen and Esquires of the Body disrobed him and put on his nightgown, which was usually white and made of fine linen or silk. A basin of water and a cloth were brought so he could wash his face and clean his teeth. His attendants combed his hair, put on his 'nightbonnet' – which might be of scarlet or black velvet, embroidered[61] – helped him into bed, and lit a night-light. Then they made obeisance and withdrew.[62] Two Yeomen of the Chamber slept on pallets outside the door, and the two Esquires of the Body were nearby in the pallet chamber. Outside in the presence chamber, the night watch of the Yeomen of the Guard had come on duty, and would be vigilant for suspicious noises or smells of burning, for in an age of candles, fire was an ever-present risk.

The King, who could now rest peacefully in the knowledge that he was well guarded, had meanwhile removed to his privy bedchamber, where he was attended by the Gentleman whose turn it was to sleep on the pallet at the foot of the bed or, on occasions, in the King's bed itself. This was not thought strange in an age in which beds were at a premium and many people shared. When Henry wanted to sleep with his wife, he summoned his Grooms of the Chamber, who brought his nightrobe and escorted him with lighted torches to the door of the Queen's bedchamber, which was reached via a private connecting gallery or stair.[63] The Grooms would wait outside the door until the King was ready to be escorted back to bed. The ceremony surrounding such an intimate event seems surprising today, but it must be remembered that the begetting of heirs to the throne was a matter of legitimate public interest, and also that it was unthinkable that the sovereign should be left unattended at any time.

10

'Innocent and Honest Pastimes'

During the summer of 1509, in the weeks after the coronation, Henry VIII indulged himself in the novel pleasures of kingship. 'Our time is spent in continuous festival,'[1] Queen Katherine wrote to Ferdinand of Aragon, while the King informed his father-in-law that he was diverting himself 'with jousts, birding, hunting and other innocent and honest pastimes'.[2] At eighteen, Henry 'was young and lusty, disposed all to mirth and pleasure, nothing minding to travail in the busy affairs of his realm',[3] and – as some English bishops pointed out to the Spanish ambassador – did not 'care to occupy himself with anything but the pleasures of his age; all other affairs he neglects'.[4] In fact, Henry was so busy enjoying himself that he would work only during Matins in the chapel royal, or late in the evenings,[5] provided he had nothing better to do.

For the first four years of the reign, the young King was reliant upon the ministers he inherited from his father. These were much older, wiser men, but this placed them at a disadvantage, since Henry always preferred to surround himself with young people. The truth was, he could not bear to be reminded of old age, illness or death.

Henry also had an aversion to paperwork. 'Writing is to me somewhat tedious and painful,' he once told Cardinal Wolsey.[6] He virtually had to be forced to write letters; Wolsey once insisted he pen a missive to his elder sister Margaret, Queen of Scots, because 'women must be pleased'.

Henry was always ready with an excuse as to why he could not attend to business, be it a headache or the fact that he was removing to another house. Once when his secretary, Richard Pace, wanted to go through some diplomatic correspondence with him, he made the excuse that he had to attend Matins. The next morning he escaped to the chase, and when he got back to find Pace waiting for him, he insisted on having supper first. Only in the evening did he begrudgingly get down to work. In 1521, poor Pace was appalled when Henry refused to put his seal to letters because he had found out that the French King did not do so; Pace had to go along with this until Henry reverted to the traditional method of signing and sealing royal letters. In 1513, a Milanese ambassador was somewhat offended when the King 'put off our discussion to another time, as he was then in a hurry to go and dine and dance afterwards'.[7]

Henry's Councillors found his lack of application to his duties disconcerting after having become used to the dedication and carefulness of his hard-working father. Fortunately, they were all experienced men who were perfectly capable of governing the country in their master's name, but this did not stop them from trying to make Henry attend to his obligations as his father had done. Because they were concerned 'lest such abundance of riches the King was now possessed of should move his young years to a riotous forgetting of himself', they constrained him to 'be present with them to acquaint him with the politic government of the realm, with which at first he could not endure to be much troubled'.[8] But Henry was impatient with them, and showed much disgust at the time they took to deliberate on affairs.

For centuries, the seat of government had been the Palace of Westminster. Here were to be found the great departments of state: the Exchequer, under the rule of the Lord Treasurer, the Chancery, headed by the Lord Chancellor, who was also Keeper of the Great Seal of England, and the Courts of Common Pleas and the King's Bench. Parliament, which was summoned and prorogued at the King's pleasure, also sat at Westminster.

Power was centred, however, upon the court, where the King was, and increasingly upon his secretariat, which travelled around with him and comprised the Lord Privy Seal and the King's 'Master Secretary' and their staffs. Together with the Lord Treasurer, the Lord Chancellor, the Lord Chamberlain, the Lord Steward and the Lord High Admiral, these officers were the foremost members of the Privy Council.[9] Next in importance came the Chancellor of the Exchequer, the Lord Warden of the Cinque Ports and the Archbishop of Canterbury.

The Privy Council, which advised the King and implemented his policies, was based at Westminster. The Court of Star Chamber, through which it exercised its legal powers, sat in the palace. The Council's seventy-odd members, who were all chosen by the King, were aristocrats, clerics, household officers and professional lawyers, but attendance levels varied. Council meetings were held in private; the King did not always attend, preferring to discuss affairs privately with individual Councillors, often whilst walking in his galleries or gardens, but all the Council's business was done in his name. Throughout Henry VIII's reign, thanks initially to the King's political indolence and later to the dominance of Wolsey and Cromwell, the Council's executive powers expanded, although it remained very much a consultative body. By 1530, it was meeting more and more at court.

In 1509, the most powerful force on the Council was Richard Foxe, Bishop of Winchester, who had been Lord Privy Seal since 1489. A sensible yet cunning lawyer and diplomatist, he seemed to the Venetian ambassador to be almost a king himself.[10] 'Here in England they think he is a fox, and such is his name,' the King told Luis Caroz, the Spanish ambassador,[11] with some truth. Foxe had enjoyed a distinguished career in the Church, and was a notable patron of learning and a humanist, who corresponded with Erasmus.

Henry's first Lord Chancellor was William Warham, Archbishop of Canterbury, who had held the post and the primacy since 1504. He too was a humanist and friend of Erasmus, who found him to be 'witty, energetic and laborious [hardworking]'; and he recorded that, although Warham gave 'sumptuous entertainments, he himself ate frugal meals and hardly ever tasted wine, but yet was a most genial host. He never hunted or played at dice, but his chief recreation was reading.'[12] In 1524, Erasmus sent the Archbishop a portrait of himself by Hans Holbein. Warham was a competent lawyer and diplomat; he and Foxe were typical career churchmen who had neglected their ecclesiastical duties in order to further their political ambitions.

The Lord Treasurer was Foxe's rival, Thomas Howard, Earl of Surrey; John de Vere, Earl of Oxford, was Lord Admiral, and the chief Secretary was Thomas Ruthal, Bishop of Durham, a capable administrator who had been in post since 1500 and who was growing rich on the proceeds of his labours. John Fisher, Bishop of Rochester, was also a prominent Councillor. There was therefore a strong ecclesiastical presence on the Council. By the end of Henry's reign, that would no longer be the case.

In November 1509, the man who would be one of the chief causes of this change, Thomas Wolsey, was appointed Lord High Almoner to the King. Wolsey was then thirty-six. The son of an Ipswich grazier and wool merchant (not a butcher, as Skelton disparagingly asserted), he had been an outstanding scholar at Oxford, graduating at only fifteen. He had taken holy orders, then risen meteorically through the Church to become, in 1507, Chaplain to Henry VII and Secretary to Bishop Foxe, who thereafter did all he could to further Wolsey's career. It was probably due to Foxe that he got the post of Almoner.

The Almoner's chief duty was to distribute the King's charity to the poor. Wolsey had a brilliant mind; he was 'very handsome, learned, extremely eloquent, of vast ability and indefatigable';[13] above all, he was a prodigiously thorough and hard-working servant. Henry soon recognised his worth, and in quick succession appointed him Dean of Hereford and Lincoln, Prebendary of York, a canon of Windsor, and Registrar of the Order of the Bath. Wolsey was already acting as an unofficial royal secretary when, in 1511, Foxe secured him a seat on the Privy Council. All this suited the Almoner very well, for he was a proud, greedy, extravagant man with ambitions well beyond his station in life. Through flattery, charm, wit and a convivial manner, he had gained the affection and respect of the King, and his fortunes were now set to prosper.[14]

With the government in the capable hands of Foxe, Warham, Surrey and Ruthal, Henry VIII considered himself free to enjoy the more pleasurable and visual aspects of sovereignty. In order to emphasise his magnificence, the King usually took his recreation in public, accompanied by appropriate ceremony. On feast days and state occasions, the Master of the Revels would devise lavish, large-scale entertainments for the court, in the manner of the festivities and pageants made popular by the Dukes of Burgundy. Many had mythical, allegorical or chivalric themes, and most had some useful propaganda value. It was the King's intention that these entertainments should not only impress beholders but also surprise them. Unlike his father, he often participated, and was almost childlike in his enthusiasm for revelry. By showing off his person, his showmanship and his prowess in pageants, dances, tournaments and sports, he could present to the world the image he wanted them to see.

And the world took notice. The King's subjects contrasted him favourably with Henry VII, who had been generally unpopular, and concluded that here was a monarch to be proud of. Ambassadors sent home glowing reports of the splendour of the English court and its ruler, and Henry's reputation as a magnificent, liberal and talented prince spread throughout Europe. At the same time, his treasury dwindled, for these entertainments were ruinously expensive, although the King no doubt felt them an expense well justified for their propaganda value alone.

Court entertainments were staged frequently during the first two decades of the reign; later on, as the King grew older and lost interest in youthful pleasures, he preferred to spend money on building or refurbishing his houses, and he also became preoccupied with the religious issues of the Reformation. Later still, his deteriorating health and thickening girth increasingly precluded his participating in revelry.

On certain holidays the public were allowed into the court to watch the entertainments; if they became too enthusiastic, the King's guard would intervene[15] – apart from one memorable occasion in 1511, of which more will be heard later.

The Master of the Revels and his staff were responsible for staging the court entertainments. They had to devise the themes of the pageants and masques, make all the costumes, scenery and props, and arrange all the seating and lighting. This was all done in close consultation with the principal participants themselves – there is evidence that some ideas came from the King himself – as well as with the Lord Chamberlain and the Dean of the Chapel Royal, which provided choristers for the pageants.

Some of the costumes and props were made of the richest materials and even embellished with gold and jewels; others were improvised, such as the papier-mâché lions made for a pageant at Greenwich. Pages and pages of costumes and props were listed by the Revels Office, including '7 masking hats, Tartary fashion, of yellow and red sarcanet [fine silk], . . . 8 satin mantles trimmed with silk, Irish fashion, . . . 8 short cloaks of scarlet with keys embroidered on the shoulders, 8 hats of crimson satin with scallop shells' – these were for 'the Palmers' masque' – plus props such as foliage with leaves of green satin and flowers of silk, antique pillars, and statuary such as 'the image of Hercules'.[16] All this implied a complicated operation involving a great amount of work, hundreds of craftsmen and many hired hands. The Revels Office also maintained and stored all the 'revels stuff', and extra accommodation had to be made available from time to time, such as the dissolved monastery at Blackfriars.[17] Another of the Master's duties was to censor any suggested entertainment that was likely to offend the King. By 1545, the post of Master of the Revels had become such an important one that the King decided to issue a patent conferring it for life; the first permanent Master was Sir Thomas Carwarden.

Early on in the reign, the chief deviser of court entertainments was William Cornish. Musician, composer, poet, playwright, actor and a Gentleman of the Chapel Royal, Cornish was a versatile genius who wrote church music in the style of John Dunstable and secular songs such as 'Ah, Robin!' and 'Blow thy horn, hunter', and he was also a virtuoso on the organ. The King, impressed by his talents, put him in charge of court entertainments. It was Cornish who was responsible for the brilliant pageants and masques of the early years of the reign, and Cornish who constituted the Children of the Chapel Royal, of whom he was appointed Master in 1509, into a dramatic company for the purposes of court entertainments. The King was particularly fond of seeing his choristers perform in plays, and often rewarded them;[18] the boys sang, danced, and often acted the female roles. Sometimes, the adult choristers and Chamber servants also participated.

Early Tudor drama consisted chiefly of mediaeval miracle and morality plays, which were rarely performed at court and went out of fashion with the Reformation; short 'interludes', which were the successors to morality plays; pageants and masques; the last two relied on spectacle, music and dance rather than plots. Hardly any play texts survive from before Elizabeth I's reign, and sophisticated dramatic works were rare. Not until 1576 was a public playhouse built in London, and until then ordinary people could only watch plays staged by travelling players in inn yards and market-places. But theatrical entertainments were popular at court. Under Henry VIII, Eltham Palace seems to have acquired a reputation as a dramatic venue. When the King was in residence, there were frequent performances in the great hall, and Londoners were admitted to watch them. Eltham was also famous for the puppet show called *The Divine Motion of Eltham*, which was performed in the palace in Henry's reign and was later mentioned by Ben Jonson.

Interludes, as the name suggests, were short plays with popular themes performed during the intervals between court entertainments. The earliest surviving example is *Fulgens and Lucrece*, written by Henry Medwell in c1486/90 for John Morton, Cardinal Archbishop of Canterbury. Modelled on an Italian play about the Roman Republic, it was aimed at educated, aristocratic audiences likely to be open to humanist influences. The young Thomas More is known to have acted in interludes whilst serving in Cardinal Morton's household.[19] William Shakespeare's *A Midsummer Night's Dream* features a typical interlude, *Pyramus and Thisbe*. Interludes were meant to mix 'mirth with modesty';[20] characters were comic or allegorical, and plots might be satirical, moralistic or farcical. The text was often written in doggerel verse.

Interludes were performed by small groups of itinerant players who visited the court, the great houses of the nobility, the universities and the Inns of Court. Up to seven different groups might perform for Henry in any one year, with many receiving rewards from him.[21] Some companies, like the King's Players and the Queen's Players, were permanently employed by the Chamber.

Apart from John Skelton, one of the finest writers of pre-Reformation interludes was John Heywood, a Londoner who married Thomas More's niece, Elizabeth Rastell, and worked for the court from 1519, initially as a singer. He also wrote music for the lute and keyboards,[22] and was no mean poet. Heywood's most famous works were *The Play of the Weather* (1533) and *The Four Ps* (c1544), in which four characters, a Palmer, Pardoner, 'Pothecary and Pedlar, all compete to tell the biggest lie. The winner was the Pardoner, who claimed he had never seen a woman out of patience. Heywood's *The Pardoner and the Friar* derived from Chaucer, and was used as a model by Christopher Marlowe for *The Jew of Malta*. Heywood is said to have narrowly escaped being executed for treason in 1544, only because the King so admired his work.

Heywood's father-in-law, John Rastell, who was married to Thomas More's sister, also wrote interludes for the court, the most famous being *The Nature of the Four Elements* (c1520). Rastell was a multi-talented lawyer who also worked as a printer, military engineer and decorative artist; in 1520, the King employed him to help embellish the temporary palace built for the Field of Cloth of Gold. It was Rastell who, in 1517, helped launch the first English expedition to America for the purposes of colonisation; sadly, it got no further than Ireland.

Pageants – the word means 'movable stage' – were entertainments involving mock battles – with knights and ladies bombarding each other with flowers, fruit and sweets – allegorical figures, and the ideals of chivalry and courtly love. They were a Burgundian innovation and afforded an opportunity for mounting dazzling spectacles featuring impressive scenery, special effects, music, poetry and dance. Pageants were performed at Christmas, Epiphany, Shrovetide and other feast-days, or for the entertainment of ambassadors, and might often be combined with tournaments. Indoors, they were usually mounted on giant wheeled pageant cars that conveyed the whole set into the great hall. The audience watched from tiered benches, set up in readiness along the walls.

'Disguisings', much beloved by Henry VIII, were often incorporated into pageants or acted out as separate entertainments. They involved the participants dressing up in disguise, with masks, and either performing incognito or taking people unawares; the King was especially fond of bursting in upon Queen Katherine and her ladies in the Queen's chamber. The denouement came when the masks were removed and the players' identities revealed. Henry took a boyish delight in these disguisings, and Katherine seemingly never tired of feigning astonishment that it was her husband who had surprised her.

Informal pleasures were often devised to break the tedium of courtier life and for 'the eschewing of idleness, the ground of all vice'.[23] Apart from daytime pastimes such as hunting, sports and tournaments (which will be discussed later), there would be dancing, gambling, board games and the antics of court jesters to while away the evenings. Many courtiers enjoyed writing poetry or making music, and there was always the intriguing game of courtly love to help pass the time.

Dancing was a popular pastime at court, if only because it afforded one of the few opportunities for men and women to enjoy physical contact in a social setting. However, one Spaniard found the English to be 'not at all graceful' and their dances to 'consist simply of prancing and trotting'.[24] Dancing was nevertheless an essential accomplishment for both men and women of gentle birth, and Henry VII had ensured that all his children were taught it well.

The dances favoured by the court were many and varied. 'Bransles', or brawls, were round dances of peasant origin that had been adopted by the aristocracy and become especially popular in England. The basse dance was so called because the feet glided slowly across the floor and were hardly lifted. Sir Thomas Elyot refers to 'bargenettes and turgions', which seem to have been spirited measures. The most stately of all dances was the majestic pavane, from Italy; its slow pace was particularly appropriate to ceremonial occasions when the dancers would be encumbered with heavy robes and long trains. The *passamezzo* was a faster version of the pavane, and was often followed by a *saltarello*, an early form of the lively, high-stepping galliard that became popular in Elizabethan times. Much Renaissance dance music survives to give us some idea of the diversity of the rhythms and forms of the dances of the period. It is clear that sixteenth-century dances were less stylised than those of later centuries, and had room for improvisation; many dances were very energetic, with much running and leaping, and in some – such as the *ronde* – the dancers sang. Nevertheless, all court dances began and ended formally with a reverence, with the dancers bowing or curtseying to the King and Queen.

Henry VIII was an expert and enthusiastic dancer. Aged ten, at the wedding of his brother Arthur, he energetically partnered his sister Margaret, and onlookers watched with delight as he flung off his coat and cavorted around in his doublet and hose.[25] As a young man, Henry 'exercised himself daily in dancing',[26] in which, wrote the Milanese ambassador in 1515, 'he does wonders and leaps like a stag'.[27] He 'acquitted himself divinely' on the dance floor, enthused one Venetian,[28] while another, the envoy Sebastian Giustinian, commented that he danced well.[29]

Katherine of Aragon also liked dancing, and often danced with her ladies in the privacy of her chamber, but in these early years she was frequently pregnant, and so Henry was usually partnered by his sister Mary, whose 'deportment in dancing is as pleasing as you would desire'.[30]

Not only the King, but the whole court, it seemed, was excessively fond of gambling: monarch, courtiers and servants would bet on any pastime that had an unknown outcome – cards, dice, board games, tennis, dog races, even whether a man could eat a whole buck at one sitting. All games of chance were organised by the Knight Marshal of the Household, who acted as a bookmaker, and the stakes would usually be high. Favourite card games – and there were many – included Mumchance, Gleek, Click-Clack, Imperial and Primero. Chess, shovelboard and 'tables' (backgammon) were popular board games; in 1539, Henry bought new chess sets from 'John the hardware man'.[31]

The King, who had been a great gambler since childhood,[32] would command the Knight Marshal to bring his cards and dice in a silver bowl, then play for hours, often with ladies of the court and sometimes with the Queen, who was especially fond of tables, cards and dice. Giustinian states that Henry risked more money than anyone else at court;[33] as King, he could have done no less, but it appears that he gambled away much of his inheritance. His Privy Purse Expenses record only his losses, and they could amount to hundreds of pounds daily; in January 1530, whilst playing with his Gentlemen of the Privy Chamber, he lost £450 (£135,000) at dominoes and £100 (£30,000) at cards and dice; in 1532, he lost £45 (£13,500) at shovelboard to Lord Rochford. We do not know how much Henry won, but between 1529 and 1532, the only years for which records are complete, he lost a total of £3,243 (£972,900), and it is clear that thousands of pounds were routinely set aside for his 'playing money'.[34]

Needless to say, moralists thundered against the evils of gambling. In 1511, there were complaints that the King had been cheated of large sums in wagers by some Italian bankers, who were immediately barred from court. In 1526 Wolsey tried to ban Chamber servants from indulging in 'immoderate and continual play of dice, cards and tables', especially in the King's presence.[35] In 1541, Henry himself forbade anyone with an income of less than £20 (£6,000) 'play any game for money',[36] making it clear that he preferred them to practise archery.

Less contentious pleasures at court included watching the comical performances of the royal jesters. Henry employed fools called Martin, Patch and Sexton, whose chief function was to make him laugh. They sang bawdy songs, made fun of anything and everyone with a nice disregard for rank or deference, and told outrageous jokes. A favourite opening line might be, 'Sir, what say ye with your fat face?'[37] Often, the King permitted his fools familiarities that no one else would have dared to attempt, and occasionally, as we shall see, they overstepped the mark.

Henry's fools wore the traditional motley-coloured livery of jesters, with horned hats, and bells tied around their knees; they carried wands with jesters' heads or pigs' bladders on strings, which they wielded to good effect, and they sometimes dressed up in ridiculous costumes. In 1529, Henry bought a periwig for Sexton,[38] and he also bought Patch

some parti-coloured hose.[39] When Sexton retired in the 1530s, he was
replaced by a youth with a wickedly inventive sense of humour.[40]
Henry's most famous fool, Will Somers, did not enter his service until
1525.

Many court pastimes were seasonal. On Midsummer Eve, it was
traditional for a bonfire to be lit in the palace grounds: Henry paid 10s.
(£150) to his gardener for arranging this.[41] In winter, the courtiers
enjoyed snowball fights;[42] in January 1519, the King joined in one,
wearing a cap borrowed from a boy to keep his ears warm.[43]

There were also occasional novelties and diversions, such as the man
who rode two horses at once, or the German who brought a lion to
court, or the fellow whose dog was trained to dance.[44] The court
attracted acrobats, jugglers, performing monkeys and even freaks such as
the 'frantic man' who turned up once at Woodstock.[45] In 1510, the King
staged a fight with battleaxes in Greenwich Park to entertain the Queen
and her ladies, and at the same time impress onlookers with the military
skills of his gentlemen. Then there was the sinister-sounding pastime
known as 'the killcalf', in which a hapless beast appears to have been
slaughtered 'behind the cloth'.[46]

The gentlest courtly pursuit was the art of poetry-writing. The King
having set the trend, there emerged several amateur versifiers, or
'makers', from amongst the nobility and gentry. Writing poetry was one
of the ways in which an accomplished knight could court his chosen
lady. These poems were copied into manuscripts and circulated amongst
the courtiers; some were later printed in Tottel's *Miscellany*. However,
little poetry of note was written in the early years of the reign; hardly
any classical verse found its way into England, the age of Chaucer,
Lydgate and Gower was long gone, and even Skelton's works, for all
their satire, were little short of doggerel. Indeed, Skelton and other court
poets were busy making money from writing poems that lovestruck
courtiers could claim as their own.

The King himself summed up the early mood of the reign, and his
love of innocent courtly pleasures, in his own verses:

> Pastime with good company
> I love and shall until I die,
> Grudge who lust, yet none deny,
> So God be pleased, thus live will I.
> For my pastance [recreation], hunt sing and dance,
> My heart is set;
> All goodly sport to my comfort,
> Who shall me let [forbid]?

Youth must have some dalliance
Of good or ill some pastance;
Company methinks then best
All thought and fancies to digest;
For idleness is chief mistress
Of vices all;
Then who can say, but mirth and play
Is best of all.

Company with honesty
Is virtue, vices to flee;
Company is good or ill,
But every man hath his free will:
The best ensue, the worst eschew;
My mind shall be
Virtue to use, vice to refuse,
Thus shall I use me.

II

'New Men' and 'Natural Counsellors'

'He is a wonderful man and has wonderful people about him,' a French ambassador once said of Henry VIII.[1] The people most about the King, and closest to him, were the members of his Privy Chamber. The privy chamber was not just a room, or suite of rooms, but a household department, set up by Henry VII around 1495 to look after the private needs of the sovereign. Under Henry VIII, the Privy Chamber would become an elite and sophisticated power base rivalling the Privy Council, rather than simply a private royal retreat.

There was rampant competition for places in the Privy Chamber. Its members were the only courtiers, apart from Privy Councillors, with a right of entry to the inward chambers, and they had daily contact with the King. They were not necessarily aristocrats – a high proportion came from the gentry – but men who could offer their master good service and congenial companionship.

All members of the Privy Chamber had to have 'a vigilant and reverend respect and eye to His Majesty, so that by his look or countenance they may know what lacketh or is his pleasure to be had or done'. They waited on him hand and foot and guarded his lodgings when he was absent, whiling away the time playing cards and dice. They were expected to be 'loving together, and not to tattle about such things as may be done or said when the King goes forth', and 'they must leave enquiry where the King is or goeth, not grudging, mumbling or talking of the King's pastime, late or early going to bed, or anything done by His Grace'.[2] All Privy Chamber staff were expected to turn their hands, when required, to music-making, singing, dancing and acting.

The senior Gentleman of the Privy Chamber was the Groom of the Stool, who ran the department and was responsible for its staff and the safekeeping of furnishings, keys and valuables; he was also Keeper of the King's Privy Purse. As we have seen, he had the dubious privilege of attending his sovereign when he relieved himself, and for this purpose was always assigned a room in the privy lodgings; no one else had access to Henry's bedchamber 'or any other secret place', unless by invitation.[3] The Groom of the Stool was usually a knight; by the end of the reign he was also a member of the King's Council.

Next in importance were the twelve gentlemen of the Privy Chamber, of whom six were on duty at any one time; at least two of them had to be in attendance on the King and sleep at night in the privy lodgings. These gentlemen were in a highly privileged and powerful position, able to advise, influence and even manipulate the King, control access to his presence, and exercise patronage. Many of them were young men, 'servants without office'[4] who were there for no other reason but that the King liked them; several had served him as Prince of Wales. The Duke of Buckingham once complained, not without reason, that the King 'would give his fees, offices and rewards to boys rather than noblemen',[5] and it is true that these non-political appointees did sometimes exercise more influence over the King than his more experienced ministers and nobles did.

There were four Esquires of the Body, proficient knights who watched over the King day and night, helped him dress, and informed the Lord Chamberlain 'if anything lack for his person or pleasaunce. Their business is in many secrets.'[6]

Four Gentlemen Ushers were responsible for ensuring that protocol was observed at all times within the Chamber. They guarded the King's door, ushered visitors into his presence and watched over his valuables.[7] The Ushers were instructed to be 'courteous, and glad to receive, teach and direct every man', and they had to 'know all the customs and ceremonies used about the King'.[8]

The Yeomen of the Chamber acted as bedmakers and torchbearers, and kept the passage leading to the privy chamber 'clear of rascals, boys and others', who often hung about there causing a nuisance.[9] Four Grooms of the Chamber carried out menial duties such as cleaning, making up fires and laying out sleeping pallets; they were helped by four Pages of Honour, or Henchmen, of gentle birth, whose duties also included waiting on their superiors and walking near the King's horse in public processions. Pages wore parti-coloured tunics with gold chains slung across the shoulder baldrick-fashion, and carried striped green and white staves on ceremonial occasions. Both Pages and Grooms slept in the presence chamber, or the pages' chamber if there was one.

Lastly, there were six Gentlemen Waiters, three Cupbearers, three Carvers, two Surveyors, three Sewers, six physicians and surgeons and Penny the barber. The King's secretaries were also members of the Privy

Chamber.[10] Most Privy Chamber staff had lodgings at court, near the royal apartments.

Amongst the gentlemen of the Privy Chamber were the King's closest friends, dashing gallants with whom he hunted, jousted, play-acted, gambled and made merry. In their company, he was more a young man bent upon having a good time than a king, and he delighted in rewarding them lavishly for the good fellowship they gave him. Henry's favourite was Charles Brandon, the son of Sir William Brandon, Henry VII's Standard-bearer, who had been cut down by Richard III at Bosworth in 1485. Brandon, whose date of birth is unknown, was admitted to Prince Arthur's household as a page and, after Arthur's death in 1502, was brought up at court with Prince Henry, with whom he struck up a lasting friendship.

In 1509, Brandon was appointed an Esquire of the Body. He was the perfect companion for the King, whom he so resembled in looks and build that some people thought he was Henry's 'bastard brother'.[11] Handsome, brave, charming and extrovert, he shared Henry's love of competitive sports, and undoubtedly owed his meteoric rise to his 'valiant' partnership of the King in the lists.[12] Soon, Henry was showering him with offices, stewardships, receiverships, wardships and licences, and in 1513 he made him a Knight of the Garter. Brandon was no intellectual match for his master, but an accomplished courtier, soldier and diplomat; and he was a loyal and congenial servant who, by sometimes compromising his principles, retained Henry's affection until he died.

As well as gaining a reputation as a womaniser, Brandon had already enjoyed a complicated matrimonial career. He had first become precontracted to Anne, sister to Sir Anthony Browne and a lady-in-waiting to Elizabeth of York. Anne bore him a daughter, but in 1506/7 Brandon wriggled out of their uncanonical union and made a more advantageous marriage with her rich forty-three-year-old aunt, Margaret Mortimer. This match was quickly annulled on the grounds of consanguinity, and in 1508 Brandon abducted and married the long-suffering Anne Browne, who bore him two more daughters before dying in 1512. In 1513, he became betrothed to his ward Elizabeth, the nine-year-old heiress of John Grey, Viscount Lisle, and assumed her father's title in anticipation of his forthcoming marriage. This betrothal was later annulled. Margaret Mortimer was still complaining that the annulment of her marriage was invalid, and it was not until the 1520s that the Pope finally declared it null and void. By then, as we shall see, Brandon was married to another lady.

The King's first Groom of the Stool was the influential William

Compton, a former ward of Henry VII who was nine years older than Henry VIII and had been his attendant since childhood. Compton came from a wealthy family and built himself a fine red-brick courtyard house, Compton Wynyates in Warwickshire, which was completed c1515/23 and still stands today. The King visited there several times; the room reputedly used by him has a ceiling decorated with royal badges and initials. Foreign ambassadors rightly regarded Compton as one of the most powerful men at court, and heaped pensions and rich gifts on him in order to secure his favour.[13]

Another of the King's boon companions was his distant cousin and Sewer,[14] Edward Neville, brother of George, Lord Abergavenny, and a relative of Warwick the Kingmaker. Like Brandon, he bore a marked resemblance to Henry – they were often mistaken for brothers, and although they were not far apart in age, a persistent rumour had it that Neville was the King's bastard; Elizabeth I later mischievously addressed his son as 'brother Henry'![15] Neville also shared his master's passion for jousting.

Sir Thomas Boleyn, an Esquire of the Body, had been at court since 1501 and was made a Knight of the Bath at Henry's coronation; he would soon be appointed a Knight of the Body, Keeper of the Exchange at Calais, joint Constable of Norwich Castle and Sheriff of Kent. The Boleyns were a rising, socially aspiring family. Thomas's grandfather, Sir Geoffrey Boleyn, had been a mercer who had prospered sufficiently to become Lord Mayor of London in 1457 and had later purchased two fine properties for himself, Blickling in Norfolk and Hever in Kent. His son, Sir William Boleyn, had made a brilliant marriage with Margaret Butler, daughter of the Anglo-Irish Earl of Ormonde, and Thomas himself had made another illustrious match with the Earl of Surrey's daughter, Elizabeth Howard.

Since his father's death in 1505,[16] Boleyn had resided at Hever Castle, his mother having inherited Blickling. Now thirty-two, he was a shrewd, able, ambitious yet miserly and unscrupulous man, greedy for power, wealth and advancement; he 'would sooner act from interest than from any other motive,' wrote a French envoy.[17] Not without personal charm, he soon proved to the King that he could be useful and trustworthy; he spoke fluent Latin, and his French was better than anyone else's at court,[18] which led to him being sent by Henry, from 1512 onwards, on several important embassies, in the course of which he displayed a sound talent for diplomacy. He was also well educated in the humanist tradition, and was praised by Erasmus as being outstandingly learned. This, and Boleyn's expertise in the tiltyard, further endeared him to Henry.

Henry Guildford, 'a lusty young man well beloved of the King',[19] was perhaps two years older than Henry; he was knighted in 1512 and remained in favour for the rest of his life, receiving several offices and grants of land. Like Boleyn, he was a cultivated humanist, and regularly corresponded with Erasmus. He also excelled in the joust and in court pageants. His brother, Edward Guildford, was another of the King's jousting partners.

William Fitzwilliam, Henry's Cupbearer, had also been brought up with the King, who was a year his junior, and shared his love of the chase. The two men always remained close: Fitzwilliam understood his master's 'nature and temper better than any man in England'.[20] In 1511 he was appointed an Esquire of the Body. He later became Treasurer of Wolsey's household for a short while, then returned to the King's service, in which he remained for the rest of his life in various household posts and on active service on sea and land. He was a dependable, solid individual, who remained aloof from factional politics and was refreshingly free of the rapacious acquisitiveness that typified most courtiers.

Henry was also fond of John Pechy, another star of the tiltyard, who served him in various administrative capacities and also invited him and Queen Katherine to hunt in his parks. Thomas Knyvet, Boleyn's militaristic brother-in-law, was another member of the young King's circle, as was his brother Charles Knyvet. Henry's other intimates included Surrey's son, Sir Edward Howard, Buckingham's brother, Henry Stafford, Earl of Wiltshire, Thomas Grey, Marquess of Dorset, and his brothers Leonard and Anthony, and John St John, a nephew of Margaret Beaufort, who had shared the King's education and would one day serve both of his daughters.[21]

During these early years, Henry was very fond of his cousin Henry Courtenay, the son of his aunt, Katherine of York, by William Courtenay, Earl of Devon. In 1509, Courtenay was only eleven; seven years earlier, his father had been sent to the Tower by Henry VII on suspicion of treason, and Elizabeth of York had taken the boy into the royal household to be brought up with the royal children. On his accession, Henry VIII freed the Earl, who died in 1511, whereupon his son inherited his title and his vast estates in the West Country.

Courtenay was an aristocrat high in the King's favour. At Henry's accession, there were 45 hereditary peers: one duke, one marquess, 12 earls and 31 barons. Between them, they owned up to 70 per cent of England; however, the power of the aristocracy had weakened since the Wars of the Roses, when several old families had died out.

Henry VII had mistrusted the nobility and created only five new peers. He restricted the numbers of liveried retainers that they might keep and forced them to enter into bonds, with ruinous penalties should they prove disloyal. Nor, being a peace-loving monarch, did he give them much scope to exercise their natural aptitude for war: since feudal times, the nobility had served the King in a military capacity as tenants-in-chief. Hence when Henry VIII came to the throne, with his grandiose ideas for reconquering England's lost lands in France, the aristocracy hailed his accession with enthusiasm. 'Now the nobility, long since at the mercy of the dregs of the population, lifts its head and rejoices in such a king, and with good reason,' wrote Thomas More in his coronation panegyric. In many ways, their expectations would be satisfied.

However, Henry VIII, like his father, was suspicious of the nobility, some of whom had royal blood and might be potential dynastic rivals. He therefore kept them busy with political and administrative affairs at court and in the shires, and rewarded them handsomely, in order to keep them faithful. Their loyalty was vital to his security, so he was careful to identify their interests with his own.

The nobility were jealous of their time-honoured right to act as the King's chief political advisers; but as far as Henry VIII was concerned, good service was as important, if not more so, than high birth, and where power had once been the privilege of the landed peerage, it was now beginning to devolve upon men who had risen through their own abilities and education rather than their pedigrees. 'We will not be bound of necessity to be served with lords, but we will be served with such men of what degree soever as we shall appoint,' Henry once stated.[22] The chief officers of the household might happen to be nobles, but their prominence at court derived from their offices rather than their birth. Like his father, Henry was also concerned to re-establish the dominance of the Crown over the nobility.

Nevertheless, the aristocracy remained a caste apart; they sat in the House of Lords, and their status was reflected in their dress, entourages and opulent way of life. Their servants wore their livery and badges, and their heraldic emblems were emblazoned on their country houses. Their privileges were enshrined in Magna Carta, and over the centuries had been further defined by tradition and sumptuary laws. For example, only a duke could sit by himself at table with the King; an earl had to have another earl with him, and his robes had one less row of ermine than a duke's. Peers surrounded the King on state occasions, their illustrious presence enhancing his majestas. Precedence governed all, and was an accepted fact of court life.

The sovereign was the fount of all honour, and only he could create peers – Henry VIII was to create thirty-seven. But noblemen were well aware that he could also unmake them, through the parliamentary process of attainder, and that their status and wealth depended on his goodwill and their good behaviour. Neither could they marry without his consent. Having set a precedent in magnificence, the King encouraged his nobles to copy his extravagant example – in an age that valued outward show, they needed little persuasion – and so distracted them from the warmongering to which they had been bred. The effort to keep up with their monarch led many to financial ruin and the consequent erosion of their power and independence, which further restricted their ability to become involved in the kind of subversive activities so feared by the King.

Henry made it clear that the court was the place to be if the nobility wished to fulfil their traditional ambitions and take their rightful place in society; their scramble for attendance upon the King, as well as their enthusiastic attempts to emulate him, are indicators of how successful Henry's controlling measures had been.

The older nobility were disparaging and resentful of those whom the Duke of Norfolk scathingly termed 'new men', men such as Charles Brandon and Thomas Cromwell, whose titles and lands were bestowed by the King as rewards for good service; the peers believed the King ought to pay heed only to themselves, who were his 'natural counsellors' by virtue of their birth.[23] The 'new men', who were mostly from the gentry and merchant classes, only fuelled their fury by flaunting their new position as landed aristocracy and affecting the manners, dress and lifestyle of the older nobility. The King had his work cut out to maintain the peace between the old elite and the nouveaux riches at court.

It was clear that what now defined a gentleman was not just the ability to 'live idly and without manual labour',[24] nor was it purely the traditional knightly virtues of military prowess, liberality, hospitality, honour, courtesy and chivalry. In Henry's reign, the definition widened.

In 1509, few aristocrats went to university, nor did they dabble in intellectual pursuits such as music and poetry; one lordly father said he would sooner see his son hanged than have him reading books. 'Before poets began to be in price,' wrote Sir Philip Sidney, 'our nation hath set their heart's delight upon action and not upon imagination.'[25] If the upper classes did read, they resorted to works that reflected the values of their caste, such as romances or books of courtesy (manners).

In Italy, however, most men of rank were also men of letters; as we have already seen, Henry VIII himself typified the Italian Renaissance ideal of the multi-talented, accomplished gentleman. His courtiers' desire to ape him, together with the spread of Renaissance influences, ensured that attitudes rapidly changed. Humanists now argued that true nobility lay in intellectual aspirations rather than in blood.

Before long, it was essential for any gentleman who wished to succeed at court to be literate, erudite and musical, and to have some knowledge of the law and theology. Sir Thomas Elyot, in his book *The Governor* (1531), also advocated artistic pursuits such as painting and carving, so that a gentleman might be able to discern 'the excellence of them which in music, statuary or painter's craft possesseth any cunning'. Music in particular, declared Castiglione, was 'not only an ornament, but necessary for a courtier'. Most aristocratic children were therefore taught to play an instrument, and many noblemen patronised musicians.

A gentleman was also supposed to conduct himself with dignity, elegance and effortless refinement, and 'to use in every thing a certain recklessness, and to do it without pain'.[26] Honour compelled him to make a brave show of his wealth, whilst affecting a certain nonchalance about it, since a preoccupation with money smacked of trade. In all he did, a gentleman was obliged to show courtesy to others and reverence towards God.

The premier peer of England was Edward Stafford, 3rd Duke of Buckingham. A descendant of Thomas of Woodstock, youngest son of Edward III, the Duke had a strong claim to the throne and his lifestyle was that of a mighty mediaeval magnate. His father, the 2nd Duke, had been executed for treason in 1483 by Richard III, and his mother, Katherine Wydeville, was Henry VIII's great-aunt; Stafford had come into his great inheritance at the age of seven; he was the richest peer in the realm, with an annual income of £6,000 (£1,800,000).

Buckingham's wife was the sister of the powerful Earl of Northumberland, and he was allied by blood and marriage to most of the older nobility. He owned vast lands in twelve counties, and had various seats including Penshurst Place in Kent, Stafford Castle, Maxstoke Castle, Kimbolton Castle and Thornbury Castle, a palatial residence that he built between 1511 and 1521 in Gloucestershire; it was said to have been modelled on Richmond.

Although Buckingham was a Privy Councillor, High Steward of England and often at court, he never became one of Henry's closest advisers. Not only was the Duke too near the throne for comfort, but he was also 'high minded',[27] haughty, aloof and not very bright. He enjoyed gambling, although he lost frequently, and was a fine jouster, which was sufficient to guarantee him a place in the King's circle; but his overweening pride in his lineage and his tendency to 'rail and misuse himself in words' made him an uncomfortable companion. He lacked the bonhomie that Henry so appreciated in those close to him, and did not condescend to acquire it; it is possible he even thought the King a parvenu.

There were other nobles who were too near the throne in blood for Henry's comfort. Several were scions of the Plantagenet House of York, which had been overthrown when Richard III was defeated and killed by Henry VII at Bosworth in 1485. There were those who believed that these 'White Rose' lords had a better claim to the throne than the Tudors, and for this reason Henry VII and Henry VIII were ever-watchful of their activities; however, where his father had been ruthless in suppressing his unwanted relatives, Henry VIII treated them well until his suspicions were aroused. Henry VII had executed Edward, Earl of Warwick, the son of Edward IV's brother George, Duke of Clarence, but Warwick's sister Margaret, widow of Sir Richard Pole, was now a close friend of Katherine of Aragon.

Edward IV's sister Elizabeth had married John de la Pole, Duke of Suffolk. Their son, Edmund, the present Earl of Suffolk, had been a prisoner in the Tower since 1506 on account of his nearness to the throne, and his younger brother Richard, a notorious political agitator, had fled abroad. Then there was Henry Courtenay, Earl of Devon, who was as yet too young to pose any threat to the King's security. In fact, for many years Henry enjoyed good relations with Devon and with Margaret Pole. He was also on excellent terms with many of the older nobility, including the Bourchiers, Nevilles, Staffords and Manners, all of whom were of Plantagenet descent. Most of the so-called 'White Rose' faction were members of the Queen's circle: their high lineage and conservative outlook appealed to her Spanish pride, and in time they came to be identified with reactionary opinion at court.

Thomas Grey, 2nd Marquess of Dorset, ranked second after Buckingham; he had no royal blood but was the grandson of Edward IV's queen, Elizabeth Wydeville, by her first marriage to Sir John Grey, and therefore the King's cousin. Dorset had inherited his title in 1501 on the execution of his father, and had been the first patron of the young Thomas Wolsey. He was now forty, of middle height with blond hair,[28] and, although of no outstanding political ability, a hero of the joust. The King liked him greatly, and in 1523 made him a Gentleman of the Privy Chamber. Dorset's wife was Margaret Wotton, who was later drawn by Hans Holbein,[29] and his seat was at Bradgate Park in Leicestershire, now famous as the birthplace of his granddaughter, Lady Jane Grey.

The most influential nobleman on the Council was the Lord Treasurer, Thomas Howard, Earl of Surrey, now aged sixty-six. The Howards had originally been East Anglian gentry, but thanks to a series of advantageous marriages had inherited the dukedom of Norfolk. Surrey's father, John Howard, 1st Duke of Norfolk, had died fighting for Richard III at Bosworth, and Surrey, who had fought with him and been wounded, had been attainted by Henry VII. The King had asked

Surrey why he had supported Richard, whereupon he staunchly replied, 'He was my crowned king, and if the parliamentary authority of England set the crown on a stock, I will fight for that stock. And as I fought then for him, I will fight for you.'[30]

Thanks to his integrity, his tenacity and his abilities as a soldier and administrator, Surrey had gradually advanced himself back into favour, had regained some of his lands – his chief seat was his palace at Kenninghall, Norfolk – and been given responsibility for guarding the northern border; but he had so far failed, for all his loyal service, to achieve his ambition of recovering the dukedom of Norfolk. By his two wives, who were both members of the Tilney family of Norfolk, Surrey was the father of a large family and related through his children's marriages to most of the English nobility. His eldest son, Lord Thomas Howard, was set for a brilliant political career at court, while his second son, the martial Sir Edward Howard, was one of the King's intimates. A kindly, dependable man of modest tastes, Surrey was a favourite of both the King and the Queen, and very popular with the people of England. He was, wrote Polydore Vergil, 'a man of the utmost wisdom, solid worth and loyalty'.

12

'All Goodly Sports'

During the heady summer of 1509, Henry VIII and his courtiers embarked upon an unceasing programme of sporting activities. The King was an energetic, vigorous man who revelled in frequent physical exercise, an unmatched sportsman whose expertise won him golden opinions in an age that valued such manly pursuits highly. Sport was, moreover, an interest Henry shared with most of the gentlemen and nobles at court. Many of them, too, excelled at it, 'but the most assiduous and the most interested was the King'.[1] He hunted, jousted, played tennis, wrestled, could throw a twelve-foot spear many yards, defeated all comers with his heavy two-handed sword in mock combats, and could draw a bow with greater strength than any man in England. The benefits of all this activity included a splendid physique, robust good health and sheer masculine strength. 'When he moves, the ground shakes under him,' observed a Venetian.[2]

Most gentlemen 'passed the summers in disports',[3] usually in the open air. Many of their traditional activities – jousting, riding, running at the ring, tilting at the quintain and archery – were essentially martial exercises, but thanks to a revival of the classical interest in physical fitness for its own sake in Italy, and Castiglione's advocacy of the social importance of sport and the opportunities it offered for the display of magnificence, attitudes were changing. In 1531, Thomas Elyot wrote: 'By exercise, the health of a man is preserved and his strength increased', and in 1542 Andrew Boorde recommended moderate exercise through 'playing at the tennis, or casting a bowl, or pairing weights in your hands'. Sport was also an effective channel for the aggression of large numbers of easily bored young male courtiers.

Nearly all sports were competitive. It was not done, however, to compete with one's social inferiors.[4] Organised ball games, such as football, were played only by the lower classes, and Parliament passed legislation restricting the playing of bowls, quoits and tennis to the upper classes only, within the privacy of their estates.[5] The King's subjects were, rather, to spend their leisure hours practising archery, which would be to the nation's profit in time of war.

In youth, the King's favourite sporting pursuits were jousting (which will be discussed separately) and hunting. Hunting was a royal and aristocratic sport, almost as prestigious as warfare, and required the same courage and skills as were needed in battle. It could also be very dangerous, as the King was to find on several occasions, and sometimes embarrassing, as when he killed the wrong buck and had to pay compensation to its owner.

The quarry, which was usually deer, was either shot with bows and arrows, tracked down by dogs, or driven into nets called 'toils', ready for the ceremonious kill. Sometimes, the deer were chased into an enclosure and the dogs let loose upon them. It was a cruel and bloody sport, but the Tudor age was not one for squeamishness.

The King was passionate about the chase. In 1520, Richard Pace told Wolsey that their master was getting up 'daily, except on holy days, at 4 or 5 o'clock, and hunts till 9 or 10 at night. He spares no pains to convert the sport of hunting into a martyrdom.'[6] 'He never takes his diversion without tiring eight or ten horses, which he causes to be stationed beforehand along the line of country he means to take, and when one is tired, he mounts another, and before he gets home they are all exhausted.'[7] When he 'hath had good sport, he will talk thereof three or four hours after'.[8]

Invariably, hunting took priority over business: the King 'was going out to have a shot at a stag',[9] or his huntsmen were waiting and 'he must needs hunt them'.[10] He was delighted when, in 1526, the King of France sent him some wild boar, which were almost extinct in England, observing that 'the hunting was very pleasant, and a King's game';[11] it was also highly risky, for boar were notoriously ferocious.

In his youth, Henry went hunting with a huge entourage of courtiers, but in 1526 numbers were restricted because their absence left the court 'disgarnished' and, through their boisterousness, 'the King's disports were hindered and impeached'.[12] After that, Henry took with him just a handful of his intimates. His inventory lists numerous items of hunting and other sporting equipment, many crammed into the cupboards in his privy lodgings. Two of his 'wood knives', or hunting swords, one etched with scenes of a boar hunt, the other damascened in gold, were crafted by the Spanish swordsmith, Diego de Çayas, and are still in the Royal Collection.[13]

Katherine of Aragon also enjoyed hunting, and was still accompanying Henry as late as 1530, at the height of their nullity suit.

Most of the royal forests, paled deer parks and hunting chases had been emplaced before 1200, many being annexed to royal castles, manors and hunting lodges. Henry's favourites were Windsor Great Park, Richmond Park, Greenwich Park, Bushy Park and Epping Forest, and he himself established several more parks and chases, including Hyde Park, Waltham Chase, St James's Park, Nonsuch Park, Marylebone (now Regent's) Park and the vast Honour of Hampton Court.[14] The royal parks and forests provided the King not only with good sport, but also with venison for his household and a substantial income from dues and fines: severe forest and venery laws imposed stiff financial or custodial penalties on ordinary people who stole the King's deer.

The hunting, or 'grass', season lasted from May or June until September or October. For part of this period the King usually went on progress, so that he could enjoy the hunting in other parts of his kingdom. Each autumn, upon his return, he would personally supervise the restocking of his parks with game, and ensure that there were sufficient hay and oats to last the deer through the winter.[15]

The King owned a fine stable of up to two hundred horses.[16] His favourites were nimble Barbary steeds or light-footed Neapolitan coursers, which he imported from Europe at a cost of up to £40 (£12,000) each. Several were gifts from princes who sought his friendship, like the bay courser sent by the Duke of Termoli. In 1509, Queen Katherine asked her father 'to send to the King my lord three horses, one a jennet, the other from Naples, and the other a Sicilian, because he desires them much, and has asked me to beg Your Highness for them, and also to command them to be sent by the first messenger that comes here'.[17]

In June 1514, Francesco Gonzaga, Marquis of Mantua, a famous breeder of horses, sent Henry a splendid 'bright bay' called Governatore and three brood mares. Henry watched 'astounded' as their trainer, Giovanni Ratto, put the mares through their paces, then asked his courtiers, 'What think you of these mares? I have never seen better animals.' After Ratto had ridden Governatore with an impressive display of Spanish dressage as a compliment to the Queen, Henry declared that this was 'the best horse' and patted the bay, murmuring 'So-ho, so-ho, my minion.' He could not have been more pleased if the Marquis had given him a kingdom, wrote a watching Venetian. Afterwards, Henry asked Ratto what the Marquis would like in return for his generosity. 'Nothing but the King's love' was the reply.[18]

Later that month Ratto informed Gonzaga that Henry was of the opinion that he had never ridden better-trained horses, and the King himself wrote an effusive letter of thanks 'for your supreme goodwill towards ourself, for those most beautiful, high-bred and surpassing steeds [that] have been sent from the very best feeling and intention. We number Your Excellency and your most noble children among our dearest friends. Farewell, with prosperity and happiness!' The next month he sent the Marquis 'some horses, saddled and harnessed in their full trappings' as a return gift.[19]

Henry was also thrilled with the mounts sent by Alfonso I, Duke of Ferrara, in 1519 and the Spanish jennets given him by the Emperor Charles V in 1520. His own courtiers were well aware that the surest way of pleasing him was to give him a horse; in 1520, for example, Sir Edward Guildford gave him two: one, a bay called Byard Hays, became one of his favourite mounts.[20]

The King, according to a Venetian ambassador, was a 'capital horseman'.[21] He would train for hours, and exercised his mounts regularly, praising them by rubbing them with his whip and crying 'Holla, holla, so boy, there boy!', or admonishing them with a sharp 'Ha, traitor! Ha, villain!' On the advice of his Italian riding masters, he preferred to encourage his horses by kindness rather than use his spurs or whip.[22]

Riding, and a knowledge of matters equestrian, were essential accomplishments for every gentleman, especially those of aristocratic birth, who were brought up to handle great warhorses whilst wearing full armour. It was Henry VIII who introduced the 'manage', the new Italian art of dressage, into England, at which he excelled above all others. This involved putting a rigorously trained horse through a series of spectacular movements by using light touches or commands. The horse might turn, rear, stop suddenly after a gallop, weave between obstacles, or perform the astonishing capriole, or 'great leap', in which all four of its hooves flew off the ground at the same time. The King would show off his skills at every opportunity, particularly at tournaments, where he would astound his audience by performing 'supernatural feats', making a succession of horses either execute 'a thousand jumps in the air' or 'fly rather than leap, to the delight and ecstasy of everybody'.[23]

Katherine of Aragon was a competent horsewoman, although she used a Spanish side-saddle shaped like a chair.

Henry also bred horses, and was constantly improving his bloodstock. He founded royal studs on the Welsh Marches, in Nottinghamshire and at Hampton Court to breed horses for hunting and even racing. It was Henry VIII, rather than Charles II, who was the first English King to race horses. He kept 'geldings that did run' and employed 'riding boys that ride the running horses'. Their livery comprised satin and fustian doublets in the Tudor colours of green and white, 'parti-hosen' and black velvet riding hats with gold buttons.[24] The King laid out a flat race course and tiltyard at Cobham in Surrey; the race course, of which traces still remain, was a mile long, and stretched in a straight line to Leigh Hill. The King himself enjoyed racing: in 1513, whilst campaigning in France, he and twenty-five companions raced their horses around the outskirts of a town.[25]

Henry became very attached to his horses. One of his favourites was Canicida, about whom his Latin Secretary, Andrea Ammonio, wrote some laudatory verses. In 1529, Henry made repeated visits to his stables just to see his favourite Barbary horse (possibly Governatore), who was enjoying a comfortable retirement. The King frequently stopped for a chat with his horsekeeper, Hannibal Zinzano, and showed genuine concern for his horses' health. His Privy Purse Expenses list several home-made cures for their ailments, and also a number of payments of 7s. (£105) for 'baths for the Barbary horse'.[26] Henry's horses were fed on bran from the royal granaries.[27]

The Master of the Horse was responsible for providing the King with horses for riding, hunting and war, and was in charge of the royal stables and conveyances as well as travelling arrangements. By virtue of the nature of his duties and of his being the third great officer of the household, he was constantly in attendance on his master, rode near him in ceremonial processions, and had the privilege of dining at his own table at court. Sir Thomas Knyvet was Henry's first Master of the Horse. The Queen had her own Master of the Horse.

The Stables were a department independent of the court, and were responsible to the King himself. They employed a large staff of squires, stable boys, farriers, jockeys and horsekeepers. The headquarters of the Stables were initially at Holborn, but when they were destroyed by fire in 1534, the department and its animals were transferred to the Royal Mews in Charing Cross, which normally housed the royal falcons.[28] Horses used by the King and court were also kept in stables at the royal palaces; some of these were built around courtyards, and a section was always partitioned off for the King's personal use. At Greenwich, there was one stable for his coursers and another for his stud mares.[29] The King's New Stable at Hampton Court, built in 1536, survives today as part of the Royal Mews on Hampton Court Green.

The Kennels were a separate department responsible for providing and housing the royal hunting packs of greyhounds, harthounds, buckhounds and harriers. They came under the jurisdiction of the Master of the Privy Hounds, Humphrey Rainsford, and their headquarters were those originally established in the fourteenth century by Edward III on the Isle of Dogs on the Thames. There were kennels at some of the palaces also, including a vast one at Greenwich. Hunting dogs were fed a diet of meat, milk and bread.

It was only as he grew older that Henry VIII grew to like hawking. His father had given him a hawk when he was nine, but as a young man he had 'no affection' for the sport, despite being coached by the court's resident expert, Sir William Tyler, a gentleman of the Privy Chamber. It was only when he reached maturity that he acquired a taste for it. In the 1520s, Thomas Heneage of the Privy Chamber reported to Wolsey from Windsor that 'His Grace, every afternoon, when the weather is anything fair, doth ride forth on hawking, or walketh in the park, and cometh not in again till it be late in the evening'.[30] In 1533, Sir William Kingston informed Arthur Plantagenet, Lord Lisle,[31] that 'the King hawks every day with goshawks, sparrowhawks and merlins, both before noon and after'. Hawking provided good sport after the hunting season was over.[32]

Hawks, notably gerfalcons, peregrines, tiercels and merlins, were extremely valuable birds and the sport was strictly an upper-class pursuit, with the ownership of certain birds being dependent upon one's rank. Henry imported hawks from Ireland, or received them as gifts from fellow rulers such as the King of France and Joachim I, Duke of Prussia. One of his hawk's hoods, fashioned of leather and what might have been embroidered crimson velvet or silk, is in the Ashmolean Museum, together with his doeskin hawking glove worked with red and gilt thread. His accounts record payments for 'jesses' (red strings attached to the hawk's legs), hoods and bells.[33]

The King's hawks were the responsibility of the department of the Toyles, which was housed in the Royal Mews at Charing Cross, where they were trained and cared for by experts in falconry who fed them on sugar comfits, horehound water and rhubarb.[34] One of the eleven falconers was Lambert Simnel, who had in childhood been set up by Yorkist sympathisers as a pretender to Henry VII's throne. The rebellion failed, and Henry had sent Simnel to work in his kitchens, whence he had worked his way up to the mews; he died in 1525. The Master of the King's Hawks headed the department; this was initially William Norris, who was succeeded by Robert Cheseman, whose portrait by Hans Holbein shows him holding a falcon.[35]

At Greenwich, Henry built a mews known as 'the cage' right next to his privy lodgings; it had racks of perches, and wooden lattices over the unglazed windows.[36] New mews were also built at lesser houses such as The More and Hunsdon.[37]

Other royal bloodsports included bear-baiting and even bull-baiting; the King had his own bear pit and bears, in the charge of the Master of the King's Bears. On Shrove Tuesday, Henry attended the traditional cockfights, for which, in 1533–4, he built new cockpits at Greenwich and Whitehall, the latter being a curious octagonal structure with a lantern roof.[38] Both had tiered rows of seating, with a special chair for the King and a viewing gallery for the Queen.[39] The fighting birds were kept in nearby coops.[40]

Henry occasionally went fishing: at Hampton Court, in 1530 and 1532, he fished in the Thames with an 'angle rod',[41] and in 1532 also he rewarded some men who had caught a prize fish at Greenwich.[42] He is also known to have fished in the moat at The More.[43]

Bloodsports were not the only sporting activities enjoyed by the King and his court. Henry was 'extremely fond of tennis'[44] and may have been taught the game by the professional players employed by his father;[45] he himself certainly retained a coach.[46] According to the Venetian ambassador Giustinian, 'it was the prettiest thing in the world to see him play, his fair skin glowing through a shirt of the finest texture';[47] for playing, he stripped to his 'slops' (drawers) and wore soft shoes, and after the game he would don a 'tennis coat' of black or blue velvet to stop him catching a chill.[48] By all accounts, even allowing for a degree of sycophantic exaggeration, he was a world-class player.

The game Henry played was not the sedate lawn tennis of today,[49] but the earlier, more aggressive version known as royal, or real, tennis, or 'palme', which derived from the mediaeval French game of _jeu de paume_ and had become a popular aristocratic sport in France and Italy. It could be played indoors or outdoors, and was a favourite winter diversion.[50]

The enclosed hard courts, or plays, had nets of fringed cord[51] and galleries for spectators, and were marked out with penthouses and chases. The walls were usually painted black and the window frames red, the windows being covered with protective wire.[52] Racquets were a recent invention; until around 1500, the ball had been caught in a gloved hand. Henry's balls were made for him by the Ironworkers' Company in London; one, of leather stuffed with dog's hair, was found embedded in the roof timbers of Westminster Hall in the 1920s,[53] and another was found in the 1960s on the site of the King's tennis court at Whitehall.

There were two versions of the game – the quarre, or minor court, and the dedans, or major court[54] – and the rules were sufficiently complicated to ensure that only educated men played. Baldassare Castiglione, author of _The Courtier_, recommended tennis as 'a noble exercise' because it afforded courtiers the opportunity to display their physical dexterity and 'nimbleness'.

Edward IV and Henry VII had built tennis plays, but Henry VIII was to build far more; notable examples are at Hampton Court and Whitehall. The Keeper of Tennis Plays was responsible for maintenance, scoring, stringing racquets with sheep-gut and coaching.[55] When the King was not playing, his courtiers were allowed to hire the plays at a rate of 2s.6d. (£37.50) a day.[56] Gambling on the outcome of a game was common, and of course there were those who grumbled that tennis was 'dangerous for the body and for the purse'.[57]

Since the fourteenth century, the long-bow had been instrumental in England's most renowned military victories, and all able-bodied men were required by law to practise shooting regularly. Sir Thomas Elyot declared that 'shooting in the long bow incomparably excelleth all other exercise'. The King, like his late brother Arthur, was a superb archer,[58] and could outshoot even the crack shots in the Yeomen of the Guard: in Calais in 1513, whilst competing with them, 'he cleft the mark in the middle and surpassed them all'.[59] Early in the reign, a new butt was set up in Tothill Fields near Westminster, and he was often to be seen shooting there; there were also butts at most of his houses, some of them – rather alarmingly – indoors.[60] Henry also enjoyed the sport as a spectator.[61]

Bowling was another sport favoured by the King in his later years, and again, he was very good at it and played frequently. There were brick-built bowling alleys, some over two hundred feet long, at several houses including Richmond, Greenwich, Hampton Court and Eltham,[62] most of them erected after 1532; and where there was no alley, a grass lawn could be used. The aim was to roll one's wheel-shaped 'ball' as close to the jack as possible. Bowling was a very popular all-weather sport, and bets were always laid on the outcome; in 1532, Henry lost £21 (£6,300) to the Duke of Norfolk.[63]

In youth, the King was always game for a wrestling match, even though this was not strictly speaking a sport for gentlemen. He was also adept at 'casting the bar',[64] which involved throwing a heavy metal beam. No feat of strength was beyond him: he once even tried his hand at labouring, sawing blocks of wood and fashioning cobblestones with steel hammers.[65]

Henry VII had copied the Burgundian precedent of building a recreational complex in his palace at Richmond: in the lower end of the gardens were to be found 'pleasant galleries and houses of pleasure to disport in at chess, tables, dice, cards, bil[liard]s; bowling alleys, butts for archers and goodly tennis plays', with space for spectators.[66] Henry VIII followed his example at many of his residences; his first project was the building of a tennis play at Westminster. These complexes, which also included tiltyards, served as sophisticated leisure centres for the King and his courtiers.

13

'Merry Disports'

In the summer of 1509, Henry informed King Ferdinand that he was about to visit different parts of his kingdom.[1] We know very little about this first progress, save that it was fairly extensive and included sojourns at Reading Abbey and the Old Hall at Gainsborough in Lincolnshire, seat of Edward de Burgh, Lord Borough, who later married Katherine Parr.

Henry went on progress almost every summer of his reign. His purpose was not only to see his realm and be seen by his subjects, but also to enjoy the hunting that was to be had in other parts. At that time of year, many courtiers had returned to their estates to oversee the harvest, so the King was usually accompanied by a smaller retinue and sometimes just by his riding household. The Queen usually accompanied him.

As he travelled, Henry distributed alms and largesse to religious houses and to individuals.[2] He always took his Chapel Royal with him, to conduct religious services and provide musical entertainment, and his hunting dogs, which were transported by cart.

Unlike his daughter Elizabeth I, Henry did not routinely seek lavish hospitality from his subjects, and his visits were never as financially ruinous to his hosts as hers were. Many of his lesser houses were progress houses, and he used them whenever possible. In the first half of the reign he lodged also in the guest houses, or in apartments especially reserved for him, at monasteries. At other times he stayed as the guest of one of his courtiers or some local worthy, becoming lord of the house for the duration of his stay, with his apartments taking on, as far as possible, the functions of the Chamber at court, and his servants having priority over the residents in the allocation of accommodation and billets.[3] Those closest to the King were assigned the rooms nearest his. If there was not sufficient space for his retinue in the house, barns and stables would be pressed into service, or tents set up in the grounds.

The Knight Harbinger was responsible for allocating accommodation to everyone, which was done strictly according to rank.[4] When the King stayed at a private residence, one of his Gentlemen Ushers would go ahead to check that the house was structurally sound, that the roof did not leak, and that there were locks on all the doors.

Progresses could last for up to two months; they usually took place between July and October, and were carefully planned in advance, with the itinerary being set out in the detailed tables called 'giests'. The King's plans were only altered when plague broke out or the weather was bad. The Master of the Horse was responsible for organising the complicated travel arrangements required to transport the court on the move, and the Board of the Greencloth for the provision of food,[5] although individual hosts would always lay on lavish hospitality for their monarch. Everything was done to make the King's transition from one house to another as smooth as possible.

Once the progress was over, the King would return to London or to his palaces in the Thames Valley, where he normally spent the winter. Late in 1509, he and Queen Katherine, who was in her first pregnancy, removed to Richmond Palace by the Thames in Surrey for the festive season.

Richmond was Henry VII's masterpiece, a large, battlemented Perpendicular fantasy modelled on the ducal residences of Bruges, and built − at a cost of £20,000 (over £6 million) − on the ruins of the mediaeval palace of Sheen, which had been destroyed by fire at Christmas 1497. The new palace, built of red brick and stone between 1499 and 1503 and renamed Richmond by royal decree after the earldom held by Henry VII before his accession, was designed on a courtyard plan. It was distinguished by vast expanses of big bay windows, fairy-tale pinnacles, and turrets surmounted by bell-shaped domes and gilded weather-vanes − there were fourteen of these on the royal apartments alone. The palace was surrounded by an extensive deer park.[6]

A contemporary described Richmond as 'an earthly paradise, most glorious to behold'.[7] There were fountains in the courtyards, orchards, and 'most fair and pleasant gardens' set with knots and intersected by wide paths and statues of the King's Beasts. Around the gardens were novel timber-framed, two-storeyed galleried walks, and nearby was the recreation complex. In the stone donjon housing the royal lodgings, the beamed ceilings were painted azure and studded with gold Tudor roses and portcullises; there were rich tapestries, panel portraits, and murals by Henry VII's painter, Maynard the Fleming, of 'the noble kings of this realm in harness and robes of gold, as Brutus, Hengist, King William

Rufus, King Arthur [and] King Henry . . . with swords in their hands, appearing like bold and valiant knights'.[8] There was a richly appointed chapel and a library established by Henry VII. A 'mighty brick wall' surrounded the palace, with a tower at each corner, and in the centre stood the main gate 'of double timber and heart of oak, studded full of nails and crossed with bars of iron'.[9] Above it were the arms of Henry VII, supported by the red dragon of Wales and the greyhound of Richmond.

Henry VIII celebrated his first Christmas as King at Richmond. It was marked by a joust before the palace gates, on what is now Richmond Green, where 'many notable feats of arms were proved'.[10] The festivities were directed by one Will Wynesbury, acting as Lord of Misrule, who impudently asked the King to lend him £5 (£1,500) on account. 'If it shall like Your Grace to give me too much,' he added mischievously, 'I will give you none again, and if Your Grace give me too little, I will ask more!' Henry thought this was hilarious.[11]

Christmas in Tudor times was a twelve-day festival, with the celebrations reaching their climax on 6 January, or Twelfth Night, which was the Feast of the Epiphany. The Advent fast ended on Christmas Eve; then there were twelve days of feasting, banqueting, pageantry, disguising and convivial merrymaking, all presided over by the Lord of Misrule, or 'Master of Merry Disports',[12] with his train of heralds, magicians and fools in fancy dress; at court, this was a time when rank took second place to revelry. Henry VIII also observed the mediaeval custom of appointing a boy bishop to take the place of his senior Chaplain: at Windsor, he once rewarded a lad called Nicholas with 10 marks for taking this role.

The court was always full at Christmas. The royal palaces, like many humbler homes, were decorated with 'holly, ivy and bays, and whatsoever the season afforded to be green',[13] and the public were often allowed in to watch the 'goodly and gorgeous mummeries'.[14] In the great hall or presence chamber, the mighty Yule log crackled on the hearth, and carols were danced and sung, 'to the great rejoicing of the Queen and the nobles'.[15]

Great feasts were served at court over Yuletide. On Christmas Day, there was always the seasonal favourite, 'seethed' brawn made from spiced boar or pork, and perhaps roast swans; the first course, however, was invariably a boar's head, which was served 'bedecked with bay and rosemary', according to the old carol printed in 1521 by the King's printer, Wynkyn de Worde. For the sumptuous banquet that marked Twelfth Night, a special cake of dried fruit, flour, honey and spices was baked, containing a pea or a bean; whoever found it would be King or Queen of the Pea or Bean for the evening; from payments made beforehand, though, it appears that at court the lucky recipients were often selected in advance, just to be on the safe side. At the void of Twelfth Night, the choir of the Chapel Royal sang as the wassail cup, which contained spiced ale, was brought in by the Lord Steward and presented to the King and Queen, then passed around the table.[16]

Christmas was also a time for solemn religious observances. Each Christmas Day, the King would hear Mass in his closet before going in procession to the chapel royal for Matins, where he actually participated in the service. This was, observed a papal nuncio, a 'very unusual proceeding', since Henry normally attended to business during public services.[17] The choir usually sang 'Gloria in excelsis' on these occasions, for which the King once rewarded them with £2 (£600). On the Feast of the Epiphany, gold, frankincense and myrrh were offered on behalf of the Queen.

Presents were exchanged, not on Christmas Day, but on New Year's Day. Not only the Queen and the royal family, but also every courtier and servant, gave the King a gift; each was presented to him by the donor or his representative in a glittering ceremony in the presence chamber, where the gifts – which might be gold or silver plate, jewellery or money – were afterwards displayed on sideboards or trestle tables for all to see. Each was then listed by the royal secretaries before being stored away. Great lords vied with each other to give the most valuable or novel items: Cardinal Wolsey regularly gave his master a gold cup worth £100 (£30,000). In return, Henry distributed gifts of plate such as cups and bowls chased with the royal cipher, each weighted according to rank, to every person at court, even the most menial members of the Household.

In January 1510, Henry staged the first of many disguisings. Early one morning, he and eleven companions dressed themselves as Robin Hood and his outlaws, donning short coats of green Kentish Kendal – a rough woollen cloth – with hoods that concealed their faces. Then, armed with bows and arrows, swords and bucklers, they burst into the Queen's chamber, at which Katherine and her ladies were much 'abashed'. Nevertheless, they agreed to dance with their visitors, and only after the dancing was finished did the King and his fellows throw back their hoods and reveal who they were, much to the astonishment of the ladies and the amusement of the men.[18]

Henry VIII's reign witnessed the Indian summer of the age of chivalry. Tournaments in the Burgundian style were hugely popular; they were staged at almost every court festival or diplomatic visit, and as regular events during May and June to provide 'honourable and healthy exercise'[19] before the hunting season began. They were essentially an

aristocratic preserve, intended to keep fighting men in the peak of
condition in peacetime, since the King was 'not minded to see young
gentlemen inexpert in martial feats'.[20] Tournaments had also become
glittering social events that afforded Henry and his courtiers the chance
to show off their wealth and prowess before visiting ambassadors.
Success in the lists was a sure route to royal favour.

There were different forms of combat: 'barriers', with opponents
fighting on foot with swords across a waist-high wooden fence; hand-
to-hand foot combats with a variety of weapons, 'in imitation of Amadis
and Lancelot and other knights of olden times';[21] the tourney, fought
out on horseback with swords; and the dramatic tilt or joust between
mounted knights with lances, thundering towards each other at either
side of a wooden palisade. In the tilt, competitors fought in pairs, in the
joust, alone. Contestants had to be courageous and strong, with a good
eye and a fine sense of timing because a high degree of risk was involved,
and men sometimes did get killed or injured; yet achieving honour in
the joust was nearly as prestigious as attaining glory in battle.

The tournament was the ultimate theatre of chivalry. Lavish
pageantry and allegory attended these events, which were watched by
spectators in covered stands. The participants would enter their names
on a 'Tree of Chivalry',[22] and they might arrive in the lists in fancy
costume – Henry once appeared as Hercules – riding on pageant cars.
Usually there was a grand procession to the tiltyard, headed by the
Marshals of the Joust on horseback, followed by footmen, drummers,
trumpeters; then came lords and knights, two by two, all splendidly
dressed and mounted, pages, the jousters, fully armed, and finally 'His
Majesty, armed cap-à-pie, surrounded by 30 gentlemen on foot, dressed
in velvet and satin'.[23] Tournaments were often held over several days.

Surviving score sheets, kept by heralds, show that marks were awarded
on a bar-gate system according to which parts of an opponent's armour
were hit – the helmet scoring highest, closely followed by the
breastplate;[24] in the tilt, the ultimate aim was to unhorse an opponent or
split his lance. Courtly love also played a role in these affairs. The
winning knight would be proclaimed the champion of the day, and
receive his accolade from the Queen or the highest-ranking lady present.
Jousts were usually held in honour of the ladies, who gave favours, such
as scarves or handkerchiefs, to their chosen knights to wear in the lists.

'The King, being lusty, young and courageous, greatly delighted in
feats of chivalry.'[25] When he was sixteen, he was reported to have
exercised in the lists every day.[26] On 12 January 1510, Henry tilted in
public for the very first time. He and William Compton appeared in
disguise in the lists at Richmond, but it was a furious contest and when
Compton, in combat with Edward Neville, was 'sore hurt and like to

die', Henry deemed it politic to leave the field. As he rode away, someone in on the secret cried, 'God save the King!', whereupon he had no choice but to 'discover himself', at which there was general amazement, for within living memory English kings had been mere spectators at such events.[27]

Compton fortunately recovered, and Henry went on to enjoy an illustrious career in the lists, much to the dismay of the 'ancient fathers' on the Council, who worried that he might injure or even kill himself. To placate them, the King began using specially made hollow lances to reduce impact, but he still took fearful risks, 'having no respect or fear of anyone in the world',[28] and was nearly killed on two occasions, as we shall hear.

Henry was literally obsessed with jousting. He trained regularly, often charging with his lance to dislodge a detachable ring from a post, or tilting at the quintain, a dummy on a revolving bar. His favourite opponents were Compton, Neville, Buckingham and above all Brandon, who was soon being made jousting clothes to match those of the King, whose regular partner he soon became.

As early as 1510, King Ferdinand's ambassador Luis Caroz observed, 'There are many young men who excel in this kind of warfare, but the most conspicuous among them all, the most assiduous and the most interested in the combats is the King himself, who never omits being present at them.'[29] A Venetian reported in 1515 that Henry jousted 'marvellously'. That afternoon the King had invited this envoy and his suite

> to see him joust, running upwards of 30 courses, in one of which he capsized his opponent, who is the finest jouster in the kingdom [Brandon], horse and all. He then took off his helmet and came under the windows where we were, and talked and laughed with us to our very great honour, and to the surprise of all beholders.[30]

On another occasion, wearing 'cloth of gold with a raised pile', he 'looked like St George in person' as he entered the lists.[31] Again in 1515, Giustinian watched enthralled as, for three hours, 'the King excelled all others, shivering many lances and unhorsing one of his opponents'.[32] A drawing of him armed for the tilt and on horseback is in the British Library.

Thanks to the King's personal involvement and enthusiasm, the English tournaments became renowned throughout Europe, where the fame of such events was regarded as crucial to the international prestige of a kingdom.

★

Life was not all heroic pleasures. In January 1510, Henry went in procession to open his first Parliament at Westminster. He looked resplendent in his crimson and ermine robes of estate with their long train, walking beneath a canopy carried by the monks of Westminster Abbey, preceded by mitred abbots, bishops, heralds, Archbishop Warham, Garter King of Arms, the royal Mace-Bearer and the Duke of Buckingham bearing the Cap of Estate; the Duke's heir, Henry Stafford, carried the Sword of Estate. After sitting enthroned through Mass in the Abbey, the King proceeded into the Parliament Chamber, where he put on the Cap of Estate. The Earls of Oxford and Surrey stood to the left of the throne as the Lord Chancellor addressed the assembly.[33]

Henry was eagerly anticipating the birth of a son and heir. He ordered a new cover for the baptismal font and linen towels to be used at the christening, as well as a sumptuous cradle of estate padded with crimson cloth of gold embroidered with the royal arms, linen for the Queen's bed, swaddling bands in which to wrap the baby, beds for the nurse and two rockers, and a 'groaning chair' for the delivery; this last was similar to a modern birthing chair, with a cut-away seat, but it was upholstered in cloth of gold and came complete with a copper-gilt bowl for receiving the blood and the afterbirth.[34]

But the Queen's pregnancy had not gone to term when, on 31 January, she went into labour; her pains were so agonising that she vowed to donate her richest headdress to the shrine of St Peter the Martyr in Spain in return for a happy outcome. Crushingly, she was delivered of a stillborn daughter. No public announcement was made, and it was four months before Katherine could bring herself to inform King Ferdinand of her loss. Despite God's failure to answer her prayers, she kept her promise to send the headdress to Spain.[35]

The King swallowed his disappointment. On Shrove Tuesday, he astonished his courtiers by publicly taking part in a revel for the first time, and thereby setting a new precedent. The occasion was a banquet held in honour of all the foreign ambassadors at Westminster. The King and Queen led their ladies and nobles into the Parliament Chamber, where Henry personally showed his guests to their seats before taking his place next to Katherine at the high table. He was soon up again, walking around the tables and chatting with his wife and the ambassadors. Then he disappeared with the Earl of Essex. Some time later they returned dressed up 'in Turkey fashion', carrying scimitars and accompanied by six gentlemen dressed as Prussians, and torch-bearers blacked up as Moors. After play-acting in these roles for a time, the King withdrew again, soon reappearing in a short doublet of blue and crimson, slashed with cloth of gold. He and the other gentlemen then danced with the ladies, Henry partnering his sister

Mary.[36] From now on, the monarch was also a showman.

The feast day of St George, the patron saint of England and of the Most Noble Order of the Garter, fell on 23 April; Henry had been proclaimed King on that date, and used it as his official birthday. St George was his hero and he had been a Knight of the Garter since the age of four. Every year on 23 April, the King held a chapter of the Order – not always at Windsor, but wherever he happened to be; during the thirty-seven years of his reign, twenty-four chapters of the Order were held at Greenwich.

Founded in 1348 by Edward III, the Garter was England's highest and most coveted order of chivalry, having been revived in imitation of the Burgundian Order of the Golden Fleece by both Edward IV, who had built St George's Chapel at Windsor, and Henry VII. Henry VIII, with his passion for ancient chivalric values and his policy of accentuating his own magnificence, would continue this tradition.

The Order comprised the sovereign and twenty-five elected Knights Companions, who were replaced only upon death or disgrace. Vacancies were filled each year at the chapter meeting. Each chapter was marked with a magnificent feast; at Windsor, this took place in St George's Hall. The Knights wore 'a blue velvet mantle with a Garter on the left shoulder, lined with white sarcanet, [and] scarlet hose with black velvet around the thighs'.[37] Each sported a light blue[38] silk garter with a gold buckle and embroidered Tudor roses round his leg – the garter being the oldest item of the insignia – and the rich gold collar introduced by Edward IV or Henry VII; Henry VIII decreed in 1510 that it consist of twelve Tudor roses set within blue garters, interspersed with twelve tasselled knots; from this collar hung a 'Great George', a jewelled pendant of St George slaying the dragon. The Knights were allowed to wear their insignia only on St George's Day and the great feast days of the court, so in 1521 Henry instituted a smaller pendant, the 'Lesser George', for everyday use. This was suspended from a gold chain or a blue ribbon, and might be set with a rare cameo. The King is known to have owned three Lesser Georges.[39]

In the roof of St George's Chapel, at the east end of the nave, is a roof boss bearing the arms of Henry VIII surrounded by the escutcheons of his Knights of the Garter; their shields also appear on stall plates in the chapel. Legend has it that the motto of the Order, 'Honi soit qui mal y pense' ('Evil be to he who evil thinks'), was first uttered by Edward III in reproof to courtiers who laughed when the garter of his mistress, the Countess of Salisbury, fell to the floor during a court dance. Whatever the truth of their origin, the words were adopted as the personal motto of the sovereign. The Garter was bestowed as a mark of great honour and friendship on foreign princes such as the Emperor Maximilian I, who usually returned the compliment: Henry VIII had been admitted to the Order of the Golden Fleece in 1505, and was painted wearing its insignia by Hans Holbein for the Whitehall mural of 1537.

Although the first chapter of the Order had been held at Greenwich in April 1509, the election of new members had been postponed until May because of the death of the late King. The first chapter proper and feast took place in April 1510.

May Day, originally a pagan fertility festival, was one of the great holidays of the year and the occasion of cheerful merrymaking at court, with the King going a-Maying with much triumph and the celebrations lasting up to four days. On 'the morn of May', everyone ventured 'into the woods and meadows to divert themselves'[40] – not always in ways of which moralists would have approved – and later there were sports, horse races, jousts, and dances around the maypole, after which it was customary for cakes and cream to be served.[41] On 1 May 1510,

> His Grace, being young and not willing to be idle, rose very early to fetch in the may and green boughs, himself fresh and richly apparelled, and all his knights in white satin, . . . and went every man with his bow and arrows shooting in the wood, and so returned to court, every man with a green bough in his cap.[42]

That month saw Henry back in the tiltyard at Greenwich. 'The King of England amuses himself almost every day of the week with running the ring and with jousts and tournaments on foot. Two days in the week are consecrated to this kind of tournament, which is to continue till the Feast of St John.'[43]

Katherine was now pregnant again, but there is evidence that Henry was straying already from her bed. On 28 May, Luis Caroz, whose account, which seems to derive from court gossip, is the only one to refer to this incident, reported:

> What lately has happened is that two sisters of the Duke of Buckingham, both married, lived in the palace. One of them is the favourite of the Queen, and the other, it is said, is much liked by the King, who went after her. Another version is that the love intrigues were not of the King, but of a young man, his favourite, by the name of Compton, who carried on the love intrigue, as it is said, for the King, and that is the more credible version, as the King has shown great displeasure at what I am going to tell. The favourite of the Queen has been very anxious in the matter of her sister, and has joined herself with the Duke her brother, with

her husband and her sister's husband, in order to consult on what should be done. The consequences [were] that, whilst the Duke was in the private apartments of his sister, who was suspected with the King, Compton came there to talk with her, saw the Duke, who intercepted him, quarrelled with him, and the end of it was that he was severely reproached in many very hard words. The King was so offended at this that he reprimanded the Duke angrily. The same night, the Duke left the palace, and did not return for some days. At the same time, the husband of that lady went away, carried her off, and placed her in a convent sixty miles from here, that no one may see her.

The King, having understood that all this proceeded from the sister who is the favourite of the Queen, the day after the one was gone turned the other out of the palace, and her husband with her. Believing that there were other women in the employment of the favourite such as go about the palace insidiously spying out every unwatched movement in order to tell the Queen, the King would have liked to turn all of them out, only that it has appeared to him too great a scandal. Afterwards, almost all the court knew that the Queen had been vexed with the King, and the King with her, and thus the storm went on between them. The Queen by no means conceals her ill-will towards Compton, and the King is very sorry for it.[44]

Buckingham had two sisters: Anne Stafford, wife of Sir George Hastings, later Earl of Huntingdon, and Elizabeth Stafford, wife of Robert Ratcliffe, Lord FitzWalter, were both ladies-in-waiting to Queen Katherine, and it is not clear from this account which of them was the object of the King's affections and which the informer. But Compton is known to have lived for a time in an adulterous relationship with Lady Hastings, and at Compton Wynyates he later founded a chantry where prayers were said daily for her soul and those of his family members,[45] so it is reasonable to suppose that it was she who was at the centre of this scandal. According to Caroz's account, though, it sounds very much as if Compton at this stage was acting as a go-between for the King and the lady; Caroz thought so, and had this not been the case, the Queen would surely not have reacted so angrily, even though she would naturally have been upset at a close attendant being so publicly disgraced, since it reflected upon her own honour and reputation. The fact that her ladies were going about the court spying on the King suggests that Katherine already had her suspicions.

It appears also that the King had not gone as far as he would have wished with the lady when the affair came to light, which would account in part for his angry reaction. He was also characteristically touchy about the matter being exposed; in all his extramarital affairs, he went to great lengths to maintain the utmost discretion, which is why the surviving evidence for them is at best fragmentary. What little we do have suggests that Henry usually strayed when his wives were pregnant, when marital intercourse would have been taboo, especially as the future security of his dynasty was increasingly at stake. This evidence reinforces the view that Henry regarded sex within marriage as being chiefly for procreational purposes; pleasure was something men pursued outside the nuptial bed.

The Stafford affair taught Katherine a humiliating lesson – that it was useless to remonstrate with her husband in such cases. Like other men of his time, Henry regarded it as his prerogative to pursue other ladies, whilst at the same time expecting his wife to stay chaste; and Katherine soon realised that, in order to preserve her dignity and avoid mortifying public rows, she should shut her eyes to his extramarital affairs and be grateful that he did not shame her by flaunting them.

That there were affairs we cannot doubt. Although the pieces of evidence are fractional, taken as a whole they are overwhelming. In 1515, Giustinian described Henry as being 'free from every vice',[46] yet in that same year a French ambassador in Rome stated that the King was 'a youngling [who] cares for nothing but girls and hunting and wastes his father's patrimony',[47] much to the distress of the English ambassador at the Vatican, who thought such words disrespectful to his sovereign. George Wyatt, the grandson of Sir Thomas Wyatt, Henry's court poet, refers to the King abandoning his pursuit of a lady when his friend Sir Francis Bryan revealed an interest in her. Henry may also have enjoyed the favours of Bryan's gorgeous sister Elizabeth, who was married to another rising courtier, Sir Nicholas Carew; the King gave her 'many beautiful diamonds and pearls and innumerable jewels' that were, strictly speaking, the property of the Queen.[48] When, some time before 1528, the King had an affair with the volatile Mrs Amadas, wife of Robert Amadas, the Master of his Jewel House, that lady, who was given to tantrums and strange visions, made no secret of the fact that William Compton had made his house in Thames Street available for their trysts[49] – a circumstance that gives credence to Caroz's assertion that Compton had acted for Henry in the Stafford affair.

In 1533, Reginald Pole, the King's cousin, would declare that Anne Boleyn, when refusing to sleep with Henry, had borne in mind 'how soon he was sated with those who had served him as his mistress'.[50] The King's physician, Dr John Chamber, described his master as 'overly fond of women' and given to 'lustful dreams'.[51] Even William Thomas, who wrote a laudatory biography of Henry VIII around the time of his death, admitted that 'it cannot be denied but that he was a very fleshly man, and no marvel, for albeit his father brought him up in good learning, yet after he fell into all riot and overmuch love of women'.

Wolsey was accused by his enemies of being 'the King's bawd, showing him what women were most wholesome and best of complexions',[52] and although he vigorously denied the charge, it is not entirely implausible. A later Catholic observer claimed that 'King Henry gave his mind to three notorious vices – lechery, covetousness and cruelty, but the two latter issued and sprang out of the former'.[53] The Elizabethan courtier Sir Robert Naunton later started what was by then well known, that Henry never spared a man in his anger nor a woman in his lust.[54]

For all this, Henry considered himself a paragon of virtue, and it is often said that, compared with other rulers such as Edward IV and Francis I, he was; but the truth is that he was an inhibited man who was far more discreet about his amours than most kings. The fact that he had separate apartments from the Queen, and only visited her bed at his own instigation, made covert infidelity that much easier. Despite what Pole claimed, some of Henry's affairs went on in private for years, as will be seen, and there is evidence that he used Greenwich Castle, the former Duke Humphrey's Tower, which he refurbished in 1526 and renamed Mireflore, as a residence for his mistresses.[55]

Henry was never coarse in speech, nor did he appreciate bawdy jokes. Once, when travelling by barge to Greenwich Castle to visit 'a fair lady whom he loved and lodged in the tower of the park' (her identity is unknown), he was 'disposed to be merry' and challenged Sir Andrew Flammock to complete a verse for him. Henry began it:

> Within this tower
> There lieth a flower
> That hath my heart . . .

Whereupon the foul-minded Flammock added:

> Within this hour
> She pissed full sour
> And let a fart.

Henry was so offended that he spluttered, 'Begone, varlet!' and waved the man out of his sight.[56] In 1542, Sir William Paget felt he ought to apologise for having to report to the King Francis I's 'unseemly' declaration that he would rather 'give his daughter to be a strumpet of the bordello' than face the Emperor in battle.[57]

This innate prudishness manifested itself in other ways. Henry, who had three of his own marriages annulled, angrily censured his sister Margaret when she divorced her husband in order to marry another man. He was harsh on the prostitutes who followed his armies, and rigorous in suppressing the brothels that had disfigured the Southwark bank of the Thames for centuries.

Henry could be openly demonstrative towards the women he loved, but never embarrassingly so. It has been suggested that he was not an inspiring or romantic lover, but his letters to Anne Boleyn (which will be quoted later) prove that he was capable of deep passion and sentimental feeling. The fact that Anne fended him off for at least six years proves, not that Henry lacked ardour, but that he was too much of a knight and a gentleman to resort to rape.

The King acknowledged only one bastard, although rumour credited him with more; this was probably down to luck or carefulness, although some writers have suggested that it implies a low level of fertility; but that does not take account of the fact that Henry repeatedly impregnated his first two wives. It has also been suggested that, given his assertion that two of his marriages were incestuous and therefore unlawful,[58] Henry was the victim of an Oedipus complex, but in fact this was a quite legitimate plea to make in each case, and not enough is known of Henry's relationship with his mother to justify such a claim.

One tale told about the King was certainly apocryphal. Sir Thomas More's nephew, William Rastell, and the Jesuit exile, Nicholas Sander, who in 1585 wrote a Catholic treatise damning Henry and his second wife, Anne Boleyn, both claimed that Anne was the fruit of an early affair between the King and her mother, Elizabeth Howard. The story was certainly current at court and in 1535 a Member of Parliament, Sir George Throckmorton, accused Henry to his face of 'meddling' both with Anne's mother and her sister Mary.

'Never with the mother,' Henry said.

'Nor never with the sister either,' lied Cromwell, who was standing by[59] and must have been well aware that the King had had an affair with Mary Boleyn (of which more will be related later). But Henry was under ten when Anne was probably conceived, and could not possibly have been her father. Yet there may not have been, in this instance, smoke without fire. Despite his denial, an early liaison, while he was perhaps in his teens, with Lady Boleyn cannot be ruled out.

14

'Rather Divine than Human'

In July 1510, Henry stayed at Windsor Castle on the first stage of his annual progress. Windsor was one of the most ancient of royal residences; it had been built by William the Conqueror around 1070, and reconstructed as a formidable stone fortress by Henry II in the twelfth century. The Plantagenet royal lodgings, laid out around three courtyards in the Upper Ward (on the site of the present state apartments), were still in use, although they had been extended and modernised in the fourteenth century by Edward III, who built the imposing St George's Hall (then half its present length) with its steep timber roof and private chapel at one end. Edward IV had modernised the royal lodgings, adding a great watching chamber amongst other improvements, and Henry VII had added a tower with more luxurious accommodation featuring oriel windows and flat battened ceilings decorated with quatrefoils and rose bosses; its first floor, much remodelled, now houses the Royal Library. In the room next to the King's bedchamber was a wall painting depicting the Knights of Malta besieging Rhodes in 1480 and 1522.[1] The adjacent Queen's range boasted a privy chamber with a ceiling studded with tiny mirrors.[2] Outside there were gardens, of which details are scarce, and a vineyard.

Windsor was still essentially a mediaeval castle rather than a Tudor palace, and for this reason Henry used it less than his more modern houses, and then only in the warmer months, when he came for the hunting in Windsor Great Park and Windsor Forest. The only major work he carried out here would be the rebuilding of the main gateway to the castle in 1510–11; it bears his arms with the pomegranate of Katherine of Aragon. He also built a tennis court, perhaps the one at the foot of the Round Tower shown in seventeenth-century views of the castle.[3]

St George's Chapel, begun by Edward IV in 1475, continued by

Henry VII, who rebuilt the adjoining Lady Chapel, and completed by Henry VIII in 1528, is one of the finest examples of late Perpendicular architecture in England, and boasts magnificent stone vaulting and outstanding stained-glass windows, one featuring seventy-five figures of saints, kings and princes. In the choir are the fine stalls of the Knights of the Garter. Those great protagonists of the Wars of the Roses, Henry VI and Edward IV, lie buried here. Henry VIII erected a richly carved timber closet with an oriel window above Edward IV's chantry chapel, from which Queen Katherine could watch services and Garter ceremonies; her pomegranate badge features in the carvings.

Whilst at Windsor, the King expended his energies in 'exercising himself daily in shooting, singing, dancing, wrestling, casting of the bar, playing at the recorder, flute [and] virginals, and in setting of songs, making of ballads, and did set two goodly masses, every one of them five parts, which were sung oftentimes in his chapel and afterwards in divers other places'.[4]

Like all the Tudors, Henry was passionate about music, which was by his time a necessary adjunct to royal magnificence. It dominated his life: wherever he went, in public or in private, at state occasions, at his entrance and departure, and especially at mealtimes, minstrels played, choirs sang or fanfares sounded. Making music was also an essential accomplishment for his courtiers, many of whom were competent composers, players or singers; a fine voice could be decisive in gaining a gentleman a post in the Privy Chamber. Many nobles employed their own bands of musicians, who performed in the minstrels' galleries above their dining halls.

Foreigners were ecstatic about the music they heard at the English court, the beautiful voices of the choristers and the virtuoso playing of the musicians, which they compared very favourably with the music at the French court, where the singing master could not read music, even when he was sober.

Much music was composed under the auspices of the Church, and it was in the sixteenth century that sacred music reached new heights of grandeur and artistic intricacy in the hands of a few gifted composers under royal patronage. Many compositions took the form of motets, Latin choral pieces in several parts, which were precursors of the anthem.

There were advances too in secular music, which was growing in popularity, yet although the Tudor age was to witness the birth of chamber music, little secular music of note survives from the period before the development of the madrigal in Elizabeth's reign. At the beginning of the century, English music still imitated the stately style of the fifteenth-century composer John Dunstable (d.1453), but thanks to the incalculable effect of Henry's interest and his generous patronage of foreign musicians such as the Italian Bassano family[5] and the lutenist Philip van Wilder, it was changing, becoming increasingly influenced by newer forms from Flanders, France and Italy. Under Henry VIII, English music progressed from the formal mediaeval style to one more florid and versatile. Most early Tudor music was polyphonic, having many voices or sounds, although traditional ballads were still very popular, and Henry himself composed them, although he disapproved of their use as a political propaganda tool.

Early sixteenth-century music was less sophisticated than that of later centuries. Few instruments survive, and sheet music is poorly annotated, so modern musicians have to 'realise' each piece on reconstructed instruments, which sometimes involves guesswork. Instruments were not as finely tuned, and modern scales were not developed until later in the century. It was during Henry's reign, in 1530, that the first book of music was printed in England, by Wynkyn de Worde; it contains various secular part-songs.[6]

Sacred music at court was the province of the highly trained, elite choir of the Chapel Royal, which sang mass daily and performed regularly for the King, especially when he wished to impress guests. Their first recorded performance for him was in 1510, in the White Hall at Westminster.[7] In 1515, when Henry invited Giustinian to attend High Mass in the chapel royal, the awestruck Italian reported that it was 'gloriously sung by His Majesty's choristers, whose voices are really rather divine than human. They did not chant but sang like angels, and as for the counter-bass voices, I do not think they have their equals in the world'.[8]

There were about a dozen boy choristers, who were headhunted by the King and William Cornish, Master of the Chapel. Since the reign of Richard III, promising boys had been impressed from cathedral schools and church choirs and expected to dedicate their lives to training their voices and learning at least one instrument. A child purchased by Henry from a stranger in 1516 for £40 (£12,000) may well have been chosen for his musical aptitude.[9]

The choristers lodged with the Master, whose duty it was to instruct them in plainchant and harmony. Since the choir did not have a regular organist, the 'Children' often sang unaccompanied. There were adult choristers too, Gentlemen in Ordinary of the Choir, whose voices had survived the transition of puberty; they took it in turns to play the organ. Boys who were unable to continue in the choir when their voices broke were found other posts or places at university. Every member of the Chapel Royal might be required to take part in court entertainments, or turn his hand to composing. Most of the music sung by the Chapel

Royal was composed by its members, notably Robert Fairfax and William Cornish, and later the great Thomas Tallis.

There was to be friendly rivalry between the choir of the Chapel Royal and Wolsey's choristers. The King, or perhaps Cornish, devised a contest after which Henry declared that Wolsey's singers had 'more surely handled it', whereupon Wolsey felt obliged to release 'young Robin', the boy with the 'craftiest descant', to his master.[10]

The King employed twenty-five well paid professional secular musicians and singers,[11] several of them foreigners whom he had enticed to England. Their expertise set the musical standards for the court. The King also retained a number of traditional minstrels, who were under the direction of Hugh Woodhouse, Master of the King's Minstrels. At least eighteen came from Flanders, Germany, France or Italy, and were paid 4d. (£5) a day.[12] One minstrel, Robert Reynolds, was Welsh, while another, Hans Nagel, is known to have acted as a spy for the King in France.[13] All royal musicians were members of the Chamber, but only a privileged few, who comprised 'The King's Musick',[14] had access to the privy chamber, where they entertained Henry in his leisure hours. The rest worked in the presence chamber.

A drawing attributed to Hans Holbein shows five royal musicians playing on a balcony: one blows a trumpet, one a sackbut (a primitive form of trombone),[15] and the others three recorders.[16] Another contemporary illustration, from Henry's illuminated psalter of c1540,[17] depicts a band of musicians playing a pipe and tabor, a trumpet, a harp and a dulcimer; such a group was known as a 'consort', an Old English word for 'concert', meaning a band of usually four to six players performing in an ensemble. A 'whole consort' was one in which all the instruments were of one kind, such as a set of viols; a 'broken consort' comprised different instruments,[18] and was the type preferred for indoor court entertainments.

Of approximately sixty musicians and minstrels on the royal payroll, sixteen were trumpeters,[19] and in 1509 a Mr Peter was Marshal of the Trumpets. Philip van Wilder, Zuan Piero of Venice and the gifted Patrec were the King's chief lutenists and 'Blind More' his harpist, while one of his favourite singers was James Hill, whom he kept always about him later in the reign.

The Dutchman Philip van Wilder was one of the most famous musicians of the period. In recognition of his skill, the King appointed him a Gentleman of the Privy Chamber and paid him a higher stipend than any other court musician. Van Wilder not only played but wrote songs, looked after Henry's musical instruments, took charge of the other musicians of the Chamber, formed his own group of 'singing men and children' and still found time to teach the royal children.[20]

Many musicians resorted to the court in search of patronage, but not all were lucky. There was the sad story of a Venetian, Zuan da Leze, who was skilled on the *clavicembalo*, a type of dulcimer. He was so certain that the King of England would want his services and remunerate him appropriately that in 1525 he purchased the best instrument money could buy and travelled to England, where he got the opportunity to play for the King. But Henry merely thanked him and sent him away with a small purse of money. Devastated, da Leze committed suicide.[21]

No other English king ever displayed such musical talent as Henry VIII. That he had real ability is patently clear. He sang 'fairly' (that is to say, well)[22] in a clear, high tenor voice; this high voice was remarked upon: in 1540, it was said that his daughter Mary 'had a voice more man-like for a woman than he for a man'.[23] In an age in which most people played music by ear, Henry 'sang from the book at sight'.[24] He once paid £20 (£6,000) to Robert Fairfax for a book of 'prick-song', or annotated music.[25]

The King and his circle of amateur aristocratic performers would often while away their leisure hours by making music in the privy chamber, but they do not seem to have performed in public because 'a gentleman singing in a common audience appaireth [devalues] his estimation'.[26] Among the most popular turns were the King's own compositions and the part songs composed by Fairfax, especially 'Behold the Sovereign Seed'. It appears that vocal music was more favoured than instrumental music, and that singers usually performed in groups, rather than solo.[27] In the British Library there is a manuscript containing a two-part double canon written in 1516 in honour of Henry VIII.[28] One favourite court song, 'My Sovereign Lord', celebrated the King's prowess in the tiltyard. Henry was also fond of duetting with Sir Peter Carew on 'freeman's songs' such as 'By the banks as I lay' and 'As I walked the wood so wild'.[29]

The King was 'a good musician'[30] who, according to Giustinian, played 'on almost every instrument', performing particularly 'well on the lute and virginals'.[31] He also played the regal, a kind of portable organ, the recorder and the cornett;[32] a picture in his psalter shows him playing the harp.[33]

Henry practised on his instruments 'day and night'.[34] His large collection was looked after by the Keeper of the King's Instruments. In 1515, Giustinian's secretary, Niccolo Sagudino was shown a room 'con-taining a number of organs, virginals, flutes and other instruments'.[35] At his death, Henry's collection included five cornemuses or drones (bagpipes), 19 viols, 20 regals, 14 virginals, two clavichords, 26 lutes, 65 flutes, seven citterns,[36] 15 shawms,[37] 10 sackbuts and 154 recorders.[38] Some instruments were adorned with precious metals and gems, and most had their own cases of leather or velvet. Henry was fascinated by the technology of instruments, and was always eager to try novel ones. In 1542, he sent to Vienna for a pair of Turkish-style drums that could be played on horseback, and he later acquired 'a virginal that goeth with a wheel without being played upon',[39] which presumably worked on a barrel-and-pin mechanism.

The King was also a 'fair' composer.[40] Thirty-three of his compositions, comprising thirteen instrumental pieces and twenty three- or four-part popular songs such as 'Pastime with good company', 'Green groweth the holly', 'O, my heart', 'Alas, what shall I do for love?' and 'Whereto should I express my inward heaviness?', were collated in the so-called 'Henry VIII Manuscript', where each is inscribed (not in Henry's hand, but probably by one of his gentlemen) 'the King, H.VIII'.[41] The manuscript was once in the possession of Sir Henry Guildford, Comptroller of the Household. All these compositions are in the mediaeval tradition and probably date from the early years of the reign; research has shown that a number of them, including the popular Flemish tune, 'Taunder Naken', are merely rearrangements of other composers' works. Nowadays, opinion is divided as to their merit, modern ears being more critical than those of Henry's courtiers. Nevertheless, in their own time Henry's songs were applauded and enjoyed widespread fame; in 1521, Dr John Longland, the Lord High Almoner, used 'Pastime with good company' as the text for a sermon.

The King's 'goodly masses' referred to by the chronicler Edward Hall have been sadly lost. His only sacred work to survive is a three-part motet, 'Quam pulchra es'. It was once thought that Henry had written the motet, 'O Lord the Maker of all Thing', but it was almost certainly composed either by William Mundy, a Gentleman of Queen Elizabeth's Chapel Royal, or by John Shepherd, organist of Magdalen College, Oxford. Nor did Henry write 'Greensleeves', which is probably Elizabethan in origin and is based on an Italian style of composition that did not reach England until after his death.[42]

From Windsor, Henry moved on to Woking, where 'there were kept both jousts and tournaments'.[43] Henry VII had acquired the fifteenth-century Woking Palace from Margaret Beaufort in 1503, and had spent £1,400 (£420,000) converting it into a sumptuous royal residence, which would be partially rebuilt and extended by Henry VIII in 1515–16 and 1532–4. The house was designed on a courtyard plan and had a gallery with a cloister beneath, both facing the River Wey, a chapel, a gatehouse, extensive royal apartments with bay windows, and a great hall built in 1508 with windows completed by the King's glazier, Bernard Flower, in 1511. There were privy gardens, orchards and some fine hunting in the surrounding park. A bowling alley was constructed in 1537.[44]

'The rest of this progress was spent in hunting, hawking and shooting';[45] it took the King into Hampshire, and to The Vyne, the house of Sir William Sandys, near Basingstoke. Sir William, now forty, was a popular and loyal courtier who had married the niece of Sir Reginald Bray, a staunch supporter of Henry VII before his accession. Sandys was one of the King's favourite companions of the chase as well as being Keeper of the royal hunting lodge at Easthampstead, twelve miles away. Henry obviously liked him because he made two return visits in later years.

From The Vyne, the King moved south to Southampton, and then east, in September, to the twelfth-century Augustinian priory at Southwick, where he made an offering at the shrine of Our Lady. This was the first of several pilgrimages Henry made to religious shrines, such as that of St Thomas Becket at Canterbury, the miraculous black cross at Waltham Abbey, Our Lady of Walsingham, St Edward the Confessor at Westminster Abbey, St Bridget of Syon and even the tomb of the uncanonised Henry VI at Windsor. His Book of Payments records huge sums donated in offerings to these and other shrines.[46]

For more than half his reign, Henry was a faithful son of the Roman Catholic Church. His piety was conventional, his charitable works legion – his annual alms amounted to £156 (£46,800) – and he enjoyed the imagery, ritual and liturgy of his religion. His rosary, made of boxwood with carved beads, one of which bears his arms, survives at Chatsworth.

Like every sovereign from Edward II to Queen Anne, Henry VIII 'touched for the King's Evil', a healing ritual believed to cure the skin disease scrofula. The divine powers conferred on an anointed King were also called into play every Good Friday, when he would bless 'cramp rings' made from the coins he had offered that day in chapel, which were then distributed to those suffering from cramp, epilepsy, palsy, labour pains or rheumatism, in the belief that the sovereign's benediction would effect a cure. On Good Friday also, 'the King's Grace crept to the Cross from the chapel door upwards, and so served the priest to mass, his own person kneeling on His Grace his knees'.[47] His attendants would smooth his path by laying down cushions.[48]

On the day before Good Friday, the King would take part in the Royal Maundy ceremony, which had its origins in the Dark Ages and is first known to have been performed by King John in 1210. In imitation of Jesus Christ at the Last Supper, wearing a voluminous white apron and armed with a towel, a basin and a nosegay to guard against infection, Henry would kneel to wash, dry, sign with a cross and kiss the fcet of a number of poor persons equal to the years of his age; to ensure that the royal nose would not be offended, the same feet had been previously well scrubbed by the Yeomen of the Laundry. The King would then give their owners gifts of bread, fish, wine and clothing, and distribute red and white purses of money. Present at the ceremony were the Lord Chamberlain, the Gentlemen of the Chapel Royal and the Yeomen of the Guard. Cardinal Wolsey often attended. The word 'Maundy' derives from the *mandatum* that Christ gave to His disciples, commanding them to love one another. Henry's queens also distributed Maundy charity in their own right.[49]

Possessing the most sensitive of consciences, and wishing to set a virtuous example, Henry was assiduous about the welfare of his soul. He was 'very religious and heard three masses daily when he hunted, and sometimes five on other days', and he usually joined the Queen for Vespers and Compline.[50] These services were conducted by his chaplains in his private closet; the King took part in services in the chapel royal only on Sundays, when he received the Eucharist,[51] and on feast-days; during daily services, which he usually attended, he worked there, secluded in his private pew.[52] In an arrangement dating from the time of Henry III, this was usually set in a gallery above the body of the chapel, facing the altar, and had a winding staircase at one end or leading from an adjoining 'holyday' closet, which Henry could use when he wished to go down and participate in services.[53] In the Black Book of the Garter (1534) there is an illumination of the King at prayer in his closet, kneeling before an altar on a cushioned prie-Dieu beneath a canopy of blue and gold.[54]

Henry was strictly orthodox. Always fierce against heresy, he had no qualms about burning those with subversive views. Nevertheless, he loved theological debate and discussion; Erasmus, who dedicated his New Testament in Latin to Henry and Katherine,[55] tells us that 'whenever he has leisure from his political occupations' – and presumably from hunting – 'he reads, or disputes with remarkable courtesy and unruffled temper', never standing upon his royal dignity.[56] Sometimes, however, Henry gave the impression that he thought he knew better than his bishops in matters of doctrine and interpretation of the Scriptures. Indeed, he was more than a match for them, being 'the most learned of kings, not only in theology, but also in philosophy';[57] he was well read in the Church Fathers and other pious works, and could cite texts; the extensive marginal notes he made in his books may still be seen in those that survive.

The responsibility for religious observances and services at court belonged to the Chapel Royal, not a building but an institution comprising twenty-six chaplains and clerks, twenty Gentlemen, the

Clerk of the Closet (who was responsible for preparing for private services in the King's closet),[58] the Serjeant of the Vestry, a Gospeller, an Epistoler, two Yeomen of the Chapel, thirteen minstrels, a watchman and the twelve choristers and their Master.[59] It had first been established in the twelfth century as the King's Chapel or the Household Chapel, its function being to provide for the spiritual welfare of the monarch, and from 1312 it was under the rule of a Dean, who was answerable directly to the Archbishop of Canterbury. The Chapel Royal performed daily services for the royal household in the royal chapels, and when the King travelled on progress or to a lesser house, a small core of its members always went with him. It cost him £2,000 (£600,000) a year to maintain the Chapel Royal.

All services were of course in Latin, and the only permitted version of the Bible was the Latin Vulgate. The calendar was full of saints' days, which were observed with various degrees of solemnity or festivity. The Church recognised seven sacraments – baptism, confirmation, marriage, ordination, penance, the Eucharist and viaticum (the last rites). Its bishops wore splendid vestments, such as the gem-encrusted mitre shown in Hans Holbein's portrait of Archbishop Warham, and lived in princely style.

To confuse matters, several of the royal chapels were known as the chapel royal, notably those at the Tower, Westminster, Eltham, Greenwich, Hampton Court, Whitehall and St James's Palace. Each household chapel was beautifully decorated, with brilliant stained-glass windows, wall paintings, statues of the Virgin and saints, and a rood screen bearing a large carving of the crucified Christ separating the nave from the chancel, which only the clergy were allowed to enter. On the altar, which was draped with an embroidered frontal, stood a crucifix and perhaps sacred relics in bejewelled reliquaries, while above hung a case called the 'pyx', which contained the Host. Most of the royal chapels had splendid organs, in which the King, who was fascinated by their workings, took an active interest. From 1514, he employed an organ-maker, William Lewes,[60] and later set up a workshop for him at Bridewell Palace.[61] It was probably Lewes who made the organ for the chapel royal at Hampton Court in 1538.[62]

15

'The Holy Innocent'

The Queen's second pregnancy progressed well, and in September 1510 preparations were made for 'the King's nursery'.[1] A Lady Mistress, Elizabeth, daughter of Sir Robert Poyntz, was appointed to take charge of the birth and care for the new baby, and the room assigned her was decorated with new hangings. A purple velvet 'bearing pane' with a long train was made for the infant.[2]

Following earlier precedents, Margaret Beaufort had laid down strict ordinances to be observed 'against the deliverance of a queen',[3] which were faithfully observed throughout her grandson's reign. 'Her Highness's pleasure being understood in what chamber she will be delivered in, the same must be hanged with rich cloth of Arras, sides, roof, windows and all, except one window, which must be hanged so as she may have light when it pleaseth her.' These tapestries were to depict innocuous scenes from romances, so that neither the Queen nor her newborn infant might be 'affrighted by figures which gloomily stare'. The floor was to be 'laid all over with carpets' before the great bed was brought in. This was made up with a mattress stuffed with wool, then a feather bed, a bolster of down, sheets of fine lawn, two long pillows and two square pillows, all filled with fine down, and a counterpoint of scarlet furred with ermine and trimmed with crimson velvet and cloth of gold. The tester and curtains were to be of crimson satin embroidered with golden crowns and the Queen's arms, the tester being edged with a silk fringe of blue, russet and gold. An altar was to be placed in the chamber, and a cupboard, covered with tapestry, for the birthing equipment. The 'rich font of Canterbury' was to be brought in specially for the occasion, in case the child was weak and needed immediate baptism.

About four to six weeks before the delivery, the Queen was to 'take to her chamber' and retire into seclusion to await the birth. On that day, she would hear Mass in a chapel 'well and worshipfully arrayed', and then host a banquet for all the lords and ladies of the court in her 'great chamber', which was also to be hung with rich tapestries and furnished with 'a cloth and chair of estate and cushions', so that the Queen might 'stand or sit at her pleasure'. 'Spices and wine' would be served, and then two high-ranking lords would escort the Queen to the door of her inward lodgings, which opened into the antechamber to her bed-chamber, where she would take formal leave of the courtiers and her male officers. As she left, her Chamberlain would desire all her people to pray 'that God would send her a good hour'. She would not be seen again in public until after the birth.

'Then all the ladies and gentlewomen to go in with her, and none to come in to the great chamber but women; and women to be made all manner of officers, as butlers, panters, sewers, etc.' No man would be allowed in, not even the King, until after the delivery. Everything that was needed would be brought to the door of the great chamber and there given to the temporary female officers.[4] As the birth approached, the Queen's chaplains would hold themselves in readiness for an urgent summons; likewise the messenger appointed to convey news of the birth to the King.[5] Childbirth was a hazardous business for both mother and child, and around a quarter of newborns were lost. The future of the Tudor dynasty hung upon a happy outcome.

In November, a tournament was held over several days, at which 'the King broke more staves than any other'.[6] Then the court moved to Richmond, where the Queen took to her chamber. At the end of December she went into labour; no more is heard of the 'groaning chair', and it appears that Katherine gave birth on 'a fair pallet bed' placed beside the great bed in her bedchamber,[7] and wearing one of the fine Holland smocks and double petticoats that were later found amongst the 'necessaries provided for what time she lay in childbed' at the Wardrobe in Baynard's Castle.[8] There was no effective pain relief. In 1512, Katherine sent the Abbot of Westminster to her pregnant sister-in-law, Margaret Tudor, with the Girdle of Our Lady, a holy relic in the possession of Westminster Abbey but loaned out to royal ladies in labour, whose sufferings were said to be relieved by its presence in the birthing chamber.[9] Perhaps we may assume that Katherine herself had found it efficacious.

In the early hours of New Year's Day 1511, the Queen was delivered of a prince, to the great jubilation of the King and the court. A royal salute was fired from the cannon ranged along Tower Wharf, all the church bells pealed out in celebration, *Te Deums* were sung by the clergy and there were triumphant processions through London. So that his subjects could share in his joy at the birth of his son and heir, Henry

ordered that bonfires be lit in the streets of London and that the Lord
Mayor arrange for the citizens to be served with free wine to drink the
Prince's health. He rewarded the midwife with £10 (£3,000) and
Mistress Poyntz with £30 (£9,000).[10]

The royal infant must have looked very tiny indeed in his vast painted
wooden cradle, which measured approximately five feet by two, and
was trimmed with silver gilt and had buckles either side to secure his
swaddling bands. He lay there, wrapped up tight, under a cover-cloth
fringed with gold and a scarlet counterpoint furred with ermine.[11] And
when he was displayed to important visitors, he was placed in an even
bigger cradle of estate, upholstered in crimson and decorated with gold
fringing, with his father's coat of arms above his head.

The Queen had now moved to a bed of estate set up in her presence
chamber, where, wrapped in a round mantle of crimson velvet, she
would receive guests and wellwishers. She would also write a letter to
her Lord Chamberlain and perhaps other officers and nobles, formally
announcing the birth.[12] It was customary for queens to lie in for up to
forty days after the delivery, before being purified in a special ceremony
known as 'churching', after which they were no longer considered
unclean and could return to their normal routine.[13] Queens did not
breastfeed; a wet-nurse was engaged for that, leaving the royal mother
free to conceive another heir for the dynasty.

When he was five days old, the Prince was christened at Richmond,
and given the name Henry. He was also styled 'Prince of Wales'. His
godparents at the font were Archbishop Warham, the Earl of Surrey and
the Earl and Countess of Devon,[14] his great-aunt and uncle, while his
august sponsors were King Louis XII of France and Margaret of Austria,
Duchess of Savoy, daughter of the Emperor Maximilian I, who both
sent expensive gifts of gold plate.

Back in his nursery, the Prince was subject to an orderly regime laid
down by his great-grandmother, Margaret Beaufort. Although royal
parents visited their children, they did not undertake their daily care,
which was left to the nursery staff. Prince Henry's Lady Mistress
supervised his wet-nurse and dry-nurse, who were assisted by four
chamberers known as 'rockers', whose chief duty was to lull their charge
to sleep by rocking his cradle. All nursery staff had to swear a special oath
of loyalty before the Lord Chamberlain, as did the Grooms, Yeomen,
Panters and Sewers who waited upon the nursery.[15] The wet-nurse had
to be of excellent moral character since 'the child suckleth the vice of
his nurse with the milk of her pap',[16] and all her food was assayed for
poison. A physician stood by to supervise every feed to make sure that
the baby was getting enough and was not being slipped any
unauthorised foods. Amongst the 'necessaries as belong unto the child',

there was 'a great pot of leather for water', 'two great basins of water' and yards of 'fine linen and blanket'. The nursery was quite luxurious, with tapestries, eight large carpets and two cushions of crimson damask, and great formality was observed within it.[17]

Royal children did not usually live at court, where the risk of infection was unacceptably high, but were assigned separate establishments and households whilst still quite young. The King immediately appointed no less than forty persons to serve his son, including a Clerk of the Signet, a Serjeant of Arms, three Chaplains, a Carver, Yeomen of the Wardrobe and the Beds, a Keeper of the Cellar and a Baker. Looking further ahead, he also designated a room in the Palace of Westminster as the Prince's council chamber.

That done, the proud father set off on a visit to the Priory of Our Lady of Walsingham in Norfolk to give thanks for the gift of a son and heir.[18] Dismounting a mile away at the Slipper Chapel, the King, like all the other pilgrims, removed his shoes and walked barefoot to the Virgin's shrine, where he lit a candle and offered a costly necklace. He also arranged, at his own expense, for the royal glazier, Bernard Flower, to make stained-glass windows for the Lady Chapel.[19]

His pilgrimage completed, Henry returned to Richmond; then, 'the Queen being churched and purified, the King and she removed to Westminster',[20] the Prince having been left in the healthier air of Richmond.

It was now time to celebrate in style. On 1 February there was a tournament at which the King, Brandon, Neville and Sir Edward Howard, all clad in 'coats of green satin guarded with crimson velvet', tilted against Essex, Devon, Dorset and Surrey's son, Lord Thomas Howard. Henry's Councillors were still trying to persuade him to watch rather than take part, 'and spake thereof as much as they durst, but his courage was so noble' that they had to give way.[21]

On 12 and 13 February, perhaps the most lavish tournament of the reign was staged at Westminster in honour of the Queen. The King took the role of Coeur Loyal – Sir Loyal Heart – and appeared in the tiltyard, wearing his wife's colours, with three other challengers on a pageant car drawn by a mock lion and antelope of damask gold and silver, and decked out as a forest 'with rocks, hills and dales'; in the midst was a golden castle, and outside the castle was 'a gentleman making a garland of roses for the Prince'. When the car stopped before the Queen, the 'foresters' on it sounded their horns, and out rode the four challengers from the castle: the Earl of Devon was 'Bon Valoir', Thomas Knyvet 'Bon Espoir' and Edward Neville 'Valiant Desire'. All presented their shields to Katherine.

The next day, the 'answerers' appeared. Charles Brandon arrived on horseback, attired as a hermit, and received the Queen's permission to accept the challenge. He then threw off his habit 'to reveal that he was fully armed', and was joined by Henry Guildford, then the Marquess of Dorset and Sir Thomas Boleyn, 'dressed like two pilgrims in black velvet tabards with pilgrims' hats over the helmets, and carrying Jacob's staffs in their hands; and their tabards, hats and cloaks were decorated with golden scallop shells', as if they had come from the shrine of St James at Compostela. Course after course was run, with the Queen bestowing the prizes; there was great applause when the King won the challenger's prize. Even after the tournament had drawn to a close, Henry insisted upon running another course with Brandon, 'for the King's lady's sake'.[22]

'The Great Tournament Roll of Westminster', a manuscript now in the College of Arms, vividly depicts the proceedings at this tournament. One scene shows Henry jousting in front of Katherine of Aragon, who sits under a canopy of estate with her ladies in a pavilion hung with cloth of gold and purple velvet embroidered with Hs and Ks, pomegranates and roses.

On the second night, there was great revelry in the White Hall, with 'an interlude of the Gentlemen of his Chapel before His Grace', in honour of the Prince, and a pageant, *The Garden of Pleasure*, in which Henry again appeared as 'Coeur Loyal' wearing a purple satin suit adorned with gold Hs and Ks. Several people, including the Spanish ambassador, would not believe they were real gold, so, during the dancing that followed, the King invited them to pull them off him to prove that they were. Unfortunately the general public, who had been allowed in to witness the festivities, mistook this as an invitation to divest the King and his courtiers of their finery for largesse, and surged into the throng of merrymakers, grabbing and pulling as they went. Henry was stripped down to his doublet and hose, as were most of his companions, while poor Sir Thomas Knyvet lost all his clothes and, stark naked, had to shin up a pillar for safety. Even the ladies who had danced in the pageant, wearing gowns of Tudor green and white, 'were spoiled likewise, wherefore the King's guard came suddenly and put the people back'. Henry passed the whole thing off as a joke, and 'all these hurts were turned to laughing and game'. The evening concluded with a banquet in the presence chamber, with everyone attending in what was left of their finery.[23] After this, security was tighter at public events.

Ten days after these rejoicings, terrible news arrived from Richmond. On 23 February,[24] the little Prince had died. The Queen was distraught, but the King, concealing his own grief, comforted her. No blame was attached to the nursery staff, and Elizabeth Poyntz was rewarded for her service with an annuity of £20 (£6,000). The Keeper of the Wardrobe supplied an elaborate hearse on which the tiny body was conveyed to London; dozens of wax candles burned around the hearse day and night while a round-the-clock vigil was kept over it by black-clad mourners in Westminster Abbey, where the Prince was afterwards buried late at night in a torchlit ceremony.[25] His soul, wrote an observer, 'is now among the holy innocents of God'.[26]

Henry made no further outward show of grief. That Easter, Pope Julius II bestowed on him a Golden Rose that he himself had blessed, and which symbolised the flowers that preceded the fruits of the Passion of Christ. Not only was this a great comfort, but also a sign of high apostolic favour, which in 1512 was followed by a Sword and Cap of Maintenance. It was also an inducement for Henry to join the so-called Holy League, an alliance between the Papacy, Spain and Venice against Louis of France, who had aggressive ambitions in Italy.

May Day was celebrated as usual. 'The King, lying at Greenwich, rode to the wood to fetch may', and for three days he, Howard, Brandon and Neville 'held jousts against all comers. Many a sore stripe was given and many a staff broke.'[27]

During his summer progress of 1511, Henry visited the Midlands, staying at Nottingham and Coventry, where he and the Queen watched part of the famous cycle of mystery plays, performed by local guildsmen. The King also indulged himself in sports and gambling, but there were complaints from his courtiers that he was 'much enticed to play at tennis and at dice' by 'crafty persons' who 'brought in Frenchmen and Lombards to make wagers with him, so he lost much money'. Fortunately, before too much damage had been done, 'he perceived their craft' and sent them away.[28] Thereafter, he would be on his guard against professional tricksters.

This same year, Henry rebuilt Sunninghill, an old royal lodge in Windsor Forest, which he intended to use as a hunting box. It was kept in repair for most of his reign, but has long since disappeared, its exact location being now uncertain.

In October, the King joined the Holy League. As a sign of solidarity with the Church, he commanded his courtiers to curb their extrava-gance and dress more soberly; he even forbade the nobility to wear silk. Instead of wasting their money on outward show, they should be spending it on the weapons and horses required for a crusade against the King of France. Henry himself put away his rich garments, donning plainer clothes, and in December, when attending Parliament, he appeared in the House of Lords wearing 'a long grey cloth gown' cut in the Hungarian fashion.[29]

This fad for austerity did not last long. The King spent Christmas at Greenwich 'with great and plentiful cheer in a most princely manner, where was such viands served to all comers of honest behaviour as hath been few times seen'.[30] The King spent over £800 (£240,000) on New Year's gifts.[31] On New Year's Night, a pageant entitled *The Fortress Dangerous* was put on in the great hall. It featured a castle with towers and a dungeon, 'garnished with artillery and weapons, after the most warlike fashion' – there was a message here for Henry's courtiers – and inside were six ladies wearing gowns of russet satin 'laid all over with leaves of gold'. Predictably, the castle was assaulted by the King and five other knights; the ladies, 'seeing them so lusty and courageous', readily yielded, and came down to dance with them.[32]

For Twelfth Night, William Cornish had devised something novel.

> The King with eleven other were disguised after the manner of Italy, called a masque, a thing not seen afore in England. They were apparelled in garments wrought with gold, with visors and caps of gold; and after the banquet [was] done, these masquers came in with six gentlemen, disguised in silk, bearing torches, and desired the ladies to dance. Some were content, and some that knew the fashion of it refused because it was not a thing commonly seen. After they danced and communed together, and as the fashion of the masque is, they took their leave and departed, and so did the Queen and her ladies.[33]

What caused all the fuss was that, rather than dancing with ladies they had rehearsed with, as in a pageant, the men were choosing their partners from the audience. Masques or 'masks' as they were known in England, were a form of drama in which the plot took second place to disguises, poetry, music and dancing, and they were usually performed by amateurs. They began with a spectacular entry, continued with a 'presentation' and ended with a dance, which was often very complicated and required skill and agility. Like pageants, many masques had allegorical or political themes. The introduction of this new form of entertainment into court festivities is an indicator that Italian influence was beginning to infiltrate the English court. The King's growing preference for masques, in which he could show off his talents to perfection, heralded the demise of the pageant, but that would not take place for several years.[34]

Henry was at Greenwich when, at the end of April 1512, the Palace of Westminster was largely destroyed by a fire that broke out in the kitchens. Westminster Hall, the Painted Chamber, the crypt of St Stephen's Chapel and the Jewel Tower luckily survived, but the rest of the royal lodgings and the service quarters were gutted. They were not rebuilt, although the hall continued to house the law courts and the Palace of Westminster remained the official seat of government. The ruins of the old palace were not finally cleared away until 1532.[35]

The loss of his chief London residence drove the King to look elsewhere for somewhere to lodge in the capital, but the two palaces available in the City, which the King immediately made use of, proved outdated, too small and insufficiently grand.

One was Baynard's Castle, a battlemented, double-courtyard house with octagonal corner towers. It was sited in Thames Street, between Paul's Wharf and Blackfriars, with a frontage facing the north bank of the River Thames. The first castle on the site had been built in the reign of William the Conqueror, and was named after its custodian, Ralph Baignard, but it had been rebuilt in 1428 by Humphrey, Duke of Gloucester, and again in 1501 by Henry VII, who made it 'beautiful and commodious'[36] for the wedding celebrations of Prince Arthur and Katherine of Aragon, who spent their wedding night there. Prior to that it had been the London residence of Cecily Neville, Duchess of York, the mother of Edward IV and Richard III. It was now the Queen's property, and used chiefly to store her Wardrobe stuff. The King found that the site was cramped and that there was no room to expand.[37]

His other London residence was, of course, the Tower of London. He used the lodgings built by his father, and erected temporary buildings near the White Tower for the officers of his household. He also rebuilt the thirteenth-century Chapel of St Peter and Vincula, which had been damaged by fire.[38] But the Tower was still too small.

Henry found that he had to compromise; if he could not live comfortably in London, he could live near it in the style to which he had become accustomed, and so he based himself chiefly at Greenwich, making use also of Richmond, Eltham or Lambeth Palace, the London house of the Archbishop of Canterbury.

Henry also began to take an interest in Leeds Castle, near Maidstone, Kent, a beautiful palace built on two linked islands in the middle of a lake. Edward I had purchased it in 1278 for his beloved wife, Eleanor of Castile, and after that it had been a dower house for the queens of England until the death in 1437 of Katherine of Valois, widow of Henry V and Henry VIII's great-grandmother by virtue of her second union with Owen Tudor. The Queen's Gallery leading to the Fountain Court was probably built for her. After her death Leeds had lost favour with royalty, but Henry VIII saw its potential. In 1512, he made Henry Guildford Constable of the castle and allowed him to live there, himself visiting from time to time. He also commissioned certain minor works, which were complete by 1515. Guildford's job was to act as overseer.

Later, between 1517 and 1523, Henry spent £1,300 (£390,000) on

Leeds. He installed bay windows in the royal lodgings in the Gloriette
tower and refurbished every room; the upper floor was fitted out for the
Queen; her bedchamber and withdrawing room, much remodelled,
remain today, and her badges may still be seen on a fireplace in her
gallery. Henry also built the Maidens' Tower to provide accommodation for her ladies, and the splendid banqueting hall, which is
seventy-five feet long and has a polished ebony floor and a ceiling of
carved oak. The contemporary fireplace, however, is French and was
installed in the twentieth century; Henry's original chimney-piece is
now in the room that has been fitted out as the bedchamber of
Katherine of Valois.

16

'A Galaxy of Distinguished Men'

In May 1512, William Blount, Lord Mountjoy,[1] a distant cousin of the King, replaced the Earl of Ormonde as Lord Chamberlain to Queen Katherine. Blount was unusual among his caste in that he had an international reputation as a humanist scholar. Having displayed an early brilliance, he had been sent by his uncle and guardian, Sir James Blount, to be educated in Paris, where the great scholar Erasmus was one of his tutors. The two struck up a friendship, and when Mountjoy was recalled to England in 1499 to consummate his marriage to the young heiress Elizabeth Say, he invited Erasmus to visit him at his house at Greenwich.

Blount was a man of many parts: a wealthy nobleman, a soldier who had fought for Henry VII in the Cornish Rising of 1497, and a man of culture. He was modest, high-minded, and had little time for gambling or idle pursuits. Erasmus held a high opinion of his learning, calling him an elegant Latinist,[2] and it was probably for this reason that Henry VII engaged him in 1499 as an academic mentor for Prince Henry; there is every reason to believe that Blount, with his powerful intellect, exerted a lasting influence over his charge. It was Blount who took Erasmus and Thomas More to visit the royal children at Eltham Palace in 1499. By 1505, Mountjoy had been made a Privy Councillor. His friendship with Erasmus drew him into the humanist circle that included Thomas More, Thomas Linacre, William Grocyn and John Colet.

Mountjoy's promotion reflected the interest of the King and Queen in learning and humanism. His family's record of impeccable loyalty to the Crown was an advantageous credential, and he was to display the same loyalty to Katherine while she was queen. He married one of her Spanish ladies, Iñez de Venegas, as the second of his four wives.

Henry VIII was keen to encourage the appointment of such men to high office. It behoved the magnificence of a Renaissance prince to be surrounded by men of learning, who would by their very presence at his court draw attention to his own erudition and thereby add lustre to his fame. His grandfather Edward IV had been 'a most loving encourager of wise and learned men',[3] and Henry VII had been 'not devoid of scholarship',[4] nor was he a stranger to humanism. Yet perhaps the most profound intellectual influence on Henry VIII was his grandmother, Margaret Beaufort, who had been an early patron of the New Learning, as humanism was beginning to be called.

The Renaissance witnessed, as its name implies, the rebirth, or rediscovery, of the classical works of ancient Greece and Rome, and those who studied these and evolved philosophies based upon them were known as humanists (from the Latin *humanitas*, then meaning 'culture'). The movement had begun with Petrarch in fourteenth-century Florence, and within a short period Italy had once more found itself at the heart of European civilisation. England being on the fringe of Europe, new ideas took time to permeate, but one of the earliest Renaissance influences was that of humanist thought, which had made its mark by the end of the fifteenth century. Most learning had until that time been the preserve of the Church, but with the spread of printing and literacy, and the growth of capitalism, laymen were beginning to take an interest in matters of the intellect, and to question the world around them.

The interest in all things classical had led naturally to a revival of the study of ancient languages. Latin, although the universal language of Europe, had gradually become debased during the Middle Ages, while Greek was little known. Humanist scholars sought to revive these languages in their ancient glory so that they could arrive at a better understanding of classical authors and indeed of the original texts of the Scriptures themselves. It was Erasmus who was chiefly responsible for the restoration of the Latin language, and also for the revival of the study of Greek. When he and friends such as Thomas More corresponded, it was in classical Latin.

Henry VIII's efforts at mastering Greek were probably halted by other demands on his time, yet he knew enough to be able to tell Bishop Tunstall that, in his reading of St Chrysostom, he had 'gathered a wrong sense upon his words'.[5] The King was fierce in his defence of Greek scholarship. When, in 1521, he learned that there was at Oxford a 'Society of Trojans' who had denounced not only the study of Greek, which they deemed impious, but also Erasmus himself, Henry invited one of its members to preach before him at Abingdon. Listening to the man ranting from the pulpit, Henry and his secretary Pace smiled meaningfully at each other. Afterwards, Henry appointed Thomas More to dispute with the preacher; the man's arguments were quickly demolished and, falling on his knees, he begged the King for forgiveness, saying his words had been prompted by a spirit.

'Nevertheless, that was not the spirit of Christ, but of foolishness,' reproved Henry. The preacher was then forced to admit he had not read any of Erasmus's works, whereupon the King retorted, 'Why then, you are a foolish fellow to censure what you never read.' This prompted the man to remember after all that he had read Erasmus's *In Praise of Folly*, at which Pace drily observed, 'Which has a great deal to do with the case, Your Majesty.' Henry gave orders that this 'Trojan' was never to preach before him again.[6]

Humanism coexisted side by side, and not always comfortably, with the old mediaeval scholasticism, which regarded the Scriptures and the works of St Thomas Aquinas and the Church Fathers as the ultimate authorities in received wisdom, and resisted any attempts at reinterpretation. Many early humanists, not to mention Henry VIII himself, were also scholastics, yet scholasticism was dying in the face of critical inquiry. As the Reformation dawned, the New Learning became increasingly identified with the forces of anticlericalism and religious reform. Not surprisingly, humanists found themselves divided in their sympathies.

In England, there were five men who, more than any others, were responsible for spreading the New Learning: Desiderius Erasmus, Thomas More, John Colet, William Grocyn and Thomas Linacre. They were not all luminaries of the court, but humanists with an international reputation for scholarship, and their influence, at court and elsewhere, was incalculable.

These early humanists advocated a Platonic society in which members of the elite laity, even princes, were educated to a high standard of erudition and eloquence as a preparation for public service. The description of the perfect courtier in Thomas More's *Utopia* (1516) could be that of the ideal Tudor gentleman. Inspired by Cicero, humanists also pressed for a more comprehensive and liberal curriculum in the schools and universities, with greater emphasis on the classics and natural science. They believed that every man had a duty to master all his God-given talents, both intellectual and physical. They demanded an end to war, and for the needs of the poor to be taken account of by the wealthy. Above all, they wanted people to take a broader view of the universe, and a less pessimistic view of man's humanity. In short, they would be the founders of a new commonwealth.

The English humanists were all friends and members of the same circle, and they were proud to count the Dutchman Erasmus as one of their number. He in turn declared that they 'have not their equal in Italy',[7] which was praise indeed, considering that Italy was the cradle of humanism.

Desiderius Erasmus had one of the greatest minds of the age. Born the bastard son of a monk around 1466 in Rotterdam, he had spent a miserable youth in holy orders, from which he was not released until 1517, and had devoted his life to scholarship. He was a brilliant writer and a passionate advocate of truth. Conscious of his own worth, he expected others to provide him with the wherewithal to continue his studies in comfort, and spent much of his life seeking wealthy patrons. The great scholar was not always easy company: although witty and erudite, he could be uncomfortably outspoken and was always complaining of his numerous ailments. His enemies were fiercely critical of him, accusing him of presumption for daring to rewrite the Gospels.

Erasmus had a high opinion of England, of its King, and also of its Queen, with whom he corresponded regularly. But he looked in vain there for patronage. He visited seven times between 1499 and 1517, sometimes as a guest of Thomas More. During these stays he attracted the attention of Archbishop Warham and Bishop Fisher, who arranged for him to lecture at Cambridge, and of Cardinal Wolsey, who gave him a pension; but the King, who may have been swayed by the anti-papal stance of *In Praise of Folly* (1511), did little for him beyond extolling his works. Erasmus settled at Basel in 1521, where he continued to write, study and correspond with his many friends and admirers. His greatest works were his translations of the New Testament and the works of St Jerome. He died in 1536.

Thomas More is the most famous of the English humanists. Born in London around 1477/8, he was the son of Judge John More who, when he discovered that his son was being taught Greek at Oxford, immediately removed him and sent him to Lincoln's Inn to learn law.[8] Later, Thomas contemplated taking holy orders, but decided he could not renounce the pleasures of the flesh, nor what turned out to be a distinguished legal career. By 1502, when he was called to the Bar, he had already earned the reputation of being one of the most brilliant classical scholars of the age, and was learned in both Latin and Greek. In 1504, he became a Member of Parliament, and in 1510 an Under-Sheriff of the City of London.

In 1505, Thomas More married Jane Colt, who bore him four children, Margaret, John, Elizabeth and Cecily, before dying in 1511, aged only twenty-three. More quickly remarried so as to provide a mother for his young children. His choice fell upon Alice Middleton, a widow who was 'aged, blunt and rude'[9] and certainly no scholar, yet despite her shortcomings she was an excellent housekeeper and More came to love her. In 1512, he purchased the wardship of an infant heiress, Anne Cresacre, who was brought up in his house and educated with his children; in 1529, she married More's son, John. More also adopted one Margaret Giggs, who later gained renown as a Greek scholar. In 1526, she married her tutor, Dr John Clement, who was also a member of More's household and later President of the Royal College of Physicians.

More's house in Bucklersbury in the City of London soon gained a reputation, not only as a meeting place for humanist scholars, but also as a haven of domestic felicity. According to Erasmus, the household 'breathed happiness'; it was run on firm Christian principles and resembled Plato's academy.[10] All More's children, even his daughters, were given a classical education, and taught Latin, Greek, logic, philosophy, theology, mathematics and astronomy. Their father exchanged letters with them in Latin, and also found time to make merry with them. He also kept a number of wild animals as pets, and an aviary.

More was a complex character, whom Richard Pace called 'a laughing philosopher'. He was calm, kind, witty and wise, a man of staunch faith who refused to compromise his principles, and something of an ascetic, despite his sensual nature. His piety was intense, and he wore a hair shirt next to his skin. He spurned fine clothing and gold chains. John Colet, who was his spiritual mentor, described him as England's only genius. More had a talent for friendship, and was essentially charming and courteous, yet he could be scathing when aroused, and over-fond of using scatological terms when reviling heretics and those of whom he disapproved. 'He had great wit,' wrote Edward Hall, 'but it was mingled with taunting and mocking.'

More is remembered not only as a martyr, but also for his writings. His first success came in 1511 when his translation of the life of the Italian humanist, Pico della Mirandola, was published. Other famous works would soon follow.

John Colet, the wealthy son of a Lord Mayor of London, had studied at Oxford, where he later lectured, as well as in France and Italy, and in 1498 had been ordained a priest. Tall, good-looking, austere in dress and lifestyle, yet of a merry disposition, he was a great scholar, a passionate lover of truth and an advocate of the integrity of the original biblical texts. 'When Colet speaks,' wrote Erasmus, 'I seem to be listening to Plato.'[11] In 1505, Colet was appointed Dean of St Paul's Cathedral in London, and four years later he founded St Paul's School. Its first High Master was William Lily, an expert linguist who pioneered the teaching of Greek and co-wrote with Erasmus a standard Latin grammar book, which formed the basis of the syntax later authorised by Henry VIII for use in grammar schools.[12] Henry had great respect for both Lily and Colet.

William Grocyn was a priest who had been educated at Winchester and Oxford, and in 1488, aged forty, had gone to Italy, where his rare knowledge of Greek qualified him to help translate the works of Aristotle. Back in England by 1491, he taught Greek at Oxford before being preferred to the living of St Lawrence Jewry in London. He died in 1519.

Dr Thomas Linacre was appointed one of Henry VIII's physicians, at £50 (£15,000) a year, in 1509. Also Oxford-educated, he had learned Greek, then gone to Padua to study medicine. His experience of Italy set him firmly in the vanguard of the humanist movement in England; Erasmus called him 'as deep and acute a thinker as I have ever met with'.[13] Linacre had translated several of the works of the ancient Greek physicians Galen and Hippocrates into Latin, taught Greek at Oxford and served for a time as physician to Henry VII and tutor to Prince Arthur. His reputation as a doctor was second to none, and he numbered among his patients Wolsey, Warham, Foxe, More, Erasmus and Colet.

Henry VIII sought to gain an international reputation as a patron of scholars, not just for the prestige they brought him, but also because he genuinely enjoyed their stimulating company and wished to encourage them to his court. Indeed, according to Erasmus, he came to prefer the company of 'a galaxy of distinguished men' to that of 'young men lost in luxury, or women, or gold-chained nobles'.[14] Where the King led, others followed, with the result that by the 1520s, the court had begun to resemble an academy devoted to intellectual pursuits. Henry, wrote Erasmus in 1519, 'openly shows himself a patron of good letters. The King's court abounds with greater numbers of the learned than any university'; it was 'a very museum of knowledge'.[15] Thomas More felt that, thanks to Henry's cultivation of all the 'liberal arts', the court had come to resemble 'a temple of the muses'.[16]

Although the King did not agree with every aspect of the New Learning – he was certainly no pacifist – he had all his children educated on humanist principles. Fortunately, most of the scholars he patronised did not live to see him squander on ruinous wars the resources that he might have spent on education and on the welfare of his subjects.

Many of those who served Henry VIII were humanists. The historian Polydore Vergil, a friend of Erasmus and native of Urbino in Italy, who had come to England around 1500 as a papal tax collector and stayed to be granted papers of denization, had been asked by Henry VII to write the history of England. It took Vergil thirty-three years to complete this great work, the *Anglicæ Historiæ* – it was published in Basel in 1534, with a dedication to Henry VIII – and his approach to it was systematic, rational and critical rather than credulous and moralistic, as the writers of history – mainly monastic chroniclers – had tended to be in the past. Predictably, his work aroused controversy: some were outraged that Vergil had dared to assert that the tales of King Arthur were partly mythical, but, although the book was biased in favour of Vergil's royal patrons, it set new standards in historical scholarship and was widely read and emulated.[17]

Cuthbert Tunstall, Bishop of Durham, who had spent six years at the University of Padua, was a humanist and a member of More's circle; in 1522, he dedicated his treatise on mathematics, *De Arte Supputendi*, to More. In 1513, the King appointed another humanist, Erasmus's friend Andrea Ammonio of Lucca, to be his Latin Secretary; it was Ammonio who, in 1516–17, helped Erasmus free himself from his monastic vows. Ammonio's kinsman and fellow humanist, Peter Vannes, became Secretary to both Wolsey and Henry VIII in turn. Richard Pace, another royal Secretary, was an outstanding humanist scholar, while Henry's Treasurer of the Chamber, Bryan Tuke, was a correspondent of Erasmus. The King promoted these men because their education and outlook qualified them to serve him better than many a nobleman with a long pedigree.

Thanks to the teachings of Erasmus and others, and the patronage of Margaret Beaufort, John Fisher and later Thomas Wolsey, who founded Cardinal College, Oxford, in 1525, humanism was already infiltrating the universities of Oxford and Cambridge. Sadly, though, Henry VIII's patronage of scholars was largely confined to the court; he showed little interest in the universities until he canvassed their support for his nullity suit in the early 1530s, and it was not until the last years of his reign that he made any foundations of his own.

Katherine of Aragon, however, was a generous patron of education. She, too, enjoyed and benefited from the company of the scholars who flocked to court, but she did not ignore the universities. In 1518, she visited Merton College, Oxford, where she was received by the students with 'as many demonstrations of joy and love as if she had been Juno or Minerva'.[18] She founded lectureships at Oxford and Cambridge, gave money to support the struggling new foundation of St John's College, Cambridge, founded by Margaret Beaufort, and, like Margaret, gave financial support to impoverished students. She also took an interest in Wolsey's college at Oxford.

Katherine had been schooled by the humanist Peter Martyr, and she was 'a rare and fine advocate'[19] of the New Learning. Many learned works were dedicated to her, and Erasmus was privately of the opinion that her scholarship was more exceptional than her husband's.[20]

*

The spread of learning, literacy and education that occurred during the Renaissance was inspired by humanism, but facilitated by the invention of printing. Since 1476, when William Caxton set up the first English printing press at Westminster, printed books and pamphlets had proliferated at a staggering rate. After Caxton died in 1491, his press had been taken over by his chief assistant, the Alsatian Wynkyn de Worde, a protégé of Margaret Beaufort; Worde moved the press to Fleet Street, and until his death in 1535 produced many important books, earning himself the title King's Printer. Among his successors to both title and press was the renowned Thomas Berthelet.

As books were expensive and only available to a wealthy few, their subject matter initially reflected the interests of the upper classes, who were to begin with no friends to the New Learning. The most popular books were devotional works and tales of chivalry. 'In our forefathers' time, few books were read in our tongue, saving certain books of chivalry,' recalled the great scholar Roger Ascham in 1570. The most popular of these was Sir Thomas Malory's *Morte d'Arthur* (written c1470, published 1485), and Ascham could only deplore the fact that 'the whole pleasure of it standeth in open manslaughter and bold bawdery'.[21] Other favourites were mediaeval romances, manuals on courtesy and hunting, and above all histories such as Robert Fabyan's *New Chronicles of England and France* (1516).

Polydore Vergil had set a new fashion in historical writing and inspired a new generation of writers. But the moralising of the past had not been forgotten. When Thomas More wrote his *History of Richard the Third* (c1514), he expected his readers to learn from it important political lessons; in many other respects, it is the first 'modern' biography.[22]

By contrast, the lawyer Edward Hall – no humanist, but an eyewitness – produced a well written but traditional chronicle of Henry VIII's reign, with vivid descriptions of pageants and state occasions; yet although it is an invaluable source for the period, its style is uncritical and adulatory.[23]

The spread of humanism led before long to changes in attitudes and the printing of more sophisticated works; some were controversial and some even heretical. Attempts to regulate the presses were not always successful, while banned books were often smuggled into England from abroad. The printed word was enormously influential in encouraging people to explore new ideas and ideologies, but they often did so at their peril.

Traditional illuminated manuscripts were still much prized, and often very valuable, and it was customary to have presentation copies of printed books illustrated by hand to make them look like manuscripts. In 1525, Henry VIII employed a 'limner of books' called Richard James.[24]

The early Tudor period produced little in the way of great literature. The age of Chaucer was long past, although his works, first printed in 1532 with a preface by the King's Treasurer of the Chamber, Bryan Tuke,[25] were still enormously popular, while the plays of Shakespeare lay decades ahead. Much of the best prose was to be found in translations of older works; it was Henry VIII who urged John Bourchier, Lord Berners, the martial Governor of Calais, to write his outstanding translation of the chronicles of Jean Froissart (1523–5), hoping that 'his worthy subjects' might be inspired to emulate the famous and warlike deeds of their ancestors.[26] Berners' other translations included a courtly romance, *Huon of Bordeaux* (c1534), for Lady Elizabeth Carew, and Antonio de Guevara's *Golden Book of Marcus Aurelius* (1535), described as 'a mirror for princes'.[27] Henry VIII also commissioned, at the time of his invasion of France in 1513, an English translation of the Latin biography of his hero, Henry V, written by the Ferrarese humanist Tito Livio da Forli in 1437–8.[28]

Henry VIII spent a fortune on illuminated manuscripts and printed books, importing many from France and Italy. He inherited some of his collection from his father and from Margaret Beaufort, who left him her copy of Froissart's chronicles. Many of his books were Bibles, classical works by Aristotle, Cicero and Thucydides, or theological tomes, such as the Church Fathers and scholastic authorities including St Thomas Aquinas, Albertus Magnus, St John Bonaventura, John of Salisbury and Peter Abelard.[29] There were also the usual romances and works of chivalry, as well as several scientific treatises.

The royal library had originally been established in the early thirteenth century by King John. It was then a collection of books that travelled with the King, but by the end of the fifteenth century, after successive monarchs, notably Edward IV and Henry VII, had added more volumes, it was housed in specially designated rooms in the royal palaces.

Under Henry VIII, the royal library expanded considerably. There were libraries at Richmond, Greenwich, Hampton Court and Whitehall, which were looked after by each respective Keeper of the Palace. There was also a resident librarian; the first to be appointed by Henry VIII was the Flemish scholar, Giles d'Ewes. These libraries were furnished with desks and lecterns, both with shelves underneath for storing books; wall-mounted shelves did not come into fashion until later in the century. The royal books were bound by the King's Bookbinder in red or black velvet or leather,[30] and they were numbered and arranged in alphabetical order.[31] Some of the King's books and manuscripts survive: several are in the British Library, while nearly a hundred duplicate volumes were donated after Henry's death to Trinity

College, Oxford; some of these had originally been acquired from monastic libraries. What was left of Henry VIII's library was to form the nucleus of the present Royal Library at Windsor.

17

'The King's Painters'

In 1511, John Browne, later the founder of Painter-Stainers Hall in London, became the first artist to be appointed to the new post of Serjeant Painter to the King, at a salary of £20 (£6,000). Browne was not employed to paint pictures, but to carry out decorative work in the royal palaces and on the King's ships and barges, and to make props and scenery for the Revels Office. He is also known to have painted flags, banners, surcoats, horse trappings and perhaps the initial letters of documents. Much of his work involved heraldic devices, and in his will he refers to three books of arms and badges which he used for reference.[1] The King owned similar pattern books, which he kept in his studies at Hampton Court and Whitehall.[2]

Until 1544, Henry's Serjeant Painters were English and members of the Painter Stainers Guild in London, which was founded by the King to provide teams of artists and craftsmen to help his Serjeant Painters carry out their duties. Henry was an exacting master who wanted work completed very quickly. As well as John Browne, he 'had in wages for limning divers other',[3] although their names are rarely recorded. Limning was the art of painting in miniature for manuscript illumination; later, the word 'limner' was used to describe a painter of miniatures.

Most English art at this time was of a decorative nature, the rest comprising crude oak-panel portraits, usually by itinerant artists; much is lost, and what does survive has often been heavily restored. There was no indigenous school of painting, and the names of few artists are known. The court's artistic inspiration came from Burgundy, but during Henry VIII's reign, Italian and French Renaissance influences became increasingly evident; most of the best artists and craftsmen working in England were foreigners imported by Henry VIII and Wolsey to reproduce the innovations that had appeared on the continent; royal agents were sent abroad to discover and recruit the most talented artificers, offering attractive rates of pay, short- or long-term contracts, and the prestige of working for the King. As has been remarked upon, there was fierce native resentment against aliens working in this field, and strict legislation controlling their activities. But the King's employees were exempt.

Edward IV and Henry VII had established royal workshops for the artists and craftsmen they employed, which Henry VIII expanded, although very little is known about how the workshops functioned. One atelier at Richmond employed illuminators, and was managed by the royal librarian, Giles d'Ewes.[4] Later in the reign, two distinct schools of craftsmen were established at court: Italian sculptors and Flemish glaziers. One of the latter was a Dutchman, Galyon Hone (or Hoon), who in 1517 succeeded Bernard Flower as 'King's Glazier', working from a new royal workshop in Southwark. Hone designed stained glass for many of the royal palaces and the Savoy Chapel before continuing Flower's work on the magnificent windows of King's College Chapel, Cambridge, with designs that were high Renaissance in concept.

Henry VIII was one of the greatest English patrons of the arts, on which he spent vast sums. Much of this went on decorative schemes and ephemeral items intended to glorify the royal image, and a great deal is lost and known only from written records. Yet there is no doubt that Henry took a keen interest in artistic developments, and was desirous of showing himself to be a European in taste. To begin with it was Wolsey who set the pace in artistic patronage, but Henry was never one to be outdone, and soon took the lead.

In Italy, the revival of classical art and architecture was facilitated by the diversity of surviving ruins and artefacts, but in England there were few such blueprints. Italian artistic influence usually reached England through trade, as well as via Englishmen who had visited Italy and Italian craftsmen who had worked in Flanders and France, and also via imported Italian books, but it was not until 1516 that the craze for all things 'antique' became fashionable and began to undermine the artistic dominance of Burgundy. Of course, Renaissance art was not unknown at court prior to that date: Henry VII had been given Raphael's *St George and the Dragon* by Guidobaldo da Montefeltro, Duke of Urbino, in return for the Order of the Garter,[5] and around 1500 the Italian sculptor Guido Mazzone had produced a bust which probably represents a smiling young Henry VIII as Duke of York. But such examples were not widely known in England.

The first great Italian artist employed by Henry VIII was Pietro Torrigiano, the Florentine sculptor. Torrigiano was a volatile man with a chequered background: he had learned his craft alongside Michelangelo in the studio of Domenico Ghirlandaio in Florence; there, Torrigiano had quarrelled with Michelangelo, and famously broken his nose. Later, after working on commissions for the Borgias in Rome, he had fought as a mercenary in the Italian wars.

It was perhaps at Wolsey's suggestion that Henry invited Torrigiano to England in 1511 to design and execute a tomb for Henry VII and Elizabeth of York, which was to be the centrepiece of the magnificent Perpendicular Henry VII Chapel in Westminster Abbey. Torrigiano worked on the tomb between 1512 and 1518. He wanted Benvenuto Cellini to assist him with the project, but Cellini refused to be associated with a man of so violent a temper, nor did he wish to live among 'such beasts as the English'.[6] In the event, Torrigiano produced the first masterpiece of Renaissance sculpture to be seen in England, with lifelike bronze effigies – the faces had probably been taken from death masks – resting on a classical marble sarcophagus, with the arms of England supported by plump putti at each end. He also completed a tomb for Margaret Beaufort, which bore a strikingly austere marble effigy of that formidable lady, based on drawings made from memory by Maynard the Fleming, and an epitaph by Erasmus. The two tombs set new precedents for English funerary monuments.

These were not the only works that Torrigiano executed in England. He produced painted terracotta busts of Henry VII and Henry VIII, which Henry VIII later displayed in his study at Whitehall,[7] and also a bust of Bishop Fisher.[8] In 1516, he sculpted a Florentine-style wall tomb for Dr John Yonge, Master of the Rolls, in the Rolls Chapel, Chancery Lane, and he may also have been responsible for the sculptured portrait roundel of Sir Thomas Lovell, Treasurer of the Household, now in Westminster Abbey. In 1517, Torrigiano began work on a marble altar with terracotta angels which was to stand before Henry VII's tomb; it was completed after his death by Benedetto di Rovezzano, but destroyed in 1644 during the Civil War; the present altar in Westminster Abbey is a 1930s reconstruction.

Another Italian who was enticed to England early in Henry's reign was Vincenzo Volpe (or Vulpe), a native of Naples, who arrived before 1512 and remained in the royal employ until 1532. The King set him to work painting heraldic designs on his ships and barges, and later commissioned him to paint maps of Rye and Hastings. He also drew up a pictorial plan of Dover harbour that was presented by the people of Dover to the King.[9]

Most pictures painted in England were portraits. Portraiture evolved considerably and became highly fashionable during Henry VIII's reign, which was when a quintessentially English style began to develop, although it was foreign artists such as Hans Holbein who made this possible. Prior to Holbein's arrival in 1526, there were few portrait painters of note working in England.

Portraits on wood were known as 'tables', while those on canvas were called 'stained cloths'. Many of those that survive from the early sixteenth century betray some Burgundian influence. Portraits were painted to order, yet there was little money to be made out of them, for in the days before Holbein they were considered to be of less value than wall hangings. There were, however, many portraits in the royal collection that were important, not so much as works of art, but as dynastic advertisements. In an age before photography, they were also tools of diplomacy, used often in marriage negotiations or as goodwill tokens between rulers.

Henry VIII owned a set of royal portraits painted by the so-called 'cast shadow workshop' around 1518–35,[10] including those of Henry V, Henry VI, Edward IV and Richard III. That of Richard III was overpainted soon after its completion, to make the image of the King look as evil as his reputation was deemed to warrant. Henry also had a portrait from life of his grandmother, Elizabeth Wydeville, dating from c1471–80, and a series of foreign royal portraits, among them Louis XII, Ferdinand and Isabella, and the three children of Christian II of Denmark.

The sitters in Tudor portraits are often identified by badges, coats of arms and inscriptions; rank and wealth were proclaimed through costume, jewellery and insignia, and elaborate symbolism, much of it still not fully understood, was used to convey more subtle messages. Full-length portraits were rare, and most were head-and-shoulders studies, with the hands sometimes resting on a shelf; some portraits were rectangular, others had arched crowns. Several versions of a portrait, of varying quality, could exist: Henry VII arranged for copies of royal portraits to hang in all his greater houses, while loyal subjects would obtain copies of portraits of the King and his family to hang in their homes.

Henry VIII's portraits were beautifully framed, some with 'black ebony garnished with silver', some of wood painted black and gilded, and others of walnut wood.[11] To prevent them from fading, brightly coloured curtains of silk, or sarcanet, were kept drawn in front of them; those at Hampton Court were yellow and green.[12]

One of the first portrait painters to be patronised by Henry VIII was Jan Raf or Rave, a master of the Painters' Guild of Bruges, more commonly known by his Latinised name, Johannes Corvus, who was working in England from c1518 until his death in 1544. One of the most famous of his surviving works is the portrait of Bishop Foxe (c1518) now in Corpus Christi College, Oxford; the portrait of Henry's sister Mary Tudor (c1529) at Sudeley Castle is similar in manner and may also be by him,[13] as may the portrait of Katherine of Aragon in the National Portrait Gallery.[14] Because his style was copied by imitators, it is often difficult to say with certainty which of the portraits ascribed to him are definitely by him.

The Renaissance portrait medal was first seen in England in Henry VIII's reign. One of the first was the medal of the King in profile, with a bonnet, straight hair and a beard, by the German master, Hans Schwarz,[15] which probably dates from the mid-1520s.

Comparatively few portraits of Henry VIII survive from the period before 1525. One at Windsor, formerly thought to portray his brother Arthur, shows Henry as an adolescent. Of three known early representations of Henry as King, one, dating from c1509, is in the Berger Collection in Denver, one is in the Fairhaven Collection at Anglesey Abbey, and the whereabouts of the third is unknown. A half-length in the National Portrait Gallery by an unknown Flemish artist, dating from c1520, is the first to show Henry bearded. The Dutch artist, Lucas Cornelisz de Koch, is said to have come to England with his large family in 1521 and to have painted the King, but his work cannot now be traced.[16]

We know something of Henry VIII's collection of paintings because inventories of his pictures were drawn up in 1542 and 1547. In 1547, twenty hung in the gallery at Hampton Court, whilst Whitehall housed 169. Many of these were portraits, but a considerable number were paintings and triptychs of religious subjects such as the 'table of Our Lady with St Elizabeth'.[17] Henry was the first English King to collect art in the modern sense, even though his purpose was invariably to use it to enhance his own glory. That he realised the value of the works he collected is apparent from the fact that some of them were hung in a gallery to which only he kept the key. Those paintings he left behind him, whose excellence he certainly appreciated, form the core of today's Royal Collection, of which he may with justification be accounted the true founder.

18

'Graceless Dogholes'

As the year 1513 dawned, Henry VIII and his allies in the Holy League were poised to go to war against France. In March 1512, Pope Julius had withdrawn Louis XII's title of 'Most Christian King' and bestowed the kingdom of France upon Henry: all he had to do was win it. A campaign was mounted that June, under the Marquess of Dorset, but had ended in ignominious failure and the death of Sir Thomas Knyvet. Now the King intended to lead an army himself against the French; it was his dream to reconquer the lands once held by Henry V but lost by the time the Hundred Years' War came to a dishonourable end in 1453. Only Calais and its Pale remained of that once vast Plantagenet empire, and Henry hoped to win glory for himself by another victory such as Agincourt. He was supported vigorously in this new enterprise by the young men of his Chamber, who, like their master, were fired by chivalrous ideals of valour in a glorious military pageant.

When it came to preparing for war, Wolsey proved his worth, undertaking a multitude of tasks with good humour and efficiency. Foreign observers noted with astonishment the sheer volume of work that he was coping with, which was sufficient to keep busy 'all the magistrates, offices and courts of Venice'.[1]

Wolsey had already shown himself to be valuable in many other ways. He was willing to implement the royal policies, to work while Henry played, and to shoulder the many administrative tasks of government. He had flattered and praised his way into favour, and hastened to act on the King's every whim. He understood that Henry wished England to become a major European power alongside France and Spain, and was prepared to do everything in his power to make that come about. He perceived that the power and majesty of the Church and the law could be enlisted to boost Henry's prestige and authority. No king could have had a servant more willing to please.

Wolsey's growing power alarmed others. The nobility considered him an upstart and deplored his arrogance and increasingly lavish lifestyle, while gentlemen of the Privy Chamber such as William Compton resented his influence over Henry. Whereas the King was coming to rely increasingly on Wolsey and regarded him as a valuable adviser whose only desire was to serve him faithfully, others perceived the massive ego and ruthlessness of the man and his desire for self-aggrandisement. But the fact remained that Wolsey was the 'most earnest and readiest among all the Council to advance the King's mere will and pleasure'. Appreciating that Henry, being young, was bored by administrative matters, he readily took upon himself 'to disburden the King of so weighty and troublesome business.'[2] Wolsey also shared the King's opulent and worldly tastes for building, art, music, learning and revelry, so they had much in common as friends.

Richard Foxe had pushed Wolsey forward to counter the influence of his rival Surrey, but by 1513 his own star was being eclipsed by the new favourite's. This did not unduly worry him, for he was not in the best of health, had no sympathy with the King's thirst for war, and was looking forward to a retirement spent looking after the spiritual needs of his diocese, which he had much neglected. He therefore encouraged Wolsey's advancement, and acted occasionally as his mentor.[3]

The King's humanist friends did not approve of his appetite for war, either. On Good Friday 1513, John Colet was invited to preach before Henry at Greenwich, and exhorted his martially inclined audience to follow the example of the Prince of Peace rather than that of heroes such as Julius Caesar or Alexander the Great. An unquiet peace, he told them, was preferable to a just war. The sermon led to an uproar, with some bishops accusing Colet of betraying the Holy League.

The King, who feared that his captains might be influenced by Colet's views, visited the Dean at the nearby convent of the Observant Friars, where he was lodging, and, dismissing his retinue, spoke with him in private. 'I have come to discharge my conscience, not to distract you from your studies,' he was heard to say. What passed between them was never divulged in detail, but Colet allowed himself to be persuaded that Henry's cause was a just one, and the King emerged beaming. Calling for wine, he raised his goblet in a toast to Colet, saying, 'Let every man choose his own doctor. This is mine!'[4]

Before he left for France, Henry looked to the security of his kingdom. Rumour had it that Louis XII intended to acknowledge Edmund de la Pole, Earl of Suffolk, the Yorkist pretender imprisoned in the Tower, as King of England. On 4 May, Henry had Suffolk beheaded, and would have meted out the same fate to his younger brother Richard, save for the fact that that young troublemaker, who liked to call himself the 'White Rose', was an exile in France and beyond Henry's reach.

Suffolk's former ducal seat, Ewelme Manor in Oxfordshire, had been in royal hands since 1504. It had been built in the 1430s by William de la Pole, the first Duke, and by 1518 Henry had converted it into a palace with a King's Side and a Queen's Side.[5] The King visited occasionally, but between 1525 and 1535 it was leased to Charles Brandon.

Henry was not unnecessarily cruel to his Yorkist relatives, and, provided they remained loyal, was often kind and generous to them. His cousin Margaret of Clarence, widow of Sir Richard Pole, was 'a lady of virtue and honour'[6] and an intimate of the Queen. In 1513, Henry created her Countess of Salisbury, in right of her mother, whose forebears had been earls of Salisbury, and restored her ancestral lands. The new Countess's country seat was Warblington Castle, Hampshire,[7] where she kept the state of a mediaeval magnate and lived a life based on piety, study and tradition. Margaret Pole's eldest son, Henry, was at the same time raised to the peerage as Lord Montague. Her daughter Ursula was married to Henry, Lord Stafford, Buckingham's heir. It was the Countess's desire to dedicate her youngest son, the intellectual Reginald Pole, now aged thirteen, to the Church, and again the King was bountiful, helping to finance Reginald's education at the Charterhouse at Sheen and at the Universities of Oxford and Padua. Henry also granted him ecclesiastical benefices so that he could live in a state appropriate to his rank.

Having put his house in order, Henry left Greenwich for Dover, accompanied by the Queen, who was to remain as Regent, and an entourage that included the Duke of Buckingham, twenty other peers, Bishop Foxe, Wolsey, heralds, musicians, trumpeters, Robert Fairfax and the choir of the Chapel Royal, six hundred archers of the Yeomen of the Guard, all in green and white liveries, and three hundred Household servants. He also took with him his bed of estate, several suits of armour and a number of brightly coloured tents and pavilions. On 30 June, the King and his great army sailed for France.

The Queen returned to Greenwich with a very depleted household. Archbishop Warham was there to offer wise advice, and she was kept 'horribly busy with making standards, banners and badges', as she wrote to Wolsey, and with her viceregal duties. In the midst of all this, she did not forget to ensure that her husband was supplied with clean body linen.

On 24 July Henry and his ally, the Emperor Maximilian, laid siege to the town of Thérouanne. On 16 August, the French were routed at the Battle of the Spurs – so called because of the haste with which they retreated – and Thérouanne fell.

Charles Brandon served as Marshal of the King's army; as second in command, he led the vanguard during the fighting, acquitting himself bravely and winning golden opinions. Henry Guildford proved his worth as the King's Standard Bearer. The only major casualty of the war was Sir Edward Howard who, having sworn to avenge the death of his friend Knyvet, was taken prisoner and stabbed to death during an attack on the French fleet off Brest, to the great grief of the King and of Brandon. William Fitzwilliam, who distinguished himself as a naval commander, was wounded in that same battle. In 1514, Henry rewarded him by making him Vice-Admiral of England.

After his victory at Thérouanne, the King and his courtiers spent three days as the guests of Maximilian's daughter, Margaret of Savoy, Regent of the Netherlands, at Lille. The Burgundian nobility hastened to be presented to Henry, and were delighted to find him 'merry, handsome, well-spoken, popular and intelligent'.[8] Although he was supposed to be taking his ease, he astonished everyone present with his energy. He jousted before the Archduchess and her young nephew, Prince Charles of Castile, in a tiltyard in which barriers of rough planks had been hastily erected. The King ran many courses against Brandon and the Emperor's champion, Guillaume de Ghislain, and broke a great number of lances, to thunderous acclaim. The Milanese ambassador was amazed at his stamina: 'He was fresher after this exertion than before. I do not know how he can stand it.'[9] The next day, a tournament was held indoors in a huge room with a black marble floor; the horses wore felt shoes to prevent them marking it.[10]

The King also excelled himself at archery. In the evenings, he played on a variety of musical instruments for the Archduchess, then, as the night wore on, he 'danced magnificently in the French style' with Margaret and her ladies, and at one point got so hot that he was obliged to throw off his doublet and shoes. The next morning he was up early, 'wonderfully merry'.[11]

Some embarrassment was caused by Henry's attempts to arrange a marriage between the widowed Archduchess and Charles Brandon. Brandon certainly entertained hopes in that direction, despite being contracted to Elizabeth Grey, and at one banquet playfully exchanged rings with Margaret. She treated the gesture as a joke, even though the King heartily recommended Brandon as a husband. When he heard, Maximilian was not pleased, and Margaret had to reassure him that the rumours about her so-called marriage plans were 'base lies'. Nevertheless, the gossip persisted, and Henry was later obliged to write to Margaret to apologise for any annoyance it had caused, and order his envoys to put a stop to it.[12]

Henry himself indulged in a flirtation with a Flemish lady, Étienne de la Baume, whom he met at Lille. According to a letter she wrote to him later, they laughed and joked together, he calling her his page, which has led to speculation that she dressed up as such so as to facilitate trysts with him. He certainly told her 'many pretty things about marriage and other things', and promised to give her ten thousand crowns when she found a husband. Soon afterwards, Étienne's father did arrange a marriage for her, and she wrote to claim her dowry. There is no record of Henry paying it.[13] In 1513, a Venetian envoy described how, 'for love of a lady', the King 'clad himself and his court in mourning'.[14] Since there exists no reference to any other mistress in 1513, this statement perhaps relates to Henry staging some elaborate charade, either during his flirtation with Étienne, or on learning that she was to marry.

Taking advantage of the King's absence, James IV of Scotland, Louis's ally, crossed the northern border and invaded England from the north, but was defeated and killed, along with the flower of the Scots nobility, by an army led by the septuagenarian Earl of Surrey at Flodden Moor on 9 September 1513. The Queen displayed the martial spirit of her mother Isabella the Catholic when she rallied the English troops with a rousing speech at Buckingham before they proceeded north. After the battle, when the body of James IV was brought south, Katherine was all for sending it to Henry in France as a trophy, but 'our Englishmen's hearts would not suffer it', she told him, so she dispatched to him a piece of James's bloodstained coat instead.[15]

Flodden was a far more significant victory than anything Henry would achieve in France, where he was still playing the conquering hero. On 21 September he took the town of Tournai, after which he knighted William Compton, Edward Neville, William Fitzwilliam and two hundred other men who had distinguished themselves during the campaign. He then spent three weeks celebrating his victories with jousts and revels.

Meanwhile, Queen Katherine, who was pregnant again, had gone to Our Lady of Walsingham, as she had promised the King she would do, to give thanks for the victory at Flodden and to pray for a son.[16] But the baby was born prematurely and did not survive.[17]

The campaigning season came to an end in the autumn, and on 22 October the King returned to England in triumph, although in fact he had achieved very little. In return for a financial outlay of nearly £1 million (£300 million) he had taken two minor towns of little significance, which some of his ungrateful subjects referred to as 'graceless dogholes'. Furthermore, he need not have gone to war at all, since Louis XII had made peace with the new Pope, Leo X, before Henry even set out. Nevertheless, Henry, who had his own political agenda, felt he had acquitted himself well, and hoped that, with the help of his allies, Ferdinand and Maximilian, he would conquer France the following year.

The King now made haste to Richmond, where Katherine awaited him; he could not wait to lay at her feet the keys of the cities he had taken.[18] Later, he commissioned artists (whose names are unknown) to paint large-scale pictures of his triumphs in France, which are still in the Royal Collection. Executed c1540–5, they show Henry's meeting with Maximilian (with the sieges of Thérouanne and Tournai in the background) and the Battle of the Spurs.

As was customary in late mediaeval warfare, noble hostages were taken to ensure that their government kept faith with the terms of the truce. As the rules of chivalry decreed, they were treated as honoured guests until the time came for them to be allowed to return home. Henry's chief prisoner was Louis d'Orléans, Duc de Longueville, who was lodged comfortably in the Tower of London with six servants. The King became very friendly with him, and often invited him to court. Henry was a remarkably generous captor, even offering to pay half the Duc's ransom himself.[19]

Soon after their arrival in England, Queen Katherine entertained the King and his hostages at Havering, Essex. There was a feast, a masque and dancing, with Henry distributing gifts 'where he liked'.[20]

The King's palace at Havering-atte-Bower had originally been built by Edward the Confessor in the eleventh century and had remained a favourite residence of English royalty ever since. The bower that gave it its name had been a garden created by King Edward on a nearby hill affording breathtaking views of the Thames Valley. Although he undertook no building works here, Henry VIII liked to visit because the palace, a great, rambling, old-fashioned building, was surrounded by an extensive deer park. A mile away, within the park, was a smaller moated house called Pyrgo, which since the time of Eleanor of Castile (d.1290) had been part of the jointure of the Queens of England; Katherine of Aragon, Anne Boleyn and Jane Seymour held it in turn, but it was not assigned to any of Henry's later wives. It was, however, to the palace that Katherine invited the French hostages.[21]

During their sojourn in France and the Low Countries, Henry and his courtiers experienced at first hand the sophisticated culture of the Franco-Flemish Renaissance and were profoundly impressed. The cessation of hostilities therefore witnessed the beginning of a craze at the English court for all things French, which would last for most of the rest of the reign. Henry himself set the trend, slavishly imitating the French King and his court in style, etiquette, fashion, food, art, architecture, tournaments and entertainment. The French language, which had recently been banned at the English court, again became a modish medium of communication for the upper classes. After seventy years, the long cultural dominance of Burgundy was at last drawing to an end.

19

'Obstinate Men Who Govern Everything'

At the end of the year 1513, 'the King kept a solemn Christmas at Greenwich to cheer his nobles'.[1] The Wardrobe issued twelve yards of yellow sarcenet to Sir Henry Guildford and Nicholas Carew, a young gentleman who was of the King's 'own bringing up', for a 'mummery', in which Brandon and Mistress Carew also took part.[2]

Nicholas Carew was rising to prominence through his expertise in the lists. The son of the Captain of Calais, whose forebears had been loyal servants of the Crown, he was a cultivated youth of about seventeen, 'well-mannered and having the French tongue'.[3] He had been placed in Prince Henry's household at the age of six, and shared his education; the King thought very well of him, and often sought his company. Carew's wife was Elizabeth, the beautiful daughter of Sir Thomas Bryan, Vice-Chamberlain to the Queen; her sister Margaret was Guildford's first wife.[4]

Soon after Christmas, Henry went down with 'a fever' which proved to be smallpox. 'The physicians were afraid for his life', but by the beginning of February he had risen from his bed, 'fierce against France'.[5] He could not wait to return to the field.

The King was still convalescent when he rewarded those who had served him so well during the campaigns of 1513. At Candlemas 1514, he created Charles Brandon Duke of Suffolk and restored to Surrey the dukedom of Norfolk. The King's cousin and Lord Chamberlain, Charles Somerset, Lord Herbert, was at the same time made Earl of Worcester. He was the bastard son of the last Beaufort Duke of Somerset, and had acquitted himself with valour in France.

The ceremony of ennoblement took place after High Mass on 2 February in the great chamber at Lambeth Palace, and followed the form laid down in the fourteenth century when Edward III had advanced his sons to the peerage. Each Duke was invested with a crimson robe and cap of estate, a coronet and sword and a gold rod. He now had the right to be styled the 'right high and mighty Prince', but was usually addressed as 'Your Grace'.[6] The ceremony was watched by the Queen and her ladies, the Duc de Longueville, and a host of peers who were in London to attend Parliament. The press of people 'was somewhat great, notwithstanding the doors were straitly kept'.[7]

The new peerage creations were not universally popular, especially that of Suffolk. 'Many considered it very surprising,' wrote Vergil. Buckingham especially was furious at the ennoblement of Brandon, whom he considered an upstart and 'not of a very noble lineage',[8] and pointedly stayed away from the ceremony. It was Buckingham's rival Wolsey who had advised the King to advance his friend, possibly with a view to offsetting the new Duke of Norfolk's influence on the Council.

When Henry granted Brandon the estates formerly held by Edmund de la Pole he became at a stroke much wealthier, and therefore more powerful, than most of the landed aristocracy. He seemed, wrote a Burgundian observer, to be 'a second King, . . . one who does and undoes'.[9] The Standard Bearer's son took it all in his stride. 'No one ever bore so vast a rise with so easy a dignity,' declared a Venetian, assuring the Senate that Suffolk was now 'the chief nobleman of England' and 'a liberal and magnificent lord'.[10] The older nobility looked askance: they were jealous of Suffolk's influence and distrusted his ambition. Erasmus spoke for them all when he wrote scathingly of the former Master of the Horse, 'The King has recently turned that new Duke from a stable boy into a nobleman.'[11]

Suffolk's power now rivalled that of the other new Duke, Norfolk, who, in recognition of his victory at Flodden, was granted the right to display the royal arms of Scotland alongside his own, with the Scottish lion impaled with an arrow, as James IV had been. He was also made Earl Marshal of England for life. Norfolk's son, another Thomas Howard, now became Earl of Surrey at the age of forty-one. In 1512, on his father's resignation, he had succeeded as Lord Treasurer of England, and in 1513 he had commanded the vanguard at Flodden. He had been married firstly to Anne of York, daughter of Edward IV, but she and their four infant children were dead by 1513, and Howard had recently married Buckingham's fourteen-year-old daughter Elizabeth. Naturally, the blue-blooded Howards had little love for Suffolk, and were poised to destroy him should the chance arise.

The King did not forget the man who had worked so hard to make the French campaign a success. On 6 February, Wolsey was appointed Bishop of Lincoln; his consecration followed on 26 March. Wolsey was to further prove his worth when, in March, Henry's allies, Ferdinand of Aragon and Maximilian, went behind his back and signed a truce with

Louis XII. The King, in truth a political innocent, was devastated at their desertion, and characteristically sought a scapegoat for this betrayal. Queen Katherine, the faithless Ferdinand's daughter, bore the brunt of her husband's anger, and suddenly ceased to be his most trusted adviser; there were even rumours in Rome that year that he intended to divorce her.

To make matters worse, Henry's sister Mary was betrothed to the Archduke Charles of Austria, Prince of Castile, the heir to both Ferdinand and Maximilian. Preparations for the wedding, which was to take place abroad before 15 May, were already well advanced. The King was fond of his sister and, at enormous cost, had provided her with a fabulous trousseau of sumptuous clothing, jewellery, furnishings and plate.[12] He had even sent fabric samples to Margaret of Austria, Charles's aunt, and asked if Mary's clothes should be made up in the Burgundian style; the Regent had simply advised that her dress should be 'queenly and honourable'.[13] Queen Katherine had appointed the Countess of Oxford as the Princess's chief lady-in-waiting, and a list of the 101 persons who would make up her retinue had already been sent for Margaret's approval.

Mary Tudor was then eighteen, 'a nymph from Heaven, a paradise'.[14] 'Nature never formed anything more beautiful,' declared Erasmus.[15] Mary was tall and graceful, with the red-gold hair of her race[16] and a fair complexion achieved without the aid of cosmetics.[17] She had a charming, lively manner, excelled at conversation, and loved dancing and music; she sang well and played several instruments. No prince could have had a more fit mate.

But now there was to be no wedding. Wolsey sought to save the King's face by advocating an alliance with France. Wolsey was no imperialist, and regarded successive emperors as his adversaries in his later quest for the papacy. Throughout the period of his ascendancy, he would remain strongly pro-French, which was one of the reasons why Queen Katherine so distrusted him.

It took a while to persuade the King to favour this new alliance, but one thing was blindingly clear to everyone, and that was that Henry had come to rely on Wolsey's judgement and advice more than anyone else's. Wolsey had become the chief Councillor, answerable only to the King, and from now on he would be all-powerful. Even Suffolk did not enjoy as much influence, so it is not surprising to find that the Duke was jealous. Hitherto, of the 'two obstinate men who govern everything', he had been the foremost in the King's counsels.[18] Now, although Henry might still be firm friends with him, he had been bested by his more able rival, and although on the surface the two remained cordial, it would be some time before he could bring himself to establish an amicable working relationship with Wolsey. Before that happened, he would have cause to be very grateful indeed to Wolsey.

There was mutual hatred between the Howards and Wolsey. The last years of Norfolk's life were overshadowed by a bitter power struggle with his adversary, who never ceased in his attempts to poison the King's mind against him; to Henry's credit, he did not let this undermine the affection and respect he had for the Duke. In 1529, Wolsey confessed to the then Duke of Norfolk (who had been Earl of Surrey in 1514) that he had been trying to destroy him for the past fourteen years; and had the Howards had the chance, they would doubtless have done the same to him. Nevertheless, they often found themselves in agreement with Wolsey's policies and working in tandem with him, whereas Buckingham and Shrewsbury were opposed on principle to everything he did.

Buckingham loathed Wolsey, and was probably his greatest enemy. He certainly led the noble opposition to the low-born arriviste who had usurped the aristocrat's traditional role of chief adviser to the King. On one memorable occasion, when the Duke had the privilege of holding a basin for the King to wash his hands in before dinner, he was shocked when Wolsey had the temerity to dip his fingers in the same water, and deliberately spilt some over Wolsey's shoes, which resulted in a very public row.[19] Buckingham had not the sense to perceive that it was his own hauteur, aloofness and sheer lack of ability that had prevented him from achieving the pre-eminence he felt ought to be his, nor the tact to hide his bitterness at being excluded from the royal counsels. Like most of his caste, he hated the French, England's traditional enemies, and could never bring himself to approve of Wolsey's foreign policy.

Whilst Wolsey negotiated an honourable peace, Henry began building the first of his recreational complexes, at Greenwich. This consisted of two high brick octagonal towers with pinnacles at either end of a gallery, overlooking a new tiltyard measuring 650 by 250 feet; from now on, a greater number of spectators could enjoy a better view of the jousts, and when not in use as a grandstand, the gallery would be utilised as a store for jousting equipment.[20] Greenwich seems to have been a favourite venue for tournaments: at least ten were held here in the decade before 1520. The tiltyard complex can clearly be seen in drawings of the palace made by Anthony van Wyngaerde around 1555–8.[21]

The new tiltyard may have been completed in time for the tournament held in May 1514, when the King and Suffolk appeared in the lists disguised as hermits, Henry in a white velvet habit with a cloak of leather and cloth of silver, Suffolk in black. Before the jousts began, both threw off their disguises and tossed them to the Queen and her ladies as largesse. Now, Henry was in black and Suffolk in white as they thundered down the field. One hundred and fourteen lances were broken in total.[22]

On 19 May, there arrived for the King from Rome a Sword and Cap of Maintenance, consecrated by Pope Leo X. The Pontiff, too, had been offended by the duplicity of Ferdinand and Maximilian, and wanted to reassure Henry of his friendship and retain his goodwill as an ally. The papal ambassador, Dom Leonardo Spinelli, was received in London with great pomp by 'sundry lords with some 400 horse'. Crowds thronged the streets, eager to see the Pope's gifts. The cap was carried aloft on the tip of the gilded sword; it was of purple satin, a foot high, with an embroidered brim and pendant tails of ermine.

Two days later, Henry, who had been staying in the Bishop's Palace by St Paul's, donned robes of purple satin chequered with gold flowers, 'a jewelled collar worth a well full of gold', a cap of purple velvet with two jewelled rosettes, and a doublet of gold brocade, then rode on a beautiful black palfrey in procession to the cathedral, surrounded by his courtiers. At the door he dismounted and walked to the high altar, where the papal envoy waited with the sword and cap. As the King knelt, two noblemen girded him with the sword and placed the cap on his head. It was too big, and covered his face completely, but he presumably adjusted it before making 'an entire circuit of the interior of the church'. After the procession, 'high mass commenced with great pomp and with vocal and instrumental music'. The King left the cathedral at 1 p.m., followed by the ambassadors and courtiers walking two by two back to the Bishop's Palace. One Venetian estimated that thirty thousand spectators had come to watch.[23]

The King had for some time been building up England's navy, of which he is with justification regarded as one of the chief founders. Henry adored ships and was fascinated by the technology of naval warfare. He had inherited only a few vessels from his father, but was determined to make his navy a power to be reckoned with on the high seas. By the end of his reign, he had built 46 warships and 13 smaller galleys, purchased 26 other ships and captured 13 more.[24] At the time, this was the greatest navy in the world: although equal in size to those of other countries, it was far better organised and disciplined.

Henry was also interested in navigation. Amongst other scientific aids, he owned a rare tidal almanack of Europe and a perpetual lunar calendar.[25] He knew more about French tidal waters than the experts did,[26] and his Lord Admirals learned to trust his encyclopaedic knowledge of naval matters.

On 13 June 1514, Henry launched his greatest ship yet, the *Henry*

Grace à Dieu, which came to be known as the *Great Harry*. The King and Queen, accompanied by the Princess Mary, various ambassadors and the whole court,[27] went in their state barges from Greenwich to Erith where the great warship lay; eyewitnesses claimed this was the greatest pageant yet seen on the River Thames.[28] The King was dressed in a vest and breeches of cloth of gold with scarlet hose, while around his neck hung a whistle on a gold chain, the insignia of the supreme commander of the navy.[29]

The *Henry Grace à Dieu* was a very large vessel with 'five decks and seven tops';[30] she had 'no equal in bulk' and 'an incredible array'[31] of over two hundred bronze and iron cannon.[32] When the King and court had boarded the splendid vessel, she was blessed with 'many masses, including high mass sung for the benediction'.[33] Then Henry conducted everyone on a guided tour of the ship.[34] He would always retain a special affection for the *Great Harry*, and when she was in dock at Rye some years later he went to view her and dined on board.

Wolsey's negotiations with France reached a successful conclusion in the summer. On 30 July, at the royal manor of Wanstead, Essex, the Princess Mary formally renounced her betrothal to Charles of Castile. A week later, the peace with France was proclaimed, and it was announced that Mary was to marry King Louis himself.

Henry showed his gratitude to Wolsey by immediately nominating him Archbishop of York, the previous incumbent, Cardinal Christopher Bainbridge, having just died in Rome. A month later, Wolsey was also made Bishop of Tournai. It seemed the King could not do enough for him. He now wrote to the Vatican, urging Pope Leo to appoint him a cardinal, 'since his merits are such that the King can do nothing of the least importance without him, and esteems him among his dearest friends'.[35]

Wolsey did not set foot in his northern diocese for many years, nor was he immediately consecrated. He was more interested in the trappings of power and status. His promotion brought him York Place at Westminster, which had been the London residence of the Archbishops of York since the thirteenth century. Wolsey immediately had it surveyed, then set about extending it in the grand manner, creating 'a very fine palace'[36] where he could entertain the King and others in princely style.[37] In 1514–15, he spent £1,250 (£375,000) on improvements.

Visitors were overawed by the splendour of York Place. Now faced with red brick and built on a courtyard plan, it had a great hall and chapel, a watching chamber, a presence chamber, a dining chamber, a gallery, an armoury and a cloister. Beneath the watching chamber was a wine cellar, which still survives.[38] Giustinian described how he 'traversed eight rooms before reaching [Wolsey's] audience chamber. They were all hung with tapestry which was changed once a week. Wherever Wolsey was, he always had a sideboard of plate worth 25,000 ducats'.[39] The palace was a monument to exquisite taste, and boasted brightly jewelled chapel plate, sets of rich tapestries and hangings, paintings of the saints, of the Emperor Trajan, 'Dame Pleasaunce' and the Duc de Berry, fine furniture of estate, jewellery, and a bedstead of alabaster bearing Wolsey's arms and gilded flowers.[40] There was also a delightful garden for the Archbishop's personal use.

With the peace about to be concluded, Henry was satisfied and Wolsey triumphant, but the royal bride was not at all happy. She had no wish to marry the ailing King Louis, who at fifty-two was thirty-four years her senior, because she was almost certainly in love with Charles Brandon. The letters that passed between Mary, Suffolk and Wolsey in 1515 reveal that, not only was the King aware of his sister's feelings, but that she had only 'consented to his request, and for the peace of Christendom, to marry Louis of France, though he was very aged and sickly, on condition that if she survived him, she should marry whom she liked'.[41] It transpired, however, that Henry had no intention of keeping his side of the bargain.

20

'Cloth of Frieze Be Not Too Bold'

On Sunday 13 August 1514, the whole court gathered at Greenwich in the great banqueting hall, which had been hung with cloth of gold embroidered with the royal arms of England and France, to see Mary Tudor married by proxy to Louis XII. The King and Queen – who was visibly pregnant and wore silver satin with a gold Venetian cap – arrived three hours late with the bride, who looked very beautiful in a purple and gold chequered gown, which matched the robes of the French King's representative, the Duc de Longueville. The couple exchanged vows, rings and a kiss before Archbishop Warham, and after the nuptial mass had been celebrated there was a banquet followed by two hours of dancing, led by the King and Buckingham. When these two set aside their long gowns and danced in their doublets, many older gentlemen present followed suit, apart from Andrea Badoer, the Venetian ambassador, who was conscious of his advancing years.

In the evening, the company proceeded into a chamber where a great bed had been prepared. The new Queen of France lay upon it in a nightgown described as 'magnificent déshabille', with one leg bared to the thigh, while the Duc de Longueville, having removed his red hose, lay beside her and touched her naked leg with his own. Warham then declared the marriage symbolically consummated, at which 'the King of England made great rejoicing'.[1]

King Louis, who was eager to see his bride, sent to England the French portrait painter, Jehan Perréal, to capture Mary's likeness[2] and help prepare her trousseau. Naturally, the trousseau provided for her marriage to Charles of Castile was not thought suitable, and the King once again opened his coffers to ensure that his sister went to France 'well and sumptuously attired'.[3] 'Merchants of every nation went to the court; the Queen of France desired to see them all, and gave her hand to each of them.'[4] Between them, they made up thirty gowns for her.

In addition, Henry supplied her lavishly with jewels and furnishings.

Mary was also to take with her to France a large entourage. Two of her youngest maids of honour were Mary and Anne, the daughters of Sir Thomas Boleyn. The Mother of the Maids was Lady Guildford, Sir Henry's mother and Mary's former governess. Most of these English attendants would be sent home by King Louis, even 'Mother Guildford', much to Mary's distress.[5]

Louis approved every name on Mary's list of attendants save one, that of Jane Popincourt, the French lady who had served Elizabeth of York and Katherine of Aragon. She was close to Mary and, together with the Duc de Longueville and the Princess's former tutor, John Palsgrave,[6] was helping her to practise conversation in French. The English ambassador in Paris, however, warned his master that Jane was leading an 'evil life' as the mistress of the married de Longueville, at which Louis declared, 'As you love me, speak of her no more. I would she were burned!' Then, claiming that his only concern was for the moral welfare of his wife, he struck Jane's name off the list.[7] Mary was quite upset.

She may have been somewhat mollified when she received Louis's chief bridal gift, the Mirror of Naples, a diamond as large as 'a full-sized finger' with a huge pear-shaped pendant pearl, which arrived in London before September, when Mary wore it for her final public appearance in London. Henry had it valued at 60,000 crowns (£4,500,000).[8]

During August, while Mary was preparing to go to France, the King set out on his summer progress. His route took him to Newbury, Guildford, and Farnham Castle, where he was the guest of Bishop Foxe; Oatlands near Weybridge, where his host was Bartholomew Reed, whose deer park would become a favourite royal hunting ground; and Croydon, where he lodged in the palace of the Archbishop of Canterbury.[9]

Mary Tudor then joined her brother and his court and proceeded to Dover via Otford, where they were entertained by Archbishop Warham, and Canterbury. The royal cavalcade was one of the longest and most richly attired ever seen. The King and Mary rode side by side, followed by the Queen in a litter and a vast concourse of nobles and knights, accompanied by their wives and wearing cloth of gold and gold chains.[10]

On 2 October, 'at the waterside' at Dover, Mary reminded Henry of their pact. He embraced and kissed her, then gave her his blessing, saying, 'I betoken you to God and the fortunes of the sea, and the government of the King your husband.'[11] Escorted by Norfolk, Mary embarked for France with a fleet of fourteen ships. She was married to Louis on 9 October at Abbeville and crowned at St Denis on 5

November. The French King was very taken with her; after their wedding night, he boasted 'that he had performed marvels'.[12]

The Duc de Longueville returned to France with Mary, bearing gifts worth £2,000 (£600,000) and the gown that Henry had worn at the proxy wedding. Several historians have suggested that Jane Popincourt, left languishing at the English court, became Henry's mistress, but there is no evidence for this. The £100 that Henry gave her when she did eventually return to France in May 1516,[13] after Louis's death, was almost certainly a reward for her years of good service to his mother, sister and wife, and it is known that Jane resumed her relationship with de Longueville when they were reunited. Moreover, by October 1514, Henry had probably embarked upon an affair with another lady.

Typically, he was taking advantage of the Queen's pregnancy, which seemed to be progressing well: on 4 October, he issued a warrant to the Great Wardrobe for a cradle upholstered in scarlet, linen and curtains 'for the use of our nursery, God willing'.[14] That same month, Suffolk, then in France, added a postscript to a letter to Henry, asking him to remind 'Mistress Blount and Mistress Carew' to reply to him when he wrote to them or sent them love tokens. This implies that the King and Suffolk were on terms of familiarity with both ladies. Indeed, they may well have shared their favours.

There is no doubt that Elizabeth Blount became Henry's mistress at some stage, because she later bore him a child which he acknowledged. She was one of the eleven children[15] of Sir John Blount of Kinlet Hall, Shropshire, by Katherine Peshall, whose father had fought for Henry VII at Bosworth. Lord Mountjoy was a kinsman, and it may have been he who secured Elizabeth – or Bessie, as she was known – a post as maid of honour to the Queen in 1513, when the girl was fifteen at most.[16] She was 'a fair damosel, who in singing, dancing and all goodly pastimes exceeded no other'.[17] She was also 'thought for her rare ornaments of nature and education to be the beauty and mistress-piece of her time'.[18]

Elizabeth Blount featured prominently in a Christmas pageant at Greenwich in 1514. She, Elizabeth Carew, Margaret, Lady Guildford and Lady Fellinger, the wife of the Spanish ambassador, all dressed up as ladies of Savoy in blue velvet gowns, gold caps and masks, and were rescued from danger by four gallant 'Portuguese' knights, played by the King, Suffolk, Nicholas Carew and the Spanish envoy. The Queen was so delighted with their 'strange apparel' that, before they all removed their masks, she invited them to dance again before her in her bedchamber. The King partnered Elizabeth Blount, and there was much laughter when the identities of the dancers were revealed. Katherine thanked the King for 'her goodly pastime, and kissed him'.[19] It is not known whether Henry and Elizabeth were lovers at this time, but if they were, they were certainly being very discreet about it.

Some writers have suggested that they were not discreet enough, and that the Queen was growing suspicious, because on Twelfth Night 1515, when the same pageant was staged once again by popular demand, Elizabeth Blount did not appear: her place was taken by Jane Popincourt.[20] However, she featured in another disguising in the company of Sir Thomas Boleyn and his young son George.[21]

We will never know whether anxiety over her husband's amours contributed to the loss of the Queen's fourth child, 'a prince who lived not long after',[22] and who was born at Greenwich in February 1515. Although a silver font was loaned by Christchurch Priory, Canterbury, for the christening, the infant's name is not recorded.[23]

Soon after Christmas, news reached England of the death of Louis XII of France and the accession of his cousin, the Count of Angoulême, who became Francis I. Henry's nose was put somewhat out of joint by the knowledge that the new French King was three years younger than he and looked set to rival him in magnificence and martial valour. France had already achieved cultural ascendancy in northern Europe, and her new monarch was to establish a court that would rapidly outdazzle those of England, Spain and the Empire. There was rivalry on a personal level as well: everything Francis did, Henry jealously copied. He could not bear to be outshone in any way, and took comfort from the fact that most people agreed that he was 'a great deal handsomer than the King of France',[24] who had a dark, saturnine complexion with the long Valois nose. Henry was also considerably more virtuous, for Francis was a notorious lecher whose court was a hotbed of sexual intrigues. But when the new King of France won a brilliant victory over the Swiss at Marignano in September 1515, Henry could not contain his jealousy. At first, he declared he did not believe it, but when Francis's envoy gave him two letters in his master's own hand, he had to. As he read them, 'it seemed tears would flow from his eyes, so red were they with the pain he suffered on hearing of the King's success'.[25]

For all his jealousy, however, Henry was to enjoy a genuine rapport with Francis. The two were much alike, 'not only in personage, but also in wisdom, delighting both in hunting, hawking, in building, in apparel, and in jewels'.[26]

Given Francis's reputation with women, Henry was concerned for his sister, who, following the custom of widowed queens of France, had donned white mourning and retired into seclusion at the Hôtel de Cluny until such time as it was certain that she was not pregnant by her late husband. There were rumours that the new King was thinking of divorcing his pregnant wife, Louis's daughter Claude, and marrying

Mary instead, but Mary seems to have believed he had designs on her virtue. This is unlikely, given who she was and the fact that, some years later, he inscribed a drawing of her 'More dirty than queenly'.

What Francis did try to bring about was a marriage between Mary and the Duke of Savoy, but Henry felt that Mary could make a more advantageous match elsewhere, and in late January sent Suffolk to France to bring her home. Knowing how matters stood between Suffolk and Mary, Henry made the Duke promise that he would not propose marriage to her. But he had not counted on Mary using every trick in the book to get Suffolk to the altar, with the result that the couple were married in secret on 3 March. Once the union had been consummated, Suffolk panicked, and wrote to Wolsey confessing all and begging the Archbishop to solicit the King's forgiveness. 'The Queen would never let me rest till I had granted her to be married,' he explained, 'and so, to be plain with you, I have married her heartily, and have lain with her insomuch I fear me lest she be with child.'[27] Henry was furious.

When his precipitate marriage became common knowledge at the English court, there were many who were outraged at Suffolk's presumption. The Privy Council, led by the Howards, urged the King to have him executed or imprisoned[28] since he had committed treason by marrying a princess of the blood without royal consent; but thanks to Wolsey's intervention and Henry's genuine affection for both Mary and Suffolk, it was agreed that they should pay him a large fine of £24,000 (£7,200,000) in instalments by way of compensation. Mary also agreed to surrender to Henry all the plate and jewels she had been given before and during her marriage, and Suffolk relinquished to his master the wardship of Elizabeth Grey, Viscountess Lisle.[29] Greatly mollified, the King graciously consented to receive the erring pair back into favour, but there were many who felt that Suffolk had got off too lightly.

In March, Francis I demanded of Mary the return of the Mirror of Naples, which was the hereditary property of the Queens of France, but she confessed that she had sent it back to her brother as a peace offering. When Henry refused to give it back, a diplomatic row ensued. Francis tried offering him 30,000 crowns for it, but to no avail. After that, there is no further mention of the Mirror of Naples in the records. There has been speculation that Henry had it recut or renamed, but descriptions of his attire in Venetian sources suggest that he wore it quite openly.

In April 1515, there arrived in England the new Venetian ambassador Sebastian Giustinian and his suite, whose members have left some of the most famous descriptions of the young Henry VIII and his court. The King wanted to impress the Venetian Senate, so on St George's Day he sent dignitaries to escort the envoy and his train in a barge fashioned like the Venetian Bucentaur (the Doge's stage barge) to Richmond, where the court was assembled. Giustinian and his colleague, Piero Pasqualigo, both left accounts of the occasion:

> Though it was before mass, they made us breakfast, for fear we should faint; after which, we were conducted to the presence through sundry chambers all hung with most beautiful tapestry, passing down the ranks of the bodyguard.
>
> We were ushered into a stately hall. At one extremity was His Majesty, standing under a canopy of gold embroidered at Florence, the most costly thing I ever witnessed. He was leaning against his gilt throne, on which was a large gold brocade cushion, where lay the long gold sword of state. [The King was resplendent in his Garter robes.] He wore a cap of crimson velvet in the French fashion; his doublet was in the Swiss fashion, striped alternately with white and crimson satin, and his hose were scarlet, and all slashed from the knee upwards. Very close around his neck he had a fine collar, from which there hung a round cut diamond, the size of the largest walnut I ever saw, and a very large round pearl [the Mirror of Naples?]. His mantle was of purple velvet lined with white satin, with a train more than four yards in length. Over this mantle was a very handsome gold collar with a pendant St George entirely of diamonds. On his left shoulder was the Garter, and on his right shoulder was a hood with a border entirely of crimson velvet. Beneath the mantle he had a pouch of cloth of gold which covered a dagger, and his fingers were one mass of jewelled rings.

Eight Knights of the Garter stood on the King's right, and to his left were a number of prelates. Also present were six officers of the Household, bearing gold rods of office, ten heralds wearing tabards of cloth of gold 'wrought with the arms of England', and 'a crowd of nobility, all arrayed in cloth of gold and silk'.

After kissing the King's hand,

> [Giustinian] delivered a Latin oration in praise of His Majesty, whom we extolled with all the eloquence we could command. This ended, we attended mass, which was chanted by the Bishop of Durham, with a superb and noble descant choir. Afterwards we accompanied the King to table, where he chose us to see the service of the courses, contained in 16 dishes of massive gold. As soon as he had commenced eating, he sent us with the Archbishop of York and the Bishop of Durham into his [presence] chamber, where a very sumptuous and plentiful dinner had been prepared for us, and

> by the King's order a repast was served for all our countrymen and
> attendants. Having dined, we remained a good while with His
> Majesty, very familiarly.[30]

Giustinian was deeply impressed by the splendour of the court, which
'glittered with jewels, gold and silver, the pomp being unprecedented',
and also by the condescension and friendliness of the King, who on one
occasion 'embraced us without ceremony, and conversed for a long
while familiarly on various topics in good Latin and French'.[31]

The foregoing describes a typical reception for a foreign ambassador,[32]
who would attend court only upon a summons from the King.
European diplomacy as we know it today was then in its infancy. For
centuries, continental rulers had sent each other envoys on specific
missions, but the concept of the resident ambassador was a new one,
instituted by some of the Italian states in the fifteenth century. The first
ambassador to be accredited to the court of England was from Venice,
in 1483. Ferdinand and Isabella sent their first resident ambassador in
1486, but there was no permanent French ambassador until 1528. From
1505, England maintained ambassadors in Spain and Rome.

Most ambassadors were of gentle birth, well educated and not easily
intimidated. They were not usually assigned lodgings at court unless the
King wished it,[33] but stayed in accommodation nearby, which was
provided for them at his expense. Giustinian and his fellows were lodged
in the Greyhound Inn and three other houses in Greenwich.[34] An
ambassador was expected to maintain an appearance that reflected his
master's status, but most monarchs kept their envoys chronically short of
funds, and they often had to make up the shortfall from their own
pockets. Henry always presented home-going ambassadors with a set of
plate for a buffet.

An ambassador bore heavy responsibilities: he had to look to his
master's interests, keep him supplied with useful, often sensitive
information in minute detail and usually in cipher, and sometimes deal
with difficult situations calling for the utmost tact. Some ambassadors
became intimately involved in the politics of their host country, and
occasionally exceeded their briefs. Nearly all employed spies and
informers to seek out state secrets or the skeletons in the closets of the
mighty. Many became involved in court intrigues, and a few found
themselves in very tricky situations, since diplomatic immunity was not
always respected. Wolsey was the worst offender: he curtly ordered
Giustinian to show him his dispatches before sending them to Venice,
and later grabbed hold of the papal nuncio, Francesco Chieregato, and
threatened to have him racked. In 1524, he intercepted the correspondence of the imperial envoy, Louis de Flandre, Sieur de Praet,

placed him under house arrest because he did not like what he read, then had him recalled.[35]

There are frequent references to Henry VIII entertaining ambassadors to dinner in the presence chamber.[36] Henry made a habit of taking foreign ambassadors into his confidence. His easy charm and unexpected familiarity ensured that some of them swallowed whole the intelligence he fed them. He once kept a Venetian envoy so long in conversation that the man had to excuse himself because he had developed a pain in his side while standing.[37] In 1509, the elderly ambassador Badoer was ill for over a month because he could not adjust to the English climate; the King, not knowing this, summoned him, then 'wept for very pity at my having come, it seeming to him that I had been taken out of my grave'.[38] As he grew older, Henry became less familiar and more inclined to brag and bluster.

Pasqualigo described the King as

> the handsomest potentate I have ever set eyes upon; above the usual height, with an extremely fine calf to his leg, his complexion very fair and bright, with auburn hair combed straight and short in the French fashion, and a round face so very beautiful that it would become a pretty woman, his throat being rather long and thick. He will enter his 25th year the month after next.[39]

On May Day 1515 there took place one of the most celebrated pageants of the reign. Pasqualigo, Giustinian and the latter's secretary, Niccolo Sagudino, all left accounts of it, describing how, early in the morning, the King sent two noblemen to conduct the ambassadors to Greenwich, where they and the 'chief lords of the kingdom' mounted their horses and escorted the Queen, who was richly attired in the Spanish style, two miles into the country to meet the King. 'With Her Majesty were 25 damsels mounted on white palfreys' with embroidered gold housings; the girls 'all had dresses slashed with gold lame in very costly trim'; their 'sumptuous appearance' made their mistress appear 'rather ugly than otherwise'. She was now approaching thirty – middle-aged by Tudor standards.

The cavalcade rode into a wood, where they found the King mounted on Governatore; he was dressed 'entirely in green velvet, cap, doublet, hose, shoes and everything', and surrounded by two hundred archers of his guard 'in a livery of green with bows in their hands'; one of them was got up as Robin Hood, and by his side stood a Mr Villiers dressed as Maid Marion in a red kirtle. A hundred noblemen on horseback were in attendance. 'Directly we came in sight the King commenced making his horse curvet, and performed such feats that I fancied myself looking at Mars.'

After a thrilling archery contest, Robin Hood asked the Queen if she and her damsels would like 'to enter the good greenwood and see how outlaws lived'. The King inquired if Katherine would dare 'venture into a thicket with so many outlaws?' Katherine answered that 'where he went, she was content to go'. Henry took her hand and led her, to the sound of trumpets, through the wood to some carefully constructed bowers or labyrinths, decorated with flowers, herbs and boughs and filled with singing birds 'which carolled most sweetly'. Within these bowers, tables had been set for 'what they call here a proper good breakfast'.

'Sir, outlaws' breakfast is venison,' Robin Hood informed the King, 'and you must be content with such fare as we use.' Henry was happy to comply, and he and Katherine were served game and wine by the archers. 'In one of the bowers were triumphal cars on which were singers or musicians, who played on an organ, lute and flutes for a good while during the banquet.'

After a time, the King came over to Pasqualigo and spoke to him in French in the most friendly fashion.

'Talk with me awhile,' he began. 'The King of France, is he as tall as I am?'

Pasqualigo replied that 'there was but little difference'.

'Is he as stout?' No, he was not.

'What sort of legs has he?'

'Spare, Your Majesty.' At this, Henry beamed and, pulling aside the skirt of his doublet, slapped a hand on his thigh, saying, 'Look here! I have also a good calf to my leg.'

Later that morning, the company proceeded homewards accompanied by 'tall pasteboard giants' of Gog and Magog on one pageant car, and singing girls dressed as Lady May and Dame Flora in another. The cars were 'surrounded by His Majesty's guard' and 'musicians sounding the whole way on trumpets, drums and other instruments, so that it was an extremely fine triumph and very pompous, and the King in person brought up the rear, in as great state as possible, followed by the Queen, with such a crowd on foot as to exceed, I think, 25,000 persons. On arriving at Greenwich, His Majesty went to Mass', having covered up his doublet with 'a handsome gown of green velvet' and 'a collar of cut diamonds of immense value'. Afterwards, 'the ambassadors had a private audience'.[40]

That afternoon, the King, Dorset and Essex were the stars of a tournament; Sagudino, watching, declared, 'The show was most beautiful. I never expected to find such pomp, and on this occasion His Majesty exerted himself to the utmost for the sake of Pasqualigo, who is returning to France today, that he may be able to tell King Francis what he has seen in England, especially with regard to His Majesty's own prowess.'[41]

During the days of jousting that followed, Henry singled out young gentlemen such as Nicholas Carew and his brother-in-law Francis Bryan to support him in the lists, lending them horses and armour, 'to encourage all youth to seek deeds of arms'.[42] Carew was an outstanding jouster who practised constantly and was renowned for his fearless daring. He became so famous that the King provided him with his own tilt at Greenwich, and a hut in which to arm himself and store his equipment. Carew was an expert at the 'manage'; once, after a tournament, he entered the lists with his horse blindfolded, so that the animal should not rear in fright when three men carried into the tiltyard a tree trunk twelve feet long and balanced it on Carew's lance rest. Carew then rode the length of the tiltyard, 'most stoutly' couching the tree like a lance, 'to the extreme adulation and astonishment of everybody'.[43] Two decades later, he was painted by Hans Holbein in full jousting armour, holding a lance.[44] Henry knighted him sometime before 1517.

Francis Bryan was a clever and versatile young man who was to gain a reputation as a rake and a hell-raiser. He became one of the King's closest companions, a fellow jouster, gambler, tennis player and, it was rumoured, accomplice in extramarital affairs. He had come 'to the court very young',[45] the son of Sir Thomas Bryan by Margaret Bourchier, a daughter of the scholarly Lord Berners. No portrait survives, so we know nothing of his appearance. Bryan was the typical Renaissance courtier, a poet[46] and man of letters who was also to distinguish himself as a solder, sailor and diplomat. His irresistible charm disguised an incorrigible intriguer who was two-faced, manipulative and promiscuous; once, on a trip to Calais, he demanded 'a soft bed then a hard harlot'.[47] He was full of pent-up energy, highly articulate, and viciously witty. Observers were astonished at the familiarity he used towards the King, both in speaking his mind and in telling jokes.[48] Bryan was no creature of principle: by altering his loyalties and opinions to conform to the King's changes of policy, he managed to remain in favour throughout the reign.

In 1515, Bryan's other brother-in-law, Sir Henry Guildford, was appointed Master of the Horse in place of Suffolk. Another rising young star was the King's cousin, Henry Courtenay, Earl of Devon, who would become closer to him when Suffolk began to have responsibilities away from court.

The fate of Fray Diego Fernandez, the Queen's confessor, was however an example of what could happen to those who fell out of favour. When several members of Katherine's household went to the

King to complain that the friar was involved in amorous intrigues with women at court, Henry summoned Fernandez and confronted him with the accusations. The friar angrily denied it, and pointedly added, 'If I am badly used, the Queen is still more badly used.' This may have been a reference to Elizabeth Blount, but even if it was not it was still impertinent, and the King, who was incensed, had Fernandez brought before an ecclesiastical tribunal, which found him guilty of fornication. Henry then had him summarily deported to Spain, with the friar indignantly protesting that 'never, within your kingdom, have I had to do with women. I have been condemned unheard by disreputable rogues.'[49] He was replaced by the Spaniard Jorge de Atheca, another Observant friar who, through the Queen's good offices, had been made Bishop of Llandaff. Atheca was a humanist and a member of Thomas More's circle.

In May 1515 Mary Tudor and Suffolk returned to England and were warmly received by the King, at whose insistence they were married a second time on the 13th of the month in the Church of the Observant Friars at Greenwich, before the whole court.[50] But the celebrations were low-key 'because the kingdom did not approve of the marriage'.[51] There were those amongst the guests who had pressed for Suffolk's execution. Public feeling was evident in one of several copies that were made of a wedding portrait of Mary and Suffolk:[52] it showed a court jester whispering to the Duke:

> Cloth of gold do not despise
> Though thou be matched with cloth of frieze;
> Cloth of frieze be not too bold
> Though thou be matched with cloth of gold.

Wolsey, by saving Suffolk's life through his intervention, had reduced his rival to the status of a client seeking patronage, and the Duke had to learn to co-operate and work more amicably with him. Yet now that he was the King's brother-in-law, 'much honour and respect are paid him', and, after Wolsey, he had 'the second seat in His Majesty's Privy Council, which he rarely enters, save to discuss matters of importance'.[53] He was often busy elsewhere, looking after the royal interests in East Anglia, which of course suited Wolsey very well.

The King, out of affection for his sister and his friend, graciously reduced their fine, but paying the balance due still strained their finances, although not as badly as many modern writers claim. From 1515 on, Suffolk was able to spend 'vast sums' on building and improving houses.[54] He raised a fine brick London residence, Suffolk

Place, on his ancestral estate by the Thames in what is now Southwark High Street, and made improvements in the antique style to his country seat, Westhorpe Hall in Suffolk, where Mary spent most of her time, attended by fifty servants.[55] He also maintained five other properties in East Anglia, Berkshire and Oxfordshire. Of the two, Suffolk was far more frequently at court, although Mary did visit from time to time; as Queen Dowager of France, she took precedence over all other ladies save Queen Katherine.

21

'The Best Dressed Sovereign in the World'

In her wedding portrait, Mary Tudor wears a nimbus-shaped French hood with her square-necked gown. Her sister Margaret Tudor appears in a similar hood in a portrait painted around the same time.[1] By 1515, French fashions were displacing Flemish and Italian influences at the English court, and would remain popular until the mid-1540s, when Spanish styles became the preferred mode. During the same period, court dress also reflected German and Swiss trends. In the sixteenth century, fashions changed far more slowly than today.

England was then entering a mini-ice-age that lasted until the late seventeenth century. 'It is always windy, and however warm the weather, the natives invariably wear furs. The summers are never very hot, neither is it ever very cold,' wrote a Venetian.[2] To cope with the climate, people wore several layers of clothing: a shirt or chemise, a doublet or kirtle, and an overgown, the top two layers often in heavy materials and always with sleeves to the wrist. The furs that lined the courtiers' gowns were sable or lynx; the seriously wealthy used egret's down.

In Tudor times, it was the court and nobility that set the trends. Clothes played an important role in proclaiming the rank and wealth of the wearer, for they could be extremely expensive. The richer the fabric and ornamentation, the higher the status. In an age that placed great stress on outward show, such things counted, and throughout the late mediaeval and Tudor periods successive governments passed sumptuary laws restricting the wearing of certain materials and colours to persons above a certain degree. Ermine, sable and miniver could be worn only by the nobility; no one under the rank of gentleman was allowed to wear any gold or silver ornament on his clothing; silk shirts were restricted to the knightly classes and above, and only earls and their superiors were permitted to sport embroideries; no commoner was to wear excessively broad-toed shoes; only dukes and marquesses might wear cloth of gold, while the colour purple was to be worn only by royalty. There were also all sorts of regulations governing the wearing of jewellery. These laws were aimed at the prosperous merchant and middle classes, who could often afford to wear the clothes reserved for their betters and frequently did so, defying the law and risking the penalty of confiscation.

Dress could also be symbolic: embroidered emblems, flowers, badges, jewellery and colours all carried their own subtle messages conveying moods, sexual innuendoes and political loyalties. Detailing was crucial to the success of an outfit, and bright colours were greatly favoured.

There was a strict line of demarcation between male and female dress. Women wore long skirts, men hose and doublets. Both sexes wore elaborate headgear, indoors and out, and broad-toed 'duckbill' shoes, sometimes with straps, while high, square-toed boots were worn for riding or hunting. Henry VIII's shoes were of soft leather or velvet, sometimes decorated with cuts or embroidered with pearls in floral designs.[3] Each pair cost about 18d. (£22.50).[4]

During Henry VIII's reign, men began to wear nightshirts and women nightshifts, or smocks, in bed, rather than sleep naked. Henry always wore a nightshirt, unless he was making love to his wife.[5] Men and women also wore nightbonnets, or 'biggins', embroidered coifs of white linen, silk or, in the King's case, velvet.[6] Older men, lawyers and academics tended to wear these under their bonnets in the daytime. 'Nightgown' was the Tudor term for a dressing-gown or housecoat.

Male fashions were more flamboyant than women's. Shirts were loose-fitting with a drawstring at the neck; early in the reign necklines were low, but later on they became high with a small frill that would later develop into the Elizabethan ruff. Hose were divided into upper and nether stocks, or breeches and stockings. Henry's hose were usually of silk, leather, velvet or satin, and were dyed in various colours such as green, white or crimson to match his shoes.[7]

The doublet was a kind of wide-shouldered waistcoat or jacket with a skirt, or 'bases', attached at the waist, and separate sleeves tied on with laces, or 'points', to eyelet holes on the shoulder. The skirt of the doublet was parted in front to reveal a prominent decorated flap, the codpiece, an overt symbol of male virility, which was tied with points. Over the doublet was worn the open-revered gown, which became shorter and wider as the reign progressed and the King's bulk increased. Cloaks or mantles were worn above this in colder weather. Men's 'bonnets' were flat caps with plumes and brims ornamented by jewels or emblems; the King's hats cost 15s. (£225) each, and were embellished by his plume-maker, Gerard van Arcle. Hair was worn in a long pageboy style, and most men went clean-shaven.

'Slashing' was a fashion peculiar to the age. It is said to have originated after the Battle of Nancy in 1477, when the victorious Swiss tore up rich materials plundered from the vanquished Burgundians and used them to patch their torn clothes. Their makeshift attire was copied by German mercenaries, and became fashionable in Germany and then France and England. Slashing involved drawing puffs of material from an undergarment through slits in an overgarment, and it was used most commonly on doublets, sleeves and breeches.

Contemporary records provide tantalising glimpses of Henry VIII's clothes. The splendour of his wardrobe reflected his regal status and left commentators striving for superlatives. 'He is the best dressed sovereign in the world: his robes are the richest and most superb that can be imagined, and he puts on new clothes every holy day,' gushed one Venetian, while Badoer was stunned at the vision of the young King dressed in a long robe of white damask glittering with diamonds and rubies.[8] Henry's Flemish tailor, Stephen Jaspar, made him doublets of blue and red velvet lined with cloth of gold, and of purple satin embroidered with gold, as well as long gowns of Venetian damask, silver tissue and cloth of gold. Some of his garments were so heavily encrusted with gems and goldsmiths' work that the material beneath could barely be seen. The King was fond of making dramatic appearances in the costume of other lands, and on various occasions wore Hungarian, Turkish, Russian, German and Prussian dress.[9] His clothes were perfumed with lavender and orangeflower water, or with his own mixture of musk, ambergris, sugar and rosewater.[10] In 1541, he received a pair of rare perfumed gloves from Italy. Normally, his gloves were ordered by the dozen.

The King spent £8,000 a year (£2,400,000) on clothes, not all of it usefully. He would order cloth of gold, which would be cut out for a new outfit, but then decide he wanted something different, so the material was wasted.[11]

In 1517, James Worsley, the Keeper of the Royal Wardrobe in the Tower of London, listed some of the items of Henry's clothing in his care, including 'mantles, gowns of cloth of gold and velvet, coats, jackets and doublets, glaudkyns [surcoats], bases, girdles, belts, furs and sables, powdered ermines, cloths of gold of divers colours, velvets, satins, damasks, sarcanets and linen cloths'. There was also a mantle of purple tinsel lined with black lambswool, a gown of green velvet lined with green satin, a surcoat of white cloth of silver lined with yellow cloth of gold, and a girdle set with Tudor roses and portcullises.[12] Henry's Inventory of 1547 lists 41 gowns, 25 doublets, 25 pairs of hose, 20 surcoats, 16 frocks (loose surcoats), 7 jerkins, 4 tuckers, 10 cassocks, 8 cloaks, 15 Spanish capes, 23 girdles and swordbelts, 3 purses, numerous bonnets, shirts, gloves and 'slops' (drawers) and the robes of the Orders of the Garter, St Michael and the Golden Fleece.

Most foreigners were of the opinion that English women dressed badly and immodestly, yet evidence from portraits suggests that necklines were no lower in England than elsewhere. Although English fashion did lag behind the rest of Europe, ladies of the court dressed sumptuously in gowns made up of at least ten yards of material. This allowed for the mandatory long trains, which were either looped up at the back to expose the kirtle, or carried over the arm.[13] Bodices were tight-fitting to the waist with wide, square necklines trimmed with goldsmiths' work or jewelled borders and tapering to a V at the back,[14] where they were laced up. Hinged corsets or 'bodies' with metal bands, covered in velvet, leather or silk, were introduced around 1530. In the 1540s, the square neckline began to give way to a stand-up collar. When pregnant, women wore bodices with front lacings that could be let out to accommodate their increasing girth.

By 1530, more women were wearing the farthingale, and skirts grew stiffer and wider; they were now worn open at the front to expose the kirtle beneath. Around the waist, ladies wore a jewelled girdle, from which hung a scented pomander on a chain. Sleeves were separate items; early in the reign they were tight to the wrist with furred or embroidered cuffs.[15] Later they became increasingly elaborate, having wide slashed interchangeable undersleeves with scalloped edges beneath long hanging oversleeves, turned back to expose the rich fabric or fur of the lining. Most women wore black knitted worsted stockings held up by garters.[16] Their only other undergarment was the chemise or smock.

As mentioned earlier, only unmarried girls were permitted to wear their hair loose, and queens on state occasions. Married women wore hoods of 'various sorts of velvet, cap fashion'.[17] The gable hood was a peculiarly English fashion that was popular from c1480 to c1540. Inspired by the five-pointed arch of late Perpendicular architecture, it framed the face and completely concealed the hair. Earlier versions had long front partlets resting on the bodice, and the twin lappets of the customary black veil hanging down at the back. By 1515, it was fashionable to loop up the partlets, and by 1536, they ended above chin level, with one lappet draped over the crown of the hood in the 'whelk-shell fashion' seen in Holbein's portrait of Jane Seymour.[18] Gable hoods were made of layers of velvet lined with silk, decorated with rich embroideries and goldsmiths' work, stiffened with metal or wire and fixed with decorative pins.[19] The method of construction of these hoods is still not fully understood and is believed to have had a symbolic significance that is only hinted at in the surviving art and literature of the period.

In the 1520s, the French hood favoured by Anne Boleyn began to be worn by ladies of fashion. This was a crescent-shaped contraption made of similar materials to the gable hood, and was worn on the back of the head over a coif of pleated linen, exposing the hair, which was parted down the middle, plaited and coiled into a bun. A black, tubular veil hung down the back. By 1540, the French hood had overtaken the gable hood in popularity, and was to remain in fashion for the next fifty years. Towards the end of Henry's reign, women also wore plumed hats resembling men's bonnets, often over coifs.

Most formal clothes were made to order by professional tailors, using fabrics and trimmings supplied by mercers and haberdashers, who usually imported their wares from overseas. They were often more expensive than the best designer clothes of today: one doublet or gown would be worth the equivalent of a labourer's annual income.[20]

The most costly, and therefore the most sought-after, materials were silk in its various forms – velvet, damask, brocade and satin – and cloth of gold and silver, which were woven with warps of precious metal, sometimes with a weft of coloured silk. These fabrics, which came mainly from Venice and Genoa, were often richly patterned with pomegranates, artichokes, pineapples, rosebuds and wreaths, using brilliant dyes. Velvet often came with a raised pile; the purple velvets worn by royalty cost a staggering 41s.8d. (£625) a yard, while silk damask cost about 8s. (£120) a yard. The most expensive material was cloth of gold, at the equivalent of £2,170 per yard. Tinsel was an inferior form of cloth of gold used for trimming garments, while tissue was a filmier type of cloth of gold, like taffeta.

Lace had traditionally been made in England for church vestments, and was sometimes imported from Flanders; Katherine of Aragon is said to have established a cottage industry in embroidery and lace-making in the Fens in the 1530s, encouraging the local women to follow her example in making Spanish 'black-work' (black embroidery on a white ground), cutwork (see below) and what is now known as 'Buckingham' lace. Lace became fashionable at court after 1533, when Catherine de' Medici introduced the Italian mode of lace-making into France.

English embroidery, once carried out mainly by nuns and chiefly on ecclesiastical vestments, had been famous for eight centuries. Elaborate embroidery was now a popular feature of upper-class dress, and was mainly produced by male professionals; by 1515, the Worshipful Company of Broderers had become rich enough to build their own hall in London. Before the end of the fifteenth century, black silk scrolled embroidery, used to decorate headdresses and the collars and cuffs of shirts and smocks, had been introduced into England from Spain and the

Low Countries.[21] Cutwork was an Italian form of highly detailed embroidery on delicate fabrics, while gold braid or cord interlaced with embroidery and even jewels became popular later in the reign.

Cotton was not known in England until the late sixteenth century, and fine linen, or 'Holland cloth', which was imported from Scotland, Ireland, Flanders and Germany, was expensive. It was used for under-garments, shirts and coifs, which were usually made and embroidered by the women in a family, queens being no exception. Katherine of Aragon was an expert needlewoman who obviously enjoyed sewing. On one occasion, she gave an audience to Wolsey and the papal legate 'with a skein of white thread about her neck'.[22] She made all Henry's fine cambric shirts, and embroidered altar cloths and church vestments.

There was a lively trade in courtiers' cast-off garments, for no one wanted to be seen too often in the same clothes, and money had to be raised to pay for new ones. Very few items of sixteenth-century dress survive today: small fragments of embroidered material, shirts, gloves – such as the gilt-embroidered gauntlets said to have belonged to Henry VIII[23] – coifs and odd accessories are the only fragile testimonials to the splendour of an extravagant, long-gone era.

During the reign of Henry VIII, mediaeval styles of jewellery gave way to Renaissance, or 'antique', designs, which featured classical cameos and engravings. The King's own signet ring was of gold and had a seal backed by an intaglio, a gem – in this case a chalcedony – with an engraved design.[24] Portrait heads appeared not only on cameos but also on medallions and in miniatures, which might be set in pendants, brooches and rings. Much jewellery featured designs from nature – flowers, birds, fish and leaves – and a lot was heavily symbolic, often embodying visual allusions or puns.

Jewellery, ever a sound investment, was even more important than dress in defining status, which was why so many items of clothing were decorated with jewels. At court, both sexes indulged in a lavish display of jewellery, most of it made by London goldsmiths or imported from Italy, Paris or Bruges. Officers of state and household wore heavy gold collars of SS links with the Tudor badges of portcullises and roses and a pendant rose, as seen in Holbein's portrait of Thomas More. Others bedecked themselves with gold chains, collars, pendants, rings and signets, carcanets, pectoral ornaments, bracelets, bejewelled girdles and buttons, aiglets, pins, brooches, pomanders, hat jewels and double pendants known as 'tablets', which opened to reveal their contents. Some items were decorated with enamels, while others reflected the tastes of the wearer: in his portrait by Holbein, Sir Henry Guildford sports a hat badge depicting mathematical instruments.

Henry VIII owned a huge collection of jewellery, greater than that of any other English king. Some of it was inherited, but many items were made to order, sometimes to Henry's own designs, by the 'King's Jewellers', Peter van der Wale of Antwerp, Hans of Antwerp and Cornelius Heyss (or Hayes), or by his goldsmith, Robert Amadas, who later became Keeper of the Jewel House. Henry also sent agents abroad to seek out fine and rare pieces. His jewels were the first in England to feature classical motifs; among them was a pendant bearing an antique face, one tablet with a representation of Hercules and another of gold antique work decorated with ten emeralds and white putti.

Some of Henry's jewels were highly detailed miniature works of art, such as the ship pendant with masts and decks of diamonds, an enamelled cap badge of St George and the dragon,[25] and 'a brooch of gold wherein is wrought and devised a tennis play and men playing at tennis with rackets in their hands', set with sapphires and rubies.[26] Some of the pendants seen in his portraits are thought to have concealed watches, which were very rare luxuries at that time.

Henry's collars were exceptionally splendid, being studded with precious stones of great price; one collar weighed over six and a half pounds. He also owned ninety-nine diamond rings. A fair number of his jewels were either stolen, 'lost off the King's back' or 'given away at pleasure'.[27] In 1546, he bought the famous 'Three Brothers', an enormous diamond surrounded by three balas rubies and four large pearls, which had once been owned by the Dukes of Burgundy, for an undisclosed price from the Fugger bank in Augsburg – much to the disgust of his Council, who thought he already had enough jewellery and had tried to prevent him from finding out that it was for sale.

A lot of the jewellery in Henry's collection was of religious significance, such as reliquaries, hat badges, crucifixes, hearts, devotional girdle books and 'IHS' or 'Jesus' pendants like that favoured by Jane Seymour, but with the advent of the Reformation such things went out of fashion. The King also owned 'a ring of gold with a death's head',[28] which typified the contemporary fashion for jewels bearing reminders of mortality.

Personalised jewellery was highly popular. Anne Boleyn owned at least three initial pendants: an AB and a B, which appear in portraits of her,[29] and an A, which is worn by her daughter Elizabeth in the Whitehall family group. Henry VIII owned a chain with Hs between the links, as well as several items of jewellery bearing his motto, 'Dieu et mon droit' and various royal badges.

The King ensured that his successive wives were lavishly supplied with jewellery. The Queen of England owned two sets: her official jewels, which were inherited from her predecessors and included some

Henry VIII in *c.*1509 (anon.)

'There is fiery power in his eyes, beauty in his face and twin roses in his cheeks.'

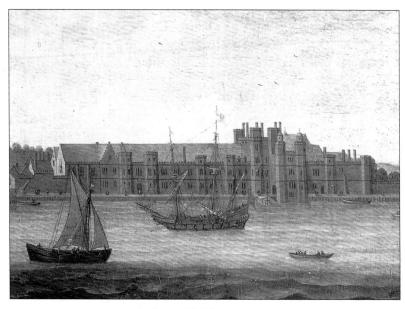

Greenwich Palace (anon.)

'Lo! With what lustre shines this wished for place,
Which, star-like, might the heavenly mansions grace.'

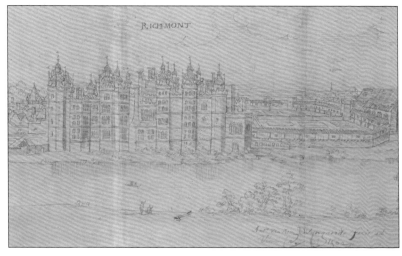

Richmond Palace (by Wyngaerde)

'An earthly paradise, most glorious to behold.'

Pastime with good
company:
song by Henry VIII

'Youth must have some
dalliance
Of good or ill, some
pastance…'

A court official (by Holbein)

The King and his Household
officers demanded a high standard
of service.

Thomas Wolsey,
Cardinal Archbishop of York (anon.)

'The Cardinal of York is the beginning,
middle and end.'

Terracotta roundel by Giovanni
Maiano at Hampton Court Palace,
commissioned by Wolsey.
The impact of the Italian
Renaissance manifested itself in
'antique' ornamental motifs.

Henry VIII's writing desk

'Writing is to me somewhat tedious and painful,' the young King once told Wolsey.

Battle of the Spurs, 1513 (detail; anon.)

Henry VIII had dreams of conquering France. Here he is shown taking the surrender of a French lord, probably the Chevalier Bayard.

Wedding portrait of Charles Brandon, Duke of Suffolk, and Mary Tudor (anon.)

One version of this portrait bore the scurrilous verse:
'Cloth of gold do not despise
Though thou be matched with cloth of frieze.'

'The Castle of Loyalty': design for a pageant at Greenwich, Christmas 1524.

Court entertainments were staged frequently during the first two decades of the reign.

Sir Henry Guildford (by Holbein)

'A lusty young man beloved of the King', he was also a cultivated humanist and able administrator.

Sir Nicholas Carew wearing jousting armour (by Holbein)

Carew was 'a most devoted servant', and an outstanding star of the tournament.

Sir Thomas More (after Holbein)

A contemporary called him 'a laughing philosopher', but his 'great wit was mingled with taunting and mocking'.

Desiderius Erasmus (by Holbein)

He had one of the greatest minds of the age, but the King did little for him beyond extolling his works.

Nicholas Kratzer (by Holbein)

He was a brilliant mathematician and astronomer and 'brimful of wit'.

Edward Stafford, Duke of Buckingham (anon.)

He was 'high-minded', haughty, not very bright, and too near the throne for comfort.

The Field of Cloth of Gold, 1520: scenes from the summit meeting between Henry VIII and Francis I (anon.)

'These sovereigns are not at peace: they hate each other cordially.'

Katherine of Aragon (by Horenbout)

'A lady of lively, kind and gracious disposition.'

Anne Boleyn (by Hoskins)

For seven years, Henry VIII urged her, 'Give yourself up, body and soul, to me.'

Jane Seymour (by Horenbout)

'A woman of the utmost charm.'

Anne of Cleves (by Holbein)

'She is nothing fair, and have evil smells about her.'

Katherine Howard (by Holbein)

'A young lady of moderate beauty but superlative grace.'

Katherine Parr (by Horenbout)

'Her rare goodness made every day a Sunday.'

very ancient and historic pieces, and her personal jewellery, which was worth a fortune.

Few items of Tudor jewellery survive. As tastes changed, pieces were melted down and refashioned, therefore most information about jewellery comes from portraits and written records.

The sixteenth century saw the design of armour reach its apotheosis. Each suit was made to be as flexible and comfortable as possible, and was beautifully engraved and damascened with precious metals. Different suits were worn for jousting, fighting on foot and fighting on horseback, and all were very expensive. Henry VIII was passionately interested in the design of armour, and amassed a large collection of it. Five of his suits of armour survive, four at the Tower of London and one at Windsor, as well as his horse armour, which is exquisitely chased with scrollwork.

Henry's interest in armour was fuelled in 1509, when the Emperor Maximilian gave him a splendid suit of gilded horse armour known as 'the Burgundian Bard', which is now in the Tower. It was probably made by a Dutch craftsman, Martin van Royne, and engraved and gilded by Paul van Vrelant of Brussels, and it was typical of the fine continental workmanship of the period. In 1514 the Emperor sent Henry a further gift, a handsome suit of jousting armour made by the greatest armourer in Europe, Conrad Seusenhofer of Innsbruck, from whom Henry had ordered two sets of armour in 1511; its grotesque helmet, with a snarling, grimacing face (said to resemble Maximilian himself) and outsize ram's-horn ears, survives in the Royal Armouries in the Tower of London; its brass spectacles are long lost.[30]

Around 1514, Henry bought a beautifully made suit of silvered armour of very advanced design from craftsmen in Flanders. It is damascened in silver and chased in gold with the legend of St George, with Hs and Ks engraved on the skirt hem; it is so well constructed that it must have fitted like a glove yet at the same time allowed unprecedented freedom of movement.[31]

England had nothing that could compete with this kind of craftsmanship, but the King determined to rectify this. In 1511, he set up an armour workshop with Milanese craftsmen at Southwark, and in 1515 he established a more important armoury near the friary at Greenwich Palace, enticing Martin von Royne to come to England as Master Armourer and supervise the eleven armourers whom Henry had imported from Germany and Flanders;[32] among them was Paul van Vrelant. This workshop, known as the 'Almain Armoury', produced superb armour of a standard to equal anything in Europe, and made for the King, among other things, two suits of foot armour, one dating from c1515–20, which was never completed, and the other, much larger,

from c1540, as well as an engraved, silver-embossed armour for the King
and his horse. All are now displayed in the Tower. The armoury also
made armour to Henry's own designs, which were 'such as no armourer
before that time had seen'.[33] Henry's armour was usually stored at
Greenwich, where it could easily be maintained. In 1521, 'Old Martin'
van Royne was succeeded as Master Armourer by Erasmus Kyrkenar.

The King was also fascinated by weapons, especially guns and cannon,
and was keen to find ways of improving their range and accuracy. He
set up a foundry in Houndsditch to make firearms to new specifications,
and restocked the arsenal at the Tower. He also designed new weapons
for his bodyguards, including an early form of bayonet and a gunshield,
both of which are in the Royal Armouries.

The King enjoyed shooting with handguns; he shot duck on
Plumstead Marshes with a party of favoured companions, or practised
firing at the wooden target shaped like a man that was made for him in
1538.[34] Unfortunately, on one of his shooting forays in the 1530s at
Greenwich, Henry underestimated the range of his firearm and blasted
off the roof of the house of his Groom of the Stool, Sir Henry Norris.[35]

Henry also collected weapons; he owned 94 swords, 36 daggers,
15 rapiers, 12 woodknives, 7 crossbows,[36] and 100 breech-loading
arquebuses; only one survives in the Royal Armouries, bearing his
monogram and the date 1537. His wooden lance, painted red, gold and
black with motifs of leaves and latticework, is also in the Tower, as is a
dagger etched with roses and pomegranates, which probably belonged
to him. Henry's crossbow, bearing the royal arms and dating from
c1527, is in Glasgow Art Gallery and Museum, while his sword and
scabbard are in the Royal Collection at Windsor.

22

'This Cardinal Is King'

In the summer of 1515, 'the King took his progress westwards, and visited his towns and castles there and heard the complaints of his poor commons; and always, as he rode, he hunted and liberally gave away the venison. And in the middle of September, he came to his manor of Woking.'[1]

Here, he was joined by Wolsey, who that month was made a cardinal by the Pope. The symbolic red hat arrived at Dover in November and was conveyed to London 'with such triumph, as though the greatest prince of Christendom had come into the realm'.[2] The new Cardinal was invested with it in a glittering ceremony in Westminster Abbey that rivalled in pomp 'the coronation of a mighty prince or king',[3] and afterwards there was a sumptuous banquet at York Place.

Wolsey aspired to a lifestyle rivalling that of the King himself. In the spring of 1515, he had begun building the most splendid palace yet seen in England. After consulting his physicians as to the most healthy site within a twenty-mile radius of London, he acquired from the Knights Hospitallers of the Order of St John of Jerusalem a lease of their manor at Hampton by the Thames, fifteen miles from Westminster.[4] It boasted a fifteenth-century courtyard house which had perhaps been built by the previous tenant, Giles, Lord Daubeney, Lord Chamberlain to Henry VII, who had visited him there with Elizabeth of York shortly before the latter's death in childbirth in 1503.

Wolsey demolished this building; the only remnant of it is the clock in the campanile above Clock Court, which bears the date 1479.[5] In its place he raised a grand red-brick double-courtyard house with mullioned windows, turrets, tall chimneys, a moat,[6] gardens, a large service complex and an advanced system of conduits and sewers. It was designed by Ellis Smith on a collegiate plan, and decorated with antique work in terracotta: there are putti supporting Wolsey's coat of arms above the clock-tower gateway,[7] and medallions of Roman emperors with exquisite decorative borders, which were carved in 1521 by the Florentine sculptor Giovanni di Maiano[8] and based on those commissioned by the Cardinal of Amboise for his palace at Gaillon, near Rouen. Hampton Court was ready for occupation by 1517, when Wolsey first entertained the King and Queen there, and finally completed in 1525. By then, it was said to contain one thousand rooms. Here Wolsey lived in princely magnificence.

The palace was entered by an imposing five-storey gatehouse with octagonal towers surmounted by lead cupolas at each corner and a large oriel window.[9] In the Base Court was accommodation for Wolsey's household and forty-five guest lodgings;[10] 280 beds with silk hangings were kept made up in readiness for visitors. A second gateway led to Clock Court, where the Cardinal's great hall, banqueting chamber,[11] gallery and chapel were located.

Wolsey spared no expense in making Hampton Court the most luxurious residence in England. His own apartments were panelled and sported moulded ceilings and rich friezes and paintings, while the outward chambers were adorned with priceless tapestries, sixty large carpets presented by the Venetian Senate,[12] and furnishings of unprecedented splendour, including five chairs of estate; one tapestry owned by Wolsey, *The Triumph of Fame over Death*, based on a work by Petrarch, still hangs at Hampton Court in the great watching chamber. A special lodging in a three-storey donjon in Clock Court was reserved for the King and Queen. The palace lay within two thousand acres of parkland surrounded by a brick wall, part of which remains today. The Kingston Road divided the park into the Home Park and Bushy Park.[13]

Wolsey had begun building another house in 1515, on land he had been granted by the King near the Dominican priory of Blackfriars in London, in the parish of St Bride. When, however, he started work on Hampton Court, he lost interest in this project and signed over the land to the King. Henry thereupon seized the opportunity of providing himself with a new residence in London to replace Westminster. He took over the building works, and built the palace of Bridewell. Constructed of red brick with octagonal towers, it stood between Fleet Street and the River Thames,[14] and was connected by a bridge across the River Fleet to the priory, which was used as an annexe whenever extra accommodation was needed. Bridewell Palace had two courtyards; in the inner one was the donjon housing the royal lodgings, which were accessed by a novel processional stair. A long gallery led to the river frontage and a watergate, and there were terraced gardens and a tennis play on the river side. There was no great hall or chapel, since both the lofty hall and the chapel in the Blackfriars convent were at the King's disposal. The palace was completed by 1522, and cost Henry £20,000 (£6 million).

On 29 October 1515, the King attended the launching of another new ship, *The Virgin Mary*, which became popularly known as *The Princess Mary* in honour of Mary Tudor. She was a huge vessel of 6–800 tons, with 120 oars, 207 guns and the capacity to carry a thousand men. Accompanied by the Queen, who was pregnant again, the Suffolks and the whole court, Henry himself, dressed in a sailor's coat and breeches of cloth of gold, piloted the ship along the Thames to the sea, blowing his large gold whistle as loudly as a trumpet. After Bishop Ruthal of Durham had celebrated mass, the vessel was formally named by the Queen; then the King hosted a feast on board.[15]

Matters of state were pressing. Archbishop Warham, who had several times clashed with Wolsey, was finding it increasingly difficult to assert his authority as Lord Chancellor and Primate of England in the face of the Cardinal's superior power and overt hostility. According to Thomas More, he was weary of public life and wished to retire to his diocese. Therefore, on 22 December 1515, he resigned his office. On Christmas Eve, at Eltham Palace, the King appointed Wolsey Lord Chancellor in his place and delivered to him the Great Seal of England.

No subject had ever before held so many high offices in both Church and state, nor commanded an income that enabled him to live like royalty. 'The Cardinal of York is the beginning, middle and end,' commented the Venetian envoy Giustinian in 1516.[16] Nevertheless, Wolsey worked hard for his rewards, being 'constantly occupied with all the affairs of the kingdom'. The King, busy amusing himself 'day and night', was happy to leave all government business to the Cardinal, 'who rules everything with consummate ability and prudence. It is essential to speak first of all serious matters to the Cardinal and not to the King.'[17]

Soon, power seemed to be centred on the Cardinal's household at York Place, where he resided during the legal term, rather than on the King's court, with visitors going to kiss Wolsey's hand before they sought an audience with Henry. Wolsey's increasing autocracy soon became evident to Giustinian, who noted that, whereas in 1515, the Cardinal would have told him, 'His Majesty will do so and so', within a year or so he was saying, 'We shall do so and so', and by 1519 it was 'I shall do so and so.' The envoy concluded: 'This Cardinal is king, nor does His Majesty depart in the least from the opinion and counsel of His Lordship.'[18] Francis I thought that Wolsey 'held the honour of his king in small account', while ambassadors felt they were dealing 'not with a cardinal but with another king'.[19]

Court factions quickly found themselves disempowered. Wolsey dominated the Privy Council and the royal household, and exercised royal patronage on the King's behalf. 'He chooses,' wrote an imperial envoy, 'to interfere in everything.'[20] Yet he remained a remote figure with whom even noblemen found it hard to obtain an audience. So complete was the King's confidence in him that none dared challenge his power. Naturally, it was bitterly resented by many.

That bitterness was fuelled by Wolsey's lavish lifestyle, which was financed by his ecclesiastical revenues and his fees as Lord Chancellor, amounting to perhaps £35,000 (£10,500,000) a year. He lived like 'a glorious peacock'[21] in luxurious palaces attended by a thousand servants wearing a crimson velvet livery emblazoned with a cardinal's hat; his cook was rumoured to dress 'daily in damask, silk or velvet, with a chain of gold about his neck'.[22]

When Wolsey went forth in procession, he was accompanied by a large entourage, preceded by silver crosses and pillars, poleaxes and a mace, and noblemen bearing the Great Seal on a cushion and Wolsey's cardinal's hat, 'raised up like some holy idol or other';[23] as he approached, his Gentlemen Ushers cried, 'Make way for My Lord's Grace!' The Cardinal, in robes of silk, velvet and ermine, and holding a pomander or an orange stuffed with spices to his nose to ward off the smell of the unwashed populace, would ride by on a mule, as churchmen did, in emulation of Christ, yet this mule was trapped in red and gold. At his table, where he dined alone beneath a rich cloth of estate, there were more dishes than were permitted to a nobleman. He dispensed alms that were far more lavish than the King's, and at New Year he sometimes outlaid greater amounts than his master did on gifts. He danced, hunted and kept – very discreetly – a mistress, one 'lusty'[24] Joan Lark, who bore him two children;[25] Queen Katherine in particular deplored his 'voluptuous life' and 'abominable lechery'.[26] Many considered his lifestyle inappropriate for a man of the Church, but there is no evidence that Henry VIII resented the splendour in which his minister lived; on the contrary, it reflected well upon his greatness to have such a distinguished servant.

Although there is evidence that Wolsey did his best to manipulate the King by distracting him with novelties,[27] Henry never fully relinquished power to him. He was happy to offload administrative affairs and routine state business onto his shoulders, but everything the Cardinal did was 'by authority';[28] the King retained his royal prerogative in having the ultimate veto, and all important decisions were made by him. Sometimes he intervened when he did not agree with the Cardinal's actions, and he frequently exhibited an incisive grasp of affairs. Wolsey kept his 'loving master' well informed, writing out summaries of the letters and documents that the King did not have leisure to read in their entirety, and even drafting replies for him to sign. Jealous of his power, the Cardinal did his best to undermine the role of the royal secretaries who had to deal with these papers, whom he perceived as threats to his position. When crossed, he could be ruthless and violent: he once hit the papal nuncio Chieregato, and swore at him. Most of the time, however, he exercised 'rare and unheard of affability'.[29]

Apart from on ceremonial occasions, king and minister met infrequently – during the legal term, Wolsey visited the court only on Sundays,[30] and he usually stayed in London while the King moved from house to house – but they remained in daily contact by letter and messenger. The Secretary Richard Pace described how Henry read each dispatch from Wolsey three times, sometimes letting his supper go cold as he did so; he would mark each item requiring attention, then dictate his responses to his secretaries, often keeping them up late in the process. He would remind Pace 'not further to meddle' with his replies in case his meaning became distorted.[31]

Wolsey laboured to a punishing schedule, often rising at 4 a.m. and sitting at his desk for twelve hours, without stopping once to eat or relieve himself.[32] Henry was aware of how hard and diligently Wolsey worked for him. 'Mine own good Cardinal,' he wrote in 1518, 'take some pastime and comfort to the intent that you may longer endure to serve us.'[33] He was genuinely fond of Wolsey, enjoyed his company, and when the Cardinal wrote to him, 'Your realm, our Lord be thanked, was never in such peace and tranquillity', was aware of to whom he had to be grateful.

23

'The Pearl of the World'

Henry spent the Christmas of 1515 at Eltham Palace, which had been one of the most favoured mediaeval royal residences since 1305. Its crowning glory was the magnificent buttressed great hall which was built by Edward IV in 1475–83 and still survives today; it measures one hundred by thirty feet and has an impressive hammerbeam roof,[1] bay and oriel windows and a minstrels' gallery. Around 1490, Henry VII refaced most of the palace with red brick, rebuilt 'the fair front over the moat'[2] and added many features, including tiled floors and new glass for the windows. The royal lodgings, which dated from the reign of Henry IV, were in a donjon in the inner or Great Court, behind which were five smaller service courtyards, and there was a separate lodging for the Lord Chancellor and a tiltyard. The whole was surrounded by a forested deer park.[3]

Eltham was one of Henry VIII's greater houses, and he used it frequently during the first half of his reign. Between 1510 and 1522, he built a new chapel with two first-floor holyday closets, and made many improvements to the royal lodgings, enlarging the Queen's Side, providing a study for himself and safeguarding his privacy with high brick walls and hedges.[4] He also had a hill flattened so as to improve the view from his windows.

At Christmas 1515, the Chapel Royal performed a comedy, *Troilus and Pandarus*, in the great hall at Eltham. This was followed on Twelfth Night by a pageant, dancing and a feast comprising two hundred dishes.[5] Temporary kitchens had had to be erected so that the Master Cooks could make jellies and gingerbread.

There were outdoor pastimes as well. The King and Suffolk amused themselves by running at the ring, Henry wearing a wreath of green satin embroidered with the Queen's pomegranate badge. He had provided all the clothes for the competitors at a cost of £142 (£42,600), and at the end of the day each man was told he might keep what he was wearing; Suffolk was also given the horse, armour and saddle he was using. The courtiers watched from elaborate pavilions with chivalric names: Flower-delice, White Hart, Harp, Greyhound, Leopard's Head and Ostrich Feather.

The King had recently acquired another house, New Hall, which stood in the village of Boreham, four miles from Chelmsford in Essex. It was a mediaeval hall house once owned by the Abbots of Waltham, which had later been acquired by Edward IV. Henry VII had granted it to Thomas Butler, Earl of Ormonde, who had entertained Henry VIII there in 1510 and again just before his death in 1515. His daughter Margaret, mother of Sir Thomas Boleyn, inherited it, and Boleyn, as Ormonde's executor, sold it to the King before January 1516 for £1,000 (£300,000).

Between 1516 and 1523, Henry converted New Hall into a sumptuous palace at a cost of £20,000 (£6 million), and renamed it Beaulieu, although the old name stuck. Faced with brick, his new residence had a gatehouse leading into a main courtyard with a fountain, a hall, a gallery, integral tennis play and chapel. A gilded and painted panel of the King's arms that once adorned its gatehouse[6] is now at Hampton Court.

The only figural window to survive from Henry's palaces was originally at Beaulieu. Crafted by Dutch glaziers, it depicts the Crucifixion with the crowned and kneeling figures of the King, Katherine of Aragon and their patron saints, and is now in the east window of St Margaret's Church at Westminster, where it was moved in the eighteenth century.[7]

The court was at Greenwich when, on 18 February 1516, after a difficult labour in which she clung to the holy girdle of her patron saint, St Catherine, the Queen at last bore a healthy child, but it was a girl, not the hoped-for son. The King, however, was delighted with his daughter. 'The Queen and I are both young, and if it is a girl this time, by God's grace boys will follow,' he told Giustinian,[8] and he gave a handsome reward to Dr Vittoria, who had assisted at the birth.

When she was three days old the infant Princess was christened in the Church of the Observant Friars and given the name Mary. The ceremonial followed the procedure laid down by the Lady Margaret Beaufort in the Household Ordinances. The silver font had again been brought from Canterbury, rich carpets were laid along the processional route and the church was hung with tapestries. The ceremony was conducted with great solemnity, the baby being divested of her rich robes and cloth of gold train furred with ermine in a specially erected closet furnished with a brazier and towels, then immersed naked into the font, which was set on a raised platform so that all the congregation could witness the baptism. After she had been anointed with holy oil, the white chrysom cloth was wrapped around her head to protect it. Then a lighted taper was put into the tiny fist and the child was carried to the high altar, where she was confirmed by Archbishop Warham. While she was being dressed, refreshments were served to her godparents, Cardinal Wolsey, the Countess of Devon and the Duchess of Norfolk, who then presented her with the usual gifts of plate. The procession re-formed, and the Princess was carried to the King and Queen, who were waiting in the latter's presence chamber, to receive their blessing. Parents were not, by tradition, expected to attend their child's christening: the mother would not yet have been churched, and it was the godparents who were central to the occasion.[9] Afterwards, there were jousts to celebrate the event, and when the Queen was up and about again she made a pilgrimage to Walsingham to give thanks for her safe and successful delivery.

The Princess Mary was immediately given into the care of a Lady Mistress, the widowed Lady Margaret Bryan, daughter of Lord Berners and mother of Francis Bryan and Lady Carew, who was granted £50 (£15,000) a year for life. Mary was not immediately assigned a separate household, but lived in her own apartments at court for the first years of her life, with her own servants, including four rockers.

Henry enjoyed showing off his daughter, carrying her about in his arms and assuring courtiers and ambassadors that she never cried.[10] She was his 'pearl of the world', he told them.[11] Mary was a bright, precocious child, 'joyous and decorous in manners';[12] she had inherited many of her parents' intellectual and musical gifts and mastered the virginals by the age of four.

By 1519, Mary had been given her own household, which cost her father £1,400 (£420,000) a year. It was based mainly at Ditton Manor in Buckinghamshire,[13] and was presided over by Margaret Pole, Countess of Salisbury, with Lady Bryan remaining as Lady Mistress. The Princess had her own Chamberlain, Treasurer, Cofferer, Clerk of the Closet, chaplains and gentlewomen. Ditton Manor was a large moated house set in a beautiful park, and had been royal property since the time of Edward IV. Henry VIII had modernised it between 1511 and 1515, possibly with a view to using it as a nursery palace.[14]

Hot upon the heels of Mary's christening followed that of the Suffolks' first son, who was born on 11 March 1516 at Bath Place in London. The King himself attended the lavish ceremony as a godfather, and the baby was named Henry in his honour. The other sponsors were Wolsey and the Countess of Devon. Henry gave his nephew a salt-cellar and cup of pure gold.

Eight weeks later, he played host to his elder sister, Queen Margaret of Scotland, widow of James IV and mother of the three-year-old James V. In 1514, Margaret had married her second husband, Archibald Douglas, Earl of Angus, but the following year the little King's cousin and heir, John Stewart, Duke of Albany, had been chosen as Regent by the Scottish Parliament and had seized custody of young James. Margaret had been driven out of Scotland and sought refuge in England; just south of the border, at Harbottle in Northumberland, in October 1515 she had given birth to a daughter, Lady Margaret Douglas.

On 3 May 1516, Margaret arrived at Tottenham in an impoverished state and suffering from sciatica. She rested in Bruce Castle[15] as the guest of Sir William Compton, until the King, whom she had not seen for thirteen years, came to escort her in a state procession into London, Margaret riding a white palfrey, which had been sent by the Queen. She was initially lodged at Baynard's Castle;[16] later that year, Wolsey arranged for her to move to Scotland Yard, once the ancient London residence of the Kings of Scotland, but now incorporated into York Place. Margaret was formally received by the King and Queen at Greenwich, and reunited with her sister Mary; she was overwhelmed by the splendour of her brother's court and 'could not take her eyes off' the gowns and gifts he showered upon her.[17] Henry was very taken with his niece, Margaret Douglas, or 'Little Marget' as he called her, and arranged for her to be brought up at court with the Princess Mary.

The rest of the month was given over to tournaments and festivities in honour of Margaret's visit. On 19–20 May, there were 'two solemn days of jousts' at Greenwich in the presence of the three Queens. On the first day, although 'every man did well, the King did best',[18] while on the second day Henry won applause when he succeeded in unhorsing Sir William Kingston, 'a very tall, strong knight' whom few had excelled. In the evening, there was 'a great banquet for the welcome of the Queen of Scots' in the Queen's apartments.[19]

But the King was not happy. Although Suffolk had performed valorously as usual in the lists, the young gentlemen who had fought against Henry had been so incompetent that he had been unable to score many blows, which he considered detrimental to his honour and reputation. In future, he announced, he would 'never joust again except it be with as good a man as himself'.[20] Thereafter, he usually chose proven men such as Suffolk or Carew as his opponents.

That May, Bishop Foxe resigned as Lord Privy Seal, and was replaced by Thomas Ruthal, Bishop of Durham. Foxe retired to his See of Winchester, 'thinking of all the souls I never see'.[21] Despite increasing blindness, he devoted the last years of his life to religion, making up for 'eighteen years' negligence',[22] and to education; he founded Corpus Christi College at Oxford and rebuilt the choir of Winchester Cathedral. He died in 1528.

The worldly influence of Wolsey was counterbalanced by the rise to power of Thomas More. Much against his inclinations, More had been persuaded to enter the King's service in 1515 after successfully completing two diplomatic missions for him. 'You would hardly believe how unwilling I am,' he told Erasmus. More was unlike most courtiers in that he was an intellectual who understood the superficiality of court life and disdained the outward trappings of wealth and power. Henry liked and respected him, valued his opinions, and would often ask him to join him in his private apartments to discuss astronomy, geometry, divinity and other subjects; sometimes at night he would take him up onto the leads of the palace, 'there to consider with him the diversities, courses, motions and operations of the stars and planets'.[23] On other occasions, the King and Queen would invite More to make merry with them, and Henry might tease him about his dislike of the court. More got on well with Wolsey, even though he may not have fully approved of him, but the contrast between the two men could not have been greater.

In 1516, More's *Utopia* was published, a book describing the ideal state, which was in fact a neo-Platonic, quasi-fascist republic with laws based on the central tenets of humanism. It was also a powerful critique of the political system in England and the vicious machinations of monarchs and courtiers, but such was More's international reputation, and the eloquence of his Latin prose, that the book won him praise everywhere. He was already working as an unofficial secretary to the King, and in 1517, his admiring master preferred him to the Privy Council.

In June, the Queen's favourite lady-in-waiting, Maria de Salinas, left her service to marry William, Lord Willougby d'Eresby, who was Master of the Royal Hart Hounds; Maria was granted letters of denization beforehand, and Katherine ensured that she was provided with a handsome dowry. The wedding took place in the Church of the Observant Friars at Greenwich. After Maria had taken up residence at Parham Park in Sussex, Queen Katherine invited her frequently to court; she may have attended the christening of Maria's son in 1517, and was probably a godmother to her daughter Katherine, who was born in 1519 and named in her honour.

After a joust on 7 July in honour of the translation of the relics of St Thomas Becket at Canterbury, the King set off on his summer progress, visiting Winchester and spending two nights at The Vyne; there he slept in a great bed hung with green velvet, which his host, Sir William

Sandys, had bought for him. In commemoration of this visit, Sandys built a long gallery lined with linenfold panelling embellished with the royal arms and the devices of Queen Katherine, and a chapel lit by windows depicting Henry VIII, Katherine of Aragon and Margaret Tudor at their devotions, with their patron saints. This glass, which was crafted in the Italian Renaissance style, appears to have been based on designs by Bernard van Orley, and was probably originally commissioned for the Chapel of the Holy Ghost at Basingstoke, which the King visited in 1516, and brought to The Vyne around 1522.[24]

Perhaps the greatest foreign musician to grace the royal musical establishment arrived at court in 1516 'to wait upon the King in his chamber'. He was Friar Dionysio Memmo, who had been organist at St Mark's Basilica in his native city of Venice. Henry VIII had invited him to England, and he brought with him a fine organ, 'at great expense'.[25] The King was enraptured at hearing him play – he had 'a greater opinion of him than words can express' – and promoted him at once to chief musician. At Henry's request, the Pope released Memmo from his vows, and he became a royal chaplain. Memmo gathered about him a group of highly talented musicians, among them a young Venetian lutenist to whom the King 'never wearied of listening', and he would entertain Henry and his court for up to four hours at a time. Knowing his own worth, Memmo composed a song with lyrics hinting that an increase in salary would be welcome; Henry took the hint, and rewarded him with the lucrative benefice of Hanbury, Staffordshire.[26] Memmo left England for Portugal in 1525, and died around 1533.

Another virtuoso organist, Benedict de Opitiis of Antwerp, joined the musicians of the Chamber at this time, at a salary of about £20 (£6,000) a year[27] – which was much more than that paid to most court musicians. Together with Richard Sampson, the gifted Bishop of Chichester, he composed exceptional sacred music for the Chapel Royal.

The Christmas of 1516, which was kept with the usual lavish festivities at Greenwich, was graced by the presence of the three Queens. Margaret Tudor, who was unable to afford New Year's gifts, was saved from embarrassment by Wolsey, who gave her £200 (£60,000) to pay for them. On Twelfth Night, there was a pageant entitled *The Garden of Esperance*,[28] with an entire artificial garden on a pageant car.

It was now nearly a year since the birth of the Princess Mary, and still the Queen had not conceived the hoped-for son. In the spring of 1517, she made another pilgrimage to Walsingham,[29] accompanied by the Duke and Duchess of Suffolk. Katherine was becoming more devout with every passing year, and with the loss of each child had turned increasingly to her faith for solace. She had aged and grown stouter, although ambassadors still remarked upon her fine complexion. She no longer participated so enthusiastically at court revels, but often withdrew early, although she never shirked her duties on state occasions. Clearly, she and Henry were growing apart.

On what would come to be known as 'Evil May Day', the King rode from London with a train of courtiers to the woods at Kensington to bring in the may. But back in the City, where resentment against aliens was seething, there were riots as large gangs of apprentices joined in a concerted rising, attacked foreign merchants and craftsmen and threatened to kill the Lord Mayor and his aldermen. There were several injuries, and many arrests; the ringleaders were executed, and on 22 May four hundred others were brought before the King and his lords in Westminster Hall, wearing halters around their necks. In a beautifully stage-managed charade, Wolsey and Queen Katherine knelt and pleaded for their lives, whereupon Henry graciously pardoned them, at which all the apprentices threw their caps in the air for joy, and their mothers called down blessings on the King's head.[30] Some modern writers assert that Henry's sisters also interceded for the apprentices, but Mary was then in Suffolk and Margaret had left for Scotland with her daughter on 18 May. Henry never saw Margaret again.

24

'Multitudes Are Dying around Us'

The spring of 1517 brought with it an outbreak of a severe epidemic of the sweating sickness, a terrifying disease that could kill with devastating speed. 'One has a little pain in the head and heart; suddenly, a sweat breaks out, and a physician is useless, for whether you wrap yourself up much or little, in four hours – sometimes within two or three – you are despatched without languishing.'[1] Apart from the violent sweats and shivering fits, the symptoms could include stomach pains, vertigo, a rash, headaches and nervous prostration. Most casualties succumbed on the first day: a man could be 'merry at dinner and dead at supper'.[2] But 'once 24 hours are passed, all danger is at an end'.[3] Many cases seem to have been purely psychosomatic: one rumour might cause 'a thousand cases of sweat',[4] and Chieregato observed that people 'suffered more from fear than others did from the sweat itself'.[5]

Tudor medicine was a mixture of the received wisdom of the ancient Greeks, superstition and old-fashioned common sense. Andrew Boorde recommended that sufferers be tucked up warmly in bed in a room with a roaring fire to sweat out the illness; other physicians recommended treacle and herbs, or exotic potions made from powdered sapphires or gold. The truth was that none of them had any real understanding of the sweating sickness, nor the slightest idea of what might cure it. The only thing they all agreed upon was that the patient should be kept awake and not allowed to lapse into a coma.

The sweating sickness had first appeared in England in 1485, when it was seen by some as a judgement of God upon Henry Tudor for usurping the throne; at that time, 'scarcely one in a hundred escaped death'.[6] There had been another, less severe, outbreak in 1508. Europeans called the disease 'the English sweat' because it was more prevalent in England than elsewhere. There were no cases after 1551, and today it is hard to be certain what the sweating sickness was. Some have speculated that it was a miliary fever – a particularly virulent form of prickly heat – others that it was a strain of influenza or typhus. Given the fact that bacteria can mutate, it was probably a simple infection which in time ceased to be fatal.

Plague in several forms, notably bubonic, was endemic in Tudor times. There were outbreaks most summers, some much worse than others, and the people who died were mainly the poor, who had not the means to escape the pest, as their betters could. Plague spread rapidly in hot, crowded, dirty cities, and London, which had about seventy thousand inhabitants crammed inside its walls, was invariably the worst-afflicted place. In 1513, three to four thousand people a day died of plague in the capital.[7]

Henry VIII was inordinately fearful of disease, and especially of any form of plague. He was 'the most timid person in such matters you could meet with'.[8] The mere words 'sweating sickness' were 'so terrible to His Highness' ears that he dare in no wise approach unto the place where it is noised to have been'.[9] No one who had been in contact with any infected person was allowed to enter his court.

In the spring of 1517, when the worst epidemic of the sweating sickness that England had yet experienced broke out in London, the King removed with the court to Richmond, where he was joined by the Suffolks, and thence to Greenwich. Whilst there, he was invited by Giustinian to a banquet on board the Venetian flagship, which lay in the Thames, and accepted the invitation on condition that most of the crew, who might be infected with plague, stayed away.

The ship's main deck had been adorned with tapestries and silk hangings, and along each side were tables bearing a lavish buffet for the King and three hundred courtiers, who were rowed out to the ship in small boats. When Henry went on board, he was conducted to the poop deck, where he was offered wine, little sponge cakes and other delicacies. He was full of praise for his hosts, and also for the sailors who performed daring acrobatic feats high up on the rigging, and was so impressed with the ship's guns that he asked to return the next day to see them all fired. At the end of the banquet, everyone was allowed to take home the exquisite Venetian glasses in which their wine had been served.[10]

Henry was now revelling in the role of international peacemaker. Having temporarily given up all idea of winning any victories against the French – he had told Giustinian he was content with what he had, and wished only to govern his own subjects[11] – he set himself to maintaining the balance of power between Francis I and Maximilian. In early July, the King received Spanish ambassadors who had come to press for a defensive alliance with the Pope and King Charles I of Spain – who had

succeeded Ferdinand the previous year – against the King of France.
The envoys were escorted to Greenwich by a deputation of four
hundred nobles, and shown every honour. At their first audience, the
whole court 'glittered with gold'.[12] The King regaled them with a
programme of masses, pageants and jousts, which culminated on 7 July
with a splendid tournament in the new tiltyard complex in front of an
audience of fifty thousand. Henry had wanted to take on all comers
separately, but was persuaded that this would take too long, so, after
giving a breathtaking display of horsemanship before his wife and his
sister, he ran eight courses against Suffolk instead, 'shivering their lances
every time, to the great applause of the spectators'.[13]

Amongst the other contestants who distinguished themselves in the
four-hour contest, in which 506 spears were broken, was a group of
young gentlemen of the Privy Chamber of whom the King had grown
increasingly fond, and who wore similar outfits to his own. One was
Nicholas Carew; it was on this occasion that he performed his feat with
the tree trunk, mentioned earlier.[14] The rest included Sir William
Compton, Francis Bryan, Anthony Knyvet and William Coffin (or
Cosyn); all were intelligent, articulate young men of gentle birth who
were inclined to intemperate and often wild behaviour; they were known
at court as 'the King's minions'. Wolsey resented this little clique because,
although they held no political offices, they had the King's ear, shared his
leisure hours and were therefore much too influential for comfort.

The tournament was followed by a banquet which lasted seven hours,
after which Henry danced with the ladies until dawn.[15] When the
ambassadors left England, the King gave them rich gifts of horses and
clothing.

By August, the plague had crept too near to Greenwich for comfort,
so Henry sent home most members of his household and moved to
Windsor, where he shut himself up with the Queen, his physician Dr
Linacre, Dionysio Memmo and only three of his favourite gentlemen:
the latter group almost certainly included Compton and Carew. No one
else was allowed to come near him, not even foreign ambassadors, and
all but the most necessary government business was held in suspension.
Meanwhile, Wolsey, who had suffered four attacks of the sweat and
survived,[16] had gone on pilgrimage to Walsingham to give thanks for his
recovery.

Although the giests had been drawn up, Henry was forced to abandon
all plans for a progress.[17] In August 1517, More wrote to Erasmus:
'Multitudes are dying around us. Almost everyone in Oxford,
Cambridge or London has been ill lately.' At Windsor, 'some of the
royal pages who slept in His Majesty's chamber' succumbed,[18] and the
King fled with his small entourage to 'a remote and unusual habitation'

which has not been identified. Thereafter, he moved from house to house to escape the contagion, but not fast enough. Lord Grey, a German servant and several of those who worked in the royal kitchens and stables caught the sweat and died, as did the King's Latin Secretary, Andrea Ammonio, three days after he had left court to seek refuge in the countryside.[19] Back in London, there was civil disorder due to the absence of both King and Cardinal.[20]

By the autumn, only a skeleton staff were in attendance upon the King. As sickness was seen as a visitation from God and a punishment for sinfulness, Henry became more assiduous at his devotions, attending Mass and receiving communion more frequently than usual.[21] He kept fear at bay by hawking, making music with Memmo or concocting his own remedy for the sweat, made up of sage, herb of grace and elder leaves infused together.

Over the years, Henry devised over thirty such remedies – medicines, plasters, lotions and ointments – using a wide range of ingredients that included plants, raisins, linseed vinegar, rosewater, worms, wines, ammonia, lead monoxide, ivory scrapings, crushed pearls, coral, marsh-mallows, 'dragon's' blood and animal fat. His 'cure' for bubonic plague consisted of an infusion of marigolds, sorrel, meadow plant, feverfew, rue and snapdragon, sweetened with sugar. He also concocted plasters that would heal ulcers, swollen ankles and sore legs, an unguent to cool inflammation and stop itching, and ointments 'to make good digestion' or 'to dry excoriations and comfort the member'.[22] It is not known whether he made up these mixtures himself in a still-room, or if he merely supervised the process.

That autumn, quacks and charlatans hovered on the fringes of the royal household, making a nuisance of themselves. One, a Spanish friar, claimed he had the power to order the seas and the weather. The King, dubious, agreed to see him, but sent him on his way with a flea in his ear after an interview lasting an hour.[23]

Henry placed his reliance on his prayers and his medical staff. Since the fifteenth century, there had been a strict division between scholarly physicians, who were often in holy orders and dealt in diagnosis, barber surgeons, who were much lower down the social scale and carried out surgery, pulled teeth and let blood, and apothecaries, who made up prescribed remedies.

The King had six physicians, the best that could be found. The chief of them, Dr Linacre, who was keen to further research into medical science, founded the Royal College of Physicians in 1518, becoming its first President, and later gave funds for two lectureships at Oxford and Cambridge. One of the first members of the Royal College of Physicians was Dr John Chamber, another of Henry's doctors, who had qualified at Padua and had been physician to Henry VII; Holbein painted his portrait in 1542, when he was seventy-two. The King's doctors all wore long furred gowns in the royal livery colours.

Henry VIII's Sergeant Surgeon was Thomas Vicary, who in 1540 became first Master of the newly formed Guild of Barber Surgeons; he is shown kneeling with his fellows in Holbein's painting depicting the King granting the Guild its charter. Vicary, who received a life pension of £26.13s.4d. (£8,000), wrote the first English manual on anatomy.[24] Sometime before 1525, Henry presented him with an instrument case enamelled with the royal arms.[25]

The King had five apothecaries, and placed much faith in their remedies, even when they made him sick.[26] At various times, he was prescribed pills to ward off plague, 'fomentations for the piles', eyebright for eyestrain, gargling mixtures for a sore throat, and rhubarb pills, herbal poultices and dragées for various other ailments.[27] Medicines for the King's use were kept with bandages and plasters in small coffers in the medical quarters of the palace service complex.

By December 1517 there were fewer cases of the sweat, but Henry 'kept no solemn Christmas'.[28] His provisions were low, and he had no wish to purchase goods that might be contaminated from markets in England. So he and his companions rode to Southampton, where they waited apprehensively for Flemish ships, which had been delayed by rough weather, to offload food supplies.[29] Wolsey, meanwhile, had spent Christmas at Richmond, well supplied with oranges, which were thought to be antidotes to the plague.

For much of 1518, the King remained on his travels. He kept in touch with Wolsey by special messengers, who took letters and messages from one to the other every seven hours.[30] In January, Henry returned briefly to Greenwich. While he was there, Wolsey, who was determined to combat the influence of the minions – whom he suspected with good reason of working against him – and had recently thwarted William Coffin's plans to marry a rich widow, found some unknown pretext for having Nicholas Carew sent away from court, replacing him with his own protégé, Richard Pace, a humanist and talented linguist who had studied at Oxford, Padua, Ferrara and Bologna before serving as secretary to both Wolsey and Ruthall. However, the Cardinal was disconcerted to hear from Pace, almost immediately, that Carew was back 'by comandment' of the King – 'too soon, after mine opinion'.[31]

Pace remained as the King's Secretary, whilst discreetly looking after Wolsey's interests. Henry was very impressed with him and appointed him at once to 'the third seat on the Privy Council'.[32] In 1519, Pace, who was a friend of Erasmus and More, succeeded Colet as Dean of St

Paul's; three years later his Latin translation of Plutarch's *Moralia* was published in Venice and became a best-seller. However, he had little leisure for study, for Henry kept him busy with correspondence or sent him on diplomatic missions abroad. Pace was a delightful man with a wonderful wit and intellect who was totally dedicated to his work. Henry looked on him as 'his very self', and it was said that, if Wolsey's hopes of being elected Pope were fulfilled, Pace would be the one to take his place.[33]

From Greenwich, Henry went to Eltham, Farnham, Reading and Wallingford. In March 1518, he was at Abingdon with the Suffolks; here he began to relax a little, since 'no man cometh to tell him of the death of any person, as they were wont daily'.[34] However, Wolsey advised him to restrict the numbers attending court at Easter, not only because of the plague, but also because he had heard rumours from abroad that some unnamed noblemen were plotting against the King. Pace wrote to Wolsey to say that 'His Highness doth give unto Your Grace most hearty thanks for your letters touching great personages, and doth right well perceive thereby, and most lovingly accept, the special regard that Your Grace hath to the surety of His Grace's person.'[35]

Taking the Cardinal's advice, Henry ordered his Privy Councillors to stay away. His inherent suspicious streak was aroused, and it may have been at this time that he wrote the undated letter warning the Cardinal to 'make good watch on the Duke of Suffolk, the Duke of Buckingham, my Lord of Northumberland, my Lord of Derby, my Lord of Wiltshire and on others which you think suspect'. The letter was intended for 'none other but you or I'.[36] No details of the supposed conspiracy are known, nor why the King had cause to doubt the loyalty of Suffolk. Northumberland had recently been in trouble for keeping too many liveried retainers, and Buckingham's open resentment of being sidelined by Wolsey was notorious, but the rest seem to have been blameless. Nevertheless, Wolsey remained vigilant.

Henry was all for returning to London, but Katherine warned him against it[37] so, after the St George's Day celebrations, the depleted court moved to Woodstock Palace, eight miles north of Oxford. This large stone house decorated with heraldic emblems had been a favourite royal residence since the early twelfth century. Henry VII had spent a great deal of money modernising Woodstock, while Henry VIII, who was attracted by the excellent hunting in the vicinity, kept it in repair and used it several times as a progress house. It could accommodate the whole court, and Henry could escape with his riding household to the greater privacy of Langley or Ewelme, which were not far off.[38]

Soon, however, there were reports of plague nearby, and the King and Queen hastened to Ewelme, where they were guests of the Suffolks, and thence to Bisham Priory in Berkshire, before moving south to Greenwich, Richmond and Esher.

In August, Henry stayed with Buckingham at Penshurst Place, then went on a hunting progress, lodging with his riding household in the houses of various noblemen. When he was reunited with the Queen at Woodstock, he was delighted to find her pregnant: 'the Queen did meet with His Grace at his chamber door, and showed until him for his welcome home her belly something great, declaring openly that she was quick with child'.[39] With hopes of a male heir revived, and the plague having at last died out, the King now deemed it safe for the court to reassemble in its entirety in London.

25

'The Mother of the King's Son'

In May 1518, Wolsey had been appointed papal legate and given unprecedented authority over the Church of England, even surpassing that of the Archbishop of Canterbury, before whom he now took precedence. Henceforth, two crosses would be borne before him in procession, and it would be said that he was 'the proudest prelate that ever breathed'.[1] It now seemed as if the Cardinal's dream of being elected pope might become reality, but he would still need the backing of the King of France or the Emperor. In order to secure such support, he determined to play an international role. Nothing, it was said, would please him more 'than to be called the arbiter of Christendom'.[2]

That same year, on behalf of Henry VIII, Wolsey negotiated the 'Treaty of Universal and Perpetual Peace' between England, France and the papacy, who by its terms resolved to persuade Maximilian and Charles of Castile to agree to maintaining a unilateral peace in Europe. To cement the concord with France, the Princess Mary was to be betrothed to the Dauphin Francis, Francis I's heir, and Henry and Francis undertook to meet the following year. Henry took the credit for arranging this ambitious alliance, even though Wolsey had done most of the negotiating – to the extent that 'the King himself scarcely knew the state of affairs'[3] – and marked 'his' achievement with a series of lavish celebrations in London, which cost him £9,600 (£2,880,000).

A French embassy, headed by Guillaume Gouffier de Bonnivet, Admiral of France, and comprising eighty fashionably dressed noblemen and their entourages, arrived in England on 25 September. When the King received them in audience, the two-year-old Princess Mary was brought in for their inspection. Catching sight of Dionysio Memmo, she cried, 'Priest! Priest!' in an attempt to make him play for her. The King caught her up in his arms while Memmo obliged, much to her delight.[4]

On 3 October, St Paul's Cathedral was filled with a vast concourse of royalty, nobles and dignitaries as the King and the ambassadors went up to the high altar, signed the Treaty of London and swore to uphold its articles. Wolsey celebrated High Mass, the solemnity being 'too magnificent for description',[5] and Richard Pace delivered 'a good and sufficiently long oration' in Latin, praising his master, who was seated before him in a throne upholstered in cloth of gold.

Afterwards, the King hosted a dinner for the representatives of his new allies in the Bishop's Palace, and in the evening, at York Place, Wolsey gave 'a sumptuous supper, the like of which was never given, either by Cleopatra or Caligula'.[6] When the feasting was over, Henry and his sister Mary led out a troupe of twenty-four masked dancers, among them Suffolk, Neville, Bryan, Carew, Guildford, Henry Norris – a popular newcomer – and the King's mistress Elizabeth Blount:[7] this was the last time she is recorded as appearing in public with Henry, although they were almost certainly sleeping together at this time. After the masque, large bowls brimming with gold coins and dice were brought to the tables so that the company could settle down to some serious gambling. 'Then dancing continued till midnight.'[8]

Two days later, the Princess Mary was formally betrothed to the Dauphin in the Queen's great chamber at Greenwich, in the presence of the King and Queen, Cardinal Wolsey, the Pope's representative Cardinal Lorenzo Campeggio, the ambassadors and the lords and ladies of the court, who were all, reported Giustinian, 'in such rich array that I never saw the like either here or elsewhere'.[9] Mary herself wore a gown of cloth of gold with a black bejewelled hood. Admiral Bonnivet stood proxy for the future bridegroom, while Wolsey lifted Mary up and placed on her tiny finger a great diamond ring that was much too large for her. The little girl asked Bonnivet, 'Are you the Dauphin of France? If you are, I want to kiss you!' – which lightened the solemnity of the occasion. The two Cardinals then blessed her and celebrated Mass 'with every possible ceremony'.[10] At the banquet that followed, the King was served by three dukes – Norfolk, Suffolk and Buckingham (who privately deplored this alliance with France) – and the Marquess of Dorset.[11] The Queen, who was heavily pregnant, retired early, but the festivities continued until 2 a.m.

On 7 October, there was a celebratory joust at Greenwich followed by a grandiose banquet and a pageant in honour of the peace and the betrothal, which featured a lady, a dolphin and the winged horse Pegasus who was to convey the glad tidings to Christendom. That evening, the King wore a long robe of stiff gold brocade lined with ermine; when Admiral Bonnivet admired it, Henry magnanimously threw it off and told him to keep it.[12]

A day or so later, the King took the visiting envoys hunting at

Richmond, after which they rode to Hampton Court, where Wolsey entertained them to a banquet of breathtaking extravagance. Neither expense nor labour was spared to ensure that the French would 'make a glorious report in their country, to the King's honour and that of this realm'.[13] The Cardinal's cooks had been at work 'day and night' to prepare the huge number of dishes that were served in surroundings of awesome splendour, and luxurious accommodation was provided for the guests. The French, it was reported, were overcome, 'rapt into a heavenly paradise'.[14] When they went home, laden with gifts, they left at Henry's court four noble hostages as a pledge for their master's good intentions.

In Bonnivet's suite there had been several 'fresh young gallants',[15] court favourites upon whom Francis I had recently bestowed the title 'Gentilhommes de la Chambre' – Gentlemen of the Chamber. During the festivities, they had been paired with the minions favoured by Henry VIII, who served in the same capacity in the Privy Chamber but had as yet no formal title. Henry, who wished to model his household according 'to the same order and state that the French King's court is at',[16] now hastened to rectify this, and in September 1518 instituted the formal post of Gentleman of the Privy Chamber.[17] He bestowed it upon the influential young men who served him there, 'who enjoyed very great authority in the kingdom' and were 'the very soul of the King'.[18] Wolsey, who controlled the court's other power centre, the Privy Council, could not but be dismayed at the promotion of his rivals, who wielded influence in a sphere to which his jurisdiction did not extend and who enjoyed the special protection of the King. He feared 'they might oust him from the government',[19] and at the first opportunity that presented itself he would bring them down.

Henry's hopes of a son ended once more in disappointment. In November, Queen Katherine bore a daughter, who died before she could be christened. Two months later there was another death, that of Maximilian, which meant that a new Holy Roman Emperor would have to be elected. Henry VIII was one of the candidates, and dispatched Richard Pace to Germany to campaign on his behalf.

In February 1519, the King spent a week as the guest of Sir Nicholas Carew at the latter's manor of Beddington Park, near Croydon in Surrey, a visit for which the local community had been preparing for a year. Carew's house had an imposing great hall with a splendid hammerbeam roof, on which the one at Hampton Court was later said to have been modelled.[20]

Around this time, another minion, Sir William Compton, who for several years had been committing adultery with Buckingham's sister,

Lady Hastings, received the King's permission to propose marriage to the Countess of Salisbury. That lady, however, turned him down, and a year or so later he was prosecuted in an ecclesiastical court for living openly in sin with a married woman.[21]

The King kept St George's Day 1519 at Windsor, 'with great solemnity'. Then he went to Richmond, 'and so to Greenwich, and there stayed all of May'.[22]

While he was there, Wolsey seized his opportunity to purge the Privy Chamber of his rivals. He told the Privy Council that 'young minions' such as Sir Nicholas Carew, Francis Bryan, Sir Edward Neville, Sir John Pechy, Sir Henry Guildford and Sir Edward Poyntz were behaving in a manner that was not commensurate with the dignity and honour of the King. They gave him 'evil counsel', encouraged him to gamble away large sums, were 'too homely with him, and played such light touches with him that they forgot themselves. Which things, although the King, because of his gentle nature, suffered them, [he] neither rebuked nor reproved them.'[23] But that was not all. Recently, during a diplomatic mission to Paris, Neville and Bryan had publicly disgraced themselves, accompanying King Francis as he rode incognito through the streets 'throwing eggs, stones and other foolish trifles at the people'. Back home, 'they were all French in eating, drinking and apparel, and in French vices and brags'; they sneeringly compared the English court with the French, poked fun at older courtiers and household officers and generally comported themselves in a reprehensible manner.[24]

Norfolk, Worcester and Boleyn spoke for the rest of the Councillors when they demanded that the King put a stop to such behaviour, since it reflected badly upon him; Henry must have seen the sense in this, as he agreed without equivocation to do what they asked. He may even have been concerned himself about the over-familiarity that he had himself permitted and even encouraged. Worcester, as Lord Chamberlain, summoned the worst offenders, dismissed them from their posts and ordered them to leave court, 'laying nothing particular to their charge'. Three, including Carew and Neville, were sent to Calais to help with its defences; the rest were told to attend to their official duties in their own counties. 'Which dismissal from court sorely grieved the hearts of these young men', but 'their fall was little mourned among wise men'.[25]

In their place, Wolsey drafted into the Privy Chamber Sir William Kingston, Sir Richard Wingfield, Sir Richard Jerningham and Sir Richard Weston, 'four sad and ancient knights'[26] who were liked by the King and could be relied upon to do the Cardinal's bidding. One young man who was allowed to remain was Henry Norris, once a Page of the

Chamber, now – thanks to Henry's favour – a Gentleman Waiter. Norris, whose elder brother John was an Usher of the Chamber,[27] was a trustworthy, thoughtful and discreet person who would become one of the King's closest intimates.

Wolsey, Norfolk and the other Councillors were gratified to hear that, freed from the influence of his favourites, Henry was resolved to lead a new, more mature, mode of life,[28] paying less attention to revelry and pastimes than to state business.

Buckingham might have made common cause with the minions against Wolsey, but failed to take the initiative. The Howards were glad to see the back of the favourites, but they would have been even more gratified to see the Cardinal cast down from his high place. Aristocratic resentment against Wolsey still festered. Norfolk was the patron of the King's former tutor, John Skelton, who around this time wrote some particularly scurrilous verses attacking Wolsey, accusing him of being ambitious, shameless and vicious, and sneering at his 'greasy genealogy'. One poem was entitled 'Colin Clout', in which all the evils in England are imputed to corrupt clergy; another was the satirical 'Speak, Parrot', and a third read:

> Why come ye not to court?
> To the King's court, or to Hampton Court?
> The King's court should have the precedence,
> But Hampton Court hath the pre-eminence.

Wolsey's wrath was such that he ordered Skelton's arrest, but the poet pre-empted him by seeking sanctuary at Westminster Abbey.

Skelton had never been afraid to speak his mind. Around c1516–19 he wrote the morality play *Magnificence*, his only dramatic work to survive. In it, a king is heavily censured for immoderate indulgence in pleasure, and advised to seek a compromise between ostentation and parsimony. But he is seen to fail because he dismisses his wise minister, Measure, and gives too much power to an extravagant one called Liberty. There was a none too subtle message here for Skelton's former pupil.

Magnificence set the tone for the court drama of the 1520s, in which satire became a popular element. Wolsey himself commissioned such plays and was also the butt of several others, although it is unlikely that these were performed at court while he was in power. Many plays were written on a classical theme, and in 1519 we have the first record of a Latin play – 'a goodly comedy of Plautus' – being acted before the King.[29] Soon afterwards, Wolsey staged a performance of Plautus's *Menaechmi*[30] at York Place.

★

In 1519, the King commissioned Pietro Torrigiano to build him a tomb at Windsor[31] that would suitably reflect the magnificence of his person and achievements. It was to be an enormous monument of white marble and black jasper, a quarter larger than Henry VII's tomb, and crowned with a triumphal arch bearing a statue of the King on horseback and surrounded by 142 lifesize gilt-bronze figures. Torrigiano undertook to complete the work within four years, for the sum of £2,000 (£600,000).

It was in 1519 also that Henry invited the celebrated German mathematician and astronomer, Nicolaus Kratzer, to enter his service. Kratzer was a brilliant man 'brimful of wit',[32] and on good terms with both Erasmus and Albrecht Dürer; More called him 'a great friend of mine', and when Kratzer came to England in 1516 to lecture at Oxford, made him a tutor to his children. He soon came to the notice of Henry VIII, who was fascinated by maths and astronomy and appointed Kratzer his official Astronomer and Horologer, in which latter capacity he designed clocks and sundials. Kratzer remained in Henry's service for the rest of the reign, although he never quite mastered English, telling the King that thirty years was not sufficient time in which to learn it.

Henry had awaited with impatience the outcome of the imperial election, which took place on 28 June 1519. He was being lavishly entertained once more by Buckingham at Penshurst Place when Richard Pace arrived with the news that Charles of Castile had been elected as the Emperor Charles V. Henry, who was playing tennis with the French hostages, received Pace 'lovingly' and took his disappointment well. When Pace told him how much money Charles had spent bribing the electors, the King said he was 'right glad that he had obtained not the same'. He insisted that Pace took supper with him, and, Pace recorded, 'spake of me many better words than I can deserve'.[33]

Henry's preoccupation with the imperial election had caused his meeting with Francis I to be postponed until the following year. In earnest of their good intentions, both monarchs agreed not to shave until they met, and Henry soon had 'a beard which looks like gold'. Queen Katherine, however, so disliked it that she 'daily made him great instance and desired him to put it off for her sake'.[34] Henry capitulated, and a diplomatic incident was neatly averted by Francis's mother, Louise of Savoy, who declared that the love the Kings bore each other was 'not in the beards but in the hearts'.[35]

Katherine clearly still had some influence over Henry, but the six-year age gap was becoming more obvious. Francis I, who had heard reports from ambassadors, referred to Katherine in 1519 as 'old and deformed',[36] while the King, according to Giustinian, was still 'much handsomer than any other sovereign in Christendom, very fair, and his whole frame admirably proportioned. Nature could not have done more for him.'[37]

Nature had in fact done more for Henry than Katherine had been able to do. Around June 1519 Elizabeth Blount bore him a son, 'a goodly man child of beauty like to the father and mother',[38] who was given the name Henry Fitzroy. The birth took place at a house known as Jericho at Blackmore, near Chipping Ongar, in Essex. It had been acquired by the King from the Augustinian Priory of St Laurence, which had been established at Blackmore in c1160; around 1527, the priory was granted by the King to Wolsey.[39] Jericho was a moated house screened by high brick walls; the moat was connected to the River Can, known locally as the River Jordan – hence the house's name. Jericho had already acquired a reputation as being one of the King's secret houses of pleasure, where he went for trysts with Elizabeth or to visit her during her pregnancy, and where 'the King's Highness have his privy chamber and inward lodgings reserved secret, at the pleasure of His Grace, without repair of any great multitude'.[40] Whilst he was there, his courtiers euphemistically referred to him as having 'gone to Jericho'.

Once his son was born, however, Henry, who had perhaps felt that his lack of a male heir was a slur upon his manhood, abandoned all discretion and openly acknowledged him. Wolsey was a godfather at his christening, and was afterwards made responsible for his care. During his earliest years, the child seems to have remained with his mother.

Elizabeth Blount, who was henceforth referred to as 'the mother of the King's son', did not return to court, nor does she appear to have resumed her affair with the King. Instead, Wolsey arranged for her to be speedily married off to one of his wards, a well-to-do young gentleman called Gilbert Tailboys, whose father Lord Kyme, 'an lunatic',[41] was in the custody of the Duke of Norfolk. His estates were being held in trust for his son by the Crown, but lands in Lincolnshire and Somerset were released to Gilbert on his marriage, while Parliament assigned Elizabeth a handsome dowry. The Cardinal's enemies made political capital out of this, accusing him of 'encouraging our young gentlemen to become concubines by the well-marrying of Bessie Blount'.[42]

Tailboys was knighted in 1525 and became the Member of Parliament for Lincoln, as well as its sheriff;[43] the marriage produced three children before his death in 1530. Four years later his widow turned down a marriage proposal from Lord Leonard Grey and wed another royal ward, Edward Fiennes de Clinton, 9th Baron Clinton,[44] who was about fourteen years her junior. She bore him three daughters, and died in 1540.

Wolsey's triumph over the minions was brief. By the autumn of 1519, Henry had overridden his protests and invited most of the dismissed

26

'The Eighth Wonder of the World'

The time was now approaching for Henry's summit meeting with Francis I, for which Wolsey, at the request of both monarchs, was making all the arrangements. The Cardinal, with the assistance of Admiral Sir William Fitzwilliam, the Earl of Worcester as Lord Chamberlain, and the Bishop of Durham as Lord Privy Seal, was overseeing every detail involved in transporting five thousand people across the English Channel. Calais, England's last remaining possession in France, was used as a storehouse and centre of operations. In Paris, England's ambassador, Thomas Boleyn, was entrusted with the diplomatic negotiations.

It was agreed that the meeting would take place six miles from Calais in a place called the Val d'Or (Golden Vale) in the open countryside between the English-held town of Guisnes, where Henry would be based, and the French town of Ardres, where Francis would stay. Guisnes Castle was, however, deemed too small for the requisite display of magnificence, so it was decided that a temporary palace connected by a private gallery to the castle should be erected in the meeting place itself. An army of six thousand labourers and craftsmen was immediately set to work to get the palace and other facilities ready in time.

Built in less than three months, the 'palace of illusions' was one of the lost treasures of Henry's reign; an Italian observer thought that even Leonardo da Vinci could not have improved upon it.[1] Designed on a 328-foot-square quadrangular plan with a gatehouse and battlements, it was built of timber on stone and brick foundations, and was covered with canvas painted to look like brickwork or masonry. The most impressive room was a dining hall with a ceiling of green silk studded with gold roses and a floor covering of patterned taffeta; there was a King's Side, a Queen's Side, a suite for Wolsey and one for Mary Tudor, who was to play a prominent role as Queen Dowager of France; all had spacious chambers decorated with gilt cornices and furnished with gorgeous tapestries, hangings of cloth of gold or silver, or of green and white, Turkey carpets, chairs and beds of estate and buffets laden with plate. The windows were glazed with diamond panes crafted by Galyon Hone, and the chimneys were of stone. There was an exquisite chapel 'painted blue and gold'[2] and hung with cloth of gold and green velvet; on the altar was a great gold crucifix, ten candlesticks and large gold statues of the Twelve Apostles, as well as many holy relics. Inside and out, the palace was skilfully decorated with Tudor roses, antique work and heraldic devices painted by artists such as the King's Serjeant Painter John Browne, More's brother-in-law John Rastell, Clement Armstrong, 'a famous designer of pageants',[3] and Vincenzo Volpe. The pitched canvas roof was painted to look like slates, and many of the ceilings were gilded. The Scots poet, Alexander Barclay, was commissioned to write mottoes and verses to be added to the decorative scheme. The palace had offices for the White Sticks, as well as its own service complex.

The gateway was surmounted by a scallop-shell pediment, the royal arms, two large Tudor roses and a golden statue of Cupid. On the lawn in front of the palace, beside a gilded pillar topped with a statue of Bacchus the god of wine, there was a fountain 'of ancient Roman work' from which flowed white wine, Malmsey wine and claret, which would be free to all comers, day and night.[4] Carved in the stonework was the invitation in archaic French, 'Faicte bonne chere quy vouldra', and chained to the fountain were silver drinking cups.[5]

The most important courtiers were to be accommodated in Guisnes Castle; the rest were supposed to occupy 2,800 gaily coloured tents set up at nearby Balinghem. But there were not enough billets for everyone: some ladies and gentlemen paid local farmers to put them up, while others had no choice but to 'lie in hay and straw'.[6]

In the Val d'Or, Richard Gibson, Master of the King's Halls, Tents and Pavilions, erected magnificent marquees for entertainments and banquets; three, for which the designs survive in the British Museum, were coloured green and white, blue and gold, and red and gold, and all were adorned with the King's badges, beasts and mottoes.[7] Henry himself had his own dining tent of cloth of gold, which housed his privy kitchen. The whole camp was laid out according to the King's wishes.[8]

Enormous quantities of livestock and foodstuffs were purchased, including 2,200 sheep, 1,300 chickens, 800 calves, 340 'beeves', 26 dozen heron, 13 swans, 17 bucks, 9,000 plaice, 7,000 whiting, 700 conger eels, 4 bushels of mustard, mountains of sugar for the subtleties that were to be made to impress the French, and gallons of cream for the King's cakes.[9] The food bill alone came to £8,839 (£2,651,700), of which £440 (£132,000) was spent on spices, while wine and beer cost £7,409 (£2,222,700).[10] A vast round brick bread oven was set up in the Val d'Or, next to cooking tents housing huge cauldrons, with serving tables outside. Some subsidiary kitchens, such as the wafery and pastry, were established in nearby houses. Extra kitchen staff were hired – among them 12 pastry cooks, 12 brewers and 12 bakers – as well as numerous pots, pans and spits, which were supplied by London cooks at a cost of £377 (£113,100).

As well as provisions, many other items had to be shipped abroad, including tapestries, furnishings and everything needful for tournaments: fifteen hundred spears from the Tower arsenal, a thousand Milanese swords, and a great number of highly strung horses. The armourers' steel mill at Greenwich was moved in its entirety to Guisnes, where it was set up alongside four forges for the repair of armour and weapons.

The French, jealously observing the English preparations from Ardres, had no wish to be outdone, but were not prepared to outlay as much money as their rivals. There was no prefabricated palace for the King of France; instead, the French court would be housed near Ardres in a little town of four hundred tents of cloth of gold and silver – the 'Camp du drap d'or'.

The Cardinal made it his job to resolve the numerous disputes that arose and laid down the rules governing matters of precedence and etiquette. It was agreed that, in order to preserve the honour of both nations, neither King would take part in any joust or combat against the other. Even the terrain itself had been flattened so as not to give either side any advantage.

Queen Katherine, naturally, was unhappy when Henry re-grew his beard in Francis's honour, but more so about this new alliance with France, Spain's traditional enemy. She had worked behind the scenes for a rapprochement with her nephew, the new Emperor Charles V,[11] who had agreed to visit England on his way home to Spain after his coronation in Aachen, before Henry left for France.

The King was to take with him to Guisnes a retinue of 3,997 persons, including 114 peers and princes of the Church, among them Wolsey, Warham, Buckingham, Suffolk and Dorset, as well as his Secretary, Richard Pace, 12 chaplains, the staff of the Chapel Royal, among them Robert Fairfax and William Cornish, all his Kings of Arms, heralds and pursuivants, 200 guards, 70 Grooms of the Chamber and 266 household officers, each with his own servants. Queen Katherine's retinue of 1,175 was headed by the Earl of Derby and included the Bishop of Rochester, the Duchess of Buckingham, six countesses, twelve baronesses and all their servants. Mary Boleyn was one of the Queen's attendants.[12]

Wolsey had his own train of 50 gentlemen, 12 chaplains and 237 servants, more than was allowed Buckingham or Warham. In total, 5,172 persons and 2,865 horses were to go to France.[13]

In May 1520, leaving Norfolk and Bishop Foxe (who had briefly come out of retirement) in charge of the government of England, and the Princess Mary keeping royal state at Richmond (where she entertained some Venetian envoys by playing on the virginals), the King and his vast entourage left Greenwich and proceeded through Kent towards Dover, where they would embark for France. They stayed first at Warham's palaces at Charing and Otford, then, on 22 May, at Leeds Castle, before arriving in Canterbury three days later in readiness for the visit of the Emperor. Henry lodged in Archbishop Warham's palace, which had been specially refurbished for the occasion.[14]

On 26 May, the Emperor's ships docked at Dover to a thunderous salute from the English fleet waiting in the straits of Dover. Charles walked ashore beneath a canopy of cloth of gold emblazoned with his badge, the black eagle, to be met by Wolsey, who conducted him to Dover Castle for the night. Informed of his arrival, King Henry arrived in haste the next morning, which was Whitsunday, and greeted Charles as he came downstairs.[15] Then Henry escorted his nephew to Canterbury, where the citizens, who hated the French, gave him a warm welcome.[16]

After the pomp and ceremony of High Mass in Canterbury Cathedral, the King and the Emperor knelt in prayer at the shrine of Thomas Becket and were shown the saint's hair shirt, his broken skull, the sword that had pierced it and other holy relics, which they devoutly kissed. Afterwards, on the marble staircase of the palace, the Emperor was presented to his aunt the Queen, who was robed in ermine-lined cloth of gold with ropes of beautiful pearls around her neck, and who wept with joy at the sight of him.[17] Dinner was a private affair, attended only by the King, the Queen, the Emperor and Mary Tudor, Duchess of Suffolk. The Duke of Suffolk had the honour of presenting the basin for washing the King's hands, Buckingham that of removing it. Later that day, Germaine of Foix, Dowager Queen of Aragon, King Ferdinand's beautiful young widow, arrived in Canterbury with a train of sixty ladies. At a banquet that evening, the three Queens sat with the King and the Emperor at the high table, and there was much merriment. The Spanish Count of Cabra got carried away and 'made love so heartily' to an English lady that he fainted and had to be carried out of the room.[18] Even the elderly Duke of Alva entered into the spirit of the occasion and led the company in some Spanish dancing. Henry danced with his sister Mary, but Charles just sat and watched.

During his visit, the Emperor, who would have preferred Henry to make an alliance with him rather than with his rival Francis, set himself to charm everybody, in particular Cardinal Wolsey, to whom he gave a handsome pension and a promise that, when Pope Leo died, he would help him secure the papacy. The King, who wanted to keep all his options open, agreed to meet with Charles again, on imperial territory at Gravelines, after he had seen the King of France.

After Charles had departed for Sandwich on the Tuesday evening, Henry and his train rode to Dover, where on 31 May they embarked for France in a fleet of twenty-seven ships. The sea was calm, and they arrived at Calais at noon that day.[19] On 3 June, the King set out with his retinue for Guisnes.

The summit meeting between Henry VIII and Francis I later came to be known as the Field of Cloth of Gold, in commemoration of the lavish display made there; some even called it the eighth wonder of the world. It cost Henry an estimated total of £15,000 (£4.5 million), while it took the French ten years to pay for their share of it.

Everyone had been ordered to attend 'in their best manner, apparelled according to their estate and degrees',[20] and Edward Hall thought it impossible to describe 'their rich attire, their sumptuous jewels, their diversities of beauties'. Bishop Fisher, appalled by the extravagance, wrote, 'Never was seen in England such excess of apparelment before.'[21] The courtiers on both sides had nearly ruined themselves buying rich materials and accoutrements, £3,000 (£900,000) being outlaid on jousting clothes alone. King Henry was his usual peacock self, and would appear each day in a series of increasingly spectacular costumes, all described in detail by Hall; for months now the King had been importing great quantities of rich fabrics, including 1,050 yards of velvet. Many lengths of cloth of gold, satin, velvet and damask had been bought for the Queen, and she took with her a variety of headdresses, including a Spanish one that left her long hair hanging loose over one shoulder and drew admiring comments.[22] Mary Tudor invariably appeared 'superbly arrayed', and looked 'scintillating in her saddle'.[23]

On 7 June, the Feast of Corpus Christi, as the cannons boomed simultaneously from Guisnes and Ardres, the two Kings, accompanied by a host of courtiers, rode from their respective headquarters to meet each other.[24] Each side secretly feared that the other would attack it, so they came in battle array. Henry VIII wore cloth of gold and silver, heavily bejewelled, with a feathered black bonnet and his Garter collar; he rode a bay horse hung with gold bells that jangled as it moved, and he was attended by the Yeomen of his Guard; Francis I, in cloth of gold and silver encrusted with gems, and sporting white boots and a black cap, was flanked by his Swiss Guards. At the perimeter of the Val d'Or, the Kings paused, then, to the sound of trumpets and sackbuts, they galloped alone towards each other, doffed their bonnets and embraced whilst still on horseback.[25] After dismounting, they linked arms and entered Francis's sixty-foot-long pavilion of gold damask lined with blue velvet embroidered with fleurs-de-lys and guarded by a statue of St Michael.[26] Here, 'they greeted each other like truly well-intentioned people, and then with evident satisfaction talked together in friendly fashion until evening',[27] sipping hippocras. Outside, their respective retinues were drinking toasts to each other: 'English and French: good friends!'

On 10 June, the King of France arrived on a mule 'to salute the English Queen' at Guisnes, and during the banquet given in his honour was entertained by the choir of the Chapel Royal. Afterwards, when 130 English ladies were presented to him he kissed them all, 'saving four or five that were old and not fair'.[28] Henry, meanwhile, had gone to Ardres to pay his respects to Queen Claude. He appeared 'entirely at ease'; his beard was 'very becoming', but an Italian observer thought him 'rather fat' – although this is not borne out by the waist measurement of his new armour, which was thirty-five inches.[29] At the end of the day, the Kings returned home, meeting one another on the way.[30]

There then followed two weeks of courtesies, feasting, jousting, dancing and 'midsummer games',[31] in which the two courts vied for supremacy. 'Everything resounded with happy voices, but it was possible to observe that not all the English viewed the French with happy minds.' Francis, observing this, half-jokingly commented to Henry, 'I fear the English even when they bring gifts.'[32] 'These sovereigns are not at peace,' commented a Venetian. 'They hate each other cordially.'[33]

Italian observers admired the wealth of gold chains worn by the English, but thought the French more elegant in dress.[34] The English were of the opinion that the dress of the French ladies was too revealing and 'singularly unfit for the chaste',[35] while the Mantuan ambassador thought the English ladies badly dressed and overfond of alcohol.[36] The visitors 'soon began to adapt the [French] mode, by which what they lost in modesty they gained in comeliness'.[37]

Between 11 and 22 June, three hundred contestants took part in the tournaments that were held in the huge tiltyard, which measured 900 feet by 320; the original design had been Henry's, but the Earl of Worcester had tactfully persuaded him to modify it, since, among other flaws, the lists were too far from the viewing gallery.[38] The jousts were organised by Suffolk and Admiral Bonnivet, and the rules of protocol agreed by a committee of English and French knights. Only blunted swords and lances were used, and even the design of the armour had been agreed beforehand by the two Kings.[39]

Two trees of honour thirty-four feet high, bearing Henry's emblem of the hawthorn and Francis's raspberry leaf, were set up on a rise at the end of the lists, and each day the challengers hung their shields on them. Henry insisted that his shield and Francis's be placed on the same level, to demonstrate their equality, and the two monarchs contrived to run the same number of courses – although not against each other – and broke the same number of spears. Their combat was so fast and furious that sparks flew from their armour[40] – the suit worn by Henry is almost certainly that surviving in the Tower Armouries[41] – and on one occasion the King caused the death of his own horse. He himself sprained his hand, while Francis sustained a black eye. One French knight died of wounds received in the lists from his own brother. Many Englishmen, notably Suffolk and Carew, gave gallant performances.

Henry and Francis observed every courtesy towards each other. When an English herald began to read out a proclamation beginning, 'I, Henry, by the Grace of God King of England and France—', using the style that English kings had used since they laid claim to the kingdom of France in the fourteenth century, the King stopped him, saying to Francis, 'I cannot be while you are here, for I would be a liar.' For the duration of the visit, he was to be simply Henry, King of England.[42]

But on 13 June, the old rivalry surfaced. After watching a wrestling match between the Yeomen of the Guard and some Bretons, Henry challenged Francis to a similar contest, and was ignominiously thrown. Honour required that he demand another round, but Francis, at the instance of his courtiers, tactfully refused.[43] Fortunately, Henry scored a victory soon afterwards in an archery contest.

Francis was, however, determined to show the English King that no slight had been intended. He ignored the advice of his lords, who thought he was putting himself at risk of some kind of treachery, and very early on Sunday 17 June, accompanied by only two gentlemen, went to Guisnes, where his brother monarch was still sleeping. Henry woke to see the King of France standing over him, offering to serve as his valet and help him dress. Henry was pleased with this mark of respect, and said, 'Brother, you have played me the best trick ever played, and shown me the trust I should have given you. From now on, I am your prisoner.' He gave Francis a fabulous collar of rubies, and received in return a bracelet worth twice as much.[44] Hurt feelings were thus soothed, and good diplomatic relations restored.

Although it was 'hotter than St Peter's in Rome',[45] the weather caused problems. Strong winds blew dust into faces and over clothing, jousters could not couch lances in the face of the gusts, and some of the tents were blown away, including the French King's vast marquee, forcing him to retreat to Ardres for shelter. Many of the local peasants and beggars got drunk on the free wine and collapsed in heaps by the fountain, and when ten thousand people turned up one day to watch the jousts, both Henry and Francis, fearful of what might happen if they too became inebriated, ordered that persons having no business in the Val d'Or should leave it within six hours, on pain of hanging.[46] Yet still the people kept coming, and the Provost Marshal of the Field was powerless to stop them.

Saturday 23 June saw the final public event. The tiltyard had been converted into a temporary chapel and there, at noon, Wolsey, assisted by five other cardinals and twenty bishops, celebrated a solemn mass before both courts. The choir of the Chapel Royal sang alternately with its French equivalent, La Chapelle de la Musique du Roi, then Richard Pace gave a Latin oration on peace to the congregation. During the service, a firework in the shape of a salamander,[47] Francis I's personal emblem, was accidentally set off, causing a hiatus in the proceedings. Another occurred when Henry and Francis strove to let the other take precedence in kissing the Gospel; similarly, neither Queen wished to be the first to kiss the Pax,[48] so they kissed each other instead.[49]

The two Kings had agreed to found and maintain a chapel to Our Lady of Peace on the site of their meeting, and after the service Wolsey laid its foundation.[50] Afterwards, there was an open-air feast and a final round of barriers, followed by the firework display. The next day saw the Kings visiting each other's Queens again. After a last feast, followed by mumming and dancing, Queen Katherine presented prizes to all those who had excelled in the jousts.

As Erasmus had predicted, very little of political significance was actually achieved at the Field of Cloth of Gold; the chapel to Our Lady of Peace was never built, the temporary palace was dismantled, and within three years England and France were at war again. The whole exercise proved to be little more than a lavish charade. Yet Henry VIII always regarded the meeting as a triumph; he was 'as well pleased with this interview as if he had gained a great realm'.[51] Years later, around 1545,[52] he commissioned, perhaps for Whitehall Palace, two large – and not entirely accurate – paintings of it from artists whose names are lost, but who were probably Flemish.[53] One shows the King's embarkation at Dover; his tiny figure is to be seen in the distance on the deck of his flagship, the *Katherine Pleasaunce*.[54] The other picture gives a composite view of the events, including the King arriving in procession[55] from Guisnes (with Calais in the distance), the meeting between the two sovereigns, a feast in a pavilion, and, in the background, one of the tournaments. Above, in the sky, appears the firework salamander.

After taking their leave of King Francis and Queen Claude on 25 June and exchanging many costly gifts, among them jewels, horses and a litter, Henry and Katherine retired to Calais, where the King thanked his courtiers for attending him and sent half of them home.[56]

On 10 July, Henry and Katherine and their reduced entourages rode to Gravelines, where they met with Charles V and the Regent Margaret. On the following day, they brought them back to Calais, where they planned to entertain them in a temporary banqueting house of canvas painted with heavenly bodies, constructed 'upon the masts of a ship, like a theatre'. Unfortunately the strong winds blew it down, so Henry and his courtiers, resplendent in their masquing gear, went to the Emperor's lodgings instead.[57] The news of these visits left Francis I somewhat uneasy, and he was further disconcerted when on 14 July Henry and Charles signed a treaty agreeing not to make any new alliances with France during the next two years. Shortly afterwards, Henry returned to England.

27

'One Man's Disobedience'

Henry spent the late summer of 1520 on progress mainly in Berkshire and Wiltshire, dividing his time between 'goodly pastimes and continual hunting'.[1] He also visited Woodstock. But he was not in a happy mood because several of the Gentlemen of his Privy Chamber had been sent by Wolsey on diplomatic errands abroad, possibly to get rid of them for a time.[2] Feeling ill-done by, Henry summoned Thomas More, Bishop Ruthal and others to attend him, so that foreign visitors to court 'shall not find him so bare without some nobles and wise personages about him'.[3]

Wolsey, meanwhile, had been keeping a close watch on Buckingham, who, in October 1520, retired from court to his palace at Thornbury. For at least two years now, the King's lack of a male heir had led people to speculate that Buckingham, a descendant of Edward III, might be named his successor, or even attempt to seize the crown for himself.[4] Henry was aware of this and it made him uneasy, hence Wolsey's vigilance. His suspicions were even more aroused when Wolsey obtained information from the Duke's servants that Buckingham was making ill-advised remarks about his proximity to the throne and had predicted that Henry would have no sons and that he himself would be king one day.[5] The Duke had also angered Henry by pressing his claim to the office of Constable of England, which had been held by his father, through the law courts, even in the face of Henry's displeasure. Buckingham's intentions may well have been sinister, but even if they were not, he certainly acted with a dangerous lack of discretion. And given his wealth, vast estates and large affinity, there is no doubt that he appeared to pose a very real threat to the King.

Buckingham seems to have been trying to lull Henry into a sense of false security when, at New Year 1521, he borrowed money from the goldsmith Robert Amadas so as to give the King a wine goblet 'of the best fashion', engraved 'With humble, true heart'.[6]

After Christmas, Queen Katherine journeyed again to Walsingham 'to fulfil a vow',[7] and also perhaps to pray once more for a son. Back at court, the King, hearing that Francis I had suffered a head injury and had to have his hair cut short, decreed that all his male courtiers were to wear their hair cropped in sympathy. Gradually, long hair for men was going out of fashion, but evidence from portraits shows that Henry grew his again, and also that at some stage he shaved off his beard. It was not until c1525 that he adopted the beard that was to remain with him until the end of his life.

During the winter, Buckingham had begun to mobilise troops, ostensibly to protect him when he toured his estates in Wales, where he was not popular, but the King feared he meant to use those troops for an entirely different, treasonable purpose. The Duke was also said to have purchased a large amount of cloth of gold and silver with which to bribe the Yeomen of the Guard. What could not be ignored was evidence that he had sworn to assassinate Henry, just as his father had planned to assassinate Richard III, coming before him with a knife secreted about his person 'so that, when kneeling before the King, he would have risen suddenly and stabbed him'.[8]

In April 1521, Wolsey moved against Buckingham. The Duke was summoned to Windsor but arrested on his way and taken to the Tower, where he was charged with imagining and 'compassing' the death of the King. On 13 May he was tried by a committee of his peers, headed by Norfolk, who, weeping, condemned him to death, the chief evidence against him being the damning testimony of his own officers, who bore grievances against him. Four days later he was beheaded. His execution caused a great stir, and he was 'universally lamented by all London'[9] because it was believed that the Cardinal, out of pure malice, had brought him down.

Skelton, Vergil and many others blamed Wolsey for Buckingham's fall, for it was well known that the two had hated each other. Charles V commented, 'A butcher's dog has killed the finest buck in England.'[10] In fact, Wolsey had advised Henry not to proceed against the Duke; it was the King who was determined to bring down this over-mighty subject,[11] and Buckingham's treacherous stupidity that enabled him to do so. Compton, who had long hated Buckingham, seems also to have been instrumental in bringing him to the block.

Those members of the older nobility who had been allied by blood ties to Buckingham, among them the Countess of Salisbury, whose daughter was married to his son and who was herself perilously near to the throne, lost favour in the aftermath of his execution. Lady Salisbury was dismissed from her post as governess to the Princess Mary, her eldest son Lord Montague spent a brief spell in the Tower, while his younger brothers Geoffrey and Reginald, the latter then a student in Venice, felt the draught of royal displeasure. George Neville, Lord Abergavenny, elder brother of the King's favourite Sir Edward Neville, was no longer welcome at court for a time.

Buckingham's extensive landed property, which was worth about £5,000 (£1.5 million) a year, was forfeited to the Crown. The King divided it up, reserving some for himself and distributing the rest amongst those lords and courtiers whose loyalty he felt he could depend on, among them Norfolk, Dorset, Worcester, the Earl of Northumberland, Sir William Sandys, Sir Thomas Boleyn, Sir Nicholas Carew, Sir Edward Neville, Thomas More, Sir Richard Weston – a member of Henry's Privy Chamber who built the great house known as Sutton Place on his share of the pickings – and Henry's cousin, the Earl of Devon, who had disdained to have much to do with Buckingham; he was elected a Knight of the Garter in his place. The office of Constable of England was allowed to lapse with Buckingham's death, which left the Duke of Norfolk as Earl Marshal supreme as Commander-in-Chief, master of state ceremonial and President of the College of Arms.

The King, who was just then laid low with the first of several bouts of malaria, granted Buckingham's widow a pension for life. At Wolsey's prompting, Henry also wrote letters of condolence to the Duchess and her son, Lord Henry Stafford.[12] Later on, Stafford Castle and some estates nearby were returned to Lord Henry.

Seven of the Duke's houses were considered suitable for the King: Kimbolton Castle in Huntingdonshire, 'a right goodly lodging' built in the fifteenth century but in need of repair; Stafford Castle and Maxstoke Castle, which also required renovation; the newly built manor house at Bletchingley in Surrey, which had a hall, chapel, chamber and a parlour lined with wainscot;[13] Writtle Manor in Essex, three miles from Beaulieu, which would be convenient as a hunting lodge if the moat were cleared of weeds;[14] Thornbury Castle and Penshurst Place. In the end, only Kimbolton, which was leased to Sir Richard Wingfield,[15] Writtle, Bletchingley, which was leased to Sir Nicholas Carew, Thornbury and Penshurst became royal property. Maxstoke was given to Sir William Compton.

The palatial Thornbury Castle in Gloucestershire was only partially built, and would never be completed. Henry used it occasionally as a progress house. Like Richmond Palace, on which it is thought to have been modelled, it had pleasant geometric knot gardens enclosed by covered galleries, an orchard and a rose garden with paths, arbours and aviaries.

Penshurst Place in Kent, a fortified house of sandstone, had been built in 1340–1 by Sir John Pulteney; it had been royal property in the early fifteenth century before being acquired by the Stafford family. It boasted a magnificent beamed great hall which still remains today, along with one of its four original corner towers. A second hall, which no longer survives, was added c1430. Henry retained Penshurst, which was managed by Sir Thomas Boleyn (who lived at nearby Hever Castle), until his death, and may have used it during his affair with Mary Boleyn. It was granted by Edward VI to Sir William Sidney in 1552.

When Henry's fever lifted, he decided to go on pilgrimage to give thanks for his safe recovery. But the Church as Henry knew it was under threat. In 1517, a monk of Wittenberg in Germany, Martin Luther, had nailed to a church door a list of ninety-five theses, attacking ecclesiastical abuses such as the sale of indulgences, and rejecting papal authority, holy relics, pilgrimages, penances and clerical celibacy. Condemned by the Pope, he refused to be silenced, and in 1521, Charles V summoned him to appear before the Diet of Worms, where again he declined to retract his protests. By then, he had attracted a strong following, in Germany in particular, where the controversies he had stirred provoked civil disorder. Luther's heresy was thereafter quickly disseminated through Western Europe, and was recognised as one of the most serious threats yet, not only to the Roman Catholic Church, but to the unity of Christendom as a whole.

What Luther advocated was a more personal kind of faith, in which a man might pray directly to God rather than through intercessors such as the Virgin Mary, the saints and priests. This rendered many priestly functions redundant, along with most of the Sacraments, of which Luther acknowledged only two, baptism and the Eucharist. Even then, he and his followers challenged the doctrine of transubstantiation, asserting that the consecrated Host did not miraculously become the actual body and blood of Christ, but merely symbolised it. Faith alone, rather than ritual and ceremonial, was the foundation of this new religion.

By 1521, Lutheranism – it was not called Protestantism until 1529 – had infiltrated England, where it would take root in fertile ground at universities and also amongst some followers of the New Learning. Heretical tracts and pamphlets were, of course, banned by the authorities, but were secretly circulated anyway, despite the fact that the penalty for heresy was death by burning.

Kings such as Henry VIII could not afford to let heresies such as Luther's take root because they encouraged social divisions, sedition and even revolution, which undermined the very body politic of Church and state. As Henry pointed out, 'By one man's disobedience, many were made sinners.' These new ideas 'robbed princes and prelates of all power and authority'.[16] In the King's opinion, religious doctrine was a matter for those best qualified to understand and interpret it, not for the man in the street. For Henry, egalitarianism was an utterly alien concept and a threat to the established concepts of order and hierarchy in a Christian society.

Both Charles V and Francis I had had special titles bestowed on them by the Pope – Charles was 'the Most Catholic King' and 'Protector of the Holy See', Francis 'the Most Christian King' – and since 1512 Henry had been dropping hints that he would like a title too. Now, alarmed by what he had read of Luther's works, he saw his chance to earn it, and in 1521, at the instance of Wolsey, he wrote a scathing attack on Luther, whom he called 'this weed, this dilapidated, sick and evil-minded sheep'.[17] It took the form of a short but succinct book entitled *Assertio Septem Sacramentorum adversus Martinus Lutherus* ('A Defence of the Seven Sacraments against Martin Luther').

The King had help from Richard Pace, who translated for his master Luther's controversial *De Captivitate Babylonica* (1520) and the subsequent papal bull excommunicating him; Thomas More served as a 'sorter out and placer of the principal matters',[18] and he, John Fisher and others gave practical assistance and advice and the benefit of their knowledge of the Church Fathers. Nevertheless, the book was from first to last the King's own, and he gave the writing of it priority over state affairs and even hunting expeditions.[19]

It was, Henry explained in his introduction, 'the first offspring of his intellect and his little erudition', and he had felt it his duty to write it 'that all might see how he was ready to defend the Church, not only with his armies but with the resources of his mind'.

'What serpent so venomously crept in as he who called the Most Holy See of Rome "Babylon" and the Pope's authority "Tyranny", and turns the name of the Most Holy Bishop of Rome into "Anti-Christ"?' Henry thundered. Thomas More urged him to tone down his polemic, on the grounds that the Pope 'is a prince as you are, and there may grow breach of amity and war between you both. I think it best therefore that his authority be more slenderly touched upon.' But Henry would not listen. 'Nay, that it shall not,' he declared. 'We are so much bounden to the See of Rome that we cannot do too much honour to it.'[20] Years later, he was to have cause to bitterly regret not taking More's advice.

The *Assertio* was completed by May 1521, when Wolsey exhibited a manuscript copy at Paul's Cross, where Luther's works were publicly burned.[21] In July, it was printed, and thirty presentation copies were sent to Rome; one, beautifully bound in cloth of gold, was intended for

Pope Leo, to whom it was dedicated by Henry in his own hand.[22]

The Pope thanked God for raising up such a prince to be the champion of the Church, and expressed astonishment that Henry had found time to write a book, which was a very unusual thing for a king to do. In gratitude, he asked the royal author what title he would like. After some discussion, in which 'Most Orthodox' and, incongruously, 'Angelic' were suggested, Henry chose 'Fidei Defensor' ('Defender of the Faith'), which was conferred on him by papal bull on 11 October 1521.[23]

In England, and abroad, the King's book was a best-seller, going through twenty editions. In February 1522 a papal legation came to England and formally presented the bull to Henry, whose title was proclaimed at Greenwich. The King then went in procession to High Mass as the trumpets sounded a joyous fanfare.[24]

But Luther was not the man to be cowed by a mere King. He responded with a fierce diatribe accusing Henry of raving 'like a strumpet in a tantrum . . . If the King of England arrogates to himself the right to spew out falsehoods, he gives me the right to stuff them back down his throat!'[25] Later, he suggested that the *Assertio* had not been written by the King at all; but Henry replied, 'However much you may pretend to believe that the book is not mine but forged in my name by cunning Sophists, yet many far more worthy of credence than your untrusty witnesses know it to be mine, and I myself acknowledge it.'[26]

He would not stoop to answer Luther's other scurrilous assertions, but delegated the task to More, Fisher and the Queen's confessor, Fray Alfonso de Villa Sancta, who all very ably refuted the reformer's arguments. In 1525, Luther, who mistakenly thought that Henry's attitude had softened, wrote him a long letter of apology, but was humiliatingly rebuffed.[27]

Perhaps in recognition of his assistance with the *Assertio*, Henry knighted Thomas More and appointed him Under-Treasurer of the Exchequer; in 1523, he was chosen as Speaker of the Commons, and in 1525 was made Chancellor of the Duchy of Lancaster. It seemed that Henry could not do enough for him. Sir Thomas, however, had already perceived that there was more to the King than most people realised, and warned Thomas Cromwell, an up-and-coming young man in Wolsey's service, to handle their master with caution, 'for if the lion knew his strength, hard were it to rule him'.

More was now a wealthy man and able to buy a fine house at Chelsea.[28] The King, 'for the pleasure he took in his company', would sometimes arrive there unannounced 'to be merry with him'. Once, he came to dinner, and 'after, in a fair garden of his, walked with him for the space of an hour, holding his arm about his neck'. After Henry had left, Sir Thomas's son-in-law, William Roper, who had married his erudite daughter Margaret, told More 'how happy he was, whom the King had so familiarly entertained, as I had never seen him do to any other except Cardinal Wolsey'. His father-in-law, although touched, replied with asperity, 'Son Roper, I may tell thee that I have no cause to be proud thereof, for if my head could win him a castle in France, it shall not fail to go.'[29] He had no illusions as to the fickleness of the King's favour.

That year, 'no great giests were appointed' for a progress,[30] but the King is known to have visited Oxford. In December, Wolsey acquired yet more offices and wealth when he was appointed Abbot of St Albans, the richest abbey in England. Earlier in the year, Robert Fairfax, the celebrated musician, had been buried there at the King's expense, although his memorial brass is sadly lost. Wolsey's abbacy brought him two substantial properties, The More and Tittenhanger, which he immediately set about refurbishing.

Yet not everything was going Wolsey's way. Henry had veered away from the French alliance the Cardinal had worked so hard to promote, and was negotiating a treaty with the Emperor. Wolsey was nevertheless content to go along with this, because Charles had promised to help make him Pope, and when Leo X died in December 1521, his hopes soared. But they were to be rapidly dashed, for instead of supporting Wolsey, the Emperor put forward his former tutor, who was elected Pope as Adrian VI. When Adrian died two years later, Wolsey was still confident of success, but again Charles failed him: the imperial candidate this time was Giulio de' Medici, who became Pope Clement VII. No one voted for Wolsey. The Cardinal never forgave Charles for his double betrayal, and thereafter became more ardently Francophile than ever.

28

'A Proud Horse Tamed and Bridled'

The Emperor, desperate for an ally, had finally weaned Henry away from Francis I with promises of a joint invasion of France, the partition of any conquests and the recognition of Henry as King of France. The new Anglo-imperial alliance was to be sealed with the betrothal of the twenty-two-year-old Charles to the Princess Mary, now six. On 2 March 1522, the King held jousts in honour of Charles's ambassadors, in which he himself rode a horse trapped in silver caparisons embroidered with a wounded heart and the motto 'Elle mon coeur a navera' ('She has wounded my heart').[1] The lady likeliest to have been the object of such overt yet mysterious symbolism was Mary Boleyn, although given the ramifications of the game of courtly love, it could have been anyone.

Two days later, on the night of Shrove Tuesday, the imperial envoys were Wolsey's guests at York Place, where was staged a pageant of some significance entitled *The Château Vert*. This was a green castle with three towers. On each flew a banner:

> one of three broken hearts, one showing a lady's hand holding a man's heart, the third depicting a lady's hand turning a man's heart. The castle was occupied by ladies with strange names: Beauty, Honour, Perseverance, Kindness, Constancy, Bounty, Mercy and Pity. All eight ladies wore Milan-point lace gowns made of white satin, and each had her name embroidered in gold on her head gear, and Milan bonnets of gold encrusted with jewels. Underneath the fortress were more ladies whose names were Danger, Disdain, Jealousy, Unkindness, Scorn, Sharp Tongue and Strangeness, dressed like Indian women [in black bonnets].
>
> Then eight lords entered, wearing cloth of gold hats and great cloaks made of blue satin. They were named Love, Nobleness,

Youth, Devotion, Loyalty, Pleasure, Gentleness and Liberty. This group, one member of which was the King himself, was led in by the man dressed in crimson satin with burning flames of gold. His name was Ardent Desire, and the ladies were so moved by his appearance that they might have given up the castle, but Scorn and Disdain said they would hold the fort.[2]

There followed the usual mock siege:

The lords ran to the castle, at which point there was a great sound of gunfire, and the ladies defended it with rose water and comfits. The lords replied with dates, oranges and other pleasurable fruits, and eventually the castle was taken. Lady Scorn and her companions fled. Then the lords took the ladies by the hands and led them out as prisoners, bringing them down to floor level and dancing with them, which pleased the foreign guests immensely. When they had danced their fill, everyone unmasked themselves. After this, there was an extravagant banquet.[3]

It was probably William Cornish who produced the pageant and played the role of Ardent Desire:[4] the chronicler Edward Hall makes it very clear that it was not the King. This was Cornish's last major pageant: he died in 1523, and was succeeded as deviser of court revels by John Rightwise, who continued in the same tradition. Rightwise, a clever Latinist, succeeded William Lily that same year as High Master of St Paul's School.

Mary Tudor, Duchess of Suffolk, led the dancers as Beauty; the Countess of Devon played the role of Honour, Mary Boleyn was Kindness, Jane Parker, the daughter of Lord Morley and shortly to be betrothed to Mary's brother George Boleyn, was Constancy, and Anne Boleyn, Mary's younger sister,[5] recently recalled from the French court because of the deteriorating political situation, was Perseverance.

Anne Boleyn was just embarking on her spectacular but ultimately disastrous career, and this was her public debut at the English court. Born around 1501,[6] she had spent her formative years firstly at the brilliant court of Margaret of Austria, then in the household of Mary Tudor during her brief reign as Queen of France, and later as a maid of honour to the pious Queen Claude. At the Burgundian and French courts, Anne had gained a fine education and learned every sophisticated accomplishment (as well perhaps as some more dubious ones), and on her return to England, her father – or possibly her sister's influence – was able to secure her a place in Queen Katherine's household. Anne stood out among the ladies at the English court because she was so French in her manners and style of dress, and therefore at the forefront of fashion.

Anne was then about twenty-one, rather old to be unmarried. For two years now, her father had been negotiating to wed her to Sir James Butler, heir to the Earl of Ormonde, to settle a dispute over the Ormonde inheritance, but the matter was dropped for reasons that are not clear.[7]

Thanks not only to Sir Thomas Boleyn's talents as a diplomat and courtier, but also no doubt to his daughter Mary's occasional occupancy of the royal bed, the Boleyns were in the ascendant and becoming very influential. Sir Thomas, now a wealthy man thanks to the lucrative stewardships that had been heaped upon him, was appointed Comptroller of the Household in 1520[8] and Treasurer of the Household in the autumn of 1522.[9] In 1523, he was made a Knight of the Garter.

Boleyn was succeeded as Comptroller by Sir Henry Guildford, whose vacated office of Master of the Horse was filled by Sir Nicholas Carew. During the decade to come, Carew would often be away from court on embassies to Paris. Still a self-avowed 'reprobate' who 'never read any book of Scriptures'[10] but enjoyed Froissart's *Chronicles*, he was nevertheless highly regarded by Francis I, who on many occasions urged Henry VIII to advance him.

In 1522, Henry appointed a new French Secretary, Bryan Tuke, a former Clerk of the Signet and Secretary to Wolsey. Tuke was a cultivated humanist and correspondent of Erasmus, and a fussy civil servant who liked things to be done the traditional way. As mentioned earlier, in 1532, he wrote an elegant preface to the first printed edition of Chaucer's *Canterbury Tales*.

There was great pageantry when, on 26 May 1522, the Emperor arrived in England on a state visit to mark the signing of the new treaty and his betrothal to the Princess Mary. After being met by Wolsey at Dover, he was conducted to the castle, where later that day the King turned up as if by chance, 'that it might appear to the Emperor that his coming was of his own mind and affection'.[11] Henry could not wait to show off his warship, the *Henry Grâce à Dieu*, and himself escorted Charles around it. The two monarchs were rowed around the harbour in a little boat, and the Emperor marvelled at the well armed English fleet.

The two royal retinues then rode via Canterbury and Rochester to Gravesend, whence they travelled in thirty barges to Greenwich; all the ships in the Thames were 'well garnished with streamers and banners, guns and ordnance', which fired a salute as the Emperor passed by.[12] At Greenwich on 2 June, the Emperor met his intended bride. 'At the hall door, the Queen, Princess and all the ladies received and welcomed him.' He knelt for Katherine's blessing, 'as is the fashion of Spain between aunt and nephew', and expressed 'great joy' at seeing her 'and in especial his young cousin Mary',[13] who gave him a gift of horses and hawks. That evening there was a great dinner, followed by dancing, with the Emperor solemnly leading out his diminutive betrothed. There was not enough accommodation in the palace for Charles's retinue, which numbered two thousand persons and one thousand horses, and many had to be billeted in the nearby houses of courtiers or in local inns.

From Greenwich, Charles made a state entry into London, where the livery and craft guilds and German merchants resident in the City accorded him a lavish welcome, with wonderful pageants – one was devised by John Rastell – and seasonal decorations; the welcoming speech was made by Sir Thomas More. Both the Emperor and the King were presented with finely crafted swords.

Charles and his suite were lodged in the Priory of the Blackfriars next to the nearly completed Bridewell Palace, and in the houses of rich citizens. Extra beds had had to be requisitioned from Richmond and the Tower.[14] The Emperor had brought with him not only the great nobles of his dominions, but doctors, surgeons, an organist, a master cook, a pastry chef and a sauce-maker. Henry provided four tuns of beer each day for his visitors, who were seen to eat heartily of the choice fare on offer.[15]

While in London, Henry took the Emperor to view the Henry VII Chapel in Westminster Abbey and Westminster Hall, during which outing they were mobbed by a crowd desperate to see and touch them. At Bridewell, the two sovereigns played tennis against each other, with William, Prince of Orange and Joachim I, Margrave of Brandenburg. 'They departed even hands on both sides after eleven games.'[16] On 8 June Henry hosted a feast for the Emperor at Bridewell Palace, and on another evening the Suffolks gave a great dinner at Suffolk Place in Southwark.

Henry next took Charles to Richmond for the hunting; then it was on to Hampton Court and Windsor, where on 10 June both monarchs signed their new treaty. During Mass, the Emperor wore his Garter robes and sat in his stall in St George's Chapel; he and Henry both swore on the Blessed Host to remain in perpetual amity, and their pact was sealed by 'great feasting'.[17] That evening, the court gathered in St George's Hall to watch 'a disguising or play' by William Cornish, in which 'a proud horse', representing Francis I, was 'tamed and bridled' by an allegorical figure called Amity. A 'sumptuous masque' and 'costly banquet' followed.[18]

The next few days were given over to the pleasures of the chase, then on 19 June the Emperor and Mary were formally betrothed. On 3 July, Henry and Charles went hunting near Winchester, and afterwards feasted in Winchester Castle beneath the Round Table, which had been repainted in honour of Charles' visit with a prominent Tudor rose in the middle.[19] Two days later they rode to Bishop's Waltham, and on the 6th the Emperor, bearing rich gifts from his host, sailed from Southampton, escorted by thirty of Henry's ships, which were then detailed to reconnoitre along the French coast.

A double portrait of Henry and Charles probably commemorates this visit. They sit at a table where lies a document – the treaty? – and above their heads is a rich canopy of estate. Each holds a sword, and there is a scene in a globe that perhaps portrays Rastell's pageant.[20]

Work had been proceeding rather slowly on the King's tomb, but in 1522, when Henry presumably complained about this or found fault with the workmanship, Pietro Torrigiano's hot temper got the better of him. Henry's wrath was such that the sculptor was obliged to flee back to Florence.[21] His compatriot and colleague, the Florentine Antonio di Nunziato d'Antonio, known as Antonio Toto, a former pupil of Domenico Ghirlandaio, remained in the service of Cardinal Wolsey. Toto, one of the most important Italian artists then working in England, initially carried out decorative work and painted scenery for pageants, but was soon executing religious pictures for Hampton Court. Later he is known to have worked on narrative paintings for the King. Giorgio Vasari, the Italian art historian, says that Toto executed 'numerous works' for Henry, 'some of which were in architecture, more especially the principal palace of that monarch [Whitehall], by whom he was very largely remunerated'.[22] In 1530, Toto was awarded an annuity of £25 (£7,500) per annum for life. Vincenzo Volpe worked as his assistant.

Work on the unfinished tomb was abandoned, and in 1528, Henry had a simple vault made ready for him in the choir of St George's Chapel.

In February 1523, the Princess Mary was seven, and it was considered time for her formal education to begin. Few women were educated at that time – Katherine of Aragon and the daughters of Sir Thomas More were outstanding but rare examples of the bluestocking – but attitudes were beginning to change. 'Erudition in women is a reproach to the idleness of men,' wrote the enlightened More, yet even he, along with most other people, still held that marriage was a woman's highest vocation, and placed great emphasis on his girls acquiring the requisite domestic skills; nor would he allow them to show off their academic talents outside their home.

Influenced by More's example, and also by the fact that Mary might well one day be Queen of England in her own right, the King and Queen were anxious for their daughter to be provided with an excellent classical education in the humanist tradition. In so doing, they set a trend which other learned or aristocratic parents would follow, so that in time the kind of formal education hitherto available only to boys came to be regarded as desirable for girls also.

Mary's first tutor, appointed in 1523, was Henry's physician, the elderly Dr Linacre, who taught her Latin and wrote for her a rudimentary grammar book before dying in October 1524. An eminent Spanish educationist, Juan Luis Vives, was then asked by the Queen to draw up a curriculum for the Princess that would prepare her for her domestic role as a wife and mother, and also for her possible public role as the future Queen of England.

Vives had been invited to England in 1523 by Cardinal Wolsey to become Reader of Rhetoric at Corpus Christi College, Oxford. Queen Katherine knew of him by repute, probably from Sir Thomas More, who had met Vives in Bruges in 1520 and had been very impressed with his ideas. In 1522, the Queen had granted Vives a pension and requested him to dedicate his translation of St Augustine's *City of God* to Henry. In 1524, Vives dedicated his treatise on female education, *De Institutione Foeminae Christianae* ('The Instruction of a Christian Woman'), to Katherine, who had herself commissioned it.

The regime drawn up by Vives was severe and demanding, suitable only for a bright child. Its objective was to inculcate in Mary the highest moral standards, to which end she was to read only the weightiest classical and scholastic authors – Cicero, Seneca, Plutarch, Plato, St Jerome and St Augustine – as well as the works of Erasmus and More, and eschew romances or any 'idle' book that might lead to wanton behaviour, since women, being feeble-minded creatures, were considered easily corruptible. Because silence was valued in the fair sex, Vives disapproved of them being taught rhetoric, and considered theology, philosophy and maths beyond their intellectual capabilities.

The Princess was to share her lessons with a handful of carefully chosen companions. All would be taught Latin, French, some Italian and Greek, grammar, music, traditional dancing, household management and good manners, and were required to read selected passages from the Bible every day. Vives himself appears to have instructed Mary in Latin; all other subjects were taught by the devout and kindly Richard Fetherston, the Queen's former Chaplain, while Katherine regularly read with her daughter and helped with her translations. Like all the Tudors, Mary was gifted with musical ability. She had been taught from a very early age to play the virginals and lute,[23] and her proud father loved to show off her precocious talent.

In May 1523, there were more lavish entertainments when King

Christian II of Denmark visited England with his wife, Isabella of Austria, sister of Charles V. Mary Tudor, Duchess of Suffolk, came to court to help Queen Katherine entertain her niece, and was given precedence over the Danish Queen at table.

That summer saw 'the high and mighty prince, Charles, Duke of Suffolk' dispatched to France with fourteen thousand men to assist Charles V in his bid to conquer French territory. Yet although Suffolk displayed 'courage and forwardness', his forces were defeated by appalling weather conditions. In December, wretched and demoralised, the Duke defied the King's order to stay where he was and returned with his army to England. Henry, hearing at first hand of their misfortunes, decided to overlook his commander-in-chief's disobedience.[24]

Back in England, Anne Boleyn had rashly become romantically involved with Lord Henry Percy, heir to the Earl of Northumberland, who was a member of Wolsey's household and would frequently 'resort for his pastime unto the Queen's chamber, and there would fall in dalliance among the Queen's maidens'. Percy, unfortunately, was already precontracted to Lady Mary Talbot, daughter of the Earl of Shrewsbury and a better match for him than Anne was. Percy had the nerve to ask Wolsey if his betrothal could be broken, but received a dressing-down for his temerity. The Cardinal sent at once for his father, who hauled his ungrateful son back up north and made immediate arrangements for his marriage to take place.

George Cavendish, who relates this tale, asserts that Wolsey had acted on the orders of the King himself, who cherished a secret desire for Anne Boleyn. There is no other evidence of Henry pursuing her before February 1526, and a furious Anne was sent home from court in disgrace after the Percy affair, vowing to be revenged on Wolsey. Had Henry been so keen on her, he would surely not have allowed her to leave court. Furthermore, in Henry's first letters to Anne, which date from c1527, he refers to having been in love with her for just over a year.

During 1523, the King was much occupied with improving or acquiring property. He spent £500 (£150,000) on works at Greenwich, improving Henry VII's riverside lodgings and enlarging the gardens. He acquired Parlaunt Manor, Gloucestershire, on the death without heirs of its owner, Sir Edward Stanley, and converted it into a keeper's lodge. In 1524, he bought the fifteenth-century hilltop castle at Ampthill, Bedfordshire, which had a fine great hall leading off a central courtyard, and several stone towers. Ampthill was renowned for its 'marvellous good health and clean air'[25] and excellent deer park, and Henry used it fairly frequently as a progress house. Between 1533 and 1547, he built extensive new royal apartments there.[26]

29

'All the Enemies of England Are Gone!'

In March 1524, Henry ordered from the Greenwich workshops 'a new harness made of his own device and fashion'. Eager to try it out, he arranged a tournament in which Suffolk was to be his chief opponent, but when they entered the lists, Henry forgot to lower his visor, and as the two charged towards each other, alarmed spectators screamed 'Hold! Hold!', for Suffolk's lance was pointed at the King's exposed face. But the Duke, who was wearing a heavy helmet, could not see or hear much; it was a miracle that, as he crashed into Henry, his lance 'struck the King on the brow right under the guard of the headpiece on the very skull cap or basinet piece to which the barbette [visor] is hinged for safety. The Duke's spear broke into splinters and pushed the King's visor so far back that all the King's headpiece was full of splinters.' Henry emerged apparently unscathed, but Suffolk was badly shaken, and swore never again to run against his sovereign. Henry reassured him that 'none was to blame but himself' and then ran six more courses just to prove that he had taken no hurt, 'which was a great joy and comfort to all his subjects present'.[1] It has been suggested, however, that the headaches from which he suffered in later life resulted from the blow to the forehead that he sustained in this accident.

The King had come literally within an inch of losing his life, and both he and his contemporaries were fearfully aware that, with no son to succeed him, England had come perilously near to civil war. For there were those who might well dispute the right of a mere girl to succeed, as well as several noblemen with Plantagenet blood who might attempt to enforce their claims to the throne.

Henry and his advisers were becoming increasingly preoccupied with the problem of the succession. It was five years since the Queen's last pregnancy and Katherine, at thirty-eight, was now going through the menopause. Since 1522, prompted by doubts raised by his confessor,

John Longland, Bishop of Lincoln, Henry had been questioning the validity of his marriage. The biblical Book of Leviticus warned that a man who incestuously married his brother's wife would be punished with childlessness, and although Pope Julius II had granted a dispensation for his marriage to Katherine, the King had begun to see his lack of sons as a judgement on him for offending God. Yet for the moment he did nothing: the Queen was much loved by his subjects, and was a virtuous woman for whom he had a deep affection; above all Henry did not wish to prejudice the imperial alliance by putting away the Emperor's own aunt.

In private, however, the King and Queen were drifting apart. In 1531 Henry claimed that, by the spring of 1525, when Katherine's periods finally ceased, although he occasionally shared a bed with her for form's sake, he had stopped having sexual relations with her, apparently because she had a gynaecological condition that repelled him.[2] However, in 1528, when he was still sleeping with the Queen, he had told Cardinal Campeggio that he had not had intercourse with her for two years.[3]

The age gap between the royal couple was never more obvious. Katherine, who had long since lost the prettiness of her youth and was now a dumpy, middle-aged matron, increasingly sought solace in the company of her daughter and her religious observances. Once, returning to Richmond with Vives by barge from Syon Abbey, whither she had gone to pray, the Queen expressed a desire for a more tranquil life than the one she now led. If she had to choose between extreme adversity and the great prosperity which she now enjoyed, she declared, she would prefer the former, since 'real loss of spiritual integrity usually visited the prosperous'.[4] Yet when called upon in the future to make such a choice, her response would be quite different.

Henry celebrated St George's Day, 1524 at Beaulieu. The following month, he found himself mourning the death of one of his most eminent Councillors, the Duke of Norfolk, who had passed away at his castle of Framlingham in Suffolk. Henry had last seen Norfolk the previous year, when they had had a brief but obviously affectionate conversation. The office of Earl Marshal had been granted to Norfolk for life only, and Henry wasted no time in conferring it upon Suffolk, something that would always rankle with the new Duke of Norfolk, another Thomas Howard, who had succeeded his father as Lord Treasurer in 1522 and served as Lord High Admiral until 1525. He was now fifty-two.

The 3rd Duke of Norfolk was short, spare and black-haired,[5] and a dour, pragmatic, sometimes brutal man whose portrait by Holbein[6] shows a face like granite with thin lips and a high-bridged, aristocratic nose. A martyr to rheumatism and indigestion, he was constantly grumbling or sighing, but he was an efficient and often ruthless military commander, and an able and polished courtier who could be liberal and affable but who had a nose for danger and a talent for survival. The guiding factor of his life was self-interest.

Now that Buckingham was dead, Norfolk regarded himself as the chief representative of the older nobility at court, and had little time for the 'new men', a term he himself coined. 'A prince may make a noble-man but not a gentleman,' he once said.[7] He was fiercely anticlerical, and hated Wolsey, which made him Suffolk's natural ally; in 1525, they joined forces in an unsuccessful attempt to bring down the Cardinal on the issue of taxation.[8] The Duke was confident, unscrupulous and, as a leading member of the Privy Council, one of the King's most powerful and willing henchmen.

Norfolk was typical of his caste in that he despised book learning, loved hunting and was energetic in the administration of his landed interests in East Anglia. He was a connoisseur of jewellery, loved ceremonial and pageantry, and was zealous for the advancement of his family. In 1525, he rebuilt his father's old manor of Kenninghall in Norfolk as a fine palace with two courts in chequered brickwork. Here he lived in great state in luxuriously appointed rooms above the chapel.[9] His tastes were rather modern for such a reactionary, for he favoured the antique and the classical in art and architecture.

Norfolk was closely related to the Boleyns, with whom he also made common cause; his sister Elizabeth was married to Sir Thomas. Their son George, who was probably no more than twenty-two at this time, was now to share in his family's advancement. This talented young man had first been brought to court by his father in 1514, when he took part in a mummery. Later he had begun his career as one of the King's Pages.[10] He was very good-looking[11] and very promiscuous. In fact, according to George Cavendish, he lived in a 'bestial' fashion, forcing widows, deflowering virgins, and apparently not even stopping at rape but taking women at will. At the end of his life, he refused to elaborate on his terrible sins because he did not wish to tempt anyone to imitate him.[12] It has been suggested that he indulged in homosexual activity too, but there is no evidence for this, although he may well have committed buggery with female partners.

Boleyn's other fault was his overweening pride, but for which – according to the poet Sir Thomas Wyatt – he would have been very popular, for he was both intelligent and witty. He was a respected poet, could compose ballads and, like his father, spoke fluent French.

Around 1524–5, George Boleyn married Jane Parker, the daughter of the erudite scholar Henry, Lord Morley, a distant cousin of the King through the Beauforts, and the translator of Petrarch. Morley, who resided at Hallingbury Place in Essex, was a Gentleman Usher of the Privy Chamber and a member of Katherine of Aragon's intellectual circle. He had been unable to meet Sir Thomas Boleyn's demand for a dowry of £300 (£90,000), but the King generously made up the shortfall.[13] He also granted George the manor of Grimston in Norfolk, perhaps as a wedding gift.[14]

At Christmas 1524 Henry, who was now thirty-three, took part for the last time in a major tournament. It was to have formed part of a great pageant, *The Castle of Loyalty*, and a castle twenty feet square and fifty high was built to the King's design in the tiltyard at Greenwich, 'but the carpenters were so dull they understood not his intent, and wrought all thing contrary'. With the structure evidently not stable enough to withstand an assault, the pageant was abandoned, but the jousts went ahead. With echoes of happier times, it began with the Queen seating herself in the model castle; there then came before her 'two ancient knights' who 'craved her leave to break spears'. When Katherine praised their courage in performing feats of chivalry at their advanced age, they threw off their disguises to reveal the King and Suffolk.[15]

A battle of a far more spectacular nature was about to take place in Italy. In February 1525, the Emperor inflicted a humiliating defeat on Francis I at the Battle of Pavia, and took him prisoner. The troublesome Yorkist pretender, Richard de la Pole, fighting for the French, was slain in battle. When a messenger brought Henry the news, the King exclaimed, 'All the enemies of England are gone!' He told the man he was as welcome as the Archangel Gabriel had been to the Virgin Mary, and ordered that bonfires be lit in the streets of London and free wine be distributed to the citizens. In March, the King went in state to St Paul's to give thanks for the Emperor's victory. Later, he commissioned a painting of the Battle of Pavia to remind him of this great triumph.

Henry might have gloated over the capture of King Francis, but he was still in thrall to French Renaissance culture and determined to rival it. In the autumn of 1526, Francis's sister, Marguerite of Valois, sent Henry three framed portrait miniatures of Francis I and his sons by Jean Clouet, the French court painter.[16] These were the first examples seen in England of the new art form called 'limning' – the word 'miniature' was not used until the seventeenth century – and they immediately set a trend at the Tudor court.

The art of miniature painting had its origins in the intricate illustrations in illuminated manuscripts, for which similar techniques had been used, and also in Italian portrait medals. Circular miniature portraits had themselves appeared in manuscripts and on official documents, but now they became popular in their own right. They were usually mounted on stiff card, painted in vivid colours against a blue background with gold lettering, and set in a frame or box, perhaps fashioned from gold or ivory. They were very expensive and therefore relatively rare and much prized.

Many of the manuscripts from which limning derived were produced in Ghent and Bruges. The most celebrated illuminators came from a family called Horenbout (a name sometimes anglicised to Hornebolte in official documents), who had been established in Ghent since 1414 and had recently worked for Margaret of Austria. Around 1524,[17] three of its members – father, son and daughter – arrived in England, probably by royal invitation. The head of the family was Gerard Horenbout, a friend of Albrecht Dürer; Gerard had been court painter to the Regent Margaret, who commissioned him to replace the missing miniatures in the famous *Sforza Book of Hours*.[18] In England, he illustrated manuscripts for Wolsey, and married one Margaret Saunders, who died in 1529.[19] From c1528 to 1532, when he disappears from English records, Gerard worked for the King in the court scriptorium before returning to Ghent, where he died in 1540.

His daughter, Susanna Horenbout, born in 1503, was also an artist, and is said to have painted miniatures, although none can now be identified. Her work must have been good because Dürer had admired it when she was just eighteen. Her connection with the court is proved by her marriages to two of its offices – John Parker, Yeoman of the Robes, and John Gylmyn, Serjeant of the Woodyard – and she remained in England until her death in 1545. There is, however, no certain evidence of her artistic activities in England, and the royal accounts do not record any separate payments to her.

Gerard's son, Lucas Horenbout, had been born around 1490/5 and trained in his father's workshop. In 1512, he had become a member of the Painters' Guild at Ghent. In September 1525, Lucas's name first appears in the royal accounts, when he was awarded a generous life pension of £33.6s. (£9,990) a year,[20] proof of the King's high regard for his talent. Lucas Horenbout was the first major portrait painter of the reign, the artist responsible for developing and popularising the art of limning in England, and in so doing setting a fashionable trend that would endure for centuries.

The King, impressed with Lucas's work as an illuminator, appears to have commissioned him to paint miniatures in the style of Clouet, which Horenbout executed with skill and delicacy. In 1527, Henry was able to reciprocate Marguerite's gesture of the previous year and send her limnings of himself[21] and his daughter Mary, which were probably by Horenbout.[22] In 1528, Lucas was promoted to 'King's Painter'.

Until comparatively recently, Lucas Horenbout's work received little recognition; now, at least seventeen important miniatures, dating chiefly from 1526–35, have been identified as his: there are five portraits of Henry VIII,[23] three of Katherine of Aragon,[24] two probably incorrectly identified as Anne Boleyn (which will be discussed later),[25] and single studies of the Duke of Suffolk,[26] the Princess Mary,[27] Charles V,[28] Henry Fitzroy,[29] Jane Seymour,[30] Prince Edward[31] and Katherine Parr.[32] It has also been suggested that the portrait of Margaret Pole[33] from the so-called 'cast shadow' workshop might be by Horenbout, and that thirteen other full-size portraits from this atelier, of lesser workmanship – with sitters including Henry V, Edward IV, Henry VIII, Jane Seymour and Prince Edward – are from his studio. Horenbout is also said to have painted a portrait of William Carey, husband of Mary Boleyn.[34]

Little is known of Henry VIII's miniature collection. Like his daughter Elizabeth I, he probably kept it in his privy lodgings. The King used miniatures as diplomatic tools – one was to play a grossly overinflated role in his courtship of Anne of Cleves – and he gave them to his courtiers as marks of high favour. The one of himself that he later gave to Jane Seymour was hung round her neck on a chain, all too visible to her jealous mistress, Anne Boleyn, who ripped it off in anger.

In 1525, Henry's most famous fool, Will Somers, entered his service. Lean and 'hollow-eyed' with a stoop, this Shropshire-born comedian is said to have come to the attention of Richard Fermour, a merchant of the Staple at Calais, who brought him to Greenwich to be presented to the King. Henry, immediately won over by Somers' wicked sense of humour, offered him a place at court. An instant rapport was struck up between the two men, and soon it was being said that 'in all the court few men were more beloved than this fool', who for the next twenty years would rule the King with his merry prattle[35] and be the constant companion of his leisure hours.

Somers was very much in demand. He had monarch and courtiers in fits of laughter as he thrust his comical face through a gap in the arras; then, with his monkey on his shoulder, he would mince around the room, rolling his eyes. The monkey might perform tricks, and Somers would tell jokes, himself laughing uncontrollably at the punchlines, or mercilessly impersonating those who were the butts of his jests. He is also believed to have appeared in the ram's-horn helmet presented to Henry by Maximilian, which was for a long time traditionally associated with him. Yet Somers never sought to capitalise on his friendship with the King, kept well in the background when not performing, and preserved his privacy.

30

'Next in Rank to His Majesty'

If Will Somers had dared, he could probably have made his audience see the comic aspects of an accident that befell the King in 1525, but in fact this was no laughing matter for, once again, Henry was nearly killed. When he was 'following of his hawk' near Hitchin in Hertfordshire, he tried to pole-vault over a ditch, but the pole snapped and he landed head first in the muddy water. Stuck fast in the clay, he would have drowned had it not been for a footman, Edmund Mody, who leapt into the stream and hauled him out.[1] This accident, like the one in the tiltyard a year before, might have accounted for the headaches he suffered later on, but its immediate effect was to bring home to the King, more forcibly than ever, the fact that the problem of the succession must be solved as a matter of urgency.

It was now known that the Queen would never bear him a son, but of course Henry already had a son, his bastard Henry Fitzroy, and it was at this time that he seriously began to consider making him his heir. Although bastardy was then a serious bar to inheritance, such children could be legitimated in certain circumstances. The first step was to bring the boy, now six and living in Durham House on the Strand, into the public eye and gauge whether or not he would be acceptable to the people.

At a chapter meeting of the Knights of the Garter on 23 April, Fitzroy was elected to the Order; he was solemnly installed on 7 June in St George's Chapel at Windsor, and given the second stall on the Sovereign's side. The Queen, who had long been aware of his existence and seems to have held no personal rancour towards the little boy, watched the ceremony from her closet above Edward IV's chantry. Then on 18 June, in the first multiple peerage creations since 1514, Henry elevated his son to the high dignity of Duke of Richmond and Somerset and Earl of Nottingham. The earldom of Richmond had been held by Henry VII prior to his accession, and the title Duke of Somerset had been bestowed by that King on his youngest son, Edmund, who had died aged fifteen months in 1500; prior to that it had been held by the Beauforts. These royal titles did not denote an heir to the throne, yet they underlined the new Duke's high status and royal blood. His coat of arms was designed by the King himself.

On the same day, the King's nephew, Henry Brandon, was created Earl of Lincoln; Henry Courtenay, Earl of Devon, was created Marquess of Exeter; Henry, Lord Clifford, became Earl of Cumberland;[2] Thomas Manners, Lord Roos, was created Earl of Rutland;[3] and Sir Thomas Boleyn, now one of the King's most influential advisers, was created Lord Rochford. The investiture of the new peers took place in the presence chamber at Bridewell Palace, where the King stood under his cloth of estate attended by Cardinal Wolsey, the Dukes of Norfolk and Suffolk, and the Earls of Arundel and Oxford. The room was packed with courtiers and it was intolerably hot. Henry Fitzroy entered first, to a fanfare, knelt before his father, and was clothed in the crimson and blue mantle, sword, cap of estate and coronet of a duke, as the patent of creation was read out. Then he took his place beside the King on the dais, taking precedence over every other peer in the room.[4]

The message was loud and clear. 'He is now next in rank to His Majesty, and might yet be easily by the King's means exalted to higher things,' observed a Venetian envoy.[5] But the Queen took great exception to the boy's promotion, seeing it as a threat to the position of her daughter, the Princess Mary.[6] The new Lord Rochford was not very happy either, for he had been forced, on advancement to the peerage, to resign his office of Lord Treasurer to Sir William Fitzwilliam without any financial compensation, for which he blamed Wolsey.

Henry Courtenay, the new Marquess of Exeter, was riding high in the King's favour. At this time he was appointed to serve as a nobleman in the Privy Chamber,[7] and made Constable of Windsor Castle and High Steward of the Duchy of Cornwall. A rich man with vast estates in the west, he lived in considerable splendour chiefly at Horsley in Surrey and at his London house, The Red Rose. His wife was Gertrude Blount, daughter of the humanist Lord Mountjoy, the Queen's Chamberlain. Gertrude, who was half Spanish, was one of the Queen's ladies, and very dear to her.

Wolsey's dominance was still unchallenged, yet his enemies were growing ever more powerful, which left him no choice but to take account of their opinions. Although he still relied heavily on Wolsey, it is possible that the King, now a mature man with a changing outlook, was beginning to look askance at the Cardinal's wealth. In June 1525, Wolsey made the grand – and politic – gesture of presenting to Henry his newly completed palace of Hampton Court with all its contents,[8] receiving in exchange Richmond Palace, which was nowhere near as big or magnificent. Apparently the King, seeing that the lodgings Wolsey had built for him at Hampton Court were far better than any in his own palaces, had dropped a few heavy hints.[9] The Cardinal, however, was still allowed to make use of Hampton Court on occasions, especially for official entertaining.

Wolsey just then had his mind on other matters. He had commissioned an imposing tomb for himself from the Italian sculptor Benedetto di Rovezzano, which was to be erected in the small chapel built by Henry VII to house the tomb of the canonised Henry VI,[10] to the east of St George's Chapel, Windsor. But Henry VI had not achieved sainthood, and Henry VIII's tomb, which was to have been built there instead, had never been finished, as noted earlier. In 1524, Henry had made the empty chapel available to Wolsey for his own tomb, which was planned to reflect the Cardinal's status and fame.

In 1525, Wolsey's foundation at Oxford, Cardinal College, opened its doors to students. Housed in splendid buildings built by master masons who had worked for the King, it was richly endowed by Wolsey from the proceeds of dissolved religious houses. The Master of the Choristers was the eminent musician and composer John Taverner, whose services were so highly valued by the Cardinal that he was to escape punishment when convicted of heresy in 1528. The Queen had taken an interest in the new college – in January Dr John Longland, the Bishop of Lincoln, had briefed her at length on its aims and functions and told her 'how it would draw students from all over England and how students and masters alike would remember to pray for her welfare'.[11]

But Katherine was no friend of Wolsey and he knew it. She blamed him for the advancement of Fitzroy. In June 1525, his spies in her household reported to him that three of her Spanish ladies were encouraging her to make a fuss about the boy's recent elevation. The Cardinal immediately had them dismissed, and when the Queen asked the King to rescind the order, he refused. Katherine, who was 'obliged to submit and have patience',[12] was thus made painfully aware of her isolated position. Nearly forty, no longer in the best of health and unable to trust her own servants, she knew that her wishes no longer counted with her husband.

To make matters worse, the Emperor had jilted her daughter. Offered the chance of marrying the beautiful Isabella of Portugal, who brought with her a dowry of £1 million, he had decided that it was not worth waiting for Mary to grow up. A coolness had naturally developed between Henry and his former ally, and Katherine's dream of a Spanish marriage for Mary seemed unlikely now to be fulfilled.

The child who was the innocent cause of her trouble was soon to be removed from the Queen's orbit. The summer of 1525 witnessed the worst outbreak of bubonic plague for ten years; in London, fifty people a day perished, and the King removed as usual to safe houses. In July, the young Duke of Richmond, who was that month appointed Lord High Admiral, Warden General of the Northern Marches and Lord Lieutenant of England with command of all military operations north of the Trent (the last two offices having been held by Henry VIII before his accession), was sent north to Yorkshire, where his quasi-royal household was established in Sheriff Hutton Castle.[13] This property had recently been granted to him along with eighty other manors scattered throughout England, which yielded a total annual income of £4,000 (£1,200,000).[14] Sheriff Hutton had been the residence of Richmond's grandmother, Elizabeth of York, before her marriage to Henry VII, and the young Duke was housed in the luxurious domestic range. His chapel was furnished at the expense of his godfather, Wolsey.[15]

His princely household comprised 245 persons, who wore his livery of blue and yellow, and was maintained by his father at an annual cost of £3,200 (£960,000). Its Master was Thomas Magnus, Archdeacon of the East Riding, who had been England's ambassador in Scotland. Sir Edward Seymour was Master of the Horse;[16] this young gentleman came from an old-established Wiltshire family. His father, Sir John Seymour, 'a gentle, courteous man',[17] was a favoured courtier of the King, whom he had attended to France in 1513 and again to the Field of Cloth of Gold in 1520; he had also been present at Canterbury during the Emperor's visit in 1522. His wife, Margaret Wentworth, to whom John Skelton had once addressed a poem, was descended from Edward III. Edward, one of their ten children, had been page to Mary Tudor when she was Queen of France, then transferred to Wolsey's service. A brave and able soldier, he had been knighted by Suffolk during the French campaign of 1523, and the following year was made an Esquire of the Body to the King. He was therefore admirably qualified for service to the young Duke.

It was not unusual for princes to advance their bastards, but there was little doubt that this boy was being groomed for kingship. He was 'well brought up like a prince's child' and kept 'the state of a great prince'.[18] He held court from a rich chair of cloth of gold set under a canopy of estate, and was addressed as royalty. Whilst in Yorkshire, he was the nominal President of the former Council of the North, now renamed the Council of the Duke of Richmond, although the actual responsibility devolved upon Thomas Magnus. Furthermore, Henry was considering marrying Richmond to a Portuguese princess.

The young Duke was also to receive a princely education. Richard Croke, an eminent classical scholar from St John's College, Cambridge – who had once given Henry lessons in Greek – was appointed his tutor, for it was the King's desire that the boy should benefit from the New Learning.

Henry cherished his son 'like his own soul', referring to him as 'my worldly jewel',[19] and the evidence suggests that Richmond loved and revered his father. The two corresponded regularly, and Henry sent gifts, among them a lute: the boy had inherited the Tudor talent for music. Richmond also wrote regularly to Wolsey, and once told him, 'I have written unto the King's Highness, making my most humble intercession for an harness to exercise myself in arms.' The letter, signed 'Harry Richmond', was perhaps written in the hope that his godfather might put in a good word for him. In his letter requesting the harness, which was addressed to 'my most dread and sovereign lord', Richmond implied that Julius Caesar would have smiled upon his request. He also stressed to Henry that 'I give my whole endeavour, mind and study to the diligent appliance of all sciences and feats of learning', and ended as usual by craving the paternal blessing.[20] History does not record whether or not he got his harness, but it seems likely that he did.

Given the Queen's dissatisfaction with his treatment of his son, Henry could do no less than provide a similar establishment for his daughter, although for Katherine this proved a mixed blessing, for it took Mary away from her. In August 1525 the Princess was sent to Ludlow Castle on the Welsh Marches, in the care of Lady Salisbury, who had regained the King's favour and been restored to her place as Lady Governess. Mary's tutor, Dr Fetherston, was among the 304 members of the Princess's household who accompanied her, many sporting her livery of blue and green.[21]

Katherine missed her child dreadfully, but kept in touch by letter, trying to be positive about the separation for Mary's sake: 'As to your writing in Latin, I am glad that you shall change from me to Master Fetherston, for that shall do you much good to learn from him to write right.'[22]

Like Richmond, Mary was to learn the art of government; in her case, she was to nominally preside over the Council of the Marches, as two Princes of Wales had done before her: Edward V and Arthur Tudor. Lady Salisbury saw that the Queen's instructions regarding her daughter's upbringing were obeyed to the letter: she was to have plenty of fresh air, 'moderate exercise', good, pure food 'served with comfortable, joyous and merry communication' and everything about her was to be 'sweet, clean and wholesome'. As well as attending to her lessons, the Princess was to have time for practising her music and dancing.[23] If she became ill, her new physician, Dr William Butts, would attend her. This Norfolk gentleman, now forty and an eminent humanist scholar, had studied at Cambridge, qualified as a doctor in 1518, and been appointed the principal of St Mary's Hostel at Cambridge in 1524. Butts wore Mary's livery and was assigned two servants and an apothecary.[24] His wife, Margaret Bacon, was also a member of the Princess's household.[25]

Mary rarely resided at Ludlow, which was the official seat of the Council of the Marches, but at the manor house of Tickenhill which stood on a hill overlooking nearby Bewdley; this was where her mother had lodged with Prince Arthur during the months before his death in 1502. The original thirteenth-century house had been updated and enlarged by Edward IV in 1473–4 for his son, the future Edward V, and further extended by Henry VII in 1490; it was put into repair and refurbished in time for Mary's arrival. Tickenhill was a timber-framed building with brick chimneys, solid oak beams and a great hall.[26]

Around this time, the King acquired another house, which would one day become one of Mary's favourite residences. Fifteenth-century Hunsdon Manor in Hertfordshire was purchased from the Duke of Norfolk as a place of retreat from the plague because of its 'wholesome air'.[27] During the next nine years, Henry would spend £2,900 (£870,000) improving it, creating a moat, building royal lodgings with heraldic windows by Galyon Hone, and partly refacing the house in brick.[28] A view of Hunsdon as it appeared in 1546 is depicted in the background of a portrait of the future Edward VI, now at Windsor.[29]

31

'The Establishment of Good Order'

Because the plague was still rampant in London, Henry did not observe the usual Yuletide festivities at the end of 1525, but spent what became known as the 'still Christmas' quietly and fearfully at Eltham with very few courtiers in attendance; no one was allowed to 'come thither but such as were appointed by name'.[1] At Richmond, however, Wolsey, well supplied with the oranges that were said to ward off infection, 'kept open household to lords, ladies and all others that would come, with plays and disguisings in most royal manner'.[2] Mary remained safe at Ludlow, far from the pestilence.

The threat of plague lasted right into the summer of 1526, and carried off at least two members of Henry's entourage. After Christmas, Wolsey joined the King at Eltham, where together they drew up the famous Eltham Ordinances, 'Articles devised by the King's Highness, with the advice of his Council, for the establishment of good order and reformation of sundry errors and misuses in his most honourable Household and Chamber'.[3] These Ordinances were aimed at reforming the royal household, saving money and eliminating waste. As far back as 1519, probably when he was feeling virtuous in the wake of the minions' expulsion, Henry had communicated to Wolsey his pleasure that his entire household 'be put in honourable, substantial and profitable order without any further delay',[4] but, as with many of his ideas, nothing had been done. Now, prompted by a looming financial crisis caused by the ruinous cost of the war with France, the King and the Cardinal had no choice but to implement drastic changes.

Servants surplus to requirements were pensioned off, and hangers-on summarily ejected; the Yeomen of the Guard were reduced to a hundred, and their court duties shared with the Gentlemen Pensioners, who were now provided with ceremonial battleaxes; tighter controls on expenditure on food and other provisions were imposed; and stricter codes of discipline and new curbs on absenteeism were introduced. Henceforth, all members of the household were to be appointed on merit, and those who gave good service would benefit from new channels of promotion.

The Eltham Ordinances not only recognised the Privy Chamber as a household department in its own right but also reformed it, and in these reforms it is possible to ascertain the extent of Henry's thraldom to Wolsey. The King had been over-generous in finding posts for his favourites and their clients, all of whom brought their own servants to court with them, and the Cardinal now seized his chance to minimise the threat to his authority posed by the one power centre at court over which he lacked influence. Numbers were cut, ostensibly in the interests of economy: the Gentlemen of the Chamber were reduced from 12 to 6, Sewers were reduced from 45 to 6, and Grooms of the Chamber from 15 to 4. 'Alas, what sorrow and lamentation was made when all these persons should depart the court,' observed Edward Hall.

The Cardinal also took measures to curb the ambitions of the members of the Privy Chamber by decreeing that they render 'humble, reverent, secret and lowly service, not pressing His Grace, nor advancing themselves, either in further service than His Grace will assign them unto, or also in suits, or intermeddle of any causes or matters whatsoever they be'.[5] Much to Wolsey's chagrin, these injunctions would be largely ignored.

Naturally, the first to go were Wolsey's enemies, among them the Groom of the Stool, Sir William Compton, Sir Francis Bryan, Sir Nicholas Carew, Lord Rochford and George Boleyn.[6] Amongst the displaced there was burning resentment against the Cardinal, and many were resolved to recover their former positions. Nevertheless, the King had allowed himself to be persuaded that their removal was for the best, although he had insisted on retaining as chief 'Nobleman of the Privy Chamber', without remuneration, his cousin Exeter, who was no friend to the Cardinal. To balance his influence Wolsey brought in his own adherent, Sir John Russell, an ambitious courtier, soldier and diplomat, who had begun his career in 1506 as Gentleman Usher to Henry VII. Henry VIII had knighted him during the French campaign of 1513, and thereafter sent him on several embassies to France and Italy. In 1522, during the war with France, Russell had lost an eye at the Battle of Morlaix. Around the time of his appointment to the Privy Chamber, he married and acquired his country seat, the fifteenth-century house known as Chenies in Buckinghamshire.

Compton was replaced as Groom of the Stool and Keeper of the Privy Purse by a man whose neutrality could be relied upon by the Cardinal, the charming and polished Henry Norris, who had become – according to Henry's own testimony – 'the best beloved of the King'[7] and was eminently fitted for this most confidential of court posts.

'At the pleasure of His Grace', Henry's inward lodgings were to be 'reserved secret, without repair of any great multitude'; no person was from henceforth to 'presume, attempt or be admitted' to enter 'other than such only as His Grace shall from time to time call for'; and strict regulations were brought in to enforce greater formality in the King's presence, and good conduct and discretion on the part of his personal servants, who were to be responsible for his 'quiet, rest and comfort, and the preservation of his health'.[8] Fifteen members of the Privy Chamber were to be in attendance on their master at any one time: Exeter, the Groom of the Stool and five other Gentlemen: Sir William Taylor, Sir Thomas Cheney, Sir Anthony Browne, Sir John Russell and William Carey; two Gentlemen Ushers, Roger Ratcliffe and Anthony Knyvet; four Grooms: William and Urian Brereton, Walter Welch and John Carey; Penny the barber and a page, fourteen-year-old Francis Weston, the son of Sir Richard Weston of Sutton Place.[9]

The Ordinances also recognised the fact that the Privy Council was meeting more and more frequently at court, and decreed that ten Councillors must always be in attendance on the King; among those so designated were John Clerk, Bishop of Bath and Wells, Sir Thomas More and the Dean of the Chapel Royal. Two at least were 'to be always present every day in the forenoon, by 10 a.m. at the furthest, and by afternoon by 2 p.m. in the King's dining chamber, or in such other place as shall fortune to be appointed for the Council chamber'.[10]

Another of those Councillors in regular attendance was Dr William Knight, who had recently replaced Richard Pace as Secretary to the King. Knight was another of Wolsey's protégés; he had been educated at Oxford, taken holy orders, and been appointed a royal chaplain in 1515. He had served on various embassies and proved his worth as a versatile man of affairs. Later, the King would appoint him Bishop of Bath and Wells.

Poor Richard Pace's career was grinding to a rather tragic halt. Wolsey, convinced that Pace was working against him, had seen to it that he was ousted from his post as Secretary and sent to Spain on an arduous diplomatic mission. In 1527, still suspicious of Pace's loyalty, he had him committed to the Tower. This was all too much for the sensitive Pace, and his mind gave way. On his release in 1530, he retired for good from public life, a broken man.

The implementation of the Eltham Ordinances called for changes amongst the chief officers of the household. The elderly Earl of Worcester, who had been ailing for some time and was to die in April 1526, was replaced as Lord Chamberlain by a man who had long enjoyed the favour of the King, William Sandys, who had been created Lord Sandys of the Vyne in 1523. He was assisted in his duties by the new Treasurer of the Household, the able naval commander and diplomat Sir William Fitzwilliam, who was elected a Knight of the Garter that year. Meanwhile Wolsey had sacked the former Cofferer, John Shurley, for taking unauthorised leave, and replaced him with Sir Edmund Peckham.

There is no doubt that the Eltham Ordinances achieved much of what they were meant to do, even though many regarded them as 'more profitable than honourable',[11] but it is not clear how stringently they were enforced, and there is evidence in royal proclamations that in several respects they were ignored. Certainly the numbers in the Privy Chamber had begun to rise by 1530, when there were 9 Gentlemen and 20 officers in total (these numbers rose to 11 and 24 respectively by 1532, and steadily increased thereafter).[12] The court remained a huge, chaotic establishment that, over the next few years, would be affected by the rule of factions and by major changes of policy, and only thirteen years would elapse before it was considered necessary to introduce another series of reforms. This all suggests that the Ordinances of 1526 did not go far enough towards stamping out waste and bad practices, and that there was insufficient provision for enforcing them.

32

'A Fresh Young Damsel'

On Shrove Tuesday 1526, there was a nasty incident when Sir Francis Bryan lost an eye in a tournament at Greenwich, necessitating his wearing an eye-patch thereafter.[1] What was more significant about this occasion, however, was the intriguing motto, 'Declare je nos' ('Declare I dare not'), which was embroidered on Henry VIII's magnificent jousting costume of cloth of gold and silver; above the words was emblazoned a man's heart engulfed in flames.[2] Such courtly devices were not uncommon, but in this case it seems that the King really had fallen passionately in love – probably for the first time in his life.

The object of the royal affections was Anne Boleyn, the younger sister of Henry's former mistress, who had at some stage resumed her duties in the Queen's household. It is not known when or where the affair began, but it had been going on for some months before it became public knowledge; the King's motto is the first evidence for it. An undated letter from Henry to Anne, which appears to have been written in 1527, refers to the King having been 'struck with the dart of love' for more than a year. Another pointer to the affair gathering momentum is to be found in the royal accounts dating from the spring of 1526, when the King ordered from his goldsmith four gold brooches: one represented Venus and Cupid, a second a lady holding a heart in her hand, a third a gentleman lying in the lap of a lady, and the fourth a lady holding a crown.[3] The symbolism was unmistakable.

Previous royal mistresses had apparently succumbed to their sovereign's overpowering charisma with indecent haste, but Anne Boleyn was different. Driven by ambition rather than virtue, she refused to become the King's lover, or even his acknowledged mistress in the courtly sense, and thereby inflamed his ardour to fever pitch. It was certainly a piquant and even humbling situation for a great King such as

Henry imagined himself to be to encounter, and intense fascination boosted his raging desire.

As usual, Henry was utterly discreet in his conduct of the affair. He must have known Anne socially before it began, and probably became close to her after losing interest in her sister. He may well have visited her at Hever Castle, using nearby Penshurst as a base, and her return to the Queen's service was perhaps engineered by him. The evidence suggests that her father, Lord Rochford, whose ambition far outweighed his moral scruples, encouraged the affair, since he had certainly profited from the King's seduction of his elder daughter; he may even have seen his younger daughter's submission as a stepping-stone to recovering his lost court posts. But Anne had no intention of being used by the King, then discarded and married off, as his previous mistresses had been.

As far as looks went, many people could not understand what he saw in her; one of her father's chaplains, John Barlow, was of the opinion that she was less beautiful than her sister or Elizabeth Blount, and a Venetian who saw her in 1532 wrote: 'Madame Anne is not one of the handsomest women in the world; she is of middling stature, swarthy complexion, long neck, wide mouth, bosom not much raised, and in fact has nothing but the English King's appetite, and her eyes, which are black and beautiful and take great effect.'[4] Another eyewitness states that those eyes 'invited to conversation'; Anne 'well knew how to use' them to effect, and 'such was their power that many a man paid his allegiance'.[5] This suggests that what Anne did have was that indefinable quality known as sex appeal, which made men find her irresistibly attractive. In addition, she had a slender 'elegant' figure,[6] a graceful carriage and long dark hair.

Anne herself was conscious of certain physical imperfections. George Wyatt, who in the 1590s wrote a laudatory memoir of her based on the reminiscences of her former maid of honour, Anne Gainsford, and on his own family traditions, stated that there was a rudimentary sixth nail 'upon the side of her nail upon one of her fingers, which yet was so small, by the report of those that have seen her, [and] which was usually by her hidden';[7] in those days, such a deformity was regarded by the devout as a sign of inner corruption or divine disfavour and by the superstitious as a witch's mark, hence the need for concealment. Catholic writers such as Nicholas Sander, who in 1585 wrote a vituperative account of Anne's life, regarded her as Jezebel personified, and made political capital out of her malformation, claiming that she in fact had six fingers. Nor was the sixth nail Anne's only blemish. George Wyatt wrote that there were said to be 'upon some parts of her body certain small moles incident to the clearest complexions', and a French eyewitness reported in 1533 that she had warts, and a large swelling on her neck.[8] Sander calls this 'a large wen', Wyatt a prominent Adam's apple.

The most famous authentic portrait of Anne Boleyn is that in the National Portrait Gallery, which is a late sixteenth-century copy of a lost original, by an anonymous artist, dating from 1533–6. The thin face, with its high cheekbones, small mouth and pointed chin, bears a marked resemblance to that of Anne's daughter, Elizabeth I. Various versions of this portrait exist: one at Hever shows Anne holding a rose and wearing a metal fillet over her French hood. The same portrait type appears in a miniature enamel of Anne set in a ring that also features a companion image of Elizabeth I, which dates from c1575 and is now at Chequers, and on a portrait medal of her, issued in 1534 and now in the British Museum.

A drawing of a lady in a gable hood by Hans Holbein at Weston Park was not identified as Anne Boleyn until 1649, and the face is different from that in the National Portrait Gallery picture. Several later painted versions of this drawing exist, notably at Hever Castle and Hatfield House. In the Royal Collection at Windsor there is another Holbein drawing of a different lady, labelled in eighteenth-century lettering 'Anna Bollein Queen'; the inscription is said to have been copied from the original one by John Cheke, who, after Holbein's death, attempted to label all his drawings. Cheke, who did not arrive at court until several years after Anne Boleyn's death, is known to have made several mistakes in his identifications; moreover, the hair of this sitter has been coloured yellow. Internal evidence suggests that this is in fact a lady of the Wyatt family.

In recent years it has been claimed that two miniatures of the same lady by Lucas Horenbout (now in the Buccleuch Collection and the Royal Ontario Museum in Toronto), formerly thought to be of Henry's third wife Jane Seymour, represent Anne Boleyn; the identification rests largely on two things: the theory that Horenbout's surviving miniatures are exclusively of royal or related persons, and the badge on the sitter's breast, which, it is claimed, is Anne's falcon badge.

There are several problems with this identification. Firstly, even allowing for traces of repainting, the sitter, with her fair hair, round face, short chin and full lips, bears little resemblance to Anne Boleyn as she appears in the National Portrait Gallery portrait. Secondly, her age is given as twenty-five. If this is Anne, and she was born around 1501 (a date now accepted by most historians), then the miniature was painted around 1526/7, when her role was little more than that of the King's low-profile inamorata, which hardly qualified her to be one of the fashionable Horenbout's first sitters. Thirdly, Anne did not adopt her crowned falcon badge until 1533, and the bird on her badge was rising to the right with wings elevated, while this bird is displayed, apparently with wings inverted. Whoever this miniature depicts – and that still remains a mystery – it was not Anne.

Anne's character has fascinated – and often eluded – historians for centuries. She was certainly ambitious, determined, tenacious and even ruthless. Her loyalty to, and pride in, her family were strong, and she seems to have been particularly close to her brother George. She was sophisticated, vivacious and witty, but could also be highly strung, sharp-tempered and vindictive. Yet her strength, boldness and courage were never in doubt. Unlike most women of her time, she had an independent spirit.

It was more than just sex appeal and wit that attracted Henry to Anne. Several writers testify to her love of fashion and her expensive tastes, which she shared with the King. Like him, she had a flair for the decorative arts and a lively interest in architecture and display. Her accomplishments were many. She was well educated, intelligent and articulate, was fluent in French and knew some Latin.[9]

Like Henry, Anne was passionately fond of music, and very talented in that sphere. 'When she sang, like a second Orpheus, she would have made bears and wolves attentive.'[10] She would accompany herself on the lute, could 'handle cleverly both flute and rebec',[11] and was competent on her clavichord, which she liked to decorate with green ribbons.[12] She could play the virginals with skill: a set decorated with the royal arms and her falcon badge, which perhaps belonged to both Anne and Elizabeth I, is now in the Victoria and Albert Museum. A beautifully crafted, nine-stringed lute, said to be Anne's but with less certainty, is at Hever Castle. Anne is believed to have composed her own songs and even written a masque, but none of her works survive.

She was also an accomplished dancer.[13] At the French court she had 'danced the English dances, leaping and jumping with infinite grace and ability. Moreover, she invented many new figures and steps which are yet known by her name or those of the gallant partners with whom she danced them.'[14] Even William Forrest, who wrote a hagiographic memoir of Katherine of Aragon, refers to Anne's 'passing excellent' skill at dancing: 'here was a fresh young damsel that could trip and go'.

Anne and her brother and their young friends were all keen poets. Anne herself 'possessed a great talent for poetry',[15] and George Boleyn was no mean versifier. He owned a manuscript of two fifteenth-century poems by the French writer Jean Lefèvre, *Les Lamentations de Mathéolus* and *Le Livre de Leesce*; the first was a cynical satire on women and marriage – which may have struck a personal chord, as later evidence suggests that Boleyn's union with Jane Parker was less than happy – the second a response. The manuscript is inscribed 'Thys boke ys myne, George Boleyn, 1526'.[16]

The most important member of the Boleyns' literary circle was the poet Thomas Wyatt, their near-neighbour in Kent. Now aged about twenty-three, he was the son of Sir Henry Wyatt of Allington Castle, a Privy Councillor and Treasurer of the Chamber; prior to 1485, Sir Henry had supported the claim of Henry Tudor against Richard III, for which he had been consigned to the Tower and tortured. He and his son were therefore held in high esteem by the King.

The younger Wyatt was a charming, intelligent man, a dreamer who preferred country life to the superficiality of the court. He was tall and good-looking with curly fair hair, and a dashing performer in the tiltyard. Women found him compellingly attractive, and he later confessed to having led an unchaste life, 'but yet I was not abominable'.[17] His father would not have agreed, for in two letters written in 1536 he referred despairingly to his son's sexual excesses and 'the displeasure he hath done to God'.[18]

However, since 1520, Wyatt had been unhappily married to Elizabeth, the daughter of George Brooke, Lord Cobham, who was notoriously unfaithful to him; they had one son, Thomas, born in 1521,[19] to whom Norfolk, Wyatt's revered patron, stood godfather. The couple had separated by 1524, and Wyatt thereafter sought solace in other women, his poetry and his career. Having come to court in 1520 as an Esquire of the Body, he had been promoted in 1524 to Clerk of the King's Jewels, probably through the influence of his father, who was then Master of the Jewel House, and had since gained favour with the King for his versifying talents, his skill with a lute, and his usefulness in devising court revels. In 1526, Henry began sending him abroad on diplomatic missions.

Wyatt was one of the greatest of English poets. He not only wrote moving poems and rondeaux,[20] witty epigrams, riddles, and satires on court life inspired by the works of Horace and Ludovico Ariosto, but was responsible for adapting the Petrarchan sonnet into English verse and introducing his own innovation, a rhyming couplet at the end, thus facilitating the composition of some of the most beautiful lyric poetry in the language. Wyatt's poems were circulated in manuscript form during his lifetime, but not published until after his death; they first appeared in print in Richard Tottel's *Miscellany* in 1557. His grandson was Anne Boleyn's biographer, George Wyatt.

Despite having been back in England for four years, Anne was still predominantly French in her ways. She was 'very expert in the French tongue'[21] and, given her graceful manners, no one would have taken her to be English, 'but a Frenchwoman born'.[22] Many of her books were in French, as were most of the love letters sent to her by Henry VIII. She preferred to dress in French fashions, in which she displayed 'marvellous taste',[23] and was largely responsible for popularising the French hood in England. Anne had long been fond of devising new modes of dress: 'every day she made some changes in the fashion of her garments'.[24] The ladies at the French court had copied her, and those at the English court would one day slavishly do the same.

However, Anne had learned more than courtly manners, deportment and culture at the promiscuous court of Francis I. We can discount Sander's malicious claim that her father had sent her to France because she had been caught in bed with both his butler and his chaplain – no other source mentions this – but other evidence of possible early sexual adventures cannot be ignored: in 1533, King Francis confided to the Duke of Norfolk 'how little virtuously Anne had always lived'.[25] Three years later, Henry himself told the Spanish ambassador that Anne had been 'corrupted' in France and that he had only discovered this when he began having sexual relations with her.[26] Later, just after her execution, when the King was offered the hand of Princess Madeleine of France, he declared 'he had had too much experience of French bringing up and manners'.[27] Anne's brother and sister were notorious for their sexual exploits, and even her mother's reputation was suspect. Given such a background, it is hard to believe that she had remained virtuous, and almost certain therefore that her calculated refusal to succumb to the King's advances stemmed from self-interest and ambition rather than her much vaunted moral principles.

33
'Master Hans'

Throughout the summer of 1526, 'the King took his pleasure hunting',[1] travelling leisurely from place to place, dispensing alms on the way, shooting venison for his hosts, and being entertained in the evenings by the jesters who had accompanied him.[2] In August, he made merry at Petworth in Sussex before riding on via Chichester to the mighty Arundel Castle, which he 'liked much'[3] and where the local gentry flocked to pay their respects. From there, ignoring the unceasing rain, Henry moved north via Winchester, Thruxton, Ramsbury, Compton, Langley, Bicester, Buckingham and Ampthill to his new palace at Grafton in Northamptonshire, which had been built in time for his arrival and stood near the parish church on land acquired by exchange from the Marquess of Dorset.

Half a mile away lay the old manor house of Dorset's ancestors, the Wydeville family; in a nearby chapel, Henry's grandfather Edward IV had secretly married Elizabeth Wydeville in 1464.[4] During the years to come, Henry would be a regular visitor to Grafton, where the hunting was very satisfactory.

The year 1526 witnessed several comings and goings at court. Lord Willoughby died, and his widow, Maria de Salinas, returned to the Queen's service. A far greater stir was caused by the parting of the Duke of Norfolk and his wife, Elizabeth Stafford, amid bitter recriminations. The Duchess moved into her dower house at Redbourne, leaving the Duke free to install his mistress, Elizabeth, or 'Bess', Holland – the chief cause of the separation – in his palace at Kenninghall. Although the Duchess described Bess as 'a churl's daughter who was but a washer in my nursery eight years',[5] she was in fact related to John, Lord Hussey, and was the sister of Norfolk's steward. The liaison had been going on for years, much to the chagrin of the Duchess, who refused to have Bess in the house. The Duke retaliated with verbal abuse and by cutting off his wife's allowance, while Bess took her own revenge: at the Duke's instance, or so the wronged wife claimed, she and her friends tied up the Duchess so tightly that 'blood came out at my fingers' ends, and [they] pinnacled me, and sat on my breast till I spit blood, and he never punished them'.[6] The Duchess also accused her husband of dragging her by the hair from the bed where she had just given birth and wounding her in the head with his dagger.

The affair was the talk of the court, and many sympathised with the Duchess, but Norfolk stoutly denied that there was any truth in what his 'wilful wife' was saying, and accused her of slander. 'He knows it is spoken of far and near,' Elizabeth Stafford wrote, but he was 'so far in doting love that he neither regards God nor his honour'.[7] In fact, the marriage had been breaking down long before the advent of Bess Holland, and it is telling that the couple's two eldest children, Henry Howard, Earl of Surrey, aged nine, and Mary, aged seven, both sided with their father. The Duchess remained bitter, and thirteen years later was still grumbling about her husband's affairs with 'that harlot' and other whores. 'If I come home, I shall be poisoned,' she declared, adding, 'the King's Grace shall be my record how I used myself, without any ill name and fortune'.[8]

In December 1526, a new Spanish ambassador, Diego Hurtado de Mendoza, arrived at court. A dignified man of integrity and astute judgement, he was one day to prove a good friend to his compatriot, the Queen. Mendoza had come to smooth over the troubled waters between Henry and the Emperor, but his arrival coincided with the King's growing inclination towards an alliance with France.

That same month, Hans Holbein the Younger, the outstanding artist who was to define the Henrician monarchy, arrived in England. A native of Augsberg, born c1497/9, he had been trained in the workshop of his father, Hans Holbein the Elder, and had worked in Basel for several years, painting murals and architectural decorations, religious pictures, altarpieces, woodcuts and portraits of local worthies, among them the humanist Erasmus, who became his friend and mentor. But with the advent of the Lutheran Reformation, commissions began to dry up, and Holbein was obliged to look around for new patrons. Erasmus suggested he try England, since Henry VIII had a reputation for encouraging foreign artists, and arranged for Holbein to lodge with Sir Thomas More at Chelsea, informing More, 'He is an excellent artist.'[9]

More was impressed. 'Your painter, dearest Erasmus, is a wonderful man,' he wrote, 'but I fear he will not find England as fruitful as he had hoped. Yet I will do my best to see that he does not find it absolutely barren.' More was as good as his word. He began by ordering portraits of himself and his family from Holbein, which were so innovative that during the next two years More was able to secure the artist commissions for portraits of his humanist friends, among them Sir Thomas Elyot, Sir John Gage and Archbishop Warham; the latter was already familiar with Holbein's work, since in 1524 Erasmus had sent him one of the artist's portraits of himself, and he wanted to send his own portrait to Erasmus in return.[10]

Holbein's formative years had been spent in a city imbued with Renaissance culture. As an adult, he had travelled in Italy and learned from the masters there. As a result, his style combined the best traditions of the Northern Renaissance with Italian influences and a strong sense of perspective. Although a gifted artist in many fields, he is now remembered as one of the greatest portrait painters of all time, a reputation derived largely from the works he executed in England, which were the most realistic and sophisticated representations of humanity yet seen in that kingdom. Holbein's skill recorded for posterity, with truth and precision, as never before, the men and women of Henry VIII's court, and set a trend for portrait painting that would persist for centuries.

So exactly delineated are these portraits that it has been conjectured that Holbein used a tracing apparatus, perhaps with a peephole. It has also been suggested that he suffered from a degree of astigmatism that resulted in his portraying people as broader than they really were, yet this is at variance with the opinion of contemporaries who knew his sitters. 'O stranger, if you desire to see pictures with all the appearance of life, look on these which Holbein's hand has created!' wrote the French humanist Nicholas Bourbon, who visited the English court in the 1530s. And in 1529, on receiving a copy of the More family portrait, Erasmus was delighted to find that it showed him the whole family 'as if I had been among you'.[11]

To make up for the previous year, the Christmas of 1526, which was celebrated at Greenwich, was a splendid affair, with banquets, masques, dancing and tournaments. On 3 January, Wolsey staged a feast which was unexpectedly interrupted by a burst of cannonfire from outside. This heralded the arrival of a troupe of visitors wearing disguises. The Cardinal, invited to guess which one was the King, incorrectly identified Sir Edward Neville as his sovereign, much to the amusement of Henry and everyone else. Nothing discomfited, Wolsey arranged for his new guests to be seated at table and, astonishing those already present, who had eaten to satiety, signalled for another two hundred dishes to be brought to table, 'to the great comfort of the King'.[12]

By Shrove Tuesday, however, Henry was in a truculent mood. News had come from Scotland that, amidst violent clashes, his sister Margaret had had her marriage to the Earl of Angus annulled on the grounds that, when it took place, Angus had been precontracted to another lady. Since Margaret had entered into the union in good faith, their daughter, Lady Margaret Douglas, was deemed to be legitimate. Henry's sister, however, was now involved in an affair with her treasurer, Henry Stewart, Lord Methven (whom she would marry the following year), and Henry chose to take a dim view of this. He pronounced that the annulment was 'a shameless sentence from Rome' and sent indignant letters lecturing Margaret on morality.[13]

Fortunately for her, Henry was soon preoccupied with negotiations for a new alliance with France, which was to be the occasion of some of the most magnificent court celebrations of the reign. At the end of February 1527, an important embassy arrived from Paris to discuss a 'Treaty of Eternal Peace', which would be sealed by the marriage of the Princess Mary to Henry, Duke of Orléans, second son of Francis I. Since Henry had no son, Orléans, it was anticipated, would one day rule England as Mary's consort. As far as the King was concerned, this was not a satisfactory solution to the problem of the succession, but it was the best he could think of in the circumstances.

The negotiations were completed by the end of April, and on 4 May the envoys made their way to Greenwich. Here, the King had ordered the construction of a grand banqueting house and a disguising house or theatre, which were built at either end of the tiltyard gallery. These houses, which were based on similar ones erected in Paris in 1518 in honour of an English embassy, were plain structures that could be embellished with stage sets, hangings and other temporary decorations that could be changed at will. Each measured 110 by 30 feet. 'The windows were all clerestories, with curious mullions strangely wrought. At one side was a haut place for heralds and minstrels',[14] lavishly embellished with a carving of the royal arms, antique busts and *trompe l'oeil* paintings of mythical beasts.

Sir Henry Guildford, who had been appointed Master of the Revels in 1526, was put in charge of the project, and Sir Henry Wyatt, Treasurer of the Chamber, was made responsible for financing it. Amongst the craftsmen who worked on these houses was Nicolaus Kratzer, who designed a complicated cosmographical ceiling, and a 'Master Hans' – almost certainly Holbein – who painted it. This was Holbein's first royal commission, probably obtained through the good offices of Sir Thomas More, for which the artist received 4s. (£60) a day, £4.10s. (£1,350) for one large painting, and £660 for designing two triumphal arches – in total, more than any other artist working on the project. To mark the occasion, Holbein painted portraits of those who collaborated with him – Kratzer, Wyatt and Guildford.[15]

Giovanni di Maiano, John Browne and Clement Armstrong, who made moulds, also worked alongside Holbein at Greenwich, crafting and painting decorative effects, which included a cornice of grotesque work. On 11 March, the King came in person to see how the work was progressing, and some of the unfinished decorations were temporarily put into place for him.

When the French and English envoys arrived at Greenwich on Saturday 5 May, they were conducted along a gallery from the Queen's apartments to the banqueting house, which was hung with tapestries depicting *The History of David* and had its timber ceiling covered with red buckram embroidered with roses and pomegranates. The room was illuminated by iron sconces and antique-style candelabra, and was dominated by a massive buffet '7 stages high and 13' long' and another cupboard nine stages high, with wonderful displays of gold and gem-studded plate.[16] At the far end of the room was an 'antique triumphal arch designed by Holbein, above which was a large painting by him of Henry VIII's victory over the French at Thérouanne, a rather tactless choice of decoration given the circumstances;[17] when Henry pointed it out to his French guests, they were somewhat offended. Holbein's picture, which is lost, was perhaps the inspiration for the large-scale anonymous painting of the battle that was commissioned later in the reign and is still in the Royal Collection.

The French envoys were 'entertained after a more sumptuous manner than had ever been seen before'.[18] On 5 May, after Mass, they were formally received by the King in the new banqueting house, where the Treaty of Greenwich was signed, Henry swearing to abide by its terms. Watching with the Queen was his sister Mary, Duchess of Suffolk.

The next day there was a splendid tournament at which the King wore a jousting costume of purple Florentine velvet trimmed with gold,[19] but he was unable to participate, having injured his foot playing tennis. It was the Master of the Horse, Sir Nicholas Carew, who triumphed that day in the lists. Afterwards, Henry hosted a lavish banquet in the banqueting house, at which sixty huge silver-gilt plates of costly spices were handed round.[20] This was followed by a recital by the Chapel Royal in the 'disguising house', which had tiered seating around three of its walls and a huge proscenium arch adorned with terracotta busts and statuary, another of Holbein's designs. The floor was carpeted with silk embroidered with gold lilies, and above was Holbein's ceiling, which depicted 'the whole earth environed with the sea, like a very map';[21] beneath this was suspended a transparent cloth, painted and gilded with the signs of the Zodiac and glittering with stars, planets and constellations. 'It was a cunning thing and a pleasant sight to behold,' enthused a rapt Edward Hall.

The recital was followed by two masques devised by John Rightwise, in one of which the King and his daughter Mary, who had returned to court in April and was 'decked with all the gems of the eighth sphere',[22] took part. As they danced, Henry could not resist pulling off her netted caul and letting her 'profusion of silver tresses' fall cascading about her shoulders for the benefit of the French ambassadors,[23] who were dutifully admiring. After the masque, the dancing went on until sunrise. Because of his injured foot, Henry was wearing black velvet slippers, and every male courtier had been required to follow suit so that their sovereign should not feel out of place on the dance floor.[24]

The celebrations continued for several days. As her parents watched from their thrones under the canopy of estate, the Princess Mary, dressed as a Roman goddess in 'cloth of gold, with so many precious stones that the splendour and radiance dazzled the sight',[25] took part in a pageant. Wolsey staged a play celebrating the alliance, which was performed by the Chapel Royal,[26] and gave a feast for the envoys at Hampton Court; one of the many fantastic subtleties served was fashioned like a chess set, and the Cardinal magnanimously presented it to a Frenchman who had admired it.

Suddenly, the festivities were brought to an abrupt halt by the dreadful news of the sacking of Rome by uncontrolled mercenary troops in the pay of the Emperor. The Pope had fled and was now a prisoner. Accounts of the atrocities were horrifying.

Everyone was in shock. The French envoys quietly returned home. By the King's order, the banqueting house and theatre were briefly opened to the public, who came in great numbers, then stripped of their decorations, which were carefully stored away.[27] From time to time over the years, Henry would use them again, furnished appropriately for each festive occasion.

34

'Noli Me Tangere, for Caesar's I Am'

For five years now, the King's ever-tender conscience had been troubling him over the validity of his marriage. As we have noted, he believed that he, good son of the Church that he was, had sinned by taking in wedlock his brother's wife, and that their lack of a male heir was proof of God's displeasure. According to Henry, the leader of the French embassy, Gabriel de Grammont, Bishop of Tarbes, had voiced doubts about Mary's legitimacy, and although the King had been able to reassure him that Pope Julius had issued a dispensation for his marriage to Katherine, he was not sure that it was valid in canon law.

Henry unburdened himself to Wolsey. The Cardinal, foreseeing a solution to the succession dilemma in a French marriage for his master, convened with Archbishop Warham an ecclesiastical court to examine the King's doubts, which met in secret at Westminster on 17 May 1527. Meanwhile, Mary was sent with her household to Hunsdon, and Henry toyed with the idea of making his son Richmond King of Ireland, so as to make him a more desirable match for Maria of Portugal, Charles V's niece. Suspecting that this might also be a preliminary to him naming the boy his heir, the Queen made very plain her disapproval.[1]

But this was nothing compared with what was to come. On 22 June, the King came to Katherine's chamber and told her bluntly that they must separate, and why, and that he had sent to Rome to ask the Pope for an annulment. This news plunged her into great grief, and drove her to seek the advice of Mendoza, the Spanish ambassador, and the aid of her nephew, Charles V.

Thus began the *cause célèbre* that became known as 'the King's Great Matter', the erroneously titled 'Divorce' that was to be one of the most infamous nullity suits in history and the catalyst for revolutionary changes both at court and in the kingdom at large. For the next decade, the Great Matter would dominate England's domestic and foreign policy and overshadow the life of the court.

There was no open rift between the King and Queen. Whilst awaiting the Pope's decision, they appeared together in public, continued to dine and spend time together in private, and showed each other every courtesy. But Katherine knew herself to be watched; several of her women were Wolsey's spies, bribed by gifts, financial inducements and even sex,[2] and every letter she sent or received was scrutinised before it reached its destination. Each attempt she made to see Mendoza in private was blocked. It was not surprising, therefore, that she incorrectly blamed Wolsey for what was happening, a view that was to be shared by many other people, notably Charles V. It was inconceivable to her that Henry himself could have instigated these proceedings.

Henry and Wolsey soon realised that the Pope, who was now the Emperor's prisoner, would be unlikely to offend Charles by annulling the marriage of his aunt. In July, therefore, Wolsey went to France to seek Francis I's support for the restoration of Pope Clement and the annulment and discuss the possibility of a French marriage for the King. As yet, the Cardinal had no idea that Anne Boleyn was anything more to Henry than his previous mistresses had been, although he feared that his enemies would be undermining his influence during his absence. In a letter to Sir William Fitzwilliam he inquired what the King was doing and who was with him. Fitzwilliam replied that the King was on progress. 'He daily passeth the time in hunting. He suppeth in his privy chamber [and] there suppeth with him the Dukes of Norfolk and Suffolk, the Marquess of Exeter and the Lord of Rochford.'[3] Wolsey cannot have been reassured.

Katherine accompanied Henry on his progress, but he did not visit her in the evenings. They put on a united front, however, when they visited Mary at Hunsdon, and when it was time to move on to Beaulieu, although Henry was 'ready to depart by a good space, he tarried for the Queen, and so they rode forth together'.[4] At Beaulieu, however, Henry was reunited with Anne Boleyn, who stayed a month, hunting with him and taking supper in his privy chamber.

Anne was still playing hard to get. When the King's ardour became too passionate, she would tactically withdraw home to Hever – presumably Katherine, who now knew what was going on, was only too happy to let her – and then Henry would have to beg her to come back. It is likely that by now Anne had realised that, if she played her cards right, she could win not just her King but also the consort's crown. Although monarchs did not normally marry commoners, there was a precedent: in 1464, Edward IV had married Elizabeth Wydeville, a knight's widow, for love.

Others were wise to the game Anne was playing. In August 1527, Mendoza reported: 'The King is so swayed by his passions. It is generally believed that, if he can obtain a divorce, he will end by marrying a daughter of Master Boleyn.'[5]

Seventeen of Henry's letters to Anne, dating from 1527 to 1529, survive in the Vatican archives; her replies are unfortunately lost. The King's letters betray his deep passion and longing to possess his elusive lady, and convey a barely restrained eroticism: 'Henceforth my heart shall be dedicate to you alone, greatly desirous that so my body could be as well,' one read, and it ended, 'Written by the hand of the servant who in heart, body and will is, Your loyal and most ensured servant, H. autre ♡ ne cherche R.' 'Give yourself up, body and soul, to me,' he pleaded, adding that he wished himself 'at this time private with you'. 'I wish you in my arms,' he declared in another letter, and then, very daring, told her he was sending her 'some flesh, representing my name, which is hart's flesh for Henry, prognosticating that hereafter you must enjoy some of mine, which I would were now . . . I would we were together an evening'. One letter was 'written with the hand of him that longeth to be yours', while another ended with him 'wishing myself, specially an evening, in my sweetheart's arms, whose pretty dukkys [breasts] I trust shortly to kiss'. Growing ever more ardent, he avowed in a later letter, 'I trust within a while after to enjoy that which I have so longed for, to both our comforts . . . I would you were in my arms, or I in yours, for I think it long since I kissed you.' One letter refers to him having had rooms prepared for Anne at court, 'which I trust ere long to cause you occupy; and then I trust to occupy yours'. It must have required all Anne's strength and presence of mind to resist such passionate addresses.

Yet resist them she did. That the affair was not consummated is attested to by the fact that in 1530, the Spanish ambassador reported that there was 'no positive proof of adultery; . . . on the contrary, several letters proving the opposite'.[6] In 1531, Henry himself would swear to Katherine that he had not committed adultery with Anne.[7] A rumour reached Rome in 1531 that Anne had miscarried a child, but there is no other evidence for this.[8]

Late in 1526, Henry had realised that he was not Anne's only suitor. The poet Thomas Wyatt was enamoured of her and one day stole her locket. Despite her protests, he would not return it, but wore it as a trophy. A day or so later, the King took one of her rings as a keepsake. Soon afterwards, Henry was playing bowls with Suffolk, Bryan and Wyatt when a dispute arose between Henry and Wyatt as to whose was the victory. Pointing with the hand on which Anne's ring was prominently displayed, Henry cried, 'I tell thee, it is mine.' Craftily, Wyatt asked permission to measure the distance and, taking off Anne's locket, used the chain to do so, saying, 'I hope it will be mine.' The King was furious and stalked off, muttering, 'It may be so, but then I am deceived.' When he questioned Anne on the subject, she denied that Wyatt meant anything to her.[9]

Anne Boleyn's relationship with Thomas Wyatt has long been the subject of controversy. George Wyatt claimed that the poet had expressed his feelings for Anne 'somewhere in his verses', and historians have searched ever since for that allusion, drawing all kinds of conclusions; but in fact only four poems could be said to be evidence for the affair, if affair it was, since all the interest seems to have been on Wyatt's side; Anne appears to have spurned his advances. The first is a riddle entitled 'Of his love, called Anna':

> What word is it that changeth not,
> Tho' it be turned and made in twain?
> It is mine Anna, God it wot,
> And eke the causer of my pain,
> Who love rewarded with disdain.

The second poem is the famous 'Noli me tangere' ('Do not touch me'), based on a work by Petrarch:

> Who list her hunt, I put him out of doubt;
> As well as I may spend his time in vain!
> And graven with diamonds in letters plain
> There is written her fair neck round about,
> 'Noli me tangere, for Caesar's I am,
> And wild for to hold, though I seem tame.'

The third poem was written after Wyatt had found a new mistress, who may have been Elizabeth Darrell, with whom he was involved as late as 1537:

> Then do I love again;
> If thou ask whom, sure since I did refrain
> Her, that did set our country in a roar.

After Anne Boleyn's execution, when it was dangerous to refer to any previous entanglement with her, Wyatt amended this last line to 'Brunette, that set my wealth in such a roar'. The fourth poem was written when Wyatt accompanied Henry and Anne on a state visit to Calais in 1532:

> Sometime I fled the fire that me brent [burned]
> By sea, by land, by water and by wind,
> And now I follow the coals that be quenched
> From Dover to Calais, against my mind.
> Lo, how desire is both sprung and spent!

The tale of Henry's altercation with Wyatt comes from the poet's grandson, George Wyatt, and was probably handed down in the family; there is no reason to disbelieve its substance, although the details may have been embroidered. This and the above poems are sufficient testimony to Wyatt's pursuit of Anne.

Some have claimed that other evidence for it lies in the so-called 'Devonshire Manuscript', a book of nearly two hundred poems composed by, and circulated within, the Boleyn circle at court.[10] In one margin are written the words, 'I am yours, An.' The handwriting is not, however, that of Anne herself, and the manuscript must date from the 1530s since the original owner, whose initials are on the binding, was probably Norfolk's daughter, Lady Mary Howard, who was only seven in 1526. Other contributors appear to have been Anne's cousin, Madge Shelton and Lady Margaret Douglas, both of whom came to court in the 1530s, but not Anne herself. A hundred and twenty-five of the poems have been attributed, some erroneously, to Wyatt, who was writing throughout that decade.

In May 1530, the imperial ambassador, Eustache Chapuys, informed the Emperor that the Duke of Suffolk had been banished from court for warning an unreceptive King that Anne was unfit to be queen because she had had 'criminal' relations with an unnamed courtier, 'whom she loves very much and whom the King had formerly chased from court for jealousy'. When Anne heard what Suffolk had said, she was fearful of the scandal being revived, and begged the King to send the unnamed gentleman away from court once more. Henry complied, but immediately regretted this decision and persuaded Anne to agree to the man's return.[11]

At that time, Suffolk, who was falling out of favour, had good reasons of his own for discrediting Anne, and Chapuys himself was not above reporting mere rumours as fact, so perhaps this tale should not be taken too seriously. Furthermore, the reports may not even refer to Wyatt, although other writers believed they did.

Three later Catholic sources, the *Spanish Chronicle* (written before 1552),[12] Nicholas Harpsfield (c1557) and Nicholas Sander (1585), all eager to defame Anne Boleyn's memory, would repeat the tale that Anne and Wyatt had been lovers. The author of the *Spanish Chronicle* gives lurid details of the affair, which is said to have begun one night at

Hever. When later Wyatt confessed all to the King, Henry refused to believe him. Harpsfield also says it was Wyatt who warned Henry that Anne was 'not meet to be coupled with Your Grace', admitting that he knew this 'as one that have had my carnal pleasure'. According to this account, Henry praised him for his honesty and told him not to repeat what he had said. Harpsfield claimed he had got his facts from a merchant, Antonio Bonvisi, who had been close to Wolsey, More and Thomas Cromwell, and had been acquainted with Wyatt. Sander states that Wyatt told the Council about his affair with Anne before he went to the King, and claims that Henry accused the poet of calumny. When Wyatt sent Suffolk to the King with a message to say he could prove what he said, Henry declined to probe further, saying that Wyatt was a bold villain who could not be trusted. It is of course possible that Anne had had an affair with Wyatt before she became involved with the King, and that in 1526 he had tried to revive it in the face of her indifference and desire to dissociate herself from a questionable past.

It would appear that Wyatt's position at court became untenable as the King's passion for Anne intensified. In January 1527, learning that Sir John Russell was about to depart on an embassy to Rome, Wyatt sought him out. 'If you please, I will ask leave, get money and go with you,' he said. Russell agreed.[13] After their return in May, Wyatt maintained a low profile and stayed away from Anne.

During Wolsey's absence in France, Anne Boleyn's influence was steadily increasing. The Cardinal did not know it yet, but his monopoly on power was being gradually eroded. Once Anne's affair with the King became public knowledge, courtiers came to view her as an important alternative source of patronage,[14] and she began immediately to use her new power to advance her family and friends. As her confidence increased, she grew 'very haughty and stout [proud], having all manner of jewels or rich apparel that might be gotten with money'.[15] With the Queen, however, her behaviour was circumspect, and Katherine treated her with distant courtesy. Yet she was not able to resist the occasional jibe. Once, when the King was playing cards with them both and Anne turned up several kings in a row, Katherine turned to her and said, 'My lady Anne, you have good hap to stop at a king, but you are not like others, you will have all or none!'[16]

Wolsey was soon to discover with a nasty jolt how things stood. When he returned from France on 17 September, he rode at once to Richmond, bearing rich gifts for the King from Francis I. As was his usual custom, he sent a message to Henry requesting a private audience to discuss his mission, asking where his master would receive him. But Anne was with the King, and before Henry could answer, she addressed the messenger in ringing tones, 'Where else is the Cardinal to come? Tell him that he may come here, where the King is.'[17] The gauntlet was thrown: from now on, there would be a bitter power struggle between the King's minister and his sweetheart.

After the treaty with France had been formally confirmed in September 1527, Henry VIII and Francis I exchanged Orders of chivalry. Henry sent Francis the Order of the Garter, and Francis bestowed on Henry the French equivalent, the Order of St Michael, which had been founded by Louis XI in 1469 in imitation of the Burgundian Order of the Golden Fleece. Each sovereign sent the other a beautifully illuminated copy of the statutes of each respective Order.[18] Henry accepted the Order of St Michael with pride, and formally promised to wear, on appropriate occasions, its collar of gold scallop shells with a pendant of the Archangel Michael, its long, ermine-lined mantle of white cloth of silver edged with gold scallop shells, and its cape and hood of crimson velvet embroidered in gold.[19]

Henry's ambassador to France, the 'comely'[20] Sir Anthony Browne, half-brother to Sir William Fitzwilliam and a Gentleman of the Privy Chamber, had been present at the chapter of the Order of St Michael that was traditionally (but not regularly) held on the feast of Michaelmas, 29 September; but he was disparaging about the ceremonies he had witnessed, and told Henry, 'They would fain follow the fashion of your Order, but they fail in everything. I think in all the world there is no such Order as yours.'[21]

On 10 November, the same day that Francis I received the Garter from Arthur Plantagenet, Viscount Lisle, Henry VIII was formally invested with the Order of St Michael. Once again, the banqueting house at Greenwich was decked out in rich tapestries, and the disguising house was adorned with a white marble fountain and two trees fashioned from silk: a Tudor hawthorn and a Valois mulberry. After the investiture, in which the King was robed in his insignia by Anne de Montmorency, Great Master of France, there was a tournament (which ended early because the autumn light was poor), a banquet and a masque. So brilliant was the occasion that the next day it seemed to have been 'a fantastical dream'.[22]

The winter of 1527–8 was exceptionally bitter – even the sea froze in places. The King kept Christmas at Greenwich, but Anne Boleyn remained at Hever. In January, probably through her influence, Sir Nicholas Carew, who was her cousin, was restored to his old place in the Privy Chamber, much to Wolsey's chagrin; but Carew was no longer the wild rake he had once been, and was now a sober politician and supporter of the French alliance.

The weather was much improved when, in March, Anne and her mother stayed as the King's guests at Windsor. Henry was attended only by his riding household, and every afternoon he and Anne went hunting or hawking in Windsor Forest, returning after dark, or walked together in the Great Park. In the evenings, they amused themselves with cards, dice and dancing, played music and recited poetry. One day the King ordered a picnic, which was held at Windsor Manor. Tables and stools were borrowed from the townsfolk of Windsor, and food and kitchen equipment was brought down from the castle. Henry and Anne and their friends feasted on plovers, partridges, larks and rabbits, as well as confections with lashings of cream, which was supplied by the park-keeper's wife.[23] On another occasion, Anne asked Thomas Heneage, one of Wolsey's servants who was about to be appointed a Gentleman of the Privy Chamber, to ask the Cardinal if he would be so kind as to send her some carps and shrimps for her table.

Anne loved hunting with Henry, because this was one of the few occasions when she could have him almost to herself, with only a few trusted companions in attendance. He was delighted to be able to share his favourite pastime with her, and bought her four French saddles of black velvet with silk and gold fringing, complete with footstools, matching harnesses and reins, as well as bows, arrows and gloves.[24] Sometimes, she would ride behind him on his own mount, using a black velvet pillion saddle – 'a most unusual procedure,' commented a scandalised imperial ambassador.[25] Anne herself ordered her palfreys specially from Ireland.[26] When they were apart, Henry would write to tell her of his successes in the chase, and send her gifts of venison. Not all of their hunting expeditions were felicitous: once, Anne's greyhound savaged and killed a cow, and the King had to pay 10s. (£150) in compensation to its irate owner. Anne was also fond of archery, and once tried her hand at bowls, although she was beaten by Richard Hill, the Sergeant of the Cellar, who was one of the King's gambling partners. Henry paid him £12 (£3,600) on Anne's behalf.[27]

Anne was 'well skilled at all games fashionable at court'.[28] She was an inveterate gambler, but often rash, so the King gave her only £5 (£1,500) at a time, often in small change, from his Privy Purse, 'for playing money'.[29] Nevertheless, his accounts show that he often lost large sums to her. One of their favourite games was 'Pope July', which appears to have been a satirical interpretation of Henry's nullity suit.[30]

Whilst she was at Windsor, Anne managed to offend Sir John Russell, an influential member of the Privy Chamber who had become involved in a bitter dispute with her cousin and client, Sir Thomas Cheney, another of the King's Gentlemen, over the marriage of Russell's two stepdaughters, who were Wolsey's wards: Cheney and another courtier,

Sir John Wallop, wanted to marry them, but Wolsey and Russell had refused their permission. On an earlier occasion, Anne had successfully intervened when Cheney had been in disgrace with Wolsey. However, this time Henry took Russell's part, and forbade Cheney to enter the Privy Chamber until he had made his peace with Russell. But the row continued, and several months later, when Wolsey banished Cheney from court, Anne summoned him back 'in spite of the Cardinal, not without using rude words to Wolsey'. At that point, Wolsey capitulated, and Cheney married his heiress.[31] The affair highlighted Anne's increasing ascendancy in the power struggle between her and Wolsey, and turned Russell into the first of the many powerful enemies she would make during the course of her career.

35

'A Thousand Cases of Sweat'

Until 1528, Henry VIII enjoyed good health, but from then on he was troubled by a series of minor ailments. He began to suffer feverish headaches and 'rheums', which could have been due to catarrh, migraine, rising blood pressure or even the head injuries he had received. In 1528 he had a bladder infection, and around the same time a sore appeared on his leg; his surgeon, Thomas Vicary, temporarily cured it, but it would later recur.

There is a persistent but erroneous belief that Henry suffered from syphilis, a disease thought to have been introduced into Europe around 1493 from the newly discovered Americas; that his so-called leg ulcer was its primary sore, which would have healed spontaneously, and that his feverish headaches were symptomatic of the disease's progress.[1] If this had been the case, the headaches would have appeared at a later stage, not at the same time as the primary sore. It is true that, after Wolsey's fall, his physician, Dr Augustine Agostini, who was almost certainly a creature of the Boleyns, stated that the Cardinal, knowing that he had 'the foul and contagious disease of the great pox', yet 'came daily' to the King, breathing in his ear and blowing upon him 'with perilous and infective breath'.[2] There is no evidence that Wolsey had syphilis, and even if he had he could not have transmitted it to Henry in this way. It has also been claimed that a portrait of Henry VIII at Hever Castle shows him with the collapsed bridge of the nose that is a symptom of the advancing disease. This portrait is in fact a poor copy of a lost original by Holbein that was painted in c1543/4; better-quality copies of the same portrait at Castle Howard and in the National Portrait Gallery, and other later representations of the King, all show him with his familiar high-bridged nose.

No hostile foreign envoy ever claimed that Henry had syphilis. In all the detailed records of purchases of medicaments by the King's doctors and apothecaries, there is not a single mention of mercury, which was the most effective treatment for syphilis and was administered over a period of six weeks with such unpleasant side effects that no ambassador could have failed to understand what ailed the King. Nor was Henry given the various remedies that were prescribed for Francis I, who did have what was known as 'the French disease', although Henry did devise for himself a plaster made from *lignum guaiacum*, a hard wood imported from the New World that was ground into ash and dissolved in water for the relief of syphilitics; however, it was, and still is, a proven remedy for gout, sore throats and pains in the leg.[3] Henry never suffered the disfiguring rash and skin eruptions of the second stage of the illness, nor the blindness, paralysis and dementia that are characteristic of its final stages: he was lucid to the end. Neither did his children show any symptoms of having inherited the disease.

The King was undoubtedly something of a hypochondriac. He considered himself an expert on diseases and ailments, and, as we have seen, was fond of devising cures for them. This concern was extended to his courtiers. When, in 1528, Sir Bryan Tuke, who had succeeded Sir Henry Wyatt as Treasurer of the Chamber, developed a painful kidney complaint, he confided in Wolsey, who in turn told the King. But somewhere along the line the information became garbled, and when Tuke next sought an audience with Henry to discuss secretarial business, the King 'began to tell me of a medicine for a tumour in the testicles. I immediately said His Highness was not well informed of my disease, which is not there but in my kidneys.' Undeterred, 'His Highness had me by and by, and gave me direct counsel, and showed me the remedies, as any cunning physician in England could do.'[4]

In an age without painkillers, Henry's minor complaints alone could have accounted for his increasing tetchiness, let alone his frustration at the delay in obtaining a decision on his marriage. For the Pope, anxious to play for time, had decided to send a legate to England to hear the King's case, but the man he had chosen, Cardinal Lorenzo Campeggio, suffered from gout and could only travel in slow stages. Henry, who was now determined to marry Anne Boleyn, was desperate with impatience.

Now Fate, it seemed, might snatch from him what he most desired, for in May 1528 the dreaded sweating sickness broke out again.[5] In great fear, the King dismissed most of his courtiers and servants and left Greenwich for Waltham Abbey in Essex, taking the Queen and Anne Boleyn with him. When news came that there was plague near Pontefract, where Richmond was staying, a worried Henry ordered his son to move further north, and sent him remedies that he himself had concocted, in case he fell ill. Fortunately, the regular bulletins on his health that reached the King were all reassuring.[6]

This visitation of the sweat proved particularly virulent, with forty thousand cases in London alone, although not all of them proved fatal. 'The term of Parliament was adjourned, and the judges' circuit also.'[7] Eighteen members of Wolsey's household died within the space of four hours, and two others succumbed after the Cardinal had sought refuge at The More.

At Waltham, two Ushers, two Grooms of the Chamber, George Boleyn and Sir William Fitzwilliam all sickened but recovered. When one of Anne Boleyn's maids fell ill in June, Henry sent his sweetheart home to Hever, then fled in terror to Hunsdon, where he 'strengthened' himself with medicines[8] made up by his apothecary Cuthbert Blackden, and remained isolated in a tower with Dr Chamber and his other physicians.[9] To begin with, he was so 'much troubled' by fear of the sweat that he ordered Sir Francis Bryan to sleep in his bedchamber with him. However, as time went by and no one in the household fell sick, the King grew 'very merry' with relief.[10]

He bombarded Wolsey with good advice, sent through Bryan Tuke: the Cardinal was to avoid any places where there was a risk of infection, and if any of his household fell ill, he was to remove with speed. 'His Highness desireth Your Grace to keep out of the air, to have only a small and clean company about him, to use small suppers and to drink little wine, and once in the week to use the pills of Rhazis', which were named after the Arab physician who had invented them. If Wolsey himself fell ill, the King had devised a posset of herbs that would bring out the sweat most profusely. Otherwise, the Cardinal was to look to his soul 'and commit all to God'.[11] Wolsey responded with news that the Dowager Duchess of Norfolk had had some success in curing a number of the sick: she made them fast for sixteen hours and stay in bed for a whole day and night, then kept them in isolation for a week, dosing them with treacle and herbs.[12]

Soon afterwards, the King received the devastating news that Anne and her father had caught the sweating sickness, and in a fever of anxiety he sent his second physician, the kindly and urbane Dr William Butts, who had formerly been in the household of the Princess Mary at Hunsdon, to attend them, with a letter to Anne 'praying God that He may soon restore your health'.[13] Butts was soon back at court with the cheerful news that Anne and her father had recovered. Soon, a relieved Henry was writing to tell her:

Since your last letters, mine own darling, Walter Welch, Master [John] Browne, John Carey, Urian Brereton and John Cocke the apothecary be fallen of the sweat in this house and, thanked be God, all recovered. As yet the plague is not fully ceased here, but I trust shortly it shall. By the mercy of God, the rest of us yet be well, and I trust shall pass it.[14]

But the King's hopes of the sweat abating were in vain, and 'for a space, he removed almost every day, till at the last he came to Tittenhanger', one of Wolsey's houses, 'where he prepared to bide the time that God would allow him'.[15] The house was 'purged daily by fires and other preservatives',[16] such as vinegar, and the King had the window in the Cardinal's closet enlarged, so as to admit more fresh air. Fearing that the plague might be a sign of divine displeasure, and realising that he should prepare for the worst, he kept the Queen with him and followed a strict devotional routine, attending Mass, taking communion more frequently than usual and going to confession daily.[17] His mornings were devoted to business, his afternoons to hunting.[18] Wolsey, meanwhile, had gone to Leeds Castle, where he spent his time dealing with the rush of requests for the offices and property of those who had died.

Back in London, the Duke of Norfolk caught the sweat and survived, but it carried off three of the King's most favoured Gentlemen of the Privy Chamber: Sir William Compton, Sir Edward Poyntz and William Carey, the husband of Mary Boleyn. Compton, who had been 'lost by negligence by letting him sleep in the beginning of the sweat',[19] left no heir; his servants stole his effects, and there was a stampede for his vacated offices. Even young Richmond wrote to his father urging that some be given to Sir Edward Seymour, 'the Master of my Horse'.[20] Compton's will bequeathed his wealth to Anne Hastings, and to the King he left personal mementoes – 'a little chest of ivory with a gilt lock' filled with jewels, a chessboard and a backgammon set.[21]

William Carey died suddenly on 22 June, aged only thirty-two. The King granted the wardship of his son, Henry Carey, to his aunt, Anne Boleyn,[22] and warned her in a letter that her sister Mary was in 'extreme necessity'; in Henry's opinion, it was her father's responsibility to support her. At Anne's request, he ordered Rochford to take her under his roof and give her succour. Later that year, at Anne's further behest, Henry himself assigned Mary an annuity of £100 (£30,000) that had formerly been enjoyed by William Carey.[23]

Carey's death left a vacancy in the Privy Chamber, which was filled three days later by Sir Francis Bryan,[24] who was another of Anne's cousins and had long desired to recover his former place. Anne's good offices may have brought this about; certainly Bryan was one of her earliest supporters. Yet for all his brilliance, the advancing years had not sobered him – unlike Carew – and although he was now an established cipherer, diplomat and courtier, he still behaved like the profligate libertine he had always been. He would now become highly influential, riding high in the King's favour: he was Henry's constant companion in the privy chamber, and his favoured opponent in gambling, bowls and tennis.

Another Privy Chamber member who was well thought of by the King was the young page, Francis Weston, a gifted lute player and a superb athlete, whom Wyatt described as a 'pleasant' individual. Henry liked his company and often chose him to sleep in his bedchamber at night.[25] Anne also favoured him; he and Bryan sometimes joined her and the King for cards.[26]

From Tittenhanger, Henry moved north to the healthier air of Ampthill, where he began to complain of pains in his head, causing a momentary panic. He was still feeling poorly when he moved to Grafton, but there the pains disappeared. What began as a flight from the plague had now turned into a progress, but the King was careful to visit various shrines and religious houses for the health of his soul.

In high summer, the sweat began to abate in England, although for the first time it was rapidly spreading across Europe. Henry, on his way to Woodstock in Oxfordshire, was met by a messenger who warned him that one of the servants of the Duke of Suffolk, who had gone ahead to prepare for his arrival, had died of the sweat some days before. The King 'could not a little marvel' that Suffolk had failed to warn him of this earlier; now the giests had to be changed at a moment's notice, much to Henry's irritation.[27] This resulted in him moving north to Old Moor Hall at Sutton Coldfield, where he stayed as the guest of John Vesey, Bishop of Exeter. Whilst hunting in nearby Sutton Chase, the King tracked down a rare boar, but it turned viciously on him and his life was saved only by the timely intervention of a local girl who, being fortuitously nearby with her bow and arrow, shot the beast dead.

In August, Henry's plans were altered again because there were still cases of plague nearer to London. A sojourn at The More was abandoned, and the King lodged at Tittenhanger instead.[28] At every stage of his journey, his officers were sent ahead to check that each house was free from infection.[29]

Around this time Jean du Bellay, Bishop of Bayonne, the first resident French ambassador to be sent to England, came to present his credentials to the King. Soon after his arrival, du Bellay noted that 'Mlle. Boleyn has returned to court', accompanied once more by her mother. It was not a long visit, but sufficient to further inflame the King's ardour after the long weeks of separation. Together, they rode out hunting daily, and du Bellay, whose master's support both Henry and Anne were keen to secure, was often asked to accompany them, a mark of signal favour.

'Madame Anne' set herself to charm him, bestowing on him generous gifts – a hunting outfit, hat and horn, and a handsome greyhound – and telling him that everything she did was 'entirely by the commandment of the King'; while Henry would often take him aside to discuss confidential affairs. The ambassador's dispatches reveal how flattered he was by this attention, but he was careful to say that it was really a sign of the King of England's love for France.[30] The King of France, no fool, would get the message.

36

'Back to Your Wife!'

The Great Matter polarised opinion amongst the elite and led to a vicious struggle for power. By 1528, three distinct factions were emerging at court, in the Privy Chamber and in the Privy Council: those who were adherents of Wolsey and supported the King, notably Sir John Russell; the aristocratic conservatives, among them Exeter, the Staffords, the Nevilles, the Poles and the Duchess of Norfolk, who discreetly supported the Queen but wanted Wolsey out of power; and the Boleyn faction, which would soon be the most powerful and was led by Anne herself, Rochford, George Boleyn and Sir Francis Bryan. The members of this group, which included Sir Thomas Cheney and his friend John Wallop, were determined to break Wolsey's monopoly on power, and seized every opportunity to poison the King's mind against him.

They were joined by the Dukes of Norfolk and Suffolk, who, although they disliked Rochford and his family, had long plotted the Cardinal's downfall, and saw in Anne Boleyn a means of achieving it.[1] Norfolk was also motivated by self-interest, since Anne was his niece and her advancement could only benefit the Howards. Anne was a willing tool: Cavendish says she was agreeable to the requests of her supporters because she had 'an inward desire to be revenged upon the Cardinal' for the breaking of her affair with Lord Henry Percy and her subsequent banishment in disgrace; but her enmity is more likely to have been fuelled by her father's removal from two very lucrative and prestigious offices.

Henry Norris, the Groom of the Stool and one of the King's chief confidants, was a loyal supporter of the Boleyns but not committed to bringing down the Cardinal. Discreet and level-headed, he did his best to strike a balance between opposing interests.

The Queen enjoyed the support of several churchmen, among them

John Fisher, Bishop of Rochester; the frail Richard Foxe, Bishop of Winchester, who made his views clear before his death that year; and her brave Chaplain Thomas Abell, who in 1530 wrote a treatise supporting her case, which Henry banned. William Warham, Archbishop of Canterbury, was also of the opinion that the royal marriage was valid, but compromised his principles by supporting the King. Another person who deeply disappointed Katherine was her protégé Juan Luis Vives, who also sided with Henry, as did many humanists, Sir Thomas More and John Fisher being notable exceptions. When Katherine asked Vives to defend her in the coming legatine hearing, he declined and left England for Bruges.[2] The Queen stopped his pension.

There is no doubt that, thanks to the influence of Anne Boleyn, Wolsey's power was declining. In August 1528, Jean du Bellay told Francis I that Wolsey no longer enjoyed the King's fullest confidence, and that Henry was taking decisions without his knowledge;[3] three months later, Mendoza reported that the Cardinal was 'no longer received at court as graciously as before'.[4]

In the past, Wolsey's power had been such that he could easily neutralise emerging factions, who had never held much sway at court because of his overriding political dominance, but that was no longer the case. Now he had to jostle for supremacy with everyone else. As his grasp weakened, the Boleyn faction flourished, and his enemies prepared to destroy him. To counteract their influence with the King, Wolsey secured the appointment of his own clients to the Privy Chamber, among them Thomas Heneage, who was on good terms with Anne Boleyn, and the Cardinal's former secretary, Sir Richard Page, who would soon switch his loyalty to the Boleyns. Wolsey also did his best to sweeten Mistress Anne with gifts and entertainments and by his strenuous efforts to obtain an annulment in the face of the Pope's stalling tactics. He knew that Anne's elevation to the consort's throne would mean his own downfall, yet he had no choice but to do the King's bidding. Relations between Anne and Wolsey were always outwardly cordial, but that deceived no one.

The King, meanwhile, had been reading up as many authorities on canon and civil law as he could lay hands on, to perfect his case in readiness for the legate's arrival. In one letter to Anne Boleyn, he claimed he was spending up to four hours each day poring through vast theological tomes, and suffering 'some pain in my head' as a result.[5] This new passion for study led to the acquisition of more and more volumes for the royal libraries, while some books were obligingly loaned to the King by the abbots of various monasteries. Henry even sent the humanist scholar Richard Croke to Italy to acquire or consult obscure works, giving him detailed instructions as to what to look for and transcribe.[6] He had convinced himself that his case was sound, and was prepared to go to astonishing lengths to prove it.

Cardinal Campeggio arrived in London in October 1528. The Pope had secretly instructed him to bring about a reconciliation between the King and Queen, but if that was not possible he was to persuade Katherine to enter a convent, thus freeing Henry to make another marriage. Campeggio soon saw that there was no chance of the former, and the Queen made it very clear that she had no vocation for the religious life: she insisted she was the King's true wife, and nothing would make her say otherwise. As for the Cardinal, who took the opposite viewpoint, Campeggio had no more success with him 'than if I had spoken to a rock'. Moreover, it soon became obvious to the legate what drove the King, and he reported to Clement: 'He sees nothing, he thinks of nothing but Anne; he cannot do without her for an hour. He is constantly kissing her and treating her as if she were his wife.' However, he was quite certain that they had 'not proceeded to any ultimate conjunction'.

Campeggio soon made it clear that Clement was prepared to offer Henry anything except the annulment he so desired, even a dispensation for a marriage between the Princess Mary and her half-brother Henry Fitzroy. He insisted that Pope Julius's dispensation was sound, but the King would not accept this. Campeggio felt that, 'if an angel were to descend from Heaven, he would not be able to persuade him to the contrary'. Wolsey, who by virtue of his own legatine powers was to work with Campeggio to reach a solution, was becoming increasingly desperate, as it became alarmingly clear that the Italian Cardinal was not to be manipulated.

The King did not help matters by installing Anne Boleyn in the palatial surroundings of Durham House on the Strand soon after the legate's arrival. But Anne was not satisfied with her new abode, and demanded something even grander. Henry arranged for her to lodge temporarily at Suffolk House in Southwark, the London home of the Duke and Duchess of Suffolk, and himself paid for the refurbishment of the rooms she would occupy, which were furnished with great splendour. Here, Anne kept regal state, attended by ladies-in-waiting, train-bearers and chaplains. Courtiers hastened there in droves to pay their respects to her, while Katherine's chamber, once the hub of courtly entertainments and gatherings, was deserted.

But this semblance of popularity was superficial. Anne and her family were never well liked at court, where they were secretly considered proud and grasping, and they were hated by the people, many of whom supported their beloved Queen. When Anne went hunting with the

King, villagers would hoot and hiss at her,[7] and on one occasion when Henry was riding alone near Woodstock, one of his subjects yelled, 'Back to your wife!'[8]

Anne cannot have been happy with the fact that Henry was still dining regularly with Katherine, and also, according to Jean du Bellay, sharing her bed.[9] On the King's own admission, he was not having sex with her, so he was probably keeping up appearances in order to impress the legate. The strain of the nullity suit had taken its toll on Katherine – Campeggio thought she was nearly fifty when in fact she was just forty-three, whereas Henry, at thirty-seven, was still in his prime.

In November 1528, the royal couple were together at Bridewell Palace; as they walked along the river gallery, they could hear a large crowd outside cheering the Queen.[10] Fearing that his popularity was at risk, the King summoned the leading citizens of London to the palace and assured them that he had instigated nullity proceedings only to set his mind at rest, and that, were he to choose again, he would take Katherine for his wife above all others.[11]

In early December, however, Henry took advantage of Katherine's temporary absence at Richmond and installed Anne at Greenwich 'in a very fine lodging which he has furnished very near his own. Greater court is paid to her every day than has been for a long time paid to the Queen.'[12] Some were scandalised by this turn of events – the Venetian ambassador spoke in such an insultingly 'lewd fashion' of the King's morals that he had to be recalled[13] – but Anne did not care. She was determined to eclipse not just Katherine, but Wolsey too. It was to Anne, rather than the Cardinal, that courtiers and supplicants now came seeking patronage.

There was a tense atmosphere at court during the Christmas celebrations. Anne kept open house in her own apartments, avoiding the official revels in the chamber 'because she does not like to meet the Queen'.[14] It was Katherine who presided over the main festivities, but she found it hard to look cheerful 'and made no joy of nothing, her mind was so troubled'.[15] The King ignored her misery; he entertained the two legates with jousts, banquets, masques and disguisings, knighted Campeggio's son, and on the Feast of St Thomas of Canterbury on 29 December appeared looking very majestic in cloth of gold lined with beautiful lynx's skins. 'All comers of any honest behaviour' were allowed to enter the great hall and partake of the 'great plenty of viands' laid out there.[16]

The Boleyns had recently taken up Holbein, who around 1528 painted portraits of several members of their faction, among them Rochford's sister Anne and her husband Sir John Shelton, and Sir John

Godsalve and his son, another John, who were members of Rochford's circle in Norfolk.[17]

Holbein had also painted the illuminated capitals for a short treatise by Nicolaus Kratzer entitled *Canones Horoptri*, which was bound in green velvet and presented to Henry at New Year 1529. The treatise described the uses of an instrument called a 'horoptrum', which had been invented by Kratzer to predict such things as the exact times of sunrise and sunset and the passage of the Sun through the Zodiac.[18] We know that Holbein had returned to Basel by August 1528, when his two-year leave of absence from the city expired, but it is possible that he came back briefly to England for the presentation of the treatise. This cannot be proved, as his movements for the next three years are unrecorded.[19]

During the early months of 1529, the legates prepared for the hearing of the King's nullity suit. Henry proposed Warham as counsel for the Queen, but Katherine had little faith in the Archbishop's ability or inclination to uphold her cause. Besides, he was Henry's subject, and therefore not impartial. She had more confidence in her other counsel, John Fisher, Bishop of Rochester, a man of greater principle.

There was a minor scandal at Easter when Anne took it upon herself to bless cramp rings, a ritual that could be performed only by an anointed king or queen. The fuss soon died down, and the court moved to Richmond to celebrate St George's Day with the usual Garter feast.

Wolsey, who had left no stone unturned to make the King's case watertight, was confident of a happy outcome when, on 31 May, the legatine court opened in the great hall of the priory of the Blackfriars in London. There was enormous public interest in the proceedings, not only because opinions ran high, but also because in England a king and queen had never before been summoned before a court. For a brief space it seemed as if the hearing might not take place after all, for when the Queen was summoned into the court she did not go to the chair of estate appointed for her, but, ignoring the legates, made her way to the King's throne and there, falling to her knees, made a dramatic plea to him to spare her the extremity of the court. She declared that she had been a true wife to him, and that when he married her she had been a virgin, 'without touch of man. And whether it be true or no, I put it to your conscience.' If, however, he persisted in his suit, then she would commit her cause to God.[20]

As the King stared straight ahead Katherine rose, curtseyed and, leaning on the arm of her Receiver General, Griffin Richards, who had served her since her marriage to Prince Arthur, she left the court, ignoring urgent calls for her return. Outside, the people cheered and clapped her. The legates, however, declared her contumacious and proceeded without her.

There followed days and days of interminable depositions and heated discussions. Much of the evidence focused on whether Prince Arthur had consummated his marriage, and several noblemen came forward to boast that they had been capable of the sex act at his age. Much of the evidence was heavily weighted in Henry's favour, but Bishop Fisher, a lone voice, spoke up for Katherine, telling the court, 'This marriage of the King and Queen can be dissolved by no power, human or divine.'[21] Henry dismissed this as the view of 'but one man'.

Campeggio listened to it all, but gave nothing away. Finally, on 23 July, he unexpectedly adjourned the case to Rome, in compliance with the Pope's secret instructions. There was a shocked silence; then, as the King walked out, his face like thunder, the Duke of Suffolk crashed his fist onto the table in front of him and shouted, 'By the mass, it was never merry in England while we had cardinals among us!' Wolsey, who was no less appalled than anyone else and doubtless believed that he now faced ruin, replied bitterly, 'Of all men in this realm, ye have least cause to be offended with cardinals. For if I, a simple cardinal, had not been, ye should have at this present no head upon your shoulders.'[22]

37

'Above Everyone, Mademoiselle Anne'

At the end of July 1529, Henry went with Anne Boleyn to Greenwich, then took her on progress, visiting Waltham Abbey, Barnet, Tittenhanger, Windsor, Reading, Woodstock, Langley, Buckingham and Grafton, where Anne 'kept state more like a queen than a simple maid'.[1] Here, in September, the two legates came, so that Campeggio could take his official leave of the King before returning to Rome.

There is no doubt that Wolsey was in disgrace, and that Anne, Norfolk and the rest of their faction were resolved to be rid of him for good. There are conflicting accounts of what happened at Grafton. Cavendish, writing many years later, claims that when the Cardinals arrived, Campeggio was led away to a comfortable lodging, but that no provision had been made for Wolsey, and he was forced to sit on his mule in the courtyard until Henry Norris came and offered the use of his own room so that the Cardinal could change out of his riding clothes before seeing the King. Another of Wolsey's servants, Thomas Alward, whose account was written five days after the event, does not mention this but states that, because Grafton was a very small house, both Cardinals were lodged at nearby Easton Neston.[2] Both are agreed that when Wolsey, full of trepidation, came into the crowded presence chamber and knelt before his master, Henry's old affection for him surfaced and, smiling, he raised him and led him to a window embrasure, where they talked for some time, much to the amazement of the onlookers.

Anne was furious. After Wolsey had gone off to eat, having arranged to meet with the King the following day, she sat at dinner with Henry and upbraided him for entertaining a man who had done him and his realm so much ill. Alward claims that Henry and Wolsey did sit in Council the next morning, and that the King went hunting after dinner, but Cavendish says Anne insisted that Henry left early with her to see a new hunting park nearby, and that Wolsey and Campeggio arrived just as the King was ready to leave, when he told them he had no time to talk and bade them farewell. Anne, who had ordered a picnic, saw to it that he was away all day. When he returned, Wolsey had gone, bound for The More.[3]

Whatever happened, Henry never saw Wolsey again. Influenced by the Boleyn faction, who were even accusing their enemy of witchcraft, he agreed that the Cardinal be indicted under the Statute of Praemunire – which prohibited papal interference in English affairs without royal consent – for receiving bulls from Rome, which Wolsey could not deny. On 17 October, he was stripped of his post as Lord Chancellor, and the Dukes of Norfolk and Suffolk triumphantly went to collect the Great Seal from him at Esher. Yet the King was merciful: when, in November, Parliament arraigned Wolsey on forty-four charges, Henry refused to proceed against him, but allowed him to retain several of his ecclesiastical properties and retire to his diocese of York.

The effects of Wolsey's fall were manifold. It unleashed a wave of anticlerical feeling, which was fed by Norfolk and Suffolk. It gave the King a useful scapegoat for things that had gone wrong in the past: he could say that Wolsey deceived him, and that many things had been done without his knowledge.[4] The Privy Council and the nobility grew more powerful now that they had no rival.

In October, the King returned to Greenwich, having seized four of Wolsey's most desirable houses – York Place, The More, Tittenhanger and Esher – along with their priceless contents, and taken full possession of Hampton Court. Building works still in progress were allowed to continue, and Wolsey's coats of arms were torn down and replaced with the King's.

On 2 November, Henry and Anne, accompanied by her mother, went by barge to view York Place.[5] This was, strictly speaking, still the property of the archdiocese of York, but early in 1530 the King's lawyers would manage to overcome this technicality.[6] Wolsey had drawn up an inventory before leaving the house, and the King and Anne inspected the piles of gold plate that had been left on trestles in the presence chamber and the sumptuous hangings that had been laid out in the long gallery.[7] Anne particularly liked York Place because it had no apartments for the Queen, and would be a house she could share exclusively with Henry. When Anne visited, she would lodge in a chamber beneath Wolsey's old library, and there was accommodation for her family also.[8]

At Hampton Court Henry was building a new private lodging for himself, the Bayne Tower, which was connected to the privy chamber by a new gallery.[9] Whilst work was in progress, he himself lodged in

Wolsey's stacked royal apartments. The Bayne Tower, which still survives,[10] is a three-storey donjon, the last of its type to be built in England: on the ground floor were the Privy Chamber office and a strong-room; the first floor housed the King's private bedchamber, bathroom (hence the name Bayne) with hot and cold taps, and study, and the top floor his library, housed in two rooms, and jewel house.[11] Henry used the Bayne Tower until 1533, when he abandoned it for more modern apartments.

His next tasks were to improve the drainage system[12] and add a second great kitchen with three huge open fireplaces and two stone hatches,[13] as well as several subsidiary kitchens and offices. Later, he extended the cellars. The service complex would then occupy over fifty rooms.[14]

Over the next year or so, the King, encouraged by Anne Boleyn, undertook other works at Hampton Court. He replaced Wolsey's wooden bridge with a stone one, guarded by statues of the King's Beasts, and set up the royal arms on the gatehouse and the inner gateway.[15] He built a new council chamber and constructed an imposing watergate down by the river, with an adjacent covered and crenellated water gallery with oriel windows. Later, he would transform the chapel, build innovative royal apartments and erect a vast great hall.[16] Altogether, in the period 1529–46, he spent £62,000 (£18,600,000) on converting Hampton Court into a magnificent show palace.[17]

Esher Palace had been built of red brick in the fifteenth century by William Wayneflete, Bishop of Winchester, and remained officially episcopal property until Henry VIII purchased it in 1537.[18] Wolsey had added a fine projecting gallery similar to that at Bridewell, which Henry had ripped out and moved to York Place whilst Wolsey was still residing at Esher, 'only to torment him'.[19]

The More, another fifteenth-century house, which stood to the south-east of Rickmansworth in Hertfordshire, had been so lavishly rebuilt by Wolsey that Jean du Bellay claimed it was finer than Hampton Court.[20] Henry initially did little to it, and by 1531 its once beautiful gardens were 'utterly destroyed'[21] and the house was deteriorating. Only in 1535 did the King make improvements, partitioning the great hall with a floor and creating new chambers above and below. Later, he entertained there several times.

Henry also took over Wolsey's unfinished tomb at Windsor, having decided that it would make an ideal sepulchre for himself. But the work proceeded in fits and starts, and the tomb, with its golden effigy on a black marble sarcophagus embellished at each corner with nine-foot bronze pillars adorned with angels bearing candlesticks, would still not be completed at the time of Henry's death.

Cardinal College, however, did not survive Wolsey's fall. Many of the lands that supported it were 'begged away to hungry courtiers',[22] and when the Master and Fellows pleaded with the King to save the rest, he gave a vague promise to found his own 'honourable college, but not of such magnificence as my Lord Cardinal intended to have'.[23] It would be seventeen years before he kept his word.

For the next two years Henry ruled England alone, determined that in future he would manage his own affairs.[24] For the first time in years he bore the sole responsibility for his kingdom, and he found it a heavy one. Initially, he told the Queen that Wolsey had left affairs in such a chaotic state that he would have to work day and night to set everything in order.[25] But it soon became clear just how many of the burdens of state the Cardinal had shouldered, and the King rapidly lost patience with his Councillors, shouting that Wolsey had been 'a better man than any of them for managing matters' and stamping out of the council chamber in disgust at their incompetence.[26]

However, ruling autonomously gave Henry a new confidence and authority, and his political and personal priorities led him to forge increasingly aggressive policies. Driven by the unshakeable conviction that he was right to demand the annulment of his marriage – 'not because so many say it, but because he, being learned, knoweth the matter to be right'[27] – he relied more and more on his own judgement and political instincts. He also paid greater attention to paperwork: Erasmus noted in 1529 that he personally corrected and amended his letters, often drafting up to four versions before he was satisfied.[28]

Wolsey's fall resulted in the promotion of several courtiers. Norfolk and Suffolk were made joint Presidents of the Council. Norfolk had envisaged that his career would flourish once the Cardinal was out of the way, but was to find himself outmanoeuvred by cleverer men. Moreover, his policies were invariably directed by his own insecurities, for it was his constant fear that the King might restore Wolsey to his former place.

Henry appointed as his Secretary a canon and civil lawyer from Cambridge, Dr Stephen Gardiner, an able but rather arrogant and difficult man[29] of about thirty-two, who had been one of Wolsey's secretaries. Gardiner was in many ways a conservative, but his overriding belief in absolute monarchical authority, and his hostility towards the Queen for defying it, made him an ideal royal servant. He was of swarthy complexion and had a hooked nose, deep-set eyes, a permanent frown, huge hands and a 'vengeable wit'.[30] He was ambitious, sure of himself, irascible, astute and worldly. Henry came to rely on him, sending him on important diplomatic missions and telling everyone that, when Gardiner was away, he felt as if he had lost his right hand; yet he was also aware that the Secretary could be two-faced.[31] Gardiner was successful in his career because he understood 'his master's nature' and knew how to manipulate him.[32]

The final, and most important, new appointment was that of Sir Thomas More as Lord Chancellor of England, on 26 October 1529; Sir William Fitzwilliam was made Chancellor of the Duchy of Lancaster in his place. Suffolk had been the King's first choice for the post of Lord Chancellor, but a jealous Norfolk opposed it on the grounds that Suffolk was powerful enough already. But More did not want to be Chancellor: he was reluctant to become embroiled in the Great Matter because he knew that his views did not coincide with the King's. Henry overruled his doubts, assuring him that he need play no part in the nullity proceedings; More might 'look first unto God and, after God, to him'. Eustache Chapuys, the new imperial ambassador who had come to replace Mendoza, declared, 'There never was nor will be a chancellor as honest and so thoroughly accomplished as he.'[33]

More cared nothing for the pomp and show of his office, and hated wearing the gold chain that went with it. When his friend Norfolk, visiting him at Chelsea, found him in a plain gown and singing with the local church choir, he tutted, 'God body, God body, my Lord Chancellor! A parish clerk! A parish clerk! You dishonour the King and his office!'[34] But More was unmoved. There were more important matters to occupy his mind, such as the Lutheran heresy that was spreading in England, which he particularly deplored. During his time as Chancellor, he would deal severely with reformers and those who spread sedition, and regarded the burning of six heretics as 'lawful, necessary and well done'.[35] William Tyndale, the exiled reformist translator of the Bible, against whom More had written a vicious diatribe, called him 'the most cruel enemy of truth'.[36]

Such was the new order, yet 'above everyone', noted du Bellay, was 'Mademoiselle Anne', whose word was law to the King.

It now seemed that the nullity suit might drag on indefinitely, yet a solution appeared to be at hand. On 29 August 1529, Stephen Gardiner and Edward Foxe, the King's Almoner, brought an obscure cleric, Thomas Cranmer, whom they had known at Cambridge, to see Henry at Greenwich. They had met him whilst staying at a house near Waltham Abbey, on their way back from Rome, and had been impressed with his views on the Great Matter. Cranmer declared that it was a theological issue that could not be dealt with under canon law, and suggested that the King canvas the universities of Europe, where were to be found the greatest experts on theology.

Henry was very impressed with the short, slight and scholarly cleric.

'That man hath the sow by the right ear!' he declared, and ordered Lord Rochford to take Cranmer into his household and appoint him his chaplain; Cranmer, in turn, was to write a treatise on his views, and in January 1530, armed with this, the King sent his envoys to every university, asking for their opinions.

Thomas Cranmer was to become one of Henry's staunchest supporters and a great partisan of the Boleyns. A keen advocate of reform, who was already secretly flirting with Lutheranism, he had won a fellowship to Jesus College but had been expelled for getting married. After his first wife, a barmaid called 'Black Joan', died in childbirth, he was re-elected to his fellowship and took holy orders; he then went to Germany, where he became involved in reformist circles and married the niece of the Lutheran theologian, Andreas Osiander; she bore Cranmer three children. During Henry's lifetime he had to keep their union secret, because in England the clergy were supposed to be celibate, and he was obliged to smuggle his wife into the country in a packing case.

By November 1529, Anne was constantly at Henry's side, acting as if she were already queen. She occupied the consort's chair at feasts and wore rich gowns of purple, a colour reserved for royalty, which the King had given her. His Privy Purse accounts show that he spent the equivalent of £165,000 on gifts for Anne during a period of three years.[37] Amongst his offerings were lengths of velvet, satin and cloth of gold for gowns, furs, fine linen for chemises, and numerous items of jewellery such as necklaces, brooches, bracelets, gold trinkets to sew on her gowns and borders of jewels and pearls to edge them, heart-shaped head ornaments, nineteen diamonds to wear in her hair, one ring set with emeralds and another with a table diamond, nineteen smaller diamonds forming lovers' knots and twenty-one rubies set in gold roses; there was even 'a crown of gold'. All were made by the King's jeweller, Cornelius Heyss.[38] Anne also owned initial pendants and rings and a bracelet set with a miniature of the King, which he had given to her early on in their courtship.[39] Her jewel box, a small bound chest, is now at Leeds Castle.

Katherine, meanwhile, was keeping mostly to her own apartments, doing her best to maintain friendly relations with Henry whenever she saw him. But when Henry dined with her on 30 November, her guard fell and she reproached him bitterly for having neglected her of late. Henry bore this patiently, but when he returned to Anne later that evening, she told him he should not argue with Katherine because she 'was sure to have the upper hand', and then began making peevish complaints about the delays in the nullity suit. She even hinted she might leave him, declaring she was wasting her youth 'to no purpose'.[40]

Soon afterwards, Anne caught a Groom of the Privy Chamber taking linen to the Queen; when tackled, he said that Katherine was going to make Henry some shirts, as she always had. Anne thereupon created a scene: an expert needlewoman herself, she was furious that Henry had not chosen to give the linen to her, but Henry was a creature of habit and insisted that it had been sent on his orders, and that he would not countermand those orders.[41] Both these quarrels ended in a passionate reconciliation.

Katherine had a staunch new champion in Eustache Chapuys, a fellow humanist and friend of Erasmus, whose zeal for her cause would often lead him to exceed his ambassadorial brief. Aged forty, he was a highly efficient canon lawyer and former ecclesiastical judge from Savoy, able, astute and never afraid to speak his mind. Yet although he spoke excellent French, Spanish and Latin, his command of English was less good, so he employed the Queen's former Usher, Juan de Montoya, who was fluent in the language, as his secretary.

Chapuys's dispatches, which are one of the chief sources for the period, were certainly prejudiced in Katherine's favour – he never referred to Anne Boleyn as anything other than 'the Lady' or 'the Concubine', even when she was Queen. He also repeated gossip or rumour as fact. Historians have therefore been cautious about accepting his reports at face value. It has even been asserted that Chapuys rarely attended functions at court, yet he dined often with the King's ministers, and had numerous influential contacts and an efficient spy network in the royal household. Very rapidly, he became a focus for those aristocrats who supported the Queen, and, on the Emperor's instructions, used all his resources to form them into an effective faction. However, the information they gave him led him to believe that support for Katherine was more widespread than it actually was, and that most of the country was prepared to rise in her favour. The King was frequently irritated by Chapuys, but genuinely liked him, sometimes confided in him, and often deliberately fed him information.[42] The Boleyns loathed him, and while some councillors believed him to be a liar and flatterer who had no regard for honesty or truth, he would probably have said the same about them.

It was to Chapuys that Sir Nicholas Carew revealed his growing sympathy for the Queen and the Princess Mary. A friend of Exeter, he had begun to feel alienated by Anne Boleyn's abuse of her position and her overbearing manner. Chapuys, realising that Carew was a powerful force in the Privy Chamber, was hopeful that he might be able to influence events, but for the present Carew preferred to keep his loyalties a secret.[43]

Anne's high-handedness was beginning to offend some of those who had hitherto supported her, but many people were concerned about her religious sympathies. She and her family were known to favour the reform of the Church and an evangelical approach to religion, which was dangerously close to what Luther preached, although some of their ideas were heavily influenced by the teachings of Erasmus. At a time when it was unthinkable that an individual should dare to interpret the Scriptures for himself, the Boleyns were therefore accused by Chapuys and others of being 'more Lutheran than Luther himself' and of supporting 'heretical doctrines and practices'. The ambassador denounced Anne herself, with good reason, as 'the principal cause of the spread of Lutheranism in this country'.[44] Anne certainly appeared to substantiate this view, which became widely accepted in the reign of her Protestant daughter Elizabeth I, by her support of various reformers who were openly challenging the traditional teachings of the Church; on several occasions she used her influence to save heretics from persecution.[45]

She even read with impunity books that had been banned in England, which she may have found in the royal library, where Henry kept them for reference. If not, they were easily come by, for Chapuys states that 'certain Lutheran books in English, of an evil sort', were always circulating at court, despite efforts to suppress them.[46] One book that Anne probably obtained from abroad was William Tyndale's *The Obedience of a Christian Man* (1528), which criticised the papacy and emphasised the authority of monarchs. She had first lent it to her maid Anne Gainsford, whose betrothed, George Zouche, had playfully snatched it from her. But he was caught with it, and Wolsey, who was then still in power, resolved to report the matter to the King. However, Anne got to Henry first and, on her knees, urged him to read the book. To his surprise he found himself agreeing with Tyndale's views, and announced, 'This is a book for me and all kings to read!' Yet it remained on the banned list because the King did not think it suitable for commoners to read.[47]

Another anticlerical book that Anne recommended to him was *A Supplication for the Beggars* (1529) by Simon Fish, a lawyer who had fled into exile after falling foul of Wolsey. Henry, who was now, perhaps understandably, becoming more receptive to criticism of the Church, again liked what he read, and thus Anne secured his protection for the author.[48]

Anne was nevertheless orthodox in the observance of her faith, and no one ever accused her of heresy. She liked the images and ritual of the Catholic Church. Before her death she had the sacrament placed in her closet 'that she might pray for mercy' with it in her sight,[49] and expressed the conviction that she was destined for Heaven 'because she had done many good deeds'.[50] Many of the devotional books she owned were written on traditional themes, such as the *Book of Hours of the Blessed*

Virgin Mary with a calendar of saints' days; Anne had written in it a message to Henry, 'By daily proof you shall me find, to be to you both loving and kind', but her signature has been cut off.[51] Some of her books were beautifully illuminated and bound, among them a fine French psalter dating from 1529 to 1532[52] and a second *Book of Hours*, printed in Paris around 1528, said to have been given by Anne on the scaffold to Wyatt's sister, Margaret, Lady Lee, and now at Hever Castle. It is inscribed in her own hand, 'Remember me when you do pray, that hope doth lead from day to day.'

However, she differed from many of her orthodox contemporaries in her belief that the Bible should be read in the vernacular. She herself owned French versions of the Scriptures: during Lent 1529, Loys de Brun, the author of a treatise on letter-writing that was dedicated to Anne, saw her reading the Epistles of St Paul in French and other translations of the Bible,[53] and there is evidence that she ordered such books from France.[54] The King was not opposed in principle to the Bible being translated into English, but disapproved of the existing reformist versions, which in his view only encouraged heresy.[55]

Anne's identification of herself with the cause of reform led to a further realignment of factions at court, which resulted in those who supported the Queen also favouring the preservation of traditional forms of religion in England. The supporters of Anne were invariably committed to reform. In this climate, on 2 November 1529, the King summoned what was to become known as the Reformation Parliament.

Henry's son Richmond was now ten. He had his father's passion for field sports, and had been delighted to receive some fine bloodhounds from his cousin James V of Scotland; smaller bloodhounds that could fit on to a man's saddle were specially bred for him at Sheriff Hutton. Richmond enjoyed hunting with the many northern nobles who sought his company, and the fellowship of his uncles, George and William Blount, who lodged permanently in his household. But the King was concerned to hear that his son was no longer applying himself diligently to his studies;[56] he therefore recalled Richmond, and made Cuthbert Tunstall, soon to replace Wolsey as Bishop of Durham, President of the Council of the North.

The young Duke was from now on based chiefly at Windsor, and John Palsgrave replaced Richard Croke as his tutor. Palsgrave, a Cambridge scholar in holy orders who had written the first French grammar book for English students, had once been French master and secretary to Henry's sister Mary. A respected humanist and disciple of Erasmus, he was friendly with More, and had a reputation for achieving success with reluctant pupils. The King himself interviewed him at

Hampton Court, saying, 'Palsgrave, I deliver unto you my worldly jewel: bring him up in virtue and learning.'[57]

Several letters from Palsgrave to the King, Sir Thomas More and Elizabeth Blount survive, giving details of how the tutor overcame Richmond's problems. He found that the boy could not pronounce Latin like a King's son because he had lost his front teeth and lisped; in addition, his diction was awful. Palsgrave's remedy was to reawaken the boy's interest by studying a funny play by Plautus. When Fitzroy wearied of study, Palsgrave would call a halt. He did his 'uttermost best to cause him to love learning and be merry at it', so much so that 'his officers wot not whether I learn with him or play with him'. Soon, Palsgrave was able to report to Elizabeth Blount that Richmond was again showing an aptitude for learning and was 'much inclined to all manner of virtuous and honourable inclinations as any babes living'.[58] He developed a fine Italianate hand and manifested the family talent for music, as well as becoming a superb horseman, like his father.

After a while, Richmond went to live with his former tutor, Richard Croke, at King's College, Cambridge, where he studied a wider curriculum under humanist disciplines in the company of other well born youths, who in their leisure time hunted with him and taught him the kind of songs that would have made his royal father blush.

The Boleyns now reigned supreme. On 8 December 1529, Anne's father was created Earl of Wiltshire and Ormonde; the former earldom had once been held by the Staffords, while the latter was granted to Boleyn after a long dispute with his Butler cousins, whose family had long held the title. His daughter was henceforth titled the Lady Anne Rochford, and took as her personal badge the black lion rampant, a device used by previous Earls of Ormonde.

On the same day, two allies of the Boleyns were also promoted to the peerage: George Hastings was created Earl of Huntingdon, and Robert Ratcliffe Earl of Sussex. At Anne Boleyn's request, George Boleyn, now Lord Rochford and an established diplomat, was around the same time restored to the Privy Chamber as one of only two noblemen, Exeter being the other. This brought him into daily contact with the King, who often lost to him at gambling, and once generously paid the arrears of rent due on Rochford's house at Greenwich.[59]

On 9 December, the King gave a lavish banquet to celebrate Wiltshire's ennoblement. Katherine did not attend, and Anne sat in the Queen's chair, next to Henry; she was thus given precedence over another Queen, Henry's sister Mary, Duchess of Suffolk, as well as over the Duchess and Dowager Duchess of Norfolk, all of whom took offence at the slight. Chapuys thought it was like a wedding feast: 'After dinner, there was dancing and carousing, so that it seemed that nothing were wanting but the priest to give away the nuptial ring and pronounce the blessing.'[60]

The Queen again presided with the King over the splendid Christmas festivities at Greenwich, while Anne was conspicuous by her absence. She was perhaps unaware, therefore, that he had sent Wolsey an intaglio portrait of himself as a sign of goodwill.[61] After the celebrations, Henry sent Katherine to Richmond and took Anne to York Place, for which he had drawn up designs for improvements that were 'expressly to please the Lady, who prefers that place to any other'.[62] It was here, on 12 January 1530, that Henry and Anne hosted a magnificent ball in honour of the departing Jean du Bellay.[63]

Twelve days later, Wiltshire was appointed Lord Privy Seal and promoted to the Privy Council, of which he became one of the most active members. The Boleyns and their allies now dominated the King, the government and the court. Even Erasmus sought their favour: it was at this time that he dedicated his commentary on the 23rd Psalm to Wiltshire and sent his portrait to Henry Norris. Yet within a short time, the power of the Boleyns would be eclipsed by a rival who was eventually to destroy them.

38

'Squire Harry Will Be God, and Do as He Pleases!'

It was around 1530 that a former servant of Wolsey's, Thomas Cromwell, entered the King's service. One of the most able ministers any king ever had, Cromwell was the son of a Putney blacksmith and had been born around 1485; his sister Katherine was the wife of a local innkeeper, Morgan Williams, and they would be the ancestors of the Lord Protector Oliver Cromwell. In youth, Thomas Cromwell had travelled in Italy, where he learned much about banking, became acquainted with the works of Machiavelli, whom he much admired, and found employment as a mercenary; he later told Cranmer 'what a ruffian he had been in his young days'.[1] When he returned home in 1512, he settled down and set himself up as a lawyer, merchant, moneylender and fuller.[2] In 1514, Cromwell had entered Wolsey's service as Collector of the Revenues of the archdiocese of York, and proved himself to be efficient and astute. From 1523, he was MP for Taunton. Around this time, he was working with Wolsey to suppress several minor religious houses in order to raise funds for Cardinal College.

Cromwell's genius for administration and finance was what endeared him to the King, who was impressed by the way he had stayed loyal to his former master and tied up his affairs. Moreover, Cromwell was pragmatic, knowledgeable, hard-headed and often ruthless; like Wolsey, he was a hard-working businessman with a talent for management. Henry quickly perceived that he could fill the gap left by the Cardinal, and, after a series of interviews, appointed him to the Privy Council.[3] Thereafter he 'grew continually in the King's favour',[4] and also became a focus for those who had supported Wolsey, such as Russell, Heneage and Page. Cromwell was not a member of the Privy Chamber, but thanks to the allegiance of such men, he was in a better position than Wolsey to lead a Privy Chamber faction.

Cromwell's portraits show a thick-set, portly man with heavy jowls, a small, severe mouth and porcine eyes. They do not reveal his hearty manner, nor his skill at dealing with people. Chapuys recorded that, in conversation, his innate reserve would give way to jovial banter and animated expressions; 'he is a person of good cheer, gracious in words and generous in actions.'[5]

Although he was not university-educated, Cromwell spoke Latin, French, Italian and some Greek, and was cultivated enough to hold his own with the likes of Kratzer, Dr Butts and, later, Holbein, who were all regular guests at his table. After the death of his wife, Elizabeth Wykes, in 1527, he never remarried, but may have taken mistresses. When he was due to stay with Norfolk at York in 1537, the Duke wrote, with wry humour, 'And if ye lust not to dally with my wife', he could supply for his guest's comfort 'a young woman with pretty proper tetins [breasts]'.[6] Yet the jovial, urbane exterior masked a calculating mind that could remain coldly detached from human considerations when making political decisions. Many of those who trusted Cromwell would live to regret it.

The Boleyns wasted no time in taking up Cromwell. He held similar religious views to theirs, and his considerable abilities and growing power could be harnessed to their advantage. As for the King, he was confident that his new adviser would be able to expedite his Great Matter.

There is no doubt that the tortuous delays in resolving his nullity suit, combined with his ever-present fears about the succession, his sexual frustration and the heady experience of autonomous government, were all responsible for the changes in Henry's character that were becoming apparent at this time. He was growing ever more suspicious of people's motives, and was so troubled about the Great Matter 'that he does not trust any one alive';[7] Erasmus and others were forcibly struck by his increasing resemblance to his father, Henry VII, in this and other respects.

Henry's virtuous conviction that he alone was right was making him supremely egotistical and sanctimonious: Luther had aptly commented, 'Squire Harry will be God, and do as he pleases!'[8] Where he had once been politically cautious, he was now prepared to be headstrong and ruthless in order to have his way. Chapuys astutely observed, 'When this King decides on anything, he goes the whole length.'[9] Henry was also turning into a master of the art of self-deception: his concept of himself as a paragon of knightly chivalry and virtue never faded, and his perception of people and events was sometimes advantageously distorted.

The young, idealistic humanist with liberal ideas about kingship was giving way to a selfish, dogmatic tyrant. Henry might still be affable and accessible, displaying a calculated bonhomie when it suited him – he would often greet Chapuys with an affectionate hug[10] – and his sense of humour was still lively, if a trifle touchy, yet he was more often the masterful embodiment of kingly authority, whose majestic and formidable presence aroused in lesser mortals both respect and fear. These days, the royal temper was more in evidence, and the King knew just when to use it to reinforce obedience. He also made no secret of his feelings: when he was pleased, his eyes glittered, when angry, he reddened, and when he was miserable, he sighed frequently or even wept.[11] As he grew older, he became ever more sentimental.

Henry was developing an increasing desire for privacy, which led him to build increasingly complex privy lodgings in his palaces, some of which – notably at Hampton Court, York Place and Greenwich – were accessed by covered galleries or stairs from private watergates, so that he could move from house to house without being seen by the public.

This growing emphasis on privacy resulted in the King abandoning his stacked lodgings in favour of the kind of apartments that Francis I was building for himself, which were all on one level, invariably on the first floor. The King's would be on one side, the Queen's on the other, and their privy lodgings were usually connected. Each suite had its own watching chamber, presence chamber and privy chamber, with the inner sanctum, or secret lodgings, beyond, accessible only to the Groom of the Stool and those specially invited. To these privy lodgings were added more and more chambers and closets, which enabled the King to withdraw completely from public life if he so desired.

Long galleries were also growing in popularity; people used them for recreation on wet or cold days, and Henry himself liked to discuss business whilst walking in them. During the next few years he was to build several fine galleries, notably at Hampton Court, Whitehall and St James's Palace, all affording good views of the gardens. Most of these galleries were private, with the King himself holding the only key. Here, he displayed his tapestries, pictures, mirrors and maps.

These changes began to take place around 1530, and resulted in some palaces falling out of favour because their stacked lodgings were considered outdated. Among them were Beaulieu, which would henceforth be used by the Princess Mary, Richmond[12] and the great palace at Eltham, which was inaccessible by river; although Henry still hunted in the park there and occasionally visited, he retained the house chiefly as a nursery palace for his children.[13] Bridewell Palace had proved too small, and was possibly subject to foul smells from the Fleet River; after 1530, Henry never used it, but lent it to the French ambassadors as their official residence.[14] He now regarded Greenwich as his chief residence, but even that would soon be superseded by York Place, which in 1529 had been designated a greater house. Greenwich would nevertheless remain one of the King's favourite country houses.

In order to keep up with the latest European architectural trends, and to satisfy a new-found greed for property that would reflect the magnificence of his status, the King now embarked, at enormous cost, on an orgy of buying and rebuilding that was to last for the rest of his reign. Hitherto, Wolsey had taken charge of royal building projects; now Henry made his own decisions, and there was no restraining him. In 1534, Thomas Cromwell lamented, 'What a great charge it is to the King to complete his buildings in so many places at once. How proud and false the workmen be; and if the King would spare for one year, how profitable it would be to him.'[15] So eager was Henry to have his new or refurbished houses finished that he paid his workforce a fortune in overtime fees, issued constant directives, and often arrived to take up residence before the paint was dry.[16] Works completed in such haste were not always executed to the highest standard, and were sometimes carried out with an appalling disregard for safety – several workmen are known to have been killed or injured.[17]

Because the King now preferred to spend his leisure in private, being entertained by his musicians and fools or gambling with favoured courtiers, there were far fewer court entertainments than there had been in the first half of the reign. It was at this time, therefore, that the recreational complexes in the royal palaces came into their own, for the diversion of courtiers who might otherwise become bored and listless.

These facilities were primarily built, however, for the King himself, who still excelled at 'manly exercise: he sits his horse well, jousts, wields the spear, throws the quoit, and draws the bow admirably. He plays at tennis most dextrously.'[18] Although he did not joust as often as in former days, he retained his passion for hunting and hawking, and continued to enjoy tennis, bowls and cockfighting. After 1530, he built new sports complexes at Hampton Court, Greenwich and Whitehall, and also at several lesser houses. The one at Whitehall would have five tennis courts or 'plays', two bowling alleys, a great tiltyard and a cockpit. At Greenwich there was another cockpit, a timber-framed tennis court, a bowling alley and a mews for hawks. Henry's covered tennis play at Hampton Court was completed in 1534 and was linked by a gallery to Wolsey's earlier court; it is not the tennis court that is there today, which dates from the 1620s, but was converted into lodgings for the future James II in the 1670s.[19] Most of Henry's tennis courts were beautiful crenellated Perpendicular buildings with buttresses, tiled floors and windows on two levels, protected by wire frames.[20] The larger courts measured eighty-three by twenty-six feet.

The King also began building a tiltyard at Hampton Court, but owing to his dwindling interest in jousting it was never finished in his lifetime, and was not used until 1604. The site is now occupied by gardens, and one of the Tudor viewing towers survives nearby. Henry also built three covered bowling alleys, two hundred feet long and twenty wide, one with windows brought from a dissolved monastic church in Oxfordshire; two of these alleys were by the river, and the third projected north from Little Chapel Court.

With the rise of heresy, there came a change in attitudes towards the New Learning, which many – at court, in the universities, and later throughout the kingdom – closely associated with the cause for reform. Many humanists were at odds amongst themselves, and the partisans of both the King and the Queen had been pressurising famous scholars for their support. The older generation, which included Fisher and More, tended to support the Queen, while the younger, led by Cromwell and Gardiner, championed the King.[21] The cause of reform attracted many radicals, if not outright heretics. Predictably, the climate in which intellectual freedom had flourished was changing to one of intolerance and censorship.

Henry tried to enlist the support of his learned cousin, Reginald Pole, who, having completed his studies in Italy, had been sent off to canvas the University of the Sorbonne in Paris; in 1530, the King recalled him and offered to make him either Archbishop of York or Bishop of Winchester. Pole, a scholar whose sympathies lay with Queen Katherine and who had no taste for public office, refused, which led to a violent quarrel in which the King barely restrained himself from punching his cousin, who emerged from the interview in tears. Amicable relations were soon restored, however, and Pole retreated to the peace of the London Charterhouse.

The Duke of Suffolk was certainly out of favour at this time, having raised the matter of Anne Boleyn's past with the King. Anne would not forgive such an insult and accused the Duke – possibly with some justification, given later events[22] – of seducing his son's betrothed, a girl of no more than eleven. For a time, Henry refused to see his old friend, but at length he prevailed on Anne to relent, and Suffolk was recalled.[23] But he was in a difficult position because his wife, Mary Tudor, loathed Anne Boleyn, and would not go to court while she was there. Suffolk, who himself secretly sympathised with the Queen, therefore, found himself the victim of divided loyalties.

Anne was now doing her best to force courtiers to abandon the Queen, threatening to have them dismissed if they did not give her their support.[24] Her adherent, William Brereton, a Groom of the Privy

Chamber, and Thomas Wriothesley, a member of the royal secretariat, were given the task of obtaining the signatures of noblemen and courtiers for a petition to the Pope, urging him to grant the King an annulment without further delay.

By 1530, a new humanist scholar had risen to prominence at court, John Leland, who had been educated at St Paul's School and the Universities of Cambridge, Oxford and Paris. He had begun his career as tutor to Norfolk's younger son, Lord Thomas Howard, had then been made a court chaplain, and had recently been appointed Keeper of the Royal Libraries. His chief task was to catalogue the many manuscripts and printed books in the King's collection. It was Leland who first suggested to Henry the idea of mapping the whole of Britain, a project that did not in fact come to fruition until Elizabeth's reign.

The summer of 1530 brought with it the plague, causing the King to flee from Hampton Court to Greenwich. Before his arrival, several poor folk were expelled from their homes as a precautionary measure; the King later compensated them for the inconvenience. During August, Henry gave himself 'entirely to hunting privately and moving from one place to another'.[25]

His son Richmond was sent back to Windsor, where Norfolk's thirteen-year-old son, Henry Howard, Earl of Surrey, was dispatched to keep him company and share his lessons. They remained there for two years, and forged a lasting friendship. Surrey, who was to become one of England's greatest poets, later looked back, when Richmond was dead and he himself in prison in Windsor Castle, upon that time of awakening adolescence as an isolated idyll, which he celebrated in one of his most moving poems, one that reveals more of Richmond's formative years than any other source:

> So cruel prison, how could betide, alas,
> As proud Windsor? where I, in lust and joy,
> With a King's son, my childish years did pass
> In greater feast than Priam's sons of Troy:
> Where each sweet place returns a taste full sour,
> The large green courts where we were wont to hove
> With eyes cast up unto the maidens' tower,
> And easy sighs such as folk drawn in love.
> The stately seats, the ladies bright of hue,
> The dances short, long tales of great delight,
> With words and looks that tigers could but rue,
> Where each of us did plead the other's right.

He recalled the two of them playing tennis under the watchful eye of a
governess, and missing the ball because their thoughts were on young
girls:

> The palm play where, despoiled [stripped] for the game,
> With dazed eyes oft we, by gleams of love,
> Have missed the ball and got sight of our dame,
> To bait her eyes, which kept the leads above.

There were happy hours spent jousting, riding and hunting, and
secret confidences shared:

> The gravel ground, with sleeves tied on the helm,
> On foaming horse, with swords and friendly hearts,
> With cheer, as though one should another whelm,
> Where we have fought and chased oft with darts.
> With silver drops the mead yet spread for ruth,
> In active games of nimbleness and strength,
> Where we did strain, trained with swarms of youth,
> Our tender limbs, that yet shot up in length.
> The wild forest, the clothed holts with green,
> With reins availed and swift, y-breathed horse,
> With cry of hounds and merry blasts between,
> Where we did chase the fearful hart of force.
> The wide walls eke, that harboured us each night,
> Wherewith, alas! reviveth in my breast
> The sweet accord: such sleeps as yet delight
> The pleasant dreams, the quiet bed of rest.
> The secret thoughts imparted with such trust,
> The wanton talk, the divers change of play,
> The friendship sworn, each promise kept so just,
> Wherewith we passed the winter nights away.
> Give me account, where is my noble fere [companion]
> Whom in thy walls thou didst each night enclose?
> To other lief, but unto me most dear.
> Echo, alas, that doth my sorrow rue,
> Returns thereto a hollow sound of plaint.
> Thus I alone, where all my freedom grew,
> In prison pine, with bondage and restraint;
> And with remembrance of the greater grief,
> To banish the less, I find my chief relief.[26]

In 1531 the King gave Richmond the early-fifteenth-century house at Collyweston, Northamptonshire, Margaret Beaufort's former residence, as his principal seat, but it appears that he rarely used it before 1533.[27]

Cardinal Wolsey, meanwhile, had retired to his See of York and was staying at Cawood Castle, preparing for his belated enthronement as Archbishop. Suddenly, in November 1530, the Earl of Northumberland – the former Lord Henry Percy, whose courtship of Anne Boleyn the Cardinal had ended – arrived at Cawood with Walter Welch of the Privy Chamber and, in the King's name, arrested Wolsey for high treason; he was charged with having attempted to enlist the support of foreign rulers in his own cause and having been in secret correspondence with Rome.

Wolsey travelled south with the Earl; they were met on the way by the Captain of the King's Guard, Sir William Kingston, with twenty-four of his men. The Cardinal knew that at the end of his journey the execution block awaited him, but he was a sick man and when they arrived at Leicester Abbey for the night, he collapsed. As he lay dying, he said, 'If I had served God as diligently as I have done the King, He would not have given me over in my grey hairs.'[28] He was buried in St Mary's Abbey in the hair shirt that he had secretly worn during the last months of his life.[29]

George Cavendish rode south to Hampton Court to inform the King of Wolsey's death, and found Henry shooting at the butts. Noticing Cavendish leaning against a tree looking pensive, the King came up and clapped a hand on his shoulder.

'I will make an end of my game, then I will talk with you,' he said. Later, Norris summoned Cavendish to the privy lodgings where the King, wearing a gown of russet velvet lined with sables, awaited him. After Cavendish broke the news, Henry spent an hour 'examining me of divers weighty matters concerning my lord, wishing that liefer than £20,000 that he had lived'.[30]

Henry kept his personal sorrow to himself, but he was determined to assert his authority over the Church that Wolsey had represented. In December 1530, spurred on by Cromwell and the rampant anti-clericalism engendered by the Great Matter, he indicted fifteen of his senior clergymen under the Statute of Praemunire for having recognised Wolsey's unlawful ecclesiastical jurisdiction.

After dropping this bombshell, Henry presided with the Queen over the Christmas celebrations at Greenwich, while Anne Boleyn made herself scarce. She had recently made a fool of herself by adopting a motto that had long been used by the Emperor's family, and ordering it to be embroidered on her servants' doublets. Given the fact that she had spent her youth at the court of Margaret of Austria, she was probably aware of what she was doing, but the defiant gesture had backfired when people began laughing at her, and she hastily had the mottoes removed.[31] Anne was back at court by New Year, however, when the King had to give her £100 to buy him a gift,[32] and she was at his side when, in February 1531, he visited Sir Nicholas Carew at Beddington Park in Surrey.

England now stood on the brink of the Reformation, and there is no doubt that Anne was using all her influence to further her own cause and that of reform by encouraging the King in his new policies.

39

'Opprobrious Language'

By early 1531, Cromwell had entered the inner circle of the Privy Council, and was heavily influencing royal policy with his ideal of a sovereign state supported by Parliament, the law and an efficient administration. In February that year, the indicted clergy submitted to the King, paid an enormous fine, and recognised him as Supreme Head of the Church of England 'as far as the law of Christ allows'; the title was suggested by Archbishop Warham, the qualification by Bishop Fisher, who was emerging as one of Henry's chief opponents. The King had not broken with Rome, but had set himself up as the temporal head of the English Church: the Pope's spiritual authority was as yet unchallenged.

Two months later, the new Supreme Head began extending and refurbishing York Place as his chief London residence, and in order to lay out spacious gardens, he acquired and demolished neighbouring properties. A crenellated gatehouse with chequered brickwork, an oriel window, Tudor badges and terracotta roundels of Roman emperors was built across the highway (the present Whitehall) that bisected the palace site. This would later be known as the Holbein Gate, although there is no evidence that Holbein ever worked on it, although he would be responsible for the ceiling of Henry's new long gallery. The privy gallery that had been brought from Esher ran across the gateway and linked Wolsey's old house with the privy chamber in the new buildings. To the north lay the privy garden, to the south an orchard. The King, who retained the Cardinal's great hall and chapel, erected new lodgings for himself, all on one level, which were completed by October 1532. Mediaeval Kennington Palace, south of the Thames, was demolished and its stonework used for York Place.

Later on, Henry had the Thames embanked along the river side of the palace and built new privy stairs for his exclusive use, and another gatehouse, the classically styled King's Gate, to the south of the highway.

He also converted Wolsey's old lodgings into a Queen's Side for Anne Boleyn.

When complete, York Place (or Whitehall, as it became known) would be the largest palace in Europe. It consisted of a rambling series of magnificent state apartments, courtier lodgings and service quarters, all ranged around a number of courtyards. The exterior walls were painted with chequers and black and white grotesque work. Henry's own lodgings, on the east side of the palace overlooking the Thames, were sumptuous: his privy chamber contained an alabaster fountain, and all the principal rooms had high bay windows, ceilings 'marvellously wrought in stone with gold' by Clement Armstrong[1] 'and wainscots of carved wood representing a thousand beautiful figures'.[2] The windows blazed with heraldic glass by Galyon Hone, and the walls were hung with royal portraits.

Inside, there were 'many and singular commodious things, most apt and convenient to appertain only to so noble a Prince for his singular comfort, pastime and solace'.[3] For the King's bedchamber, a 'great bed of walnut tree'[4] gilded by Andrew Wright, one of Henry's decorative artists, was constructed over ten months at a cost of £83.3s.10d. (£24,957.50). Lucas Horenbout is known to have carried out commissions for the King at York Place in 1531–2, as did another eminent painter and engraver, John Bettes the Elder, who helped paint a mural of Henry's coronation.[5] There was probably another mural in the Adam and Eve Chamber, depicting the Fall of Man.

Much of this was done 'to please the Lady',[6] but the truth was that Anne Boleyn no longer pleased many of her former supporters. In June 1532, she quarrelled violently with Sir Henry Guildford, who had dared to praise the Queen in her hearing, and 'threatened him most furiously' that, when she became Queen, she would have him punished and dismissed from his office of Comptroller. In scathing tones he told her that she need not wait so long, and immediately resigned. The King urged him to reconsider, advising him he 'should not mind women's talk', but although Chapuys says Guildford refused, he must at some stage have relented because he certainly remained in office until his death.[7]

During June and July 1531, Henry and Anne spent their time hunting, accompanied only by Sir Nicholas Carew and two other attendants.[8] Up until this time, the King and Queen had made a point of visiting each other every few days for the sake of appearances; Henry always treated Katherine 'with respect, and occasionally dines with her'.[9] But now he decided that they must separate for good. On Friday 14 July, he rode out from Windsor with Anne and Carew and went to Woodstock, leaving

Katherine behind without saying farewell. He simply left orders that she was to remove with her household to The More and not write to him or see her daughter Mary.

At The More Katherine continued to enjoy the state of a queen, with a household that numbered two hundred, but few courtiers came to pay their respects. An Italian visitor, Mario Savorgnano, who went there that summer to see her dine, reported that she had 'always a smile on her face' and that thirty maids of honour were standing around her table.[10] One of those maids was Wyatt's mistress, Elizabeth Darrell, who would remain with Katherine until her death. Another was Jane Seymour,[11] whose brother Edward was now an Esquire of the Body to the King.

The Princess Mary was then residing at Richmond. At fifteen she was 'not very tall' but had 'a pretty face' and was 'well-proportioned with a very beautiful complexion'.[12] Her adolescence had been marred by the rift between her parents, which caused her untold misery and was to have an indelible effect upon her health. Although she loved her father, it was her mother whom she staunchly supported, and it was for this reason that Henry refused to allow the two to meet, in case they might plot against him.

Henry was forty in June 1531. Later that year, an Italian visitor, Lodovico Falier, would say of him, 'In this eighth Henry, God has combined such corporeal and intellectual beauty as not merely to surprise but to astound all men. His face is angelic rather than handsome, his head imperial and bold, and he wears a beard, contrary to English fashion.'[13] His hair was now worn cropped close to his head. Savorgnano described Henry as 'tall of stature, very well formed, and of very handsome presence . . . Nature, in creating such a prince, has done her utmost to present a perfect model of manly beauty, in favour both with God and man . . . I never saw a prince better disposed than this one. He is also learned and accomplished, and most generous and kind.'[14] 'You never saw a taller or more noble looking personage,' wrote the reformer Simon Grynaeus, who visited England that year.[15] In 1532, Falier wrote a confidential dispatch stating that the King had 'a very well-proportioned body of tall stature and an air of royal majesty such as has not been witnessed in any other sovereign for many years'.[16]

During the summer of 1531, the King travelled to Sandwich to inspect the defences there, and later took Anne Boleyn to visit Lord Sandys at The Vyne. In the autumn, he was hunting again, then in November he and the Queen hosted separate banquets for the Lord Mayor and the citizens of London in adjoining rooms at Ely Place in Holborn. Henry and Katherine managed to avoid meeting each other on this, the last state occasion in which the Queen would take part.

Katherine's departure from court undermined the power of her faction. Leave of absence was never refused to those who took her part, and in the Privy Chamber Exeter, whom Katherine had described to Chapuys as a good friend of hers, and his friend Carew found their influence undermined by Cromwell's allies. The Duchess of Norfolk, who supported the Queen on principle since the Duke was an ally of Anne Boleyn, openly impugned Anne's ancestry, quarrelled bitterly with her over Anne's interference in the marriages of the Duchess's children, and smuggled letters to the Queen in oranges; Anne found out what was happening and warned her aunt, in very 'high words', to desist, but the Duchess defiantly continued to act as a go-between for Katherine and Chapuys. Inevitably, the King discovered what was going on, and banished her from court.[17]

As the influence of the Boleyns and Cromwell increased, so that of Norfolk and Suffolk declined; realising that they had brought down the Cardinal only to have someone else take his place, rather than themselves, both Dukes were implacably hostile to Cromwell, whom they regarded as an upstart, although they were wise enough to establish good working relationships with him. Cromwell, however, was no fool: he knew that Norfolk in particular could 'speak fair to his enemy as to his friend',[18] and young Surrey was not above openly referring to Cromwell as 'that foul churl'.[19] Gardiner, who was appointed Bishop of Winchester in December 1531, was Norfolk's ally, but Anne was becoming suspicious of them both. Norfolk crossed swords with his niece on several occasions, but Gardiner was too wily to give her any cause for complaint. Norfolk and Suffolk were themselves at odds, both in the Council chamber and in their local jurisdictions in East Anglia, and the men of their affinity were now forming themselves into antagonistic rival bands.

The atmosphere at Greenwich that Christmas was subdued: 'there was no mirth because the Queen and the ladies were absent'.[20] Anne was now installed in the Queen's lodgings, 'accompanied by almost as many ladies as if she were queen',[21] but she did not preside with the King over the festivities, which were devised to impress the new French ambassador, Giles de la Pommeraye.[22] The Queen kept Christmas at The More, and made good cheer for the sake of her ladies, while Mary was at Beaulieu. Her cousin Margaret Douglas had recently joined her household and was sharing her education; the two girls, who were almost of an age, became very close friends.

At New Year, Anne presented Henry with some darts (probably boar spears) wrought 'in the Biscayan fashion, richly ornamented', while he gave her a set of rich hangings of cloth of gold, silver and crimson satin, lavishly embroidered, and a bed hung with cloth of gold and silver.

Although he had sent a gift to Mary, Henry did not purchase one for Katherine, yet she sent him an exquisite standing, or ornamental, cup. Angry with embarrassment, he refused to receive it, then changed his mind in case her messenger should return later in the day to present it in front of the whole court. Recalling the messenger, he took the cup and had it discreetly placed among his other gifts on a sideboard in the presence chamber. In the evening he returned it, sending orders that neither Katherine nor Mary were to send him gifts in future.[23]

By 1532, Henry was heartily sick of the Pope's procrastination, which in his opinion was bringing the Church into disrepute, and was beginning to contemplate a complete break with Rome. Anti-papal feeling was widespread in England, especially in the south-east, and there was bitter resentment against the tithes that had to be paid to an already wealthy Church and the corruption of many of its clergy. If Henry broke with Rome, the revenues of the English Church would be his, and his power and jurisdiction immeasurably increased. But it was a huge step to take after a thousand years of unity, and the King wavered, hoping that, even after all this time, the Pope would pronounce in his favour.

Others, however, had seen which way the wind was blowing. Reginald Pole went into self-imposed exile in Italy rather than stay in England to face a conflict of loyalties, and other members of the Queen's faction realised that they would soon be embroiled in a clash of ideologies.

The man who would mastermind the English Reformation, Thomas Cromwell, was appointed Master of the Jewel House in April 1532 and soon afterwards emerged as the King's chief minister. He would never be another Wolsey, for he was essentially a bureaucrat, not a prince of the Church, and there was no danger of him forming a rival court to challenge the ascendancy of the King's because his tastes were modest and middle-class, compared with those of the Cardinal. He lived in a well appointed house in London, dressed well but soberly, owned a fine collection of jewellery, enjoyed hunting, bowls and gambling, and gave generously of his wealth for the relief of the London poor. Cromwell did not have Wolsey's monopoly on power, but had to share it with Anne Boleyn and her faction, with whom he was allied against the court conservatives. However, he had 'risen above everyone except the Lady, and the world says he has more credit with his master than ever the Cardinal had. Now there is not a person who does anything except Cromwell.'[24] The King, however, did not leave all the decision-making to Cromwell: the policies were essentially Henry's but the means of carrying them out efficiently were devised by his brilliant minister.

During the next two years, Cromwell would amass a number of prestigious and lucrative offices, the most important being that of Chancellor of the Exchequer, to which he was appointed in 1533.

Under Cromwell's auspices, Parliament would introduce a series of measures designed to limit papal power in England and bring the Great Matter to a satisfactory conclusion. The first of these, the Annates Act, passed in April 1532, effectively deprived the Pope of the first fruits of all English benefices.

At Easter, the provincial of the Observant Friars, William Peto, was invited to preach before the King and court, but caused a sensation when he warned a glowering Henry that any marriage with Anne Boleyn would be unlawful. If, like Ahab in the Bible, he committed this dire sin, the dogs would one day lick his blood, as they had Ahab's. Furious, Henry ordered one of his chaplains, Richard Curwen, to preach a retaliatory sermon the following Sunday, but he was heckled by another Observant Friar, Henry Elston. Both Peto and Elston were arrested.

That April, in defiance of the Duchess of Norfolk's wishes, Anne Boleyn used her influence to bring about the marriage of the Earl of Surrey to Frances de Vere, daughter of the Earl of Oxford, a young lady of impeccable ancestry but no fortune. Anne's choice of a bride for his son nevertheless came as a relief to Norfolk because she had recently toyed with the idea of marrying Surrey to the Princess Mary, with whose cause Norfolk had no desire to be identified.

The King's sister Mary, Duchess of Suffolk, had no qualms about declaring where her loyalties lay. That same month, she publicly referred to Anne Boleyn in 'opprobrious language',[25] which sparked a fight between the Duke's retainers and those of Norfolk; one of Suffolk's men, Sir William Pennington, was killed whilst seeking sanctuary in Westminster Abbey by two of Norfolk's followers, Richard Southwell and his brother, at which the enraged Suffolk broke into the Sanctuary 'to remove the assailants by force'. For weeks afterwards, 'the whole court was in an uproar'. The Suffolks withdrew to their estates, but their followers were still in a bullish mood, and the King and Cromwell had to intervene to prevent any further affrays.[26] Soon afterwards, Henry visited his sister and Brandon, but it took all his powers of persuasion to make the Duke return to his duties. Southwell was later pardoned after paying a fine of £1,000 (£300,000).

Anne had also incurred the enmity of her former supporter, Sir Nicholas Carew, by her treatment of his friends Suffolk and Guildford, and he would from now on work stealthily against her. Guildford died in May 1532; after his death, the King appropriated some of his plate to give to Anne Boleyn.[27] The passing of Guildford, which was quickly followed by the deaths of John Rightwise, who had worked with him devising court entertainments, and the King's Serjeant Painter, John Browne, who had been responsible for much of the scenery and props, brought to an end of the golden era of the Revels Office.

Guildford was succeeded as Comptroller of the Household by Sir William Paulet,[28] a friend and neighbour of Lord Sandys of The Vyne; Paulet lived at Basing House, which he rebuilt around this time. A cautious, astute man who changed his views as expediency dictated and thereby remained in favour and amassed a fortune, he was already a member of the Privy Council and Master of the King's Wards.

Revolutionary changes were afoot. When Parliament threatened the autonomy of the ecclesiastical courts, the convocations of Canterbury and York hastily surrendered them into the hands of the King, and formally conceded that they held their authority at his pleasure. Gardiner was one of the few who dared to protest against this, but in doing so provoked the King's anger and was forced to retire to his See.

Sir Thomas More was another who could not countenance this erosion of the privileges of the Church, and on 16 May, the day after the submission of the clergy, he resigned as Lord Chancellor. Despite his earlier promise, the King made no secret of the fact that he wanted More's approval of his nullity suit and his legislation, for the endorsement of one of the finest and most respected minds in Europe would add immeasurable weight to his cause; but More could not in conscience give it. His position had become untenable, and he surrendered the Great Seal with relief. Four days later, Sir Thomas Audley, one of Cromwell's lawyer friends and a loyal but pliable royal servant who had been Speaker of the Commons since 1529, was appointed Keeper of the Great Seal in More's place; he would be made Lord Chancellor the following January.

40

'The Lady Marquess'

In the summer of 1532, the King presented to Anne Boleyn the royal manor house at Hanworth, near Hounslow in Middlesex, which had been rebuilt by his father on the site of an older house; Henry now extended the property and had it remodelled in the Renaissance style with terracotta roundels of goddesses by Giovanni di Maiano,[1] and completely refurnished. The house stood to the south of the present parish church, and was connected by bridges over the moat to the beautiful gardens laid out by Henry VII with ponds, strawberry beds, an orchard and an aviary. Beyond was a park where the King 'took great delight' hunting 'buck and hare'.[2] Anne was also given the royal manor of Ditton Park at this time.

Another major building project on which the King embarked in 1532 was the embellishment of the chapel of King's College, Cambridge. He paid for a superb rood screen, organ loft and stalls, which were wonderfully carved by Italian craftsmen with Henry and Anne's initials and devices. The King later provided the magnificent stained-glass windows, which were the work of his glaziers, Galyon Hone and Bernard Flower. These works are some of the most outstanding examples of English Renaissance art to survive from this period.

The improvements at Hampton Court were progressing rapidly. In 1532, work was begun on the vast great hall – 106 feet long, 40 feet wide and 60 high – on the site of Wolsey's old hall, from which the large oriel window by the dais may be a survival. 'The King's new hall' was built of brick and stone in the Perpendicular style, with buttresses surmounted by octagonal turrets bearing the King's Beasts and gilded vanes; erected at first-floor level, above the cellars, it was designed as the first of the outward apartments, and was accessed by a processional stair. When completed, it would have a tiled floor[3] and a fine minstrels' gallery above an oak screen; crowning all was a magnificent hammerbeam roof designed by the King's Master Carpenter, James Nedeham, which was decorated with red, blue and gold badges and initials – among them those of Henry VIII and Anne Boleyn – as well as figures, antique scrollwork and putti, and elaborate pendants, all carved by the royal joiner, Richard Ridge of London. A three-tiered, hexagonal, domed louvre in the roof let out the smoke from the central hearth. The hall, completed in 1535, was hung with the tapestries depicting the story of Abraham, which are still there today.[4]

The hall at Hampton Court was the only one of its type built by Henry VIII, and, although calculated to impress, it was already outdated by the time building work commenced. At several other houses, Henry was demolishing his great halls and replacing them with an outward first-floor chamber accessed by a great processional – or 'halpace' – stair from the courtyard, an arrangement that would endure in English palaces for three hundred years.

Work at York Place was forging ahead. In 1531 the King had acquired the old leper hospital of St James, which stood in open countryside nearby, and had pensioned off its three remaining inmates and had the old buildings demolished. Between 1532 and 1540 he erected there 'a magnificent goodly house'[5] as 'a residence for the royal children',[6] which was known as St James's House or St James's in the Fields. Ranged around four courtyards, it was approached via a mighty gatehouse embellished with octagonal turrets and decorated with a Tudor rose and the initials H and A. The new palace boasted fine royal lodgings, a tennis court, a tiltyard and a beautiful chapel,[7] but no great hall. Out of sixty acres of nearby marshland, which he had drained, the King created St James's Park and stocked it with deer for his 'greater commodity and pleasure';[8] to this he added a hunting chase for his own exclusive use, which stretched as far as Hampstead Heath and Islington. Henry himself rarely stayed at the palace, and it was used mainly as a London residence for the Duke of Richmond.

In the summer of 1532, Henry's new mania for building was extended to the Tower, which he wanted refurbished in time for Anne Boleyn's coronation, an event which he confidently expected would take place in the near future. At a cost of £3,500 (£1,050,000), Cromwell arranged for the old royal apartments to be gutted, and their walls and ceilings decorated in the antique style. A new Queen's lodging was built in the Inner Ward, north of the Lanthorn Tower, with a presence chamber, a dining chamber, a bedchamber with a privy, a gallery that led to the King's apartments, and a bridge across the moat leading to a private garden. A novel 'mantel of wainscot with antique' was installed in the dining chamber, and Henry was so pleased with the effect that he began tearing out fireplaces in his other houses and replacing them with similar antique-style mantels. Back at the Tower, St Thomas's Tower was converted into new lodgings for court officials, and the White Tower was put in repair.[9]

In 1532, Andrew Wright replaced John Browne as Serjeant Painter to the King. Essentially a decorative artist, he had commended himself by his work on royal ships, carriages, banners and pageant scenery. Another artist who may have worked for Henry at this time was one 'Ambrose', who may be identified with Ambrosius Benson, a Lombard who had been a member of the Painters' Guild of Bruges since 1519. Benson is known for his religious pictures and portraits, and almost certainly painted Lord Berners, the translator of Froissart, and perhaps Berners' friend, George Hastings, Earl of Huntingdon, but no royal commissions can be traced.[10]

The work of such artists was soon to be utterly eclipsed by that of Hans Holbein, who returned to England in 1532 and settled in London, where, since his former patron, Sir Thomas More, was no longer in a position to help him, he made a living painting the portraits of the German merchant community. But Holbein's links with the court were by no means broken, and within a year his growing reputation would ensure that he would be again in demand.

In the field of music, as in art, there were rising stars at court. One was a 'very handsome'[11] young man called Mark Smeaton, who was appointed a Groom of the Privy Chamber in 1532.[12] Not only was he a gifted player of the lute, virginals and portable organ, but he was also an excellent singer and dancer. His talents had been spotted while he was quite young, and he had joined Wolsey's choir, transferring to the Chapel Royal after the Cardinal's fall. It was talent alone that accounted for his rise, not birth, since he was merely the son of a carpenter and a seamstress, with whom he now disdained to have much contact.[13] He also dressed badly, usually in 'yerns' (which have been improbably identified as jeans), and the King occasionally provided him with shirts, hose, shoes and bonnets.[14] People addressed him as 'Mark', which indicates his lowly status within the Privy Chamber.[15]

Smeaton, whose name was later to be irrevocably and tragically linked with Anne Boleyn's, was soon taken up by Lord Rochford, through whom he became associated with the Boleyn circle at court. His signature – 'A moi, M. Marc S.' – appears at the bottom of Rochford's manuscript of Jean Lefèvre's poems; this manuscript later came into the possession of Wyatt whose name is written in it, along with a number of proverbs on the fly-leaves.[16] There is no evidence that Rochford and Smeaton were ever involved in a homosexual relationship, as has recently been suggested.[17]

Mark Smeaton has also been associated with a music book written for Anne Boleyn.[18] His signature on the Lefèvre manuscript has been identified with the handwriting in this book, from which it has been inferred that he wrote it, but this is by no means certain. The music book is a collection of thirty-nine Latin motets and five French *chansons*, all written before 1515; among them are works by the great French composer Josquin des Prés, with which Anne had probably become familiar in Burgundy and France. One initial letter depicts what has been described as Anne's armorial falcon, pecking at a pomegranate – the badge of Katherine of Aragon – which, if correct, would date the book's completion to 1533 at the earliest, which was when Anne adopted her falcon badge. However, this bird bears no resemblance to Anne's crowned falcon. Thomas Boleyn's motto, 'Now thus', also appears, as does a reference to 'Mres. [Mistress] A. Bolleyne', which indicates that the manuscript was begun before December 1529, in which case it cannot have been Smeaton's work. Anne may even have brought it home with her from France in 1522.

In the summer of 1532, the King and Anne Boleyn left Hampton Court on a progress to Woodstock and Abingdon,[19] but this was curtailed for fear of demonstrations against Anne.[20] In August, on his return south, Henry visited Waltham Abbey[21] and was then entertained by Sir Thomas Cheney, now Lord Warden of the Cinque Ports, at Shurland House on the Isle of Sheppey in Kent, which had been extended and improved in honour of the King's coming.[22] The King and Anne spent the rest of the summer hunting at Hanworth.

Throughout the progress, Giles de la Pommeraye was at the King's side; he had come to negotiate a new treaty of friendship between Henry and Francis I and to discuss Henry's forthcoming visit to France, during which the King hoped to persuade Francis to intercede on his behalf with the Pope. In order to win over the French, Henry demonstrated great favour to the ambassador, personally showing him the improvements he had made at the houses they visited,[23] singling him out as his sole companion on hunting expeditions and inviting him to partner Anne Boleyn in archery contests. When Anne hosted a feast for the King at Hanworth, de la Pommeraye was guest of honour.[24]

Henry was feeling far from well at this time. He was suffering from chronic toothache and sinus trouble, as well as gout, which was probably the result of eating too much rich food. Nevertheless, he did not let his ailments interfere with his enjoyment of the progress nor his plans for the French visit. A majority of the universities had declared in his favour, and he was confident that pressure could be brought to bear on Clement to give the right decision. If not, it was open to him to take the ultimate step and break with Rome.

Then, opportunely, on 22 August, Archbishop Warham died, aged eighty-two. As his long life drew to a close, his conscience had finally moved him to condemn the King's nullity suit and state his intention of opposing any legislation that might be injurious to the Church. Henry had angrily threatened him with the Statute of Praemunire, but by then the Archbishop was too ill to leave his bed and past worldly considerations. Now he was dead, and the King could choose in his place someone who would prove more amenable to his will. Henry opted for Thomas Cranmer, who was duly elected Archbishop of Canterbury, unopposed by an unsuspecting Clement.

The King was optimistic that Anne would soon be queen, and on Sunday 1 September 1532, in order to increase her status and give her equal rank with some of the noble ladies whom she would meet in France, he took the unusual step of creating her a peeress – Lady Marquess of Pembroke – in her own right, in a glittering ceremony at Windsor. Before Mass, wearing a gown of crimson velvet 'completely covered with the most costly jewels',[25] and with her hair loose about her shoulders, Anne was escorted by the Countesses of Rutland and Sussex into the presence chamber. The Duchess of Norfolk appears to have refused to attend,[26] so her daughter, Lady Mary Howard, followed behind, carrying a crimson velvet mantle and gold coronet. Anne knelt before the King, who was attended by the Dukes of Norfolk and Suffolk and Giles de la Pommeraye, and he invested her with the mantle and coronet as the Patent of Creation, which also granted her £1,000 a year 'for the maintaining of her dignity', was read aloud by Bishop Gardiner. Then the new Lady Marquess rose, curtseyed and thanked the King before retiring, to the sound of trumpets, to her chamber.

After Mass in St George's Chapel, the King and Giles de la Pommeraye both swore to abide by the terms of the new Treaty of Windsor, after which the ambassador was again the guest of honour at a state banquet held in celebration of the new alliance and Anne's ennoblement.[27]

41

'The Triumph at Calais and Boulogne'

It appeared significant to some that the Patent of Creation, when referring to the new Lady Marquess's heirs male, omitted the usual words 'lawfully begotten'. Was Anne's ennoblement a reward for her surrender and a way of ensuring that any child, legitimate or otherwise, born of her body, was sufficiently provided for? It would seem so. For it is almost certain that, once Warham was dead, Anne, confidently anticipating that she would soon be married, became the King's mistress in the fullest sense.

Henry was determined that she should be at his side throughout the visit to France, a queen in all but name. He demanded that Katherine surrender the official jewels of the Queens of England, so that Anne could wear them, but Katherine indignantly declared that she would not give up what was rightfully hers to adorn 'a person who is a reproach to Christendom and is bringing scandal and disgrace upon the King through his taking her to such a meeting as this in France'. But the King insisted, and she had no choice but to obey.[1] Most of the jewels, which included four bracelets with eighteen table rubies, twenty other rubies and two diamonds, were then reset for Anne.[2]

Anne was determined to have all the trappings of queenship. Without telling the King, she ordered her Chamberlain to seize the Queen's barge, a fine vessel with twenty-four oars, and have its coat of arms burned off and replaced with her own; the barge was also painted in Anne's colours, blue and purple. Chapuys made a formal protest to the King, who angrily censured the Chamberlain.[3]

Anne then ruffled feathers by ordering some gowns in the French fashion; the historian Polydore Vergil condemned the modes she had copied from the 'wanton creatures' at the French court as being 'singularly unfit for the chaste'. The French, however, were to be impressed by Anne's wardrobe, which included a gown of cloth of gold spangled with diamonds, and several items with which the King had provided her: a green damask gown, a gown made entirely of gold-embroidered velvet which cost £74 (£22,200), silks, furs, and the more intimate gift of a nightgown (the Tudor equivalent of a dressing-gown) made of fourteen yards of black satin lined with taffeta, banded with velvet, and with the upper sleeves stiffened with buckram; it cost him over £10 (£3,000).[4]

For all Anne's grand preparations for the coming visit, no royal lady of the French court could be found to receive her. Henry had no wish to meet Francis's second queen,[5] Eleanor of Austria, who was the Emperor's sister, and Francis's own sister Marguerite refused to receive 'the King's whore'.[6] Henry was horrified when it was suggested that Francis's mistress, the Duchess of Vendôme, should do the honours. It was decided, therefore, that Anne should remain in Calais whilst Henry travelled alone to meet Francis. On 7 October they left Greenwich; amongst Henry's retinue of 2,139 persons[7] were Richmond, Norfolk, a reluctant Suffolk, whose wife had refused to accompany him,[8] Cromwell, Wyatt and the Gentlemen of the Privy Chamber.[9] Anne was attended by thirty ladies, summoned by the King to accompany his 'dearest and most beloved cousin'.[10] While the main personnel of the court went on ahead to Calais, the royal party spent one night at Stone, the home of one of Anne's closest friends, Bridget, Lady Wingfield,[11] another at Shurland as the guest of Sir Thomas Cheney, and a third at Canterbury in the house of Sir Christopher Hales. Then they rode to Dover.[12]

At 5 a.m. on 11 October, the King and his sweetheart set sail in the *Swallow*; the wind was fair, and they were in Calais by 10 a.m. After being received by the Mayor and Lord Berners, the King's Deputy, and riding in torchlit procession to the Church of St Nicholas to hear Mass, they were lodged at the Exchequer,[13] a great mansion that had been enlarged against their coming. It boasted two privy gardens for the King and Queen, a tennis court and a long gallery. Henry's bed had been sent ahead from England and set up in his lodgings, which were hung with green velvet. Anne was assigned a suite of seven rooms, and a connecting door linked her bedchamber to the King's;[14] a French source states they were living openly together.[15] Anne was certainly accompanying Henry to Mass and everywhere else, just as if she were Queen already, and there was speculation that Henry would secretly marry her whilst they were in Calais.[16] Anne had hinted as much to her sister back in August, when she wrote bidding Mary prepare to attend her to Calais, where 'that which I have so long wished for will be accomplished'.[17]

In Calais, Henry and Anne spent ten days at leisure, hawking, inspecting the town's defences, gambling with Norfolk and other courtiers,[18] and feasting on gifts of food sent by Anne de Montmorency, now Constable of France: carp and porpoise, venison pasties, choice pears and grapes.[19]

By mutual agreement, the coming visit was to bear no resemblance to the Field of Cloth of Gold: Henry insisted there must be 'no precious apparel of gold, nor embroidery, nor any other sort of nonsense'.[20] Each King was to be attended by his household only and six hundred men-at-arms. It had also been decided that Henry and Francis would each bear the cost of entertaining the other. In the event, most of these strictures were ignored, and both sovereigns spent lavishly on their attire and on the entertainments: Henry is estimated to have outlaid over £6,000 (£1,800,000).

On 16 October, Norfolk and Montmorency met to finalise the details, and on the 19th King Francis arrived at Boulogne, where he set up court in the Abbey of Notre Dame. Two days later the two Kings were embracing at St Inglevert, then known as Sandingfield, near the border of the Calais Pale. Henry, who wore russet velvet with borders of goldsmiths' work and pearls, had with him an escort of 140 velvet-clad lords and gentlemen, forty guards and six hundred horse. For a mile, Henry and Francis rode hand in hand, then stopped to drink a toast to one another near the French border. Hawking along the way, they proceeded towards Boulogne, outside which they were met by the Dauphin Francis and his two brothers, wearing black velvet edged with silver, who were accompanied by four cardinals and a thousand horse. Henry kissed Francis's sons on the mouth and embraced them fondly,[21] then kissed each of the French lords present. A thousand cannon sounded a deafening salute – which could be heard twenty miles away – as the royal procession entered Boulogne.

Here, Henry lodged with Francis in the Abbey of Notre Dame, in a suite of four chambers hung with cloth of silver and tapestries depicting Ovid's *Metamorphosis*. Every day, he and Francis attended Mass in the abbey church, kneeling in separate oratories, and ate in great splendour in the refectory, which had been adorned with tapestries portraying the story of Scipio Africanus. A vast buffet had been set up there, displaying plate glittering with precious gems.

During the four-day visit, an observer noted that the French 'far surpassed the English in apparel'. Francis himself once appeared in a doublet 'overset with stones and rich diamonds, valued at £100,000 (£30 million),[22] and Henry VIII wore an outfit that Francis gave him, a crimson satin doublet encrusted with pearls beneath a long gown of white velvet embroidered in gold.

On the first day, after Mass, Henry and Francis talked of going on a

joint crusade against the Turks, and then went on to discuss the Great
Matter. Francis promised to use his influence with the Pope to achieve
a favourable outcome, and undertook to dispatch two cardinals to
Rome to inform Clement of the alliance and assure him that he need
not fear the Emperor.[23]

The weather remained fine. In the afternoons, Henry watched
Francis's sons playing tennis, and laid bets on the outcome; one day, he
lost £157 (£47,100).[24] He made an offering at the shrine of Our Lady
of Boulogne,[25] and entertained the French nobles to a sumptuous feast.
There was no jousting and no dancing, since there were no ladies
present. Henry lavished gifts on his host, among them fine horses,
mastiffs, falcons and jewels, and gave the Dauphin and his brothers
300,000 gold crowns.[26] His gifts were so generous that Francis had to
borrow funds in order to present Henry with six horses – and he also
gave him his own bed, hung with crimson velvet.

On 24 October, Francis invested Norfolk and Suffolk with the Order
of St Michael. The next day, he left for Calais with Henry, who was
resplendent in a cloth-of-gold gown over a slashed doublet ornamented
with diamond and ruby clasps. Outside Calais, Francis was greeted by
the Duke of Richmond, 'a goodly young prince full of favour and
beauty';[27] three thousand guns sounded another salute as the royal
cavalcade rode into the town and through streets lined with English
soldiers and serving men.[28] Francis was lodged in great state, at the
expense of the Calais merchants, at their headquarters, the Staple Inn,
where 2,400 beds and stabling for 2,000 horses had been made ready for
his retinue. That evening, the French King sent the Provost of Paris to
Anne Boleyn with a costly diamond as a token of his esteem.

On the Sunday evening, there was bull- and bear-baiting in the
courtyard of the Staple Inn, and a huge variety of meat, game and fish
at supper. This was served in the banqueting hall, which had been hung
with silver and gold tissue adorned with gold wreaths which sparkled
with precious stones, reflecting the light from twenty silver chandeliers,
each bearing a hundred wax candles. A seven-tier buffet groaned under
the weight of the Tudor gold plate. Henry appeared in purple cloth of
gold with a collar of fourteen rubies, the smallest the size of a goose's
egg, and two rows of pearls from which hung the Black Prince's ruby.[29]

After supper, Anne Boleyn and seven other ladies, including Lady
Mary Howard, Lady Rochford and Lady Fitzwalter, all masked and
clothed in unusual outfits of cloth of gold and crimson tinsel with gold
laces, danced before the two Kings. Then they led out the gentlemen,
Anne herself partnering Francis. Henry could not resist pulling off her
mask to show the French King who he was dancing with,[30] but Francis
rose to the occasion superbly, and after the dance had ceased, sat chatting

with Anne in a window seat for an hour.[31] The evening ended with Henry escorting his brother monarch to his apartments.

On the 28th, Henry held a chapter of the Order of the Garter, which Francis attended, wearing his Garter robes. Here, the two Kings made a solemn pledge to go on crusade against the Turks. Later that day, they watched wrestling matches between Henry's Cornish champions and the French, which the Cornishmen won.[32] Francis invited Richmond and Surrey to visit his court to complete their education, and it was agreed that they should accompany him back to France, where they would remain until September 1533.

At the end of the visit, on 29 October, Henry accompanied Francis onto French soil, and there the two monarchs said farewell with 'princely countenance and hearty words';[33] a stronger rapport had been established between them, and Henry was confident that Francis would prove a supportive friend.

After the King returned to Calais, violent storms lashed the Channel coast, and he and Anne were obliged to remain where they were for nearly two weeks. When the tempest had abated, fog set in, but the King insisted on sailing back to England at midnight on 12 November. He and Anne then took a leisurely route through Kent, staying at Leeds Castle, and again at Stone on the 20th; they arrived at Eltham Palace on the 24th.[34] Soon afterwards, the King made a state entry into London and gave thanks at St Paul's for the success of his visit and his safe return.

In December, Henry escorted Anne and Giles de la Pommeraye to the Tower of London. After they had inspected the building works, the King allowed his guests the rare privilege of entering his treasure chamber, where he presented a beautiful gold cup to the ambassador as a token of his gratitude. He also gave Anne a cupboard, and she selected gilt cups, flagons, basins and candelabra for her New Year's gifts.[35] Christmas was spent at Greenwich, with such a lavish banquet being served on Twelfth Night that temporary kitchens had to be built in the grounds. Soon afterwards, Anne realised she was pregnant.

42

'Anna Regina Angliae'

Henry had to move quickly if his expected son was to be born in wedlock. With the weight of scholarly opinion in his favour, he now considered himself a free man. Leaving Archbishop Cranmer to sort out the formalities later, he secretly married Anne Boleyn. Edward Hall gives the date as 14 November 1532,[1] which was the one accepted by later writers, but Cranmer, in a letter, refers to the ceremony having been performed on or about the Feast of the Conversion of St Paul, 25 January 1533.[2] The wedding is said to have taken place before daybreak in 'the high chamber' over the Holbein Gate at York Place.[3] The officiating priest was either Dr Rowland Lee, the King's Chaplain,[4] or George Brown,[5] Prior of the Austin Friars in London,[6] a vocal supporter of the nullity suit. The King apparently pretended that the Pope had sanctioned the union.[7] There were few witnesses:[8] Sir Henry Norris, Thomas Heneage, Anne Savage, a client of William Brereton,[9] and a Groom of the Privy Chamber, perhaps Brereton himself.[10]

Their marriage might have been secret, but both Henry and Anne took great delight in dropping hints about it. In late January, people applying for places in Anne's household were assured that they would not have long to wait until she was queen.[11] In February, 'amidst great company', Anne told 'one she loved well, and who was formerly sent away from the court by the King out of jealousy, that she had had a furious hankering to eat apples, and the King had told her that it was a sign she was pregnant'.[12] The man she spoke to may have been Wyatt, who was appointed to the Privy Council around this time. Then, on 24 February, Anne hosted a banquet for the French ambassador in her apartments at York Place. Henry was embarrassingly attentive to her and her ladies, largely ignored Suffolk, Audley and the other guests, and got so drunk that he became either incoherent or indiscreet. Waving a hand at the rich hangings and plate, he asked the Dowager Duchess of

Norfolk, 'Has not Madame la Marquise a grand dot [dowry] and a rich marriage, as all that we see belongs to her?'[13] The court was abuzz with speculation, but hardly anyone guessed the truth.

That month, Queen Katherine, who had been staying at Easthampstead, was ordered to move to Ampthill Castle with a reduced household. Her staunch friend, Maria de Salinas, Lady Willoughby, had already been dismissed in August 1532, and it was probably at this time that some of the Queen's thirty maids of honour, among them Jane Seymour, were sent home.

On 30 March 1533, Thomas Cranmer was consecrated Archbishop of Canterbury. There was great mutual liking, trust and respect between the King and his new Primate, even though they did not always agree on theological matters; Henry realised how much Cranmer was sacrificing to serve him, for the Archbishop would greatly have preferred a life of study to one at the centre of public affairs. He had no love for pomp and ceremony, but was a simple, charitable man with a high regard for the truth, a zealous reformist who was unswervingly loyal to the King, yet vulnerable to the vicious machinations of his enemies on the other side of the religious divide. In the years to come, Henry would on several occasions intervene to protect Cranmer from those who would have destroyed him.

At his consecration, Cranmer took the traditional vow of allegiance to the Pope, but added that he would not be bound by any authority that was contrary to the law of God or of England. Cranmer was aware of the King's secret marriage to Anne Boleyn, and was ready to take radical steps to put it on a legal footing, whatever the Pope might say. To this end, in April, Parliament passed the first – and arguably the most important – of several pieces of revolutionary legislation that would bring about the Reformation of the Church in England, the Act of Restraint of Appeals. This Act stressed the sovereign authority of the English state: its preamble majestically proclaimed, 'This realm of England is an empire, governed by one Supreme Head and King having the dignity and royal estate of the imperial crown,' who owed submission to no one but God. This was the first direct challenge to the Pope's jurisdiction over the English Church; in future, final appeals in spiritual matters would be heard, not in Rome, but in England, where the King was from now on to enjoy 'plenary, whole and entire power, pre-eminence, authority, prerogative and jurisdiction'. The Act not only created an autonomous Church of England with the monarch as its governor, but effectively prohibited the hearing of the King's nullity suit by the Pope, and barred Katherine from appealing to the Vatican against any decision that an ecclesiastical court in England might take.

No English sovereign had ever before been granted such power, nor would again. The King had been exalted above other mortals, not only as a temporal ruler whose authority was now defined for the first time by the language of empire, but as the spiritual leader of his people, strong in virtue and righteousness. It was a vindication of everything that Henry had striven for during these last years, and now he basked in the knowledge and conviction that not only Parliament, but also God Himself, were on his side.

Few spoke out against the new order. Fisher secretly wrote to the Emperor, begging him in vain to use force to bring Henry to his senses. More, far from enjoying a quiet retirement, was actively encouraging those who supported the Queen. Katherine's former confessor, Friar John Forrest, was imprisoned for speaking out in her favour. Sir John Gage, Henry's rather unworldly Vice-Chamberlain, dared to voice his misgivings to the King, only to be banished from court.[14] But these were lone voices among a silent majority.

On Easter Eve, 12 April 1533, Anne Boleyn appeared in public as Queen for the first time; wearing cloth of frieze and diamonds, and preceded by trumpeters, she went to Mass in the chapel royal attended by sixty ladies; Lady Mary Howard carried her train. The King observed his astonished nobles closely to ensure that they were paying his wife the respect due to her rank, and after Mass 'begged the lords to go and visit and make their court to the new Queen'. Even Anne's supporters were taken aback by her sudden elevation, and did not know whether to laugh or cry.[15] On Easter Sunday, in churches all over the land, she was publicly prayed for as Queen by bewildered subjects who were under the impression that the King was still married to his first wife.

Anne was assigned a household of two hundred persons, all appointed or approved by the King, who was present when they took their oaths of allegiance. Thomas de Burgh, Lord Borough, was appointed Chamberlain, but was replaced later that year by George Brooke, 9th Lord Cobham; Sir James Boleyn, Wiltshire's brother, was Chancellor; Sir William Coffin, a Gentleman of the Privy Chamber, was Master of Horse; John Uvedale, late of Richmond's Council of the North, was the Queen's Secretary, while George Taylor, who had served her father, was her Receiver General; Richard Bartlett, late of Wolsey's household, was her physician, and Nicholas Shaxton her Almoner. Among her chaplains were William Latimer, John Skip and William Betts, who would be replaced on his death in 1535 by Matthew Parker; all were evangelicals, and the Queen expected them to instruct her household 'to embrace the wholesome doctrine and infallible knowledge of Christ's Gospel'.[16]

Anne's ladies-in-waiting included Lady Margaret Douglas, Lady Mary Howard, Mary Boleyn, Lady Rochford, the young Countess of Surrey, Lady Berkeley, Elizabeth, wife of Sir James Boleyn – whom Anne 'never loved'[17] – and Elizabeth, Countess of Worcester. A Mistress Marshall was Mother of the Maids, and among her charges were the Queen's cousin, Margaret Shelton,[18] Norfolk's mistress Elizabeth Holland, Anne Saville, Anne Gainsford, now Lady Zouche, Grace Parker, and Jane Seymour, whose post had been secured for her through the good offices of Sir Francis Bryan; her name was amongst those ladies who received a New Year gift from the King the following January. The Queen employed both male and female fools.[19] There was such a frantic demand for places in her household that many were disappointed. Lady Lisle tried for years to have her daughter Katherine Basset accepted, begging anyone with any influence at court to help and sending the Queen a succession of gifts, but ultimately to no avail.[20]

Anne's servants all wore her livery of blue and purple, and their doublets were embroidered with her new motto, 'La plus heureuse' ('The most happy');[21] she outlaid £1,000 (£300,000) a year on their wages and tips,[22] and there were rich pickings to be had from clientage and patronage: the evidence shows that the members of Anne's household were particularly assertive in seeking favours and advancement for themselves and their clients.

According to William Latimer, who wrote his laudatory chronicle in Elizabeth's reign, the new Queen was determined to set a high moral standard for her household, probably with a view to outrivalling her predecessor and giving the lie to those who believed she was of bad character. One of her first acts was to summon her council of officers and instruct them in their duties. They were to be honourable, discreet, just and thrifty in their conduct, and a godly 'spectacle' to others, attending Mass daily and displaying a 'virtuous demeanour'. On pain of instant dismissal and perpetual banishment from court, 'to their utter shame', they must not quarrel, swear or frequent 'evil, lewd and ungodly disposed brothels'.[23] It would appear that these austere rules were generally observed: years later, Anne's silkwoman, Jane Wilkinson, told John Foxe she had never seen 'better order amongst the ladies and gentlewomen of the court than in Anne Boleyn's day'.

The Queen's ladies were required to be above reproach. Anne gave each of them a little book of prayers and psalms that could be hung from a girdle. In order to prevent them from getting into mischief through idleness, she made them devote hours of their time to sewing garments for the poor, for distribution by the Queen on progress.[24] Anne did her share; she particularly enjoyed needlework, and by all accounts was very good at it. She made some of her own clothes – an embroidered headpiece and coif said to have been worked by her are at Hever Castle – as well as hangings and household embroideries. George Wyatt relates that Hampton Court was made sumptuous by 'rich and exquisite works wrought by her own hand and needle, and also by her ladies'; in 1598, a German traveller, Paul Hentzner, saw there an exquisite tester that Anne had made for Henry VIII's bed. Even in the late seventeenth century, Anne's needlework was still on show, with that of Mary II, although none of her pieces at Hampton Court survives today.

Anne was generous in her charities. George Wyatt estimated that her annual charitable donations amounted to £1,500 (£450,000). She also set intellectual standards for the court by sponsoring scholars and reformers, who were brought to her attention by her chaplains and also by Dr William Butts,[25] who was now 'a considerable man of affairs' at court[26] and even more radical than Anne in his religious views; he was responsible for the preferment of several young men from his old college at Cambridge, Gonville Hall, where Shaxton and Skip had also studied. It was Butts who secured chaplaincies to the Queen for William Latimer and William Betts, who had once been arrested for circulating forbidden books at Oxford. Anne also gave financial support to the universities, and funded the studies of poor scholars, among whom was Wolsey's bastard son, Thomas Winter.[27]

Anne's heraldic emblem as Queen of England was a white falcon with a crown and sceptre standing with wings elevated on a tree stump covered with Tudor roses.[28] This badge, and her initials and coat of arms, replaced Katherine's in all the royal palaces.[29] The King gave Anne Baynard's Castle and Havering, which had once been assigned to Katherine of Aragon, as part of her jointure. Baynard's Castle remained a store for her large and valuable collection of Wardrobe stuff, much of which she had inherited from Katherine.[30]

The Boleyn faction was at the zenith of its power. In order to justify his marriage, Henry would use religion, art and every aspect of court culture to exalt Anne's image and emphasise the legitimacy of her title. Next to the King, she was the greatest fount of patronage in the kingdom, and she would zealously utilise her influence to promote the King's religious policies and the cause of reform. Of the ten bishops who were appointed during the period 1532–6, seven were her clients. In defiance of the law, she kept an English Bible in her apartments for all to read, and openly debated its contents with the King at dinner.[31] In public, she was rarely seen without a book of devotions in her hands.

Several pious works that Anne owned as Queen survive, some of them beautifully illuminated manuscripts with decorative borders in the French Renaissance style. The Bible that she kept on display may have been her presentation copy of Tyndale's New Testament of 1534, which is bound in black leather and bears the name ANNA REGINA ANGLIAE in faded red lettering on the gold page edges.[32] Anne also owned a French translation of the Bible by the humanist Jacques Lefèvre d'Étaples, which was printed at Antwerp the same year and dedicated to Henry VIII and herself: their initials and crowned Tudor roses appear on the binding.[33] Her manuscript of Clément Marot's sermons on the Good Shepherd came from one of the foremost workshops in France, and has her arms and falcon badges emblazoned on the frontispiece;[34] it may have been a gift from Francis I. At Christmas 1532, Lord Morley had given Anne his translation of *The Epistles and Gospels for the LII Sundays in the Year*.[35] Another important illuminated manuscript owned by her was 'The Ecclesiaste', which has the King's arms impaling hers on the front cover, and a binding of black velvet with brass corners.[36]

Anne and Cromwell were natural allies, both through self-interest and through their religious and political views, although they both acted independently of each other. Cromwell helped Anne to assist several reformers who had fallen foul of the law and sought her protection; he also helped to administer her household, and used his influence to secure preferment in it for his clients.[37]

Anne's family certainly benefited from her elevation. Her father was now one of the most important men in the kingdom, while in 1533 her brother Rochford was made a baron in his own right. Master of the Buckhounds, Lord Warden of the Cinque Ports and Master of the Bethlehem (Bedlam) Hospital for the insane. During the next three years he would be entrusted with several important diplomatic embassies to France.

In 1533, 'the King kept St George's Day at Greenwich, with great solemnity, and the court was greatly replenished with lords, knights, ladies and gentlewomen, to a great number, with all enjoyment and pleasure'.[38] Most were doubtless agog to see their new Queen. In May, the King attended the wedding of his niece, Lady Frances Brandon, to young Henry Grey, 3rd Marquess of Dorset. It was a spectacular event, held at Suffolk Place, and cost the bride's father £1,666 (£499,800). As the Duke and Duchess of Suffolk were hosting the event, the Queen, mindful of the Duchess's hostility, did not attend. This was Mary Tudor's last public appearance. She was ailing, and would soon return to Westhorpe in Suffolk for good.

That month, Archbishop Cranmer convened an ecclesiastical court at

Dunstable Priory, where on the 23rd he pronounced the King's union with Katherine null and void; five days later he declared that Henry's marriage to Anne Boleyn was valid and lawful. 'The King, in his blindness, fears no one but God,' Chapuys observed.[39]

43

'Here Anna Comes, Bright Image of Chastity'

The King was determined that Anne's coronation should outrival any of those of her predecessors in splendour. On the day after Cranmer pronounced judgement, she donned cloth of gold and proceeded in the former Queen's barge from Greenwich to the Tower of London, attended by Wiltshire, Suffolk and a host of nobles and bishops, and escorted by the Lord Mayor, Sheriffs and Aldermen with music, fireworks, pageantry and a 'marvellous' salute of cannonfire. At the Tower, Henry greeted her most affectionately, openly cupping her pregnant belly with his hands. The next day he dubbed eighteen Knights of the Bath, among them the Earls of Dorset and Derby and Francis Weston; most had Boleyn connections.[1]

Two days later, on Saturday 31 May, wearing white cloth of gold and ermine with her hair loose beneath a coif with a jewelled circlet, Anne made a ceremonial entry into London, travelling in procession from Cheapside to Temple Bar in a litter draped with white cloth of gold, drawn by two palfreys caparisoned in the same. Above it was borne a canopy carried by four knights. The half-mile-long procession was led by the French ambassador and his suite, followed by ladies, gentlemen, knights, judges, bishops, crimson-clad nobles, squires, heralds, ambassadors and the Queen's servants dressed in scarlet. Then came Suffolk, wearing bejewelled robes of crimson velvet,[2] who had been appointed High Constable of England just for this occasion and had left his desperately sick wife to attend; and Lord William Howard, acting as Earl Marshal in place of his half-brother Norfolk, who was in France with Rochford on official business. Thanks to his niece's influence, Norfolk had recently been able to wrest the office of Earl Marshal from Suffolk, who had held it since the death of the 2nd Duke of Norfolk in 1524; Cromwell had mollified Suffolk by telling him that the King thought his enforced surrender of the office imputed 'much honour' in him and was grateful to him for nourishing 'kindness and love between my Lord of Norfolk and you'.[3] Norfolk was represented at the coronation by his son Surrey, who had returned briefly from Paris for the occasion.

The streets of London were freshly gravelled and gaily decorated with tapestries and rich hangings, and Anne's falcon badge was everywhere to be seen. In Gracechurch Street, the German merchants of the Steelyard had erected a triumphal arch designed by Holbein, upon which was a tableau of Apollo on Mount Parnassus surrounded by the four Muses, all 'playing on several sweet instruments'.[4] Beneath was a white marble 'fountain of Helicon', from which flowed Rhenish wine for all comers.[5] At various places en route, the Queen paused to listen to Latin orations and angelic-sounding choirs, or to watch pageants mounted in her honour, which had been commissioned and paid for by the City companies and devised by Nicholas Udall, an erudite but vicious paedophile who became Provost of Eton in 1534; he was assisted by John Leland, the King's librarian, and Richard Cox, a Cambridge humanist. These pageants lauded the new Queen's chastity and expressed the hope that she would bear sons to continue the Tudor dynasty.

Late in the afternoon, Anne arrived at Westminster Hall. There, standing beneath a cloth of estate, she took spices and hippocras before changing out of her robes and leaving secretly by barge for York Place, where the King awaited her. Tradition decreed that he play no part in her triumph – it was to be hers alone. Yet Anne was dissatisfied with her reception, which, according to Chapuys, had been more appropriate to 'a funeral rather than a pageant'.[6] Few citizens in the huge crowds had doffed their caps or cried 'God save the Queen!', and Anne's fool had yelled at them, 'I think you all have scurvy heads, and dare not uncover!' At the sight of the royal couple's entwined initials, several wags had dared to laugh, 'HA! HA!' Some even said that the crown did not become Anne.[7] Nevertheless, the King commissioned his printer, Wynkyn de Worde, to publish a pamphlet commemorating her triumph.

On Sunday 1 June 1533, Anne was attired for her coronation in a kirtle of crimson velvet, over which was a traditional sideless surcoat of purple velvet furred with ermine; on her head she wore a caul of pearls beneath a rich coronet. Walking beneath a cloth-of-gold canopy, with the Dowager Duchess of Norfolk carrying her train, she went in procession from Westminster Hall to the nearby Abbey, attended by thirteen mitred abbots, the monks of Westminster, the entire Chapel Royal, the bishops and clergy, and the lords in their robes of estate. Sir Thomas More, the Duchess of Norfolk and the Exeters were conspicuous by their absence, much to the King's chagrin.

Seated in St Edward's Chair, which was draped in cloth of gold, Anne was crowned by Archbishop Cranmer with the same formalities as if she had been a queen regnant. St Edward's Crown was placed on her head – it was later replaced by a smaller crown specially made for her[8] – and she was invested with the sovereign's two sceptres. The choir then sang *Te Deum* in celebration.

Afterwards, eight hundred people sat down to a sumptuous banquet in Westminster Hall; up to thirty dishes were served at each course, to the sound of trumpets,[9] as well as marvellous 'subtleties and ships made of wax, gorgeous to behold'.[10] The Duke of Suffolk, as Steward, rode up and down between the tables on his courser, overseeing everything, while Sir Nicholas Carew acted as the Queen's Champion. Anne sat on the King's throne at the high marble table on the dais, twelve steps up, served by eight nobles and attended by the Countesses of Oxford and Worcester, who from time to time held a rich cloth in front of her face 'when she list to spit or do otherwise at her pleasure'.[11] The King, attended by several ambassadors, watched the proceedings from a latticed closet in the cloisters of St Stephen's Chapel. At the end of the afternoon, the Queen was served spices presented by her Sewer and hippocras from a gold cup offered by the Lord Mayor, before departing at 6 p.m. to spend the night at York Place.

'The English sought unceasingly to honour their new Princess, not because they wanted to, but in order to comply with the wishes of their King.'[12] On 2 June, jousts were held in honour of the coronation in the new tiltyard at York Place. Henry did not take part, and Carew led the answerers, but few spears were broken.[13] There followed 'a goodly banquet in the Queen's chamber'.[14] The next few days were given over to hunting, dancing and feasting, then the King and Queen moved to Greenwich, where the festivities continued on a smaller scale. Sir Edward Baynton, Anne's Vice-Chamberlain, informed Lord Rochford that, 'as for pastime in the Queen's chamber, [there] was never more'. If any man had gone away leaving at court a lady who might 'mourn at parting, I can no whit perceive the same by their dancing and pastime they do use here'.[15] For all her efforts to occupy the moral high ground, Anne was to preside over a court bent on pleasure: a year or so later Margaret Roper was to tell her father, Sir Thomas More, that there was 'nothing else in the court but sporting and dancing'.[16] Anne often entertained the King at feasts and 'fine mummeries',[17] and was even known to dance with her ladies and favoured gentlemen in her bedchamber.[18]

Most of the gentleman were members of the King's Privy Chamber. Anne enjoyed their witty and stimulating company, chose them as hunting companions and gambling partners, flirted openly with them and exchanged gifts of money and trinkets, all in accordance with the accepted conventions of courtly love.[19] Most people, including the King, were happy for her to do so, but Chapuys and others looked askance at such familiarity.

One of the gentlemen most favoured by Henry and Anne was Sir Henry Norris, upon whom had been showered numerous offices – amongst other things he was Black Rod in the Parliament House, Chamberlain of North Wales and High Steward of Oxford University – and generous grants of land. As Groom of the Stool, Norris was the King's most intimate associate, and much trusted by him; it was to Norris, rather than Cromwell, that petitioners took their requests. Another member of the charmed circle was Francis Weston, now a Gentleman of the Privy Chamber, a renowned lutenist, and a frequent partner of the King at tennis and of the King and Queen at cards.[20] When Weston had married Anne Pickering in 1532, the King had given him ten marks and wished him better fortune in marriage than he himself had had. An up-and-coming favourite was William Brereton, for whom Anne had recently secured a post as Page of the Chamber. Henry liked him, and was to promote him to Gentleman of the Privy Chamber and grant him lands and offices in Wales worth £1,200 (£360,000) a year.[21] Brereton, who often accompanied Henry and Anne to the hunt, was a noted seducer of women[22] and a client of both Richmond and Norfolk.

The death of Mary Tudor, Duchess of Suffolk, at Westhorpe on 25 June caused hardly a ripple in the merrymaking. Suffolk had hastened to her bedside after the coronation, bearing a conciliatory message from the King, which healed the rift between brother and sister. Mary was buried in the Abbey of Bury St Edmunds in Suffolk with all the honours due to a queen, and her daughter Frances, Marchioness of Dorset, as chief mourner.

On 28 June, there arrived at Greenwich a sumptuous litter and three mules, a wedding gift from Francis I to the new Queen, who was so delighted with it that she insisted on being taken for a three-mile ride there and then.[23]

As Queen, Anne was enjoying a sumptuous lifestyle. In every royal house, Katherine of Aragon's devices were being replaced, at enormous cost, by her successor's arms, initials and falcon badges.[24] At Hampton Court, work was progressing rapidly on new, luxurious, first-floor lodgings for Anne and the King, which ran at right angles to each other above Cloister Green Court and were connected by private galleries.[25] A staircase led to a new privy garden, and there was a balcony from which the Queen and her ladies could watch the hunting in the park.

Anne's rooms were decorated in the antique style by a German craftsman[26] and had mirrors set into the ceilings. Grotesque work adorned the outer walls of her bedchamber.

Anne's furnishings were the best that the age could provide. Her elaborately carved headboard, bearing the royal arms of England, is now at Hever Castle; she owned another of gilded walnut. One of her beds was hung with red sarcanet with a matching canopy stiffened with blue buckram; another, smaller bed of green satin had crimson and orange curtains. She owned six chairs of estate, variously upholstered in cloth of gold, green silk or crimson and purple velvet, with silk and gold fringing and gilded and enamelled pommels.[27]

At Hampton Court, Antonio Toto was commissioned to paint religious pictures, decorative panels and shields to adorn the new royal apartments; Robert Shynk made the moulds for the antique work, and Henry Blankston of Cologne carried out much of the decorative painting and gilding – 'all the walls of the palace shine with gold and silver'.[28] Galyon Hone spent ten years working on the heraldic glass at Hampton Court, where many of the windows were glazed with crystal. The King's presence chamber was known as the Paradise Chamber, and was one of the wonders of the palace for many years. Here, 'everything glitters so with silver, gold and jewels as to dazzle one's eyes'.[29] Persian tapestries hung on the walls, and there was a beautiful painted ceiling and a cloth-of-gold canopy of estate above the throne on the dais.[30] Henry's privy chamber had an alabaster fountain set into the wall, as at Greenwich, a black leather desk and a clock stand. Many rooms were 'adorned with tapestries of gold, silver and velvet'.[31]

The elaborate gardens that Henry VIII created at Hampton Court in the 1530s have long vanished, although their layout can still be seen. The walled privy garden had square railed beds laid to lawn or sanded, with flowers round the edges, and green and white striped posts bearing painted statues of the King's Beasts. Painted and gilded rails also surrounded the ornamental fishponds in the Pond Gardens, which were laid out in 1536[32] near the site of the present Banqueting House, built in 1700 on the site of one of Henry's banqueting houses, of which there were several in the grounds. One, built on a circular plan with a dome, stood high up on an artificial mound in what was known as the Mount Garden, and afforded excellent views of the gardens, park and river. Elsewhere in the gardens there were crenellated box hedges, fantastic topiary in the shapes of men and centaurs, arbours, fountains and sundials. There was a herb garden, and two orchards, one of which provided fruit exclusively for the King; the other was adorned with five hundred red rose bushes.

The Queen's gabled first-floor apartments at Greenwich were also being renovated at this time: the ceiling of her presence chamber was decorated with gilded bosses on a lattice of white battens; expensive Seville tiles were laid in the chimney grates, and cheaper green and yellow Flanders tiles in every alcove.[33] Five new doors were hung in her great bedchamber, new rush matting was laid in the passage to her robing room, and new transoms were installed in the great bay window between her bedchamber and her presence chamber, which overlooked the elaborate classical conduit in the inner court. Two folding tables in antique style were made for her, with inlaid tiles: one was a 'breakfast table', the other was a gaming table 'for Her Grace to play on'.[34]

The King's other major building project at this time was at Windsor, where he erected a wooden platform that later became known as the North Terrace along the clifftop beneath the royal apartments in the Upper and Middle Wards. It gave him access from his lodgings to the Little Park, via an outside stair; 'every afternoon' that summer, 'when the weather is anything fair, His Grace doth ride forth on hawking, or walketh, and cometh not in again till it be late in the evening'.[35] He was in a buoyant mood, for he was confident that he would soon, at long last, be the father of a prince.

44

'The High and Mighty Princess of England'

In 1533, Hans Holbein painted a splendid double portrait of the French ambassadors Jean de Dinteville – who begged to be recalled after only one stormy audience with Henry VIII, in June of that year, from which he emerged visibly shaking[1] – and Georges de Selves; it was a picture that was laden with symbolism, dark hints of mortality and religious discord.[2] It was probably this masterpiece, almost certainly painted at Bridewell Palace, that led to Holbein gaining the patronage of Cromwell, who appreciated his genius and meant to exploit it in the service of the King. After Cromwell had sat for him,[3] Holbein soon found himself in demand as a fashionable portrait painter, working on commissions from important people at court.

Many of his portraits survive, some as drawings,[4] others as finished works; some, of husbands and wives, were in pairs. Several are known to be lost. These portraits constitute the most important and extensive visual record of any sixteenth-century court, and are important source material for costume and jewellery. Holbein must have set up a large studio with several students assisting him and reproducing his works in order to keep up with the demand for them.

Holbein also produced exquisite miniatures, having learned the art of limning from 'the famous Master Lucas', who was almost certainly Lucas Horenbout, whom Holbein 'as far excelled in drawing, arrangement, understanding and execution as the sun surpasses the moon in brightness'.[5] Fifteen of his miniatures survive, five in the Royal Collection.

It has been suggested, on good evidence, that Holbein worked as a spy for Cromwell.[6] As a fashionable artist, it was easy for him to obtain an entrée to the houses of those whose loyalty to the new regime was suspect: it is surely no coincidence that several of the portraits he painted at this time were of persons about whom Cromwell wanted information, such as George Neville, Lord Abergavenny, Sir Nicholas Carew and Sir John Russell, none of whom had much liking for Anne Boleyn.

Holbein appears to have found a royal patron in Anne, whose religious views he shared. He designed for her an antique-style standing cup and cover decorated with an imperial crown and her falcon badge supported by satyrs,[7] as well as the metalwork on the binding of her book, the *Ecclesiaste*. He also designed monogram jewellery for Anne and Henry, and executed a set of portrait drawings of the young women of the Queen's circle, all similar in composition. However, no certain portrait of Anne by him survives, and it may be that any that did exist were destroyed after her death.

On 3 July 1533, Katherine of Aragon's erstwhile Chamberlain, Lord Mountjoy, was sent to Ampthill to inform his former mistress of the King's marriage to Anne Boleyn and order her to relinquish the title of Queen. Staunch in her conviction that she was the King's true wife, Katherine refused, despite being threatened by the Privy Councillors present with an indictment for treason. Knowing of Anne Boleyn's spite towards her, she believed that Henry was being influenced against his true nature to set her aside. Henry had his revenge later that month, when he moved Katherine to a less comfortable residence, Buckden Towers in Huntingdonshire, with a household that had again been reduced in size; of her thirty maids of honour, only ten remained.

That July, Henry set off on a progress which was restricted to the London area because of the Queen's advancing pregnancy; all was progressing well, and at Wanstead the royal couple were reported to be very merry.[8] At the end of the month, not wishing to upset his wife at this time, Henry left her at Windsor, saying he was going hunting, when in fact he was meeting with his Council to discuss grave news from Rome:[9] the Pope, having learned of the King's remarriage, had threatened to excommunicate him if he did not repudiate Anne by September. Henry refused to be intimidated, nor did he perceive the hand of a vengeful deity in the deaths of two members of his household from plague at Guildford, but moved with his Privy Chamber to Sutton Place, the home of Sir Francis Weston, which was mercifully free of contagion.[10]

This was not just a hunting progress, but an exercise in public relations, for during it the King attempted to win over those whom he suspected of having become disaffected by recent events. He visited Exeter at his house at Horsley in Surrey, where he was entertained with a lavish banquet of twenty-nine dishes,[11] and Sir John Russell at Chenies in Buckinghamshire, where he slept on a gold and silver bed with the royal arms embroidered on its tester. On 6 August, Russell wrote he had never seen 'His Grace merrier of a great while than he is now'; at the houses they had stayed in there had been 'the best pastime in hunting red deer that I have seen'.[12]

A week later Henry returned to Windsor, then removed with Anne to York Place and Greenwich, where she took to her chamber on 26 August;[13] her Chamberlain had been briefed by Lord Mountjoy as to the arrangements made in the past for Queen Katherine's confinements.[14] The King had taken from his Treasury a 'rich and triumphant bed', which had been part of the Duc de Longueville's ransom in 1515, and had it placed in Anne's bedchamber, next to a pallet bed with a crimson canopy, on which she would actually be delivered. A new state bed had been built in her presence chamber, where she would receive well-wishers after the birth.[15]

But while these preparations were being made, Anne found out that Henry was being unfaithful to her, a common failing of his when his wives were pregnant, as we have seen. The name of his inamorata is unrecorded, but Chapuys described her as 'very beautiful' and added that 'many nobles are assisting him in the affair', presumably to dis-countenance the Queen. Unlike Katherine, Anne created a scene, using 'certain words which the King very much disliked', but he brutally told her that she must 'shut her eyes and endure as her betters had done', and that she ought to know that he could humiliate her as quickly as he had raised her; it was as well she had her bed already, because he would not give it to her now. For two or three days, the royal couple maintained a frosty silence, then there was a grudging reconciliation. Chapuys dismissed this as 'a love quarrel', but it is an indication that Henry's passion for Anne had subsided somewhat.[16] Nevertheless, it was being said abroad that he was still so infatuated with her that court discipline was becoming very lax.[17]

The King was planning jousts, banquets and masques to celebrate his son's imminent birth: he had consulted his physicians and astrologers, and all had assured him that the child would be male. The royal father had not yet made up his mind whether to call the boy Edward or Henry, but had asked the French ambassador to hold him at the font at his baptism.[18] Letters announcing the birth of a prince were awaiting dispatch to the English shires and foreign courts.

At last, on 7 September, in a chamber hung with tapestries depicting the legend of St Ursula and her eleven thousand virgins, Anne Boleyn gave birth, not to the expected son, but to a healthy, red-haired daughter who much resembled her father.[19] 'God has forgotten him entirely,' commented Chapuys,[20] but the King, although disappointed, was confident that sons would soon follow. After the word 'prince' had been changed to 'princess', the letters announcing the birth were sent off[21] and *Te Deum* was sung in St Paul's for the Queen's safe delivery.[22] But the planned jousts and entertainments were cancelled.

On 10 September, when she was only three days old, the King's daughter was given a splendid christening in the Church of the Observant Friars at Greenwich. The church and the gallery that led to it were both hung with rich arras, and the silver font placed on a high railed platform. The royal infant, wearing a mantle of purple velvet furred with ermine, with a long train, was carried in procession to the church by the Dowager Duchess of Norfolk under a crimson canopy borne by four earls; Anne had wanted her borne upon the christening cloth that had been used for the Princess Mary, but Katherine of Aragon refused to relinquish it on the grounds that it was her personal property, brought from Spain.[23] Archbishop Cranmer stood godfather at the christening, while the Dowagers of Norfolk and Dorset were godmothers, and the baby was baptised Elizabeth by John Stokesley, Bishop of London. Immediately afterwards, Cranmer confirmed her, with a reluctant Lady Exeter as sponsor.[24] Then Garter King of Arms cried, 'God of His infinite goodness send prosperous life and long to the high and mighty Princess of England, Elizabeth!' and the trumpets sounded a fanfare. In the flickering light of five hundred torches, Elizabeth was borne back in procession to the Queen's bedchamber, where she received her mother's blessing. The King was not present, but commanded Norfolk and Suffolk to thank the Lord Mayor and his brethren for attending. That evening, bonfires were lit and free wine flowed in the City.[25]

At Greenwich, on the same day that the Princess Elizabeth was born, the Duke of Suffolk, a widower of just ten weeks, married his ward Katherine, the fourteen-year-old heiress of Lord Willoughby. This brilliant, spirited, sharp-witted young lady had been betrothed to his son, Henry Brandon, Earl of Lincoln, but Suffolk had had the betrothal annulled in order to marry her himself. Chapuys commented, 'The Duke will have done a service to the ladies when they are reproached, as is usual, with marrying again immediately after the death of their husbands!'[26]

Given that the new Duchess's mother was Maria de Salinas, this marriage involved Suffolk in yet another conflict of loyalties, yet it also rescued him from financial ruin and brought him the greater part of his lands and wealth, as well as a new country seat, Grimsthorpe in Lincolnshire, which was part of his wife's dowry.[27]

Despite the thirty-five-year age gap, and the fact that the Duke was growing fat and was no longer the splendid knight who had once excelled in the tiltyard, the marriage was successful. Katherine Willoughby, whose portrait sketch by Holbein is in the British Museum, bore the Duke two sons, Henry in 1534, to whom both the King and Cromwell were godfathers, and Charles in 1537/8; Holbein painted their miniatures in 1541.[28] Her former betrothed, Lincoln, is said to have been so upset at losing her to his father that he died of sorrow, and Anne Boleyn, who had little love for Suffolk, is reported to have declared, 'My Lord of Suffolk kills one son to beget another.'[29] However, Lincoln did not die until March 1534, and had been in failing health for some time, which probably explains why Suffolk had married Katherine himself.

On 1 October, the King's daughter Mary was informed that she must no longer style herself 'Princess'. She was told that the King had appointed her a new household of 162 persons, headed by her beloved governess Lady Salisbury, but it would only be hers in return for her acknowledgement of her diminished status. The next day, Mary wrote to her father, defiantly refusing to relinquish her title and censuring him for his conduct in such strong terms that even Chapuys felt she had gone too far.[30] A furious Henry abandoned his plans for her household and ordered her to leave Beaulieu, where she had been residing and which he was now going to lease to Lord Rochford,[31] and go to Hertford Castle. Mary obeyed, but her health had been broken by the strain of the conflict of loyalties that had been forced upon her, and for the rest of her life she would suffer headaches, toothache, palpitations, depression and amenorrhoea.

On 25 November, the Duke of Richmond, lately returned from Paris, was married to Norfolk's daughter, Lady Mary Howard, a union that firmly allied him to the Boleyn faction. The bride was a member of the Queen's household and a staunch advocate of reform, and Fitzroy was a close friend of her brother Surrey. The marriage was a triumph for Anne Boleyn and a slap in the face for the Duchess of Norfolk, who had opposed it. However, it was never consummated,[32] and it may be that the Duke, now fourteen, was already showing signs of the tuberculosis that was to kill him, and that the King, mindful of the fate of his own brother Arthur, whose death was said to have been hastened by too much early sexual activity, had ordered the young couple to wait.

There was little love lost between the Queen and Norfolk. The Duke had had enough of his niece's malice towards him and her insufferable pride, and had clashed with her on several occasions. Once she used 'more insulting language to Norfolk than one would to a dog, such that he was obliged to leave the room'. The Duke was so offended he publicly heaped abuse on her: 'one of the least offensive things he called her was "the great whore" '.[33] Privately, he was of the opinion that she would be the ruin of his House.[34]

In December, when the Princess Elizabeth was three months old, she was assigned her own household and sent to live at Hatfield in Hertfordshire. Margaret, Lady Bryan, who had had charge of the Princess Mary in infancy, was appointed her Lady Mistress; the Lady Margaret Douglas, late of Mary's household, was her first lady of honour, while Blanche Parry, who was to stay with Elizabeth for fifty-seven years, was a rocker in the nursery. Sir John Shelton, the Queen's uncle, was Steward of the Household. The King and Queen were distant parents, making only occasional visits to their daughter,[35] although Anne was kept informed of her progress by Lady Bryan.[36] When Elizabeth was thirteen months, the Lady Mistress applied to Cromwell for permission to wean her; the request was passed on, then Sir William Paulet, Comptroller of the Household, informed Lady Bryan that the King and Queen had consented.[37]

On 14 December, the household of the Lady Mary, as the former Princess was henceforth to be known, was disbanded; when Lady Salisbury refused to surrender Mary's jewels to the Queen, she was summarily dismissed. Mary was sent to live in her half-sister's establishment, where she was assigned the meanest chamber in the house. Her new governess, Anne, Lady Shelton, the Queen's aunt, did her best to make her life a misery, and Mary went in fear that the Boleyn faction would try to poison her. She was missing her mother dreadfully, but the King would not let them meet, even when Mary fell seriously ill. Instead, he sent his own physician to her, and allowed Katherine to send hers. Thanks to the good offices of Chapuys, Katherine managed to smuggle heartening letters to Mary.[38] But her father, in thrall to her jealous stepmother, refused to see her when he visited Elizabeth,[39] who took precedence over Mary in everything.

Very few now dared speak out in favour of the former Queen and her daughter. The Marquess of Exeter, whose sympathies lay with Katherine and who loathed Cromwell and deplored the King's new religious policies, remained sitting on the fence, but his wife was so active and vociferous in Katherine's favour that Henry warned them both that they 'must not trip or vary for fear of losing their heads'.[40] After that, Lady Exeter kept quiet. Chapuys thought that aristocratic opposition to the Boleyn marriage was far more cohesive and widespread than it actually was, but although Katherine and Mary had several influential supporters, it is clear that there was no organised court faction acting on their behalf.

45

'The Image of God Upon Earth'

The Christmas of 1533 was spent at Greenwich, where 'the King's Grace kept great court, as merry and lusty as ever'[1] – as well he might be, for Anne was once again pregnant.[2] Her gift to him at New Year 1534 was an exquisite table fountain of gold, studded with rubies, diamonds and pearls, from which 'issueth water at the teats of three naked women standing at the foot of the fountain';[3] it was probably designed by Holbein.

In January, still in pursuit of places for her daughters in the Queen's household, Lady Lisle sent Anne a rare breed of toy dog, which was entrusted to Sir Francis Bryan. He told Her Ladyship that 'the Queen liked [it] so well that she took it from me before it had been an hour in my hands'. Anne called the dog Little Purkoy (or Pourquoi), and 'set much store' by him. Later that year, Lady Lisle sent Anne a caged linnet and eighteen dotterells, a small breed of plover; the latter were slaughtered at Dover, brought to court by Lord Rochford and served to the Queen six at a time. She liked them 'very well', and assured Lady Lisle that the linnet was 'a pleasant singing bird, which doth not cease to give Her Grace rejoicing with her pleasant song'.[4] But there was no offer of a place for either of Lady Lisle's daughters.

Cromwell's influence was steadily growing. In 1534, he was appointed Master of the Rolls and Chancellor of the University of Cambridge, and in April finally succeeded in ousting Gardiner, who never forgave him, and replacing him as principal Secretary to the King, an office that would become of supreme political importance during his tenure. In this new capacity Cromwell wielded power by charming people into his confidence, or intimidating them with the threat of treason – overtly or, more often, by implication. Through his many contacts and a network of paid informers and numerous grateful clients, he gained access to a great deal of confidential and sensitive information that was stored for future reference and sometimes used against those whom the King or Master Secretary wanted out of the way.

It was essential that opposition to the King's new marriage be crushed, and on 23 March 1534 an Act of Parliament settling the succession upon the Princess Elizabeth and disinheriting the Lady Mary was passed; the Act laid down that every loyal subject, when so required, should swear an oath recognising its provisions. Most people complied, but there were notable exceptions. Katherine and Mary both refused to take the oath, and the King knew better than to use force, for the Emperor was Katherine's nephew and a powerful deterrent.

Both Sir Thomas More and Bishop Fisher also declined to swear, and were committed to the Tower for their disobedience. When More was questioned by Cromwell, he declared, 'I am the King's faithful subject. I say no harm, I think no harm, but I wish everybody good. And if this be not enough to keep a man alive, in good faith, I long not to live.'[5] Through several interrogations, he responded to all demands to take the oath with uncompromising silence, and reminded his distraught daughter and family that he had always looked first upon God and then upon the King, 'according to the lesson His Highness taught me at my first coming to his noble service'.[6] His silence spoke volumes, and Henry feared it would serve as a battle cry for those who opposed him. 'By the mass, Master More,' commented Norfolk, 'it is perilous striving with princes.'[7] More did not need his old friend to remind him of the peril in which he had placed himself.

Fisher was not so reticent; he had stated categorically, 'The King our Sovereign Lord is not the Supreme Head on earth of the Church of England.' Now he was refusing to acknowledge Henry's marriage. His defiance could only be construed as treasonous.

Once again, the King was confident that he would soon have a son whose birth would bring such rejoicing that few would even think of questioning his legitimacy. To mark this pregnancy, he ordered a medal of Anne to be struck, inscribed with her portrait in relief and the legend, 'A.R. THE MOOST HAPPI'.[8] Every care was taken of the expectant mother: when her morning rest was disturbed by the noise made by Henry's peacocks and pelican, which had been a gift from the 'New Found Land' (America) and now had the run of the gardens at Greenwich, he arranged for Sir Henry Norris to remove them to his own house nearby, and paid for three timber coops to be built for them there.[9]

The Queen's apartments at Eltham were converted into a nursery 'against the coming of the prince', with a great chamber, a dining chamber, an arraying chamber and a bedchamber, in which was a cradle covered with a canopy of iron. The roof timbers were all painted yellow ochre.[10] The King ordered his goldsmith, Cornelius Heyss, to make a silver cradle of estate, which may have been designed by Holbein. It had pillars adorned with Tudor roses, precious stones set in a gold border around the rim, and gold figures of Adam and Eve crafted by Heyss and painted by Holbein. The bedding was embroidered with gold, and cloth of gold was purchased for a layette.[11]

In April 1534, doubtless anticipating that there would soon be a new Knight of the Garter, the King commissioned a magnificent new register of the Order, called the *Liber Niger* or *Black Book of the Garter* after its black velvet binding; in it were enshrined the Order's statues, its history, and the records of its ceremonies. The *Black Book* survives today,[12] a beautifully illuminated manuscript which contains illustrations of the enthroned King surrounded by his Knights, and of him bringing up the rear in a Garter procession.

On 22 June, the artist Lucas Horenbout, who had worked with others on the *Black Book of the Garter*, became a naturalised subject of Henry VIII, and was appointed King's Painter for life. He was assigned a tenement at Charing Cross in which to set up his studio, and licensed to employ four foreign journeymen.[13] One of his first commissions in his new role was a miniature of the fifteen-year-old Duke of Richmond,[14] which shows Fitzroy in an open-necked nightshirt and embroidered nightcap, further evidence that he was known to be terminally ill. The miniature bears out a Venetian envoy's statement that the Duke greatly resembled his father in looks, although his nose is bigger than Henry's. In the 1930s it was thought that the anonymous full-length portrait in the Royal Collection of a Tudor courtier dressed entirely in scarlet was Richmond, but the costume is of a later date.

Henry had planned another visit to Calais in the summer of 1534, but postponed it until the following April because the Queen's pregnancy prevented her from accompanying him. Instead, he went on progress, staying at The More, Chenies, Woking and Eltham, where he visited his daughter Elizabeth. On 28 July he arrived at Guildford, where Anne had planned to join him, but it is not known if she actually did so. Henry stayed there until 7 August, then rode north to tour the Midlands.[15]

Chapuys, who had accompanied the court, reported from Woodstock on 23 September that the Queen was not after all to have a child, and that the King had begun to have doubts as to whether she had ever been pregnant at all.[16] This sounds rather like a face-saving, damage-limitation exercise on Henry's part, since it would have been virtually impossible for Anne to keep up the deception of a false pregnancy for eight months – in June, she had had 'a goodly belly'[17] – and what probably happened is that sometime in July or early August, she lost the child she was carrying, or it died soon after birth. It was not usual for royal stillbirths or miscarriages to be publicly announced, but an even stricter veil of secrecy seems to have been drawn over this event than had been the case with Katherine of Aragon's lost babies. That Anne's infant was born prematurely may be inferred from the fact that she did not formally take to her chamber preparatory to the birth.

According to Chapuys, the outcome of this tragedy was that the King 'renewed and increased the love that he had had previously towards another very beautiful maid-of-honour of this court'. Her identity is unknown, but she was almost certainly the mistress he had dallied with before the birth of Elizabeth in 1533, because she was similarly concerned to befriend the Lady Mary. She was certainly not Jane Seymour, because Chapuys did not consider Jane a beauty.[18]

Frustration and resentment over his continuing lack of a legitimate son, coupled with fear for the health of his illegitimate one, made the King more determined than ever to justify himself to the world and even less tolerant of those who opposed him. In October 1534, Henry suppressed the Order of Observant Friars at Greenwich,[19] whose members had consistently spoken out against the nullity suit and the King's supremacy. The friary church was converted into a mill for the royal armoury.

In November, a new Act of Supremacy enshrined in law the King's title of Supreme Head of the Church of England, finally severing the latter from the Church of Rome. Henceforth, ecclesiastical matters and doctrine would be the responsibility of the sovereign, who now regarded himself in every respect as God's deputy on Earth, a latter-day King David or King Solomon, responsible for the temporal and spiritual welfare of his subjects. From now on, according to Richard Sampson, Bishop of Chichester, who wrote a treatise on the subject, 'The word of God is to obey the King, and not the Bishop of Rome.'[20]

The advocates of reform, such as Queen Anne, Cranmer and Cromwell, applauded the King for leading his people out of darkness into the light. Those bishops who were reluctant to accept the change were intimidated into doing so by Cromwell, who jurisdiction over spiritual affairs was second only to the King's, and whose pursuit of the Reformation was so relentless that Reginald Pole called him an emissary of Satan. Anything that smacked of popery was suppressed. Hardliners even condemned the Order of the Garter and its patron saint St George as suspect, but these were dear to the King and were allowed to remain.

To the end of his life, Henry VIII remained a devout Catholic who deplored Lutheran and other heresies, but he had to maintain a balance between the radical evangelicals at his court, who were pressing for even

wider reforms and secretly flirting with Protestantism, and the conservatives, who would have given anything to put the clock back. The
King had always been interested in theology, but now he devoted more
time than ever to reading up on doctrinal issues and making copious
marginal notes. He would then lend the books he had read to
Gentlemen of the Privy Chamber of opposing viewpoints, and ask for
their comments before making up his own mind.

Because of diplomatic considerations and pressure from factions at
court and from foreign princes, Henry was not always consistent in his
religious policies. He was unwavering in his adherence to the doctrine
of transubstantiation, believed in purgatory and clerical celibacy, and
insisted on maintaining the Latin rituals and ceremonies he had grown
up with; he was no iconoclast, and his closets and chapels were full of
painted and graven images.[21] His Chapel Royal remained largely
unaffected by the religious changes he had effected. But he was not in
favour of extreme unction, individual confession or the traditional
mystical concept of ordination to the priesthood. He burned Lutherans
for heresy and papists for treason,[22] preferring to forget that he himself
had once written a tract defending the Pope's authority. He never lost
an opportunity to proclaim 'his zeal for the faith with all the resources
of his mind and body',[23] and one of his gold chains bore the inscription
'PLUS TOST MORIR QUE CHANGER MA PENSEE' ('I
PREFER TO DIE RATHER THAN CHANGE MY MIND').[24]

At court, religious observances remained largely unchanged, although
more emphasis was laid on preaching. At York Place, the King built a
special open-air pulpit in the shape of a Renaissance-style loggia in the
former privy garden, now a cobbled courtyard. Four times as many
courtiers could attend as could fit into the King's chapel.[25] Some
windows of the royal lodgings faced the 'preaching place', and the King
and Queen would watch from what appears to have been the council
chamber.[26] Archbishop Cranmer advised preachers new to the court
that they should avoid controversial issues and preach for no more than
one and a half hours, 'for the King and Queen may perhaps wax so
weary that they shall have small delight to continue throughout with
you to the end'.[27] Henry particularly enjoyed the sermons of the ardent
reformist Hugh Latimer, Bishop of Worcester, and on several occasions
entered into theological debates with him.[28]

Henry and Cromwell mobilised every resource and propaganda tool at
their disposal to promote and glorify the so-called 'New Monarchy' that
evolved in the wake of the Act of Supremacy and became a focus for the
heightened English nationalism of the period. Henry's enhanced status
was reflected in the words of Lord Morley, who described him as 'the

noblest King that ever reigned over the English nation, the father of our country, an ark of all princely goodness and honour, one by whose virtue, learning and noble courage England is newborn, newly brought from thraldom to freedom'.[29]

It was by clever management that Cromwell enabled the King to rule like a virtual despot. He manipulated the machinery of government to serve his master's will, and ensured that the Upper Chamber of Parliament was packed with lords loyal to Henry and that MPs sympathetic to the new order – of which there were many – were elected to the Commons, so that there would be little opposition to the momentous legislation that was passing through Parliament's hands. Thus the monarch, the peerage and Parliament became allies in the new order, sharing a common aim and interests. Against such an alliance protest was virtually useless.

The symbolism of empire was again brought into play. A new coinage was issued bearing the image of the King as Roman Emperor, and a third Great Seal in the Renaissance style was made, featuring the King on an antique throne and bearing the title of Supreme Head; this image was probably designed by Lucas Horenbout, whose portraits of the King it greatly resembles.[30] An imperial crown was added to the royal arms to signify that Henry recognised no higher power than his own save God.[31] There was a deliberate revival of the cult of King Arthur, from whom the Tudors claimed to be descended, and who was said to have owned a seal proclaiming him 'Arthur, Emperor of Britain and Gaul'.[32] Henry VIII, it was claimed, was merely reviving his ancestor's title and dignity. It was also asserted that England's sovereignty had for a thousand years been mistakenly subinfeudated to Rome by the King's predecessors: now he had redeemed it.[33]

No English king before Henry VIII had been so concerned to magnify and disseminate his public image. Under Cromwell's auspices, there was a flood of tracts and pamphlets proclaiming Henry's heroic virtues and moral superiority. Preachers, artists, craftsmen, writers, poets, playwrights and historians such as Polydore Vergil were called upon to use their talents to advertise and glorify the New Monarchy. Propagandists such as Gardiner portrayed Henry VIII as semi-divine, calling him 'the image of God upon Earth' who 'excelled in God's sight among all other human creatures.[34] A correspondent of Sir Anthony Browne declared that the King's subjects 'had not to do with a man but with a more excellent and divine estate', in whose presence one could not stand without trembling.[35]

The effect of all this was to turn Henry into an imperious and dangerous autocrat who became mesmerised by his own legend. In 1536 he wrote, 'God has not only made us King by inheritance, but has given us wisdom, policy and other graces in most plentiful sort, necessary for a prince to direct his affairs to his honour and glory.'[36]

The New Monarchy found its visual expression in art. It was state policy to ensure that images of the King and the symbols of monarchy proliferated. Henry had always been fond of giving portraits of himself to those he favoured, but it now became *de rigueur* for his subjects to proclaim their loyalty by displaying the image of the sovereign in their houses, thus instituting a tradition that would continue for three hundred years.

The artist chiefly responsible for creating the iconography of the New Monarchy was Holbein. In 1534, he painted a miniature of Solomon receiving the Queen of Sheba:[37] the figure of Solomon almost certainly represents Henry VIII – this is the first known painting of him by Holbein – and he appears enthroned in a magnificent Renaissance setting, highlighted in gold; above are the words 'Blessed be the Lord thy God, which delighteth in thee to set thee on His throne, to be King for the Lord thy God.' The message is unmistakable and powerful. The Queen of Sheba, kneeling in homage, can be symbolic of no other but the Church of England. This miniature may have been commissioned by Cromwell for presentation to the King.

The Reformation had a profound impact on art in England. As portrait painting became enduringly fashionable, religious paintings and images began to appear outdated and contentious, and biblical scenes gradually featured less and less as subjects for tapestries and pictures, often being replaced by classical themes. Artistically, England became isolated from the European mainstream.

At court, art was a useful propaganda tool, although few examples survive. Around 1535, the Flemish artist Joos van Cleve painted a portrait of Henry VIII[38] which shows him holding a scroll on which appears a Latin text from St Mark, chapter 16: 'Go ye into the world and preach the Gospel to every creature.' These, perhaps coincidentally, were the words that appeared on the title page of Miles Coverdale's banned English Bible of 1535. It has been suggested that the portrait was painted before the break with Rome, in which case the inscription must proclaim the King's loyalty to the Catholic Church, but it cannot, on the evidence of costume, be dated earlier than 1530, at which time Henry's relations with the Pope were rapidly deteriorating. The painting must therefore belong to the period of the Reformation, for which its text is apposite.

In c1538–40, Henry commissioned from Girolamo da Treviso a painting of the Four Evangelists stoning the Pope, which was executed in grisaille highlighted in gold. It hung in the King's privy gallery at Hampton Court, and still hangs in the palace today. Treviso had been one of Raphael's students in Rome before working for the Gonzaga at the court of Mantua. Henry retained him not only for his artistic talent, but also for his skills as a military engineer and architect. The King's enhanced prestige had also given impetus to his programme of building, restoring and acquiring houses, since the royal palaces were now to be the magnificent, glittering setting for the New Monarchy, and craftsmen like Treviso would be much in demand.

The royal supremacy was not without its critics at court. The conservative Gardiner initially led a clerical party opposed to the new order, and stoically endured a period out of favour. Norfolk, another reactionary conservative, had mixed feelings, having little time for priests yet scorning humanist tenets. 'I have never read the Scripture, nor never will read it,' he declared. All the same, 'it was merry in England afore the New Learning came up; yea, I would all things were as hath been in times past'.[39] Nevertheless, he was the King's man through and through, and Henry did not question his loyalty, although Cromwell remained suspicious of him and did all he could to oust him from court. After Master Secretary, Norfolk was the most experienced and respected member of the Council, but he represented the old feudal order, and there could never be anything but rivalry between him and the upstart he had helped to power. Norfolk's other rival, Suffolk, had still not recovered his former eminent position, declined to become involved in factional politics, and supported the Reformation, even though his formidable mother-in-law was in the opposite camp.

In November 1534, Norfolk was deputed to receive Francis I's special envoy, Philippe Chabot de Brion, Admiral of France, who had come to help restore good relations between England and France, which had deteriorated of late. The Admiral was lodged at Bridewell Palace, entertained by Norfolk and Suffolk, and invited to dine with the King at court.[40] The Queen, who had met de Brion in Calais in 1532, was offended when he failed to follow the practice of previous French ambassadors and send her a courteous message of goodwill, for she had planned to give a banquet in his honour. But the Admiral did not request an audience. The King noticed the omission, and dropped a heavy hint that the envoy should pay his respects to the Queen, but de Brion was chillingly aloof in her presence and did not participate in the dancing and tennis she had arranged for him. Instead, he struck up a friendship with Chapuys, which alarmed Anne greatly.

Worse was to come. The Admiral proposed a marriage between the Lady Mary and the Dauphin, ignoring the Princess Elizabeth entirely, then stated that, if Henry would not agree to this, his master would marry his son to the Emperor's daughter, an alliance that would leave

England, at this critical time, isolated in Europe.[41] Henry and Anne were mortified, and the King angrily repudiated the proposal, suggesting instead that Elizabeth be betrothed to Francis's third son, Charles. The French were unmoved.

Anne was under immense strain at this time. The King of France was no longer her friend, she had failed to give Henry the son he so desired, and she was miserable at his continued involvement with his unnamed mistress. She had enlisted Lady Rochford's help in getting rid of her rival, but the King intervened and icily told Anne that 'she had good reason to be content with what he had done for her for, were he to begin again, he would certainly not do as much, and that she ought to consider where she came from'. Lady Rochford was temporarily banished from court. When Anne dared to complain to the King in front of several courtiers that the maid of honour he had seduced was rude and disrespectful to her, he stormed out of the room in a temper.[42]

The King invited a number of beautiful ladies to court for the Admiral's visit, among them his mistress. 'He is more given to matters of dancing and ladies than he ever was,' observed Chapuys. At the beginning of December, de Brion was seated with the King and Queen at a court ball held in his honour, watching the dancing, when Henry rose and went to fetch the Admiral's secretary, Palmedes Gontier, saying that he wished to present him to Anne. The Admiral noticed the Queen's anxious eyes following Henry as he moved through the crowds in the presence chamber, then suddenly she burst out laughing hysterically. When the astonished envoy coldly inquired if she were 'mocking' him, she looked at him with tears in her eyes and replied, 'I could not help laughing at the King's proposition of introducing your secretary to me, for whilst he was looking out for him, he met a lady, who has made him forget the matter!' Sir Nicholas Carew told Chapuys at this time that the King was growing tired of Anne's complaints.[43]

Anne had cause for further sorrow that December when Little Purkoy suffered a fall and died of his injuries. None of her attendants dared tell her, so the King took it upon himself to break the news.[44] Then to sadness was added anger and humiliation when the Queen's sister Mary appeared at court noticeably pregnant and revealed that she had married – for love – a landless nobody called William Stafford, a distant cousin of the late Duke of Buckingham, and a soldier serving at Calais. So furious were the Boleyns at this *mésalliance* that they persuaded the King to forbid the disgraced couple the court. When Wiltshire cut off her allowance, Mary wrote in despair to Cromwell, begging him to intercede with the Queen and other members of her family on her behalf, but to no avail: she would never again be received at court.[45] She and her husband retired into obscurity in the country. Later, Wiltshire relented and allowed them the use of Rochford Hall in Essex, which remained their chief residence until Mary Boleyn died on 19 July 1543.[46]

At Christmas 1534, the King and Queen kept 'a great house'.[47] The King displayed 'his most hearty manner',[48] but the tension at court was palpable.

46

'That Thin Old Woman'

The court had now taken on a new character: the emphasis was no longer on chivalry and revelry but on religion and factional interests. Funding the New Monarchy posed problems, but the Church of which Henry was now Head possessed untapped wealth. Early in 1535, the King made Cromwell his viceregent in spiritual matters, and ordered him to make a survey of all the religious houses in England in order to discover any abuses within them, and – more importantly – to establish the possessions of each. The results of the survey, which took many months to complete, were written down in a great book known as the *Valor Ecclesiasticus*;[1] on its title page is a miniature of Henry VIII enthroned, executed by Lucas Horenbout.

Suppressing monasteries was no new thing. Henry V had done it in the early fifteenth century, as had Wolsey, and before the break with Rome Pope Clement had intended to sanction the closure of some English abbeys. The monastic orders were in decline – no new house had been founded since Syon Abbey in 1415, apart from the six friaries of the Observant Franciscans in the period 1482 to 1507.

Henry VIII's commissioners exposed much laxity and several cases of fraud, such as the much celebrated Holy Blood of Hailes, which turned out to be the blood of a duck, renewed regularly by the monks. Several communities opposed the royal supremacy. Queen Anne went in person to Syon Abbey and lectured the 'prostrate and grovelling' sisters on 'the enormity of their wanton incontinence', and ticked them off for reciting by rote Latin prayers that they did not understand. Before she left, she gave each one a prayerbook in English.[2] But Anne did not agree with Cromwell that the religious houses should all be closed down. She did her best to spare those that received a good report, and suggested that reform was a better alternative than closure.

Cromwell, however, wanted to make Henry 'the richest King that ever was in England'.[3] With the wealth and vast lands of the monasteries in his possession, he could not only fill his depleted treasury but also reward those who had shown their loyalty to the new order, thus transforming it into a popular movement.

Once the decision was taken to suppress the monasteries, Henry took steps to preserve their literary treasures, and commissioned his librarian, John Leland to 'peruse and diligently to search all the libraries' belonging to the religious houses and colleges, make a survey of their books and manuscripts, and find texts that would emphasise the royal supremacy and the New Monarchy. Leland set out to perform his mammoth task in 1535; he would not complete it until 1543. As he travelled around England, he 'conserved many good authors, the which otherwise had been like to have perished', and removed many works, which ended up in the royal libraries.[4] He also made copious notes on the places he visited, their customs and legends, and the people who lived there. These notes were later collated and published in 1710–12 as Leland's *Itinerary*.

By February 1534, the King had tired of his unnamed mistress and begun courting one of the Queen's cousins, either Madge Shelton or her sister Mary.[5] Madge was softly spoken and pretty, with dimpled cheeks and a fair complexion. Unlike her predecessor, the Queen's cousin (whichever she was) had no intention of espousing the cause of Katherine and Mary, but Anne resented Sir Francis Weston and other Gentlemen of the King's Privy Chamber paying court to her.[6] Moreover, the girl was a frivolous creature. When the Queen discovered that she had written 'idle poesies' in her prayer book, she 'wonderfully rebuked her' for defacing it with 'such wanton toys'.[7]

Anne's determination to play the virtuous queen found further expression at Easter 1535, when she distributed larger purses of Maundy money than any queen had hitherto given.[8] The King also permitted his former wife Katherine to perform the traditional Maundy Thursday rites; she had 'kept a Maundy' the previous year, and he had not objected because his grandmother Margaret Beaufort had set a precedent for royal ladies other than queens presiding, and Katherine was now officially Princess Dowager of Wales.[9]

On 5 May, the Boleyn contingent was out in force at Tyburn to witness the first executions of those who had refused to swear the oath to the Act of Succession, among whom were John Houghton, Prior of the London Charterhouse, and Richard Reynolds, a monk of Syon Abbey, who were both renowned throughout Europe for their learning and integrity. Wiltshire, Rochford, Norfolk and Richmond stood 'quite near the sufferers', looking on as the dreadful sentence of hanging, drawing and quartering was carried out. Rumour had it that Henry himself would have liked to be present, 'which was very probable, seeing that nearly all the court were there'. Some courtiers, however, had come masked or disguised as Scotsmen.[10] Afterwards, shock waves reverberated around Christendom at the enormity of what the King had done.

When one of the Queen's ladies contracted measles that spring, Henry mistook it for plague and hurried away with Anne to Hampton Court. But plague did break out in London soon afterwards, and a proclamation was issued forbidding the citizens to approach the court.[11] The King spent the late spring and summer months hunting well away from the capital before departing on progress.

During May, the celebrated French humanist and poet, Nicholas Bourbon sought asylum at the English court after falling foul of the French authorities for his evangelical reformist beliefs; when his plight had been drawn to the attention of Henry VIII and Anne Boleyn by the French ambassador, Jean de Dinteville, and Dr William Butts, with whom Bourbon corresponded regularly, they secured his release from prison, and were now happy to extend to him their patronage. Bourbon, a friend of Erasmus, was lodged at first in Dr Butts's house at the Queen's expense; Butts, he said, was like a father to him. Later, he lived with the King's goldsmith, Cornelius Heyss. Anne also secured for Bourbon a post as tutor to her nephew and ward, Henry Carey, Sir Henry Norris's son and Edmund, son of Sir Nicholas Harvey, another reformist courtier in the Queen's circle.[12] During his stay in England, Bourbon – who wrote under the name Borbonius – sat for Holbein, whom he called 'the incomparable painter'; he also befriended Cromwell whom he described as being 'aflame with the love of Christ', Nicolaus Kratzer and Archbishop Cranmer, who was 'a head of his people'.[13]

In 1535, Miles Coverdale's English translation of the Bible was published in Zürich. It was dedicated to Henry VIII and his 'dearest wife and most virtuous princess, Queen Anne', but was never officially sanctioned in England. Its frontispiece, which is attributed to Holbein, shows an image of Henry VIII as an Old Testament king, perhaps King David, enthroned above the lords spiritual and temporal, holding a sword and a Bible, which he is handing down to three kneeling bishops. This image was revolutionary for its time, in that it had hitherto been bishops who had conferred spiritual authority on kings. Anne Boleyn owned the copy that is now in the British Library; her initials are embossed on the binding.

In June 1535, a satirical play parodying the Apocalypse was performed before the King at court. After the Reformation, drama became increasingly politicised, and was under the control of one of Cromwell's masters of propaganda, Richard Moryson. Cromwell advised the King that plays were an ideal means of setting forth 'lively before the people's eyes the abomination and wickedness of the Bishop of Rome, monks, friars, nuns and suchlike, and to declare and open to them the obedience that your subjects, by God's and man's laws, owe to Your Majesty'.[14] In the late 1530s, a number of such plays were performed at court, including perhaps John Bale's *King John*, which was not only the first historical play in English but also a clever piece of propaganda that refuted the Pope's claim to hold jurisdiction over the English Church. 'Bilious Bishop Bale', as he was called – he was Bishop of Ossory, in Ireland – was a closet Protestant and playwright who, under Cromwell's patronage, had his own touring company of players which he used to promote the Reformation and the New Monarchy. Another of his plays was called *The Whore of Babylon* (c1546). However, given the sensitive climate of the times, there was a limit to what was acceptable at court: anti-papal thrusts could all too often be misconstrued as attacks on the Catholic faith itself.

Drama was ever popular at court. In the year 1537–8, for example, seven companies of players were working for the King, the Queen, the Lord Chamberlain, Lord Chancellor Audley, Suffolk, Exeter and the Lord Warden of the Cinque Ports, whose names they bore. These companies were amateur dramatic groups formed by members of the royal household and the households of the nobility. Amongst the productions they mounted were old favourites such as *Fulgens and Lucrece*, and *The Pardoner and the Friar* adapted by John Heywood from Geoffrey Chaucer's *Canterbury Tales*; Christopher Marlowe later based *The Jew of Malta* on this work.

Henry was now moving nearer to an alliance with the Emperor, despite the fact that seemingly insurmountable obstacles stood in its way. Yet Renaissance princes often took a pragmatic approach to such things, and Charles V can only have been relieved that Henry's friendship with Francis I had begun to cool. The King had been angered by the refusal of the French to consider the Princess Elizabeth as a bride for Francis's son, and at the same time concerned that, because she was a bastard in the eyes of Catholic Europe, she would be of little value to him in the marriage market. In June, the new French ambassador, Antoine de Castelnau, Bishop of Tarbes, took offence at the King's refusal to allow him to use Bridewell Palace as an embassy, as his predecessors had done, and was further put out when Cromwell pointedly avoided him. To make matters worse, Henry had begun to make a great fuss of the imperial ambassador Chapuys, inviting him to join him in the chase and generally courting his goodwill.[15]

Yet Henry's persecution of eminent Roman Catholics continued to threaten the fragile beginnings of an entente with the Emperor. In June, Bishop Fisher was tried and condemned to death for treason. 'A very image of death'[16] after long months of rigorous confinement, he emerged on 22 June to kneel at the executioner's block on Tower Hill, wearing his finest clothes, for this, he declared, was his wedding day. On the scaffold, he insisted that he was dying to preserve the honour of God, and was then decapitated with a sword. Some time earlier, word had come from Rome that the Pope had made him a cardinal and that his red hat was on its way. The King had commented grimly that he would have to wear it on his shoulders. There was widespread outrage at the butchering of such a saintly man.

The trial of Sir Thomas More followed on 1 July, and he was condemned to death on the evidence of Richard Rich, one of Cromwell's henchmen. On 6 July, while the King hunted at Reading,[17] More was beheaded on Tower Hill, claiming he died 'the King's good servant, but God's first'.[18] His execution provoked even greater shock than Fisher's had, but few were brave enough to follow his example. The King soon regretted More's death, and accused Anne Boleyn of having been the cause of it. Anne sought to distract him by arranging feasts and revels.[19]

Lady Rochford was now back at court, but was no longer the Queen's friend and ally. Since her banishment the previous year, something had occurred to alienate her from her sister-in-law. Perhaps she blamed Anne for her disgrace, or had become jealous of the close bond between the Queen and Lord Rochford. The evidence suggests that the Rochfords' marriage was not happy, and Jane may have resented Anne's influence over her husband. What happened next suggests that there was now a serious rift between the two women, for in July, Lady Rochford was one of several ladies involved in a demonstration at Greenwich in support of the Lady Mary, and ended up in the Tower with the other ringleaders, among them Katherine Boughton, wife of Lord William Howard, and the wives of some leading citizens of London.[20]

Will Somers, the King's fool, was also in disgrace, for that same month Sir Nicholas Carew had dared him to declare that the Queen was 'a ribald' and the Princess Elizabeth 'a bastard'. Great licence was normally allowed the royal jesters, but on this occasion, according to Chapuys, the King threatened to kill Somers with his own hand, and he had to go into hiding in Carew's house at Beddington until his master's wrath had cooled.[21]

Henry's mood improved as the summer progressed. In July, he was happily 'feasting ladies', and perhaps going further than that, since

Chapuys commented that his 'amorous' reputation was now notorious.[22] At forty-four, he was beginning to put on weight and now sported cropped hair and a permanent, short, square beard, which he expected others to copy. John Stow claims that, on 8 May 1535, the King had 'commanded all about his court to poll their heads, and to give them example he caused his own hair to be polled, and from henceforth his beard to be knotted and no more shaven'. His later portraits bear this out.

Henry's mania for property had not abated. In 1535, he acquired five new houses. He bought moated Chobham Park in Surrey from Chertsey Abbey, and immediately began extending it and creating royal lodgings.[23] He gained possession of manor houses at Hackney, near London, and at Leconfield, Humberside, the latter by exchange with the Earl of Northumberland,[24] who also sold the King Petworth House in Sussex.[25] Lastly, Henry got a house at Mortlake in Surrey by exchange with Archbishop Cranmer.

In 1535–6, the King converted what had possibly been Wolsey's dining hall into the great watching chamber at Hampton Court, which still survives with its beautiful oriel window and ceiling ornamented with a geometric lattice of gilded battens, drop pendants and leather-mâché roundels bearing 130 devices and badges of the King and Jane Seymour, in whose time the ceiling was finished.[26] This was the first of the outward chambers of the King's apartments, but those beyond its door no longer survive.

Henry was also carrying out works at Greenwich at this time. His refurbished privy chamber on the first floor of the donjon had bay windows overlooking the Thames, tapestried walls, grotesque decoration and carpets on the floor. Its antique-style ceiling was patterned with timber battens with gilded lead leaves at the intersections; it was made by the King's joiner, Richard Ridge, who had carved the decorations on the ceiling of the great hall at Hampton Court.[27]

In the summer of 1535, the King embarked on one of the most important progresses of his reign. This was not just an elaborate hunting jaunt, but a public relations exercise 'with a view to gaining popularity with his subjects'[28] and promoting the recent religious reforms. Not only courtiers who had supported the King's policies were favoured with visits, but also traditionalists whose goodwill he wished to retain. During this progress, Gardiner, who had now had leisure to revise his views, secured his return to favour by publishing a timely treatise entitled *De Vera Obedientia*, which strongly endorsed the royal supremacy. The King rewarded him with the post of ambassador to France.

On 5 July, attended by a vast train of courtiers, servants and baggage, Henry and Anne travelled west from Windsor to Reading, Ewelme, Abingdon, Woodstock, Langley and Sudeley Castle, where they stayed a week. Cromwell joined them here on the 23rd; he had come to arrange for the King's commissioners to visit all the religious houses in the West Country.

By late July, Henry had reached Tewkesbury. He then rode south to Gloucester; he and the Queen lodged at nearby Painswick Manor, which afforded excellent hunting. They were at Berkeley Castle from 2 to 8 August, then moved on to Thornbury; Henry had intended to visit Bristol, but had been deterred by reports of plague. Instead, a delegation of leading citizens waited upon him at Thornbury. At Iron Acton he stayed at Acton Court, where Sir Nicholas Poyntz had built a lavish new Renaissance-style eastern range especially for the King's visit.[29] The Poyntzes were a notable courtier family: Nicholas's grandfather, Sir Robert Poyntz, had been Vice-Chamberlain to Queen Katherine, while his uncle, Sir John Poyntz, was a member of Queen Anne's household and a friend of Wyatt, who dedicated to him two of his satires on the superficiality of life at court. Nicholas himself was a reformist and a member of Cromwell's circle.

From Iron Acton, Henry moved on to Little Sodbury and Bromham, where two fervent supporters of reform, Sir John Walsh and Sir Edward Baynton, the Queen's Vice-Chamberlain, were respectively hosts to their sovereign. Afterwards, the King made his much celebrated visit to Wulfhall,[30] the home of Sir John Seymour, where he stayed three nights.[31] Some writers date the commencement of his affair with Jane Seymour to this visit, but while this may be true, there is no evidence for it.

During October there were reports that the King and Queen and all the nobles were merry and in good health, and hawking daily.[32] Yet Anne again had cause for concern, for early that month the French ambassador reported that the King's love for her was diminishing daily since he had 'new amours'.[33]

Henry had lost interest in Madge Shelton (or her sister); Madge was now being courted by the widowed Sir Henry Norris, to whom she would be betrothed in 1536. The King was presently pursuing Sir Edward Seymour's sister Jane, who was one of the Queen's maids of honour. At twenty-seven, Jane was rather old to be unwed, but it appears that her father could not afford to dower her richly. She was neither accomplished nor pretty. 'She is no great beauty,' observed Chapuys. 'Her complexion is so fair that one would rather call her pale.'[34] Her portraits by Holbein[35] bear out the French ambassador's opinion that she was plain, and show a wide, angular face with compressed lips, little eyes and a large nose. Polydore Vergil called Jane 'a woman of the utmost charm', and although it is not evident in her portraits this was perhaps the quality that attracted the King. She was also the complete antithesis of Anne Boleyn – quiet, demure, subservient and discreet, characteristics the King had come to appreciate in a woman. She could read and sign her name, but if she was as intelligent as her champions claimed, she hid it well. The King confided to Chapuys that she had a gentle nature and was 'inclined to peace'.[36] Her behaviour in the coming months suggests, however, that she was also a tough, ambitious woman of ruthless determination.

In October, the court spent four days in the familiar surroundings of The Vyne in Hampshire, where Lord Sandys extended to his sovereign his usual warm welcome. The King returned to Windsor at the end of the month,[37] and soon afterwards the Queen discovered that she was pregnant again.

By the autumn of 1535, Henry's relationship with Anne had deteriorated significantly, despite their outward show of cheerfulness. Anne was no longer the alluring young woman who had captured his heart: a portrait of her at Nidd Hall, which must date from c1535–6, shows that she was ageing, while Chapuys was soon to refer to her as 'that thin old woman', and one courtier described her as 'extremely ugly'.[38] The King was by now 'tired to satiety' of her;[39] she had never learned the discretion or decorum befitting a queen, and still upbraided him for his infidelities. She dared to argue with him in public, laughed at his clothes and his poetry, and even appeared bored in his company.[40] She remained unpopular and controversial, and her very existence was a barrier to a closer understanding with the Emperor. She exercised so much influence over public affairs that it was said that she wielded more authority than Henry or Cromwell. 'The King dares not contradict her,' wrote Chapuys. 'The Lady well knows how to manage him.'[41] Henry was probably a little in awe of this formidable woman with her strident opinions and inflammable temper, and certainly resentful towards her. However, she was his queen and hopefully he would soon honour her as the mother of his son. Nevertheless, by December, the couple were barely on speaking terms, and in February 1536, Chapuys claimed Henry had had little to do with Anne for three months.[42]

At court and in the Privy Chamber, the Boleyn faction was still powerful. It included Wiltshire, Rochford, Archbishop Cranmer and Lord Chancellor Audley. Cromwell was still, on the surface at least, an ally of the Queen, although they had quarrelled in June 1535, when he told Chapuys that she had threatened to have him beheaded.[43] Another ally, Gardiner, was in France. Norfolk had long since been alienated by

Anne, and was more of an enemy than a friend. However, there was little apparent opposition. Of the former Queen Katherine's English supporters, only Exeter, Bryan and Carew remained at court, and they were quiescent. But in December 1535, Henry made it clear which way the wind was blowing by receiving Chapuys at Greenwich with calculated courtesy, putting his arm around the ambassador's neck and walking with him for some time 'in the presence of all the courtiers'.[44] Henry knew now that another obstacle in the way of an alliance with the Emperor would soon be removed, for he had received news that the Princess Dowager was dying.

For some time now, Katherine of Aragon had been suffering from what proved to be terminal cancer of the heart. Confined to one room in Kimbolton Castle in the Fens, she was attended only by her physician, her confessor, an apothecary and three women, who cooked and tasted her food in her presence, for fear of poison. Maria de Salinas, Lady Willoughby, was with Katherine during her last illness, and at her side when she died on 7 January 1536. Amongst several items forwarded to Henry was a final letter from his former wife, vowing that 'mine eyes desire you above all things'; it was signed, defiantly, 'Katherine the Queen'.

Although he wept when he read the letter,[45] the King was greatly relieved to be freed from the threat of war with the Emperor, who had staunchly upheld Katherine's cause to the last. Henry and Anne appeared at court in satin outfits of yellow, the colour of royal mourning in Spain at that time, and also in purple mourning, according to one imperial source; yet the atmosphere was one of triumph rather than grief, as the King carried his daughter Elizabeth into chapel for a solemn Mass, to the sound of trumpets, then proudly showed her off to his courtiers at a banquet, which was followed by dancing and jousting.[46]

At forty-four, Henry still jousted occasionally, but his career in the lists came to an abrupt end on 24 January 1536 when, during a tournament at Greenwich, wearing full armour, he was unhorsed by an opponent. As he toppled to the ground, his armoured steed collapsed on top of him. The King lay unconscious for two hours. 'He fell so heavily that everyone thought it a miracle he was not killed,' reported Chapuys.[47] At one point it was feared that he was dead, and the Duke of Norfolk hastened to the Queen to break the news to her. But Henry recovered and 'sustained no injury'.[48] Although his jousting days were over, he continued to enjoy riding and walking a great deal.

Some modern authors[49] have suggested that this fall resulted in brain damage that affected the King's judgement and behaviour during the rest of his life, but there is no evidence to support the theory that there was a sudden change in his character. Had there been, contemporaries would surely have remarked upon it. However, the fall may well have exacerbated the ulcer or osteomyelitis in the King's leg, or may have caused a varicose vein to burst and later become thrombosed. As he had already suffered problems in one leg, this may account for the condition that would soon appear in the other.

Henry was still recovering when, on 29 January, Katherine of Aragon was buried in Peterborough Cathedral. Frances Brandon, Marchioness of Dorset, was chief mourner, supported by Lady Willoughby and her daughter, the young Duchess of Suffolk. The King wore black on that day, and attended a requiem Mass at Greenwich.

On the same day, Anne went into premature labour. That morning, Chapuys was told by one of Exeter's servants that a distraught King had confided to one of his Gentlemen that he had been 'seduced by witchcraft' into marriage, 'and for this reason considered it null. It was evident because God did not permit them to have any male issue, and he believed he might take another wife'.[50] After the Queen's baby had been aborted, Chapuys learned that it 'had the appearance of a male of 15 weeks' growth', and stated that it was generally held that Anne had a 'defective constitution' that would prevent her from bearing healthy children.[51] Some even believed she had never been pregnant at all.[52]

The loss of their son was a crushing disappointment to both Henry and Anne. Anne attributed it to the shock she sustained when Norfolk told her that the King was dead and her distress over Henry's infidelities.[53] When he visited her, Henry said bitterly, 'I see that God will not give me male children. When you are up, I will speak to you.'[54]

47

'Thunder Rolls around the Throne'

The King left Greenwich early in February and went to York Place for the Shrovetide celebrations and the final session of the Reformation Parliament, which lasted from 4 February to 14 April. Both the Queen and Jane Seymour remained at Greenwich, but Anne had removed to York Place by 24 February, when she and Henry celebrated the feast day of St Matthias there. Chapuys claims that the King had been sufficiently moved by Anne's distress over his affair with Jane to forsake Jane's company for hers on this occasion.[1] Thereafter, however, he visited Greenwich frequently to pay court to Jane, for whom his passion was growing. Chapuys, however, placed little reliance on rumours that he wanted to marry her.[2]

On 3 March, Sir Edward Seymour was appointed a Gentleman of the Privy Chamber. He and his brother Thomas were looking forward to many more honours and spoils through their sister's liaison with the King, and both they and their conservative friends, Sir Nicholas Carew, Lord Montague and his brother, Geoffrey Pole, the Marquess of Exeter and Sir Thomas Elyot, urged Jane not to submit to her royal lover but to wrest every advantage from the relationship. There is little doubt that the Seymours and their allies, who were also Anne's enemies and Mary's supporters, meant to use Jane to topple the Queen and further their own interests. Jane, who was of an orthodox religious persuasion, and sympathetic to the Lady Mary, was a willing tool.

She had seen how similar tactics benefited Anne Boleyn, and now played the role of modest virgin to perfection. When, in March, the King sent her a letter with a purse of gold sovereigns, she knelt, kissed the letter, and returned both to the messenger, declaring that she could only accept a dowry from the King when she found a husband.[3] Impressed by her virtue, Henry promised that he would not visit or speak to her 'except in the presence of one of her relatives'.[4] In March,

Cromwell vacated his rooms at Greenwich, which afforded secret access to the privy lodgings, and Sir Edward and Lady Seymour were installed there, to act as chaperones when the King came 'through certain galleries without being perceived' to pay his chaste addresses to Jane.[5]

Yet even this degree of privacy did not prevent the truth leaking out. At the end of March, Cromwell, smiling meaningfully, reassured Chapuys that, 'although the King has formerly been rather fond of the ladies, I believe he will henceforth live more chastely, and not change again'. But by then the ambassador knew all about Jane Seymour, whom he regarded as just another in a long line of royal mistresses. Although he referred to her as 'the lady whom [the King] serves', which suggests a courtly rather than a sexual relationship, he had no great opinion of her virtue, writing to the Emperor, 'You may imagine whether, being an Englishwoman, and having been long at court, she would not hold it a sin to be still a maid.' He added that there were 'plenty of witnesses to the contrary'.[6]

Far from being the doomed heroine portrayed by many biographers, Queen Anne's position was surprisingly strong during February, March and April 1536. Rather than having caused a rift between the royal couple, her miscarriage appears to have excited the King's sympathies towards her, and he clearly had no real intention of ridding himself of her at this time; on the contrary, when it came to the imperial alliance, he would be hot in defence of her position as Queen.

During these months, Anne spent lavishly on clothing and other items for herself and her two-year-old daughter. Among her purchases were fabrics and trimmings for gowns: purple cloth of gold, black and tawny velvet, black damask, carnation and white satin, lambskin and miniver; she ordered thirteen kirtles of white satin and damask, eight nightgowns, including one of orange tawny silk, one trimmed with miniver and another edged with Venice gold braid; three cloaks of black satin, embroidered tawny satin and black cloth; black velvet for shoes and slippers (which were made up by her shoemaker, Arnold), ribbon for putting up her hair, tassels and fringing of Florence gold for her 'great bed', decorative attachments for her saddles, leading reins for her mule, caps for her female fool and green ribbon to adorn her clavichords. For Elizabeth, there was an orange satin gown, a russet velvet kirtle and pretty embroidered caps. The fabrics were supplied by William Loke, the King's mercer, and the garments – which cost Anne an average of £40 (£12,000) a month – were made up by her tailor, John Matte.[7]

The Boleyn faction was still dominant at court, still entrenched at the centre of the web of patronage. In March, Wiltshire's lease of Crown property at Rayleigh, Essex, was extended with a rebated rent, and

Rochford was made joint tenant. After an Act of Parliament separated the town of King's Lynn from the diocese of Norwich on 14 April, the King granted the town to Wiltshire, along with two dissolved abbeys.[8] Around this time, the King gave his approval for his son Richmond, who was now very ill and residing at St James's Palace, to give his manor of Collyweston to Queen Anne in exchange for Baynard's Castle and Durham House.[9]

The Emperor was now so eager to conclude an alliance with Henry VIII that he was prepared to be conciliatory. He had recently prevented the Pope from publishing the sentence of excommunication that would deprive Henry of his throne and, now that his aunt Katherine was dead, he was willing to offer the King his support for 'the continuation of this last matrimony' with Anne Boleyn, 'or otherwise', in return for Katherine's daughter Mary being declared legitimate.[10] Cromwell was convinced that, given the threat of excommunication, an imperial alliance was vital to England's security, and even the Boleyn faction had resolved to abandon their hopes of a new entente with France and support an understanding with Charles.[11]

Late in March, Chapuys had heard that Cromwell had fallen out with the Queen, probably because of his compliance in vacating his rooms for the Seymours. Cromwell confirmed the rift to Chapuys on 1 April, asserting that Anne hated him and wanted to have him executed. He asked Chapuys how Charles V would feel if the King remarried. Chapuys insisted that the world would never recognise Anne as Henry's true wife, but might accept another lady.[12]

Henry and Anne, however, were determined to secure the Emperor's acknowledgement of her as Queen and, having granted Chapuys an audience for Easter Tuesday, 18 April, the King arranged matters so that the ambassador, who had hitherto refused to pay Anne the courtesy of kissing her hand, would have every opportunity of paying his respects to her.

When Chapuys arrived at Greenwich on the 18th, he was warmly welcomed at the gates by Rochford. Cromwell then came forward with a message from the King, inviting him to visit Anne and kiss her cheek – a great honour conferred only on those in high favour. Chapuys managed to ignore this summons, but allowed himself to be escorted by Rochford to Mass in the chapel royal. When the King and Queen descended from the royal pew to make their offerings, Anne espied the ambassador standing behind the door and turned, 'merely to do me reverence'. He bowed in response. Anne hoped to speak with Chapuys at the dinner she was to host in her apartments, but after she had left the chapel with the King she was dismayed to see that the ambassador was not among those who were waiting at her door.

'Why does he not enter, like the other ambassadors?' she asked.

'It is not without good reason,' replied Henry, who had in fact decided to approach Chapuys himself during the coming audience. After dining with Anne, he went to his presence chamber, where Chapuys had eaten in the company of Rochford, and spoke with the ambassador in the privacy of a window embrasure. During the conversation, the King showed himself unexpectedly cool towards the mooted alliance, and insisted that the Emperor apologise for his past behaviour to Henry and acknowledge Anne as Queen – all in writing. Cromwell, who had certainly exceeded his brief in the negotiations with Charles, and was heavily committed to the alliance, watched in consternation, knowing that the Emperor would never agree to such humiliating terms. The Secretary realised that Anne herself was behind Henry's stand, and afterwards attempted to remonstrate with the King. In vain. Henry was so angry and obstructive that Cromwell deemed it politic to withdraw from court and feign illness.[13]

He knew now that, while Anne was in power, the Spanish alliance, which he believed was vital to the security of the realm and his own future, would be in jeopardy. Anne was now his enemy and the greatest threat to his career, even his life, and her hold over the King was still considerable. It was at this point, as he would tell Chapuys on 6 June, that he decided she must be eliminated.[14]

During the last two weeks of April, in the privacy of his London house, Cromwell hatched the plot that would not only bring Anne down but also purge the Privy Chamber and the court of her supporters. He even made common cause with the Seymours, Carew, Exeter, Montague and Sir Francis Bryan, who had recently returned to court and was a staunch ally of the Seymours. This unlikely alliance between the champions of conservatism and the chief architect of reform would until recently have been unthinkable, but they now shared a common aim, and Cromwell realised that supporting Jane Seymour offered him his best chance of political survival. Another ally was Chapuys, who obtained the Lady Mary's qualified approval of the plot.[15]

On 23 April, the King, Norfolk, Wiltshire and the ailing Richmond were among those who attended the annual chapter meeting of the Order of the Garter at Greenwich. A vacancy had arisen, and in honour of a promise he had made to Francis I, Henry chose Sir Nicholas Carew rather than the other candidate, Lord Rochford. Chapuys mistakenly interpreted this as a sign that the Boleyns were losing favour.[16]

On that same day, the Queen took it upon herself to reprove Sir Francis Weston for flirting with Madge Shelton, and speculated as to why Sir Henry Norris had not yet married Madge. Weston pointed out,

'Norris comes more into your chamber for Your Grace than he does for Madge.' Anne ignored this, although she did not forget it, and told Weston she had heard he did not love his wife, Anne Pickering. Teasingly, she asked if he was in love with Madge.

'I love one in your household better than both,' he answered meaningfully.

'Who is that?' Anne asked.

'It is yourself,' he declared. The Queen 'defied him' and indicated that their talk was at an end.[17] Reported conversations such as this enabled Cromwell to construct a case against Anne.

The next day, Lord Chancellor Audley authorised Cromwell and Norfolk to head a commission to investigate unspecified cases of treason and other offences committed in Middlesex and Kent;[18] it is unlikely that, at this stage, the King was aware that his wife was the object of an inquiry, or that he knew about the patent of oyer that Cromwell had obtained, since the issue of such documents was routine.

In fact, contrary to the opinion of nearly every modern historian, Henry had every reason to be pleased with Anne, for the evidence strongly suggests that she was pregnant again. Just as she had conceived rapidly after the birth of Elizabeth, so her reconciliation with the King after the miscarriage in January had quickly borne fruit. Henry made what was probably an oblique reference to her pregnancy that April, when he rounded on Chapuys for suggesting that God had not thought fit to send him male issue because He had ordained that England should have a female succession. 'Am I not a man like other men? Am I not? Am I not?' shouted Henry. 'You do not know all my secrets.' On 25 April, in a letter sent to his ambassador Richard Pate in Rome and duplicated to Gardiner and Wallop in France, Henry announced 'the likelihood and appearance that God will send us heirs male', implying that 'our most dear and entirely beloved wife the Queen' was once more expecting a child.[19] Had Anne conceived towards the end of February, it would have been possible for the King to state this with some certainty, and clearly he was eager to do so. In the past, royal conceptions had not normally been the subject of official announcements, but the urgent resolution of the succession problem was a matter of vital national importance meriting widespread publicity. On a personal level too, the King was anxious to show the world that he was capable of fathering an heir, and also to justify his marriage to Anne. It is unthinkable therefore, if there had been no certain hope of a child, that he, a normally discreet man in such matters, would have made such a statement, knowing that his ambassadors would make it public.

The news that the Queen might yet bear a son and so render herself invincible must have caused Cromwell considerable alarm, and gave him the impetus to bring her down while he had the chance. He was keeping all his options open: towards the end of April, he and his fellow conspirators were still discussing the possibility of the royal marriage being annulled.[20] But the Queen was in a very strong position: only the most damning charges against her would now suffice to destroy her.

On the 29th, a conversation that Anne had with the musician Mark Smeaton was reported to Cromwell. Smeaton had enjoyed more success than most people of his 'poor degree'[21] ever dreamed of, but he was acutely aware of being outside the charmed circle that surrounded the Queen, whom he evidently admired. Anne now came upon him standing dejectedly in the 'round window' in her apartments.

'Master Smeaton, why are you so sad?' she asked.

'It is no matter,' he replied dejectedly.

Anne answered haughtily, 'You may not look to have me speak to you as I would to a nobleman, because you be an inferior person.'

'No, no, a look sufficeth me,' Smeaton assured her, 'and thus fare you well.'[22] He was to have bitter cause to regret his words.

The King had been planning for some time to revisit Calais, and intended to depart with the Queen on 2 May, after the May Day jousts. Before crossing the Channel, they would stop in Dover to inspect the fortifications.[23]

But the visit would never take place. It is clear that Anne's fall from favour was sudden. On 30 April, as the Queen watched a dog-fight in Greenwich Park, Cromwell laid before the King shocking and seemingly incontrovertible evidence that she had seduced Smeaton and other members of the Privy Chamber, including her own brother; furthermore, she had plotted regicide,[24] with the intention of marrying one of her lovers and ruling as regent for the child she was carrying. The evidence was sufficiently strong and convincing to cast serious doubt on the paternity of her baby, and to utterly alienate the King from her. With devastating clarity, he saw now that all along he had nourished a viper in his bosom: not only had she deceived and humiliated him, both as a husband and as her sovereign, but – more seriously – she had put the succession in jeopardy and committed the worst kind of treason by plotting the King's death.

Most modern historians are of the opinion that Anne was not guilty of any of the twenty-two charges of adultery laid against her; eleven of them can be proved false. It is unlikely that she would have schemed to kill the King, who was her chief defender and protector. The circumstances of her fall suggest strongly that she was framed; even Chapuys thought so[25] and, on the eve of her death, Anne herself would swear on the blessed sacrament that she was innocent. However, her reputation, her flirtatious nature, her enjoyment of male company and her indulgence in the amorous banter and interplay of courtly love all made the charges against her believable. Not only the King, but many other people, thought her guilty.

Anne was doomed. In the normal course of justice, her pregnancy would have saved her from a death sentence, or at least postponed it, but this child could never be allowed to live, because the King would not dare risk a disputed succession. Nor, however, could he be seen as a monarch who put an innocent baby to death, which is perhaps the reason why some of the documents relating to Anne's trial were destroyed. No further mention is made of her pregnancy, and it is perhaps significant that she was not made to undergo an examination by a panel of matrons before her execution, as Lady Jane Grey did in 1553. Anne herself never mentioned her condition whilst in the Tower, but neither did she make any reference to her daughter Elizabeth. In both cases, she must have realised that to do so would be futile, for Henry had hardened his heart against her.

Cromwell had obtained most of his evidence by questioning the members of Anne's household, particularly the ladies of her Privy Chamber, who, he claimed, were so shocked by her crimes that they could not conceal them.[26] What he uncovered was described at her trial as 'bawdy and lechery',[27] and only fragments of it survive, but they suffice to suggest that the whole fabric of the case against Anne was constructed on the basis of innuendo and inference. It was enough, however, to convince an overly suspicious man like the King.

On 30 April, after Henry's fateful interview with Cromwell, the King and Queen were observed at a window overlooking the courtyard at Greenwich. Anne was holding Elizabeth in her arms, and seemed to be pleading with Henry, who appeared to be angry. The Council sat until dark in 'protracted conference', and a crowd gathered at the palace, realising that 'some deep and difficult question was being discussed'.[28]

During that day, Anne had tackled Sir Henry Norris about his failure to marry Madge Shelton; he said he wished to 'tarry awhile', but she interpreted his evasive reply as implying that it was because of her.

'You look for dead men's shoes!' she told him. 'For if aught came to the King but good, you would look to have me.'

Norris was appalled at her indiscretion and infringement of the rules of courtly love, which required the man to set the pace, and stoutly declared that, if he ever thought such a thing, 'he would his head were off'. Anne was amused, and said she could undo him if she wished to, but then realised that others were listening to their conversation, and made Norris go to her Almoner, John Skip, to swear on his oath that she 'was a good woman'.[29] Within three days the gossip-mongers had spread her words round the court.

That evening, whilst dancing, Anne learned that Mark Smeaton had been arrested.[30] She was also informed, at 11 p.m., that the coming visit to Calais had been postponed for a week.[31]

Smeaton was taken to the Tower on the morning of 1 May.[32] There, probably under torture,[33] he confessed to committing adultery with the Queen on three occasions in the spring of 1535[34] – the only one of the men accused with her to admit his guilt. His inclusion among her alleged lovers was doubtless intended to show how low she had stooped to gratify her lust, and so further inflame public opinion against her. Anne herself later insisted that Smeaton had been in her apartments only twice – on 29 April, and at Winchester in 1535, when he played the virginals for her.[35]

The May Day jousts went ahead as planned. Sir Henry Norris led the defenders while Rochford was the leading challenger. When Norris's steed became uncontrollable, the King lent him one of his own horses.[36] But before the tournament ended, to everyone's astonishment, especially the Queen's,[37] Henry left abruptly with less than six attendants,[38] probably because Cromwell had sent word that he had Smeaton's confession to hand and that Norris also was under suspicion.[39] If he was indeed manufacturing evidence, Cromwell was taking a risk here, because Norris was one of the King's closest friends and intimate associates, and enjoyed far greater influence with Henry than Cromwell did. But the King chose to believe his Secretary, which suggests that the evidence against Norris was seriously compelling. Norris was summoned to accompany his master to York Place, and during the journey Henry personally accused him of committing adultery with the Queen as far back as October 1533,[40] which Norris vehemently denied. All the same, he was taken under guard to the Tower at dawn the next day.[41]

Anne was not to be kept in suspense for long. After watching a game of tennis on the morning of 2 May,[42] she was arrested and conveyed by barge to the Tower; here she was comfortably lodged in the rooms she had occupied before her coronation, in the custody of the Constable of the Tower, the kindly Sir William Kingston. Her brother Rochford was also committed to the Tower that day. The accusation of incest was the vilest of the charges against Anne, calculated to arouse the deepest public revulsion, especially in view of the fact that, in late 1535, when her affair with her brother was alleged to have taken place, she was pregnant. The implication, of course, was that the child was not the King's.[43] It was on the evidence of Lady Rochford alone that the charge of 'undue familiarity' between her husband and his sister was made,[44] although Rochford received a message through Carew and Bryan that his wife planned to intercede with the King on his behalf. There is no record of her doing so. It was believed at the time that Lady Rochford was motivated by 'envy and jealousy' of the close relationship between Rochford and Anne.[45]

On the evening following Anne's arrest, the King broke down. Once again, his hopes of an heir had been cruelly frustrated, and he was by now ready to believe anything of his wife. When Richmond came to bid him goodnight and ask his blessing, he clasped him to his breast and began weeping, declaring 'that he and his sister [Mary] were greatly bound to God for having escaped the hands of that accursed whore, who had determined to poison them'.[46] Henry's state of mind at this time has been largely ignored by many writers, who forget that his only son was obviously dying, a fact that was no doubt responsible in part for the King's uncertain temper, emotional reactions and phases of almost desperate gaiety. Jane Seymour, calm and sympathetic, must have offered a welcome refuge from the horrors that had invaded Henry's existence.

The atmosphere at court was tense as people wondered who would be arrested next. Anne's Receiver General, George Taylor, and her Sewer, Harry Webb, went in fear of their lives.[47] Even Francis Bryan was questioned by Cromwell,[48] but this may have been a charade to lend credibility to the other arrests, since Bryan was unquestionably Anne's enemy and in fact profited from the fall of her co-accused. In a letter to Gardiner informing him of Bryan's cold-blooded abandonment of his cousin, Cromwell refers to him as 'the Vicar of Hell', a name which stuck.[49]

Sir Francis Weston was the next to be arrested, and around 4/5 May, William Brereton was also committed to the Tower. The charges against him were not made public, but probably included adultery with the Queen. There is good evidence that Cromwell resented his territorial influence in North Wales and Cheshire, where he served as Richmond's deputy, and wanted him out of the way.[50] Cavendish says he was executed 'shamefully, only of old rancour'.[51] Brereton's distraught wife and family pleaded his innocence, but to no avail.

By 8 May, another Gentleman of the Privy Chamber, Sir Richard Page, was in the Tower,[52] along with Sir Thomas Wyatt. Wyatt believed that Suffolk had been the cause of his arrest; it is unlikely that his friend Cromwell would have ordered it. Given Henry's earlier suspicions of Wyatt, and Suffolk's accusations, Wyatt may well have been correct in his assumption. He was deeply affected, not only by his own plight, but also by that of Anne and the men accused with her, and during his imprisonment he wrote poignant verses expressing his misery. Entitled 'Circa Regna tomat' ('Thunder rolls around the Throne'), they began,

These bloody days have broken my heart,
My lust, my youth did then depart,
And blind desire of estate.
Who hastes to climb seeks to revert.
Of truth, circa regna tomat.

It is not known when Henry decided to marry Jane Seymour, but few doubted that she would soon be queen. Sir Nicholas Carew had offered her a temporary refuge at his home at Beddington,[53] but she did not remain there long since it was inaccessible by river and the King naturally did not wish to be seen riding abroad in public at this time. Carew therefore found her lodgings near Hampton Court, where Henry could visit her by barge.

During the Queen's sojourn in the Tower, the King continued to keep a low profile. He did not venture beyond the gardens of York Place, save for short jaunts along the Thames in the evening, banqueting with the ladies in his barge and returning after midnight. 'Most of the time he was accompanied by various musical instruments and by the singers of his chamber.' He was behaving, according to Chapuys, 'like a man who had rid himself of a thin, old and vicious hack in the hope of getting again a fine horse to ride'.[54]

One evening, Henry had supper at the house of John Kite, Bishop of Carlisle, 'and showed an extravagant joy' as he dined in the company of many ladies. The Bishop afterwards told Chapuys that the King told him he believed more than a hundred men 'had had to do' with the Queen, 'and said he had long expected the issues of these affairs, and that thereupon he had before composed a tragedy, which he carried with him. And so saying the King drew from his bosom a little book written in his own hand, but the Bishop could not read the contents. It may have been certain ballads that the King had composed, at which the whore and her brother laughed as foolish things'.[55]

On 12 May, Norris, Weston, Brereton and Smeaton were arraigned at Westminster Hall; all were condemned to death. The trial of the Queen and Rochford, who by virtue of their rank had the privilege of being tried by their peers, was held three days later in the great hall within the Tower. They too were sentenced to die, despite their protestations of innocence. Rochford caused a sensation at his trial when, passed a paper by Cromwell and told to respond without revealing what was written there, he read out what his wife had alleged – that the Queen had revealed to him that the King was impotent. Given that Anne had probably conceived four times in three years, this was unlikely. When asked if he had expressed doubts that Elizabeth was Henry's child, Rochford refused to answer and incriminate himself.[56]

That evening, Sir Francis Bryan brought news of Anne's condemnation to Jane Seymour at Hampton, and soon afterwards the King himself arrived for dinner, having been conveyed along the Thames with an almost festive air of pageantry.

After her trial, Anne was moved to two panelled rooms on the first floor of the newly constructed Lieutenant's Lodging opposite Tower Green, which is now known as the Queen's House.[57] She would remain here until her execution, and from her windows would have been able to see the scaffold being built.

On 17 May, the Queen's alleged lovers were beheaded on Tower Hill. All except Smeaton stressed their innocence, and Rochford warned the onlookers to beware of 'the flatteries of the court'.[58] That same day, Archbishop Cranmer pronounced Anne's marriage to the King null and void and her daughter Elizabeth a bastard. The next day, he issued a dispensation for the King to remarry within the third degree of affinity. No such relationship existed between Henry and Jane Seymour, who were far more distant cousins, and it may be that the King had been involved in an unrecorded sexual relationship with somebody closely related to Jane,[59] or that Jane herself had once been the mistress of one of Henry's cousins.

Anne Boleyn met her death with such dignity and courage that even Cromwell was impressed:[60] she was executed with a sword on Tower Green at 9 a.m. on Friday 19 May, and was buried in the afternoon in the Chapel of St Peter ad Vincula within the Tower. Richmond and his friend Surrey were among the crowd that witnessed the execution. The King's household expenses for that day were lower than for any other day that year, which suggests that he spent it in seclusion. On the following Sunday, Ascension Day, he made the gesture of wearing white mourning.[61]

There had been no precedent for the trial and execution of an English Queen, and Anne Boleyn's fall with its attendant purge of the Privy Chamber had been nothing less then sensational. At a stroke, Cromwell had eliminated a whole faction, and many were touched by the tragedy. Anne's daughter Elizabeth, not yet three, was at Hunsdon when her mother perished, and remained there in the care of Lady Bryan. That redoubtable lady was soon having to beg Cromwell to replace the clothes her charge had outgrown. The child herself, sharp for her age, was soon openly wondering why people had ceased to address her as 'My Lady Princess' and were now calling her 'My Lady Elizabeth'. No one knows when and how she discovered what had happened to her mother.

Anne's father, the Earl of Wiltshire, was immediately deprived of his lucrative office of Lord Privy Seal and all his lands in Ireland,[62] but he retained his place at court, and when his wife died in April 1538, there was talk that he might marry Lady Margaret Douglas. When he passed away in March the next year, the King ordered masses to be said for his soul.[63] He was buried in Hever Church, where a fine brass marks his resting place.

Lady Rochford retired from court after her husband's fall; her husband's possessions had been confiscated by the Crown, and she was reduced to begging Cromwell for financial help, signing herself 'a power [-ful] desolate widow'. Her jointure was not restored to her until after Wiltshire's death.[64]

Shortly after Anne's execution, Cromwell secured the release of Wyatt and Page. The King would have received Page back into favour, but Page had decided it was safer to stay away from court.[65] Wyatt, also bitterly disillusioned with a courtier's existence, returned to his father's castle at Allington, Kent, for a time.

Despite his affinity with the Boleyns, Archbishop Cranmer survived the purge and continued to promote the cause of reform. Norfolk, who had presided at Anne's trial and passed sentence, retained his post of Lord Treasurer, but deemed it politic to retire to Kenninghall for the present. His absence from court enabled the Seymours to establish political ascendancy there, and so initiated the bitter rivalry between them and the Howards that was to endure for the rest of the reign.

Cromwell was careful to ensure that Norris's office of Groom of the Stool was filled by his own man, Thomas Heneage, while Bryan became chief Gentleman of the Privy Chamber.

Anne Boleyn had been one of the most powerful women ever to wear the consort's crown, yet her rapid and cataclysmic fall illustrates just how fragile was the balance of power at the English court.

48

'Bound to Obey and Serve'

On 20 May 1536, the day after Anne Boleyn's execution, Jane Seymour was brought by barge to Hampton Court, where she and the King were formally betrothed. Soon afterwards, Henry took her to York Place, which in 1536 was officially renamed 'the King's Palace of Westminster' and designated by statute as the principal residence of the sovereign and the seat of government, in place of the former Westminster Palace;[1] from the late 1530s it was popularly and commonly known, however, as Whitehall Palace, a name that may have derived from the pale ashlar stone used to build Wolsey's great hall. The remaining buildings of the mediaeval palace were incorporated into the complex, and sometimes used on state occasions. Henry VIII had spent over £8,000 (£2,400,000) on Whitehall, and it was now the largest palace in Europe, and a fitting setting for the New Monarchy.

Henry and Jane were quietly married by Bishop Gardiner in the Queen's closet at Whitehall on 30 May. Later that day, Jane was 'set in the Queen's seat under the canopy of estate royal'.[2]

At forty-five, the average age of male life expectancy in Tudor times, the King still boasted an impressive physique: that year, his armourers found his waist to measure thirty-seven inches and his chest forty-five. He remained active, continuing to enjoy hunting, riding and dancing. But foreign observers no longer praised his good looks. He was growing bald on top, and his face had aged into the familiar mould depicted in his later portraits, with narrow eyes, heavy jowls and a small, tightly pursed mouth. The frustrations and stresses of the last decade had left their mark, not only upon his appearance but also upon his character. Where he had once been open-handed, liberal and idealistic, he was now contrary, secretive, dogmatic and unpredictably changeable. 'Such are the King's fickleness and natural inclination to new or strange things that I could not find words to describe it,' declared Chapuys. 'His natural inclination is to oppose all things debatable, taking great pride in persuading himself that he makes the world believe one thing instead of another.'[3] His egotism was supreme: 'He never forgets his own great- ness, and is silent as to that of others,' observed a French envoy.[4] His temper was feared by all.

It has been suggested that this was all a front put on by an ageing man to mask his disappointment and shame at not having an heir, and perhaps also his increasing impotence. But the evidence for this is slender. In the August following his marriage to Jane Seymour, the King, perhaps disappointed that his bride was not yet pregnant, confided to Chapuys that he felt himself growing old, and doubted whether he would have any children by the Queen.[5] This cannot be taken as conclusive proof of sexual difficulties, since Henry had said as much when addressing Parliament in 1532,[6] and Anne Boleyn conceived probably four times during their subsequent marriage; then, four months after Henry's conversation with Chapuys, Jane herself conceived. Apart from the suspect evidence produced at Rochford's trial, that Anne Boleyn had told him Henry was unable to copulate with her and had neither skill nor staying power in bed,[7] there is nothing else to suggest that the King was actually impotent. Indeed, Cromwell may well have manufactured this evidence in order to portray Anne as a wife who had no respect for her husband and sovereign, and who pretended that he was impotent in order to gratify her own lusts.

In fact, there is evidence that in his later years Henry was still indulging his sexual impulses. Many of his contemporaries referred to his predilection for female company – Norfolk, who knew Henry well, asserted that he was 'continually inclined to amours'[8] – and in Europe his reputation as a libertine was notorious: Charles V told Chapuys that it was well known that Henry was 'of amorous complexion'.[9] In 1533, one observer had predicted that the Princess Elizabeth would be a weakly child because of her father's 'complexion and habits of life':[10] it was widely accepted that a man's promiscuity affected his offspring.

In 1535, John Hale, Vicar of Isleworth, confided to a priest, Robert Feron, that the King indulged in 'foul pleasures' and was mired in vice: 'If thou wilt look deeply upon his life, thou shalt find it more foul and more stinking than a sow, wallowing and defiling herself in any filthy place. For how great soever he is, he is fully given to his foul pleasure of the flesh and other voluptuousness.' Hale claimed that Henry had violated most of the women of his court, and married Anne Boleyn out of sheer 'fornication, to the highest shame and undoing of himself and all this realm'. He had also learned that 'our sovereign lord' kept his own brothel, which Hale described as 'a short of maidens over one of his chambers at Farnham'.[11]

There is plenty of evidence, as we have seen, that the King had a wandering eye. Soon after his marriage to Jane Seymour, he noticed two beautiful young women at court, and 'said and showed himself sorry that he had not seen them before he was married'.[12]

Other evidence, despite being fragmentary, bears out Hale's assertions. In the late 1530s, a man called William Webbe complained that, whilst he was riding in broad daylight with his mistress near Eltham Palace, they encountered the King, who took an immediate fancy to the 'pretty wench', pulled her up on his horse and rode off to the palace, where he ravished her and kept her for some time. Webbe was furious, and swore he would have his revenge, but could do little but recount his grievance to all and sundry.[13]

There is a curious story, which must date from after 1536, that while Holbein was painting a portrait of an unidentified lady that had been privately commissioned by the King, a 'nobleman' – perhaps a rival for her favours – burst into the room. Mindful of the discretion required of him, Holbein, without any compunction, pushed him out and threw him down the stairs. He then locked up his house, hastened to the King, fell on his knees and begged to be pardoned for committing an assault within the Verge of the Court. Hot on the artist's heels came the nobleman to give his version of events. But Henry's jealousy got the better of him and he lost his temper, telling the man, 'You have not to do with Holbein, but with me. I tell you, of seven peasants I can make as many lords, but not one Holbein.'[14]

Such was Henry's reputation for lechery that in 1537 it was being said that all it took to please him was 'an apple and a fair wench to dally withal'.[15] The King's discretion, along with a natural reluctance on the part of observers to commit what they knew to paper, may account for the paucity of evidence, but enough survives to suggest a healthy sexual appetite rather than impotence.

On 2 June 1536, Jane Seymour dined in public with the King for the first time, and her servants all took their oath of allegiance. Later that day the court moved to Greenwich, where, two days later, at Whitsuntide, Jane was proclaimed Queen 'and went in procession, after the King, with a great train of ladies following her, and also offered at mass as Queen, dining in her chamber of presence under the cloth of estate'.[16]

Jane's elevation brought her brother Edward to prominence at court. On the day she was proclaimed Queen, he was created Viscount Beauchamp of Hache, Somerset, and appointed Governor of Jersey and Chancellor of North Wales. Now the most important Gentleman of the Privy Chamber, he enjoyed great influence with his brother-in-law the

King and was therefore able to ensure that his allies and clients were appointed to key posts in the royal household.

Seymour was a haughty, reserved man, somewhat under the thumb of his volatile second wife, Anne Stanhope, whom he had married in c1534/5; his sister Jane had been godmother at the baptism of their eldest son in February 1536. Although cultivated and astute, Seymour was too much of an idealist to make a great politician, but his ambition and status overrode such a minor consideration, and his loyalty to the Crown was never in doubt. A humanist, he was sympathetic to the cause of reform, but 'so moderate that all thought him their own'.[17] His greatest talent was as a military commander: even Norfolk was impressed with him, and his recommendation later led to Seymour's successful command of the royal forces in the North of England.

On 7 June, the King and Queen came by barge from Greenwich to Whitehall, attended by great pageantry. As they passed the Tower, where Anne Boleyn had lain in her grave for less than three weeks, four hundred guns sounded a salute; 'all the Tower walls towards the water-side were set with streamers and banners'.[18] At Radcliffe Wharf the royal barge halted so that Chapuys could pay his respects; surrounded by his velvet-clad gentlemen and wearing purple satin, he stood bowing under a tent embroidered with the imperial arms, then gave the signal for three small boats laden with musicians playing trumpets, shawms and sackbuts to escort the King and Queen to Westminster. After they had dis-embarked, Henry and Jane walked in procession to Westminster Abbey and attended High Mass.[19]

The next morning, Jane stood in the gallery above the Holbein Gate at Whitehall, and waved Henry farewell as he rode off in procession to open Parliament.

As Queen, Jane proved herself to be entirely subservient to the King's will; Chapuys discovered that she was not to be drawn into discussions about religion or politics.[20] She was compassionate and pious, but made a point of distancing herself from her inferiors, and thus appeared 'proud and haughty'.[21] Because she was only a knight's daughter and lacked Anne Boleyn's confidence, she seems to have felt it necessary to emphasise her new status, and was consequently strict with regard to protocol and etiquette.[22] Chapuys had cause to revise his earlier opinion of her, and reported that she bore her royal honours with dignity.[23]

Meanwhile, throughout the royal palaces, an army of masons, carpenters, painters, glaziers and embroiderers had been hastily replacing Anne Boleyn's initials, mottoes and badges with Jane's;[24] at Hampton Court, the entwined initials H and I may still be seen in the great watching chamber. Jane's badge was her family emblem of a phoenix rising from a flaming castle, and her heraldic beast was the panther. The motto she had dutifully chosen was 'Bound to obey and serve'. Jane was given Baynard's Castle and Havering-atte-Bower as part of her jointure. The Queen's lodgings at Hampton Court, begun for Anne Boleyn, were completed for her. Her bed boasted a wooden roundel painted with her arms.[25]

Henry ordered a stained-glass window depicting St Anne, his former wife's patron saint, to be removed from the chapel at Hampton Court.[26] Miles Coverdale, who had been about to dedicate the latest edition of his translation of the Bible to Anne, hastily inserted Queen Jane's name before it went to the printer.[27]

The King was planning a splendid coronation for Jane, which was to take place in October. A great barge, built along the lines of the famous Bucentaur of the Doges of Venice, was to be constructed, which would bring the Queen from Greenwich to London, where she would be received with magnificent pageantry and music and thus proceed to Westminster.

Many of Anne Boleyn's officers and servants transferred to Jane Seymour's household of two hundred persons. Some were replaced by clients of the Seymours. Before 1536 was out, Lady Rochford had returned to court as one of the new Queen's ladies-in-waiting. Mary Zouche, who had also served Anne Boleyn, was a maid of honour, and is perhaps to be identified with the 'Mrs Zouche' who was presented with jewel-encrusted neckline borders by Queen Jane and who later attended the Queen's funeral; in 1542, the King awarded her a pension of £10 (£3,000) in consideration of her good service to Jane and himself. A Holbein sketch of a lady identified as 'M. Souch' survives: it may be of Mary Zouche, or of Anne Boleyn's former maid of honour, Anne Gainsford, who became Mistress Zouche upon her marriage to George Zouche of Codnor.[28]

Other ladies who served Jane Seymour included Anne Parr, the wife of William Herbert, later Earl of Pembroke; her sister Katherine would become Henry VIII's sixth wife. Elizabeth Darrell, Wyatt's mistress, who had served with Jane in the household of Katherine of Aragon and had attended that lady to the end, was saved from destitution by her new appointment. Sketches by Holbein survive of two more of the Queen's ladies: Suffolk's daughter (by Anne Brown), Mary Brandon, Lady Monteagle, to whom Jane gave gifts of jewellery, and Grace, Lady Parker, Lady Rochford's sister-in-law.[29]

Jane was determined to enforce high moral standards in her household. She laid down strict rules governing not only the behaviour but also the dress of her attendants: her ladies were to be sumptuously but modestly attired and had to wear trains three yards long and girdles set with a regulation number of pearls. One girl was told that a girdle embroidered with 120 pearls was not sufficiently grand to wear before the Queen.[30] Although Jane herself dressed magnificently, she left little mark upon fashion except to popularise nightgowns and caps edged with gold and silver embroidery. The King showered her with jewels, including a large IHS pendant studded with black diamonds, which she wears in Holbein's portrait, and there is evidence that some of them were designed for her by Holbein, among them the emerald and ruby pendant surrounded by gold acanthus leaves that appears in the portrait, for which a similar design by him survives.

Holbein also designed an exquisite gold Renaissance-style drinking cup for Jane, perhaps a wedding gift from the King. It was decorated with her motto around the stem and on the cover, with the initials H and I entwined in true lovers' knots, four antique medallion heads, and the Queen's arms supported by dolphins and cherubs and surmounted by a crown.[31] Few items of English goldsmiths' work achieved such a standard of perfection.

By 1536, thanks to Cromwell's influence, Holbein was working as King's Painter from a studio in Whitehall Palace on a salary of £30 (£9,000). Henry was in no doubt that here was an exceptional artist worthy of his patronage, who would create the iconography of the New Monarchy, and amongst his first commissions were portraits of himself and Queen Jane.[32] That of Henry VIII, a small panel of astonishing power and presence highlighted in real gold leaf, is the only original painting of the King by Holbein to have survived. Those on display in the Galleria Corsini in Rome, at Belvoir Castle, the Walker Art Gallery in Liverpool, Warwick Castle, Hever Castle and Castle Howard are all copies of lost originals by the artist.

Henry also commissioned Holbein to design jewellery, clocks, plate, seals, ceremonial garters, hat badges, book clasps, daggers and swords,[33] as well as decorative schemes in the royal palaces. Some of these items were probably made up by Cornelius Heyss, the King's goldsmith, others by Holbein's friend, the celebrated Hans of Antwerp, who also enjoyed Henry's custom. In 1537, Hans was admitted, on Cromwell's recommendation, to the Goldsmiths' Company in London.

Jane Seymour enjoyed simple pleasures. She owned a white poodle, which appears in a seventeenth-century copy of Holbein's Whitehall mural of the Tudor dynasty.[34] The royal accounts testify to her love of gardens; Master Chapman, her head gardener at Hampton Court, was quite famous.[35] She was an expert needlewoman, whose work was on display in the royal palaces more than a century after her death. She also liked field sports, and followed the hunt whenever she could.

The summer of 1536 was given over to celebrations and entertainments, with masques, hunting trips, river pageants and a firework display, and on 3 July a banquet and tournament were held to mark the triple wedding of the Earl of Westmorland's three children, at which the King appeared disguised as the Sultan of Turkey. He did not, however, take part in the joust. On 15 June, Henry and Jane went again in procession to Westminster Abbey, to observe the feast of Corpus Christi; Jane's train was carried by Lady Margaret Douglas. On St Peter's Night, 29 July, the royal couple stood at a window of the Mercers' Hall in Cheapside to watch the annual torchlit procession of the scarlet-clad Marching Watch of the City of London.

During that year the King acquired yet more magnificent properties. Suffolk gave him the sumptuously appointed Suffolk Place in Southwark in exchange for Norwich House on the Strand, which would henceforth be known as Suffolk House.[36] Lord Sandys gave Henry the riverside manor house at Chelsea, which partly occupied the site of the present Cheyne Walk, also as part of an exchange; Henry built a bijou palace there with beautiful gardens, which later became the home of Katherine Parr and, later on, of Anne of Cleves.[37] In July 1536, the King annexed Durham House on the Strand to Whitehall Palace. The former London residence of the Bishops of Durham, dating from the thirteenth century, had at various times accommodated Katherine of Aragon and Anne Boleyn, and had been refurbished for Anne.[38] Henry acquired it by exchange with Cuthbert Tunstall, Bishop of Durham.

Around this time, the King was given the hunting lodge of Copt Hall in Essex by the Abbot of Waltham, in the vain hope that his gift would remove the threat of dissolution that hung over his abbey.[39] Another monastic property acquired by Henry, from the Abbot of Westminster, was the 361-acre manor of Hyde, which Henry emparked as a royal hunting ground and which now survives in part as Hyde Park in London.

49

'The Suppression of the Religious Houses'

In June 1536, the alliance between Cromwell and the conservatives fell apart. The Queen wanted the Lady Mary to return to court and bear her company, but the King would not allow it until Mary had acknowledged that her mother's marriage had been incestuous and unlawful. Between alternately cajoling and bullying Mary to submit to her father's will, Cromwell again found himself in opposition to the conservatives who supported her and were hoping to see her restored to the succession. In the end, after initially defying the King and suffering much agony of mind, Mary capitulated, but she would never forgive herself for betraying her mother's memory and the principles she had stood for.

The Queen now stepped in to bring about a reconciliation between Henry and his daughter. On 6 July, the royal couple visited Mary at Hackney, and the King showed himself affectionate and generous. Soon he was sending her gifts of money, while the Queen sent court gowns and Cromwell a fine horse. Meanwhile, Mary's household was reassembled[1] and her former governess, Lady Salisbury, was welcomed back at court. Through the Queen's good offices, the Lady Elizabeth was also allowed to visit the court that summer, although she did not dine at the same table as her father and stepmother. Nevertheless, Henry was 'very affectionate' towards her and the French ambassador was certain that 'he loves her very much'.[2] The little girl did not remain long at court, however, and spent her childhood mainly in the pleasant nursery palaces of the Thames Valley.

In July 1536, a new scandal enthralled the courtiers, when it was discovered that the King's beautiful and strong-willed niece, twenty-one-year-old Lady Margaret Douglas, had been conducting a secret love affair with Norfolk's much younger brother, Lord Thomas Howard;

several poems relating to this liaison survive in the 'Devonshire Manuscript', some written by Margaret herself. When Henry learned that the young couple had contracted to marry each other without seeking his permission, his wrath was terrible: Margaret was near in blood to the throne, and Howard's presumption amounted in Henry's view to treason. The unhappy lovers were sent straight to the Tower, where Margaret was imprisoned in the rooms Anne Boleyn had occupied in the Lieutenant's Lodging. Lord Thomas solaced himself by writing poignant verses to her:

> My love truly shall not decay
> For threatening nor for punishment;
> For let them think, and let them say . . .[3]

A clause was added to the Act of Succession making it treason 'to espouse, marry or deflower' any woman of the royal family, and Lord Thomas was attainted by Parliament and sentenced to death. Lady Margaret might have faced the same fate, but fortunately, according to Chapuys, 'copulation had not taken place'.[4] Although he did not execute her lover, the King could not forgive her. Five months later, he was still complaining to his sister, Margaret's mother, that 'she hath behaved herself so lightly as was greatly to our dishonour', [5] which led to Margaret Tudor threatening to disinherit her daughter if she did not obey the King.

In the autumn of 1537, both Margaret and Howard contracted fever. The King relented a little and, on 29 October, released Margaret into the care of the Abbess of Syon. Two days later, Thomas Howard died in the Tower; in one of his poems, Surrey refers to his uncle as a 'gentle beast' who ended his life 'in woe' and willingly sought his death 'for loss of his true love'. Soon afterwards, having written several times to assure Cromwell that her 'fancy' for Howard was dead, Margaret, now recovered, was finally allowed to return to court.

In July 1536, Thomas Cromwell had been knighted and created Baron Cromwell of Wimbledon. He also succeeded Wiltshire as Lord Privy Seal and was formally appointed Vicar General and Viceregent of the King in Spirituals, with responsibility for the dissolution of the monasteries. His success was reflected in the marriage of his son Gregory to the Queen's sister, Elizabeth Seymour.[6] Cromwell was now in control of the major administrative departments, which enabled him to effect the sweeping reforms that would facilitate the bureaucrats in the government secretariats functioning independently of the King and his household, thus freeing his grateful master from many of the chores of personal rule and laying the foundations of the future Civil Service. Thanks to his mastery, the office of Principal Secretary now embraced all aspects of the administration, while in the Council, Cromwell's influence was paramount.

Cromwell could not, however, have functioned thus without the support and approval of the King, whose wishes certainly prompted the reforms he carried out and whose authority was increased rather than reduced by them. Henry held the upper hand in the relationship, and he was no easy master. Once when he was in a bad mood, he told Cromwell that his birth made him unfit 'to intermeddle with the affairs of kings', and in 1538, George Paulet, brother of William, Comptroller of the Household, wrote, 'The King beknaveth him [Cromwell] twice a week, and sometimes knocks him well about the pate; and yet when he hath been well-pummelled about the head and shaken up as it were a dog, he will come out of the great chamber shaking off the bush with as merry a countenance as though he might rule all the roost.' On another occasion, the King 'called my Lord Privy Seal villain, knave, bobbed him about the head, and thrust him from the privy chamber'.[7] Cromwell bore this with unfailing humour and patience, knowing it was a small price to pay for his position, and that, for all his irascibility, the King liked him.

Gardiner was another at whom Henry lashed out on occasions.[8] There was no love lost between Gardiner and Cromwell, and Gardiner strongly disapproved of the Secretary's interference in church affairs. Theirs was not just a professional feud, but an acrimonious personal conflict, and each was awaiting the chance to bring down the other. Gardiner, a religious conservative despite his acceptance of the royal supremacy, did not have much time for Cranmer either.

In 1536, under the guidance of the King, Convocation laid down the Ten Articles of doctrine for the Church of England, treading a middle road between the teachings of the Catholic Church and the more radical beliefs of the reformers. The Dissolution of the Monasteries began, and within four years every religious house in England – 563 in all – would be closed and their inmates pensioned off, changing the landscape of England for ever. When the Queen begged the King to reconsider, he sharply told her to desist if she wished to avoid Anne Boleyn's fate. In July 1537, however, when Jane was pregnant and he desired to humour her, he refounded Bisham Priory as an abbey and established a convent at Stixwold, Lincolnshire, for his own soul and the Queen's; neither survived the Dissolution.

Cromwell, who masterminded the Dissolution, was assisted in his task by men such as Richard Southwell, an unprincipled thug who had been Surrey's mentor in youth, had risen at court and become Sheriff of Norfolk and Suffolk in 1534–5. The fact that he had been convicted of murder in 1532, and later been pardoned on payment of a fine, hardly mattered. Southwell had been instrumental with Richard Rich, another of Cromwell's acolytes, in securing Sir Thomas More's condemnation. Rich, who was of merchant stock, was an ambitious lawyer who had married a wealthy wife who bore him fifteen children. In 1533, he had been made Solicitor General. All in all, Southwell and Rich had proved very useful to Master Secretary.

The vast revenues of the abbeys were diverted into the treasury, doubling the royal income and commensurately increasing the King's power and authority. They would finance, amongst other things, his building projects and the acquisition of new property. Henry also appropriated wagonloads of jewels removed from crucifixes, relics, shrines and altar ornaments, and a wealth of plate. Among the gems were the ruby donated by Louis VII of France in 1179 to adorn the tomb of St Thomas Becket at Canterbury – Henry VIII had it set in a thumb ring – and a great sapphire from Glastonbury.

The Crown also took possession of monastic lands worth £120,000 (£36 million) a year, one fifth of the kingdom's landed wealth. The King redistributed a third of this land in order to secure the support and loyalty of influential men, and in late 1536 a new Court of Augmentations, under Cromwell's control, was established to implement this policy. Richard Southwell was its first Receiver, then its Solicitor and lastly its Chancellor. Most large grants of land went to important courtiers: 124 to the lords temporal and spiritual, 183 to knights and gentlemen, and 147 to household officers. The rest went to merchants, lawyers, doctors and yeomen, enabling the rising middle class to become landed gentry and thus binding them to the King in gratitude and loyalty. Most beneficiaries had to pay for the privilege, although there were some free grants, mainly to Gentlemen of the Privy Chamber. Most men of affairs were prepared to compromise their principles for the sake of gain, and readily identified themselves, through their new vested interests, with the royal supremacy; opposition to the King's religious reforms, particularly in the south, was therefore minimal.

There was hardly a peer who did not benefit from the Dissolution. Many converted monastic buildings into fashionable and showy stately homes, of which a number survive today, including Audley End at Saffron Walden, originally built by Lord Chancellor Audley,[9] Battle Abbey, acquired by Sir Anthony Browne,[10] and Woburn Abbey, initially leased by Sir Francis Bryan but later owned by the Russells, who built the present house. Some are in ruins, such as the abbeys of Beaulieu and Titchfield, converted by Thomas Wriothesley, the future Lord Chancellor; Waverley Abbey, the home of Sir William Fitzwilliam; Netley Abbey, the seat of William Paulet; Mottisfont Abbey, which

Lord Sandys acquired from the King in exchange for the manor of Chelsea; and Leez Priory, Essex, owned by Richard Rich. Cromwell himself was granted St Osyth's Priory in Essex, the house of the Greyfriars in Yarmouth and monastic estates in Leicestershire and Sussex.

Henry kept only a small number of monastic properties for himself, and converted several into palaces. The most important were those houses conveniently situated on the route between London and Dover, in which he had in the past maintained lodgings for himself. He now had them radically altered in order to provide both a King's Side and a Queen's Side, with the usual arrangement of outward and inward chambers. Henry acquired St Augustine's Abbey in Canterbury in 1538, and it was ready in time for the arrival of Anne of Cleves in December 1539. The Abbot's lodging was converted into apartments for the King, while a new range of brick and timber, overlooking a garden, was built for the Queen; the whole was to be called 'the King's Palace'.[11]

In 1538, Dartford Priory in Kent – where his aunt, Bridget of York, had been a nun – fell into Henry's hands. He demolished most of it, and built a luxurious palace at a cost of £6,600 (£1,980,000). It too was completed in time for the coming of Anne of Cleves, and had a great court from which a processional stair led to the royal apartments, which were ranged around the old cloisters. The staircase was flanked by pillars supporting the Welsh dragon and the English lion, and paved with nine thousand tiles.[12]

Other monasteries redeveloped by the King were on popular progress routes. In 1538, Henry acquired Dunstable Priory, Reading Abbey and St Albans Abbey. He visited Dunstable occasionally, but only minor works were carried out there.[13] After the defiant Abbot of Reading had been hanged at the gates of his monastery, his lodging was converted into a palace 'wholly reserved to the King's use'.[14] The Abbot's house at St Albans was kept in repair for Henry's occasional visits. In 1539, three more important monasteries reverted to the Crown. A royal lodging with a garden, built at Henry's own expense, already existed at the Dominican friary at Guildford, and the King now extended it, although he rarely visited.[15] Syon Abbey was left virtually untouched until 1542, when it was converted into an ordnance factory. The London Charterhouse was used by the King as a store for his tents and garden equipment.

In March 1540, Henry took possession of Rochester Cathedral Priory, where royal lodgings had been maintained since the fourteenth century for the benefit of regal travellers. The King now converted one of the cloister ranges into a royal residence, which he first visited in March 1541.[16]

★

The young Duke of Richmond died at St James's Palace on 22 July 1536, aged seventeen.[17] The cause of death is thought to have been tuberculosis. His passing was deliberately kept secret: the King commanded Norfolk, Richmond's father-in-law, to have the body wrapped in lead, hidden under straw and conveyed with only two attendants in a farm wagon to Thetford Priory in Norfolk for burial.[18] The secrecy was to avoid fears over the succession; opinion at court had long held that, despite his bastard status, Richmond, a male nearly grown to maturity, had a better chance of succeeding his father than either of Henry's daughters, who had both been disinherited. Cromwell himself later confirmed that the King 'certainly intended to make the Duke his successor, and would have got him declared so by Parliament'.[19] But Richmond's death left the succession open. Nevertheless, the news got out, and Chapuys was soon reporting that 'the party of the Princess Mary is naturally jubilant at his death'.[20]

After the funeral, Henry had one of those alarming changes of heart that characterised his later years, and openly berated Norfolk for not burying his son with the honours due to him.[21] When Norfolk heard later that he might be imprisoned or executed, he wrote angrily to Cromwell that he was 'full, full, full of choler and agony', and scornfully declared, 'When I deserve to be in the Tower, Tottenham shall turn French!'[22] Eventually the King's anger dissipated. After the Dissolution, Richmond's body was moved to Framlingham Church in Suffolk, where many of the Howards were buried. His widow, Mary Howard, whom he left a virgin, now faced a long struggle to obtain financial help from the King, growing increasingly bitter with her father, Norfolk, for his lack of support. Her brother Surrey keenly mourned the death of his friend, and wrote poignant verses in his memory.

After Richmond died, Henry departed with Jane on his long-planned visit to inspect the defences at Dover, visiting Rochester, Sittingbourne and Canterbury on the way. They stayed a week at Dover Castle, where Galyon Hone had just inserted stained-glass windows bearing 'the Queen's badge' at a cost of £200 (£60,000).[23] Chapuys noticed that the King was depressed, not only because of his bereavement but also because Jane was not yet pregnant.

The royal couple spent the rest of the summer hunting, enjoying 'good sport'. On 9 August, they killed twenty stags.[24] Henry's spirits revived as he immersed himself in plans for Jane's coronation,[25] which was to be either at Michaelmas[26] or at the end of October.[27] Chapuys was told that the King intended 'to perform wonders'.[28] Henry had already spent £300 (£90,000) and selected the furnishings he would provide for Jane's sojourn in the Tower before her state entry into London, and his carpenters were hard at work preparing Westminster Hall for the coronation banquet. Then plague broke out in London, and the ceremony was indefinitely postponed. The court moved to Windsor for safety.

In October, the Lady Mary returned to court,[29] where she was accorded precedence as 'the first after the Queen, and sits at table opposite her, a little lower down, after having first given the napkin for washing to the King and Queen'.[30] The latter would take Mary by the hand and walk with her as an equal, refusing to go first through a doorway. Jane persuaded Henry to assign Mary lodgings at Hampton Court (in the Base Court), Greenwich and various lesser houses,[31] but Mary did not live permanently at court, although she was to spend more time there in the next few years than at any time in her youth. Otherwise, she resided at Hunsdon, Tittenhanger or Hertford, and was occasionally visited by her half-sister Elizabeth, of whom she was dotingly fond.

The trauma of her parents' 'divorce' and her forced submission, and her frustrated desire for a husband and children had made Mary increasingly neurotic and prone to vague but debilitating illnesses and menstrual irregularities. Her bastardy stood in the way of a grand foreign marriage, yet there was little likelihood of her father allowing her to marry a commoner, and Mary now faced the fact that, while the King lived, she would be 'only the Lady Mary, the unhappiest lady in Christendom'.[32]

Nevertheless, she could not but rejoice at the reversal in her fortunes. Whereas she had hitherto had to make over old gowns, she was now provided with the sumptuous clothes in which she delighted. She had money to dispense on charitable donations and on rewards and gifts to those who had done her kindnesses. She could indulge her pleasure in hunting, gambling, dancing and music. And Jane, her woman fool with the shaven head, made her laugh.[33]

Mary was still an innocent where men were concerned. When Henry was told she knew 'no foul or unclean speech, he would not believe it', and arranged for Sir Francis Bryan to test her virtue by using a sexual swear-word whilst dancing with her during a masque. Both men were astonished when Mary, who had never heard it, failed to react[34] – which is a measure of how cynical the courtiers had become with regard to the virtue of women.

Henry Howard, Earl of Surrey, now nineteen, was a rising man. With his erudition, his expansive personality, his talent in the lists and his aristocratic bearing, he was held by the King in high affection and esteem. Yet Surrey's character was marred by fatal flaws: overbearing arrogance, instability, a hot temper and an ungovernable wild streak. He had little political sense and no business acumen, being profligate with money. He had an inflated view of the Howards' importance and status, and his actions were dictated by family pride. Through his mother's Stafford blood he had inherited Buckingham's claim to the throne, and behaved, and was often deferred to, as if he were a prince of the blood. He commissioned more portraits of himself from Holbein than any other sitter; in a full-length portrait painted probably by Guillim Scrots in c1546–51 and now at Arundel Castle, Surrey appears with a shield blatantly displaying the royal arms of England.[35] The King was for years unusually tolerant of Surrey's vagaries, for he had been much beloved by Richmond, and it appears that in some ways Henry's thwarted paternal feelings found an outlet in this 'foolish proud boy'.[36]

Surrey had travelled in Italy, seen the glories of the Renaissance at first hand and learned the techniques of Italian and French poetry, which he would later put to good use. He also returned to England 'French in his living',[37] like his cousin Anne Boleyn, whom in many ways he resembled.

Like her, he had a talent for making enemies. He hated the Seymours, whom he regarded as low-born upstarts, but was not above paying passionate addresses to Anne Stanhope, the wife of Edward Seymour, Lord Beauchamp. His audacity caused much resentment, especially since his feelings were not returned, and he had no choice but to withdraw, writing of his renunciation in a poem. By then, the damage had been done, and Seymour's anger and jealousy, together with Surrey's disdain and enmity, would fuel an acrimonious and lasting feud, sowing the seeds of a bitter harvest.

50

'The Most Joyful News'

The great rebellion known as the Pilgrimage of Grace, a well organised, armed reaction to the King's religious policies, broke out in October 1536 in Lincolnshire and the North, where the old ideas remained more entrenched among the gentry, to whom the court was a distant place. This was the most serious threat to his authority that Henry had yet faced, and he prepared to lead an army against the rebels in person. At Greenwich, the tiltyard was converted into a workshop, where his armourers were set to repairing his rusted old armour that had been in storage at the Crowned Key Inn in Southwark. However, as the rebellion spread, the King realised that he did not have sufficient forces to deal with it, and he decided to play for time. He sent north an army under the command of Norfolk and Suffolk, with instructions to use conciliatory measures. The coronation of the Queen was again postponed.

Fortunately, most lords rallied to the support of the Crown, demonstrating that the Reformation and the Dissolution had become largely populist movements. In December, a truce was reached, with Norfolk, in the King's name, agreeing to all the rebels' demands, among them a request that the Queen be crowned at York, and dangling before them a royal pardon which Henry had no intention of putting into effect.

The King had remained at Windsor. Among his attendants was an upcoming young secretary, Thomas Wriothesley, who had entered the royal service in 1530 as a Clerk of the Signet. Wriothesley, now thirty-one, was a member of a distinguished family of heralds; his father, William Wryth, York Herald, had changed his name, with a view to bettering himself, to Wriothesley (pronounced 'Risley', as his family relatives phonetically spelt it). Young Thomas had been taught law by Stephen Gardiner at Cambridge, but had left early to pursue a career at court, where he attracted the attention of Cromwell. His loyalties, however, would always lie with Gardiner. Wriothesley was able, enterprising, tenacious and ruthless, yet insufferably overconfident and egotistic. Henry liked him, however, rewarded his diligence with substantial grants of monastic lands and sent him abroad several times as an ambassador.

It was upon such men that the King relied at times of crisis. Until now, his advisers had urged him to deal gently with the rebels, but he had no intention of keeping his promises, although he lured Robert Aske, one of the leaders of the rebellion, to spend Christmas at court, there to be lulled into a sense of false security.

It was a bitter winter, so cold that the Thames froze. Henry and Jane, swathed in furs, rode on horseback through the gaily decorated streets of London to a service in St Paul's Cathedral, then galloped across the ice-clad river to Greenwich instead of travelling by barge,[1] much to the delight of the crowds who came to see them. Christmas was kept with wonderful solemnity and splendour, marred only by news of the death of the Queen's father, Sir John Seymour, on 21 December at Wulfhall. Both the King's daughters were at court, and at New Year Mary was the recipient of many expensive gifts from her father and stepmother, and from Cromwell.

Aske went back north convinced that his sovereign was on his side, but in January 1537, another rising broke out in Yorkshire. This time, the King was prepared, and bent on vengeance. Martial law was imposed in the North, and Suffolk set about suppressing the rebels with grim ferocity.

The King's anger had been fuelled by news from Rome that his cousin, Reginald Pole, had not only accepted a cardinal's hat from the Pope, but had also published a vicious tract[2] condemning Henry, who had been generous to him in youth, as a heretic and adulterer. Worse still, the Pope had appointed Pole to co-ordinate a European offensive against Henry whilst he was occupied with the rebellion. This was treason of the worst kind, and all those linked by blood to Pole, who was out of reach of Henry's justice, suffered the consequences. Cromwell had warned the King that Lady Salisbury and her sons might unite with the Exeters and other conservatives against him, and that now seemed all too credible, despite Lady Salisbury's condemnation of her son's book. From now on, the Poles and the Courtenays were under suspicion. 'The King, to be avenged of Reginald, will kill us all,' they predicted.[3]

God, it appeared, was on the King's side, for at the end of February Queen Jane revealed that she was at last to bear him a child. There was no more talk for the present of her coronation, for Henry wished to spare her any undue strain that might threaten her precious burden, and was happy to postpone the ceremony until after the birth.[4] In March, the Queen stood sponsor at the christening of her brother Edward's daughter, who was named in her honour; Mary and Cromwell also attended. The following May, the baby's father, Lord Beauchamp, was admitted to the Privy Council.

That spring, the Pilgrimage of Grace was finally – and ruthlessly – suppressed, which the King and many others took as a sign of divine approval. Two hundred rebels, including Aske, were executed, and Henry emerged stronger, more powerful and more respected than ever before. Norfolk and Suffolk were restored to high favour, while other magnates such as the Earls of Rutland and Shrewsbury and Sir John Russell, who had been especially proactive on the Crown's behalf, basked in the King's gratitude. Henry also dubbed forty-eight new knights. Hard on the heels of the rebellion, Cranmer published, on the King's instructions, a book outlining the doctrines of the Church of England. Entitled *The Institution of a Christian Man* but known as *The Bishops' Book*, it marked a return to more orthodox beliefs.[5]

Spring brought warm weather. Henry told Norfolk that he had intended to go north to overawe the subjects who had dared rebel against him, but confessed, 'To be frank with you, which you must keep to yourself, a humour has fallen into our legs, and our physicians advise us not to go far in the heat of the year.'[6] He was suffering from 'a sore leg that no man would be glad of',[7] perhaps a recurrence of the ulcer or abscess that had first troubled him in 1528, which may have been triggered by his fall in January 1536. Now both legs were affected, one worse than the other, and henceforth Henry would be subject to attacks of unbearable pain and suffer intermittent problems with mobility and consequent weight gain, which only exacerbated the problem. His condition would also have an incalculable effect on his increasingly irascible temper, for he found it hard to be incapacitated after leading such an active life, and drove himself when it would have been better to rest. But, as a ruler, he could not afford to be seen to be losing his grasp.

The condition Henry suffered from was probably osteomyelitis – a septic infection of the bone resulting from an injury that had caused splinters of bone to break away. When, from time to time, they worked their way through the skin, there would be sudden swelling accompanied by agonising pain, which was only relieved by a discharge of pus and the removal of the bone shard. It could also have been a varicose ulcer, perhaps made worse by a fall, or thrombosed or infected varicose veins. It has recently been suggested that the King's sore legs were due to scurvy, contracted as a result of following a diet too high in protein,[8] but there is plenty of evidence that Henry like fruit and vegetables.

This attack was severe enough to confine the King to his chambers: 'he seldom goes abroad because his leg is something sore'.[9] His physicians tried many remedies, including herbal baths, and Henry devised some of his own, but to little effect.[10] For such a fastidious man, the condition was distasteful and humiliating. It is said that his fool, Will Somers, was the only person who could keep his spirits up when his leg was paining him, which would account for the close friendship between these two very different men. During the King's period of seclusion, there was much speculation at court as to the severity of his illness. Lord Montague privately observed, 'He will die one day, suddenly. His leg will kill him, and then we shall have jolly stirrings!'[11]

Henry's low spirits were evident one day when a French merchant brought to court the latest velvet bonnets, lace trimmings and other luxuries from Paris. Henry refused to see him, saying he was 'too old to wear such things'. However, he later changed his mind and bought a rich collar, a hat, some fur, some linen and a mirror.[12] In fact, he would continue to adorn himself magnificently, and set fashion trends, until the end of his life.

When Henry recovered, he took Jane on a short pilgrimage – his last – through Kent, visiting Rochester, Sittingbourne and Canterbury, where they made offerings at the shrine of St Thomas Becket, which would be destroyed the following year. After a brief visit to Dover, the royal couple made their leisurely way to Hampton Court. Whilst in Kent, they may have taken the opportunity to visit three former archiepiscopal residences that the King had acquired from Cranmer that year, having decided that the Archbishop, who owned sixteen houses, had too much property in Kent.

Charing Palace had been built around 1300, and a stone gatehouse and hall survived from that time, but Archbishop Morton had converted the other buildings into a brick courtyard house at the end of the fifteenth century.[13] Knole, which the King liked for its 'sound, perfect and wholesome situation',[14] had been built as a private residence by Archbishop Thomas Bourchier in 1456–60, and on his death in 1486 had passed to the See of Canterbury. Henry enlarged the house and park, building the battlemented west front with its gatehouse, King's Tower and octagonal chimney-stacks, and constructing or extending the Green Court[15] to house his retinue. He also installed plasterwork ceilings, marble chimney-pieces and carved panelling, examples of which survive.

Otford, which Henry disliked because it was low-lying and 'rheumatic', was acquired as a satellite house for Knole, of which Henry said, 'If I should make abode here, as I do surely mind to do now and then, I will live at Knole, and most of my house shall live at Otford.'[16] History, however, does not record that Henry spent very much time at Knole at all. Otford, despite its situation, was one of the most splendid palaces in England. Warham had rebuilt much of the original moated manor house – reputedly erected by Thomas Becket in the twelfth century – in c1514–18, retaining only the hall and chapel. His new palace was vast – the brick outer court measured 270 feet by 238 – and ornamented with gilded carvings; it was surrounded by beautiful gardens with topiary, herbs, rare fruits and high hedges. The King had on several occasions been entertained there. He now ordered some rebuilding,[17] but made only one recorded visit thereafter.

In 1537, Henry offered one William Reed the suppressed priory of Tandridge in exchange for the manor of Oatlands at Weybridge, Surrey, which he later incorporated into the Honour of Hampton Court.[18] During the next eight years, the King was to spend £16,500 (nearly £5 million) on constructing a large palace around the core of the old moated house; it was built of brick and stone around three courts, one of them irregularly shaped with an octagonal tower, and the royal lodgings were gabled rather than crenellated. Outside there were terraced gardens with fountains, a pleasance and a deer park, which incorporated the site later occupied by Brooklands Racing Track. The fruit trees for the orchards, like the stone of the fabric, came from nearby Chertsey Abbey.[19] The royal lodgings were hung with fine French tapestries, the floors laid with Turkey carpets, and the furniture upholstered in velvet and cloth of gold. Oatlands, which covered ten acres, was designated a greater house, and Henry regularly used it as a hunting lodge.[20]

That same year, to mark the renewal of his hopes for an heir, the King commissioned Holbein to paint a vast mural of the Tudor dynasty in the privy chamber at Whitehall Palace. This magnificent work – which perhaps measured twelve by nine feet – depicted the full-length, almost life-sized figures of Henry VII and Elizabeth of York standing on marble steps draped with a Turkey carpet behind Henry VIII and Jane Seymour, in a splendid antique setting with a classical roundel, grotesque pillars and friezes, trompe l'œil decoration and shell-shaped niches, which perhaps reflected the architecture and decor of the privy chamber. The painting, which was by then deteriorating, was lost when the palace was destroyed by fire in 1698, but is known through two small copies commissioned by Charles II in 1667 from a mediocre Dutch artist, Remigius van Leemput.[21] Holbein's full-sized cartoon of the two Kings survives, however,[22] although it shows Henry VIII facing sideways rather than forwards, as in the finished mural. The dominating figure of the King was so realistic and majestic that visitors approaching the throne below the mural claimed they felt 'abashed and annihilated'[23] by its power. This was the definitive image of Henry VIII from which many subsequent portraits derive – feet firmly apart, hands on hips, gazing with steely authority at the viewer – and was in fact the first English state portrait, launching a royal tradition that continues to this day. The deliberate dissemination of this image may well have been government policy, but the evidence suggests that after the Reformation there was a popular demand for portraits of the King.

At Hampton Court, work was continuing on the royal apartments. The so-called Wolsey Closet, reconstructed in Victorian times from surviving fragments of Tudor interiors, gives some idea of the decor in the privy lodgings, with its plain stone fireplace, oak linenfold panelling, carved Renaissance frieze bearing mermaids, dolphins, urns and Wolsey's motto, painted panels depicting Christ's Passion, and a chequered, gilded ceiling studded with Tudor roses, sunbursts and Prince of Wales' feathers, which must date from after 1537.

The Queen's pregnancy progressed well. Late in May she appeared at Hampton Court in an open-laced gown, and on Trinity Sunday *Te Deum* was sung in St Paul's and other churches throughout the realm 'for joy of the Queen's quickening of child'.[24] But in June, there occurred another, more virulent outbreak of plague, which drove the court to Windsor and a fearful Jane to an over-rigorous observance of holy days and fast days, much to everyone's concern. Lord Hussey wrote to Lady Lisle, 'Your Ladyship could not believe how much the Queen is afraid of the sickness.'[25] In London, the pestilence was killing off a hundred victims every week, and the King forbade anyone from the City to approach the court. He cancelled his plans for a large-scale hunting progress, concerned that the Queen, 'being but a woman, upon some sudden and displeasant rumours that might by foolish or light persons be blown abroad in our absence, being so far from her, might take to her stomach such impressions as might engender no little danger or displeasure to the infant'.[26] Instead, he confined himself to short hunting trips, staying at houses within a sixty-mile radius of his wife. His companions found him in good spirits, behaving 'more like a good fellow than a king'.[27]

Meanwhile, Surrey was diverting the waiting court with his escapades. According to the late-sixteenth-century poets Thomas Nashe and Michael Drayton, whilst visiting the Lady Mary at Hunsdon in 1536 he had met a young maid of honour, Lady Elizabeth FitzGerald, the penniless ten-year-old daughter of the late Earl of Kildare. Surrey immediately conceived a romantic yet platonic affection for this child,

and immortalised her in a sonnet as 'Fair Geraldine', in imitation of
Petrarch's love poems to Laura. The courtiers were intrigued by this odd
affair, but even more amused when they learned that the hotheaded
young Earl had been imprisoned at Windsor for punching Lord
Beauchamp in the face within the Verge of the Court. Beauchamp had
provoked the attack by suggesting that Surrey was sympathetic to
Robert Aske and his rebels; thanks to the intervention of Cromwell, and
the fact that the Earl was known to be loyal, the King was inclined to be
sympathetic. Surrey remained in confinement for only two weeks, and
spent the time writing verses, among them the poignant poem recalling
his years at Windsor with Richmond.

Lady Lisle, who had been unsuccessful the previous year, was still
desperately trying to get her daughters, Anne and Katherine Basset,
accepted in the Queen's household. To this end, she assiduously
dispatched braces of the quails Jane was craving from Calais.[28] Whilst
eating some at dinner one day, the Queen told the Lisles' agent, John
Husee, that she would take one of Lady Lisle's girls as a maid of honour,
but wished to seen them both before deciding which. They were to
travel from Calais and present themselves, suitably dressed, at court. The
girl chosen must be 'sober, sad, wise and discreet, and lowly above all
things, and be obedient, and governed and ruled by my Lady Rutland
and my Lady Sussex, and serve God and be virtuous, and be sober of
tongue'.[29]

The Queen ceremonially took to her chamber at Hampton Court on
16 September. To minimise the risk of plague, Henry moved with his
riding household to Esher, where he would await news of the birth.[30]
From there, he issued orders for a Garter stall to be prepared at Windsor
for the expected prince.

On the 17th, Lady Lisle's daughters arrived, and Jane chose the
younger, Anne Basset, who had been educated in France and was highly
accomplished. She was 'a pretty young creature', 'fair, well-made, and
behaveth her self so well that everybody praiseth her that seeth her'. The
Queen had her sworn in, and commanded her mother to provide her
with a new wardrobe – no French hoods or low necklines – and a maid.
Anne was to become a popular figure at court, highly regarded by the
King, and never lost her good reputation.

The Queen's labour was long and hard, but at the end of it, at 2 a.m.
on 12 October 1537, she gave birth to the long-awaited Prince. The
King was jubilant, weeping with joy as he held his son for the first
time,[31] and the country erupted in celebration. Hugh Latimer wrote,
'We all hungered for a prince so long there was so much rejoicing as at
the birth of John the Baptist.' *Te Deum* was again sung in St Paul's, a
two-thousand-gun salute resounded from the Tower, church bells

pealed out, bonfires were lit, free wine was distributed in London, and there were processions, street parties and civic banquets. Meanwhile, royal messengers sped off to all parts of the realm with 'the most joyful news that has come to England these many years'.[32] The kingdom had an heir, and the Tudor dynasty was assured. The spectre of civil war, which had threatened for so many decades, retreated into oblivion.

The Prince was to be christened in the new chapel royal at Hampton Court. In 1535–6, the King had converted Wolsey's old chapel into a lavish Perpendicular masterpiece with Renaissance details, and had installed a beautiful oak fan-vaulted ceiling, carved by Richard Ridge and another master craftsman, Henry Corren,[33] and painted blue and gold, with drop pendants, piping putti and the King's motto, 'Dieu et mon Droit', on the arches. There were new stained-glass windows, carved choir stalls and benches, paintings, tapestries, a black and white chequered floor and an organ. Pews for the King and Queen were set in a gallery above the main body of the chapel; this gallery had crystal windows and was approached through two richly appointed 'holyday closets' with battened and gilded ceilings.[34] The arms of the King and Queen were set in stone plaques either side of the chapel door, where they may be seen today.

The Prince was brought here on the evening of Sunday 15 October in a magnificent torchlit procession, led by knights, ushers, squires and household officers, followed by bishops, abbots and the clergy of the Chapel Royal, the entire Privy Council, foreign ambassadors, and many lords, among them the Earl of Wiltshire. Then came the Lady Elizabeth, just four, borne in the arms of Lord Beauchamp and carrying her new brother's richly embroidered white baptismal robe and the chrysom oil. The Prince followed, on a cushion held by the Marchioness of Exeter, with Norfolk supporting his head and Suffolk his feet, all walking under a canopy of cloth of gold carried by four Gentlemen of the Privy Chamber. The Prince's long velvet train was carried by the Earl of Arundel, who was followed by the baby's nurse, Sybil Penn, and the midwife who had delivered him. The Lady Mary, who was to be the Prince's godmother, walked behind, attended by many ladies. Although there were four hundred people present, numbers had been restricted for fear of plague.

In the chapel royal, at midnight, Archbishop Cranmer baptised the Prince with the name Edward, after St Edward the Confessor, in the silver-gilt font which had been set up on a dais draped with cloth of gold; nearby was a cubicle formed of tapestries, in which was set a basin of perfumed water and a charcoal brazier, so that the infant should not catch cold when he was undressed. Suffolk, Norfolk and Cranmer were godfathers. Garter King of Arms then cried, 'God, of His almighty and infinite grace, give and grant good life and long to the right high, right excellent and noble Prince Edward, Duke of Cornwall and Earl of Chester, most dear and entirely beloved son to our most dread and gracious lord, King Henry VIII!'

After the final *Te Deum*, the procession re-formed and, to the sound of trumpets, the Prince was borne back to the Queen's apartments, where his parents were waiting to receive him and their guests. The Queen, wearing a mantle of crimson velvet lined with ermine, was lying on a rich pallet bed, propped up on cushions of crimson damask and cloth of gold, with the King sitting beside her. After Jane had given her son her blessing, the King took him in his arms and, weeping for joy, blessed him in the name of God, the Virgin Mary and St George. The young Duchess of Suffolk then took the baby back to his nursery, and refreshments were served: there were hippocras and wafers for the nobility, and bread and wine for the rest. Henry then gave alms to be distributed amongst the poor who had gathered at the palace gates. It was nearly morning before the guests kissed the hands of the King and Queen and departed.[35]

Three days later, on 18 October, Prince Edward was proclaimed Prince of Wales,[36] although he would never be formally created such. On the same day, several lords were ennobled. The Prince's uncle, Lord Beauchamp, whose future prominence and influence were now assured, was created Earl of Hertford, and Sir William Fitzwilliam was promoted to Earl of Southampton. He had been appointed Lord High Admiral in place of Richmond in 1536; a portrait of him holding his staff of office, painted by Holbein in 1542, hung in his house at Cowdray, near Midhurst, Sussex.[37]

The King also knighted several courtiers, notably Thomas Seymour, Hertford's younger brother, an ambitious but dangerous hothead who had until recently been in the service of Sir Francis Bryan. Henry now promoted him to the Privy Chamber, and used him on several diplomatic missions. Seymour was a lusty man, in great favour with the ladies, but shallow and unscrupulous, and ever jealous of his elder brother, in whose shadow he was doomed to live.

Thomas Wyatt was also knighted, and given the dissolved abbey of Boxley, Kent, which he made his country seat; in 1537, his marriage to Elizabeth Brooke was finally dissolved, and he married Jane Haute, a distant connection of the King's grandmother, Elizabeth Wydeville, queen of Edward IV. Despite his aversion for court life, Wyatt now made a career of diplomacy, and from 1537 to 1539 served as ambassador to Charles V.

Another rising courtier who was dubbed knight was William Parr, son of Sir Thomas Parr, a former Comptroller of the Household, and brother of the future Queen Katherine. Born in 1513, he had been educated at Cambridge, then, thanks to the influence of his uncle, William, Lord Parr of Horton, who made suit to Cromwell, was admitted to the Privy Chamber. Both Cromwell and Norfolk recommended him for a knighthood. In 1526, Parr had married Anne, heiress of the last Bourchier Earl of Essex, whose title and vast estates Parr was to inherit.[38] A close ally of the Seymours, Parr was an amiable man with a 'florid fancy and wit'.[39] He loved music and poetry, and aspired to be a soldier, but never showed much aptitude for a military career.

In the royal household, Sir William Paulet was now made Treasurer, while Sir John Russell was appointed Comptroller in his place.

Before her son was many days old, Queen Jane contracted puerperal fever, probably as a result of unhygienic obstetric methods employed during her confinement. Her attendants swathed her in furs and gave her the rich foods she asked for,[40] but her condition grew worse, and on 24 October she died. The King was at Hampton Court at the time, having postponed a hunting trip to Esher to be at her side. After her death, he immediately left for Whitehall, and shut himself away to mourn in private.[41] Kings did not customarily attend the obsequies of their spouses.

Henry had observed only perfunctory mourning for his two previous wives, and since full-scale court mourning for a queen had not been decreed since the death of Elizabeth of York in 1503, Norfolk, who was in charge of the Queen's obsequies because the King was 'too broken' to order them, was obliged to ask Garter Herald to study precedents. The wearing of mourning garments was governed by sumptuary laws and complex household ordinances, many of them laid down by Lady Margaret Beaufort, who specified the length of trains, the size of hoods (which must not cover the face) and the width of mourning barbs (which could only be worn over the chin by ladies of noble estate).[42] Mourning was issued to everyone in the royal household by the Great Wardrobe, in materials appropriate to the degree of the wearer. Kings wore purple or white mourning; everyone else wore black.

Jane Seymour's solemn obsequies lasted for three weeks. Because long periods usually elapsed between the death and the burial of a royal personage, the corpse was always embalmed. In 1503, the body of Elizabeth of York had been treated with certain chemicals, wrapped in seventy-five yards of waxed and spiced Holland cloth, then sealed in a lead coffin draped with black velvet pall with a white damask cross. Queen Jane's body was dressed in gold tissue and laid out in her presence chamber, with a crown on her head and rings on her fingers. The Lady Mary, who was chief mourner, and the ladies of the Queen's household, took turns to keep perpetual vigil on their knees beside the bier, which was surrounded by twenty-one wax tapers, while dirges were sung and masses offered for the soul of the departed. The body remained in the presence chamber for a week before it was embalmed, coffined and moved to the chapel royal, which had been hung with black cloth and decorated with rich images. Around the hearse were banners depicting the Queen's noble lineage. A herald required all present, 'of their charity', to pray for their late mistress's soul. Priests watched over the corpse by night, Mary Tudor and the ladies by day.

Regal funerals, like every other aspect of royal life, were occasions for magnificent display, designed to impress upon observers, through ceremonial processions, pageantry, heraldry and pomp, the high status of the deceased, which was also reflected in elaborate tombs. It was customary for a wax effigy of the dead king or queen, complete with crown and sceptre, to be placed on the bier; such an effigy was carried at Jane Seymour's funeral.

On 8 November, 'in presence of many pensive hearts', the body of the Queen was taken in a solemn procession to Windsor 'with all the pomp and majesty that could be'; on 12 November, it was buried in a vault in the choir of St George's Chapel. Norfolk ordered twelve thousand masses to be said in London churches for her soul,[43] while the King arranged for twelve to be said privately. Henry planned to raise a splendid tomb to his wife's memory, bearing an effigy of Jane sweetly sleeping, surrounded by marble figures of children with baskets of the flowers she had loved so much,[44] but it was never built.

The Queen's household, which, since her death, had been subject to the rule of the Lady Mary, was disbanded soon afterwards,[45] and her official jewels returned to the Jewel House; her personal jewellery was given to her family or distributed among her ladies. Mary herself returned to Hunsdon later in November, and for the next two years would be an infrequent visitor to court, since there was no queen to act as her chaperone.

Court mourning was decreed for a period of three months, until the day after Candlemas Day, 3 February 1538, when the King and everybody else appeared again in normal clothes.[46] After the funeral, Henry emerged from seclusion and was reported to be 'in good health and merry as a widower may be'.[47] Already, he was considering taking another wife.

51

'The Very Pearl of the Realm'

In November 1537, Cromwell began searching for a foreign bride for the King, having persuaded a grieving Henry to 'frame his mind' to a fourth marriage. Given that the hazards of infancy could carry off the Prince at any time, it was prudent to safeguard the succession by remarrying and providing other sons.

Since his birth, Edward had remained at court in the care of his dry-nurse, Sybil Penn, and a wet-nurse, Mother Jack. In March 1538, the King established a household for his son at Hampton Court, which cost £6,500 (nearly £2 million) to administer in the first year. Suffolk's cousin, Sir William Sidney, brother-in-law of Sybil Penn and a member of the Privy Chamber, was appointed Chamberlain to the Prince. The redoubtable Margaret, Lady Bryan transferred from the Lady Elizabeth's household to act as Lady Mistress; she was replaced by Katherine Champernowne,[1] who took charge of Elizabeth's elementary education. Lady Bryan was now responsible for the 'nurture and education'[2] of the Prince. In this she was assisted by Sybil Penn, who remained on the staff after the wet-nurse's services had been dispensed with in October 1538. Dr Butts was Edward's physician. In 1539, Dr Richard Cox, a renowned Cambridge scholar, was appointed his Almoner.

The apartments created for Prince Edward at Hampton Court were in the north range of Chapel Court and were linked by a gallery to the now deserted Queen's apartments; they had a similar layout to those of the King. In the presence chamber was the magnificent cradle of estate in which the heir to England was shown off to privileged visitors, who approached via a processional stair and a heavily guarded watching chamber. The privy chamber served as a day nursery. In the bed-chamber, or 'rocking chamber', was the cradle in which the Prince actually slept, protected from the sun by a canopy,[3] while next door was a bathroom, and a garderobe which may still be seen. The Prince had his own privy kitchen, where his food was prepared.[4]

Henry's increasing paranoia is evident in the strict ordinances he imposed on the Prince's household, which were designed to eliminate all risks to his son's health and safety. It was not only the myriad illnesses to which Tudor babies were prone to succumb that Henry feared, but also poison or the assassin's dagger. Even dukes had to obtain a written authority from the King before approaching the Prince's cradle. No member of his household was to speak with persons suspected of having been in contact with the plague, nor were they permitted to visit London without permission during the summer months, for fear they might themselves act as carriers. Any servant who did fall ill was to leave the household at once. The Prince's Chamberlain was to supervise the robing of his charge, his daily bath, the preparation of his food and the washing of his clothes. All Edward's food was tasted for poison. The walls and floors of the rooms, galleries, passages and courtyards in and around the Prince's apartments had to be swept and scrubbed with soap thrice daily. Members of his household were to observe stringent standards of personal hygiene, everything that might be handled by the baby had to be washed before he came into contact with it, and no food or dirty utensils were to be left lying around. There were no pages in Edward's household because the King held that boys were careless and clumsy; dogs and beggars were also rigorously excluded.[5]

Henry would have preferred to have his precious son under his eye at court, but the crowded court was often an insanitary place where infection might breed, and it was felt that the purer country air would be a far healthier environment. The Prince's establishment was therefore moved from Hampton Court to Havering-atte-Bower in November 1538, and thence to Hunsdon the following year. Whilst he was there, the Privy Council were invited to inspect his progress; Lord Audley declared he had never seen so goodly a child for his age, 'for he shooteth out in length and waxeth firm and stiff, and can steadfastly stand'.[6] Later, Edward settled for a time at Ashridge, near Berkhamsted. The King also created lodgings for him next to his own at Greenwich, and at Enfield, Tittenhanger and Hatfield.[7] No accommodation was prepared for him at Whitehall, probably because St James's Palace had been designated his London residence; parts of it were still referred to as 'the Prince's lodging' in Elizabethan times.[8]

The King doted on his son, and visited him whenever he could. In May 1538, Edward was brought to him at the hunting lodge at Royston in Hertfordshire. Henry played with him and cuddled him 'in his arms a long space', then held him up at a window so that the crowds outside could see him.[9] A delightful cameo of the King and the infant Prince survives as testimony to Henry's joy in his son.[10] Lady Bryan sent regular reports on Edward's progress to Cromwell. Chapuys thought the Prince 'one of the prettiest children that could be seen anywhere'.[11] He was strong, healthy, adventurous and given to normal temper tantrums. There was nothing to suggest that this precious child would not live beyond his sixteenth year.

Although the court was in mourning over the Christmas of 1537, which was spent quietly at Greenwich,[12] an account survives of the gift-giving ceremony on New Year's Day. When John Husee presented himself in the presence chamber to deliver Lord Lisle's offerings, he found the King leaning against a cupboard as the courtiers came forward in turn to give their presents to him. Beside Henry stood Cromwell and Hertford, and behind were two Gentlemen of the Privy Chamber, Sir William Kingston and Sir John Russell. At the other end of the cupboard stood Bryan Tuke, Henry's Secretary, recording the gifts on a scroll.

When he saw Husee, Cromwell beamed. 'Here cometh my Lord Lisle's man,' he said. Husee did not catch Henry's reply, but the King looked pleased, smiled warmly as the gift was presented, and seemed to take longer than usual to express his thanks, inquiring about the health and activities of Lord and Lady Lisle. All the King's gifts were displayed on trestle tables, and included a clock fashioned like a book (from Suffolk), pictures, velvet purses full of coins, carpets, coffers, dog collars, embroidered shirts, hawks' hoods, a gold trencher, six cheeses from Suffolk and even a marmoset.[13]

Henry had sometimes made use of the stately episcopal palace at Hatfield, Hertfordshire, and in 1538 it finally came into his possession. Built of red brick around a large courtyard by John Morton, Bishop of Ely (and future Archbishop of Canterbury), in the 1480s, it was essentially a mediaeval house with towers, buttresses, gables and twisted chimneys. In 1538 the King visited Hatfield to escape the plague in London, nervously complaining to Sir Nicholas Carew, his Master of Horse, that his head hurt. However, the country air had a beneficial effect, and he was soon in a merry mood.[14] Henry kept Hatfield in good repair, using it chiefly as a nursery palace for his children, and it will be forever associated with his daughter Elizabeth, who in 1558 received the news of her accession in the park there.[15]

The King acquired two other houses at this time: Henham Hall, a newly built courtyard house in Suffolk, which came to him through an exchange with the Duke of Suffolk;[16] and a former Austin friary at Newcastle that came to be known as the King's Manor, which Henry never visited but retained for the use of the Council of the North.[17]

Henry was now about to embark on the most innovative and adventurous building project of his reign: a purpose-built palace incorporating the very latest trends in architectural design, which would rival Francis I's great palace of Chambord on the Loire. Plans were drawn up for such a house to be built at Waltham-in-the-Forest,[18] but were soon abandoned. Instead, the King acquired the village and church of Cuddington, near Ewell, Surrey, and razed them to the ground. In their place arose the most amazing palace ever to be constructed in England. Because no one had yet seen anything like it, it was called Nonsuch.

Nonsuch was essentially a small hunting lodge and private pleasure house, built around two courts; it was designed by James Nedeham, Surveyor of the King's Works. Some of the building materials came from the suppressed Merton Priory. The outer court was constructed in the conventional Tudor style, with turrets and battlements, but the inner court was flanked by two large, octagonal, pinnacled towers; they, and the outer walls of the court, were decorated with gilded plasterwork panels carved with elaborate Renaissance reliefs. Figures of Roman emperors adorned the gateway that led from the outer court to the inner, while a massive statue of the King enthroned dominated the inner court, where the royal apartments were situated. The lower walls of this courtyard were of stone, but the upper sections were of plaster and covered 'with a variety of pictures and other antique forms of excellent workmanship' in mezzo-relievo stucco bordered by guilloche carving in slate, mounted on timber battens.[19] They illustrated heroic tales from history and mythology, and were chosen to reflect the noble virtues of the King. The artists responsible were Nicholas Bellin of Modena, William Cure of Amsterdam and Giles Goring.

We know relatively little about the interior of the palace. Much of it was decorated by Nicholas Bellin, who had worked with Francesco Primaticcio at Fontainebleau before entering Henry's service in 1537, at a salary of £20 (£6,000) plus 20s. (£300) for clothing. There was no great hall, just a dining hall large enough to seat the King's riding household, and the usual ranges of first-floor inward and outward chambers, each with twelve rooms. The royal lodgings were accessed by 'generous winding steps, magnificently built'.[20] French Renaissance influence seems to have predominated; Bellin built huge stucco chimney-pieces, like those that dominated the chambers of Francis I. In the privy chamber, there was a fountain in the form of a silver serpent caught in the paws of a lion.

Other artists known to have worked at Nonsuch were the Florentine Bartholomew Penni, a portrait painter who had also produced narrative paintings for the King, and Antonio Toto, who had executed frescos at

Hampton Court. Toto is believed to have painted the wooden and canvas wall panels now at Loseley House near Guildford, which may have come from Nonsuch. They bear grotesque motifs, *trompe l'œil* designs, mythological figures, classical urns, putti, the King's portcullis badge and motto, the Prince of Wales' feathers, and the cipher and badge – a maiden issuing from a Tudor rose – of Katherine Parr, which dates them to 1543 at the earliest. Also at Loseley is a marble table carved with a Tudor rose and a Scottish thistle, thought to have been made for Henry VIII at the time he was hoping to marry Prince Edward to the young Mary, Queen of Scots, and to have come from Nonsuch. Portraits of Henry, Katherine of Aragon, Anne Boleyn and Mary I, said to have been found in the cellars of the old palace, now hang in Nonsuch Mansion, a Georgian house in Nonsuch Park, which also boasts another relic of the palace, a stone plaque dated 1543, which adorns its porch wall. A fragment of glass bearing the arms of Henry VIII and Jane Seymour, probably from Nonsuch, is now in the Victoria and Albert Museum.

The palace stood in a two-thousand-acre park stocked with a thousand deer. To the south-west was a two-storey timber banqueting house, which had a viewing platform on the roof from which the King could watch hunts in the park. A little way off there was another, smaller banqueting house. The gardens of Nonsuch, laid out by French experts, became famous for their groves, fountains, rockeries, stone carvings, marble pillars, aviaries, trellised walks, orchards and vines, and there was a maze in the privy garden.[21]

Work on Nonsuch began in April 1538, with five hundred and twenty labourers and craftsmen working round the clock and camping in tents, yet their task was complicated and demanding. The inner court was virtually complete by 1541, but the outer court was still unfinished at the time of Henry's death. By then, he had outlaid £24,536 (about £7.5 million) on the project.[22]

Not for nothing was Nonsuch called 'the very pearl of the realm'. One Jacobean observer wrote:

> Here, Henry VIII, in his magnificence, erected a structure so beautiful, so elegant and so splendid that, in whatever direction the admirer of florid architecture turns his eyes, he will say that it easily bears off the prize. So great is the emulation of ancient Roman art, such are its paintings, its gilding and its decoration, that you would say that it is the sky spangled with stars.[23]

52

'A Sort of Knaves'

In April 1538, the ever-simmering tensions at court erupted into violence. One of Lord Hertford's retainers killed a man in a duel within the Verge of the Court, then fled to sanctuary in Westminster Abbey. In another incident, a courtier was found murdered, while soon afterwards a brawl between the servants of the Earl of Southampton ended with one being brutally slain. Then Sir Gavin Carew and one of his men picked a fight with one of the Serjeants of the Household and his Yeoman, which left the Yeoman dead and the Serjeant badly wounded. Cromwell's own henchmen then weighed in against Carew, who was arrested, and the quarrel spread amongst the servants of the various lords of the Council, leading to a riot involving forty gentlemen and their retainers.[1] There is no record of what happened next, and no one is known to have been punished.

This may have been due to a more urgent crisis intervening. In May that year, the King fell desperately ill. The abscess or ulcer on his leg closed up and 'the humours which had no outlet were like to have stifled him'. It appears that a blood clot from his diseased leg broke loose and caused a blockage in a lung, which rendered him black in the face and speechless with pain. For twelve days, he was 'in great danger' and his courtiers, expecting him to die, began to debate whether their allegiance would then lie with the infant Edward or the adult Mary. Then the King suddenly rallied, and by the end of the month was well again.[2] From now on, however, his physicians would endeavour to prevent the suppurating wound in his leg from closing.

It was now more imperative than ever that the King remarry, and soon. Various brides were under consideration: it was thought that some of the highborn ladies of France might prove suitable, but Henry, who was proving particularly choosy, was taking no chances, and demanded that seven or eight of them be brought to Calais for his inspection. On the instructions of an outraged King Francis, the French ambassador, Gaspard de Coligny, Sieur de Castillon, replied, 'It is not the custom of France to send damsels of noble and princely families to be passed in review as if they were hackneys for sale.' Why could not His Majesty send envoys to report on their appearance and demeanour?

'By God!' retorted Henry, 'I trust no one but myself. The thing touches me too near. I wish to see them and know them some time before deciding.'

Castillon impudently responded, 'Then maybe Your Grace would like to mount them one after the other, and keep the one you find to be the best broken in. Is that the way the Knights of the Round Table treated women in your country in times past?' The King had the grace to look ashamed: 'he laughed and blushed at the same time', then quickly changed the subject.[3]

Henry liked Castillon's racy humour. In recommending Louise de Guise, the ambassador said, 'Take her, she is still a maid, and you will be able to shape the passage to your measure.' The King laughed heartily, clapping Castillon on the shoulder.[4]

Another candidate for the consort's throne was Charles V's niece, the beautiful Christina of Denmark, who had married Francesco Sforza, Duke of Milan, but been left a widow at only sixteen. She was said to have resembled Madge Shelton in looks, and Holbein was dispatched to Brussels to paint her portrait.[5] The King was entranced, and began to act the ardent swain, ordering his musicians to play love songs deep into the night and having masques staged constantly at court, but his potential bride was somewhat less enthusiastic, despite being informed by Thomas Wriothesley that his master was 'a most gentle gentleman, his nature so benign and pleasant that I think till this day no man hath heard many angry words pass his mouth'. If she had two heads, Christina declared, one of them would be at His Majesty's disposal.[6]

In July, Henry departed on his usual hunting progress, making a detour to the south coast 'to visit his ports and havens'.[7] Upon his return in the autumn, he staged an unprecedented public debate in the great hall of Whitehall Palace with a radical Lutheran, John Lambert, who had been arrested for heresy. Eager spectators crowded onto the tiers of scaffolding that had been specially erected along the walls so that all might hear their sovereign defend the doctrines of his Church. The King, dressed entirely in white silk, was seated under his canopy of estate, flanked on one side by purple-clad bishops and on the other by lords, judges and the Gentlemen of the Privy Chamber, as Lambert was brought before him, under guard. He spoke genially enough to the prisoner, saying, 'Ho, good fellow, what is thy name?'

Lambert told him it was John Nicholson, but that he was known as Lambert. The King, his 'brows bent unto severity', replied, 'I would not trust you, having two names, although you were my brother.' When Lambert tried to flatter him, he interrupted, 'I did not come hither to hear mine own praises!' and asked Lambert if he believed in the doctrine of transubstantiation. Lambert, after some prevarication, stated, 'I deny it.' Henry warned him he would be condemned to the stake if he persisted in this opinion, but remained arguing with him for five hours in an attempt to save him. In the end, seeing it was futile, he asked, 'Wilt thou live or die? Thou hast yet free choice.' Lambert would not recant, so the King, rising, told him, 'That being the case, you must die, for I will not be a patron unto heretics.' Six days later Lambert was burned over a slow fire at Smithfield.[8]

Ever since Reginald Pole's attack on the King in 1536, the members of his family had been watched. Cromwell, who viewed these reactionary scions of the House of Plantagenet as an ever-present threat to the new order and his own position, had now accumulated a formidable amount of evidence against them, sufficient to convince an already suspicious King that his life and throne were under threat. Some of the most damaging information came from Lord Montague's brother, Geoffrey Pole, who turned King's evidence to save his own skin. There is little doubt that there was a conspiracy of sorts, and that its members were exceptionally incompetent and indiscreet, but it seems unlikely that they were as malicious and as organised as they were made out to be.

In November 1538, Cromwell struck, bringing down the entire White Rose faction, all of whom were closely related to the King. Exeter was sent to the Tower on a charge of compassing Henry's death and plotting to usurp the throne; Lady Exeter was arrested with her husband for carrying on a treasonable correspondence with the imperial ambassador Chapuys; Cardinal Pole's brother, Lord Montague, their mother, Lady Salisbury, and Sir Edward Neville, the King's former jousting companion and an enemy of Cromwell, were also imprisoned for conspiring with Exeter. Most had been in regular contact with Cardinal Pole. Even the innocent young sons of Exeter and Montague were confined in the Tower.[9]

The King was fond of Neville, and had warned him against associating with Montague, but was angered when he learned that Neville had been overheard making disparaging remarks about the Privy Chamber. 'God's blood!' Neville had said, 'I am made a fool amongst them, but I laugh and make merry to drive forth the time. The King keepeth a sort of knaves here, that we dare neither look nor speak, and if I were able, I would rather live any life in the world than tarry in the Privy

Chamber.' This, apparently, was enough to convince Henry of Neville's disloyalty.

On 9 December, Exeter, Montague and Sir Edward Neville were beheaded. Lady Exeter would later be pardoned, but her son, Edward Courtenay, and young Henry Pole remained in the Tower, along with Lady Salisbury, who with the rest of her unfortunate family was attainted for treason by Parliament in 1539.[10]

The Christmas of 1538 was observed quietly at Greenwich. Soon afterwards came the news that Pope Paul III, shocked at the King's treatment of his kinsmen, had ordered the Bull of Excommunication drawn up by his predecessor in 1533 to be put into effect. This effectively isolated Henry from his Roman Catholic neighbours in Europe, who were now called upon by the Pope to dethrone him. Ominously, on 12 January 1539, those former enemies, Charles V and Francis I, signed the Treaty of Toledo, agreeing to make no further alliances with England. Henry immediately took measures to resist an invasion, strengthening defences and ordering musters up and down the land.

Cromwell now moved against other leading conservatives. His attempt to discredit Sir Anthony Browne failed since the King refused to hear any ill of his former minion, but he succeeded in ousting Sir Francis Bryan from his post as chief Gentleman of the Privy Chamber – to Bryan's great distress – and having him replaced by his own candidate, Anthony Denny. The son of a London lawyer who was related to the late William Carey,[11] Denny was a highly educated, serious-minded humanist with a 'sincere affection to God and His holy word'.[12] He lived in Aldgate, where Holbein, to whom he would be a generous patron, was his neighbour; Holbein painted Denny in 1541.[13] Denny was ambitious and self-seeking: although he had begun his court career in Bryan's service, he did not flinch at supplanting him. In time, he would make himself indispensable to his sovereign.

The biggest fish Cromwell netted was Sir Nicholas Carew, who had already fallen out of favour with the King after a game of bowls, when Henry had made insulting remarks, only half in jest, to him, and Carew had rashly responded in anger.[14] When Cromwell produced apparently treasonable letters written by Carew at his home, Beddington Park, the King was easily persuaded that he had been involved in the Exeter conspiracy.

Sir Nicholas was arrested on 14 February and executed on 3 March. Chapuys was of the opinion that it was his devotion to the Lady Mary that had brought about his fall, rather than any treasonable intent,[15] but it appears that the King coveted his estates in Surrey, where he was in the process of creating a vast hunting domain. Beddington Park also came to Henry on Carew's death.[16]

In March, Sir Anthony Browne was appointed Master of the Horse in place of Carew. Sir William Paulet, a Privy Councillor whose influence was rapidly increasing, was created Lord St John of Basing, while Sir John Russell, now an important member of the Privy Council and the Privy Chamber, was created Lord Russell of Chenies.

Regardless of the Pope's censure, Henry VIII pressed on with his Reformation. In the spring of 1539, after a heated debate between Cranmer and Cromwell on one side and Norfolk and Gardiner on the other, Parliament passed the Act of Six Articles, enshrining the doctrines of the Church of England in law. The King had realised that his subjects were 'more inclined to the old religion than the new opinions', and the Act reflected this conservatism, boosting Henry's popularity; but although it was meant to put an end to debate, it found no favour with the radicals, who referred to it as 'the whip with six strings'. Two bishops even resigned.

Although the new Act prescribed the death penalty for anyone denying the sacraments, it did authorise an English Bible to be chained in every parish church. For the first time in history, ordinary people would be able to read and interpret the Scriptures for themselves, without fear of persecution – a new freedom that was to have the most profound effects on every aspect of daily life. The first authorised version was the Great Bible of 1539–40, based on the translations by Coverdale and Tyndale. Its title page, by an unknown artist, shows Henry VIII enthroned, handing down the Word of God to his subjects, amongst whom Cranmer and Cromwell are prominent.[17] This powerful image of the King as the fount of all secular and spiritual virtue and authority was the first example of mass-produced propaganda in England.

Cromwell might have steered the kingdom through the Reformation and the turbulent politics of the 1530s, but by the summer of 1539 his work was almost completed and he was losing his ascendancy. He had made many enemies along the way, and incurred the jealousy and resentment of many at court who coveted his power and sneered at his lowly birth, yet feared what he knew about them. Norfolk and Gardiner had already tried to bring him down in Parliament; the people of England hated him; and the King, dismayed at his support for religious radicals, was losing confidence in him. Cromwell's only true ally, aside from the fawning clients who looked to profit from his patronage, was Cranmer.

It was Cromwell who pressed the King to marry Anne of Cleves. To counterbalance England's political isolation from the great European powers, he believed that an alliance with one of the Lutheran German states would be wise. William, Duke of Cleves, had two unmarried sisters, Anne and Amelia; Anne, Cromwell had heard, excelled Christina of Denmark in beauty 'as the golden sun did the silvery moon'.[18] Envoys were duly dispatched to Düsseldorf, along with Hans Holbein, who had been commissioned to paint the two princesses. His portrait of Amelia is lost, or unidentified, but that of Anne is now in the Louvre. Holbein also painted a miniature of her, the only one of its period to survive in its original ivory box, which was in the shape of a Tudor rose.[19] According to the English envoy Nicholas Wotton, Holbein 'expressed their images very lively'.[20] The King liked what he saw, and instructed Cromwell to proceed with the marriage negotiations.

Henry was in jovial spirits that summer, and on 17 June staged a river pageant at Whitehall with a markedly antipapal theme. There was a mock battle between two barges, 'one for the Bishop of Rome and his cardinals, and the other for the King's Grace', which ended with the former being tipped into the Thames. None were drowned, for the chosen actors could all swim and the King's barge lay nearby to pick them up. Henry and his courtiers watched the 'triumph' from the leads above the privy stairs, seated under a canvas canopy decorated with roses and green bows. The riverbank was crowded with small craft filled with ladies and gentlemen, while two other barges conveyed musicians up and down the river.[21]

In 1539, Henry VIII created the vast Honour of Hampton Court, an enclosed royal hunting domain that stretched across thirty-six square miles of the Surrey countryside, from Weybridge to Thames Ditton, and from Battersea and Balham to Epsom, Coulsdon and Mortlake. The first royal forest for two centuries, it was intended to facilitate easier sport for the King, who was growing 'heavy with sickness, age and corpulency of body, and might not travel so readily abroad, but was constrained to seek his game and pleasure ready at hand'.[22] The new Honour was centred upon Hampton Court Chase. Several royal houses came within its compass, and there was provision for the days on which the King was unable to ride: then, the deer were driven through two lines of nets past a small timber-framed building called a 'standing', which had a high gallery from which he and his companions could shoot them. The ladies would often come to watch, and refreshments would be served. Henry had several of these standings built in his later years. At the royal palaces, mounting blocks were raised so that he could mount and dismount easily, and elsewhere bridges were built over marshland for his safety whilst riding.[23]

By 1541, the King owned eighty-five hunting parks and forests, and was to create two more: Nasing Park, Essex, in 1542, and Marylebone Park (now Regents Park), north of London, in 1544.

Henry's mania for acquiring property did not abate. Seven houses came into his possession in 1539, three of them intended as residences for his children. Ashridge, formerly a thirteenth-century monastery with a collegiate church, was renowned for its healthy air and was used frequently by Edward and Elizabeth.[24] They also stayed often at Elsynge Hall, north of Enfield, Middlesex, which had been built before 1524 by Sir Thomas Lovell and already had a suite of chambers for the use of the King. Henry reconstructed the outer court, which boasted a covered gallery, and updated the royal apartments. There was a well stocked deer park, which bordered Enfield Chase; in the chase was a royal hunting lodge called 'Camelot', but virtually nothing is known about it. The King came to Elsynge occasionally, received ambassadors, and once held a Council meeting there.[25] Nearby was the fourteenth-century fortified manor house at Enfield, which reverted to the Crown on the death of Lady Wingfield. Henry created apartments for all his children here, but they lodged more frequently at Elsynge, which was larger and grander.[26]

The King obtained Halnaker House, Sussex, by exchange with Lord de la Warre; he also purchased a fourteenth-century hunting lodge at Bagshot, which he refurbished but rarely used,[27] and two houses in the North, Hull Manor and the King's Manor at York, which he intended to visit on a future progress.

53

'Nourishing Love'

The Duke of Cleves, eager to form an alliance with Henry VIII, signed the marriage treaty on 4 September 1539. Later that month, his envoys arrived in England to conclude the alliance. During the eight days they spent at Windsor, the King laid on feasts and hunting expeditions in their honour, then took them to Hampton Court, where he ratified the marriage treaty on 8 October. After the envoys had left, Henry began preparing for the arrival of his bride.

Cromwell, whose credit with his master had been somewhat restored as a result of these successful negotiations, now turned his attention to bringing about major reforms to the royal household. The Eltham Ordinances of 1526 had failed to eliminate extravagance and waste, and economy dictated that more stringent measures be imposed. The Greenwich Ordinances that Cromwell drew up, which came into effect on 24 December 1539, provided for the entire household to be placed under the control of a Lord Great Master, to whom the Lord Chamberlain would be subordinate. Since the ageing Lord Sandys was often absent from court, there was no danger of a power struggle, and when Sandys died in 1541, the office of Lord Chamberlain was left vacant for three years. The post of Lord Steward was abolished; the Earl of Shrewsbury, who had occupied it since Henry's accession, had just died, so this was an opportune moment to make the change. The office of Lord Great Master was based on that of the 'grand maître d'hostel du roi' of the French court, and the first to be appointed to it was the Duke of Suffolk.

Cromwell also streamlined household administration and cut down numbers in every department but the Chamber, where the King insisted on an increase in staff; his Gentleman now numbered sixteen. The Household servants were reduced from 500 to 230. Each person's duties were laid down in writing, along with comments about their performance, and records of attendance were strictly kept. Stern measures were taken to keep out unauthorised retainers, beggars, boys and animals, while tight spending controls were imposed, each department being made accountable to the Board of the Greencloth, which was presided over by the Lord Great Master assisted by four Masters of the Household, the Cofferer and the White Sticks (the six chief household officers). The emphasis was on efficiency and good service, which the King prized very highly. So effective was Cromwell's system that it survived, in essence, until the nineteenth century.[1]

Cromwell's reforms also extended to the King's Council, where he designated nineteen of the most active and influential Councillors as the Privy Council, a name that had hitherto been used for those Councillors who were especially close to the King. The new Privy Council would, much later, evolve into the Cabinet. Naturally, Cromwell dominated this privileged group, much to the chagrin of Norfolk and other lords, but both the King and Cromwell held that promotion to it depended on merit, not birth. Their views were enshrined in an Act of Precedence that ranked the eleven great officers of state and household above the nobility, however ancient their title. However, as many of these offices were normally held by peers, there was always an aristocratic majority on the Council, which increased during the 1540s. Members of the Council were from now on to meet at court rather than at Westminster, and would enjoy the privilege of lodging there and dining in their council chamber.

The King's own powers were now extended: his proclamations were to have the same force as an Act of Parliament, and his authority was to encompass doctrinal issues. Thomas Wriothesley and Ralph Sadler were appointed his joint Principal Secretaries of State early in 1540, Wriothesley acting as Secretary to the Council and Sadler as Secretary to the King. The King had rewarded Wriothesley's good service with the dissolved abbey of Titchfield, which Wriothesley was busily converting into his country seat. He easily dominated Sadler, and by 1542 it was being said that he 'almost governed everything'.[2] Ralph Sadler had graduated from Cromwell's household and, having impressed the King by his performance as an envoy in Scotland, was now embarking on a career as a politician and diplomat that would span four reigns and make him one of the wealthiest commoners in England. In 1540, Henry granted him land at Standen, Hertfordshire, where he built a fine courtyard house.

The Gentlemen Pensioners were refounded in 1539, under the Greenwich Ordinances, as an elite guard for the King, keeping watch in the presence chamber. Now numbering fifty well-born young men,[3] under the captaincy of Sir Anthony Browne, they were expected to provide their own weapons – a poleaxe, a dagger and a sword – and wear dark velvet doublets or a livery of red and yellow damask, but were given a gold medallion of office which was worn on a chain round the neck. This may be seen in the portrait of one Gentleman Pensioner, William Palmer, painted by Gerlach Flicke in c1546, and in Holbein's drawing of William Parr, who was appointed their second Captain in November 1541.[4] So many gentlemen wished to join that the King later created a separate band of Gentlemen at Arms, whose numbers had risen to forty-one by the end of the reign; there were then a hundred and fifty Gentlemen Pensioners.[5]

Henry's devoted fool, Will Somers, who enjoyed the status of a Chamber servant, remained untouched by the reforms. Cromwell liked him, and had applauded the way in which he had, on many occasions, jokingly drawn the King's attention to the abuses within his household. Somers was that rare creature at court, a man of integrity and discretion, who refused to become embroiled in factional politics and who never took advantage of his privileged position. He remained one of the King's closest companions during Henry's later years: an illustration in the King's Psalter (c1540–2) shows him listening while Henry plays the harp.[6] Somers may also be the male figure standing on the right of the Whitehall family portrait referred to earlier.[7]

Somers was always on hand to offer comfort whenever the King's leg gave him trouble and forced him into tedious inactivity, as it did in the winter of 1539, when George Constantine confessed to a friend that it grieved him 'to see His Grace halt so much upon his sore leg'.[8] Henry was also suffering from constipation at this time, which did not help matters. [9] But he was in high spirits, for his bride was at last on her way to England.

Everything was ready for the arrival of Anne of Cleves. The Queen's apartments at Hampton Court and elsewhere had been redecorated and put in repair. Two of the King's richest beds had been sent to Rochester and Dartford in Kent, where the Princess would stay on her way to Greenwich. The King planned to marry her there at the start of the Christmas season, and then enjoy twelve days of lavish celebrations. Anne would make her state entry into London on 1 January, and be crowned at Westminster Abbey on Candlemas Day, 2 February. Many courtiers had already ordered rich fabrics and garments for these coming events.

The new Queen's household was ready and waiting, with Rutland and Baynton restored to their offices of Chamberlain and Vice-Chamberlain, and Sir John Dudley as Master of the Horse. There had been the usual stampede for places, more so because the King had limited the numbers to 126. The six ladies-in-waiting, who were now to be called 'the great ladies of the household',[10] were Lady Margaret Douglas, the Duchesses of Richmond and Suffolk, the Countess of Sussex, Lady Howard and Lady Clinton – the King's former mistress, Elizabeth Blount.[11] Norfolk secured posts for his nieces, Katherine Howard and Mary Norris, and his great-niece, Katherine Carey (daughter of Mary Boleyn), as maids of honour. Katherine Howard was the daughter of Norfolk's ineffectual brother, Lord Edmund Howard, who had recently died after spending several unprofitable years as Controller in Calais. She had been raised, in the company of several other well-born girls, in the household of the Dowager Duchess of Norfolk at Horsham in Norfolk and at Lambeth, where discipline had been so lax that she had compromised herself with two young men – one her music master, Henry Manox, when she was just eleven, the other her distant cousin, Francis Dereham, with whom she had been more deeply involved. Now aged about fifteen, she was tiny in stature, very pretty, and old in the ways of love.

Lady Lisle, having made certain of a post as maid of honour for Anne Basset, pleased with the King to find one for her other daughter, Katherine. Henry, who had recently presented Anne with a fine horse and saddle, prompting rumours that she was his mistress, told Lady Lisle he had not yet decided how many maids the Queen would need, but he meant to ensure that they were all 'fair, and meet for the room'.[12] The Mother of the Maids was the strict Lady Browne, wife of Sir Anthony, who would not have allowed any levity, however fair the girls.

The Princess Anne had left Cleves in November, but was delayed in Calais by fierce December gales. Lord Lisle entertained her with banquets and tournaments, while Lady Lisle wrote to her daughter Anne Basset that the new Queen would be 'good and gentle to serve and please'.[13] Soon, the Lord High Admiral, the Earl of Southampton, arrived to escort Anne to England. With him were the Seymour brothers, Sir Nicholas Poyntz, Gregory Cromwell and a young member of the Privy Chamber called Thomas Culpeper, to whom the King had recently shown special favour. Henry had instructed Southampton to 'cheer my lady and her train so they think the time short',[14] so, with the help of an interpreter since Anne had little English, the Admiral taught her to play 'Sent' and other card games that Henry enjoyed, with Gregory Cromwell joining in.

After Christmas, the storms abated and the Princess of Cleves was able to cross the channel to Deal in Kent, arriving on 27 December. The Duke and Duchess of Suffolk were waiting to receive her, and they escorted her to Dover Castle, where she slept that night.

Anne brought with her a retinue of three hundred and fifty Germans, of whom a hundred were her personal servants, notably her ladies, household officers, a cook called Schoulenburg, a physician, Dr Cornelis, a secretary, a footman named Engelbert, thirteen trumpeters, two drummers and the artist Susanna Horenbout. Her escort was formed of noblemen and ambassadors. It had been agreed that most of these people would return to Cleves after the wedding.[15] The appearance of Anne's twelve German maids caused great amusement in Calais and England, for they 'dressed after a fashion so heavy and tasteless that it would make them appear frightful even if they were beauties'.[16] In charge of them was a formidable matriarch called Mother Lowe, who effectively ruled the whole household.

On the 29th, Anne arrived in Canterbury, where she was welcomed by Archbishop Cranmer. After a night in the new Queen's lodgings in the former abbey of St Augustine,[17] she rode to Sittingbourne, and thence, on the 31st, was escorted by Norfolk to the Bishop's Palace at Rochester. Here she was received by Lady Browne, who was dismayed at what she saw. The King, she predicted, could never love Anne, for there was in her 'such fashion and manner of bringing up so gross and far discrepant from the King's Highness' appetite'.[18]

Anne had been educated by her mother at a cultural backwater of a court where it was considered immodest for a woman to sing, play an instrument, dance or be in any way learned.[19] Nor was it thought necessary for her to speak any language other than German. Instead, Anne had been taught reading, writing and needlework; Nicholas Wotton noted that she spent most of her time sewing.[20] She had never been hunting, and her preferred exercise was a sedate walk in the gardens. Now she would be expected to preside over one of the most brilliant and cultivated courts in Europe; it is not surprising that Lady Browne had reservations.

Yet Anne did have excellent personal qualities. 'Her manner was like a princess',[21] but she was kind and good humoured, and amiable without being over-familiar. She was anxious to please the King: at twenty-four she was no giddy girl, and had been trained to do her humble duty as a wife, although she was entirely innocent of sexual matters. The Duchess of Cleves had not thought it necessary to enlighten her.

The King spent Christmas at Whitehall; the court was exceptionally crowded because so many people had come to greet the new Queen, although Mary, Elizabeth and Edward all kept the festival at Hertford Castle. Because of the delays in Anne's journey, the wedding had been deferred and was now due to take place as soon as she arrived.

On New Year's Day, Hans Holbein presented the King with a superb portrait of the two-year-old Prince Edward, wearing a wide-brimmed bonnet and clutching a gold rattle. The Prince appears in a solemn, mannerist pose, gazing steadily at the artist with all the gravity of an adult ruler, which is what the portrait was intended to convey. Below the portrait are verses written by Richard Moryson, Cromwell's propagandist, exhorting the boy to 'equal your renowned father in greatness; no man can wish for more'.[22] A delighted Henry gave Holbein a silver-gilt covered cup made by Cornelius Heyss.

Later that day, having learned that Anne of Cleves was at Rochester, the impatient King left the festivities and galloped off with a few gentlemen and a gift of furs to greet his bride and 'nourish love'.

54
'Displeasant Airs'

When the King and five of his Gentlemen presented themselves at Anne of Cleves' lodgings at Rochester on 1 January 1540, they were all dressed alike in marbled coats and hoods. Henry did not identify himself, but embraced Anne, saying he had come with gifts from the King. After he had carried on this charade for a short time, he revealed who he was, much to her discomfiture: she had not the English to greet him properly, but indicated the window, outside which a bull-baiting was taking place. Henry took an instant aversion to her and left as soon as courtesy permitted, taking the furs with him. On the way back to Whitehall, he complained to Sir Anthony Browne, 'I see nothing in this woman as men report of her, and I marvel that wise men would make such reports as they have done.'[1]

It is clear from Wotton's reports[2] that Holbein had made a good likeness of Anne of Cleves, but he painted her full-faced, making the best of her looks. Another portrait of her, attributed to Barthel Bruyn the Elder and now in the possession of St John's College, Oxford, is a sideways view and shows her long nose to disadvantage; recent X-rays of the portrait reveal an even longer nose. The French ambassador, Charles de Marillac, described Anne as 'tall and thin, of middling beauty, with determined and resolute countenance'; she was 'not so young as was at first thought, nor so handsome as people affirmed', since her skin was pitted by smallpox scars. Nor did her charm of manner compensate for 'her want of beauty'.[3] But it was not just Anne's looks that revolted the King: he later told Cromwell she was 'nothing fair and have very evil smells about her' and that he could 'have none appetite for displeasant airs'.[4]

Back at Whitehall, Cromwell asked him how he liked the Queen. Henry snapped, 'Nothing so well as she is spoken of. If I had known as much before as I know now, she would never have come into this realm.' He was referring not only to Anne, but to the fact that Francis I had recently sent him a gift of boar pâté for Christmas, an indication that he wished to renew his friendship with England, which would obviate the need for an alliance with Cleves.

On 2 January, a glowering Henry moved with the court to Greenwich, where the wedding was to take place. Anne herself travelled to the newly converted Dartford Palace, where she spent the night before riding in procession to Shooters Hill. Here, she was welcomed by her Chamberlain, the Earl of Rutland, and the officers and great ladies of her household, who kissed her hand then escorted her into one of several rich pavilions that had been set up at the foot of the hill. Here, she was robed in a round gown of cloth of gold cut in the Dutch fashion without a train, a pearl-embroidered caul and bonnet, and a partlet of rich stones, ready for her official reception by the King at Blackheath, which was to be the last great state occasion of the reign.

On Blackheath, the Mayor and Corporation of London and the German merchants of the Steelyard stood waiting as hundreds of knights, soldiers, liveried servants and the newly reformed Gentlemen Pensioners arranged themselves into orderly ranks. At noon, to the sound of trumpets, the King, attended by Norfolk, Suffolk and Cranmer, rode through Greenwich Park towards the waiting crowds, preceded by his household officers, the Gentlemen of the Privy Chamber, barons, bishops, earls, foreign ambassadors, Lord Privy Seal Cromwell, Lord Chancellor Audley, the Kings of Arms and a host of lords and bishops. Henry was 'mounted on a goodly courser, trapped in rich cloth of gold, pearled on every side, the buckles and pendants all of fine gold'. He wore 'a cloak of purple velvet made like a frock, all over embroidered with flat gold of damask with gold laces and tied with great buttons of diamonds, rubies and orient pearl. His sword and swordgirdle [were] adorned with stones and emeralds, his nightcap garnished with stone, but his bonnet was so rich of jewels that few men could value them.' He also wore, baldrick-fashion, 'a collar of such ballasts and pearl that few men ever saw the like', while 'about his person ran ten footmen, all richly apparelled in goldsmiths' work'.[5]

Henry was followed by the Lord Chamberlain, the Master of Horse leading the King's horse of estate, the Pages of Honour and the Yeomen of the Guard. He halted some way short of the pavilions, and waited. Presently, Anne emerged on a richly trapped steed and rode towards Henry, who 'put off his bonnet and came forward to her, and with most lovely countenance and princely behaviour saluted, welcomed and embraced her, to the great rejoicing of the beholders'. Anne, in turn, 'with most amiable aspect and womanly behaviour, received His Grace with many sweet words and great thanks and praisings'.[6] The royal couple then rode back to Greenwich, followed by their vast retinues. As they approached the palace they could see the citizens and guilds of London, rowing up and down the river in gaily bedecked barges from which issued music and singing, 'which sight and noise they much praised'.

Henry and Anne alighted in the outer court of Greenwich Palace, where 'the King lovingly embraced and kissed her, bidding her welcome to her own, and led her by the arm through the hall, and so brought her up to her privy chamber, where he left her for that time'. Meanwhile, 'a great peal of guns' issued from Greenwich Castle.[7] That evening, there was a sumptuous banquet in Anne's honour.

Henry had behaved impeccably, although he was still doing his best to wriggle out of the alliance with Cleves. But it was too late to do that without giving great offence and provoking a hostile reaction, so he unwillingly faced the fact that the marriage must go ahead. On the morning of 6 January, before he emerged from his privy lodgings for the ceremony, he told Cromwell, 'If it were not to satisfy the world and my realm, I would not do that I must do this day for none earthly thing.'[8] At 8 a.m., wearing 'a gown of cloth of gold raised with great flowers of silver, furred with black', beneath a cloak of crimson satin embroidered with large diamonds, and with a rich collar about his neck,[9] he summoned his nobles and proceeded to the gallery that led to the royal closets. There he waited, having dispatched some lords to fetch the Princess, whose bridal attire was 'a gown of rich cloth of gold set full of large flowers of great Orient pearl, made after the Dutch fashion', with a jewelled collar and belt. Her long fair hair was loose beneath a gem-studded 'coronal of gold' with trefoils fashioned to represent sprigs of rosemary.[10]

Escorted by two German lords and preceded by the English nobles, she came to the gallery, where she made three low curtseys to the King. Then Henry led her into the Queen's closet, where they were married by Archbishop Cranmer. Around the new Queen's wedding ring was engraved the legend 'God send me well to keep'. Once the nuptials were completed, Henry and Anne proceeded hand in hand into the King's closet, where they heard Mass. Afterwards, spices and hippocras were served, then Henry went off to his privy chamber to change while Anne was escorted by Norfolk and Suffolk to hers. She was still in her wedding gown when, at nine, Henry rejoined her in a robe of rich tissue lined with crimson velvet. Then, 'with her serjeant-of-arms and all her officers before her, like a queen, the King and she went openly in procession' into the King's closet, where they made their offerings. Afterwards, they dined together. In the afternoon, Anne changed into 'a gown like a man's, furred with rich sables' with long fitted sleeves, and a headdress encrusted with stones and pearls. Thus attired, she accompanied the King to Vespers and supped with him. Afterwards there were 'banquets, masques and divers disports till the time came that it pleased the King and her to take their rest'.[11]

There was no public bedding ceremony, but the bed in which the royal couple almost certainly slept, which bears the initials H and A and the date 1539, had an antique headboard adorned with erotic polychrome carvings, one priapic cherub and one pregnant one, intended to inspire lust and promote fertility.[12] But the King, who felt he had been ill advised by Cromwell and cheated by Southampton, who had praised Anne's looks, was in no mood to consummate the marriage. In fact, during the days that followed, he appeared to take an almost perverse pleasure in proclaiming his impotence. He told Cromwell that, although he had done 'as much to move the consent of his heart and mind as ever man did', he had not 'carnally known' the Queen because he did not like her body and could not therefore become aroused. In fact, 'he mistrusted her to be no maid, by reason of the looseness of her breasts and other tokens, which, when he felt them, struck him so to the heart that he had neither will nor courage to prove the rest [and] left her as good a maid as he found her'; nor could he tolerate her rank body odour.[13]

He poured out his woes first to Anthony Denny, then to Dr Chamber, claiming that Anne's body was so 'disordered and indisposed' that he 'could not overcome the loathesomeness' of it, 'nor in her company be provoked or stirred to that Act'. Dr Chamber soothingly advised him 'not to force himself' in case he caused an 'inconvenient debility' of the sexual organs. The King then sought out Dr Butts, confiding to him that, although he had not been able to do 'what a man should do to his wife', he had had two wet dreams in his sleep on his wedding night and thought himself 'able to do the Act with other than with her'. Butts was told to make this known at court, to counteract growing rumours that the King really was impotent. In fact, as Chamber and Butts suspected, there was probably nothing wrong with him:[14] the logical conclusion is that he had purposefully avoided consummating the marriage so that it could be annulled when the time was ripe.

Henry and Anne shared a bed every night for four months, but never achieved 'true carnal copulation'; in fact, after the first four nights, Henry gave up all pretence of trying,[15] and made it known he had never even taken off his nightshirt. Anne herself was so innocent that she did not realise there was anything wrong. Having revealed to her ladies that all the King did was courteously wish her goodnight and good morning, she reacted with alarm when told that there must be more than that if she was to bear a Duke of York, and said she was happy she knew no more.

*

Anne did her best to please Henry. Although her brother was inclined to Lutheranism, she dutifully observed all the rites of the Church of England[16] and gave the King a German Book of Hours dedicated in his honour.[17] She learned English rapidly and well. She began wearing gowns in the English fashion, mostly of black satin or damask so that she could show off her jewels to greater effect. Some of those jewels were designed by Holbein, and featured the entwined initials H and A.[18] The King, however, did not lavish jewels on her as he had done his previous wives; Anne herself purchased one of her richest pieces, a diamond brooch with miniature scenes from the life of Samson.

For her jointure Anne was given Baynard's Castle only, Havering having been reserved for the use of Prince Edward. She used both the ducal coronet and the swan of Cleves as her badge. Her very presence in a court that had not had a queen for over two years enabled her to attract 'a great court of noblemen and gentlemen',[19] all avid for her patronage. Eleanor Paston, Countess of Rutland, Jane, Lady Rochford and Winifred, Lady Edgecombe, were high in her favour, as were the only two of Anne's German maids who had been allowed to stay in England, Katherine and Gertrude. However, when the King's dislike for Anne became known, many people deserted her chambers.

Although she never learned to sing or play, Anne soon came to share the King's love of music, and employed her own musicians to entertain her. Among them were several members of the Jewish Bassano family, whom Cromwell's agents had discovered in Venice, where they were hiding from the Inquisition. Offered asylum in England, they arrived at court in the spring of 1540. The Bassanos were skilled recorder players, and they and their descendants would faithfully serve the Crown until the reign of Charles I.

Anne's other pleasures were chiefly domestic. She took a delight in the palace gardens, and rewarded the gardeners generously for their services. She spent hours at her needlework, working in a form of cross-stitch called 'opus pulvinarium' on cushion covers and mats, and was responsible for introducing some German Renaissance designs into England. She enjoyed gambling with cards or dice with her ladies in her privy chamber, or watching the feats performed by a visiting acrobat. She is known to have owned a parrot, and is said to have introduced the liver-and-white toy spaniel into England.

On 11 January, Henry and Anne presided over a tournament in honour of their nuptials, the Queen appearing for the first time in English dress, with a French hood.

The King had already abandoned plans for her coronation, but he did arrange for her to make a state entry into Westminster on 4 February, sailing with her in the royal barge from Greenwich, attended by the nobility and guildsmen in a flotilla of smaller barges. The new Queen received a thunderous salute from the Tower guns as she passed, and the banks of the Thames were crowded with cheering citizens. At Westminster stairs, the King helped Anne out of the barge, and they walked in procession to Whitehall Palace.[20]

Nearby, the state apartments of St James's Palace were now finished, and the chapel royal nearing completion. Its magnificent ceiling, painted by Holbein, was probably inspired by the decor of the ambulatory vault of St Costanza in Rome and the entrance hall to the Palazzo de Té in Mantua, and commemorates the marriage of Henry VIII and Anne of Cleves, whose initials, badges and mottoes, with the date 1540, were incorporated into the design. Tapestries hung beneath the clerestory windows, and the high altar was lavishly adorned. The new chapel would from now on be the official home of the Chapel Royal.[21]

In February, the ever optimistic Lady Lisle sent a large bribe to Mother Lowe in the hope of getting her daughter Katherine accepted into the Queen's household, only to be told that the King had decreed that no new maids be appointed unless one of the existing ones left to get married. Undeterred, Lady Lisle insisted that an unwilling Anne Basset approach Henry himself, armed with a gift of his favourite quince marmalade. Anne reported to her mother that 'His Grace does like it wondrous well, and gave Your Ladyship hearty thanks for it', but added that she had dared not ask for a place for her sister 'for fear lest how His Grace would have taken it'. Later, when she did find courage to broach the subject, Henry told her that Sir Francis Bryan and others had asked him the same favour for their friends, and that he would 'not grant me nor them yet'.[22] The following month, Lord Lisle was found to have grossly mismanaged the King's affairs in Calais, and was sent to the Tower, where he died two years later. Henry had a soft spot for Anne Basset, and allowed her to remain at court, but there was no hope of her sister joining her.

Any romantic feelings that Henry may have cherished for Anne were extinguished that spring when he began pursuing Katherine Howard. By Easter, his passion for her was notorious, and the Catholic party at court, led by Norfolk and Gardiner, hastened to capitalise on their good fortune. Norfolk, who apparently knew nothing of her past, extolled his niece's 'pure and honest condition', while Gardiner 'very often provided feastings and entertainments' for the King and Katherine at Winchester Palace in Southwark.[23] Henry showered his new love with jewels and other gifts, and was rejuvenated by her youth, her prettiness and her vivacity. He was 'so marvellously set upon [her] as it was never

Thomas Boleyn,
Earl of Wiltshire (by Holbein)

'He would sooner act from interest than
any other motive.'

Mary Boleyn (anon.)

'A great whore, the most
infamous of all.'

Sir Thomas Wyatt (by Holbein)

One of the greatest of English poets,
his association with Anne Boleyn is
surrounded in mystery.

Thomas Howard,
3rd Duke of Norfolk (by Holbein)

Efficient and often ruthless, he had a nose
for danger and a talent for survival.

Thomas Cranmer,
Archbishop of Canterbury (by Flicke)

'The greatest heretic in Kent.'

Edward Seymour, Earl of Hertford (anon.)

He was 'so moderate that all thought him
their own'.

Thomas Cromwell,
Earl of Essex (after Holbein)

'Who shall Your Grace trust hereafter if
you may not trust him?'

Henry Fitzroy, Duke of Richmond,
bastard son of Henry VIII (by Horenbout)

The King called him 'my worldly jewel'.

Standing cup designed by Hans Holbein
for Jane Seymour

Few items of English goldsmiths' work
achieved such a standard of perfection.

Fragments of a leather-mâché frieze of putti from Henry VIII's long gallery at Hampton Court

The interior décor of the period was rich, vivid, even gaudy.

Whitehall Palace (by Wyngaerde)

The largest palace in Europe, it was designated by statute in 1536 as the principal residence of the sovereign.

HENRY VIII SPENT THE EQUIVALENT OF £19 MILLION ON MAKING
HAMPTON COURT A MAGNIFICENT SHOW PALACE.

The vanished Tudor royal lodgings on the south front of Hampton Court Palace (by Danckerts).

The great hall, Hampton Court Palace.

The chapel royal, Hampton Court Palace.

(*Facing page*)
Holbein's lost Whitehall mural of
the Tudor dynasty; copy by Remigius
van Leemput

The figure of the King was so
majestic that observers felt 'abashed and
annihilated' by its power.

Henry VIII dining in the privy chamber (anon.)

The King's meals were always conducted with great ceremony and formality.

Sir William Butts (by Holbein)

As royal physician and a great reformist, Butts was one of the most influential people at court during Henry VIII's later years.

Nonsuch Palace (Flemish School)

'You would say that it is the sky spangled with stars.'

The Whitehall Family Group (anon.)

A masterful piece of dynastic propaganda.

Sir William Paget
(attr. to the master of the
Statthalterin Madonna)

He was an honest and able man
who had 'one foot in every
pageant'.

Henry Howard, Earl of Surrey
(attr. to Scrots)

'The most foolish, proud boy that is in England.'

Henry VIII reading in his
bedchamber (from the
King's Psalter)

Once thought to be the
invention of a fanciful
artist, this room may really
have existed, perhaps at
Nonsuch Palace.

known that he had the like to any woman'.[24]

Charles de Marillac, the new French ambassador, described Katherine's countenance as 'delightful',[25] but there is no certain portrait of her. Two almost identical miniatures by Holbein, thought to be of Katherine, survive today.[26] They show a plump girl with auburn hair and the Howard nose, which bears out Marillac's assertion that she was 'a young lady of moderate beauty but superlative grace, of small stature, of modest countenance and gentle, earnest face'.[27] The miniature was first identified as Katherine in 1736, probably correctly, given the rich clothing of the sitter and the fact that she is wearing the same pendant that appears in Holbein's portrait of Jane Seymour; the wide jewelled border edging the low neckline of her gown may be the 'square containing 23 diamonds and 60 rubies with an edge of pearl' that Henry VIII gave Katherine in 1540.[28] A drawing at Windsor of a sitter with similar features may also represent Katherine Howard, but was not identified as her until 1867. It has recently been suggested that Katherine was the model for the figure of the Queen of Sheba in a stained-glass window in King's College Chapel at Cambridge, which was crafted, probably by Galyon Hone, while she was Queen; King Solomon bears a resemblance to Henry VIII. A Holbein portrait at Toledo, Ohio, now thought to be of Elizabeth Seymour, was erroneously identified as Katherine Howard in 1898.

Katherine was frivolous, flighty, pleasure-loving and sensual. Chapuys thought her 'imperious and wilful',[29] which was perhaps the result of the King overindulging her. Although her religious views were certainly orthodox, she was not noted for her piety.

Henry was now resolved to rid himself of Anne of Cleves, and by April was 'declaring before God he thought she was not his lawful wife'.[30] Apprised of the King's wishes, Parliament petitioned him to look into the circumstances of his marriage since they doubted its validity.

On 17 April, Cromwell was raised to the peerage as Earl of Essex and appointed Lord Great Chamberlain of England, but while he was in London dealing with Parliament, Norfolk and Gardiner had the King's ear at Greenwich, and were busily poisoning Henry's mind against him; Norfolk in particular resented the fact that Cromwell had been given an earldom that had been held until recently by the Bourchiers, who were descended from Edward III.

That month, the King held the annual chapter of the Order of the Garter at Windsor. Several of its members had been executed for treason, mainly in the wake of the Exeter conspiracy, and it was suggested that their dishonoured names be deleted from the register. Henry, however, did not wish to deface the records, and ordered that the names should remain but that next to each were to be written the words, 'Vah, proditor!' ('Oh, traitor!').[31]

On May Day, the King and Queen watched the customary jousts from the new gatehouse at Whitehall. Amongst the challengers was Henry's new favourite, Thomas Culpeper, who had the misfortune to be unhorsed. Lady Lisle, who, like many women, was susceptible to the charms of this 'beautiful youth',[32] had sent him her colours to wear, with a message that 'they are the first that ever I sent to any man'.[33]

Culpeper was ambitious, wealthy and of good birth. He had been brought up in the privy chamber, starting as a page and rising to the position of Gentleman, and now 'ordinarily shared [the King's] bed'.[34] By 1537, his influence with his master was considerable enough for Lady Lisle to send him a fine hawk in return for his patronage.[35] Yet there was a ruthless, violent side to Culpeper. In 1539 he had brutally raped the wife of a park-keeper while 'three or four of his most profligate attendants' held her down at his bidding; he then murdered one of the villagers who tried to arrest him. The King, not wishing to forgo the young hothead's company, pardoned him.[36] Culpeper was also greedy: he and his brother, another Thomas who served in Cromwell's household, were forever seeking to acquire grants of monastic land, court offices and pensions.[37]

The tournament lasted five days, and when it ended, Henry and Anne attended a banquet at Durham House, to which the public were admitted so that they could watch the victors of the jousts receiving cash prizes and grants of houses from the King. This was Anne of Cleves' last public appearance as Queen.

Cromwell, the man who had helped to make her Queen, who believed he was at the pinnacle of his career, was arrested without warning on 10 June. As he entered the council chamber at Westminster, the Captain of the Guard apprehended him, and Norfolk and Southampton triumphantly stripped him of his Garter insignia and seal. Shouting that he was no traitor, Cromwell was then hustled off to the Tower. On 29 June, Parliament passed an Act of Attainder condemning him to death as a traitor and heretic: he was said to have denied the Real Presence in the Mass, a charge that was calculated to alienate the King. He was also accused of presuming too far above his 'very base and low degree'. Sir Richard Rich was one of those who testified against him, and Norfolk was undoubtedly instrumental in his fall.

The King was so appalled by the evidence laid before him that he did not think to question it, and paid no heed to Cranmer, who bravely ventured to ask, 'Who shall Your Grace trust hereafter if you may not trust him?'[38] Yet he did not put Cromwell to death immediately because, even now, he could prove useful by providing information that would help secure an annulment of the Cleves marriage. Cromwell readily complied, but it did not save him. Henry ignored his last letter, which ended with the desperate plea, 'Most gracious Prince, I cry for mercy, mercy, mercy!'

Cromwell was beheaded on 28 July 1540 on Tower Hill, protesting that he died a faithful Catholic. The people of England, who did not understand his worth, rejoiced in his death, and the King's popularity soared. Henry also acquired a convenient scapegoat for the failure of his marriage to Anne of Cleves.

The Catholic faction at court were jubilant. 'Now is the false churl dead, so ambitious of others' blood,' sneered Surrey. 'Now he is stricken with his own staff.' He was referring to the process of attainder, whereby so many of Cromwell's victims had come to grief. Southampton, who had once been Cromwell's friend but had distanced himself from him after the Cleves marriage, now replaced him as Lord Privy Seal, with Lord Russell becoming Lord High Admiral in his place. Cromwell's fall also represented a victory for religious orthodoxy, and drove many radical reformers underground. Even Holbein, whose career had been advanced by Cromwell, fell out of favour and received no royal commissions for two years.

Yet the conservatives' victory was incomplete: many of those who had been Cromwell's men remained in post, and Cranmer, who held similar religious views to the late Lord Privy Seal, retained the King's confidence and could not be unseated. Although the influence of Norfolk and Gardiner increased after Cromwell's fall, neither was ever to achieve the political dominance he had enjoyed. And never again would the King rely on any one minister, as he had on Wolsey and Cromwell. From now on, he would rule alone, maintaining a balance of power between the rival factions at court.

On 24 June, Henry sent Anne of Cleves to Richmond Palace, ostensibly 'for her health, open air and pleasure'.[39] The next day, a deputation of Councillors came to inform her that her marriage had been found to be invalid. She made no protest, and in return was rewarded with a generous financial settlement of £500 (£150,000) a year, Richmond Palace, Hever Castle and Buckingham's former manor of Bletchingley, as well as the right to call herself the King's sister, with precedence over all the ladies in England after the Queen and the King's daughters. She was also allowed to keep all her jewels, plate, clothes and hangings, and allocated a suitable household comprised mainly of her German servants. Her marriage was annulled by convocation on 9 July, on the grounds of the King's lack of consent to it and Anne's alleged precontract with the son of the Duke of Lorraine.

Anne told her brother, 'God willing, I purpose to lead my life in this realm.' Freed from the ties that had bound him to her, Henry discovered that he quite liked her, and invited her to court on several occasions. He also visited her at Richmond. Anne made the most of her independence, looking more 'joyous' than ever and putting on a new gown every day, 'each more wonderful than the last'.[40] In the years to come, she would establish a considerable reputation as a good hostess, and entertained many courtiers at Richmond. Rarely had a royal divorce had such a happy outcome.

55

'I Have Been Young, and Now Am Old'

On the day Cromwell died, 28 July 1540, the King secretly married Katherine Howard at Oatlands Palace, with Edmund Bonner, Bishop of London, officiating. The wedding night was spent in an ornate 'pearl bed', which Henry had specially commissioned from a French craftsman,[1] and there were no more consultations with the royal doctors about impotence. The marriage was made public on 8 August, when Katherine was 'showed openly' and prayed for as Queen in the chapel royal at Hampton Court.[2]

Henry was besotted with his young bride, and 'so amorous of her that he knows not how to make sufficient demonstrations of his affection, and caresses her more than he did the others'.[3] He showered her with gifts, including lands that had once belonged to Cromwell, took delight in showing her off, and indulged her every whim: 'the King had no wife who made him spend so much money in dresses and jewels as she did, and every day [she had] some fresh caprice'.[4] He seemed like a man reborn: his health improved, and so did his temper.

Whether Katherine was as enamoured of Henry is another matter, for at forty-nine, his increasing infirmity, bouts of enforced inactivity and addiction to rich food had made him old before his time and grossly overweight.[5] Suits of field and, optimistically, tilt armour made for him at Greenwich in 1540[6] have a chest measurement of 57 inches and a waist measurement of 54–17 inches greater than it had been in 1536. Despite his obesity and his sore legs, he rode or hunted whenever possible, and still dressed in gorgeous clothes, although his accounts show regular payments to his tailors for letting out doublets and jackets.[7] It now became fashionable for gentlemen of the court to affect bulky styles of dress in emulation of their sovereign, wearing puffed and padded short gowns that were almost as wide as they were long.

The French ambassador, Marillac, accurately summed up the King's

character in middle life, or in what Henry himself was soon to refer to
as 'old age':

> This Prince seems tainted with three vices: the first is that he is so
> covetous that all the riches of the world would not satisfy him.
> Thence proceeds the second, distrust and fear. This King, knowing
> how many changes he has made, and what tragedies and scandals he
> has created, would fain keep in favour with everybody, but does
> not trust a single man, expecting to see them all offended, and he
> will not cease to dip his hand in blood as long as he doubts his
> people. The third vice [is] lightness and inconstancy.[8]

To these three Marillac might have added deviousness and perversity,
for his predecessor Castillon had written of Henry: 'He is a wonderful
man and has wonderful people about him, but he is an old fox.'[9] Secrecy
and surprise were his watchwords; he kept his own counsel, spun his
own webs of intrigue, set traps, then pounced on the unsuspecting. He
ruled on the precept that fear engenders obedience.

Henry's seventeenth-century biographer, Lord Herbert of Cherbury,
who had access to several lost sources, described the King as
'opinionated and wilful' and highly suggestible, 'inasmuch as the
impressions given him by any court whisperer were hardly or never
effaced. This wilfulness had a most dangerous quality annexed to it,
especially towards his later end, being an intense jealousy of all persons
and affairs, which predisposed him to think the worst.' Advancing
paranoia and attacks of excruciating pain permanently soured Henry's
temper, and he was given to such unpredictable and terrifying
explosions of rage that those about him concluded they had to deal with
'the most dangerous and cruel man in the world'.[10] On days when he
was in an irritable mood, his courtiers had to keep their wits about them,
for 'when he came to his chamber he would look [around] angrily, and
after fall to fighting'.[11] Few dared contradict him, since his egotism was
such that he was unable to conceive that he might be in the wrong.

No one at court ever felt truly safe, for the King had amply demonstrated that he 'never made a man but he destroyeth him again, either
with displeasure or with the sword'.[12] Even his outward bonhomie could
be sinister, for he often showed a smiling face to those whom he meant
to destroy. Abroad, he was known as 'the English Nero',[13] and it was said
that 'in England, death has snatched everyone of worth away, or fear has
shrunk them up'.[14] Despite Henry's enduring popularity among his
subjects, a growing number were becoming disaffected: a man arrested in
Kent for slandering him was not exaggerating when he said, 'If the King
knew every man's thought, it would make his heart quake.'[15]

There were still flashes of the golden youth Henry had once been. He could yet exert his famous charm, or show kindness and generosity. If he felt he had been over-harsh with his ministers, he would summon them into his privy closet and reassure them that it was the matter under discussion, and not they themselves, that had aroused his anger.[16] Even if he did not live up to them, his ideals of kingship are evident in the passages he marked in his copy of *The Book of Salamon*: 'Let mercy and faithfulness never go from thee', and 'Cast down the people whose delight is to have battle.' As we have seen, he was not devoid of emotion, and when touched, would weep openly. His sentimentality, mentioned earlier, became more overt with the advancing years.

Although Henry had become more diligent at attending to business than he had been in his earlier years, and was now an exceptionally hard-working monarch, he still hated making decisions, insisting on taking a long time 'to maturely advise and peruse instructions'. 'As ye know,' Ralph Sadler had written to Cromwell, 'His Grace is always loath to sign.'[17] Incompetence irritated the King: Norfolk was reprimanded for sending useless letters full of 'extreme and desperate mischiefs and remiss in honest remedy',[18] and Sir William Petre for failing to go into sufficient detail in his dispatches from France,[19] while Cranmer was praised for his directness and brevity. The King outlaid large sums of money on efficient postal messenger services: dispatches sent from Calais reached court and were dealt with by the end of the following day.[20] An astonished Marillac reported that Henry 'speaks as if he had men all over the world who did nothing but write to him'.[21] Certainly he was better-informed than most European monarchs.

His role as Supreme Head of the Church had made the King more sanctimonious and high-minded than ever, and more certain of his special relationship with God. Marillac observed that he had become 'not only a King to be obeyed on Earth, but a veritable idol to be worshipped'.[22] Demonstrating how self-deluded he could be, Henry constantly compared his own honesty, openness, simplicity and chivalry with the perfidy and deceit of others. For him, as for many middle-aged people, there was no middle ground, only moral absolutes.

The King still remained devout in his religious observances. Once, when his leg was paining him, it was put to him that he need not kneel to 'adore the body of Our Saviour', but could receive the sacrament sitting in a chair. He refused, saying, 'If I lay not only flat on the ground, yea, and put myself under the ground, yet in so doing I should not think that I have reverence sufficient unto His blessed sacrament.'[23] He insisted on creeping painfully on his knees to the Cross every Good Friday until 1546.

Yet he was reluctant to abandon the title Fidei Defensor, even though it had been conferred upon him by the Pope, and in 1543 Parliament passed the Act of the King's Style, making the title an hereditary one, 'annexed for ever to the imperial crown of this His Highness's realm of England'.[24]

The books purchased by Henry VIII in the 1540s were chiefly bibles, devotional works and scholastic texts.[25] A beautiful psalter was commissioned by him in c1540–2 from the French illuminator Jean Mallard, who had once worked for Francis I. It contains seven exquisite miniature scenes, two of which portray the King in his favourite role as King David: in one he is slaying Goliath, and in the other he appears as a penitent. Other miniatures show him playing the harp with Will Somers in attendance, and reading in his bedroom. More of Henry's annotations appear in the margins: against verse 25 of Psalm 37 – 'I have been young and now am old, yet have I not seen the righteous forsaken' – he wrote in Latin, 'Dolus dictum' ('A painful saying').[26]

If the young Queen felt any distaste for her ageing husband, she hid it well, and played the role of dutiful, loving wife to perfection. Each evening at 6 p.m., Sir Thomas Heneage, Groom of the Stool, brought her news of the King,[27] to her evident satisfaction. Her days were one long round of pleasure: she did 'nothing but dance and rejoice'.[28] She was too young and inexperienced to concern herself with state or administrative matters. The only book dedicated to her as Queen was Richard Jonas's tract on midwifery. *The Birth of Mankind*.[29] Although her education had been neglected, she could read and write, and the dubious Manox had taught her to play the virginals.

The King made no plans for Katherine's coronation. She made a state entry into London by river, arriving in her new barge, which was manned by twenty-six bargemen and strewn with rushes scented with rosemary. The Lord Mayor and Corporation rode out in their own craft to welcome her, and a salute of guns echoed from the Tower.

Henry settled Baynard's Castle on Katherine as her jointure. Many of those who had served Jane Seymour and Anne of Cleves were appointed to her household, along with a horde of her Howard relatives. Lady Margaret Douglas was senior Lady of the Privy Chamber, and under her were the Dowager Duchesses of Richmond and Norfolk; Katherine's aunt and namesake, the Countess of Bridgewater; her widowed step-mother, Lady Margaret Howard; her sisters, Margaret, Lady Arundel, and Isabella, who was married to the Queen's Vice Chamberlain, Sir Edward Baynton; Lady Rochford; Jane Seymour's sister, Elizabeth; Lady Cromwell; Lady Rutland, wife of the Queen's Chamberlain; Lady Edgecombe and William Parr's sister, Katherine, wife of John Neville, Lord Latimer. Among the maids of honour were his other sister, Anne

Parr, Anne Basset and Surrey's favourite, Lady Elizabeth FitzGerald. Joan Bulmer, Margaret Morton, Katherine Tilney and Agnes Restwold, who had been with Katherine in her grandmother's household and were all privy to the secrets of her past, were found posts as chamberers. There is some evidence that Bulmer, at least, used blackmail to obtain her post. Katherine's household cost Henry £4,600 (£1,380,000) a year to maintain.

Katherine dressed 'after the French fashion', and insisted that all the other ladies at court did so too.[30] Every day she appeared in a new gown. The jewels Henry lavished on her were magnificent, and included a gold brooch with scenes from the life of Noah picked out in diamonds and rubies, a rich collar with her initial set in diamonds, heavy gold chains, ropes of pearls, gem-studded crosses, a necklace of table diamonds, black-enamelled gold beads, emeralds set in gold lozenges, pomanders, clocks and a jewellery casket. The King also gave her a black velvet muff lined with sables and ornamented with rubies, hundreds of pearls and tiny gold chains; it hung round her neck from a gold and pearl chain.[31]

Katherine's personal badge was a crowned rose. She adopted as her device the motto 'Non autre volonté que la sienne' ('No other will than his'), and had it embroidered in gold around her sleeves.[32] The King ordered that her badge and other emblems be set up in place of those of Jane Seymour and Anne of Cleves in the royal palaces.

The Howards, led by Norfolk, now dominated the court. Katherine's brother Charles was appointed to the Privy Chamber, where her uncle, Lord William Howard, was already influential as one of the King's Gentlemen. Norfolk's brother-in-law, Robert Ratcliffe, Earl of Sussex, was given Cromwell's former office of Lord Great Chamberlain and thus gained control of the Chamber. Surrey, despite his youth, became a Knight of the Garter.

The ascendancy of the conservatives provoked great resentment and jealousy on the part of their enemies, who were mostly of the reformist persuasion, and gave rise to the most vicious factional divisions of the reign. Two distinct parties emerged at this time: the conservatives, led by the reactionary Gardiner and Norfolk, who were supported when in the ascendant by the self-seeking Wriothesley, and wished to see a return to more traditional forms of religion; and the reformists, headed by the autocratic Hertford and backed by Cranmer, William Parr and Hertford's staunch friend and political ally, the honest and able Sir William Paget (who became the first ever Clerk to the Privy Council in 1540). This party was keen to see even more change. Surrey sided with his father and, like him, hoped to bring about the overthrow of upstarts like the Seymours, but he was a liability, not only because of his wild, unpredictable streak, but also because his religious views were probably more radical than Hertford's. In the reformist party, there were frequent squabbles on account of the unpopular Hertford's high-handedness and criticism of his colleagues.[33] Suffolk, meanwhile, managed to remain on good terms with both Norfolk and Hertford.

The dominance of first Wolsey and then Cromwell had prevented the emergence of such factions in the past, but now that there was no chief minister there was nothing to stop them from attempting to gain ascendancy in Council, achieve control of the Privy Chamber, and manipulate an over-suggestible King. The power struggle between these factions, which was to dominate the 1540s, was essentially political, but was fought over religious differences.

Later writers, such as John Foxe and Nicholas Sander, would claim that Henry was easily led by these parties; Sander even went so far as to claim that they waited to approach him 'in the evening, when he was comfortably filled with wine, or when he had gone to the stool, for then he used to be very pleasant'. Even though some historians still accept this view today, the evidence is largely against it. It is true that, while Henry played off rival factions against each other and manipulated individuals for his own ends, following a policy of divide and rule, his apparent mastery hid a degree of 'irresolution and despondency',[34] but this was because he was unsure whom he could trust. He also suspected that Lutheran ideas were taking hold in the minds of some of those around him, under the cloak of an interest in reform. Furthermore, there was the problem of an age difference: many men now in power at court were of a younger generation, ambitious and aggressive,[35] and although Henry like to surround himself with youth and bask in its reflected glamour, the age gap was too wide to be easily breached.

On the other hand, neither faction could ever be sure of the King, who in 1540 was burning both Catholics, for supporting the Pope, and Protestants, for heresy. Although there was a clear logic in this, many took it to mean that Henry was unsure of his religious position, and sought to influence him, with only varying degrees of success, since he was ever watchful for courtiers who tried to blind his 'eyes with mists' or manipulate him 'for their own profits'.[36] Nor, according to Chapuys, was it usual for Councillors to enter into 'secret communication' with each other, for it was something they 'were not accustomed to do, even in matters of no importance or suspicions'.[37] In the main, Henry remained firmly in control of affairs until his death, and his authority was absolute and final. Jealous of his prerogative, he kept his own counsel and would allow no man or faction to rule him. Rival parties did manage to sway him on occasion by exploiting his suspicious nature and poisoning his mind against their enemies, which was what had brought about the falls of Anne Boleyn and Cromwell, but in each case they had presented convincing evidence. They even encouraged him to marry their own candidates, although he allowed none of his last four wives to wield any political influence. As will be seen, more often than not, Henry knew what his courtiers were up to, and sometimes turned the tables on them.

During these latter years, the King was more politically active, powerful and despotic than at any previous time, and kept a firm grip on administrative matters, scrutinising state documents, dispatches, letters, accounts, service records and check rolls, and making numerous notes in the margins and changes where necessary: his secretaries were instructed to leave two-and-a-half-inch margins and one inch between lines to enable him to do so.[38] Each Sunday evening, Henry was given a list of the matters to be discussed by the Council in the coming week, and always drew up the agenda himself. Every Friday, his Principal Secretary would write a summary of the meetings, which was presented on Saturday for Henry's decisions or approval. If a decision was needed more urgently, the Lord Chancellor would seek audience of the King in the privy lodgings.[39]

Very little escaped Henry's notice – 'there is not a single bruit anywhere which he does not hear among the first, even to little private matters, which princes care but little to hear'.[40] Sir William Paget later revealed that, in diplomatic reports, he was always careful to include 'matters of no great importance', since he felt it 'meet that His Majesty should know all'.[41] Henry's encyclopaedic memory, which could retain details of every grant made to numerous petitioners,[42] stored up every snippet of information that might prove useful in the future. Thanks to his experience, his eye for detail, his erudition and his sharp mind, he was able to dominate those who sought to influence him.

The summer of 1540 was very hot; no rain fell between June and October, and there was plague in London. In August, the King took his young bride on a honeymoon progress, an extended hunting trip through Surrey into Berkshire, where they stayed at Reading before moving north to Ewelme, Rycote, Notley, Buckingham – where the King held a Council meeting at the Old Castle House, which dated from Saxon times – and Grafton, arriving on the 29th. A week later, the King began riding south towards Ampthill, where he stayed for a fortnight until 1 October. Here, Katherine's Vice-Chamberlain, Sir Edward Baynton, disgraced himself by appearing drunk in the King's presence, which prompted Henry to issue a stern injunction to all household servants 'concerning the sober and temperate order that His

Highness would have them use in his chamber of presence and the Queen's'.[43]

Whilst at Ampthill, Henry fell sick with a tertian fever – probably malaria – and his legs became infected. His doctors expressed great concern, but he suddenly rallied. Then it was on to Dunstable, for another Council meeting, and The More, and so back to Windsor on 22 October. Prior to the King's arrival, persons who had been in contact with the plague were made to leave the town, and although they were promised compensation by the Privy Council, payment was long deferred.

During this progress, the King had some traders who had followed the court put in the pillory for overcharging for food. Henry was equally wrathful, on his return, to hear gossip that his niece, Lady Margaret Douglas, had become involved in yet another clandestine affair, this time with the Queen's brother, Charles Howard. Upon finding out that it was true, he packed Margaret off to the recently dissolved Syon Abbey at Isleworth in Middlesex for 'over much lightness', and warned her that she would stay there until she had learned to 'wholly apply herself to please the King's Highness'.[44] Margaret remained at Syon for a year, and would only be released to make way for a far more important prisoner.

56

'Is Not the Queen Abed Yet?'

After the progress, the King seemed a new man. At Woking in December, he rose between 5 and 6 a.m., attended Mass at seven, and rode out early to hunt, returning at ten for dinner. In the afternoon, he attended to business. He told Marillac that he felt better in the country than when he stayed all winter in London, and that his leg was much better. The ambassador was of the opinion that he had adopted his 'new rule of living' in order to lose weight.[1]

Henry's desire for increasing privacy, which was exacerbated by increasing ill health, was becoming an obsession and leading to significant changes within the inward lodgings. Recently, it had resulted in many of the functions of the presence chamber and council chamber being shifted to the privy chamber, which meant that the presence chamber was used only on rare state occasions, and that the privy chamber was now frequently crowded and no longer a place to which the King could withdraw into seclusion with his favoured intimates. By 1540, access to the privy chamber was no longer the prize it had once been, because the King was extending his inward lodgings to accommodate his need for privacy and spending more time in them, allowing only Gentlemen and Grooms of the Chamber to serve him there.[2] Those who were permitted beyond the privy chamber door were privileged indeed. By the end of his reign, a new sub-department was emerging, the Bedchamber, upon which the King's private life now increasingly centred.

Henry's so-called secret lodgings were aptly named, for access was so restricted that very little information about them survives. The plans that survive for the works carried out at Hampton Court, Whitehall and Greenwich show a network of small rooms beyond the King's bedchamber, with some leading off his privy gallery. It is clear that at some lesser houses there was only one such room. The evidence for secret lodgings for the Queen and Prince Edward is sparse, but suggests that their apartments were extended in line with the King's.

At Hampton Court, the new secret lodgings led off a ground-floor gallery on the east side of Cloister Green Court; the King's presence and privy chambers remained on the first floor of the south side, while the Queen's apartments were extended on the north side. Eventually the first floor of the connecting east range was converted into a private suite with bedchambers and reception rooms for the royal couple to share. At Whitehall, the new secret lodgings were off the privy gallery, which was henceforth out of bounds to courtiers.[3]

The King might remain in his secret lodgings for days on end; when he was ill, no one would be any the wiser or doubt he was retaining his grip on affairs. He had also ceased to be as accessible to petitioners, insisting that 'they should no longer molest his person with any suit' and send all claims in future in writing to the Privy Council.[4]

By 1540, Whitehall was badly in need of refurbishment. The tiltyard and gardens were overgrown, the Queen's apartments needed redecoration, and the tapestries and hangings were either moth-eaten or 'foul and greasy'.[5] After his marriage to Katherine Howard, Henry embarked upon a programme of improvements, building a new east front along the river side, a privy lodging above for the Lady Mary, a banqueting house, the 'preaching place' and the King Street Gate at the palace's southern approach. He also laid out an orchard and a great garden, and refurnished the palace from the spoils of Acts of Attainder, among them purple velvet counterpanes and bed-hangings from Beddington Park, the former house of Sir Nicholas Carew, and embroidered cushions from the house of Lord Montague. Many of Wolsey's furnishings were still in use. An elaborate design, attributed to Holbein, for a massive, richly carved classical chimney-piece with antique and heraldic details,[6] once thought to have been built at Bridewell Palace or Nonsuch, was probably commissioned for Whitehall, given its estimated scale – 14 feet high and 9 feet 6 inches wide – which suggests that it was destined for a great outward chamber; its Tuscan and Ionic pillars bear similarities to those in the Whitehall family group painting. Nicholas Bellin of Modena is known to have worked on the banqueting house, preaching place and gardens at Whitehall, and to have built chimney-pieces there based on those in Francis I's gallery at Fontainebleau.[7]

By the time of the King's death, although the works he had begun were unfinished, the Whitehall Palace site would extend over twenty-six acres as a result of further compulsory purchases of property from local residents and the reclamation of 12,600 square yards of the Thames foreshore.[8]

At Hampton Court, in 1540, Henry VIII set up the famous astronomical clock, which was designed by Nicolaus Kratzer and made by a Frenchman, Nicolas Oursian, Deviser of the King's Horologies.[9] It shows not only the hours, but the month, the date, the number of days since the beginning of the year, the phases of the Moon, the movement of the constellations in the Zodiac, and the time of high water at London Bridge – useful in the days when most courtiers travelled to London by barge. The clock also shows the Sun revolving around the Earth, a mediaeval theory that was yet to be debunked by Copernicus and Galileo. In an age not renowned for precision in timepieces, visitors were astounded by this remarkable piece of technology.

In 1540, John Ponet, a fellow of Queen's College, Cambridge, and future Bishop of Winchester, presented the King with a marvellous sundial he had himself designed, which showed 'not only the hour of the day, but also the day of the month, the sign of the moon, the ebbing and flowing of the sea, with divers other things as strange'.[10] This, too, was installed at Hampton Court.

Henry acquired only one new property in 1540, and that was the ancient castle at Westenhanger, near Folkestone in Kent, which he got by exchange with Sir Thomas Poynings. The castle had long been famed for its romantic association with Rosamund de Clifford, the mistress of Henry II, but Henry VIII used it only rarely, although he kept it in repair and built a new lodging for his daughter Mary.[11]

The Christmas revels of 1540, held at Hampton Court, were exceptionally magnificent. At New Year, the King lavished gifts on his young wife, among them two pendants containing 26 'fair table diamonds', another with 27 diamonds, 158 'fair pearls', a rope of 200 large pearls and 26 clusters of pearls.[12] On 3 January, Anne of Cleves arrived at court, bringing with her two superb horses caparisoned in purple velvet for the King and Queen. There was no rancour between her and her successor or her former husband: the King greeted her with a fraternal kiss, and the Queen welcomed her warmly, as Anne knelt respectfully before her. That evening, after they had supped together and the King had retired to bed, Anne and Katherine 'danced and drank together'. The next day, when Anne dined with the King and Queen, there was a great deal of 'conversation, amusement and mirth'. Henry presented Katherine with a ring and two lap-dogs, then looked on with approval as she gave them to Anne. That night, Katherine and Anne danced together again.[13]

In January 1541, the conservative faction pounced on three respected courtiers who had been closely associated with Cromwell, whose activities they had been doggedly investigating. Sir Thomas Wyatt, who had been away on a diplomatic mission to the Low Countries in 1540, was arrested, bound and borne off to the Tower along with Ralph Sadler and Sir John Wallop, himself a conservative. The King had been persuaded that all three held subversive religious views – Wyatt was said to be a Lutheran, while Wallop had praised the Pope – and that they had all been guilty of treasonable misconduct whilst serving on embassies abroad. There seems to have been little basis to the charges, and in March, after the Queen had interceded for them, all three were freed, Wyatt on condition that he take back his first wife, Elizabeth Brooke. Soon, they were restored to favour, although Wyatt never fully regained the King's trust. Sadler, however, was knighted later that year and admitted to the Privy Council.

Another courtier who incurred the royal displeasure was a Serjeant Porter, Sir Edmund Knyvet, who in February 1541 assaulted and injured Thomas Clere, one of Surrey's retainers, during a fight in the royal tennis court at Greenwich. Knyvet had been brought by the Knight Marshal before the Court of the Verge in the great hall of the palace, where the White Sticks sentenced him to lose his right hand and forfeit his lands and possessions for having drawn blood within the Verge of the Court.

On the day the sentence was to be carried out, a grim pageant of household officials gathered with awesome ceremony designed to impress upon the watching courtiers that breaching the King's peace within the precincts of his palace was a very serious crime indeed. The Serjeant Surgeon, who was to amputate the hand, arrived with his instruments, followed by the Serjeant of the Woodyard with a mallet and block and the King's Master Cook with a sharp knife. It would be the duty of the Serjeant of the Larder to position this on the prisoner's wrist. After the sentence had been carried out, the wound would be seared with irons provided by the Serjeant Farrier and heated by a Yeoman of the Scullery in a firepan, while a Yeoman of the Chandlery would be ready with sear-cloths with which to dress the stump, assisted by a Yeoman of the Ewery, who had with him a basin, ewer and towels. For some obscure reason, the Serjeant of the Poultry arrived with a live cockerel, 'which shall have his head smitten off on the same block with the same knife'. Finally, the Serjeant of the Cellar brought wine, ale and beer to be served to those who had come to view the gruesome spectacle.

When all were assembled, the Knight Marshal brought in Knyvet, who confessed his crime and threw himself on the royal mercy, begging that someone go and ask the King if he might lose his left hand rather than his right, 'for if my right hand be spared, I may hereafter do much good service to His Grace'. The proceedings were halted while a messenger sped off to the privy lodgings, then returned with the joyful news that the King had been so impressed by Knyvet's loyalty and courage that he had graciously pardoned him. Knyvet, who was 'more frightened than hurt',[14] was restored to his former post and held it till his death five years later. In 1542, Parliament passed 'an Act for Murder and Malicious Bloodshed within the Court', making the sentence of amputation mandatory, although noblemen who drew blood whilst chastising their servants were exempt.[15]

Masques were staged at Hampton Court on 21 and 22 February, but the King did not attend. To his 'great alarm', the ulcer on his leg had suddenly become 'clogged', leaving him feverish and black in the face, and his doctors feared for his life. The surgeons had to drain off fluid to relieve the swelling, but this was a painful process and Henry's temper suffered accordingly. He snapped irritably at everyone, grew morose and depressed, and 'formed a sinister opinion of some of his chief men', declaring bitterly that 'he had an unhappy people to govern'. He accused many of his Councillors of being lying time-servers and flatterers who looked only to their own profit, adding that he knew what they were plotting, 'and if God lent him health, he would take care that their projects should not succeed'. He mourned the loss of Cromwell, having perceived that his Councillors, 'upon light pretext, by false accusations, had made him put to death the most faithful servant he ever had'. His misery was so great that he would not even listen to music, and remained shut away in his lodgings. Court life ground to a standstill, and so many members of the household were sent home that the court 'resembled more a private family than a King's train'. For over ten days, Henry even refused to let the Queen visit him in his pitiable state, which gave rise to gossip that there was a rift between them.[16]

By Easter, which fell on 19 March, Henry's leg was better, and his depression beginning to lift. On 22 March, he was at Rochester, inspecting the work on the converted priory and no doubt expressing his dissatisfaction, since less than a year later the great hall that had been fashioned from the monks' refectory was rebuilt as two great chambers. The King moved on via Otford and Knole – his only recorded visits after he acquired these houses – to Penshurst. On his return to court, he appears to have had good cause for rejoicing, for on 10 April, Marillac reported that 'the Queen is thought to be with child, which would be a very great joy to this King, who, it seems, believes it and intends, if it be found true, to have her crowned at Whitsuntide. The young lords and gentlemen of this court are practising daily for the jousts and tournaments to be then made.'[17]

Even hopes of an heir did not mitigate Henry's savage reaction to news of a minor rebellion against his religious policies in Yorkshire, led by a scion of the Nevilles, which gave him the excuse he needed to eliminate yet another of his Plantagenet relatives. Margaret Pole, Countess of Salisbury, still languished in the Tower under sentence of death, but despite her great age – she was sixty-eight – and the fact that she had nothing to do with the rebellion, the King ordered her execution. The headsman was inept, and the Countess was butchered in the most slovenly fashion.[18] One Londoner wrote, 'I do not hear that any of the royal race are left, except a nephew of Cardinal [Pole] and the son of the Marquess of Exeter. They are both children, and in prison and condemned.'[19] Even Henry VIII did not stoop to executing children, and the boys remained in the Tower.

Either Katherine had had a false alarm, or her pregnancy ended in a miscarriage. By the end of June, as preparations went ahead for the long-deferred progress to the North, the King was displeased with her, 'avoiding as much as possible her company' and seeking his pleasures elsewhere, while the Queen kept to her lodgings. Marillac still believed her to be pregnant and, having learned that Henry was taking with him to the North his richest clothing and the most sumptuous tapestries and plate from Whitehall, surmised that Katherine was to be crowned at York, since the citizens were eagerly anticipating the birth of a duke of York, the title customarily given to the second son of the monarch.[20]

This all fitted in with the King's stated purpose of reinforcing the royal authority in the areas of his realm that had been infected with rebellion, and where, never having visited these parts, he was just a name to the people. This was not to be just a hunting progress, but a display of calculated magnificence and majesty designed to overawe and impress disaffected subjects; and in case that were not enough, Henry was taking with him such a strong military presence that his train seemed 'more like a military camp' than a court.[21] Not since the Field of Cloth of Gold, twenty-one years earlier, had the King amassed such a retinue. There were five thousand horses, a thousand soldiers, most members of the court and two hundred tents and pavilions in which to accommodate those for whom there was no room in the houses where the King was to stay. The Queen and the Lady Mary were of the company, as were several ambassadors, but Prince Edward was left behind, and Cranmer, Audley, Hertford and Sadler remained in London to attend to matters of state.

On 30 June, the King led his vast company northwards towards Hatfield, Dunstable, Ampthill and Grafton, hunting and hawking on the way. At every town and city he visited, people flocked to see him in gaily bedecked streets, and there speeches, lavish receptions and banquets. Henry won hearts by exerting his compelling charm and making himself accessible to all who 'grieved for lack of justice'.[22] On the road, food provided by the various Household departments, supplemented by game, fish and fowl caught by the hunting parties, was prepared in field kitchens. Progress was slow and initially hampered by stormy weather: the roads became impassable, the baggage carts got stuck in the mud, and the Queen was unwell for a time.[23] It took the court almost three weeks to reach Grafton, but after that the weather cleared, and the vast train was able to press on to Northampton at a faster pace.

On 9 August, after visiting Stamford and staying with the Suffolks at Grimsthorpe Castle, Henry arrived at Lincoln wearing a suit of Lincoln green, preceded by his archers marching with drawn bows, the Yeomen of the Guard with their pikes and axes, and trumpeters and drummers. Having changed in a pavilion into splendid outfits of cloth of gold and silver, the King and Queen went in procession up the hill to the cathedral, where Henry formally pardoned the citizens for their disobedience during the Pilgrimage of Grace and *Te Deum* was sung in celebration.

Then it was on to Boston, and so into Yorkshire. At Hatfield Chase, the King and his companions shot nearly four hundred deer in two days and enjoyed a picnic in the open air.[24] Having visited Doncaster and Pontefract, the royal entourage moved towards York, and was welcomed there on 16 September by the Archbishop of York and three hundred clergy. Then two hundred men who had rebelled against the King and been pardoned came to make further submission, kneeling in the street before him and offering purses stuffed with gold.[25] While in York, Henry stayed in a house now known as the King's Manor, which either had been specially built for him next to the former abbot's lodging of St Mary's Abbey, or was a refurbished building of the erstwhile Benedictine monastery.[26] An army of fifteen hundred workmen had rebuilt the great hall of the abbey and furnished it with the tapestries and plate from Whitehall, in readiness for the arrival of James V, King of Scots, who had arranged to meet his uncle in York. Tents had been erected in the grounds of the abbey to accommodate the members of both courts.[27]

Henry waited in York until 29 September, but James, who did not trust his uncle, never showed up, much to his chagrin. Apart from this, the progress had been a triumphant success,[28] and the King, generally well satisfied, moved east to Hull to plan fortifications. He stayed there five days in Hull Manor House, which he had had converted into a small palace,[29] then returned south via Kettleby, Grimsthorpe, Collyweston, Ampthill, The More and Windsor to Hampton Court, arriving on 30 October.

He would have been horrified had he known what the Queen had got up to during the progress. During the King's illness in the spring,

Katherine had rashly begun a secret flirtation with Thomas Culpeper, which soon developed into something more serious. At every stop made by the court on progress, they contrived to meet, after Katherine had made a point of 'seeking for the back doors and back stairs herself'.[30] This was done with the connivance of Lady Rochford, who acted as a bawd, and some of the Queen's maids of honour. At Hatfield, Margaret Morton saw such significant 'looks pass between the Queen and Culpeper' that she thought 'there was love between them'.[31] At Lincoln, Katherine 'went two nights out of her chamber, when it was late, to Lady Rochford's chamber'. Margaret Morton acted as lookout, and did not retire until 2 a.m., when Katherine Tilney awoke and asked, 'Jesus! Is not the Queen abed yet?'[32] All these women must have been aware of the danger they were courting: at Pontefract Castle, they were thrown briefly into a panic by unfounded fears that the King had discovered what was going on and had ordered his guard to watch them.

On 27 August, while the court was still at Pontefract, the net tightened around Katherine still further when her former lover, Francis Dereham, came to her seeking employment, with a recommendation from the Dowager Duchess of Norfolk. Perhaps bowing to blackmail, the Queen made him her Private Secretary and Usher of her Chamber, but he proved a liability because he was prone to boasting arrogantly that, if the King died, he was certain that Katherine would marry him. He also hinted at the favours she had already granted him,[33] thus arousing Culpeper's jealousy. Dereham had a violent temper: he attacked another Gentleman Usher, John Fell, who had objected to his remaining seated at table after the Queen's Council had risen, and laid him out. It was fortunate for Dereham that this escaped the attention of his superiors. However, it would not be long before he was in more serious trouble than he could ever have imagined.

57

'Little Sweet Fool'

Whilst the King was away, Prince Edward had fallen ill with a fever, possibly malaria, but was now, to his father's immense relief, completely recovered.[1] To minimise the risk of further infection, Henry sent the boy to Ashridge, having imposed strict limits on the number of servants that his attendants were permitted.

During the progress, the King's delight in his young wife had been reawakened, and at his instance, on All Saints' Day, 1 November, special services were held up and down the land to give thanks for 'the good life he led and trusted to lead' with this 'jewel of womanhood'.[2] On that day, however, as Henry arrived in the royal pew in the chapel royal to render thanks, he found a sealed letter awaiting him.

Amongst the women of the Duchess of Norfolk's household was a chamberer, Mary Lassels, who had been overlooked when her companions had been found places in the Queen's household. Festering resentment drove Mary Lassels to complain to her brother John, an ardent reformist who would one day be burned for his Protestant beliefs, and reveal to him what she knew of Katherine Howard's promiscuous past. Seeing an opportunity of bringing down the Catholic Queen and her party, Lassels went straight to the Council and divulged what he had been told.

Archbishop Cranmer, who also wished to see the conservative faction toppled from power, immediately laid the sordid facts before the King – in the letter discreetly left in his pew. When Henry read it, his first reaction was one of disbelief. But when, during a Council meeting at Winchester Palace in Southwark, incontrovertible evidence was laid before him, he called for a sword so that he could slay the Queen, then broke down in tears, complaining of his misfortune in meeting with 'such ill-conditioned wives'[3] and blaming the Council, who had 'solicited' him to marry her, for what had happened.[4]

The Queen and Lady Rochford were both placed under house arrest at Hampton Court, Katherine being told it was 'no more the time to dance'. [5] There is a poignant tale that she broke free of her guards and ran to intercept the King when he attended Mass in the chapel royal, but was caught and dragged screaming back to her apartments. This incident is said to have happened in the so-called Haunted Gallery, but recent research has shown that Katherine would not have taken this route from her apartments to the chapel,[6] so the tale is certainly a romantic fabrication. However, there is plenty of evidence that she was in an hysterical state during the days after her arrest and the interrogations conducted by Cranmer.

The King left Hampton Court, without seeing Katherine, on 5 November, to solace himself with hunting, and returned before the 8th, when Marillac observed him putting on a brave front, 'socialising with the ladies, as gay as I ever saw him'.[7]

So far, however, the evidence pointed only to misconduct before marriage, which was not a crime and had occurred before Henry began paying court to Katherine. But Cranmer, backed by Hertford, the Howards' bitter enemy, would not let the matter rest there. Dereham, taken to the Tower, would only admit that he and Katherine had been precontracted. Since a precontract was as binding as a marriage, and could only be annulled by an ecclesiastical court, this would render Katherine's marriage to the King invalid.

Katherine might have escaped the fate awaiting her had she admitted to the precontract, but, in a futile effort to save herself, she denied that one had ever existed, although she confessed that she had had intercourse on many occasions with Dereham during their affair, and that she had practised some form of birth control. When Dereham was questioned again, he was asked if he had had sexual relations with the Queen since her marriage, but denied it, asserting that Thomas Culpeper 'had succeeded him in the Queen's affections'.[8] When, on 10 November, the King was informed that his beloved Culpeper was under suspicion, he left Hampton Court 'suddenly after dinner' and rode to Whitehall, a broken man.[9] The court followed soon afterwards, leaving the Queen behind in the deserted palace.

Now in much greater peril, Katherine was asked about her relationship with Culpeper, but would only admit that she had flirted with him, met him by the back stairs, given him gifts and called him her 'little, sweet fool'.[10] Although she had signed a letter she sent him with the words 'Yours as long as life endures',[11] she firmly denied having committed adultery with him, and accused Lady Rochford of having encouraged her to do so, then of having spread the vile rumour that they had been lovers.[12] When questioned, Lady Rochford denied this and, throwing Katherine to the wolves, stated her belief that adultery had indeed taken place. The couple had met in her rooms with her standing guard, and also in the Queen's apartments. Once, when the King came to claim his marital rights and found the door locked, Lady Rochford kept him waiting until Culpeper had escaped down the backstairs.[13]

Under interrogation, the Queen's maids gave detailed depositions of what had been going on both before the marriage and during the progress, but none had actually been a witness to any act of adultery. However, when one revealed that Katherine and Culpeper had resorted to meeting in the Queen's stool chamber, the Council naturally believed the worst. Culpeper, when arrested and questioned under the threat of torture, agreed that he and the Queen had met in secret on many occasions, but insisted that they had never 'passed beyond words',[14] although 'he intended and meant to do [so] with the Queen, likewise the Queen so would to do with him'.[15] Hertford observed that his evil intent constituted in itself high treason. Culpeper insisted that Katherine had been the prime mover in the affair, while Lady Rochford had encouraged it and acted as a procuress. According to Margaret Morton, Lady Rochford was 'the principal occasion of the Queen's folly'.[16] Historians have endlessly speculated as to her motives, but the only plausible inference is that she obtained a vicarious thrill through her involvement in this illicit liaison.

On 13 November, Wriothesley went to Hampton Court and summoned all the members of the Queen's household into the great chamber, where, having declared to them their mistress's offences and announced that she had forfeited her title of Queen, he discharged most of them.[17] Only Anne Basset was allowed to remain at court; as her stepfather Lord Lisle was in prison, the King had undertaken to arrange a suitable marriage for her.[18] The Queen's coffers and chests were sealed and placed under guard while an inventory was taken; Sir Thomas Seymour later came to collect the Queen's jewels and return them to the King. In 1542, Katherine's emblems would be removed from all the royal palaces.

On the morning of the 14th, the former Queen, henceforth to be known as the Lady Katherine Howard, was taken to Syon Abbey, accompanied by Sir Edward and Lady Baynton, three gentlewomen, two chamberers and a confessor, who would 'wait on her until the King's further pleasure'.[19] Lady Margaret Douglas, who had been languishing in disgrace at Syon, had been sent with the Duchess of Richmond to Kenninghall. That same day, Lady Rochford and Culpeper also left Hampton Court, bound for the Tower,[20] where Lady Rochford found the strain of repeated interrogations so great that she suffered what seems to have been a complete nervous collapse – her contemporaries concluded that she had gone mad. Thanks to this 'fit of frenzy', she could not legally stand trial, but the King was determined to have his revenge, and sent his physicians to her every day to treat her and report on her progress.[21]

After Katherine had gone to Syon, Henry returned to Hampton Court. When Anne of Cleves heard the news of the Queen's fall, she moved immediately to Richmond to be near at hand in case Henry should wish to take her back, but the only messenger who came was a Privy Councillor who had been ordered to retrieve the ring that Katherine had given her.[22]

On 1 December, Dereham and Culpeper were arraigned at the Guildhall for high treason and condemned to death. The King commuted the sentence of hanging, drawing and quartering to decapitation, and they were both beheaded on the 10th of the month. Their heads were set on spikes on London Bridge, where they remained until at least 1546.[23]

Few members of the Howard family escaped the King's displeasure. Charles Howard was dismissed from the Privy Chamber. The Dowager Duchess of Norfolk, Lord William Howard and his wife Margaret, Katherine, Countess of Bridgewater, and Anne, wife of Henry Howard, the former Queen's brother, were all tried and imprisoned for misprision of treason, having been found guilty of concealing the Queen's misbehaviour; they were also sentenced to forfeiture of their possessions. Within a year, however, the King had pardoned and released all of them. Norfolk and Gardiner, who had done more than anyone else to promote the King's marriage to Katherine Howard, escaped censure, although Norfolk would never again stand so high in the King's favour. Prudently, he retired from court for a time to attend to affairs at Kenninghall, whence he wrote grovellingly to the King, deploring the misconduct of his niece and other relatives, and begging for 'some assurance of favour'.[24] His son, Surrey, remained untouched by the scandal, and continued to bask in Henry's love and esteem.

The eclipse of the conservatives left the Privy Chamber firmly under the control of the radical reformist party led by Hertford and Anthony Denny, who would remain the dominant faction for most of the rest of the reign.

During these terrible weeks, Henry could tolerate 'no company but musicians and ministers of pastime, and spent most of his time hunting, seeking to forget his grief'.[25] He would not stay in one house for long, but moved about restlessly. Christmas at Greenwich was a dismal affair, with only a small company in attendance. The King, observed Marillac, was 'sad, and disinclined to feasting and ladies', while his Councillors were 'pensive and melancholy'.[26]

In January 1542, Henry was looking 'old and grey, after the mishap of the last Queen'. Chapuys reported that he had never seen him 'so sad, pensive and sighing'.[27] Clues to his state of mind may be found in the passages he marked in his devotional books, all of which refer to the folly of becoming involved with loose women; one, in the Book of Proverbs, reads, 'My son, why wilt thou have pleasure in a harlot?'

The King, who had rapidly gained weight after the tragedy of Jane Seymour's death, was solacing his grief over Katherine Howard's perfidy by indulging in what Marillac called 'marvellous excess' in eating and drinking. Already 'very stout', he was 'daily growing heavier', and beginning to look more and more like his maternal grandfather Edward IV, who had been similarly given to overindulgence.[28] Soon, it would be said that 'the King was so fat that three of the biggest men that could be found could get inside his doublet', while during 1542 his great bed of walnut wood at Whitehall was enlarged to measure 7 feet 6 inches long and 7 feet wide, to accommodate his increasing bulk.[29]

The physician Andrew Boorde – known as 'Merry Andrew' because he believed that laughter was the best medicine – saw Henry in 1542 and reported that his hair was still plentiful and red, although thinning on top, that his pulse was strong and regular, and that his digestive system was functioning well. Yet Boorde was concerned about the King's excessive overeating and obesity, while some of the royal doctors were of the opinion that he was 'not of constitution to live long'.[30]

When Parliament met in January 1542, it passed an Act declaring it treason for an unchaste woman to marry the King without first revealing her past.[31] 'Few, if any, ladies at court would henceforth aspire to such an honour,' commented Chapuys acidly.[32] Yet the King was soon in better spirits and once more 'feasting ladies'. On 29 January, the day Parliament introduced the Act of Attainder that would condemn Katherine Howard to death, he entertained twenty-six of them to supper, with thirty-five more at another table, making them 'great and hearty cheer'[33] and paying marked attention to Wyatt's estranged wife, Jane Haute, and to Anne Basset, 'a pretty young creature with wit enough to do as badly as the others, if she were to try'.[34]

Meanwhile, Katherine Howard had been keeping up her spirits at Syon, although she had no illusions as to what her fate would be. But after the Act of Attainder against her was passed in February, and the lords of the Council came to escort her to the Tower, she panicked and had to be manhandled into the waiting barge. Once in the fortress, however, she regained her composure and asked that the execution block be brought to her room so that she could practise making a good death. On the morning of 13 February, so weak with fear that she could hardly stand, she was decapitated with an axe on Tower Green, where her cousin Anne Boleyn had died less than six years before. Amongst the crowd of onlookers was another cousin, the Earl of Surrey.

Lady Rochford followed Katherine to the block. Seeing no improvement in her hysterical state, the King had demanded that Parliament pass an Act making it lawful for him to execute an insane person who had committed treason. However, by the time Lady Rochford reached the scaffold, she was calm and resigned, and confessed her faults.[35]

Katherine, who was probably no more than seventeen at the time of her execution, was buried near Anne Boleyn beneath the altar pavement in the chapel royal of St Peter ad Vincula within the Tower; the Victorian historian Lord Macaulay would later call this 'the saddest spot on earth'.

58

'A Nest of Heretics'

By March 1542, the court was returning to normal. Within a week of Katherine Howard's execution, the King was hosting pre-Lenten banquets for his Privy Councillors, nobles and men of law. One such banquet was given for a number of ladies, whose company Henry appeared to relish 'as a man nurtured among them'. On the morning beforehand, he personally inspected the lodgings that had been prepared at court for the ladies, going from chamber to chamber checking the hangings and bed-coverings to ensure they were the best that could be provided. When his guests arrived, he received them 'with much gaiety' and 'made them great and hearty cheer, without showing special affection to any particular one'.[1]

In July, the court was diverted by news that the volatile Earl of Surrey had challenged Sir John Leigh, one of the King's servants, to a duel, provoking an angry Henry to consign him to the Fleet Prison in London. A fortnight later, after writing an abject letter to the Council admitting that 'the fury of restless youth' had got the better of him, and pointing out that he was 'not the first young man to have enterprised matters that he afterwards regretted', Surrey was released on a surety of the huge sum of £6,666 (nearly £2 million).[2]

The young Earl was soon to replace Wyatt as the premier English poet. Wyatt, who was elected a Knight of the Shire for Kent in 1542, had gown weary of the diplomatic service, and longed to retire to the peace of his Kentish home, but in the autumn of 1542 the King sent him to Falmouth to welcome an imperial emissary and escort him to court. Wyatt never reached Falmouth: in October, he died of pneumonia at Sherborne, Dorset.

Few mourned him more sincerely than his fellow poet, Surrey, who wrote in an epitaph:

A tongue that serv'd in foreign realms his King,
Whose courteous talk to virtue did influence
Each noble heart; a worthy guide to bring
Our English youth by travail unto fame.[3]

Surrey's works were already much admired at court. His broad knowledge of classical and Renaissance literature lent his writing an elegance and form not yet seen in England. Surrey popularised the Petrarchan sonnet, adapting it to his own purpose as Wyatt had done, wrote a rhyming version of the Book of Ecclesiasticus as well as graceful love poems, and made a brilliant translation of Virgil's *Aeneid*, in which he introduced blank verse into the English language. His genius was to inspire the works of later generations of poets, among them Sir Philip Sidney, William Shakespeare and John Milton.

In November, the Lady Mary presided over court feasts 'in default of a queen'.[4] The King, however, was preoccupied with deteriorating relations with Scotland, and in November sent north a military force under Norfolk to prevent James V and his army from crossing the border. This was the Duke's chance to regain his sovereign's confidence, and he and his son Surrey, who was seeing military service for the first time, acquitted themselves well.

During the campaign, one of the friends of Henry's youth, William Fitzwilliam, Earl of Southampton, was killed fighting the Scots. His heir was his half-brother, Sir Anthony Browne, who inherited Southampton's house at Cowdray, Sussex. Sir Anthony, an ageing widower, celebrated his good fortune by marrying the fifteen-year-old Lady Elizabeth FitzGerald – 'Fair Geraldine' – much to Surrey's distress,[5] and began converting Cowdray into a great palace.[6]

Lord Russell had succeeded Southampton at Lord High Admiral in 1540, but was himself replaced in 1542 by John Dudley, Viscount Lisle, the son of Henry VII's unpopular minister Edmund Dudley, whom Henry VIII had executed as a sop to popular opinion in 1510. Dudley, now forty, had been restored in blood during youth and brought up by Sir Edward Guildford, whose daughter Jane he married, and in 1542 he inherited the Lisle title from his mother. He had hitherto served the King mainly in a military capacity; an excellent soldier, whose daring and horsemanship had made him renowned, he was now a Warden of the Scottish Marches alongside Suffolk. A pragmatic man of cold, calculating ambition, his able, sometimes devious, mind had impressed the King, who would in 1543 admit him to the Privy Council and Privy Chamber.

On 24 November 1542, the English won a great victory over the

Scots at Solway Moss; Norfolk was quick to point out to his master that this was due to his own expert leadership, although Hertford, who had also been given a leading command, deserved some of the credit. The King was jubilant, and the court gayer than at any time since Katherine Howard's fall.[7] News of the death of James V on 14 December gave even further cause for rejoicing, because his heir was a week-old girl, the infant Mary, Queen of Scots. Scotland would be subject to yet another weakening regency – it had endured six during the past hundred and fifty years – and should give no further trouble. Henry now conceived the idea of marrying Queen Mary to Prince Edward and uniting the two kingdoms under Tudor rule, a plan the Scots were to violently resist.

The court was merry again that Christmas. Scottish nobles, taken hostage during the campaign, were honourably entertained at court, but not set free until they had sworn on oath to further the proposed marriage alliance.[8]

Early in the new year of 1543, Surrey disgraced himself again. In February, after arriving back south, he stayed in London with two companions, Wyatt's son Thomas and William Pickering, who would later become a distinguished Elizabethan courtier. One night, whilst celebrating the recent victory, they went on a drunken spree, outraging the citizens by rampaging through the streets, smashing the windows of churches and aldermen's houses, and throwing stones at passers-by. The next night, they took a boat out on the Thames and shot pellets at the whores on Bankside. They were also seen eating meat during Lent, which was strictly forbidden to Catholics.

Surrey's friend, George Blagge, a religious radical, warned him what people might infer from this, but the Earl complacently replied, 'We shall have a madding time in our youth, and therefore I am very sorry for it.' The Lord Mayor, however, complained to the Council, and the three miscreants were hauled before it at St James's Palace. Surrey admitted breaching the King's peace by his misdemeanours, but pleaded in mitigation that he had only broken the windows of papists. He was nevertheless sent once more to the Fleet to learn to control his 'heady will'. The King was exasperated, referring to Surrey as 'the most foolish proud boy that is in England', but his fondness for the young man was unabated.[9] By the middle of May, Surrey was a free man, and doing his best to regain his master's favour. However, he never forgave Gardiner, Wriothesley, Browne and Russell for their part in his interrogation, nor Sir Thomas Seymour who had sanctimoniously pressed for a stiffer sentence.[10]

By February, the King had begun to betray an interest in Katherine Parr, the wife of John Neville, Lord Latimer. She was no giddy young girl, but a mature, well educated woman of about thirty whose intellectual gifts may have attracted Henry as much as her comely person. He had probably known her all her life: her father, Sir Thomas Parr, had served Katherine of Aragon until his death in 1517, her brother William was a prominent courtier, her sister Anne had waited on Katherine Howard, and Lady Latimer herself had visited court with her husband. Henry's first recorded gift to her – a package of 'pleats and sleeves' – was paid for on 16 February, while her ailing husband was still alive. It was followed by presents of fashionable gowns, cut in the Italian, French and Dutch styles, and French hoods.[11] Lord Latimer, who had been ill for some time, died on 2 March.

The Parrs were an ancient Westmorland family, distantly related to the Plantagenets and Tudors. Katherine had been born at Kendal Castle in 1511/12, but had been brought up in London. She had now buried two husbands, the first having been the elderly Edward de Burgh, Lord Borough, whom she had married in 1526. He died in 1528 and she married Lord Latimer around 1530. There were no children from either marriage.

Katherine was 'of small stature'[12] and, although not beautiful, had a 'lively, pleasing appearance'.[13] She was dignified, 'graceful and of cheerful countenance, and is praised for her virtue'.[14] The half-length portrait of her now in the National Portrait Gallery shows a pleasant-faced matron with auburn hair[15] and hazel eyes, wearing a rich red gown with stand-up collar and jaunty feathered cap. She was kind, warm-hearted, generous and intuitive, although given to occasional rash impulses. In his Will, the King praised her for her devotion, obedience, chastity and wisdom, but beneath the virtuous and godly exterior there beat a passionate heart.

There has been much recent scholarly debate as to the extent of Katherine's intellectual capabilities. There is no doubt that she was intelligent and well read, but she was pious rather than intellectual. She was well educated for a woman of her time, imbued with the New Learning, and is known to have written at least two rather erudite devotional books. A good conversationalist, Katherine was fluent in French and Italian, could read and write Latin and understood some Greek; she had been taught French as a child by her mother, and learned the other languages later in life. Her handwriting was in the new Italianate style. Katherine had the utmost respect for scholarship, was well aware of her own shortcomings, and constantly sought to improve herself.

The King's interest in Lady Latimer may well have accounted for the preferment of her brother William, Lord Parr, to the Privy Council in

March and his election as a Knight of the Garter the following month. The King also appointed him Warden of the Scottish Marches. Around this time, however, Parr's wife, Elizabeth Bourchier, deserted him, and he discovered that her children had been fathered by other men. Incensed, he urged the King to have her executed, which was the prescribed penalty for the adulterous wives of peers. Thanks to Katherine Parr's intercession with the King, Lady Parr escaped death, but Parliament granted her husband a divorce on 17 April and declared her children bastards and unfit to inherit the Essex estates, which were instead entailed upon Lord Parr.

Although Latimer had been a conservative, his widow held radical, if not Protestant, religious views, and had to be careful. The reformers Miles Coverdale and Hugh Latimer were guests at her house near the former London Charterhouse, but so also was the staunchly Catholic Lady Mary, who may have known Katherine Parr from childhood and was a good friend.

It was a dangerous time to hold Lutheran opinions. Led by the energetic Gardiner, ably supported by Wriothesley, the conservative faction, in order to regain its ascendancy and discredit its rivals, was ruthlessly seeking out heretics and traitors within the royal household. In March 1543, they 'uncovered a nest of heretics'[16] amongst the musicians of St George's Chapel at Windsor. The gifted organist, composer and Master of the Choristers, John Marbeck, a secret Calvinist, was sentenced to be burned at the stake after heretical writings were found in his house, but the King valued his playing so highly that he pardoned him.[17] Three other members of the Chapel Royal were not so lucky.[18]

In April, Gardiner struck at Archbishop Cranmer, whose primacy he coveted, and had him accused of heresy. But the King again intervened. He arrived at Lambeth Palace in his barge and sent a message inviting Cranmer to accompany him on a trip along the Thames. When the Archbishop appeared, Henry said jovially, 'Ah, my chaplain, I have news for you. I now know who is the greatest heretic in Kent.' He also hinted that he knew Cranmer had a wife. The Archbishop was thoroughly frightened, but the King, who was very fond of his primate, even though he must have suspected his Protestant sympathies, made it clear that he meant to protect him from his enemies, and authorised him to preside over the inquiry into his own alleged heresy. When the conservatives approached the King for permission to arrest Cranmer, he granted it, but then privily summoned the Archbishop and gave him a ring as a token of his favour, which the primate was to produce when the Council came for him. The next day, Cranmer was able to confound his enemies, and was supported by Henry, who delivered a stern homily on the evils of faction politics and commanded the rival parties to make their peace.[19]

The King also taught a lesson to Sir Thomas Seymour, who had accused the Archbishop of not maintaining a household, or entertaining in a style appropriate to his dignity, and urged that his vast revenues be diverted to the Crown and replaced with a salary. After the heresy scandal had died down, Henry, probably having warned Cranmer what he was about, ordered Seymour to present himself at Lambeth Palace one afternoon. Seymour was astonished to find a lavish meal awaiting him. When he arrived back at Whitehall, the King asked him, 'Had my lord dined before ye came? What cheer made he you?' A shamefaced Seymour had to admit that he had 'abused Your Highness with an untruth'. Henry, who had personal reasons for wishing to discountenance Seymour, lectured him, then warned, 'There shall be no alteration made while I live.'[20]

Later that year, the King sanctioned the return of Mistress Cranmer, who had been living in Germany, and in 1544 and 1545, he would again intervene to save Cranmer from those who wished to destroy him.

Thwarted of bigger fish, the conservatives next struck at the Privy Chamber, and draft indictments were drawn up by Gardiner's protégé, Dr John London, against eleven of its members, among them the Master of the Revels, the diplomat and scholar Philip Hoby, Master Penny, the King's barber, and the royal cook. But Henry was not impressed or pleased: he ordered the arrest of London and pardoned those under suspicion. London was found guilty of perjury, made a public example of, then imprisoned in the Fleet, where he died the next year.[21]

But the defeated Gardiner and his party remained undaunted and determined to rid the court of reformists and closet heretics, intending that, when the King eventually died, the Catholics would be in control. For the present, however, the reformists were dominant at court, and among them were several rising 'new men'. In April 1543, the shrewd and competent William Paget replaced Sir Ralph Sadler as Principal Secretary to the King. Paget, an ally of Hertford who wisely kept his religious views to himself, was a man who 'will have one foot in every pageant'.[22] He enjoyed immense influence with the King, and his fellow Councillors often used him to convey messages and requests to Henry.[23] Paget was therefore able to exercise extensive patronage, dabble in a little blackmail, and grow rich: he built himself a fine mansion at West Drayton, Middlesex.[24] Paget screened most of the documents and information intended for the King, as well as those sent out by Henry, but there is little evidence that he ever tampered with them; either he was honest, or he covered his traces well.

William Petre was appointed Secretary of State and knighted in 1543. An erudite lawyer and Fellow of All Souls College, Oxford, he was to retain his post until 1566 and serve four Tudor monarchs. Petre built a splendid house at Ingatestone in Essex, which survives today. In 1543 also, William Paulet, Lord St John, was appointed Chamberlain of the Household.

Anthony Denny's influence with the King was growing steadily. At the centre of a humanist circle, he was 'a favourer of good learning'[25] and furthered the careers of scholars such as Sir Thomas Elyot, John Cheke and Roger Ascham, who in turn filled the 'tuneful court' with 'resonant hymns praising his universal popularity'.[26] Denny, who was knighted in 1544, not only managed the Privy Chamber administration, but also acted as confidential adviser to the King. A man of great personal charm, his painstaking devotion to his duties endeared him to the ageing Henry, for whom he acted as a buffer against a clamorous world. He fielded petitioners for his master and even wrote out their suits for them, 'which, considering his attendance upon the King and other business, is very much for him to do'.[27] Yet there was a high degree of self-interest involved, because in so doing Denny created a vast web of patronage with himself at its centre. He was therefore a very busy man, and willingly delegated some of his less pleasant duties to his unscrupulous brother-in-law, Sir John Gates, who was also a member of the Privy Chamber. Denny's genuine but radical religious convictions – he spoke out bravely against the persecution of Protestants – and his closeness to the King aroused the bitter resentment of the conservatives, but for all their efforts they were powerless to dislodge him.

Sir Francis Bryan, who had once supported the imperialists at court, now aligned himself with the reformist faction through his friendship with William Parr, to whom he dedicated his translation of Antonio de Guevara's *A Dispraise of the Life of the Courtier*. Bryan was now around fifty, but had lost none of the restless energy of his youth, which is why the poet Surrey, a kindred spirit and fellow poet, sought his friendship, transcending the enmities of courtly factions.

Catholics and reformists might wrangle and jostle for power, but the King, who had become 'very stern and opinionated',[28] was the ultimate authority in religious matters. Although largely orthodox in his views, he retained the humanist ideals of his youth and respect for the New Learning, and liked to surround himself in his later years with people who shared these interests, perhaps little realising that most held extremely radical, and possible heretical, religious views.

In 1543, the so-called 'King's Book', written under Henry's direction and partly in his own hand,[29] was published. Its true title was *The Necessary Doctrine and Erudition of Any Christian Man*, and it was the most orthodox and reactionary statement yet of the creed of Henry's Church. But it was too late to put back the clock. The availability of the Bible in English had encouraged the King's subjects to think for themselves, and many had gone way beyond the unquestioning obedience expected of devout Catholics, who Henry liked to think formed the majority of his people. Some reformists even dismissed the King's Book, with its paternalistic dogmatism and assumption of widespread traditional morality, as being not worth 'a fart'.[30]

Paget had reassured Henry that eleven twelfths of his subjects were of an orthodox persuasion, but for Gardiner this was not enough, and he urged the King to clamp down on wholesale reading of the Bible. Henry, too, thought it dangerous, and in 1543, Parliament passed the Act for the Advancement of True Religion, which condemned 'crafty, false and untrue' translations, including Tyndale's, and restricted the reading of the Scriptures to the upper and middle classes.[31]

The King was not the only man in pursuit of Katherine Parr. Sir Thomas Seymour was also paying court to the wealthy widow and, years later, she admitted to him, 'As truly as God is God, my mind was fully bent, the time I was at liberty, to marry you before any man I know.' But she was to be 'overruled by a higher power', for in May, the King, who would brook no rival, sent Seymour on an embassy to Brussels, which was followed by a military command under Sir John Wallop in the Low Countries.

Katherine bowed to her fate. By the middle of June, she and her sister Anne, the wife of William Herbert, an Esquire of the Body, were frequent visitors at court, and there was little doubt in anyone's mind that the King would soon make her his sixth wife.

59

'The Good Expectations of the King's Majesty'

Henry VIII and Katherine Parr were married by Bishop Gardiner on 12 July 1543 in the Queen's holyday closet at Hampton Court, with 'none opposing and all applauding'.[1] Among the twenty guests were the King's two daughters, the Lords Hertford and Russell, and William – soon to be Sir William – and Anne Herbert. Lady Margaret Douglas, restored to favour, carried the bride's train.[2] The new Queen was not crowned probably because the treasury could not bear the cost. The motto she adopted, 'To be useful in all I do', was an apt one.

As with all Henry's queens, the composition of Katherine's household reflected her family loyalties and ideological affiliations. Sir Anthony Cope, an erudite humanist scholar, served briefly as her Chamberlain, before being replaced in December 1543 by her uncle, Lord Parr of Horton. Sir Thomas Tyrwhit, her stepson by marriage, was Steward. The Queen's sister Anne became her chief lady-in-waiting; her other ladies included Katherine Willoughby, Duchess of Suffolk; the Countesses of Hertford and Sussex; Honor Greville, Lady Lisle; Joan Champernowne, wife of Sir Anthony Denny; the Queen's cousin, Maud, Lady Lane, and her stepdaughter, Elizabeth, Lady Tyrwhit. Another stepdaughter, Margaret Neville, was a maid of honour, as was Anne Basset.[3] In 1546, Lord Dorset's daughter by Frances Brandon, Lady Jane Grey, the King's learned little niece, came to serve the Queen as maid of honour. Elizabeth Billingham, an old friend of Katherine's, was Mother of the Maids. The Queen appointed George Day, Bishop of Chichester, as her Almoner, while among her chaplains were noted radicals such as Miles Coverdale and John Parkhurst, later Bishop of Norwich. Another member of the Queen's household was the young Nicholas Throckmorton, later to be one of the luminaries of Queen Elizabeth's court; his brother Clement was Katherine's Cupbearer.

Katherine was 'quieter than any of the young wives the King had, and as she knew more of the world, she always got on pleasantly with the King and had no caprices'.[4] Many writers portray her as little more than a nurse to an increasingly incapacitated husband, but the evidence shows that, apart from the times when his bad leg laid him low, the King and Queen were an active couple and constantly on the move. Right up to the last few months of his life, Henry refused to give in to the illnesses that at times threatened to overwhelm him. There is no evidence that Katherine found him offensive or disagreeable; on the whole, they seem to have enjoyed a harmonious relationship: the Queen confided in a private letter to her brother that this third marriage was 'the greatest joy and comfort that could happen to her'. Even Wriothesley had to admit that Katherine was 'a woman, in my judgement, for certain wisdom and gentleness most meet for His Highness; and I am sure His Majesty never had a wife more agreeable to his heart than she is'.[5]

From the first, Katherine exerted a benevolent influence over the court. Not since the days of Katherine of Aragon and Anne Boleyn had a queen patronised humanist scholarship so enthusiastically. Katherine welcomed men of learning to her court and drew extensively on her privy purse to fund the studies of poor students. One of the Queen's chaplains, Francis Goldsmith, who owed his promotion to her generosity, declared that 'her rare goodness has made every day a Sunday, a thing hitherto unheard of, especially in a royal palace'.[6]

In her religious observances Katherine was outwardly orthodox, and her writings display a personal piety that had more in common with the teachings of Erasmus than those of Luther. Her prayerbook, dated 1534, is at Sudeley Castle, and she owned a beautiful manuscript of the Epistles in Latin and English, as well as a French version of the New Testament; both were illuminated by William Harper, Clerk of the Closet.

Yet the Queen's private views seem to have been as radical as Cranmer's, and the members of her circle were mostly of like mind. As well as her ladies-in-waiting, they included Lady Elizabeth Hoby, Jane, Lady Lisle, and Margaret, Lady Butts, all of whom held dangerously Lutheran opinions. The Duchess of Suffolk, who had enthusiastically embraced the new faith, dared openly to criticise the Catholic bishops, and mischievously named her pet spaniel Gardiner, taking pleasure in calling him sharply to heel. [7]

Katherine's chamber became a haven for those with radical opinions. There were sermons by reformist preachers such as Nicholas Ridley, Hugh Latimer and Nicholas Shaxton, and readings from the Scriptures which were often followed by impassioned debate. Much time was devoted to self-improvement and pious devotion, and Nicholas Udall, visiting the court, was impressed to see the Queen and her ladies absorbed in 'virtuous exercises, reading and writing, and with most earnest study, applying themselves to extending knowledge. It is now no news in England to see young damsels in noble houses and in the courts of princes, instead of cards and other instruments of vain trifling, to have continually in their hands either psalms, homilies or other devout meditations'.[8] This all gave a tremendous boost to the cause of reform, but it was fraught with risks, not least because it aroused the resentment and suspicions of the conservative faction.

Katherine certainly discussed religious issues with Henry,[9] but John Foxe, looking back from the Protestant perspective of Elizabethan England, may have been exaggerating when he wrote that she never ceased urging the King 'zealously to proceed in the reformation of the Church'. Although he enjoyed debating theology with his wife, Henry allowed her little political influence, and she never actively involved herself in factional politics. Her family were content with their advancement and did not seek to rule the King. However, since most members of her household and circle were of the reformist persuasion, she was identified with the interests of that party, and thus further incurred the enmity of the conservatives.

In 1543, the King began building new lodgings for Katherine Parr at Hampton Court, in the south-east corner of the Base Court, and a new barge was constructed for her by a Lambeth shipwright. Katherine's life was not totally centred on scholarship and religion, and she pursued other, more traditional pleasures. She loved clothes, especially in the Italian and French fashions. Most of the silk for her dresses came from Antwerp, yet there were complaints that the Queen was often slow to pay for her purchases. She was, however, less extravagant than the King's previous wives: many of the gorgeous bejewelled gowns made for Katherine Howard and kept in storage at Baynard's Castle were altered to fit her. But she had a weakness for shoes, and once purchased forty-seven pairs in one year. Among them were velvet court shoes trimmed with gold at 14s. (£210) a pair, six pairs of cork-soled shoes, and 'quarter shoes' which cost 5s. (£75) a pair and wore out very quickly.[10]

Katherine adored flowers: the chamber accounts record daily payments for floral arrangements for her apartments and for 'perfume for the chamber', her favourite scents being juniper and civet.[11] She was an accomplished needlewoman and produced exquisite embroideries, of which examples survive at Sizergh Castle in Westmorland. She retained several fools, including a dwarf and a woman called Jane, for whom she bought a red petticoat. She kept greyhounds and parrots as pets.

Katherine also enjoyed dancing and shared the King's passion for music. She maintained an Italian consort of viols, whose members

received 8d. (£10) a day. She once sent a letter to the Lady Mary by the
hand of a musician, 'who will be, I judge, most acceptable, from his skill
in music, in which you, I am well aware, take as much delight as
myself'.[12]

Katherine doubtless appreciated the music of the great composer,
singer and organist, Thomas Tallis, who had joined the Chapel Royal in
1542 after serving as a lay clerk at Canterbury Cathedral, having been
made redundant when Waltham Abbey, where he had been organist
and master of the choristers, was dissolved in 1540. The King had
admired his work since hearing him sing at Waltham. Tallis, who has
been called 'the Father of English Music', was to enjoy a long and
distinguished career in the Chapel Royal until his death in 1585. Under
his auspices, English church music would reach an unprecedented
zenith. During Henry VIII's reign, he wrote five antiphons, three
masses, the motet 'Miserere Nostri' and – perhaps at this time – another
Latin motet for forty voices, all in a restrained mediaeval style; it was his
later works, composed during the reign of Elizabeth I, that were his
greatest achievement.

There was plague in London that summer, and the King issued
proclamations forbidding either the citizens to approach the court or the
courtiers to go to the City.[13] In July, Henry left with his bride and his
elder daughter on a long hunting progress that would take them via
Oatlands to the south and west of England. After a short stay at Wulfhall,
the court moved north to Woodstock, Langley and Grafton, then
homewards via Dunstable and Ashridge.[14] This was the last time the
King would ever venture so far afield. In future, he would confine his
travels to the Thames Valley, and ensure that facilities at his riverside
palaces were improved and adapted to his increasing bulk and periods of
restricted mobility.

During 1543, the King built 'the Great Standing' – now known as
'Queen Elizabeth's hunting lodge' – in a park called Fairmead in Epping
Forest, two miles north-east of Chingford. Of timber construction and
L-shaped, it had an open gallery on the upper floor from which the King
could shoot game or just watch the hunt with his companions.[15]

There was still plague in London in the autumn when the King returned
from his progress, and sometime between 7 October and 29 November,
it claimed the life of Hans Holbein. Holbein had recently recovered
some of the King's former favour, and Katherine Parr had commissioned
circular portraits of Henry's three children, of which only those of
Edward and Mary survive. Holbein's last work, a vast painting of Henry
VIII presenting a charter to the Barber Surgeons Company of London,

a commission that was obtained through the good offices of Dr Butts, was left unfinished.[16] Holbein died at his house in the parish of St Andrew Undershaft and was buried in the Church of St Catherine Cree. He left money for the maintenance of two bastard children, whose mother had perhaps also been a victim of the plague. There was nothing for the family he had abandoned in Basel. Holbein's many drawings were left in his studio at Whitehall and appear to have passed into Henry VIII's art collection.

No one could replace the genius of Holbein. Lucas Horenbout's grant of office as King's Painter, which referred to the King's long acquaintance with 'the science and experience' in his 'pictorial art', was renewed in 1544, but he died soon afterwards in London. In 1547, his wife Margaret received a payment of 40s. (£600) for a portrait of Katherine Parr; whether she painted it herself or whether it was in settlement of an outstanding debt to her late husband is not known.[17]

Henry's Serjeant Painter, Andrew Wright, had died in 1543, and was succeeded in the post by Antonio Toto, who was to remain in office until the next reign. Toto was the first foreign artist to be appointed Serjeant Painter, and undoubtedly the most competent so far.

The King now began to seek out new artistic talent. Several of those who worked for him cannot now be identified, such as the master who painted the Whitehall family group, which was executed around this time, but others became famous. Holbein's most important successor was the gifted Hans Eworth, who came to England from Antwerp in 1543 and is said to have finished off portraits that Holbein had left incomplete. Eworth attracted the patronage of Katherine Parr, who commissioned from him miniatures of herself and the King, costing 30s. (£450) each. Another follower of Holbein known only as 'Master John', is known to have painted portraits of Katherine Parr (full length) and the Lady Mary, which were picked out in gold leaf.[18]

Perhaps the most prominent artist in Henry's last years was the Dutch master Guillim Scrots, who had been chief painter to Mary of Hungary, Regent of the Netherlands, since 1537. In the autumn of 1545, the King persuaded him to come to England with the inducement of a high salary of £62.10s. (£18,750). Scrots introduced novel Renaissance elements into English painting, such as classical statuary, putti, masks and heraldic escutcheons. These are evident in the masterful full-length portrait attributed to him of the Earl of Surrey, painted in c1546. Scrots also introduced into England the northern Renaissance obsession with costume detail, which he painted with consummate skill whilst making little attempt to convey the character of the sitter. This style was to dominate English portraiture until the early seventeenth century. One of Scrots's most famous works – and the only one signed by him – is the anamorphosis (or distorted perspective) of Prince Edward (1546), which was hung in Whitehall Palace and was the kind of novelty appreciated by Tudor courtiers.[19] Many paintings have been attributed to Scrots, but few can be said with certainty to be his original work. He is thought to have painted the three-quarter-length portraits of the Prince of Wales and the Lady Elizabeth which are still in the Royal Collection and date from c1545-6.

John Bettes the Elder, whose work suggests that he was trained in Holbein's studio, was a competent painter, miniaturist and engraver. He had worked on the mural depicting the coronation of Henry VIII at Whitehall in 1531-3, and had also painted decorative heraldic pictures for the palace. Katherine Parr paid him £3 (£900) for miniatures of herself and the King and six other pictures in 1546-7, and he is also known to have painted the likenesses of several courtiers.[20] Sadly, none of his miniatures can now be identified.

Henry VIII also employed a female artist, Levina Teerlinc, the daughter of Simon Benninck, one of the foremost masters of the Ghent/Bruges school of illuminators and limners. Levina, who was married to George Teerlinc of Blankenberg, entered Henry's service in 1546 and was granted an annuity of £40 (£12,000);[21] her husband was made a Gentleman Pensioner. Teerlinc is thought to have been influenced by Horenbout, but her work is known only through later miniatures, which are poor in quality and draughtsmanship, and portray sitters with disproportionately tiny bodies and stick-thin arms.

The obscure John Shute also painted portraits of courtiers. Another artist who was on the fringe of the court was Gerlach Flicke, who came from Osnabrück in Germany and settled in London around 1545. His most famous work is his portrait of Archbishop Cranmer,[22] but it is of mediocre quality, and although he received commissions from courtiers, he did not attract royal patronage.

Katherine Parr was a kind and supportive stepmother to the King's three children, who all came to love her. She was already close friends with the Lady Mary, who was only four years her junior, and she now declared that it was her pleasure rather than her duty to establish affectionate relations with Edward, now six, and Elizabeth, who was ten.[23] To this end, she encouraged all three to come to court whenever circumstances and their father permitted, and maintained a warm correspondence with them when they were absent; Edward wrote to her in Latin, and Elizabeth, on one occasion at least, in Italian. She exchanged gifts and kindnesses with them, worried about their health and welfare, gave them money, bought clothes for them – Edward received outfits of crimson velvet and white satin – and encouraged them in their studies.

It was Katherine who, in 1544, encouraged Mary to translate Erasmus's *Paraphrases of the Gospel of St John* into English. Mary made a good start, but achieved little further progress because of intermittent ill-health, so the Queen called in Nicholas Udall to finish the project, and also met the costs of publication.

Mary, who now came to court more often than ever before, already had lodgings in several of the royal palaces, but it was not until Henry married Katherine Parr that Elizabeth was allocated any; they were next to the Queen's own apartments at Greenwich and Whitehall. Both princesses had their own chamber servants. Edward, like his sisters, had his own establishment, but as the King feared him risking infection by coming to court often, Katherine saw less of her stepson than she would probably have wished. However, she did sometimes arrange for the family to be together when she and the King visited one of the lesser houses, such as Hanworth, and in 1543–4 Henry created a lodging for the Prince with a bedchamber next to his own at Greenwich.[24]

The King was fond of all his children, although Edward, the precious, long-awaited son, was naturally his favourite. Edward was small for his age with one shoulder higher than the other and was short-sighted, but he was an attractive child with blond hair and grey eyes. His early portraits show an elfin face with a pointed chin like his mother's, but his resolute, direct gaze was his father's. As he grew older, he consciously aped the King's mannerisms and posed for artists in the classic Henrician stance, feet firmly apart, hand on hip or dagger.

It was drilled into the Prince from birth that he must 'satisfy the good expectations of the King's Majesty',[25] a lesson he learned so well that, in a letter written later to his father, he vowed he would be 'worthy to be tortured with stripes of ignominy if, through negligence, I should omit even the smallest particle of my duty'.[26] When, in 1546, Henry presented his son with jewels from the suppressed monasteries, Edward took it as a sign of the King's great love for him, 'for if you did not love me, you would not give me these fine gifts'. When he wrote to Henry, the Prince addressed him as 'Most noble Father and most illustrious King'.[27] Although Henry was an affectionate father, he was also a distant and awe-inspiring one.

As soon as he was six, Edward was breeched, taken from Lady Bryan and his nurses, who were pensioned off, and given into the care of male tutors. For a long time, historians believed that it was Katherine Parr who took the responsibility for his education, but recent research suggests that it was in fact the King who made the decisions and arrangements. Katherine's role was to encourage and support the boy in his studies.

Edward now began a rigorous classical education under renowned

humanists, who were all followers of Erasmus, Vives and More. He was
to learn languages, including Latin and Greek, Scripture, classics,
philosophy, astronomy and 'all liberal sciences'.[28] It was fortunate that
the boy was highly intelligent and loved books. His studies were
supplemented by more traditional lessons in horsemanship, archery,
fencing, tennis, music and dancing, all of which he much enjoyed,
although he was never to be a sportsman like his father. So that he
should not learn in isolation, the King founded a select palace school,
choosing fourteen aristocratic boys to share his education: they included
Suffolk's son, the learned Henry Brandon, Surrey's son, Lord Thomas
Howard, Lord Lisle's son, Robert Dudley, John, Lord Lumley, Lord
Mountjoy, Henry, Lord Hastings, and Barnaby Fitzpatrick, a sprig of the
Irish nobility who was unfortunate enough to be appointed the Prince's
whipping boy, yet became a close friend. It is also possible that the
prodigious Lady Jane Grey shared Edward's lessons.

The men who were given responsibility for the Prince's education
were among the most brilliant scholars of their day. Dr Richard Cox,
Edward's former Almoner, who had worked with Henry on the King's
Book and later became Provost of Eton and Bishop of Ely, was the
Prince's first tutor. Although he did his best to make learning enjoyable,
and resorted less frequently than most Tudor teachers to the rod, he is
known to have beaten Edward on occasion.

John Cheke, the first ever Regius Professor of Greek at Cambridge
and one of the most outstanding minds of his day, joined Cox in 1544,
having probably been recommended to the King by either Sir William
Butts or Anthony Denny, who were both his patrons. Edward became
very fond of Cheke, who soon took over from Dr Cox as senior tutor.

Cheke is said to have brought from Cambridge two men of high
reputation to help with Edward's education. The humanist Sir Anthony
Cooke, who, like Thomas More, had four learned daughters, and whose
translation of St Cyprian's treatise on the unity of the Church was
dedicated to Henry VIII,[29] may indeed have tutored the Prince,
although the evidence is conflicting. Roger Ascham, later schoolmaster
to the Lady Elizabeth, taught Edward penmanship. In 1545, the eminent
William Grindal was brought in to help with the teaching of Greek.
There was also a German tutor called Randolph; there is no evidence
that Edward ever learned German, so perhaps he taught another subject.

Edward's tutors were mostly Cambridge men, committed scholars
imbued with Erasmian teachings; all later emerged as Protestants, as soon
as it was safe to do so, although there is no evidence that they held such
views during Henry's reign. Cheke, for one, was no religious fanatic.
The King would never have allowed anyone tainted with the merest
hint of heresy near his heir. The Prince's tutors gave Henry no cause for

suspicion, and succeeded well in teaching Edward what they were employed to teach. The fact remains, however, that as soon as Edward came to the throne, he embraced the Protestant faith with alacrity, which suggests that there had been a degree of subtle indoctrination.

In 1546, a Frenchman, Jean Belmaine, was engaged to teach French to Edward and Elizabeth. Belmaine was a follower of John Calvin, the Swiss reformer who preached an extreme form of Lutheranism, but he knew better than to make his opinions known at the English court.

Edward, like all his race, loved music, and was taught to play the lute by Philip van Wilder. There is little evidence to support the claim that the renowned composer Christopher Tye, choirmaster of Ely Cathedral, was the Prince's music master.

Elizabeth had received her early education from her governess, Katherine Ashley; the princess was bright, sharp-witted and old for her years, and showed early signs of fulfilling Wriothesley's prediction, made when she was six, that she would be an honour to her sex. As well as rapidly becoming proficient on the lute and virginals, she proved so precociously able in languages and the classics that the King, perhaps at the behest of Katherine Parr, arranged for her to be taught by William Grindal. From about 1545, Roger Ascham, then based in Cambridge, acted as her educational mentor. After Henry's death, he became her tutor.

It was probably due to Katherine Parr's influence that the King invited all three of his children to spend Christmas at court in 1543. The festivities began on 23 December, when William Parr was solemnly created Earl of Essex, and his uncle made Lord Parr of Horton, in a glittering – and now rare – ceremony in the presence chamber at Hampton Court. Having been robed in the pages' chamber off the great watching chamber, the two men were invested by the King, who was enthroned under the cloth of estate.[30] Later that day, Henry convened a chapter of the Order of the Garter and admitted Sir John Wallop to the Order, 'to the joy of all present'.[31] The court then moved to Greenwich for Christmas.

At New Year, Anthony Denny presented the King with a clock salt he had commissioned from Holbein. Henry loved technical novelties, and this exquisite piece, fashioned in the Italian Renaissance style, was not simply a combined clock and salt-cellar but cunningly concealed an hour-glass, two sundials and a compass. Nicolaus Kratzer had assisted Holbein with the design.[32]

Elizabeth gave her new stepmother her own 117-page translation, from French verse into English prose, of Marguerite of Navarre's lengthy devotional poem, The Mirror, or Glass, of the Sinful Soul, for

which she had also embroidered the blue binding with a knotwork
pattern in silver thread, encompassing Katherine's initials.[33] She warned
the Queen that she might have to 'rub out, polish and mend the words,
which I know in many places to be rude',[34] but Katherine doubtless
appreciated the hours of work that had gone into the making of the gift.
It was the measure of the impact her kindness had made on three
motherless children.

60

'The Enterprise of Boulogne'

Henry VIII's final years were overshadowed by financially ruinous wars with France and Scotland that would leave England crippled with debt. By 1544, relations between England and France had deteriorated sufficiently for the threat of war to become a reality; the King had built a ring of defensive castles along the south coast in anticipation of a French invasion, and was now planning to invade France himself.

In February of that year, Parliament passed a new Act of Succession, so that there should be no disputes over who would succeed Henry were he not to return alive from France. The Act settled the succession firstly on Prince Edward and his heirs, secondly on the Lady Mary and her heirs, thirdly on the Lady Elizabeth and her heirs, and finally on the heirs of Henry's younger sister, the late Mary Tudor, Duchess of Suffolk.[1] The heirs of his elder sister, Margaret Tudor, who had died in 1541, were passed over because Henry had no intention of uniting England and Scotland under Stewart rule, but was still aggressively pursuing his intention of marrying Edward to the little Scots Queen. The arrangements made in this Act reflect the fact that Henry's authority was now so absolute as to override the long-established laws of primogenitural succession. They may also reflect the benign influence of Katherine Parr.

In February, as preparations for war went ahead, the King's leg swelled up and laid him feverishly low again, confining him to bed for eight days and leaving him 'a little indisposed' for a while afterwards. In order to nurse and cheer him, the Queen had her own bed moved into a closet leading off his bedchamber,[2] and she was seen sitting with his bad leg on her lap. Her accounts show payments to the royal apothecaries for suppositories, liquorice pastilles, cinammon comfits, plasters and sponges.[3] When Henry eventually emerged from his privy lodgings in March, he was 'so weak on his legs that he could hardly stand'. Chapuys believed that his 'chronic disease and great obesity' were putting his life at risk and should be urgently remedied, 'yet no one dares to remonstrate with him'.[4]

On 17 February, while the King was ill, there arrived at court the Spanish Duke of Najera, a special envoy from Henry's ally, Charles V, who was graciously received by the Queen and the Lady Mary, to whom he was conducted by Chapuys. Najera's secretary, Pedro de Gant, left an account of the visit, and describes Katherine's rich gown of crimson and cloth of gold with a golden girdle and a train two yards long, which was set off by two crucifixes and a jewel set with magnificent diamonds, all hung about her neck; there were 'a great number of splendid diamonds in her head-dress also'. The Lady Mary looked splendid in cloth of gold and purple velvet.[5]

After the Duke had kissed the Queen's hand, she led him into another chamber where he was entertained for several hours with music and 'much beautiful dancing'. Although the Queen was feeling unwell herself, she danced 'very gracefully, for the honour of the company' with her brother Essex, while the Lady Mary partnered Lady Margaret Douglas and then paired up with some gentlemen of the court, one of whom, a Venetian, danced galliards 'with such extraordinary activity that he seemed to have wings on his feet'. As the evening drew to a close, the Queen summoned a Spanish-speaking nobleman to present her gifts to the Duke, then rose and offered Najera her hand to kiss. 'He would have kissed that of the Princess Mary, but she offered her lips, and so he saluted her and all the other ladies.'[6]

A day or so later, Najera received a summons to attend upon the King in his privy lodgings at Whitehall.

> Before the Duke arrived at the King's chamber, he passed through three salons hung with tapestry, in the second of which [the watching chamber] were stationed in order on either side the King's bodyguard, dressed in habits of red and holding halberds. In the third salon [the presence chamber] were nobles, knights and gentlemen, and here was a canopy made of rich, figured brocade, with a chair of the same material. Here, the brother of the Queen and other noblemen entertained the Duke for a quarter of an hour until it was announced that we should enter the chamber of the King [the privy chamber].

Pedro de Gant was mortified when only two Spanish nobles were permitted to accompany Najera 'and no one else, nor did they permit us even to see the King'.[7]

*

As the future King's uncle, the Earl of Hertford was one of the most important men at court, but he lacked the qualities that made a good political leader. By 1544, he had alienated many: Norfolk, Gardiner and Wriothesley had long been his enemies, but he had also managed, through his high-handedness and lack of tact, to incur the enmity of most members of his own faction. In March, he quarrelled with Lord Russell, whom he accused of failing to act in his interests with the King, concluding that Russell, 'a feigned friend', must bear him 'malice or grudge'. Thanks to the efforts of Paget and Wriothesley, a reconciliation was effected, but resentments still simmered beneath the surface.[8]

It was as well, therefore, that, in the spring, Hertford – on Norfolk's recommendation – was given joint command with Lisle of the King's armies and sent north to force the Scots to agree to the proposed marriage alliance; after they had sacked Edinburgh and ruthlessly laid waste the Scottish lowlands, the campaign became known as 'England's rough wooing'.

On 22 April, Lord Audley died. The following month, the able but unscrupulous Wriothesley was chosen to replace him as Lord Chancellor, and was invested with the Great Seal of England by the King in a ceremony in the privy chamber. Henry perhaps chose Wriothesley because he knew him to be vigorously opposed to heresy, and because he hoped this would counterbalance the influence of the powerful reformist party. His appointment came at a time when Gardiner's supremacy had been weakened as a result of his having shielded his papist nephew, Germain Gardiner, from prosecution. After Germain had been executed, Suffolk persuaded the King to proceed against Gardiner as a traitor, but the Bishop's friends in the Privy Chamber, 'suspecting the matter, sent him word thereof'. Gardiner hurried to the King, confessed all, begged for forgiveness, and was pardoned.[9] This is a typical example of Henry playing off one faction against the other.

In 1544, the King conceived the idea of an English Litany, and commanded Archbishop Cranmer to prepare it. The ultimate result, which Henry did not live to see, would be the beautifully written Book of Common Prayer, still used on occasions by the Church of England today. In May, the Queen published a book called *Psalm Prayers*, selected and paraphrased by herself, which was printed by Thomas Berthelet and bound with gilded leather. Her Almoner, George Day, was to use it regularly.

Henry was determined to lead the invasion of France himself, and as the time for his departure drew near, he seemed to be invested with a new zest for life. There were a few details that needed to be attended to before he left, however. At the end of June, he and the Queen were present at the wedding of his niece Lady Margaret Douglas to Matthew Stewart, 4th Earl of Lennox, in the chapel royal at St James's Palace. This marriage had been arranged because Lennox was one of the few Scots peers who supported Henry's plan to ally the two kingdoms under Tudor rule. After the wedding, Lennox returned to Scotland to plot on Henry's behalf, but was discovered, attainted and exiled to England, where he lived with his wife at Temple Newsham House near Leeds. Their first son, born there in 1546, was named after the King.[10]

On 7 July, Henry appointed Katherine Parr Regent of England in his absence, and settled upon her the manors of Hanworth, Chelsea and Mortlake.[11] Hertford, who would have preferred to make peace with France, was to remain in England and serve in a subordinate role as Lieutenant of the Realm; he later joined the King at Boulogne.

On the 14th, Henry sailed for Calais, having made detailed plans for the campaign and sent ahead maps and instructions for his captains. His broad knowledge of fortifications, projectile warfare and military strategy would serve his armies well. His armour had been burnished to perfection by his Master Armourer, Erasmus Kyrkenar.[12] The war was popular with his courtiers, many of whom had already received knighthoods and prestigious military commands and so had a vested interest in it.

Privately briefed by Chapuys, Charles V had been certain that Henry's bad leg and unwieldy bulk would prove drawbacks, but the King was feeling reinvigorated at the prospect of taking the field again, and displayed much of his old energy, riding from Calais into French territory at the head of his army, 'armed at all pieces upon a great courser', with a heavy musket laid across his saddle; behind rode an officer carrying the royal helm and lance. Henry's gun and lance were later displayed in the Tower armoury, and those who saw them marvelled that any man could lift a lance of such huge dimensions. At the siege of Boulogne which followed, Henry remained active from dawn until dusk. Prior to his departure, Hertford had found him 'merry, and in as good health as I have seen His Grace at any time this seven year',[13] while Chapuys confessed himself staggered by Henry's unexpected stamina.[14] From England, the Queen wrote, 'I rejoice at the joyful news of your good health.' Nevertheless, it was quite an operation to winch Henry, in full armour, onto his horse, and during the siege of Boulogne his leg became so painful that his armour had to be cut away to relieve the pressure.

While Henry was in France, he exchanged regular and affectionate letters with Katherine, who was staying at Hampton Court with his children. She kept him up to date with news of their progress, assuring him they were all, 'thanks be to God, in good health', and asked for his approval for the replacement of certain ladies of her household 'that cannot well give their attendance by reason of sickness'. Henry felt that the substitutes she had suggested were in equally frail health and not really suitable for royal service, 'yet we remit the accepting of them to your own choice. You may, if you think so good, take them into your chamber to pass some time with you at play or otherwise to accompany you for your recreation.'

There was another outbreak of plague in London that summer, so the Queen and her stepchildren departed on a short progress, staying at Enfield en route for Oakham Castle, where they were the guests of the Countess of Rutland, who was thrown into a panic at the prospect of their coming and begged her father to send her fresh fish, 'as here is small store, and the court is merry!'[15] No one who had been in contact with the plague was permitted anywhere near anyone from the court, 'under the Queen's indignation and further punishment at her pleasure'.[16] Fortunately, this was a mild epidemic, and Katherine was able to return to Greenwich in August.

While the King acted as Commander-in-Chief, the redoubtable Duke of Norfolk, aged seventy-one, served as Lieutenant-General of the army in France, and Suffolk, now sixty, was given command of the forces that besieged Boulogne, amongst whom were the Gentlemen Pensioners. John Dudley, Lord Lisle, also distinguished himself during the campaign, enhancing his already formidable reputation as a soldier. Surrey, who had seen active service in the Emperor's army the previous year and had rashly exposed himself to enemy fire so as to boost his chivalrous reputation,[17] served as Marshal when Norfolk besieged Montreuil, and again made a bid for glory, narrowly escaping death when he led what was meant to be a decisive assault on the town. His rival, Sir Thomas Seymour, served as Lord High Admiral. The artist Girolamo da Treviso was killed during the siege of Boulogne, where he was employed as a military engineer.

Boulogne fell on 14 September, followed soon afterwards by Montreuil. A sword made for Henry by the Spanish craftsman Diego de Çayas, in commemoration of his victory at Boulogne, is still in the Royal Collection at Windsor.

The campaigning season over, the King returned in triumph to England on 30 September. On his way home, he was reunited with the Queen at Leeds Castle in Kent and held a meeting of the Privy Council there, at which the Emperor's special envoys formally took their leave of him. His glazier Galyon Hone had made decorative glass for the banqueting hall, private apartments and chapel in readiness for this visit.[18] Henry then spent what was left of the autumn hunting.

61

'The Worst Legs in the World'

Around 1544–5, the famous Whitehall family group portrait, a masterful piece of dynastic propaganda, was painted by an unknown artist. At the centre is the dominating figure of the King, enthroned in a magnificent setting with a richly decorated battened ceiling, wall panelling and pillars embellished with antique grotesque work, a painted floor and an embroidered cloth of estate. Prince Edward stands at his knee, while to the right sits, not Katherine Parr, but Jane Seymour, who had borne the King an heir; her figure was probably copied from Holbein's mural. On the far left stands the Lady Mary, and on the far right the Lady Elizabeth. Through two open arched doorways to either side of the dais can be caught tantalising glimpses of the Great Garden of Whitehall with the King's Beasts mounted on columns, and in the background the Lady Mary's lodging with its grotesque decoration, the Westminster Clockhouse, a turret of the great close tennis court, and part of the north transept of Westminster Abbey, as well as the figures of a man and a woman who are thought to represent Will Somers and Jane the Fool. The picture was probably painted for the presence chamber at Whitehall, where it is known to have been hanging in 1586–7.[1]

The image of the King in this picture derives directly from Holbein, and is intended to show a great ruler at the zenith of his power. But other representations of Henry dating from the last years of his reign show a prematurely aged and bloated human being. One of the best-known portrait types from these years is that at Castle Howard, which is one of several versions of a lost portrait by Holbein and dated 1542. The King faces forwards, in the pose adopted for the Whitehall mural, but his face is fatter and he leans on a staff. Other versions are at Hever Castle, the National Portrait Gallery and St Bartholomew's Hospital, London.

Cornelis Matsys, who lived and worked in Antwerp, made an engraving of the King in 1544.[2] This is one of the most famous yet grotesque depictions of Henry VIII in later life, with its slitted eyes and heavy jowls, but it may not have been taken from life, since there is no record of Matsys ever visiting England. A medal of Henry wearing a skull-cap and bonnet, which is of more realistic proportions yet still shows a bloated, ageing face, is perhaps a better representation.[3]

The King had more leisure for his intellectual interests during his latter years, since his bad leg and huge bulk did not permit him to indulge as frequently as hitherto in the physical pursuits he had once loved. Confined more often to his secret lodgings, he read extensively and made prolific marginal notes. His accounts record payments for books, calendars, almanacs, writing paper and a globe.[4] He now needed spectacles – known then as 'gazings' – for reading, and ordered ten pairs at a time from craftsmen in Germany. The frames were made of gold or silver and clipped onto the nose rather than the ears, while the lenses, cut from rock crystal, came from specialists in Venice.

Between March and June 1545, Henry was ill again. He had 'a burning fever for several days, and subsequently the malady attacked the leg'.[5] He remained behind closed doors and the true state of his health was deliberately not made public, but there was naturally speculation, and Gardiner expressed the fear that the King would not live until 'my Lord Prince may come to man's estate'.[6]

When Henry finally did emerge, he told Chapuys that he had felt 'ten times better in France' than he had since his return. The ambassador was shocked to see him 'much broken down' and very depressed. He spent his days in his chair, locked in melancholy, dressing only to attend Mass and sometimes rousing himself to play cards with Hertford or Lisle.[7] Henry was having to come to terms with the fact that he would be a semi-invalid for the rest of his life, a bitter prospect for a man who had once been such an active and renowned sportsman. He lamented the fact that time 'is of all losses the most irrecuperable, for it can never be redeemed for no manner price nor prayer'.[8]

Exacerbated by inactivity and pain, the King's temper became more irascible than usual, and he was 'often of one mind in the morning and of quite another after dinner'.[9] Yet soon his iron will asserted itself, and he would force himself to carry on as normal, riding out, hunting, hawking and playing bowls as often as his health permitted, and moving from house to house with relentless frequency. Chapuys thought it remarkable that he could get about at all, since he had 'the worst legs in the world' and was now of very weak constitution.[10]

This is borne out by the fact that more and more apothecaries were employed to assist the King's Gentleman Apothecary, Thomas Alsop, during the years 1540–6. Sometimes, apothecaries from outside the court were paid to make up medicines for the King. Expenditure on these preparations rose steadily.[11] It was the apothecaries who determined what he should be given, rather than the physicians, whose role was now subordinate. The latter's task was to monitor Henry's health, measuring his urine against his fluid intake and examining his stools. It is fortunate that none of his medical staff resorted to the drastic, painful and usually useless remedies employed by some Tudor doctors, although it is clear that they could do little to relieve his symptoms. 'At the last, by reason of his sore leg, the anguish whereof began more and more to increase, he waxed sickly, and therewithal froward and difficult to be pleased.'[12] When he was in this mood, those around him knew 'it was high time for us to get clear of him, in order to avoid offending him or irritating him further, having regard to his malady'.[13]

The King's doctors, being so frequently in attendance, were now amongst the most influential people at court, and none more so than Sir William Butts, in whom Henry had special confidence. Butts was a great evangelical and perhaps a closet Protestant, and is known to have used his influence to protect others of like mind. Once, when Henry was determined to punish one Richard Turner, a young reformist, for inciting a Kentish community to anti-papist demonstrations, Butts waited until the King was having his beard trimmed, and 'with some pleasant conceits to refresh and solace' him, 'pleasantly and merrily insinuated unto the King the effect of the matter'; after which Henry 'so altered his mind that, whereas before he commanded the said Turner to be whipped out of the country, he now commanded him to be retained as a faithful subject'.[14] Butts exercised vast powers of patronage, being sought out by clients who wanted their suits laid before the King, but he remained discreet and entirely trustworthy. During these final years, it was to Butts, Cranmer and Somers, more than anyone else, that Henry confided his secrets and unburdened his mind.

Chapuys was also in very poor health, due to gout, and had to be carried about in a chair. In May 1545, he told the King he would shortly be departing from England for good. Soon afterwards, as he sat enjoying the sunshine in the garden facing the Queen's lodgings at Whitehall, Katherine Parr approached with her ladies and told him how sorry she was to hear that he was leaving, for Henry had told her 'that I had always performed my duties well, and the King trusted me; but on the other hand, she doubted not that my health would be better on the other side of the sea'. The Queen insisted on taking him to say farewell to the Lady Mary, whose champion he had been for so many years. During his retirement, Chapuys would keep abreast of affairs in England and write succinct and insightful commentaries on them.[15] Soon after his departure, the Emperor replaced him with a new ambassador, Francis van der Delft.

The war between England and France continued. Hertford had been left in command at Boulogne, and in January, using brilliant military tactics, had successfully repelled an onslaught by the French.[16] Later that year, Henry was to replace him with Norfolk and give him a command in the North against the obdurate Scots.

In July, French ships harried the south coast. The King went down to Portsmouth to review his fleet and oversee operations. On the 19th, as the French lay off the Isle of Wight, Henry was standing on the battlements of Southsea Castle, watching the *Great Harry* lead his ships out of the Solent to do battle. Suddenly, the *Mary Rose*, with all hands on board, keeled over and sank. More than six hundred men drowned, and their cries could be heard by the horrified King.

'Oh, my gentlemen! Oh, my gallant men!' he exclaimed, then turned to comfort Lady Carew, the wife of Sir George Carew, Vice-Admiral of the Fleet, who had gone down with the stricken ship.[17] The loss of the *Mary Rose* was a terrible blow to Henry, yet despite it the English fleet still managed to trounce the French and send them packing.

Afterwards, Henry departed on a hunting progress, feeling so confident of the 'valour and affection of his subjects' that he could safely leave the defence of his kingdom to them, having arranged for regular reports to be sent to him.[18] He stayed three nights at Nonsuch, inspecting works he had ordered to be carried out in May, when he had complained that the workmen were making slow progress with completing the palace. This time, he was here with the court, and a forest of tents sprang up in the gardens to accommodate everyone, while furnishings and tapestries were brought from Whitehall to make the house fit for the King.

Dwindling funds had brought to a halt the King's passion for property acquisition. The last house Henry acquired was Apethorpe Hall in Northamptonshire, which he purchased from Charles Blount, Lord Mountjoy, in 1543.[19]

On 22 August, whilst the court was at Guildford, the Duke of Suffolk, who had accompanied the King on progress, died unexpectedly. Henry was stricken at the loss of one of his oldest and most loyal friends, and arranged for the Duke to be buried in St George's Chapel, Windsor, at his own expense. He told the Council that, for as long as Suffolk had served him, he had never betrayed a friend or knowingly taken unfair advantage of an enemy. None of those present could say as much, he added, his gaze bearing down on them. Young Henry Brandon, now eleven, succeeded his father as Duke of Suffolk, while the late Duke's widow, Katherine Willoughby, continued to rule over his vast estates in Lincolnshire. William Paulet, Lord St John, Chamberlain of the Household, was promoted to Lord Great Master in Suffolk's place.

Norfolk had taken over Hertford's command in France, but quickly proved so incompetent that the King recalled him and gave him perhaps the most blistering dressing-down of his career, accusing him of acting 'clean discrepant from our commandment', and warning him that in future he must 'study and seek our honour, herein somewhat touched, redubbed'.[20]

Surrey was chosen to replace his father in France. For a year now, the Earl had been occupied with the building of a fine new mansion, Mount Surrey, near Norwich.[21] In September 1545, he was appointed the King's Lieutenant General in charge of all the land and naval forces in France. Once installed at Boulogne, he served the King with such ostentatious valour that both Henry and Paget felt obliged to rebuke him for putting himself at unnecessary risk.[22] The Council were not so impressed by Surrey's lavish overspending, nor by the inefficiency of his administration.[23]

On 6 November 1545, Katherine Parr published her second book, a devotional work entitled *Prayers or Meditations, wherein the Mind is Stirred Patiently to Suffer all Afflictions*, which was printed by Thomas Berthelet. Although strongly evangelical in tone and content, it did not overstep the bounds of orthodoxy, and appeared with the King's full approval. It was very rare in early Tudor England for a woman to publish a book: only seven others did so during the reigns of the first two Tudors.[24] Katherine's book immediately became very popular, especially among her own sex, and went through nineteen editions in the sixteenth century. On the strength of its reputation, the Universities of Oxford and Cambridge both asked the Queen to become their patron, an honour she took pleasure in accepting, and Nicholas Udall dedicated to Katherine his translation of the Gospel of St Luke.

In 1544, Roger Ascham had completed his brilliant satirical treatise *Toxophilus*, which was ostensibly about archery – 'a pastime honest for the mind, wholesome for the body, fit for every man, vile for no man' – yet also contained a pithy summation of the state of the realm and a plea for English to replace Latin as the language of humanism. Ascham had long hoped to present his work to the King, but the French war had intervened, and it was not until 1545 that he obtained – probably through the good offices of his friend and patron, Sir Anthony Denny – an audience with Henry, who received him in the gallery at Greenwich and 'did so well like' the book that he immediately awarded Ascham a pension of £10 (£3,000), thus opening the way to further court patronage.

Henry – and the reformists – lost another supportive friend in November 1545 when Sir William Butts died. Dr Thomas Wendy replaced him, but he lacked the intellectual stature of Butts, whose ministrations were greatly missed when, in the winter, the King suffered yet another bout of illness. Van der Delft reported on Christmas Eve that he was 'so unwell that, considering his age and corpulence, fears are entertained that he will be unable to survive further attacks'.[25]

Nevertheless, on that same day, the King went to Westminster and addressed Parliament for what was to prove the last time. With unusual humility, he thanked the Speaker for his speech reminding him of his duty as sovereign, 'which is to endeavour myself to obtain and get such excellent qualities and necessary virtues as a prince or governor ought to have, of which gifts I recognise myself both bare and barren. But for such small qualities as God has endowed me with, I render to His goodness my most humble thanks.' After complaining that 'that most precious jewel, the Word of God, is now disputed, rhymed, sung and jangled in every alehouse and tavern', he exhorted his subjects, 'Be in charity one with another, like brother and brother. Love, dread and serve God, the which I, as your sovereign lord, exhort and require you; and then I doubt not but that love and league shall never be dissolved nor broken between us.'[26] His speech had a profound impact on his listeners: one MP commented, 'To us that have not heard him often, it was such a joy and marvellous comfort as I reckon this day one of the happiest of my life.'[27]

It was in 1545 that, so as not to weary the ailing King with routine business, a 'dry stamp' bearing his signature was brought into use, for validating official documents.[28] The stamp left an imprint of the royal signature, which was inked in by persons authorised to forge it, namely Sir Anthony Denny, Sir William Herbert, Sir William Paget, Sir John Gates and William Clerk, all trusted members of the Privy Chamber. Only three of these men were permitted to use the stamp at any one time, while the other two were designated to act as witnesses. Initially, the King himself kept the stamp, but he later gave it, in its black bag, to Gates for safe-keeping.[29]

62

'Painful Service'

On 1 January 1546, the antiquary John Leland presented Henry VIII with 'A New Year's Gift', a written summary of his researches into the treasures of England's religious houses and the antiquities of England. 'I have conserved many good authors,' he wrote in his dedication, 'the which otherwise had been like to have perished; of the which, part remain in the most magnificent libraries of your royal palaces.' Henry had already rewarded Leland with ecclesiastical offices, but the antiquary preferred to stay in London and preserve his links with the court whilst writing up his notes. Sadly, his mind gave way under the strain of his work and he became insane. Death came mercifully quickly the following year.[1]

Another of Henry's New Year's gifts was the Lady Elizabeth's elegant translation into Latin, French and Italian of Katherine Parr's *Prayers and Meditations*.

That January, the King appointed Cranmer to head an ecclesiastical commission to examine the validity of certain church ceremonies, himself recommending that several time-hallowed rituals be abolished as superstitious and smacking of papistry, among them the ringing of bells on the Eve of All Souls and 'the greater abuse of creeping to the Cross on Good Friday'. However, after Gardiner wrote a long letter to Henry protesting about the changes, the King changed his mind. When Sir Anthony Denny presented the final list to him for signing, Henry declined to do so. 'I am now otherwise resolved,' he said.[2] To the end, he would uphold his own brand of orthodoxy.

It was now that, thanks to the influence of Katherine Parr and John Cheke, Henry finally gave his attention to the universities, which had suffered during the Reformation. At Oxford, he refounded Wolsey's Cardinal College and renamed it Christ Church. The college, which was to teach theology, Greek and Hebrew, was more richly endowed than any of its rivals, and its chapel was to serve as a cathedral for the newly founded See of Oxford. The first Dean was Dr Richard Cox, Prince Edward's tutor, and the King himself was to act as Visitor. At Cambridge, Henry founded and endowed Trinity College, replacing three mediaeval colleges, Michaelhouse, King's Hall and the Physwick Hostel. Henry's statue may still be seen above the entrance gate to Trinity College. Back in 1540, he had endowed five Regius professorships at Cambridge in Greek, Hebrew, civil law, divinity and medicine.

Henry's courtiers, who had been covetous of university land since the Dissolution, 'gaped after' the extent of the landed endowments that he gave to his colleges; but he rebuked them, saying, 'I tell you, Sirs, that I judge no land in England better bestowed than that which is given to our universities, for by their maintenance our realm shall be well-governed when we be dead and rotten.'[3]

Early in 1546, Surrey, acting with his usual rashness, lost fourteen of his captains and several English standards to the French in a skirmish at St Étienne outside Bolougne. In a wrathful mood, Henry summoned him home and replaced him, to his bitter and loudly expressed chagrin, with his enemy, Hertford. Paget urged Surrey to seek a lesser post in which he might redeem his honour, but the hotheaded Earl ignored this wise advice, and plotted instead how to wreak vengeance on Hertford.[4]

In February, the King was again laid low with a fever, which confined him to his apartments for three weeks. By 10 March, he was out of bed and losing money at cards to Lisle and others.[5] Soon afterwards, making light of his weakness, he announced that he intended shortly to visit the furthest parts of his realm, and when he met with envoys from Charles V on the 22nd he told them that, although his leg was still a little painful, his strong constitution had aided his recovery. His face, however, bore the hallmarks of suffering, and the envoys concluded that his illness had been worse than he pretended.[6]

The Queen spent these weeks nursing her husband; she may also have been writing her new devotional work, a 120-page book entitled *The Lamentations of a Sinner*, in which she depicted the King as Moses, leading his people out of 'captivity and bondage'. Henry, she asserted, had shown her a holier way of existence and delivered her from 'the ignorance of her blind life'. In placing the emphasis on personal faith, the Queen was edging dangerously close to the Protestant ethos, which may be why the book was never printed during Henry's lifetime. Eventually published in 1548, it was to become Katherine's most famous work.

Katherine's enemies in the conservative faction had long suspected her of heresy. Above all, they resented and feared her influence with the King and the Prince of Wales. It was now becoming clear that Henry would not live to see Edward attain his majority, and the rival factions were girding their loins for a power struggle over the regency. Gardiner, Wriothesley and their Catholic followers were determined to purge the court of heresy, and were even prepared to eliminate the Queen, just as Cromwell had got rid of Anne Boleyn when she became a threat to his position. In the case of Katherine Parr, the conservatives had no doubt that evidence of heresy could be found, if they were watchful.

Matters played into their hands. During Lent, Norfolk's younger son, Lord Thomas Howard, took exception to the orthodox themes of the sermons by the royal chaplains, and openly criticised them 'in the Queen's chamber and elsewhere in the court'. Hauled before the Privy Council, he was given a severe reprimand.[7] In May, a fashionable court preacher, Dr Edward Crome, who was also a leading member of a secret Protestant circle based in London, was arrested for heresy. Under interrogation, he revealed the names of his associates, amongst whom were several courtiers and a Lincolnshire woman, Anne Askew. Anne, a self-confessed Protestant, had connections at court and was acquainted with some of the Queen's ladies, and the conservatives were convinced that she could give them useful evidence about Katherine Parr. When Anne refused to talk, she was put on the rack, and when she bravely maintained her silence and the Lieutenant of the Tower refused to torture her further, Lord Chancellor Wriothesley and Sir Richard Rich themselves turned the wheel, but to no avail. Anne was returned to prison, her body broken but her integrity intact.

Dr Crome had named several members of the Privy Chamber, and in June, Gardiner had them all arrested, namely Surrey's friend, the poet Sir George Blagge, a page, Master Wourley, a Sewer, John Lassels, who had been instrumental in bringing about Katherine Howard's fall, and one William Morice. The King was 'sore offended' when he learned that Blagge had been arrested without his knowledge and sentenced to burn for heresy, for he had a great affection for the young fool, whom he had nicknamed his 'pig'. Summoning Wriothesley forthwith, he berated him 'for coming so near him, even to his Privy Chamber', and made him draw up a pardon there and then. When he next saw Blagge, Henry cried, 'Ah, my pig! Are you safe again?'

'Yes, Sire,' answered Blagge, 'and if Your Majesty had not been better than your bishops, your pig had been roasted ere this time!'[8]

The conservatives next attempted to accuse Sir Anthony and Lady Denny of heresy, but without success. The Queen was another matter.

Early in July, Henry was again in low spirits. On the 4th, 'although dressed to go to mass, he did not go, nor did he go into his gardens, as his habit is in the summer'.[9] Two days later, he moved from Greenwich to Whitehall, then fell 'ill with colic'.[10] Since the conservatives were now in the ascendant, he had with him Gardiner, Wriothesley, Norfolk, Paulet, Petre and Sir Anthony Browne.

According to the Elizabethan writer John Foxe, who is the only source for what is said to have happened next, the Queen angered Henry one day by becoming too opinionated whilst they were debating a theological matter. When Katherine had gone, Henry grumbled to Gardiner that it was 'nothing much to my comfort in mine old days to be taught by my wife'. Gardiner sympathised, then took a great risk in venturing to suggest that the Queen might be harbouring views of which Henry would not approve. The King gave him permission to investigate further: the books in Katherine's closet were examined, and her ladies questioned. They gave away nothing, so Wriothesley obtained Henry's signature on a warrant for Katherine's arrest, in order for her to be questioned also. Fortuitously, the warrant fell from the pocket of a Councillor's gown and was found by a member of the Queen's household, who took it straight to her. Horrified at what it portended, Katherine took to her bed and began screaming in panic. In his apartments, the King heard her hysterical cries and sent his physician, Dr Wendy, to discover what was wrong. When Katherine told him, he urged her to compose herself and dress, then go to the King and plead for forgiveness.

Katherine took his advice. She told Henry that, if she had dared dispute with one whom Nature had so patently formed for superiority, it was only to divert him in his illness. 'Is that so, sweetheart?' asked a mollified Henry. 'Then we are perfect friends again.'

The next day, as the King and Queen sat together in the privy garden, Lord Chancellor Wriothesley arrived with a detachment of guards to arrest the Queen. Henry rose angrily, soundly berated him, and beat him about the head, shouting, 'Arrant knave! Beast! Fool!' The Chancellor made a hasty and somewhat undignified exit.[11]

Foxe's tale sounds contrived, yet it was characteristic of Henry to behave in this way, testing the loyalty of those around him and playing them off against each other, much as he had done in the past with Cranmer and Gardiner.

Katherine Parr was safe, but Anne Askew and John Lassels were not so lucky. On 16 July, they were burned at Smithfield.

The collapse of the plot against the Queen, and the return to court of Hertford in June, signalled the end of the conservatives' brief period of ascendancy, and also brought to a halt the witch-hunt for heretics. Soon afterwards, Hertford formed a powerful alliance with Lord Lisle. Their ultimate aim was to secure control of the government after the King's death, and to this end they took care to lean 'neither on one side or the other' of the religious divide.[12] Both owed their power to their military achievements, while Hertford was in a strong position as the uncle of the future King. Supported by the influential and efficient Paget, who until the summer had appeared to favour the conservative faction,[13] they formed a formidable coalition.

Norfolk, careful of his own interests and aware that his influence was dwindling, now swallowed his pride and attempted to ally himself with the Seymour faction. But, having obtained the King's approval for a marriage between his daughter Mary, Richmond's widow, and Sir Thomas Seymour, the Duke met with furious opposition from his son, Surrey, who also refused to countenance a match between one of his own daughters and Hertford's son. Nor was Mary Howard in favour of the marriage proposed for her. However, Surrey believed he could use it to his family's advantage, and told Mary that, when the King sent for her to congratulate her on her betrothal, she should use her feminine wiles on him, become his mistress and wield as much influence upon him 'as Madame d'Étampes doth about the French King'. Mary was outraged and cried that she would 'cut her own throat' rather than 'consent to such a villainy'.[14] At this, she and her brother fell out, a rift that was to have tragic consequences.

Because of his failing health, the King now spent most of his time in the privacy of his secret lodgings, 'and used seldom, being not well at ease, to stir out of his chamber', unless it was to walk in his privy gardens. His temper was now more volatile than ever, for his legs gave him so much pain 'that he became exceedingly perverse and intractable',[15] and was inclined to lash out on the slightest provocation. Apart from his Gentlemen and Chamber servants, the only persons admitted to see him were the Queen, selected Councillors 'by special commandment', and, on occasion, foreign ambassadors. Henry did not want the world, or indeed the courtiers who waited outside in the presence chamber, to think he was losing his grasp on affairs.

But speculation about his health was rife, while those close to him wondered how many more physical crises he could survive. Yet he would not give in, 'was loath to hear any mention of death',[16] and behaved as if he still had many years ahead of him, ignoring the pain in his legs and bravely driving himself to lead as normal a life as possible. Addressing the problem of mobility, he had two invalid 'chairs called trams' made for him, 'for the King's Majesty to sit in to be carried to and fro in his galleries and chambers at Whitehall'. One was covered in quilted tawny velvet, the other in gold velvet and silk, and both had embroidered foot-rests and shafts like sedan chairs. They were kept with the King's maps and pictures in his 'secret study', which now became known as the 'chairhouse'.[17]

According to the chronicler Edward Hall, 'the King was now overgrown with corpulency and fatness, so that he became more and more unwieldy. He could not go up or down stairs unless he was raised up or let down by an engine.' Norfolk, too, claimed that Henry 'could not go up and down the stairs, and was let up and down by a device',[18] and although there is no record of any mechanical pulley, hoist or lift in any of his palaces, this does not mean that such a contraption did not exist.

It was clear to his advisers that the King could not last long, and the power struggle for the regency intensified, with each faction competing for supremacy. According to the new imperial ambassador Francis van der Delft, self-interest and fear held men together.[19] The conflict was bitter, and the mounting tension such that heated quarrels were liable to break out on the slightest pretext. Nor would the matter be resolved until blood had been shed.

In one camp were Hertford, Lisle, Paget, Denny, Gates, Essex and other reformists; in the other were Gardiner, Wriothesley, Rich, Norfolk, Surrey, the ailing Browne and their conservative partisans. The Seymour–Dudley party was easily the dominant faction, and Chapuys and others were of the opinion that no one was fitter or better suited to govern the Prince than his uncle Hertford,[20] but the opposition was not giving in without a fight. Surrey, however, seemed to have his own agenda, and in some ways to have lost touch with reality: he struck Lisle, insulted Rich and warned that Hertford would 'smart' for usurping his command in France.[21] He also fell out with George Blagge, who opposed Surrey's obsessive determination to gain control of the Prince after the King's death. In Surrey's opinion, Norfolk was the man best suited to be Edward's guardian. Blagge said he would rather stab Surrey than see the government in the hands of the Howards.[22]

Hertford was suspected by many, with good reason, of holding radical views, and in September 1546, van der Delft expressed concern about the number of his clients and supporters that were constantly about the King.[23] Hertford was on poor terms with everyone except Lisle and Paget, and at particular loggerheads with Wriothesley, who had switched factions as soon as he realised the conservatives were losing ground. In October, Lisle struck Gardiner during a fierce dispute 'in full Council meeting', and was expelled from the court, but in November he was back, unrepentant; soon afterwards he and Hertford were overheard using 'violent and opprobrious' words against Gardiner and Wriothesley.[24]

The King struggled to maintain control over the warring factions, but his refusal to confront the issue at stake only exacerbated the tension. Each Councillor was fearful lest his enemies should try to blind Henry's eyes 'with mists' or calumny.[25] The court began to seethe with mounting anxiety, which was tangible to both the French and Spanish ambassadors, who found their sources of information drying up as men refused to talk to them, fearing accusations of treasonable plotting.[26]

The last important state pageant of the reign took place in August 1546, when Claud d'Annebaut, Lord High Admiral of France, came to England with two hundred gentlemen to ratify a treaty of peace between England and France. Because of the King's infirmity, Prince Edward, with an escort of eight gold-clad gentlemen and eighty Yeomen of the Guard, rode out to greet the Admiral at Hounslow. The French were impressed no less by the boy's horsemanship than by his Latin speech of welcome, which radiated 'high wit and great audacity'.

Having conducted the Admiral to Hampton Court, where he was received by Lord Chancellor Wriothesley and the Privy Council, Edward was to deputise for his father on several occasions during the ten days of receptions, banquets, masques, dances and hunting trips that followed, and would also show off his skill on the lute.[27] The Admiral's retinue were accommodated in tents of cloth of gold and velvet in the palace gardens, where two new banqueting houses had been erected and hung with tapestries threaded with gold and jewels.

On the second morning of the visit, d'Annebaut was received by the King in the presence chamber and accompanied him to Mass in the chapel royal. Another time, the King was present at an open-air reception, standing under a marquee, but observers noticed him leaning heavily on the shoulders of the Admiral and Archbishop Cranmer. He is said to have startled the Admiral by suggesting that 'the mass in both realms' be changed 'into a communion service'.[28] It sounded as if the King was flirting with Lutheranism, but he was probably just being provocative. Alternatively the tale could be retrospective wishful thinking on the part of the man who wrote it, John Foxe.

At the end of their stay, the French were sent home with fine gifts of plate, horses and dogs.[29] Prince Edward then stayed briefly at Durham House before taking up residence at Hunsdon, where he was to remain for much of the rest of the year.[30]

The King departed on his usual hunting progress, but he did not go beyond the Thames Valley and kept to 'houses remote from towns'. He stayed firstly at Oatlands, where he shot from a standing as the deer were driven past him, and on one occasion rode with the hounds after a stag at Chertsey, shooting with darts and spears. For three days he was 'always at the chase'.[31] A ramp had been built at Oatlands to enable him to mount his horse with ease, while the mounting blocks had been raised at other palaces.[32] Later in August, Henry was hunting at Chobham, Surrey, where his courtiers were housed in tents.[33] In September he set out for Guildford, but his exertions had been too much for him, and he was forced to retire to Windsor. The progress was abandoned.

Wriothesley announced that the King had a cold, but van der Delft later discovered that he had actually been in 'great danger' and that the royal physicians had given up 'all hope of recovery'.[34] Yet against the odds, Henry recovered once more. By early October, he was out hunting and hawking again, and as much in command of affairs as ever. He received van der Delft at Windsor and, on learning that the ambassador himself had been ill, offered him the services of his own physician. However, he was not well enough to give audience to the new French ambassador, Odet de Selve, and Paget had to deputise for him.[35]

In October, Sir Anthony Denny succeeded Sir Thomas Heneage as Groom of the Stool. Heneage had served the King for twenty years, and the reasons for his dismissal are unclear; he appears to have left court under a cloud.

Denny was now in daily close proximity to the King, and in overall control of the Privy Chamber, the secret lodgings and the dry stamp, and his influence became dominant during the closing months of the reign. Whichever faction he supported was likely to gain control of the regency, and he was a close ally of the Seymours. Denny's job was no sinecure, however. After Henry's death, Paget referred to his 'painful service',[36] indicating that his dealings with the ailing King had not been easy or pleasant. But Denny had the support of his brother-in-law, Sir John Gates, who carried out his orders and bullied the rest of the Privy Chamber into submission. Gates was also Keeper of Pyrgo Park at Havering, where he resided, when not at court, in regal luxury. Gates's subordinates were William Clerk, who also had authority to use the dry stamp, and an accountant, Nicholas Bristow.

Paget, Hertford's friend and mentor, was also enormously influential. As Principal Secretary to the King, he controlled all the letters and information entering and leaving the privy lodgings, and was in overall control of the government when Henry was ill. It was Paget who helped forge the alliance between Denny and the Seymour faction, which made Hertford, the potential future *de facto* ruler, the most important man at court. Paget boasted of his own confidential relationship with the King, asserting that Henry 'opened his pleasure to me alone in many things'. However, Denny and Sir William Herbert insisted that Henry would always, 'when Mr Secretary was gone, tell us what had passed between them'.[37] This was yet another instance of Henry's policy of divide and rule.

The conservative faction was dealt a blow in November when Gardiner, who as recently as August had been described by van der Delft as one of the King's chief advisers,[38] incurred Henry's displeasure by refusing to exchange some episcopal lands with him. When Henry barred him from entering the privy chamber, Gardiner concluded that Hertford had been working against him, and blamed him for his exclusion. He asked Paget to intercede for him, but the King refused to grant him an audience.

In the middle of November, Henry moved to Whitehall to take 'preparative medicine for certain medicinal baths which he usually has at this season'.[39] Gardiner haunted the outward chambers of the palace, but Henry still would not see him, and he was reduced to ensuring that he was seen in the company of Councillors who were in favour, so that people should not know of his disgrace. On 2 December, he wrote to the King, craving an audience and offering to agree to the exchange of lands after all, but a terse note in reply informed him that His Majesty could see 'no cause why you should molest us further' and instructed him to arrange the transfer of property through government officials in London. The letter bore the sign manual, or dry stamp, and had been witnessed by Denny and Gates.[40] Gardiner would probably have been correct in concluding that his enemies were working to destroy him.

Soon afterwards, Henry went to stay at Oatlands.[41] There were rumours in London about his failing health,[42] but he was out taking exercise on 7 December. However, it would be for the last time.

63

'The Rarest Man that Lived in His Time'

On 10 December 1546, whilst he was still at Oatlands, Henry was laid low with a fever, and for thirty hours his doctors battled to keep him alive.[1] To their relief, he rallied, and when van der Delft next saw him, he told the ambassador he was completely recovered; but van der Delft could see from his appearance that he was a sick man. His face was ashen, his body 'greatly fallen away', and although he was up and dressed, he was very weak. Norfolk had told the ambassador that Henry 'could not long endure'.[2]

'In case any light bruit may rise to the contrary', the Council instructed English ambassadors abroad to give out that the King's fever had been merely the result of 'some grief of his leg'; they were to stress that he was now, 'thanks be to God, well rid of it, and would be better of it [for] a great while'.[3]

With their ambitions about to reach fruition, the Seymour faction now moved to destroy their enemies, the Howards. Van der Delft had no doubt that Hertford and Lisle were the prime movers in the plot against them,[4] and Gates was certainly active in the matter.[5] Norfolk was no real threat to Hertford's supremacy: he was ageing, he had failed to live up to his reputation as a military commander, and he had alienated so many Councillors by telling tales about them to the King that they had used their influence to have him excluded from the inner circle of the Privy Council. Surrey, however, was a real danger, for he had made no secret of his determination to secure the regency and the person of the Prince on the King's death.

Yet this was not all. Surrey's former friend, Sir Richard Southwell, had betrayed him by laying before the Council evidence about the Earl 'that touched his fidelity to the King'. The Duchess of Richmond had revealed that her 'rash' brother had said of the Seymours that 'these new men loved no nobility, and if God called away the King they should smart for it'. Then she added the most damaging testimony of all: that Surrey had replaced the coronet on his coat of arms with a crown, flanked by the initials HR – for Henricus Rex. Government agents searched Mount Surrey and found armorial glass, paintings and plate bearing the arms of Edward the Confessor, which Surrey claimed he bore by right of descent, even though Garter King of Arms had ruled 'that it was not in his pedigree'.[6] It seemed clear that the Earl had schemed to be king, but it is more likely that he was underlining – in his usual foolish way – his superior claim to head the regency; he had already asked Paget to be Lord Chancellor in his government.[7] Nevertheless, the Council were satisfied that Surrey had conspired to murder them all, depose the King and 'take possession of the kingdom'.[8]

On 12 December, Norfolk was arrested, and Surrey followed him to the Tower the next day, having been apprehended at Whitehall during dinner.[9] While Henry had good cause to proceed against Surrey, 'his inexcusable severity' to Norfolk was hardly justified, but Hall imputes it to the effects of illness and pain. From his prison, Norfolk protested to the Council, 'I have always shown myself a true man to my sovereign,' and added, 'I think surely there is some false man that have laid some great cause to my charge, or else I had not be sent hither. I have had great enemies.'[10]

With the fall of the Howards and Gardiner's disgrace, the conservative faction was finished, leaving Hertford's party in a position of unchallenged dominance, both on the Privy Council and in the Privy Chamber. Van der Delft was in no doubt that 'the custody of the Prince and the government of the realm' would be entrusted to Hertford, who had 'obtained authority with the King'.[11] It was significant that during December and January, Council meetings would be held at Hertford's London house rather than at court.

Once he was able to travel, the King moved in slow stages to London, lodging on the way at Esher, Nonsuch and Wimbledon, before arriving at Whitehall. After making short visits to Ely Place in Holborn and Hampton Court, he stayed at Greenwich for the last time on 22 December, then finally returned to Whitehall, plainly very ill. Whereas, in August, he had paid less than £5 (£1,500) for medicines and sick-room comforts, in December the bill rose to £25 (£7,500).[12] This included purchases of perfume to sweeten his chambers and sheets, 'two pairs of slippers newly devised to warm feet', and a new close stool upholstered in black velvet edged with a black silk fringe, with arms and a lifting seat.[13] The treatments prescribed by Henry's doctors included applications of rosewater and 'eyebright water', ointments for haemorrhoids and the stomach, comfits of cinammon and green ginger, and regular blanket baths by the barber-surgeons.[14]

On Christmas Eve, the Queen and the King's daughters left Whitehall on his orders, to spend Christmas at Greenwich. Prince Edward was at Ashridge in Hertfordshire, and at New Year Katherine sent him a double portrait of herself and the King, urging him to 'meditate upon the distinguished deeds of his father' whenever he looked at it.[15] The Prince wrote Henry a letter in Latin, assuring him he would strive to follow his example 'in virtue, wisdom and piety'.[16] It is unlikely he was aware of how ill the King was.

Henry spent the festive season in total seclusion; the court was closed and only 'a handful of councillors and three or four Gentlemen of the Chamber' were allowed access to the King.[17] They kept at bay those who might exert undesirable influence over him, and ensured that little information about his condition reached the outside world, with the result that we know very little about what was happening to him during these final weeks. Nevertheless, van der Delft, and many others, guessed that Henry was dying: he was said to be 'in great danger', and his physicians were in despair.[18]

Before he left for Boulogne in the summer of 1544, the King had drawn up his Will, in which were enshrined the provisions of the recent Act of Succession. On the evening of 26 December 1546, he summoned Hertford, Paget, Lisle and Denny to his chamber, and asked for the Will to be read to him. He then drew up a list of sixteen Councillors of the reformist persuasion to serve on a Council of Regency, but made it clear that this was to be an equal coalition and that no one man was to wield power. Hertford, Dudley, Paget, Sadler, Cranmer and Russell were included, but Henry refused to have Gardiner because 'he was a wilful man and not meet to be about his son', and of so troublesome a nature that no man but himself could rule him.[19] In choosing the rest, Henry, unwittingly or not, prepared the way for the establishment of a radical Protestant government.

Of course, the King's arrangements for the regency ran contrary to Hertford's expectations. Paget, who was 'privy in the beginning, proceeding and ending of the Will', wrote it out himself, and although it was said to be signed 'with our own hand in our Palace of Westminster' on 30 December in the presence of eleven witnesses, the dry stamp was used, as Paget later admitted.[20] Furthermore, it must have been used after 23 January, because the Will refers to Sir Thomas Seymour as a Privy Councillor, and he was not admitted to the Privy Council until that date. The Will is said to have been given to Hertford on 30 December for safe-keeping, but it appears that Paget had it in a box and Hertford kept the key.[21]

Henry, therefore, did not sign the Will at all; in order to retain control over his Councillors, he may have deferred doing so until the last possible moment, and then left it too late, giving his Councillors no choice but to use the sign manual. It is also possible that, without the King's knowledge, they altered the Will before the dry stamp was applied, but dated it to a day when Henry had been well enough to sign it.[22] However, had this been done, one would have expected the provisions to be more heavily weighted in favour of Hertford's leadership; on the other hand, the motive may have been merely to increase the size of individual bequests. Whatever the circumstances, no one thought to question the validity of the King's Will at the time.

Henry was stricken with fever again on 1 January 1547.[23] On the 8th, there were rumours that he was dead, because, 'whatever amendment is announced, few persons have access to his chamber'.[24] Two days later, the ulcer on his leg had to be cauterised, an agonising process in the days before anaesthetics. De Selve commented, 'Whatever his health, it can only be bad, and [he] will not last long.'[25]

On 10 January, Queen Katherine and the Lady Mary returned to Whitehall. Although Henry was a little better, they were not allowed to see him for the present;[26] it is not clear whether it was Henry, or his doctors, or the Seymour faction who kept them away.

The Queen was not included in the Council of Regency, probably because Henry disapproved of women interfering in politics. However, he left her handsomely provided for, with £3,000 (£900,000) in plate, jewels and furnishings, and £1,000 (£300,000) in cash, in recognition of 'the great love, obedience and chastity of life being in our wife and Queen'.[27]

Surrey was tried at the Guildhall for high treason on 13 January, and spoke up vigorously in his own defence, but his case was prejudiced from the start because, the day before, Norfolk had formally admitted his guilt in concealing his son's treason. The King, although confined to his sickroom, followed reports of the proceedings closely, and noted on one memorandum, 'If a man presume to take unto his arms an old coat of the Crown, which his ancestors never bore, nor he of right ought to bear, can he use it without offence?' Elsewhere, he wrote, 'If a man compassing himself to govern the realm do actually go about to rule the King, and should for that purpose advise his sister to become his harlot, what this imparteth?'[28] It imparted, of course, that Surrey was guilty as charged, and his peers, on receiving a note to that effect from the King, accordingly condemned him to death. A triumphant Hertford was among them. On hearing his fate, Surrey shouted at him, 'The King wants to get rid of the noble blood round him and employ none but low people!'[29]

After the trial, Henry's health improved a little. He ordered French saplings for his garden, evidently hoping to be around to see them grow into trees,[30] and on 17 January he gave audience to both the Spanish and French ambassador and said he was sorry that his incapacity had prevented the speedy dispatch of their business. When van der Delft and de Selve congratulated him on his recovery, he admitted that his suffering had been prolonged and severe. The ambassadors had been warned not to tire him, but he seemed 'fairly well' and in good spirits, and spoke lucidly of international affairs, military matters and a 'closer amity' with France. However, he deferred frequently to Paget, who gave the impression of being better informed.[31] This was to be the last time Henry would appear in public, and henceforth access to his rooms would be severely restricted. But he was not yet at death's door, and on 19 January was planning Prince Edward's investiture as Prince of Wales.[32]

A Bill of Attainder against both Norfolk and Surrey was introduced into Parliament on that day; this would sentence them to forfeit not only their lives, but also their lands and possessions to the Crown. The King told Paget that these would be 'liberally disposed and given to his good servants', and he drew up a list of those who were to benefit, which he 'put in the pocket of his nightgown'; but despite excited speculation in the Privy Chamber, it was never found after his death.[33]

On 21 January, Surrey, who had made a frantic but abortive attempt to escape from the Tower through his privy,[34] was beheaded on Tower Hill.[35]

After 19 January, Henry had had a relapse, and it was now obvious that he was dying. Even his musicians had been dismissed, and it was Paget who sat with him through the long winter nights, deep in conversation.[36] Later, Hertford and other Councillors took their turn.

Clearly, Henry was losing his grip on affairs. On the 23rd, when it was suggested to him that Sir Thomas Seymour be made a Privy Councillor, he cried out from his sick bed, though his breath was failing him, 'No! No!' But Hertford pressurised him into agreeing.[37]

Three days later, his strength ebbing away, Henry summoned the Queen to his bedside. 'It is God's will that we should part,' he began, but was too choked to go on and, weeping, sent her from him.[38] In a less sympathetic mood, he dictated a farewell letter to Francis I, who was dying of syphilis, and reminded him that he too was mortal.[39] Even *in extremis*, the old rivalry simmered.

On 27 January, the dry stamp was applied to the Howards' attainder, the royal assent having been given by commission in the House of Lords, as the King was too ill to attend.[40] Norfolk's execution was set for the following day. But the Duke was not to die, for the King had other, more urgent concerns, and may have decided that enough blood had been spilt. It is often said that Henry died before he could sign the death warrant, but his assent to the Act of Attainder would have been sufficient authority for the execution to go ahead. And if, as Odet de Selve later suggested, Hertford had applied the dry stamp without the King's knowledge, he would surely have seen that the sentence was carried out. So the likelihood must be that Henry ordered that Norfolk be reprieved.[41]

On the morning of 27 January, the King saw his confessor and received holy communion. Later that day, he was well enough to discuss state affairs with his Councillors, but by the evening he was failing fast. The Council, knowing that his death was near, ordered that all the ports be closed.

No one, even his doctors, had as yet plucked up the courage to warn Henry of his imminent demise. He had always been loath to hear any mention of death, and Edward Hall states that 'his servants scarcely dared speak to him to put him in mind of his approaching end, lest he, in his angry and imperious humour, should have ordered them to be indicted', for it was treason to predict the King's death. Yet it was also unthinkable that a man should be denied time to prepare his soul, so Sir Anthony Denny boldly ventured to warn his master that 'in man's judgement, he was not like to live' and should remember his sins, 'as becometh every good Christian man to do'. Henry said he believed that the mercy of Christ would 'pardon me all my sins, yea, though they were greater than they be'.[42]

Denny asked Henry if he would like to speak to any 'learned man'. He replied that 'if he had any, it should be Dr Cranmer, but I will first take a little sleep, and then, as I feel myself, I will advise upon the matter'. These were his last known words. A messenger was at once dispatched to Croydon to summon the Archbishop, but when Cranmer arrived in the early hours of Friday 28 January, the King was beyond speech, and when the primate asked him to give some sign that he died in the faith of Christ, he 'did wring his hand in his as hard as he could'. Cranmer and the Councillors present took this for hearty assent.[43]

Shortly afterwards, at around 2 a.m.,[44] Henry VIII gave up his long struggle and quietly slipped from this world.

The cause of the King's death is uncertain, thanks to the secrecy that surrounded his final illness, but it is likely to have been a pulmonary embolism. For two days his passing was kept secret, and his body lay undisturbed in his bedchamber while outside court life went on as normal, with the King's meals being brought to his lodgings with the usual flourish of trumpets.[45]

On the day Henry died, the Earl of Hertford rode to Hertford Castle to secure the person of the nine-year-old Prince and pay homage to him as King. Once this was accomplished, he sent Paget the key that would unlock the casket containing the old King's Will. The next day, Lord Chancellor Wriothesley, so overcome with weeping that he could barely speak, announced Henry VIII's death to Parliament, where there were great demonstrations of grief. The young Edward VI was brought to the Tower on 31 January, and there proclaimed King, with the heralds crying, 'The King is dead! Long live the King!'

The next day, in defiance of his late master's wishes, Hertford was named Lord Protector and appointed to head the Council of Regency.[46]

Meanwhile, Henry's body had been embalmed and encased in lead, and laid in state in the presence chamber at Whitehall, surrounded by burning tapers. After a few days, it was moved into the chapel.

There were solemn dirges and tolling bells in every parish church in the land, in memory of the late King. In Paris, Francis I ordered a Requiem Mass at Notre Dame. On 14 February, Henry VIII's body began its journey from Whitehall to Windsor, where it was taken in a solemn procession stretching for four miles. Antonio Toto and Nicholas Bellin helped to produce the heraldic escutcheons and painted banners that were carried about the hearse.

The vast coffin, covered with palls of blue velvet and cloth of gold, lay on a chariot drawn by black-caparisoned horses, who drew it along roads that had been swept and even widened for the occasion. On top of the coffin was a wax effigy of the King, carved by Nicholas Bellin and clad in crimson velvet trimmed with miniver; on its head was a crown atop 'a night cap of black satin, set full of precious stones'. It wore jewelled bracelets and velvet gloves adorned with rings. Even in death, Henry was magnificent.

The cortege rested that night at Syon Abbey. The next day, it reached Windsor, where, in accordance with his Will, the King was buried in the vault in the choir of St George's Chapel, next to 'his true and loving wife, Queen Jane', the mother of his heir. Sixteen strong members of the Yeomen of the Guard carried the coffin into the black-draped church and lowered it into the vault. Gardiner, who would not recover royal favour until the reign of Mary I, preached the sermon and conducted the Requiem Mass, while the Queen watched from Katherine of Aragon's closet. At the end of the ceremony, the chief officers of the household signified the termination of their service by breaking their white staves of office and casting them into the vault after the coffin, as the trumpets sounded 'with great melancholy and courage, to the comfort of them that were present'.[47] The King had left money for daily masses for his soul to be said for him at the altar 'while the world should endure',[48] but the new Protestant ruling caste put a stop to them after a year.

The magnificent Renaissance tomb that Henry had taken over from Wolsey was never completed. Work on it ceased with the death of Edward VI in 1553, probably due to lack of funds. It was partially dismantled by the Commonwealth in 1649, and in 1805 the sarcophagus was used as the base of Lord Nelson's tomb in the crypt of St Paul's Cathedral. One candlestick, the only surviving example of the fine metalwork on the tomb, most of which was sold off or melted down under Oliver Cromwell, now reposes in Ghent Cathedral. The chapel which had housed the tomb was completely refurbished by Queen Victoria in memory of the Prince Consort, and is now known as the Albert Memorial Chapel.

Henry VIII's unmarked vault was discovered in 1813, quite by chance; his coffin had partially fallen away, and his skeleton could clearly be seen. Jane Seymour's coffin was undisturbed. Also in the vault was the lost coffin of Charles I and that of an infant of Queen Anne, both placed there in the seventeenth century. In 1837, a slab of black marble was placed on the tomb on the orders of William IV.

Writing in the year of Henry VIII's death, his earliest biographer, the admiring William Thomas, declared that the King

> was undoubtedly the rarest man that lived in his time. I say not this to make him a god, nor in all his doings I will not say he has been a saint. He did many evil things, but not as a cruel tyrant or as a hypocrite. I wot not where in all the histories I have read to find one king equal to him.[49]

Henry was a legend in his own time, and under the reigns of his children, all of whom revered his memory, the legend became embedded in the national consciousness; during Elizabeth's time, 'Great Harry' was especially lauded for having brought the English Church out of the tyranny of Rome. That he had caused intolerable religious divisions, executed hundreds of his subjects,[50] nearly bankrupted his treasury on ruinous wars, destroyed the glories of hundreds of abbeys and churches and debased the coinage of the realm seemed of little import beside such an achievement. And indeed it is true that, besides founding the Church of England and steering his realm courageously through a religious revolution, he promoted parliamentary government, immeasurably enhanced the standing of the monarchy, overhauled the machinery of the state, changed the face of the English landscape for ever, patronised the arts to lasting effect and created the most magnificent court in English history, setting a pattern for future centuries. Henry began his reign in a mediaeval kingdom; he ended it in a modern state.

In the seventeenth century, however, when the long and brilliant reign of the Tudors was over, the verdict of historians on Henry VIII was harsher. Sir Walter Raleigh wrote of him: 'If all the pictures and patterns of a merciless prince were lost in the world, they might all again be painted to the life out of the story of this King.' Since then, Henry VIII has become a caricature of his former self, with the real man submerged beneath the popular image of the bloated, self-willed monster who changed wives and chopped off heads with gleeful alacrity.

Thanks to a wealth of modern research, however, the genuine Henry has been allowed to emerge once more, imperious and autocratic as ever, magnificent in his person, yet all too human in the minutiae of his daily life. After more than four hundred and fifty years his charisma still has the power to intrigue us, and whatever judgement we may make of him, we may well agree with Francesco Chieregato that he excelled all who ever wore a crown.

Abbreviations used in the Notes and References

BL   British Library
CP, ed. Kaulek   *Correspondance politique*, ed. Kaulek
CSP: Milanese   *Calendar of State Papers: Milanese*
CSP: Spanish   *Calendar of State Papers: Spanish*
CSP: Venetian   *Calendar of State Papers: Venetian*
Four Years   *Four Years at the Court of Henry VIII*
Inventory   Inventory of the goods of Henry VIII (see n. 32, p. 507)
L&P   *Letters and Papers of the Reign of Henry VIII*
PPE   *Privy Purse Expenses of Henry VIII*
PRO   *Accounts of the Chamber and the Great Wardrobe* (Public Record Office)

Note: Authors of Primary Sources are listed by their full names; authors of Secondary Sources are listed by surname only.

Notes and References

1. 'A MOST ACCOMPLISHED PRINCE'

1   L&P
2   George Cavendish
3   Erasmus : *Epistles*
4   B. L. Cotton MSS. Titus
5   *CSP: Spanish*
6   Polydore Vergil
7   *CSP: Venetian*
8   *CSP: Milanese*
9   L&P
10 *CSP: Venetian*
11 *CSP: Milanese*
12 *State Papers*
13 L&P
14 George Cavendish
15 Thomas Stapleton
16 cited by Froude: *History of England*
17 *Original Letters* ed. Ellis
18 see John Leland: *Collectanea*
19 Erasmus: *Epistles*
20 *CSP: Venetian*
21 Ibid.
22 cited by Bruce: *The Making of Henry VIII*
23 Erasmus: *Epistles*
24 *CSP: Milanese*
25 William Thomas
26 Erasmus: *Opus Epistolarum*
27 cited by Erickson: *Great Harry*
28 *CSP: Venetian*
29 Ibid.
30 cited by Richardson: *Mary Tudor*
31 William Thomas
32 An inventory of the goods of Henry VIII was drawn up after his death in 1547. The first part, entitled 'The first part of the inventory of the jewels, plate, stuff, ordnance, munitions and other goods belonging to our late sovereign lord King Henry the Eight' comprises MS. 129 of the Society of Antiquaries of London. The

second part is in B.L. Harleian MS. 1419, vols. A and B.

33   *L&P*
34   Now in the National Maritime Museum, Greenwich.
35   Inventory
36   Ibid.
37   B. L. Cotton MSS. Augustus
38   B. L. Royal MSS.
39   Erasmus: *Opus Epistolarum*
40   *CSP: Spanish*
41   Huizinga: *Erasmus*
42   *CSP: Spanish*
43   Ibid.
44   *L&P*
45   *CSP: Spanish*
46   Ibid.

2. 'THE TRIUMPHAL CORONATION'

1   Erasmus: *Opus Epistolarum*
2   Ibid.
3   *CSP: Venetian*
4   Edward Hall
5   *CSP: Spanish*
6   Ibid.
7   Edward Hall
8   *CSP: Spanish*
9   *CSP: Venetian*
10   Ibid.
11   Henry Clifford: *Life of Jane Dormer*
12   *Original documents relating to Queen Katherine of Aragon*
13   *CSP: Spanish*
14   *L&P*
15   Henry Clifford: *Life of Jane Dormer*
16   *Excerpta Historica*; B. L. Additional MSS.
17   *History of the King's Works*
18   William Lambarde
19   John Leland: *Itinerary*
20   see Thurley: *Royal Palaces*
21   *History of the King's Works*
22   Rawlinson MSS., Bodleian Library
23   John Leland: *Itinerary*. Greenwich remained a favourite royal residence until the reign
      of Charles I (1625-49). Under the Commonwealth, the state apartments were turned
      into stables and the palace was allowed to fall into decay. In 1662, Charles II
      demolished most of the remains and began building a new palace on the site, which
      later became the Royal Naval College. Charles II also landscaped Greenwich Park.
      The Tudor great hall survived until 1866, and the chapel, which had been used as a
      store, until the late 19th century. Apart from an undercroft built by James I in 1606
      and one Henry VIII's reservoir buildings of 1515 (now part of The Chantry in Park
      Vista), nothing survives of Greenwich Palace today.
24   cited by Aslet
25   *History of the King's Works*; Newcastle MSS., Nottingham University Library
26   John Leland: *Collectanea*
27   *L&P*; *Receipt of the Lady Katherine*
28   *Songs, Ballads etc. of Henry VIII*
29   cited by Erickson: *Great Harry*

30   *CSP: Spanish*
31   cited by Erickson: *Great Harry*
32   *CSP: Spanish*
33   George Cavendish
34   Edward Hall
35   cited by Bayley
36   see Thurley: *Royal Palaces*
37   B. L. Cotton MSS. Tiberius
38   Edward Hall
39   For the coronation see Edward Hall and the *Great Chronicle of London*
40   Edward Hall
41   B.L. Cotton MSS. Titus
42   This crown was melted down with most of the royal regalia in the 17th century under the Commonwealth. The present St Edward's Crown was made in 1661 for Charles II.
43   Anthony Wood, 17th century antiquarian
44   *L&P*; this crown was also melted down under the Commonwealth.
45   *Great Chronicle of London*
46   cited by Neville Williams:*Henry VIII and his Court*
47   Edward Hall
48   Ibid.
49   Ibid.
50   cited by Plowden: *House of Tudor*
51   Edward Hall
52   *L&P*

3. 'A PRINCE OF SPLENDOUR AND GENEROSITY'

1   *CSP: Venetian*
2   cited by Kelso
3   Stephen Gardiner: *De Vera Obedientia*
4   cited by J. Scarisbrick
5   Stephen Gardiner: *De Vera Obedientia*
6   William Tyndale: *Obedience of a Christian Man*
7   *Acts of the Privy Council*
8   Ibid.
9   Henry VIII: *Letters*
10   *L&P*
11   Sir Thomas Smith: *De Republica Anglorum* (ed. L. Alston, Cambridge, 1906)
12   Elton
13   Gabriel Tetzel: *Travels of Leo of Rozmital* (tr. and ed. M. Letts, Hakluyt Society, 108, 1965)
14   The last Valois Duke of Burgundy, Charles the Bold, had been defeated and killed in 1477 at the Battle of Nancy, when the region that is today known as Burgundy was annexed by France. When Charles's sole heiress, Mary of Burgundy, married the Emperor Maximilian, the more important county of Burgundy, which was part of the Low Countries, was absorbed into the Holy Roman Empire.
15   cited by M. L. Bruce: *The Making of Henry VIII*
16   cited by Morris
17   *CSP: Milanese*
18   *L&P*
19   Niccolo Machiavelli: *The Prince* (ed. W. K. Marriott, London, 1940)
20   *CSP: Venetian*
21   Ibid.
22   Ibid.

23   CSP: Milanese
24   L&P; PPE
25   Ibid.

4. 'THIS MAGNIFICENT, EXCELLENT AND TRIUMPHANT COURT'

1   Sir John Fortescue: *The Governance of England* (ed. C. Plummer, Oxford, 1885)
2   Louis le Brun: *Ung Petit Traicte de Francoys* (B. L. Royal MSS.)
3   *L&P*
4   *Collection of Ordinances*
5   *Tudor Royal Proclamations*
6   *L&P*
7   Loades: *Tudor Court*
8   Henry VIII: *Letters*
9   *English Historical Documents*
10   Sir Thomas Wyatt's satire 'How to use the Court and Himself therein', dedicated to Sir Francis Bryan; cited by Neville Williams:*Henry VIII and his Court*
11   cited by Starkey: *Henry VIII*
12   CP ed. Kaulek
13   *L&P*; *Lisle Letters*
14   *L&P*
15   CSP: Spanish
16   Ibid.
17   CSP: Venetian
18   *L&P*
19   Ibid.
20   CSP: Spanish
21   Ibid.
22   Ibid.
23   George Cavendish
24   *Collection of Ordinances*
25   *Rutland Papers*
26   George Cavendish
27   *Collection of Ordinances*
28   *L&P*
29   *Rutland Papers*
30   Thurley: *Royal Palaces*
31   *L&P*; Nottingham University Library MSS.
32   *History of the King's Works*
33   cited by Loades: *Tudor Court*
34   *Collection of Ordinances*
35   Ibid.
36   *L&P*
37   John Skelton: *Complete Poems*
38   cited by MacDonagh
39   Incontri; Jesse
40   cited by MacDonagh
41   Inventory. One of Henry's dog collars was exhibited in the 17th century in the Tradescant Museum, Oxford, but has since been lost (*Tradescant's Rarities*).
42   *L&P*
43   CSP: Venetian
44   *Collection of Ordinances*
45   CSP: Spanish
46   *L&P*

47   cited by Richardson: *Mary Tudor*
48   William Forrest

5. 'A PERFECT BUILDER OF PLEASANT PALACES'

1   Amongst the many sources used for this chapter, and the next, I am especially
     indebted to the researches of Simon Thurley (*The Royal Palaces of Tudor England*),
     David Loades (*The Tudor Court*), Maurice Howard (*The Early Tudor Country House*)
     and Peter Brears (*All the King's Cooks*).
2   In 1550, Langley Manor was granted to John Dudley, Earl of Warwick; in the 17th
     century it decayed, and was largely rebuilt in the 19th as a farmhouse. The north walls
     are part of the original manor house, and feature carvings of a Tudor rose and the
     initials of Henry VII and Elizabeth of York.
3   In 1603, Minster Lovell Hall was sold to Sir Edward Coke. It is now a ruin.
4   By 1660, Wimbledon had been alienated from the Crown.
5   By the reign of Elizabeth, Windsor Manor was no longer a royal residence, but was
     used as a keeper's lodge.
6   Easthampstead Park was alienated from the Crown in 1628. It was rebuilt in the 19th
     century and is now a college.
7   Wanstead was granted to Lord Rich in 1549. During Elizabeth's reign it was a
     favoured residence of Robert Dudley, Earl of Leicester. It was rebuilt in the 17th
     century.
8   Elizabeth I leased the ruins of Berkhamsted Castle to Sir Edward Carey, who used its
     stones to build a new house nearby. Very little remains of the castle today.
9   Hertford Castle was ruinous by 1609. The walls and towers that survive today have
     been incorporated into a building housing the local council offices.
10   Externally, Warwick Castle remains very much as it was in Henry's day, but the
     interior was restored in 1871 after a fire.
11   cited by Steane
12   Kenilworth Castle was alienated from the Crown in 1553 and was later the chief
     residence of Robert Dudley, Earl of Leicester, who lavishly entertained Elizabeth I
     here in 1575. Although the castle was wrecked and dismantled during the Civil War,
     extensive ruins remain today.
13   The ruins of Sheriff Hutton Castle survive today in private farmland.
14   Pontefract Castle was dismantled during the Civil War and is now a ruin.
15   Only ruins remain from Henry's time. Much of Sudeley Castle was reconstructed in
     1858 by Sir Gilbert Scott.
16   William Thomas
17   William Harrison
18   Ibid.
19   cited by Sturgis
20   *History of the King's Works*; PRO
21   Inventory
22   Ibid.; B. L. Additional MSS.
23   PRO
24   Ibid.
25   Henry VII had spent only £29,000 (£8,700,00) on his greater houses. A number of
     Henry VIII's houses and estates are still in the hands of the Crown, although many
     were alienated after his death by his heirs and, later, by the Commonwealth. By 1649,
     only 23 of his houses remained, and by the 18th century many of those had been either
     demolished or largely remodelled to conform to Georgian tastes.
26   *L&P*
27   *Collection of Ordinances*; *L&P*
28   *Collection of Ordinances*
29   i.e. a picture

30   a type of musical instrument
31   i.e. a backgammon board
32   Inventory
33   Under succeeding monarchs, the largely unchanging pattern of court life, as it had been established by Henry VIII, ensured that the design and layout of his houses remained a blueprint for English royal palaces until the 19th century.
34   PRO
35   Inventory
36   Inventory; B. L. Egerton MSS.
37   *L&P*
38   Richard Hakluyt: *The Principal Navigations, Voyages and Discoveries of the English Nation* (1589; 12 vols., ed. W. Raleigh, Glasgow, 1903-5)
39   Rawlinson MSS., Bodleian Library
40   Inventory
41   *Antiquarian Repertory*
42   see *Rivals in Power*, ed. Starkey

6. 'THE KING'S HOUSE'

1   *L&P*
2   *History of the King's Works*
3   Maurice Howard: *The Early Tudor Country House*
4   See Thurley: *Royal Palaces*, for a fuller discussion of the development of grotesque decoration.
5   Thurley: *Royal Palaces*
6   See the Whitehall family group painting, and Hans Holbein's miniature *Solomon and the Queen of Sheba*, which almost certainly portrays Henry VIII enthroned in a typical presence chamber. Both are in the Royal Collection.
7   Thurley: *Royal Palaces*
8   Inventory
9   Ibid.
10   Ibid.
11   This set was sold off by the Commonwealth, and is now in Spain.
12   Rawlinson MSS; Bodleian Library
13   Ibid.
14   Nottingham University Library MSS.
15   Inventory
16   PRO
17   B. L. Royal MSS.
18   cited by Bruce: *The Making of Henry VIII*
19   *CSP: Venetian*
20   *L&P*
21   Ibid.; *Collection of Ordinances*
22   Thurley: *Royal Palaces*
23   Inventory
24   Ibid.
25   PRO
26   Inventory
27   *Collection of Ordinances*
28   Ibid.
29   *PPE*
30   Ibid.
31   B. L. Additional MSS.
32   Mary I's x-frame chair, made for her marriage to Philip of Spain in 1554, is still to be seen in Winchester Cathedral.

33 Inventory
34 Ibid.
35 B. L. Additional MSS.
36 Both seals are in the Public Record Office.
37 *Collection of Ordinances*
38 *History of the King's Works*
39 Inventory
40 PRO
41 This bed was sold off by the Commonwealth and is last recorded in 1674 (Longleat MSS.)
42 PRO
43 Inventory. Tissue was a rich material of gold or silver, but thinner than cloth of gold.
44 Ibid.
45 It was sold in 1649 by the Commonwealth, and is now in the possession of the Worshipful Company of Goldsmiths, London.
46 It was given away by James I in 1604, and is now in the British Museum.
47 Now in the Schatzkammer of the Residenz, Munich.
48 cited in *Henry VIII: A European Court in England*
49 *L&P*
50 Now in the Church of St John the Baptist, Cirencester.
51 *L&P*
52 Inventory
53 Nottingham University Library MSS.
54 PRO
55 Now in the Victoria and Albert Museum, London.
56 PRO
57 Inventory
58 *PPE*
59 Inventory
60 Letter from Henry Huttoft, Surveyor of Customs at Southampton, to Thomas Cromwell, cited by Glasheen: *Secret People*
61 Inventory
62 *Collection of Ordinances*
63 B.L. Harleian MSS.
64 Bodleian Library MSS.
65 Rawlinson MSS., Bodleian Library
66 Now in the British Library.
67 French inventory of Mary Tudor's trousseau, cited by H. Norris
68 Bodleian Library MSS.
69 Thomas Platter: *Travels of England* (London, 1599); PRO
70 Accounts of Henry Courtenay, Earl of Devon and Marquess of Exeter, in the Public Record Office
71 cited by Thurley: *Royal Palaces*
72 *Original Letters*, ed. Ellis
73 *Collection of Ordinances*
74 cited by L. B. Smith: *Henry VIII, The Mask of Royalty*
75 *Collection of Ordinances*
76 Rawlinson MSS., Bodleian Library
77 Ibid.
78 Bodleian Library MSS.
79 *Collection of Ordinances*
80 Ibid.
81 Ibid.
82 Ibid.
83 Ibid.

84   Ibid.
85   *L&P*; Longleat MSS.
86   PRO
87   Ibid.; B. L. Additional MSS; Thurley: *Royal Palaces*
88   Andrew Boorde; Bodleian Library MSS.
89   *Collection of Ordinances*; *Early English Meals and Manners*
90   *Collection of Ordinances*; Thurley: *Royal Palaces*
91   Erickson: *Great Harry*
92   Ibid.; *The Babees' Book*
93   Thurley: *Royal Palaces*
94   Steane; Thurley: *Royal Palaces*
95   Sturgis
96   Andrew Boorde
97   Rawlinson MSS., Bodleian Library
98   Ibid.
99   *Tudor Royal Proclamations*

7. 'THE WORSHIP AND WELFARE OF THE WHOLE HOUSEHOLD'

1   *Collection of Ordinances*; Myers; Loades: *Tudor Court*; Thurley: *Royal Palaces*. Much of the material for this chapter is drawn from *Collection of Ordinances and Regulations for the Government of the Royal Household*; amongst the many other sources consulted, David Loades' *The Tudor Court* proved an indispensable mine of information.
2   *Collection of Ordinances*
3   cited by Loades: *Tudor Court*
4   *Collection of Ordinances*
5   Ibid.
6   cited by Loades: *Tudor Court*
7   *Collection of Ordinances*. Prior to Henry VIII's reign, the monarch's washing had been done by the Yeoman of the Laundry.
8   *Collection of Ordinances*
9   James Howell: *Londinopolis* (London, 1657)
10   cited by Erickson: *Great Harry*
11   *PPE*
12   *Collection of Ordinances*
13   Ibid.
14   cited by Bowle
15   B. L. Arundel MSS.
16   State Papers in the Public Record Office; B. L. Harleian MSS.
17   Sim
18   *L&P*
19   Now in the Metropolitan Museum of Art, New York; a similar miniature is in the Kunsthistorisches Museum, Vienna.
20   cited by Erickson: *Great Harry*
21   *Collection of Ordinances*; B.L. Cotton MSS. Vespasian.
22   *Collection of Ordinances*
23   Ibid.
24   *L&P*
25   Ibid.
26   *Collection of Ordinances*
27   Ibid.
28   The Board of the Greencloth still survives today as a department of the Royal Household; it meets at Buckingham Palace, and its members still sit at a table covered with a green cloth.

29   *Collection of Ordinances*
30   B.L. Additional MSS.; PRO
31   Loades: *Tudor Court*
32   *L&P*; *Collection of Ordinances*
33   Brears
34   cited by Mackie
35   *Four Years*; *CSP: Venetian*
36   Jacobus Francisca
37   *Collection of Ordinances*; B.L. Royal MSS.
38   Public Record Office
39   Marino Sanuto
40   cited by H. Norris
41   H. Norris
42   *L&P*
43   John Stow: *Annals*
44   *State Papers*
45   B.L. Additional MSS.
46   PRO
47   Bodleian Library MSS.
48   cited by Erickson: *Great Harry*
49   Ibid.
50   Charles Wriothesley
51   *L&P*
52   Rawlinson MSS., Bodleian Library; PRO
53   *PPE*
54   *L&P*; Brears; Thurley: *Royal Palaces*

8. 'SUCH PLENTY OF COSTLY PROVISION'

1   Seymour Papers
2   *Collection of Ordinances*
3   *Rivals in Power*
4   Cardinal Wolsey built the original kitchens at Hampton Court, but much of what remains today is Henry VIII's work. His kitchens were partitioned in the 17th century, and last used in the 18th. They were altered in the 19th century, and imaginatively restored between 1978 and 1991. They are now the best surviving example of 16th century service quarters. Only a small part of the complex, centred on Fish Court, is open to the public. The rest is used as offices, apartments and self-catering accommodation. The Boiling House is the only one of Henry's subsidiary kitchens to survive at Hampton Court.
5   *CSP: Spanish*
6   for this chapter and the next, I have relied heavily on the *Collection of Ordinances and Regulations for the Government of the Royal Household*. I am also deeply indebted to the researches of Peter Brears (*All the King's Cooks*), Alison Sim (*Food and Feast in Tudor England*), Sarah Paston Williams (*The Art of Dining*), Matthew Sturgis (*Hampton Court Palace*), Elizabeth Burton (*The Early Tudors at Home*), and Simon Thurley (*The Royal Palaces of England*)
7   Brears; Thurley: *Royal Palaces*; Rawlinson, MSS., Bodleian Library; B.L. Additional MSS.
8   *Collection of Ordinances*; *L&P*
9   *Collection of Ordinances*
10   Sim
11   *L&P*; Pero Doux's name is also given as Perot le Doulce.
12   *L&P*
13   Seymour Papers

14 *L&P*
15 *Collection of Ordinances*
16 These five departments had the largest staff after the Great Kitchen.
17 Brears; *L&P*
18 Andrew Boorde; Thomas Elyot: *The Castle of Health*
19 *L&P*
20 Thurley: *Royal Palaces*
21 Bowle
22 It was called hippocras because it was strained through a bag known as a Hippocrates Sleeve.
23 B. L. Additional MSS
24 *Collection of Ordinances*
25 Alexander Barclay
26 *Collection of Ordinances*
27 PRO; B.L. Royal MSS.
28 *L&P*
29 William Harrison
30 *L&P*
31 *Collection of Ordinances*
32 Thurley
33 Brears
34 *Collection of Ordinances*
35 Brears
36 *Collection of Ordinances*
37 *PPE*
38 Ibid.
39 *Collection of Ordinances*
40 Marzipan made with rosewater.
41 *Collection of Ordinances*
42 *CSP: Venetian*
43 *Collection of Ordinances*
44 Ibid.
45 Ibid.; Neville Williams: *Henry VIII and his Court*; Loades: *Tudor Court*
46 *Collection of Ordinances*
47 Ibid.
48 Ibid.; Glasheen: *Secret People*; Richardson: *Mary Tudor*
49 Hibbert: *Court at Windsor*
50 *Collection of Ordinances*
51 Andrew Boorde
52 Pewter plates were first recorded in 1553, but are almost certainly depicted in the anonymous painting of the Field of Cloth of gold, which dates from the 1540s and is now in the Royal Collection (Paston Williams).
53 Inventory
54 Paston Williams; Brears
55 Inventory
56 *Collection of Ordinances*; Brears
57 *Collection of Ordinances*
58 *The Babees' Book*
59 *Collection of Ordinances*

9. 'ELEGANT MANNERS, EXTREME DECORUM AND VERY GREAT POLITENESS'

1 John Skelton: *Speculum Principis*
2 The coronations were those of Henry himself (1509) and Anne Boleyn (1533); the

summit meeting was the Field of Cloth of Gold (1520); the state visits were that of the Emperor Charles V to England (1522) and that of Henry VIII to France (1532); Anne of Cleves' reception was in 1540.

3 Thurley: *Royal Palaces*
4 John Leland: *Collectanea*
5 *Collection of Ordinances*
6 Hibbert: *Court at Windsor*
7 Sturgis
8 cited by Erickson: *Great Harry*
9 George Cavendish
10 Elias Ashmole
11 *CSP: Venetian*
12 *L&P*
13 Inventory
14 cited by Sim
15 Inventory
16 *Collection of Ordinances*
17 Ibid.
18 *Collection of Ordinances*; *Antiquarian Repertory*
19 *Collection of Ordinances*
20 Ibid., *PPE*
21 *Collection of Ordinances*
22 Ibid.; *Antiquarian Repertory*
23 Inventory; 'a tassel of hair to make clean combs' is also listed.
24 *Collection of Ordinances*
25 *L&P*
26 B. L. Additional MSS,; Rawlinson MSS., Bodleian Library; B. L. Harleian MSS.; Thurley: *Royal Palaces*
27 Thomas Platter; Thurley: *Royal Palaces*
28 Inventory; Thurley: *Royal Palaces*
29 Ibid.
30 Thurley: *Royal Palaces*; Rawlinson MSS., Bodleian Library; Inventory
31 *L&P*
32 Inventory of Mary Tudor's trousseau, cited by H. Norris
33 Inventory
34 Bodleian Library MSS.; Rawlinson MSS.; Bodleian Library; Thurley: *Royal Palaces*
35 cited by Sturgis
36 *L&P*
37 Ibid.; *CSP: Spanish*
38 Thurley: *Royal Palaces*
39 *Collection of Ordinances*
40 Sturgis
41 Rawlinson MSS., Bodleian Library
42 cited by Erickson: *Great Harry*
43 Starkey: *Henry VIII; Collection of Ordinances*
44 H. Norris
45 *Collection of Ordinances*
46 Inventory
47 Ibid.; Brears
48 *Collection of Ordinances*
49 *PPE*
50 Letter of Henry Huttoft, surveyor of Customs at Southampton, to Thomas Cromwell, 1539.
51 This drawing was once attributed to Holbein, but more recent historians have suggested that it dates from the late 16th or early 17th century. There is, however,

internal evidence that it may be contemporary. For a fuller discussion of this, see Thurley: *Royal Palaces*, and *Henry VIII: A European Court in England.*

52 *Collection of Ordinances*; Inventory; Brears
53 Inventory; *Sotheby's Concise Encyclopaedia of Glass*; Sim, Henry's Inventory lists 600 items of glass.
54 *Collection of Ordinances*
55 Letter of Bryan Tuke to Cardinal Wolsey, *L&P*
56 Henry VIII: *Letters*; *CSP: Spanish*
57 cited by Erickson: *Great Harry*
58 Inventory
59 *Collection of Ordinances*; Bowle; Neville Williams: *Royal Residences*
60 Ralph Sadler to Thomas Cromwell, *L&P*
61 PRO
62 Hibbert: *Court at Windsor*; Chapman: *Sisters of Henry VIII*; Prescott: *Mary Tudor, Early English Meals and Manners*
63 *L&P*; *CSP: Spanish*

10. 'INNOCENT AND HONEST PASTIMES'

1 *CSP: Spanish*
2 Ibid.
3 cited by Richardson: *Mary Tudor*
4 *CSP: Spanish*
5 Ibid.; *L&P*
6 cited by J. Scarisbrick: *Henry VIII*
7 *CSP: Milanese*
8 Stow: *Annals*
9 Starkey: *Henry VIII*; Loades: *Tudor Court*
10 *CSP: Venetian*
11 *CSP: Spanish*
12 Erasmus: *Opus Epistolarum*
13 *Four Years*
14 Much of our information on Wolsey comes from the biography by his Gentleman Usher, George Cavendish, published in 1557.
15 cited by Mackie
16 *L&P*; Edward Hall
17 *L&P*
18 *PPE*
19 William Roper
20 Nicholas Udall: *Ralph Roister Doister*
21 B. L. Additional MSS.
22 Ibid.
23 *L&P*
24 *CSP: Spanish*
25 *Antiquarian Repertory*
26 cited by Rowse: *Windsor Castle*
27 *CSP: Milanese*
28 *CSP: Venetian*
29 *Four Years*
30 cited by Perry
31 B. L. Additional MSS.; *PPE*
32 *Privy Purse Expenses of Elizabeth of York*
33 *Four Years*
34 *PPE*; *L&P*
35 *Collection of Ordinances*

36   *L&P; Statutes of the Realm*
37   cited by Stevens
38   *PPE*
39   PRO
40   *L&P*
41   Ibid.
42   Accounts of Henry Courtenay, Earl of Devon and Marquess of Exeter, in the Public Record Office
43   *L&P*
44   *PPE*
45   Ibid.
46   cited by Loades: *Tudor Court*; Emmison: *Tudor Food and Pastimes*

11. 'NEW MEN' AND 'NATURAL COUNSELLORS'

1   cited by Neville Williams: *Henry VIII and his Court*
2   *Antiquarian Repertory*
3   *Collection of Ordinances*
4   cited by Starkey: *Henry VIII*
5   cited by Loades: *Tudor Court*
6   cited by H. Norris
7   *Collection of Ordinances*
8   Ibid.
9   Ibid.
10   Ibid.
11   cited by Richardson: *Mary Tudor*
12   Edward Hall; according to a tradition dating from Elizabethan times, the 'Brandon Lance' in the Royal Armouries once belonged to Charles Brandon.
13   *CSP: Venetian*, for example
14   *L&P*
15   cited by J. Scarisbrick: *Henry VIII*
16   *L&P*
17   cited by Erickson: *Great Harry*
18   *L&P*
19   cited in the *Leeds Castle Guidebook*
20   *CSP: Spanish*
21   He became guardian of the Princess Mary and, much later, Lord Chamberlain to Elizabeth I (epitaph in Bletsoe Parish Church, Bedfordshire).
22   cited by Loades: *Tudor Court*
23   cited by Morris
24   Sir Thomas Smith
25   cited by Morris
26   Baldassare Castiglione
27   William Fitzwilliam, cited by Fraser
28   His body was discovered in an excellent state of preservation when his tomb in the collegiate church at Astley, Warwickshire, was opened in 1608.
29   now in the Royal Collection
30   William Camden

12. 'ALL GOODLY SPORTS'

1   *CSP: Spanish*
2   *CSP: Venetian*
3   cited by Bowle
4   Baldassare Castiglione

5   *Statutes of the Realm*
6   *L&P*
7   *CSP: Venetian*
8   Letter from Sir William Fitzwilliam to King Francis I of France, 1521, cited by Bowle
9   *L&P*
10 *State Papers*
11 *L&P*
12 *Collection of Ordinances*
13 *Henry VIII: A European Court in England*
14 see Thurley: *Royal Palaces*
15 PPE
16 Numbers fluctuated throughout the reign; shortly before his death, the King owned only 80 mounts.
17 *CSP: Spanish*
18 *CSP: Venetian*
19 Ibid.
20 *L&P*; the other horse was given by Henry to Sir Nicholas Carew.
21 *CSP: Venetian*
22 see Erickson: *Great Harry*, for a very good account of the King's horses.
23 *L&P*; *CSP: Venetian*; Erickson: *Great Harry*
24 PPE; *Great Tournament Roll of Westminster*
25 *CSP: Milanese*
26 PPE
27 *L&P*
28 The move, meant to be temporary, became permanent. Nevertheless, the name 'The Royal Mews' was retained.
29 PRO
30 *L&P*
31 *L&P*; *Lisle Letters*; Lord Lisle was a bastard son of Edward IV, and therefore the King's cousin; he served as Governor of Calais.
32 *L&P*
33 Ibid.
34 Ibid.
35 Now in the Mauritshuis, The Hague.
36 Rawlinson MSS., Bodleian Library; State Papers of Henry VIII in the Public Record Office
37 Rawlinson MSS., Bodleian Library
38 see Thurley: *Royal Palaces*. A drawing of the cockpit, dated 1606, is in Sir John Soane's Museum, London.
39 Rawlinson MSS., Bodleian Library; Thurley: *Royal Palaces*. The Queen at that time was Anne Boleyn.
40 Rawlinson MSS., Bodleian Library; Thurley: *Royal Palaces*
41 PPE
42 Ibid.
43 Rawlinson MSS., Bodleian Library
44 *Four Years*
45 Loades: *Tudor Court*
46 B. L. Additional MSS.
47 *Four Years*
48 PRO; H. Norris; Inventory
49 Lawn tennis is first recorded in 1591, and is said to have been invented to divert Elizabeth I; see Loades: *Tudor Court*
50 Accounts of Henry Courtnay, Earl of Devon and Marquess of Exeter, in the Public Record Office.
51 The modern type of net first appeared in the 17th century.

52   Thurley: *Royal Palaces*
53   Now in the Museum of London.
54   See Antonio Scaino, de Luze and Thurley: *Royal Palaces* for a fuller discussion of the rules of tennis.
55   *L&P*; Nottingham University Library MSS; *PPE*; Thurley: *Royal Palaces*
56   *CSP: Venetian*
57   *L&P*
58   *A Relation . . . of the Island of England*
59   *L&P*
60   Ibid.; B. L. Additional MSS.
61   *PPE*
62   *PPE*; Loades: *Tudor Court*; Rawlinson MSS., Bodleian Library; Thurley: *Royal Palaces*. There were three bowling alleys at Hampton Court.
63   *PPE*
64   Edward Hall
65   Rawlinson MSS., Bodleian Library; Thurley: *Royal Palaces*
66   *Receipt of the Lady Katherine*

13. 'MERRY DISPORTS'

1   *CSP: Spanish*
2   *PPE*
3   see Maurice Howard: *Early Tudor Country House*
4   *Collection of Ordinances*; *L&P*; *Archaeologia*
5   *Collection of Ordinances*
6   Richmond Park was remodelled into its present form by Charles I and Charles II in the 17th century.
7   College of Arms MS.
8   Ibid.
9   The description of Richmond Palace is drawn mainly from the *Antiquarian Repertory* and *The Receipt of the Lady Katherine*. The only remaining parts of the palace are the gatehouse, some Tudor brickwork in the heavily restored wardrobe building, and fragments of masonry in nearby buildings. Much of the fabric was destroyed by the Commonwealth in 1649. What was left was granted by Charles II to his mother, Queen Henrietta Maria, upon the Restoration in 1660, but was too ruinous to be habitable or restored. It was broken up into tenements, but the Tudor buildings had largely disappeared by 1690. The present Old Friars stands on the site of the convent of the Observant Friars.
10   cited by Benton Fletcher.
11   cited by Neville Williams: *Henry VIII and his Court*
12   John Stow: *London*
13   Ibid.
14   Edward Hall
15   Ibid.
16   *Collection of Ordinances*
17   *CSP: Venetian*
18   Edward Hall
19   *L&P*
20   Ibid.
21   *CSP: Spanish*
22   *L&P*
23   *Four Years*
24   College of Arms MS.
25   Edward Hall
26   *CSP: Spanish*

27 Edward Hall
28 cited by Bowle
29 *CSP: Spanish*
30 *CSP: Venetian*
31 Ibid.
32 *Four Years*
33 The procession for the Parliament of 1512: MS in Trinity College, Cambridge
34 *L&P*
35 *CSP: Spanish*
36 Edward Hall
37 *L&P*
38 It remained light blue until the reign of George I, when the darker blue was introduced.
39 Diana Scarisbrick; H. Norris
40 John Stow: *London*
41 Sim
42 Edward Hall
43 *CSP: Spanish*
44 *CSP: Spanish*
45 see Mathew
46 *Four Years*
47 *L&P*
48 *CSP: Spanish*
49 Bernard: *Rise of Sir William Compton*. When Henry VIII married Anne Boleyn in 1533, Mrs Amadas got into trouble for making malicious prophecies about them (*L&P*). Her prediction that Anne would be burned at the stake within six months was perhaps born of jealousy.
50 *L&P*
51 *CSP: Spanish*
52 *L&P*
53 B. L. Sloane MSS.
54 Sir Robert Naunton: *Fragmenta Regalia* (published 1653; ed. Edward Arber, London, 1879, 1896)
55 Benton Fletcher. Greenwich Castle stood on the hill now occupied by the Royal Observatory.
56 George Puttenham: *The Art of English Poesie*. Puttenham was the nephew of Sir Thomas Elyot, Henry's learned courtier and author of *The Governor*. Although not published until 1589, his *Art of English Poesie* was probably compiled twenty years earlier. The offending verse was not printed in this work, but appeared in a Jacobean play about Henry VIII, *When You See Me, You Know Me*, by Samuel Rowley (1605).
57 *State Papers*
58 Flügel
59 *L&P*

14. 'RATHER DIVINE THAN HUMAN'

1 Rawlinson MSS., Bodleian Library
2 *History of the King's Works*
3 Very little remains at Windsor of the royal apartments Henry knew. They were extremely remodelled by Charles II in the 1670s, and even more drastically altered by George IV in the 1820s. The fire of 1992 revealed a great deal of valuable information about the mediaeval palace; see Brindle and Kerr: *Windsor Revealed*.
4 Edward Hall
5 The Bassanos founded a musical dynasty that endured at the English court until the Civil War.

6   Now in the British Library. Only the base part survives.
7   Edward Hall
8   *Four Years*
9   *L&P*
10 Ibid.
11 *L&P*. Their numbers fluctuated. This figure relates to the latter part of the reign.
12 B. L. Lansdowne MSS.
13 *L&P*
14 The post of Master of the King's Musick was not created until the reign of Charles I.
15 A primitive form of trombone.
16 British Museum
17 B. L. Royal MSS.
18 Scholes
19 *L&P*
20 PPE; B.L. Additional MSS; Loades: *Tudor Court; Henry VIII: A European Court in England*
21 *CSP: Venetian*
22 *Four Years*
23 *L&P*
24 *CSP: Venetian*
25 *L&P*
26 Thomas Elyot: *The Governor*
27 John Leland: *Collectanea*; Stevens
28 B. L. Royal MSS.
29 cited by J. Scarisbrick: *Henry VIII*
30 *CSP: Venetian*
31 *Four Years*; virginals were an early form of harpsichord.
32 An ancient woodwind and brass instrument, not to be confused with the later cornet.
33 B. L. Royal MSS.
34 *CSP: Venetian*
35 Ibid.
36 An ancient stringed instrument played with a plectrum. It is mentioned by Chaucer and Shakespeare.
37 An early type of oboe, usually an accompaniment to the sackbut.
38 Inventory
39 Ibid.
40 *Four Years*
41 B. L. Additional MSS.; Stevens; *Songs, Ballads and Instrumental Pieces* etc. There are 109 pieces in the manuscript, including works by William Cornish and Philip van Wilder.
42 *Henry VIII: A European Court in England*
43 Edward Hall
44 Maurice Howard: *Early Tudor Country House*; Palmer: *Royal England*; Loades: *Tudor Court*; Thurley: *Royal Palaces*; *History of the King's Works*. See also the following articles in *Surrey Archaeological Collections*: R.A.C. Godwen Austen: 'Woking Manor' (7, 1880); D. J. Haggard: 'The Ruins of Old Woking Palace'; (55, 1958); N. Hawkins: 'Woking Palace or Old Hall, Old Woking' (77, 1986), as well as the *Victoria County History of Surrey*, Vol. III. Woking Palace was alienated from the Crown in 1620, after which it fell into decay. All that remains are some brick and stone foundations and the vestiges of a moat.
45 Edward Hall
46 *L&P*
47 Ibid.
48 B.L. Additional MSS.
49 *Original Documents relating to Katherine of Aragon*; *CSP: Spanish*; *L&P*; William Latimer;

Rawlinson MSS., Bodleian Library
50 *Four Years*; *L&P*; PRO
51 Stephen Gardiner: *Letters*
52 *L&P*
53 *History of the King's Works*. This arrangement may be seen in the chapel royal at Hampton Court; the gallery was originally built by Henry VIII, but the throne and fittings date from the reign of William III.
54 MS. in the collection of the Dean and Canons of Windsor. The artist was perhaps Lucas Horenbout.
55 *Calendar of the Manuscripts . . . at Hatfield House*
56 Erasmus: *Opus Epistolarum*
57 *L&P*; William Thomas echoes this, calling Henry 'a perfect theologian, a good philosopher'.
58 *Collection of Ordinances*
59 Ibid.; Myers
60 PRO
61 Rawlinson MSS., Bodleian Library
62 PRO; for a full discussion of royal chapels and organs, see Thurley: *Royal Palaces*

15. 'THE HOLY INNOCENT'

1   cited by Erickson: *Great Harry*
2   *L&P*
3   John Leland: *Collectanea*; *Collection of Ordinances*; Trinity College Dublin MSS.
4   Ibid.
5   *Collection of Ordinances*
6   Edward Hall
7   *Collection of Ordinances*. The source is Lord Mountjoy, Katherine's Chamberlain, who in 1533 informed Lord Cobham, Lord Chamberlain to Katherine's successor, Anne Boleyn, of the procedure to be followed at royal confinements, so that the same could be observed for Anne.
8   *Original Documents relating to Katherine of Aragon*
9   *L&P*
10 Ibid.
11 *Original Documents relating to Katherine of Aragon*; John Leland: *Collectanea*
12 B.L. Harleian MSS.; *State Papers*
13 John Leland: *Collectanea*; *Collection of Ordinances*
14 Edward Hall
15 *Collection of Ordinances*; Plowden: *Tudor Women*; John Leland: *Collectanea*
16 Sir Thomas Elyot: *The Governor*
17 *Collection of Ordinances*; Plowden: *Tudor Women*; John Leland: *Collectanea*
18 Edward Hall
19 Steane
20 Edward Hall
21 Ibid.
22 Ibid.
23 Ibid.
24 The date is sometimes given as 22 or 24 February, but Hall says the Prince died on the Eve of St Matthias, whose feast day is 24 February.
25 Neville Williams: *Henry VIII and his Court*; Erickson: *Great Harry*; Fraser
26 cited by Saunders
27 Edward Hall
28 Ibid.; *L&P*
29 *CSP: Venetian*; Erickson: *Great Harry*
30 Edward Hall

31 *L&P*
32 Edward Hall
33 Ibid.
34 Loades: *Tudor Court*; Erickson: *Great Harry*; *Oxford Companion to English Literature*; Scholes
35 The Painted Chamber was destroyed in the great fire that ravaged the Houses of Parliament in 1834. The present Palace of Westminster was rebuilt between 1840 and 1852. All that remains from Henry VIII's time are Westminster Hall, the crypt of St Stephen's Chapel and the Jewel Tower.
36 John Stow: *London*
37 Baynard's Castle would be held by each of Henry's wives in turn. It was burned down in the Great Fire of 1666, after which the land it had occupied was used to build wharves and warehouses. In 1972-3, when the site was being cleared for the building of the new City of London School; the foundations of the towers and river frontage of Baynard's Castle were revealed.
38 Much of what remains today was built by Henry VIII, although the chapel was restored by Queen Victoria.

16. 'A GALAXY OF DISTINGUISHED MEN'

1   Pronounced 'Montjoie'.
2   Erasmus: *Opus Epistolarum*
3   *The Croyland Chronicle Continuation, 1459-1486* (ed. N. Pronay and J. Cox, Gloucester, 1986)
4   Polydore Vergil
5   cited by Erickson: *Great Harry*
6   Erasmus: *Opus Epistolarum*
7   Ibid.
8   William Roper; Nicholas Harpsfield; Erasmus: *Opus Epistolarum*
9   cited by Strong
10 Erasmus: *Opus Epistolarum*
11 Ibid.
12 It remained in use for centuries; after 1758, it was known as *The Eton Latin Grammar*.
13 Erasmus: *Opus Epistolarum*
14 Ibid.
15 Ibid.
16 More: *Correspondence*
17 The 1534 edition ended with the death of Henry VII; Vergil later extended his history to 1537. He returned to Urbino in 1553 and died there three years later.
18 cited by Mattingly: *Catherine of Aragon*
19 Erasmus: *Opus Epistolarum*
20 Ibid.
21 Roger Ascham: *The Schoolmaster*, in *Whole Works*
22 It was first published in 1543 by Richard Grafton.
23 It was published by Richard Grafton in 1548 as *The Union of the Two Noble and Illustre Families of Lancaster and York*; the main section was entitled *The Triumphant Reign of King Henry the Eighth*.
24 *Henry VIII: A European Court in England*
25 It was printed by William Thynne, and a copy is now in Clare College, Cambridge. Another late mediaeval classic, John Gower's *Confessio Amantis*, was printed the same year by Thomas Berthelet.
26 cited by L. B. Smith: *Henry VIII: The Mask of Royalty*; Ferguson: *Indian Summer of English Chivalry*.
27 *Henry VIII: A European Court in England*
28 The name of the English translator is unknown.

29   B.L. Additional MSS.
30   Inventory
31   Inventory of the Whitehall library, 1542, in the Public Record Office. There were
      over 900 volumes in the 'upper library' alone (Inventory). There were also over 300
      books in the library at Greenwich (*PPE*).

17. 'THE KING'S PAINTERS'

1   Nichols: *Notices*; Thurley: *Royal Palaces*
2   Inventory
3   cited by H. Norris
4   Loades: *Tudor Court*
5   Now in the National Gallery, Washington.
6   cited by Neville Williams: *Henry VIII and his Court*
7   The bust of Henry VII is now in the Victoria and Albert Museum, London, while
      that of Henry VIII is in the Metropolitan Museum of Art, New York.
8   Now in the Metropolitan Museum of Art, New York.
9   It is probably the plan of Dover in B.L. Cotton MSS. Augustus.
10   The date has been determined by dendrochronological analysis. These portraits are
      still in the Royal Collection.
11   Inventory
12   Ibid.; PRO; *L&P*; H. Norris; Thurley: *Royal Palaces*
13   Its original frame, now lost, recorded her age as 34. Both portraits now have frames
      inscribed JOHANNES CORVUS FLANDRUS FACIABAT (Richardson: *Mary
      Tudor*).
14   Another, almost identical, version is in the Museum of Fine Arts, Boston.
15   Now in the British Museum.
16   Karel van Mander
17   Inventory; Thurley: *Royal Palaces*

18. 'GRACELESS DOGHOLES'

1   *CSP: Venetian*
2   George Cavendish
3   Richard Foxe: *Letters*
4   Erasmus: *Opus Epistolarum*. A year or so later, Colet retired to the Charterhouse
      monastery at Sheen. He died in 1519 and was buried in St Paul's Cathedral in a tomb
      decorated with a bust by Torrigiano. This was lost in the Great Fire of 1666, but a
      contemporary copy of the bust survives at St Paul's School. Hans Holbein based his
      portrait drawing of Colet on Torrigiano's original bust.
5   Ewelme was decaying by 1558 and in ruins when most it was demolished in the 17th
      century. A Tudor range survived into the 18th century, when the present manor
      house, which incorporated part of the original brick walls, was rebuilt.
6   *CSP: Spanish*
7   All that remains of this moated brick courtyard house today is a ruinous five-storey
      octagonal tower by the entrance gate.
8   *L&P*
9   *CSP: Milanese*
10   Ibid.
11   Ibid.
12   *L&P*
13   Ibid.; *CSP: Venetian*; Erickson: *Great Harry*; Fraser. Étienne married Jean Neufchâtel,
      Seigneur de Marnay, in October 1514.
14   *CSP: Venetian*
15   *L&P*; B.L. Cotton MSS. Vespasian

16 B.L. Cotton MSS. Vespasian
17 The premature birth is inferred from the fact that there is no record of any preparations being made for the Queen's lying-in, nor of her taking to her chamber.
18 Edward Hall
19 *CSP: Venetian*
20 cited by Benton Fletcher
21 Henry VIII later used Havering as a nursery palace for his children. It remained a royal residence until the Civil War, but decayed during the Commonwealth. Pyrgo was demolished in 1770 and the palace in 1814. Hardly any traces remain of either building.

19. 'OBSTINATE MEN WHO GOVERN EVERYTHING'

1 Edward Hall
2 PRO
3 *L&P*
4 She died before 1521. Guildford later married Mary Wotton, the 'Lady Guildford' painted by Holbein. For the Bryan family, see *The Spear and the Spindle: Ancestors of Sir Francis Bryan* by T.A. Fuller (T. Anna Leese), Maryland, 1993.
5 *L&P*; *CSP: Venetian*
6 *Rivals in Power*
7 cited in *Rivals in Power*
8 *CSP: Venetian*
9 *L&P*
10 *CSP: Venetian*
11 Erasmus: *Opus Epistolarum*
12 B.L. Cotton MSS. Vitellius; Edward Hall
13 *L&P*
14 *CSP: Venetian*
15 Erasmus: *Opus Epistolarum*
16 When Mary's body was exhumed in 1784, her hair was found to be reddish gold and nearly two feet long. A lock has been preserved in Moyse's Hall Museum, Bury St Edmunds. It was probably the same colour as Henry VIII's hair.
17 Peter Martyr, cited by Perry and in Neville Williams: *Henry VIII and his Court*
18 *L&P*
19 Fiddes
20 PRO; *History of the King's Works*; Anglo; Thurley: *Royal Palaces*
21 Now in the Ashmolean Museum.
22 Edward Hall
23 *CSP: Venetian*
24 *Henry VIII: A European Court in England*
25 Now in the National Maritime Museum.
26 *L&P*
27 *CSP: Spanish*
28 cited by Benton Fletcher
29 Today, boatswains wear similar whistles in commemoration of this event.
30 *CSP: Venetian*
31 *L&P*
32 *CSP: Venetian*
33 Ibid.
34 *L&P*
35 cited by Neville Williams: *Henry VIII and his Court*
36 *CSP: Venetian*
37 Despite Wolsey's extensive rebuilding programme, York Place was still not large enough to accommodate the King and his entourage overnight, and Henry is known

to have spent only one night there during Wolsey's tenure (Thurley: *Royal Palaces*).

38   This 70 foot cellar, known erroneously as 'King Henry VIII's Wine Cellar' was discovered in 1935 when the present Ministry of Defence offices were built in Whitehall; because it was in the way of the new foundations, it was moved in its entirety 43 feet along, 23 feet down, and then along again to its present position.

39   *CSP: Venetian*

40   *L&P*

41   Ibid.

20. 'CLOTH OF FRIEZE BE NOT TOO BOLD'

1   For the proxy marriage see *CSP: Venetian*; Edward Hall; B.L. Harleian MSS.; *L&P*

2   The portrait he painted is probably that in the National Gallery.

3   cited by Neville Williams: *Henry VIII and his Court*

4   *CSP: Venetian*

5   *L&P*

6   *CSP: Venetian*

7   *L&P*

8   *CSP: Venetian*

9   Now the Old Palace School of John Whitgift. Only one range remains of the original moated courtyard house.

10   *CSP: Venetian*

11   Edward Hall

12   cited by Brewer

13   *L&P*

14   *State Papers*

15   The effigies of the five boys and six girls appear on the sides of the tomb of Sir John Blount and his wife in the church of St John the Baptist at Kinlet, Salop. The nearby manor house was demolished in the 18th century; Moffats School now occupies the site.

16   Her exact date of birth is not known, but her father was only 36 in 1519 (*Inventories of Henry Fitzroy*; Fraser).

17   Edward Hall

18   Herbert of Cherbury

19   Edward Hall; *Inventories of Henry Fitzroy*

20   Edward Hall

21   *L&P*

22   *CSP: Spanish*

23   PRO; *CSP: Venetian*

24   *CSP: Venetian*

25   cited by Seward

26   *State Papers*

27   *L&P*

28   Ibid.

29   The wardship was bought by Katherine of York, Countess of Devon, who shortly afterwards married Elizabeth to her son, Henry Courtenay. Elizabeth died young without issue.

30   *CSP: Venetian*; *Four Years*

31   *Four Years*

32   Cf the account of another Venetian envoy, Andrea Trevisano, who described how the King received him 'in a small hall hung with handsome tapestry, leaning against a tall gilt chair covered with cloth of gold. His Majesty wore a violet gown lined with cloth of gold and a collar of many jewels, and on his cap was a large diamond and a most beautiful pearl.' (Is this another reference to the Mirror of Naples?) (*CSP: Venetian*)

33   *Collection of Ordinances*
34   PRO
35   *L&P*; *CSP: Spanish*; *CSP: Venetian*; Mackie
36   *L&P*
37   *CSP: Venetian*
38   Ibid.
39   Ibid.
40   Ibid.; *Four Years*; Edward Hall
41   *CSP: Venetian*
42   cited by Starkey: *Henry VIII*
43   *CSP: Venetian*
44   Now in the collection of the Duke of Buccleuch.
45   Francis Bryan: Introduction to his translation of Antonio de Guevara's *A Dispraise of the life of the Courtier* (cited by Starkey: *Henry VIII*)
46   Although his work is said to have featured in Tottel's *Miscellany*, his poetry is either lost or cannot now be identified; it was much admired by his contemporaries.
47   *L&P*
48   Ibid.
49   *CSP: Spanish*
50   In view of Suffolk's previous matrimonial entanglements, the validity of his marriage to Mary was affirmed in 1524 by a papal bull, which also declared their children legitimate.
51   *CSP: Venetian*
52   One version is at Woburn Abbey, another is in the collection of the Earl of Yarborough.
53   *CSP: Venetian*
54   Polydore Vergil
55   Westhorpe Hall was near Frimingham, 12 miles from Bury St Edmunds. It was demolished in the 18th century. A farmhouse now stands on the site; above the door is a pediment bearing the arms of Mary Tudor.

21. 'THE BEST DRESSED SOVEREIGN IN THE WORLD'

1   A full-length copy by the 17th century artist Daniel Mytens of a lost original is at Holyrood Palace, Edinburgh; Scotland and France were ancient allies.
2   *CSP: Venetian*
3   *L&P*; PRO
4   PRO
5   Ibid.; *L&P*
6   *L&P*
7   *L&P*
8   *CSP: Venetian*
9   Ibid.; Edward Hall
10   PPE
11   *L&P*
12   B. L. Harleian MSS.
13   *CSP: Venetian*
14   cf Holbein's sketch of a lady in the British Museum; this is the best back view of an early Tudor gown.
15   *CSP: Venetian*
16   Ibid.; silk stockings were not invented until the reign of Elizabeth I.
17   *CSP: Venetian*
18   Now in the Kunsthistorisches Museum, Vienna.
19   A carved ivory pin-head in the form of a gable hood was found during excavations at Whitehall.

20   Sim

21   It was not introduced into England by Katherine of Aragon, as several writers have stated.

22   George Cavendish

23   Now in the Victoria and Albert Museum.

24   Ibid.

25   Now in the Royal Collection.

26   cited by Diana Scarisbrick

27   cited in *Henry VIII: A European Court in England*

28   Inventory

29   One portrait is in the collection of Viscount Mountgarret at Nidd Hall and the other is in the National Portrait Gallery.

30   The rest of this suit of armour was sold as scrap metal in 1649 by the Commonwealth.

31   Now in the Royal Armouries, Tower of London.

32   These workshops survived into the 17th century.

33   *L&P*

34   Nottingham University Library MSS.; Thurley: *Royal Palaces*

35   Rawlinson MSS., Bodleian Library; Thurley: *Royal Palaces*

36   Inventory

22. 'THIS CARDINAL IS KING'

1   Edward Hall

2   cited by Neville Williams: *Henry VIII and his Court*

3   cited by Starkey: *Henry VIII*

4   It was formerly a preceptory dating from the 13th century. A manor house had stood on the site since Saxon times.

5   The bell was made by the 15th century founder, Thomas Harris, whose initials it bears. It used to chime the hours, but is now only rung at funerals. Traces of the manor house's foundations were uncovered in the 1970s during excavations in Clock Court, where their position is marked out on the paving stones (Sturgis).

6   The moat, reputed to be the last one dug in England, was filled in by Charles II, but re-excavated in the 19th century, when the stone bridge to the gatehouse was uncovered.

7   The Cardinal's arms were later removed by Henry VIII; they were rediscovered and restored to their original place in 1845.

8   He was paid £2. 6s. 9d. (over £700) each for them. Some of Maiano's work, such as the *Histories of Hercules* carved on the oriel window of the gatehouse (which Henry VIII removed), is lost. Maiano later worked for the King: two of his roundels were discovered at Windsor in 1882.

9   By 1770, the gatehouse had become much decayed and there were fears that it would collapse. In 1771-3, it was partially demolished and rebuilt on a smaller scale, with only three storeys. The leaden cupolas on the turrets were never replaced. In 1882, the gatehouse was refaced with new red bricks.

10   Base Court remains much as it was in Wolsey's day, despite some Victorian restoration. The rest of the palace has been greatly altered, and all the Cardinal's private apartments have disappeared. The so-called Wolsey Closet is a 20th century reconstruction.

11   Wolsey's banqueting hall may have been on the site of the present great watching chamber. The existing oriel window was perhaps constructed to lighten the cardinal's table.

12   *CSP: Venetian*

13   Sturgis

14   Today, Unilever House occupies the site.

15   *CSP: Venetian*; *L&P*

16   *Four Years*
17   *CSP: Venetian*
18   *Four Years*
19   *CSP: Venetian*
20   *CSP: Spanish*
21   Polydore Vergil
22   George Cavendish
23   Polydore Vergil
24   John Skelton
25   His daughter Dorothy became a nun at Shaftesbury Abbey, Dorset. His son, Thomas Winter, took holy orders whilst still very young, and received, through Wolsey's influence, thirteen lucrative benefices and offices. Joan Lark was the daughter of a Thetford innkeeper; her brother, who was Master of Trinity Hall, Cambridge, was Wolsey's confessor. Wolsey arranged for Joan to be married to a gentleman, Mr Legh; it is not known whether Wolsey continued having relations with her after the marriage.
26   cited by Perry
27   Polydore Vergil
28   cited by Mackie
29   cited by Erickson: *Great Harry*
30   George Cavendish
31   *L&P*
32   George Cavendish
33   Henry VIII: *Letters*

23. 'THE PEARL OF THE WORLD'

1   This is the third largest hammerbeam roof surviving in England, after those in Westminster Hall and Christ Church, Oxford.
2   William Lambarde
3   *History of the King's Works*
4   PRO
5   Edward Hall; Raphael Holinshed; Brewer
6   This coat of arms may be seen in situ in an engraving of 1786 by George Vertue (Society of Antiquaries of London).
7   Watercolours of the stained glass portraits of Henry and Katherine were painted in 1737 by Daniel Chandler (Society of Antiquaries of London).
8   *Four Years*
9   John Leland: *Collectanea*; B.L. Cotton MSS. Julius; *Collection of Ordinances*
10   *CSP: Venetian*
11   cited by Erickson: *Great Harry*
12   Richard Sampson, Bishop of Chichester, cited by Saunders
13   The Princess also spent some time at Hanworth; she was there at New Year, 1522, when she received a gift of 12 pairs of shoes from Sir Richard Weston.
14   *History of the King's Works*. A 19th century house now occupies the site.
15   The present Bruce Castle is a Jacobean building erected on the foundations of the Comptons' house.
16   *L&P*
17   cited by Bowle
18   Edward Hall
19   Ibid.
20   cited in *Henry VIII: A European Court in England*
21   Richard Foxe: *Letters*
22   Ibid.
23   William Roper.
24   Although The Vyne was remodelled in the classical style in the 17th and 18th

centuries, the Tudor gallery and chapel remain.
25   cited by Neville Williams: *Henry VIII and his Court*
26   *CSP: Venetian; L&P*
27   *L&P*
28   Edward Hall
29   *L&P*
30   Edward Hall; *CSP: Venetian*

24. 'MULTITUDES ARE DYING AROUND US'

1   cited by Neville Williams: *Henry VIII and his Court*
2   Edward Hall
3   *CSP: Venetian*
4   *L&P*
5   *CSP: Venetian*
6   Polydore Vergil
7   *CSP: Venetian*
8   *Ambassades de Jean du Bellay*
9   Stephen Gardiner: *Letters*
10   *Four Years*
11   Ibid.
12   *CSP: Venetian*
13   Ibid.
14   Ibid.; Edward Hall
15   *CSP: Venetian*
16   *L&P*
17   Edward Hall
18   *CSP: Venetian*
19   *L&P*
20   *Four Years*
21   *CSP: Venetian; State Papers; L&P*
22   *L&P*; Horace Walpole: *Correspondence*; B.L. Sloane MSS.
23   *L&P*
24   *A Treasure for Englishmen concerning the Anatomy of Man's Body*, published 1577. Vicary lived from 1495 to 1561.
25   Now owned by the Worshipful Company of Barber Surgeons. The original instruments contained in the case are long since lost.
26   *CSP: Spanish*
27   *L&P*
28   Edward Hall
29   *CSP: Venetian*
30   *L&P*
31   Ibid.
32   *CSP: Venetian*
33   *L&P*
34   Ibid.
35   Ibid.
36   B.L. Additional MSS. The letter is catalogued under 1519 in *L&P*, and some historians have attributed it to 1520, but it fits in very well with the scenario at Easter 1518.
37   *L&P*
38   Woodstock was decaying by the time the future Elizabeth I was under house arrest there in 1554-5. It was largely demolished during a siege in 1646, and the ruins were cleared away in 1705 when Blenheim Palace was built nearby. The architect Sir John Vanbrugh used some of its masonry to build a bridge. The site of the palace is marked by a column.
39   cited by Erickson: *Great Harry*

25. 'THE MOTHER OF THE KING'S SON'

1   cited by Neville Williams: *Henry VIII and his Court*
2   *CSP: Venetian*
3   Thomas More, in *L&P*
4   *CSP: Venetian*
5   *L&P*
6   *Four Years*
7   Ibid.; Edward Hall
8   *Four Years*
9   Ibid.
10 Ibid.
11 *L&P*
12 *CSP: Venetian*
13 George Cavendish
14 Ibid.
15 cited by Richardson: *Mary Tudor*
16 *L&P*
17 Until 1520, the French version of the title was used.
18 Edward Hall
19 *Four Years*
20 Beddington Park is now known as Carew Manor. Although much of the house was remodelled in the 18th century, the great hall remains. The building is now a school and is owned by the London Borough of Sutton.
21 *L&P*
22 Edward Hall
23 Ibid.
24 Ibid.
25 Ibid.
26 Ibid.
27 They were probably related to William Norris, who was Master of the King's Hawks in 1509.
28 *Four Years*
29 cited by Halliday
30 This was the play on which Shakespeare based *A Comedy of Errors*.
31 At a chapter of the Order of the Garter held at Greenwich in 1517, Henry had declared that is was his intention to be buried at Windsor. He probably chose St George's Chapel rather than the Henry VII Chapel in Westminster Abbey because of its associations with the Order of the Garter, and also because there was no room for his tomb in the chapel dominated by his father's monument at Westminster.
32 Nicholas Burton.
33 *State Papers; L&P*
34 *Four Years*
35 cited by Lacey
36 *CSP: Venetian*
37 *Four Years*
38 cited by Bowle
39 The priory church survives today as the Parish Church of St Laurence. Nearby is a Georgian brick house built upon the foundations of a Tudor house that may have been Jericho. The moat still survives, but the encircling walls have been rebuilt. A long, low Tudor building, now an inn, is reputed to have been Henry VIII's stable block.
40 cited by Benton Fletcher
41 cited by Morton Bradley
42 cited by Childe-Pemberton

43   *L&P*
44   Elizabeth I created him Earl of Lincoln in 1572.
45   *L&P*. Some sources give the date incorrectly as 1521. Ives, Starkey and Warnicke all agree that the marriage took place in 1520.
46   The picture of Mary Boleyn is a companion to a portrait said to represent her sister, Anne Boleyn, which derives from Holbein's portrait sketch of an unknown lady at Weston Park, which was not called 'Anne Boleyn' until 1649. No source is known for the Mary Boleyn portrait.
47   It was later sold by their son, Henry Carey, to Lord Rich, who greatly enlarged it. The house has been considerably altered since then.
48   *L&P*
49   Brantôme: *Oeuvres complètes*
50   cited by Ashdown
51   *L&P*
52   Ibid.
53   Ibid.
54   Ibid.

26. 'THE EIGHTH WONDER OF THE WORLD'

1   *CSP: Venetian*
2   cited by Neville Williams: *Henry VIII and his Court*
3   cited by Richardson: *Mary Tudor*
4   Edward Hall
5   *L&P*
6   Edward Hall
7   B.L. Cotton MSS. Augustus
8   Letter from the Earl of Worcester to Henry VIII in *L&P*
9   *L&P*
10   Ibid.
11   Charles was the son of her elder sister, Juana the Mad, former Queen of Castile, by Philip the Handsome, Duke of Burgundy. Philip was the son of the Emperor Maximilian and the brother of Margaret of Austria.
12   *Chronicle of Calais*; *Rutland Papers*
13   Neville Williams: *Henry VIII and his Court*
14   The Old Palace where Henry stayed was rebuilt in 1896, using some materials from the earlier building.
15   Edward Hall
16   Ibid.
17   *CSP: Venetian*
18   Ibid.
19   Ibid.
20   cited by Richardson: *Mary Tudor*
21   John Fisher
22   *CSP: Venetian*
23   cited by Richardson: *Mary Tudor*
24   For the meeting, see principally *L&P*, *CSP: Venetian*, and Edward Hall. A stone relief in the Hôtel de Bourgtheroulde in Rouen, carved soon after 1520, commemorates the event.
25   Edward Hall
26   *Les Mémoires de Martin et Guillaume du Bellay*
27   Polydore Vergil
28   Fleuranges. Robert de la Marck, Seigneur de Fleuranges (1491-1537) took part in the jousts at the Field of Cloth of Gold.
29   *CSP: Venetian*
30   Polydore Vergil

31   John Fisher
32   Polydore Vergil
33   *CSP: Venetian*
34   Ibid.
35   Polydore Vergil
36   *CSP: Venetian*
37   Ibid.
38   Anglo: *Hampton Court Painting*
39   *L&P*
40   *CSP: Venetian*
41   It was probably hastily made to comply with the new rules governing the design of armour laid down by Francis I in March 1520. This suit incorporates the requisite skirt, or tonlet, and a great helmet called a basinet. It is etched with Tudor roses, the Garter collar and the figures of St George and the Virgin and Child.
42   Fleuranges.
43   Ibid. No English source mentions this incident.
44   Fleuranges.
45   *CSP: Venetian*
46   Edward Hall
47   Some sources refer to it as a dragon, but it is more likely to have been a salamander in Francis' honour.
48   The Pax was a crystal box containing the consecrated Host.
49   *L&P*
50   *CSP: Venetian*
51   cited by Erickson: *Great Harry*
52   The date is indicated by the mid-16th century uniforms of the Yeomen of the Guard, other costume details, and the portrayal of the King, which derives from Holbein's portraits. The white greyhounds shown in the painting were probably those given to Henry by Suffolk in 1536.
53   Both are still in the Royal Collection.
54   Commissioned in 1518, she had panelled state rooms for the King and Queen, and was a forerunner of the royal yachts.
55   A few of the people in the procession have been identified: Wolsey rides beside the King, Suffolk and Essex ride behind. Henry is preceded by Dorset, carrying the Sword of State, and Sir Thomas Wriothesley, Garter King of Arms. Neither Katherine nor Mary Tudor can be seen in the procession but may be among the female figures in the banqueting tent, in litters or on horseback. Queen Katherine and Queen Claude may be seen watching the jousting from the stands in the distant tiltyard.
56   Edward Hall
57   Stow: *Annals*; Anglo

27. 'ONE MAN'S DISOBEDIENCE'

1   Edward Hall
2   Polydore Vergil; John Palsgrave
3   cited by Neville Williams: *Henry VIII and his Court*
4   *CSP: Venetian*
5   *L&P*
6   *Original Letters*, ed. Ellis
7   *CSP: Venetian*
8   *L&P*
9   *CSP: Venetian*
10   cited by Neville Williams: *Henry VIII and his Court*
11   *L&P*
12   Ibid.

13 Ibid.
14 Ibid.
15 It reverted to the Crown on his death in 1525.
16 Henry VIII: *Assertio*
17 Henry VIII: *Letters*
18 William Roper
19 *L&P*
20 William Roper
21 *CSP: Venetian*
22 *L&P*
23 The title is still used by the Queen today, even though the faith she defends is that of the Protestant Church of England, not the Catholic Church of Rome. Eleven presentation copies of Henry's book survive. One is in the Vatican, another, autographed, is in the Royal Library at Windsor.
24 Edward Hall
25 cited by Funck-Brentano
26 Henry VIII: *Letters*
27 Doernberg; J. Scarisbrick: *Henry VIII*
28 The house has long since disappeared, and its exact location is not known, although it was probably near Chelsea Old Church.
29 William Roper
30 Edward Hall

28. 'A PROUD HORSE TAMED AND BRIDLED'

1   *L&P*
2   Ibid.; Edward Hall
3   Ibid.
4   Anglo: *Spectacle*; Ives: *Anne Boleyn*
5   Evidence that Anne was the younger sister is outlined by Gairdner in *English Historical Review*
6   For the evidence for Anne's birthdate, see Paget: *Youth of Anne Boleyn*
7   *L&P*
8   *State Papers*
9   *L&P*
10 cited by Michell
11 cited by Bowle
12 cited by Fletcher
13 Edward Hall
14 *Rutland Papers*
15 Ibid.
16 Edward Hall
17 Ibid.
18 Ibid.
19 The Round Table now hangs in the 13th century Great Hall, which is all that remains of the royal castle. In Henry's time, it was believed that the table was the genuine article, although it is now known to be a mediaeval fabrication.
20 See Anglo: *Spectacle*, and *Henry VIII: A European Court in England*, in which the picture is reproduced. It was never recorded in the Royal Collection.
21 Later that year, Torrigiano moved to Spain, where, learning that the Inquisition suspected him of heresy, he committed suicide.
22 Giorgio Vasari: *Lives of the Most Excellent Architects, Painters and Sculptors* (Florence, 1550)
23 *L&P*
24 Edward Hall
25 *History of the King's Works*

26 Ampthill Castle was partially demolished in 1567 and ruinous by 1605. Its remains were completely dismantled in 1649, and at the end of the 17th century Ampthill Park was laid out on the site. A stone cross marks the place where the castle once stood.

29. 'ALL THE ENEMIES OF ENGLAND ARE GONE'

1 Edward Hall
2 *L&P*
3 Ibid.; *CSP: Spanish*
4 Juan Luis Vives
5 *CSP: Venetian*
6 This portrait, which dates from c1540, is now in the Royal Collection.
7 cited by Bowle
8 *L&P*
9 Only one brick range with some original windows survives, and is now a farmhouse.
10 *L&P*
11 Anthony Wood
12 George Cavendish: *Metrical Visions*
13 *Original Letters*, ed. Ellis
14 *L&P*
15 Edward Hall
16 These are now lost. The miniature of the Dauphin Francis by Jean Clouet in the Royal Collection was acquired in the 19th century.
17 The first identifiable English work by one of them, Lucas Horenbout, is the King's portrait in an initial letter on a patent dated 28 April 1524 (sold at Sotheby's in 1983 and now in a private collection), which is certainly by the same hand as Lucas's miniature of Henry VIII in the Fitzwilliam Museum, Cambridge.
18 B.L. Additional MSS.
19 A brass dated 1529 marks her tomb in Fulham Parish Church, London.
20 B.L. Egerton MSS.
21 This was probably the miniature discovered in France in 1994 and auctioned in Paris in November that year. It is now in the Louvre.
22 *L&P*
23 Two are in the Royal Collection, the others are in the Fitzwilliam Museum Cambridge, the Buccleuch Collection, the Louvre and a private collection. They probably date from 1526-7. The King is shown clean-shaven or bearded, with bobbed hair, and looks as if he is putting on weight.
24 They are in the National Portrait Gallery, the E. Grosvenor Paine Collection and the Buccleuch Collection; in the last the Queen is shown with a pet monkey.
25 They are in the Buccleuch Collection and the Royal Ontario Museum.
26 Now in the collection of Louis de Wet Esq.
27 On loan to the National Portrait Gallery from a private collection.
28 Now in the Victoria and Albert Museum.
29 Still in the Royal Collection.
30 Now at Sudeley Castle.
31 Now in the Buccleuch Collection.
32 See Strong: *English Renaissance Miniature*
33 Now in the National Portrait Gallery.
34 Ives: *Anne Boleyn*
35 cited by Benton Fletcher

30. 'NEXT IN RANK TO HIS MAJESTY'

1 Edward Hall
2 Clifford, who had begun his career as a Page of the Chamber, later distinguished

himself in defending the northern border against the Scots. He married the King's niece Eleanor Brandon, younger daughter of the Duke of Suffolk by Mary Tudor.

3   He was the grandson of Anne Plantagenet, sister of Edward IV, and had been a favourite of Henry VIII since the French campaign of 1513. His country residence was Belvoir Castle.

4   *L&P*; the patent of creation stipulated that he was to take precedence over all dukes except those legitimately born to the King or to his heirs male.

5   *CSP: Venetian*

6   Ibid.

7   *L&P*; *Collection of Ordinances*

8   *CSP: Spanish*; John Stow: *Annals*

9   George Cavendish; Edward Hall

10 The first chapel on this site was built by Henry III and later added to by Edward III. Rebuilt by Henry VII, it was extensively altered in the 19th century, when it was used as a temporary mausoleum for the Prince Consort, and is known today as the Albert Memorial Chapel.

11 *L&P*

12 Ibid.

13 The ruins of the castle survive today on private farmland. The massive ditch of the double moat may still be seen.

14 *L&P*

15 Ibid.

16 Ibid.

17 cited by Fraser

18 *CSP: Venetian*

19 Ibid.

20 Letter in the Public Record Office

21 *L&P*

22 B.L. Cotton MSS. Vespasian

23 *L&P*

24 Ibid.

25 Ibid.

26 The house survives today in a much altered state, although its Georgian facade conceals substantial Tudor remains.

27 cited by Erickson; *Great Harry*

28 *L&P*

29 Hunsdon House was granted by Elizabeth I to her cousin, Henry Carey, later Lord Hunsdon, in 1559. It was largely rebuilt in the 19th century, leaving only one of the original turrets, and is now a private residence. The house has recently been the subject of an archaeological excavation.

31. 'THE ESTABLISHMENT OF GOOD ORDER'

1   Edward Hall

2   Ibid.

3   *Collection of Ordinances*. The original vellum MS. is in the Bodleian Library.

4   *L&P*

5   *Collection of Ordinances*

6   *L&P*

7   cited by Starkey: *Henry VIII*

8   *Collection of Ordinances*

9   B.L. Cotton MSS. Vespasian.

10 *Collection of Ordinances*

11 Edward Hall

12 Loades: *Tudor Court*

32. 'A FRESH YOUNG DAMSEL'

1   Edward Hall
2   Ibid.
3   *L&P*
4   *CSP: Venetian*
5   Lancelot de Carles
6   Ibid.
7   George Wyatt of Boxley Abbey, Kent (1554-1624) was the son of the rebel and traitor, Sir Thomas Wyatt the Younger, and the grandson of the poet Sir Thomas Wyatt the Elder. George's life's work, the memoir of Anne Boleyn, was written in response to the Jesuit Nicholas Sander's attack on her in his treatise of 1585.
8   *L&P*
9   B. L. Sloane MSS.
10 Brantôme; even William Forrest, a partisan of Katherine of Aragon, states that Anne had a pretty singing voice. See also Lancelot de Carles and B. L. Sloane MSS.
11 Brantôme; Nicholas Sander
12 *L&P*
13 Lancelot de Carles; Nicholas Sander; B. L. Sloane MSS.
14 Brantôme
15 Ibid.
16 B. L. Royal MSS.
17 cited by Muir
18 *L&P*
19 In 1554, Sir Thomas Wyatt the Younger was executed for leading a major rebellion against Mary I.
20 A rondeau was a French poem, 10 or 13 lines long, with just two rhymes repeated throughout and the first words used twice as a refrain.
21 William Latimer. Latimer was Anne Boleyn's chaplain, and wrote a highly sympathetic biography of her after her death.
22 Lancelot de Carles
23 Brantôme
24 Nicholas Sander
25 *L&P*
26 *CSP: Spanish*
27 *L&P*

33. 'MASTER HANS'

1   Edward Hall
2   *PPE*
3   cited by Bowle
4   Only fragmentary remains of one of the service courts survive today; these are situated to the south of the present manor house.
5   *L&P*
6   Ibid.
7   Ibid.
8   Ibid.
9   Erasmus: *Opus Epistolarum*
10 Holbein's portrait of Archbishop Warham is in the Louvre. A version is at Lambeth Palace.
11 Erasmus: *Opus Epistolarum*
12 George Cavendish
13 Henry VIII: *Letters*
14 Edward Hall. These houses survived for at least 80 years, but although they have long

vanished, there are detailed descriptions of them, and their contents, in PRO, *L&P* and B.L. Egerton MSS.

15   The portrait of Nicolaus Kratzer, which shows him surrounded by mathematical instruments, is in the Louvre; a copy is in the National Portrait Gallery. Copies of Holbein's portrait of Sir Henry Wyatt are in the Louvre and the National Galleries of Scotland. The portrait of Sir Henry Guildford is in the Royal Collection, and shows him wearing his Garter collar (he had been admitted to the Order in 1526) and holding his white wand of office as Comptroller of the Household. Attached to his hat is a badge decorated with mathematical instruments.

16   Edward Hall

17   *CSP: Venetian*. The tapestries may be identified with the ten-piece set now in the Musée de la Renaissance at the Château d'Écouen in France.

18   Edward Hall

19   *L&P*

20   Edward Hall

21   Ibid.

22   *CSP: Venetian*

23   Ibid.

24   Ibid.

25   Edward Hall

26   PRO; B.L. Egerton MSS.

27   Rawlinson MSS., Bodleian Library

34. 'NOLI ME TANGERE, FOR CAESAR'S I AM'

1   *CSP: Spanish*

2   William Tyndale: *Works*

3   *L&P*

4   Ibid.

5   *CSP: Spanish*

6   Ibid.

7   Ibid.

8   Ibid.

9   George Wyatt

10   B.L. Additional MSS; the manuscript was once at Chatsworth.

11   *CSP: Spanish*

12   *Crónica del rey Enrico*

13   George Wyatt: *Papers*

14   *L&P*

15   George Cavendish

16   George Wyatt

17   *CSP: Spanish*

18   An illuminated copy of the Statutes of the Order of St Michael is now in the Public Record Office; the copy of the Garter Statutes sent to Francis I is among B.L. Additional MSS., and features a miniature of the Princess Mary dressed as 'Concord'.

19   Edward Hall. For the exchange of these Orders, see *Henry VIII: A European Court in England*

20   Edward Hall. A portrait of Sir Anthony, which probably dates from this time, since he is wearing French costume, is in the National Portrait Gallery.

21   The Order of St Michael was abolished in 1578 because the admission of too many knights had debased it. Henry III of France founded in its place the Order of the Holy Spirit.

22   George Cavendish

23   *L&P*; Erickson: *Great Harry*

24   *PPE*

25   Ibid., *CSP: Spanish*
26   *L&P*
27   *PPE*
28   Brantôme
29   *PPE*
30   Ibid.
31   *L&P*; *Ambassades de Jean du Bellay*

35. 'A THOUSAND CASES OF SWEAT'

1   This theory was first propounded in 1888 by A. S. Currie in 'Notes on the Obstetric Histories of Katherine of Aragon and Anne Boleyn', and given widespread circulation by means of an anonymous article, 'Some Royal Deathbeds', which appeared in the *British Medical Journal* in 1910. It was refuted by Frederick Chamberlain in *The Private Character of Henry VIII* (1932), J. F. D. Shrewsbury in *Henry VIII: A Medical Study* (1952), and B. Deer in *Carnivore King: The Main Course of History* (1989).
2   *L&P*
3   Ibid.; Brewer; *CSP: Spanish*
4   *L&P*; *State Papers*
5   This was the last, and worst, major outbreak of the sweating sickness. It returned for one final time in 1551, then disappeared.
6   *L&P*
7   Edward Hall
8   *Henry VIII: Letters*
9   *L&P*
10   Ibid.
11   Ibid.
12   Ibid.
13   *Henry VIII: Letters*
14   Ibid.
15   Edward Hall
16   Ibid.
17   *CSP: Venetian*; *State Papers*; *L&P*
18   *L&P*
19   *State Papers*
20   *L&P*
21   Ibid.
22   Ibid.
23   Ibid.
24   Ibid.; *State Papers*
25   *CSP: Spanish*
26   *PPE*
27   *L&P*
28   *Original Letters*, ed. Ellis
29   *Excerpta Historica*
30   *Ambassades de Jean du Bellay*; *L&P*

36. 'BACK TO YOUR WIFE!'

1   George Cavendish; *CSP: Spanish*; Starkey: *Henry VIII*
2   Shortly afterwards Vives found a new patron, John III, King of Portugal. He died in 1540.
3   *L&P*
4   *CSP: Spanish*
5   *L&P*; *Henry VIII: Letters*

6   *L&P*
7   *CSP: Spanish*
8   Ibid.
9   *L&P*
10   *CSP: Spanish*
11   Edward Hall
12   *L&P*
13   *CSP: Venetian*. After this, Venice sent no ambassadors to England for 60 years.
14   *L&P*
15   Edward Hall
16   Ibid.
17   Wilson: *Holbein*
18   The 16-page MS. on vellum is now in the Bodleian Library.
19   Wilson: *Holbein*
20   George Cavendish
21   *L&P*
22   George Cavendish; Edward Hall

37. 'ABOVE EVERYONE, MADEMOISELLE ANNE'

1   George Cavendish
2   *Original Letters*, ed. Ellis; *CSP: Spanish*
3   George Cavendish
4   *CSP: Spanish*
5   Ibid.
6   George Cavendish
7   Ibid.
8   *CSP: Spanish*; *L&P*
9   PRO
10   The Bayne Tower was partially refaced in the 19th century, and its windows replaced with Tudor-style replicas, but survives otherwise intact. Considering the fact that none of Henry VIII's private apartments survive anywhere else, it is surprising that the Bayne Tower, which is of enormous historical interest and significance, is not open to the public but is used as accommodation for palace staff.
11   Sturgis
12   The great arched conduits he built, 14 feet high and 10 feet wide, which carried kitchen waste under the moat to the Thames, still survive today.
13   The storage platforms in Henry VIII's Great Kitchen were built in the 17th century.
14   The Boiling House is the only one of Henry's subsidiary kitchens to survive today. Only a small area of the service complex, around Fish Court, is open to the public.
15   The originals have long since disappeared; the King's Beasts that we see today are 20th century reconstructions, as is the royal coat of arms on the gatehouse.
16   See Chapter 40.
17   More than 10,000 pages of accounts detailing Henry's works at Hampton Court survive in the Public Record Office.
18   In 1553, Mary I restored Esher to the diocese of Winchester. The house was decayed by 1660, and thereafter fell to ruin, but the great gatehouse and a tower still survive.
19   George Cavendish
20   The More was leased in 1576 to the Earl of Bedford, but was ruinous by 1598. No trace of the house remains today. The present Moor Park was built in 1727.
21   cited by Fraser.
22   cited by Neville Williams: *Henry VIII and his Court*
23   Ibid.
24   *CSP: Spanish*
25   Ibid.

26 *L&P*
27 Ibid.
28 Erasmus: *Opus Epistolarum*
29 State Papers in the Public Record Office
30 John Ponet, Bishop of Winchester, cited by Neville Williams: *Henry VIII and his Court*
31 C. R. N. Routh
32 *CSP: Spanish*
33 Ibid.
34 Nicholas Harpsfield: *More*
35 Thomas More: *English Works*
36 William Tyndale: *Works*
37 *PPE*
38 Ibid.; *L&P*
39 Henry VIII: *Letters*
40 *CSP: Spanish*
41 *L&P*
42 *CSP: Spanish*
43 Ibid.; *L&P*
44 *CSP: Spanish*
45 See *L&P*; John Foxe; William Latimer; Dowling: 'Anne Boleyn and Reform'
46 *CSP: Spanish*
47 John Foxe; John Strype; *Narratives of the Reformation*, ed. Nichols; George Wyatt; *Tudor Royal Proclamations*
48 John Foxe. Fish was later reconciled to the Church. He died of plague in 1531.
49 *L&P*
50 Ibid.
51 B.L. King's MSS
52 Sold at Sotheby's to a private collector in 1982.
53 B.L. Royal MSS.
54 B.L. Additional MSS.; *L&P*
55 *L&P*
56 Ibid.
57 Ibid.
58 Ibid.
59 George Cavendish; *PPE*. Cavendish says Rochford was not yet 27.
60 *CSP: Spanish*; *L&P*
61 *Henry VIII: A European Court in England*
62 *CSP: Spanish*
63 *L&P*

38. 'SQUIRE HARRY WILL BE GOD, AND DO AS HE PLEASES'

1   cited by Mathew
2   A cloth-dresser. The Cromwell family had owned a fulling mill at Putney for 50 years.
3   George Cavendish
4   Ibid.
5   *CSP: Spanish*
6   *L&P*
7   Ibid.
8   Ibid.
9   *CSP: Spanish*
10 Ibid.
11 Ibid.
12 Much of Richmond Palace was destroyed under the Commonwealth, and its contents

13   sold. In 1660, what remained was given to Queen Henrietta Maria, but it was barely
      habitable. By 1690, nearly all the buildings had disappeared. All that remains of the
      palace today is the gateway bearing Henry VII's arms, which overlooks Richmond
      Green, and two heavily restored dwelling houses, the Old Palace and Wardrobe
      Court, which incorporate some of the Tudor fabric. Trumpeter's House stands on the
      site of the chapel and great hall. The remains of the cellars are nearby.

13   Much of Eltham Palace was demolished under the Commonwealth, when the park
      was destroyed. In 1656, the diarist John Evelyn described the palace as 'miserable
      ruins'; the great hall was in use as a barn and the chapel decayed. Eltham was alienated
      from the Crown when Charles II granted it to Sir John Shaw in the late 17th century.
      Major restoration works were carried out in the 1930s and the 1990s. Today, the great
      hall remains, along with part of its screens passage, as well as the Chancellor's Lodging,
      built by Henry VIII, a bridge over the moat, the arched gate to the vanished tiltyard,
      and a courtier lodging.

14   It was the earliest embassy building in England, and continued as such until 1553,
      when Edward VI established a House of Correction for the vagrant poor in the palace.
      Such houses were thereafter known as Bridewells. The royal apartments were burned
      down in the Great Fire of 1666, but many of the Tudor buildings survived until the
      19th century. The House of Correction was finally demolished in 1864. The site was
      excavated in 1978.

15   *L&P*

16   Bodleian Library MSS.; Thurley: *Royal Palaces*

17   Ibid.

18   *CSP: Venetian*, 1532

19   Thurley: *Royal Palaces*. Only the external brickwork of Henry's tennis court remains.
      Wolsey's play was demolished in the late 17th century.

20   Nottingham University Library MSS.

21   McConica.

22   *L&P*. See Chapter 44.

23   *CSP: Spanish*; *L&P*

24   Ibid.

25   *CSP: Spanish*

26   Richard Tottel: *Miscellany*

27   John Leland: *Itinerary*. Collyweston was granted to the future Elizabeth I in 1550, but
      alienated from the Crown in 1625. It was in ruins by the 18th century. Today, only
      a few terraced foundations remain.

28   George Cavendish

29   Ibid.

30   Ibid.

31   *CSP: Spanish*

32   *PPE*

39. 'OPPROBRIOUS LANGUAGE'

1   PRO

2   cited by Erickson: *Great Harry*

3   Ibid.

4   PRO

5   Ibid.

6   *CSP: Spanish*

7   Ibid.; *L&P*

8   Ibid.

9   *CSP: Venetian*

10   Ibid.

11   Charles Wriothesley

12 *CSP: Venetian*
13 Ibid.
14 Ibid.
15 *Original Letters relative to the English Reformation*
16 *CSP: Venetian*
17 *L&P*
18 Ibid.
19 cited by Neville Williams: *Henry VIII and his Court*
20 Edward Hall
21 cited by Neville Williams: *Henry VIII and his Court*
22 *CSP: Spanish*; *L&P*
23 Ibid.
24 *CSP: Spanish*
25 *CSP: Venetian*
26 Ibid.; *L&P*
27 *L&P*
28 Ibid.

40. 'THE LADY MARQUESS'

1   Hanworth, which remained royal property until Elizabeth I sold it to Francis, Lord Cottingham, burned down in 1797. Only two of the roundels survive in the remains of the gardens, along with a carving of the royal arms, two Tudor chimneys, part of the moat and a five-step mounting block. Fragments of heraldic stained glass survive in Hanworth Rectory. The old trees were cut down in the 18th century, and the park reduced in area. The wall that marks the extent of the original gardens was built in the 17th century.

2   *L&P*; William Camden. It is sometimes stated that Gardiner presented the house to Anne Boleyn, but it is clear that it was still in royal hands in 1532, and that it was Henry who granted the house to Anne.

3   Laid in October 1532 (PRO).

4   The great hall was restored in 1770 and again, more extensively, in the 1840s, when new stained glass windows depicting the royal descents of Henry VIII and his wives and children were installed in place of the long-vanished Tudor glass. At the same time, the moulded polychrome cornice was added. In the 1920s, the louvre was removed from the roof, and the Tudor paint stripped away from its timbers. Some of Anne Boleyn's initials and badges survive on the ceiling; others, more accessible, were replaced by those of Jane Seymour.

5   *L&P*

6   *CSP: Spanish*

7   See Chapter 57. Three of the four courtyards of St James's Palace survive today, among them Friary Court. The only other remains from Henry VIII's original house are his watching chamber and presence chamber in the state apartments, each with a fireplace carved with lovers' knots encasing the initials H and A, the chapel royal and the great gatehouse.

8   Raphael Holinshed

9   *L&P*; *History of the King's Works*; Thurley: *Royal Palaces*. The royal lodgings in the Tower were demolished in the 17th and 18th centuries.

10 A portrait attributed to Ambrosius Benson in the collection of the Earl of Ashburnham has sometimes been incorrectly identified as Katherine Parr.

11 Henry Clifford

12 PPE; *CSP: Spanish*; Edward Hall

13 George Cavendish: *Metrical Visions*

14 *PPE*

15 *L&P*

16   B.L. Royal MSS.; *L&P*
17   Warnicke: *Anne Boleyn*
18   See Lowinsky: *A Music Book for Anne Boleyn*. The MS. is in the Royal College of Music.
19   *L&P*
20   *CSP: Spanish*
21   *L&P*
22   All that survives of Shurland House is the ruined entrance facade.
23   Hamy; *L&P*
24   *CSP: Spanish*; *L&P*; *CSP: Venetian*
25   *CSP: Venetian*
26   *L&P*
27   For the investiture and banquet see Milles: *Catalogue of Honour*; *L&P*; B. L. Harleian
      MSS.; *CSP: Venetian*; *Calendar of the Manuscripts at Hatfield House*; *CSP: Spanish*;
      Edward Hall

41. 'THE TRIUMPH AT CALAIS AND BOULOGNE'

1   *CSP: Spanish*; *L&P*
2   *L&P*; B.L. Royal MSS.
3   *CSP: Spanish*; *L&P*
4   *PPE*; *L&P*
5   Claude of France had died in 1524.
6   cited by Perry
7   Seymour Papers
8   *CSP: Spanish*
9   *L&P*
10   *CSP: Spanish*
11   *PPE*. She was the widow of Sir Richard Wingfield, K.G., who died in 1525. Stone is
      20 miles north of Hever Castle.
12   For the French visit see *The Manner of the Triumph at Calais and Boulogne*; *L&P*;
      Edward Hall; *CSP: Venetian*; *CSP: Spanish*; *Chronicle of Calais*; *An English Garner*;
      Hamy; Knecht
13   Edward Hall
14   *History of the King's Works*
15   *L&P*
16   *CSP: Venetian*
17   Ibid.; *CSP: Spanish*
18   *PPE*
19   Ibid.
20   cited by Seward
21   *CSP: Venetian*
22   Ibid.
23   *L&P*
24   *PPE*
25   Ibid.
26   Ibid.
27   *L&P*
28   Edward Hall; *CSP: Venetian*
29   *L&P*
30   Ibid.; Edward Hall; *CSP: Spanish*
31   *L&P*
32   Ibid.
33   cited by Bowle
34   *CSP: Spanish*; *L&P*
35   Ibid.; *PPE*

42. 'ANNE REGINA ANGLIAE'

1   Ives speculates that 14 November 1532 may be the date on which Henry and Anne began sleeping together after contracting themselves to each other before witnesses, a procedure that was as binding as a canonical marriage in the early 16th century; however, the evidence strongly suggests that they were already having sexual relations before that date (see Chapter 41).

2   Thomas Cranmer: *Miscellaneous Writings and Letters*

3   B.L. Sloane MSS.

4   Later Bishop of Coventry and Lichfield.

5   Later Archbishop of Dublin.

6   *CSP: Spanish; L&P*

7   B.L. Sloane MSS.; Nicholas Harpsfield: *Pretended Divorce*; Nicholas Sander

8   *CSP: Spanish*

9   She shortly afterwards married Thomas, Lord Berkeley.

10 *L&P; Letters and Accounts of William Brereton*; Nicholas Sander

11 *CSP: Spanish; L&P*

12 Ibid.

13 Ibid.; *CSP: Venetian*

14 Gage talked of renouncing the world and entering a monastery, but later changed his mind and became a loyal supporter of the King. He was allowed to return to court and in 1540 was appointed Comptroller of the Household. Later, he held military commands in Scotland and France.

15 *CSP: Spanish; L&P; CSP: Venetian*

16 William Latimer; Dowling: 'Anne Boleyn and Reform'. Shaxton became Bishop of Salisbury, Skip became Bishop of Hereford, and Parker became Queen Elizabeth's first Archbishop of Canterbury.

17 *House of Commons*

18 Daughter of Sir John Shelton by Anne Boleyn, Wiltshire's sister.

19 For Anne Boleyn's household see *L&P; Lisle Letters; CSP: Spanish*; Friedmann; *House of Commons*

20 *Lisle Letters*

21 *CSP: Spanish; L&P*

22 *L&P*

23 William Latimer; John Foxe

24 George Wyatt

25 Matthew Parker: *Correspondence*

26 cited by H. Norris

27 William Latimer; Dowling: 'Anne Boleyn and Reform'

28 This badge was derived from the falcon crest of the Butler Earls of Ormonde; it was later used by Elizabeth I.

29 *CSP: Spanish*

30 *L&P*

31 William Latimer

32 Now in the British Library.

33 Now in the British Library.

34 B.L. Royal MSS.

35 B.L. Harleian MSS.

36 Now owned by the Duke of Northumberland.

37 *L&P*

38 Edward Hall

39 *CSP: Spanish*

43. 'HERE ANNA COMES, BRIGHT IMAGE OF CHASTITY'

1   For Anne Boleyn's coronation, see chiefly Edward Hall; *L&P*; Charles Wriothesley; *The Noble Triumphant Coronation of Queen Anne*
2   *L&P*
3   cited in *Rivals in Power*
4   Edward Hall. Holbein's design is now in the Staatliche Museen Preussischer Kulturbesitz in Berlin.
5   Edward Hall
6   *CSP: Spanish*
7   *L&P*; *Crónica del rey Enrico*
8   *L&P*
9   B.L. Cotton MSS. Vespasian
10 Edward Hall
11 Ibid.; *L&P*
12 Lancelot de Carles
13 Edward Hall; *The Noble and Triumphant Coronation of Queen Anne*
14 Edward Hall; *CSP: Venetian*
15 *L&P*
16 William Roper
17 cited by Bowle
18 *Calendar of State Papers, Foreign, Elizabeth I*
19 Charles Wriothesley, *CSP: Spanish*; *L&P*; *CSP: Venetian*
20 *PPE*; Lancelot de Carles
21 *CSP: Spanish*; *Letters and Accounts of William Brereton*
22 Muir; Thomson: *Wyatt*; *Letters and Accounts of William Brereton*
23 *L&P*; *CSP: Spanish*; *CSP: Venetian*
24 *History of the King's Works*; *CSP: Spanish*
25 *History of the King's Works*
26 Ibid.
27 *L&P*
28 Paul Hentzner
29 Ibid.
30 The Paradise Chamber was demolished with most of the rest of these royal apartments in 1689-91 by Sir Christopher Wren. The present Cumberland Suite occupies the site of Henry VIII's privy chamber. Henry's lodgings were replaced by the present King's Apartments, built for William III.
31 Paul Hentzner
32 Sunken gardens created in the 1950s in the Tudor style now occupy the site of the Pond Gardens.
33 *History of the King's Works*
34 Rawlinson MSS., Bodleian Library
35 cited in *Windsor Castle: The Official Guide*. The North Terrace was rebuilt in stone by Elizabeth I. Henry VIII's private apartments at Windsor were extensively remodelled by Charles II in the 1670s, and again under George IV in the 1820s. The present State Apartments occupy the site.

44. 'THE HIGH AND MIGHTY PRINCESS OF ENGLAND'

1   *L&P*
2   Now in the National Gallery, London.
3   Holbein's original portrait of Cromwell is lost. The best copy is in the Frick Collection in New York, and there are two other copies in the National Portrait Gallery in London. On one of the latter there is an inscription referring to Cromwell

as Master of the Jewel House, which must date the sitting to 1533/4.

4   After Holbein's death, many of his drawings remained in the Royal Collection, but were sold in 1553 to Henry FitzAlan, Earl of Arundel. They passed in 1590 into the collection of his son-in-law, John, Lord Lumley, by which time they had been bound into a book. On Lumley's death in 1609, the book was acquired by Henry, Prince of Wales, son of James I. His brother Charles I later gave it to the Earl of Pembroke, who sold it to Thomas Howard, Earl of Arundel, before 1642. The drawings were purchased by Charles II prior to 1675, and have remained in the Royal Collection ever since. In 1727, the book of 87 drawings was found by Queen Caroline of Ansbach in a bureau in Kensington Palace. The pictures were then extracted and framed. George III had them rebound in two volumes, and they were moved to Windsor in the 19th century, where they remain today, remounted and preserved between acrylic sheeting. 85 of the pictures remain, 80 of which are signed by Holbein; several have deteriorated and/or been retouched. 69 have been identified, but some are incorrectly labelled. In 1590, the Lumley inventory noted that the names on the pictures had been subscribed by Sir John Cheke, Secretary to Edward VI, who had first come to court in 1542 and may not have known all the sitters. It is unlikely that any of the existing labels are his: they were probably copied in the 18th century.

5   Karel van Mander

6   see Wilson: *Holbein*

7   Holbein's design for the cup is now in the Öffentliche Kunstsammlung Kupferstichkabinett, Basel.

8   *L&P*

9   Ibid.

10 Ibid.

11 Ibid.

12 *Lisle Letters*

13 Ibid.; *L&P*

14 John Leland: *Collectanea*; *Lisle Letters*

15 *CSP: Spanish*; Rawlinson MSS., Bodleian Library

16 *CSP: Spanish*; *L&P*

17 *L&P*

18 *CSP: Spanish*; *L&P*

19 Lancelot de Carles

20 *CSP: Spanish*

21 One is in the B.L. Harleian MSS.

22 *L&P*; Edward Hall; Charles Wriothesley; *CSP: Spanish*

23 *CSP: Spanish*. A lace-trimmed christening robe, said to be Elizabeth's, is at Sudeley Castle, but probably dates from the 17th century.

24 Lancelot de Carles

25 For the christening, see Edward Hall; *L&P*

26 *CSP: Spanish*

27 Suffolk renovated and modernised Grimsthorpe, and some of his works can still be seen there.

28 Both are in the Royal Collection.

29 *Crónica del rey Enrico*

30 *CSP: Spanish*

31 In 1573, Beaulieu was granted by Elizabeth I to the Earl of Sussex, who rebuilt it. The north wing of his house still survives. The only remains of Henry VIII's palace are in the cellars, apart from an oriel window which is now in St Margaret's Church, Westminster. Beaulieu was largely rebuilt in the 18th century, and in 1798 became a Catholic convent school. It was badly damaged by enemy action in 1943, but the Elizabethan façade has been restored.

32 *L&P*

33 Ibid.; *CSP: Spanish*

34 Ibid.
35 *State Papers*; *L&P*
36 *L&P*
37 Ibid.; *Lisle Letters*
38 B.L. Arundel MSS.
39 *CSP: Spanish*
40 Ibid.; *L&P*; quote cited by Bowle

45. 'THE IMAGE OF GOD UPON EARTH'

1   *Lisle Letters*
2   She had probably conceived in November 1533: her pregnancy was reported in Rome on 23 January 1534, the news having been presumably conveyed by her uncle, Lord William Howard, the newly arrived English ambassador.
3   *L&P*; *Lisle Letters*. The New Year gift roll for 1534 survives in the Public Record Office and lists all the gifts given and received by the King.
4   *Lisle Letters*; *L&P*
5   cited by Neville Williams: *Henry VIII and his Court*
6   Letter of Sir Thomas More, cited in Reynolds: *The Field is Won*
7   William Roper
8   Only one example of this medal survives, in the British Museum. The nose is somewhat mutilated, yet the face shape is recognisably Anne's.
9   Rawlinson MSS., Bodleian Library; *PPE*; *History of the King's Works*
10 PRO; Rawlinson MSS., Bodleian Library
11 *L&P*
12 Now in the possession of the Dean and College of Windsor
13 Foister; *Dynasties*
14 Now in the Royal Collection
15 *L&P*; *CSP: Spanish*
16 Ibid.
17 *L&P*
18 *CSP: Spanish*
19 *History of the King's Works*
20 Strype
21 PRO
22 The Catholic Church today recognises 50 Henrician martyrs, among them More, Fisher, Margaret Pole, 33 monks and 11 priests
23 *L&P*
24 Ibid.; it was commissioned in 1535.
25 John Stow: *London*; PRO
26 John Foxe. This preaching place was demolished in 1649 under the Commonwealth.
27 *L&P*
28 Ibid.; William Latimer.
29 cited by Neville Williams: *Henry VIII and his Court*
30 This seal is now in the Public Record Office
31 An example is in the British Museum.
32 *CSP: Spanish*
33 Polydore Vergil
34 Stephen Gardiner: *De Vera Obedientia* (1535)
35 *L&P*
36 Ibid.
37 Now in the Royal Collection.
38 Now in the Royal Collection. Henry also owned portraits of Francis I and Eleanor of Austria by Joos van Cleve, which are still in the Royal Collection.
39 cited by Neville Williams: *Henry VIII and his Court*

40 *L&P; CSP: Spanish*
41 Ibid.
42 Ibid.
43 Ibid.
44 *L&P; Lisle Letters*
45 *L&P; CSP: Spanish; Letters of Royal and Illustrious Ladies*
46 *L&P*
47 Ibid.; *Lisle Letters*
48 *Lisle Letters*

46. 'THAT THIN OLD WOMAN'

1   Now in the Public Record Office
2   William Latimer
3   John Bale: *The Laborious Journey and Search of John Leland for England's Antiquities* (London, 1549)
4   Ibid.
5   *CSP: Spanish*; William Latimer identifies her as Mary Shelton, who married Sir Anthony Heveningham in 1546 and is the subject of a portrait sketch by Holbein (Royal Collection).
6   *CSP: Spanish*
7   William Latimer
8   Ibid.
9   *L&P; CSP: Spanish*: Warnicke: 'The Lady Margaret'
10 *CSP: Spanish; L&P*; Henry Clifford
11 *L&P; Tudor Royal Proclamations*
12 William Latimer; Nicholas Bourbon; *L&P*
13 Nicholas Bourbon
14 cited by Anglo; Loades: *Tudor Court*
15 *L&P; CSP: Spanish*
16 cited by Neville Williams: *Henry VIII and his Court*
17 *L&P*
18 More and Fisher were both canonised in 1935.
19 *CSP: Spanish; L&P*
20 *L&P*
21 *CSP: Spanish; L&P*
22 Ibid.
23 Chobham Park was sold by Mary I to Nicholas Heath, Archbishop of York in 1558. Nothing remains of the house today.
24 The manor of Hackney was later granted by Edward VI to Sir William Herbert.
25 Parts of Henry's house were incorporated into the present Petworth House when it was built at the end of the 17th century.
26 The fireplace, doors and cornice were replaced by Wren in 1700, and the original roundels were replaced with copies in the 19th century. The stained glass in the oriel window dates from 1841.
27 PRO; Rawlinson MSS. Bodleian Library; Inventory. A lead leaf and a Tudor rose were found during excavations at Greenwich, and are now in Nottingham University Museum.
28 *CSP: Spanish*
29 see *Henry VIII: A European Court in England*
30 The present Wulfhall is mainly Elizabethan, but incorporates some early 16th century work. Tudor chimneys and mullioned windows can be seen in a house opposite, and may have come from Sir John Seymour's house.
31 *L&P*; Seymour Papers
32 *L&P*

33   Ibid.
34   *CSP: Spanish*
35   A sketch of Jane by Holbein is in the Royal Collection at Windsor. His finished
      portrait is in the Kunsthistorisches Museum, Vienna, while what is thought to be a
      studio copy hangs in the Mauritshuis in the Hague. Holbein's likeness is echoed in
      Lucas Horenbout's miniature of Jane at Sudeley Castle.
36   *CSP: Spanish*
37   *L&P; Henry VIII: A European Court in England*
38   *CSP: Spanish*
39   *CSP: Venetian*
40   *CSP: Spanish; L&P*
41   Ibid.
42   Ibid.
43   Ibid.
44   Ibid.
45   Polydore Vergil
46   *CSP: Spanish*; Edward Hall; Polydore Vergil; *L&P*; Herbert of Cherbury; Henry
      Clifford
47   *CSP: Spanish; L&P*
48   Ibid.; Charles Wriothesley also says Henry 'had no hurt'.
49   chiefly MacNalty
50   *CSP: Spanish*
51   Ibid. There is no contemporary evidence to support Warnicke's elaborate theory that
      the foetus was deformed. Chapuys' sources gave him a detailed description of it, and
      he would not have hesitated to make political capital of any abnormality.
52   *L&P*
53   *CSP: Spanish*
54   Ibid.

47. 'THUNDER ROLLS AROUND THE THRONE'

 1   *CSP: Spanish*
 2   Ibid.
 3   *L&P*
 4   cited Neville Williams: *Henry VIII and his Court*
 5   *L&P*
 6   *CSP: Spanish*
 7   Loke: *Materials*
 8   *L&P; CSP: Spanish*
 9   *Statutes of the Realm*
10   *L&P*
11   *CSP: Spanish; L&P*
12   Ibid.
13   Ibid.
14   Ibid.
15   Ibid.
16   Ibid.
17   *L&P*; Strype; B.L. Cotton MSS. Otho; B.L. Harleian MSS.
18   Charles Wriothesley
19   *CSP: Spanish; State Papers; L&P*
20   *CSP: Spanish; L&P*
21   Thomas Wyatt: *Collected Poems*
22   *L&P*
23   Ibid.; *Lisle Letters*
24   For the indictment, see *L&P*. Warnicke has suggested that the men accused with

Anne Boleyn were all known to have indulged in criminal perversions and thus easily framed, but there is no real evidence to support this theory.

25   *CSP: Spanish*; *L&P*
26   *L&P*
27   cited by Starkey: *Henry VIII*
28   *CSP: Foreign, Elizabeth I*; letter from Alexander Aless to Elizabeth I, 1 September 1559, now in the Public Record Office.
29   *L&P*; Strype; B.L. Cotton MSS. Otho; B.L. Harleian MSS
30   *L&P*
31   Ibid.
32   George Constantine. Constantine was Norris's servant, and had known Brereton since their youth.
33   Ibid.; *Crónica del rey Enrico*
34   *Reports of Sir John Spelman*; *L&P*
35   *L&P*; Strype; B.L. Cotton MSS.; Otho; B.L. Harleian MSS.
36   George Constantine
37   Edward Hall
38   Ibid.
39   Sander says that Henry left in a rage after Anne dropped her handkerchief to Norris as a favour. Norris's use of it to wipe the sweat from his face was seen by the King as evidence of intimacy. No contemporary source mentions this incident.
40   *L&P*
41   Ashmole MSS., Bodleian Library
42   *L&P*; Strype; B.L. Cotton MSS. Otho; B.L. Harleian MSS.
43   *State Papers*; George Constantine; *L&P*
44   Lancelot de Carles; Henry Clifford; Herbert of Cherbury; Gilbert Burnet
45   *Excerpta Historica*
46   *CSP: Spanish*; *L&P*
47   *L&P*; *Lisle Letters*; *PPE*
48   *L&P*
49   Ibid.
50   *Letters and Accounts of William Brereton*
51   George Cavendish: *Metrical Visions*
52   *L&P*; *Lisle Letters*
53   *CSP: Spanish*; *L&P*
54   Ibid.
55   Ibid.
56   Ibid.
57   Now the official residence of the Governor of the Tower. The Queen's House is not called after Anne Boleyn, but is known as the King's House or the Queen's House according to the gender of the current monarch. The rooms occupied by Anne have been preserved; a carving of her first name is to be seen in the stonework of the fireplace in her bedchamber.
58   *Chronicle of Calais*; *Excerpta Historica*; William Thomas; Charles Wriothesley
59   see Loades: *Tudor Court*
60   *CSP: Spanish*
61   Edward Hall
62   *L&P*; *CSP: Spanish*
63   *L&P*
64   B.L. Cotton MSS. Vespasian; *Original Letters*, ed. Ellis; *L&P*
65   *L&P*; *Lisle Letters*

48. 'BOUND TO OBEY AND SERVE'

1   *Statutes of the Realm*

2   Charles Wriothesley
3   *CSP: Spanish*
4   *L&P*
5   *CSP: Spanish*
6   Edward Hall
7   *CSP: Spanish*; *L&P*
8   *L&P*
9   *CSP: Spanish*
10 *L&P*
11 Ibid.
12 *CSP: Spanish*; *L&P*
13 *L&P*
14 This tale was recounted by the 18th century antiquary and art historian, George Vertue, who had access to sources now lost to us, and is recorded by Horace Walpole in *Anecdotes of Painting in England*
15 *L&P*
16 Charles Wriothesley
17 cited by L. B. Smith: *Henry VIII: The Mask of Royalty*
18 cited by Neville Williams: *Henry VIII and his Court*
19 Charles Wriothesley
20 *CSP: Spanish*
21 Ibid.
22 *Lisle Letters*
23 *CSP: Spanish*
24 Rawlinson MSS., Bodleian Library; PRO. Some of Anne's emblems were too inaccessible to remove, or were overlooked: her initials, entwined with Henry's, are still to be seen on the vaulted ceiling above the entrance to Anne Boleyn's Gateway at Hampton Court and in the roof timbers of the great hall, and her falcon badge survives in the rood screen in King's College Chapel, Cambridge
25 PRO
26 B.L. Additional MSS.
27 Inventory
28 Now in the Royal Collection.
29 Both sketches are in the Royal Collection.
30 *Lisle Letters*
31 This cup was recorded in royal inventories until the reign of Charles I, who, in 1629, had it melted down to raise funds. Holbein's preliminary design is in the British Museum, and his more elaborate finished presentation drawing is in the Ashmolean Museum, Oxford.
32 Jane's portrait is in the Kunsthistorisches Museum, Vienna; Henry's is in the Thyssen Collection at Lugano. The portraits may have formed a diptych: one of Henry VIII and Jane Seymour is recorded in the King's Inventory. However, they are not a matching pair, and it may be that one or the other was part of the diptych, and that the corresponding portrait is now lost.
33 More than 250 of his designs survive in the British Museum, the Ashmolean Museum and at Basel.
34 see below, Chapter 50.
35 *L&P*; *Privy Purse Expenses of the Princess Mary*
36 Suffolk Place was given by Mary I to the Archbishop of York in 1556. Few traces of the house remain today.
37 Anne of Cleves died there in 1557. In 1639, Chelsea Palace was alienated from the Crown. Nothing remains of it today.
38 Durham House was kept in repair throughout the Tudor period, but demolished in the mid 17th century.
39 Copt Hall was given by Edward VI to Mary Tudor in 1548. It was rebuilt in 1758, but later destroyed by fire. Only ruins remain.

49. 'THE SUPPRESSION OF THE RELIGIOUS HOUSES'

1   *L&P*; B.L. Cotton MSS. Vespasian
2   *L&P*
3   cited by Muir and Mason
4   *CSP: Spanish*
5   cited in *The Hamilton Papers*, ed. J. Bain, Edinburgh, 1890–92
6   A portrait by Holbein of a lady thought to be Elizabeth Seymour that descended in the Cromwell family and is now in Toledo, Ohio, was in the 19th century incorrectly identified as Katherine Howard. A copy is in the National Portrait Gallery.
7   *L&P*; *State Papers*
8   John Foxe
9   The present house is a 17th century reconstruction on a much larger scale. Audley also converted an Augustinian Friary in Aldgate into a London town house, but this has long since disappeared.
10 Browne was also granted the Priory of St Mary Overy in Southwark (now Southwark Cathedral), which he converted into a town house.
11 *History of the King's Works*. The gateway and ruins of the royal apartments have survived. In 1896, the Old Palace at Canterbury was built by Archbishop Temple using building materials from Henry VIII's palace, which had been alienated from the Crown in 1612.
12 Rawlinson MSS., Bodleian Library. Dartford was granted to Anne of Cleves on Henry's death, and to Robert Cecil, Earl of Salisbury, in 1606. A brick gate and part of the outer court are all that survive.
13 It was sold by Mary I in 1554.
14 *Letters to Cromwell*. Reading remained in use as a royal residence until the reign of Charles I. It was mostly destroyed in 1643, during the Civil War, but a few ruins remain in Forbury Gardens, while the gatehouse is used as a museum.
15 *History of the King's Works*. It stood on the present Friary Street, but was ruinous by 1603 and demolished in 1607.
16 Edward VI granted it in 1548 to George Brooke, Lord Cobham, but it had been demolished by 1558.
17 *L&P*; B.L. Additional MSS.; PRO; John Stow; Charles Wriothesley
18 *L&P*
19 Ibid.
20 *CSP: Spanish*
21 *L&P*
22 Ibid.
23 Newcastle MSS., Nottingham University Library
24 *L&P*
25 Ibid.
26 Ibid.
27 Charles Wriothesley
28 *CSP: Spanish*
29 There is a later story that she was publicly received back at court on 17 December, but since it is clear that she returned in October, this must be apocryphal (*CSP: Spanish*).
30 *L&P*
31 Rooms were set aside for Mary at Ampthill, Enfield, Guildford, Woking, Otford and Westenhanger. *L&P*; *CSP: Spanish*; Rawlinson MSS., Bodleian Library; B.L. Cotton MSS. Vespasian
32 cited by Neville Williams: *Henry VIII and his Court*
33 *Privy Purse Expenses of the Princess Mary*
34 Henry Clifford
35 Later versions are at Knole, Parham Park and Castle Howard.

36   cited by Robinson: *Dukes of Norfolk*
37   CSP: *Spanish*

50. 'THE MOST JOYFUL NEWS'

1   Edward Hall
2   *De Unitate Ecclesiae*
3   cited by Neville Williams: *Henry VIII and his Court*
4   *L&P*
5   B.L. Cotton MSS. Cleopatra
6   *L&P*
7   Ibid.
8   Kybett
9   *L&P*
10   Ibid.; Brewer
11   *L&P*
12   Ibid.
13   Charing was not used by Henry VIII or his successors. It fell into neglect and was alienated from the Crown in 1629. The remains of the palace may be seen near the parish church.
14   *Knole: Official Handbook*
15   It is not certain whether this court and the tower were first built by Archbishop Morton, Archbishop Warham or Henry VIII. Under Mary I, Knole passed to the Sackville family. It was vastly extended and remodelled by Thomas Sackville, 1st Earl of Dorset, in 1603–8, and is now the largest private house in England.
16   *Knole: Official Handbook*
17   Otford rapidly decayed after Henry's death; by 1549, the lead had already been stripped from the roofs of the hall, presence chamber and privy chamber. It was sold by Elizabeth I to a local gentleman. Parts of the north entrance range of the outer court remain, consisting chiefly of a 3-storey, red-brick, hexagonal tower that stood on the north-west corner of the palace complex and now rises stark, roofless and derelict in the middle of a field. Its floors have long disappeared, but the fireplaces on each storey may be seen through the windows. Some other buildings have been incorporated into nearby Castle Farm; part of Archbishop Warham's cloistered gallery with its red brick floor has been converted into cottages. Otford has been the subject of an archaeological excavation.
18   see below, Chapter 52.
19   PRO
20   Oatlands remained a favourite royal residence until the reign of Charles I, but was sold and largely demolished under the Commonwealth. In 1660, the remaining buildings were given to Queen Henrietta Maria, who converted them into a lodge, which was destroyed by fire in the 18th century. Some foundations remain underground, beneath the council housing estate that now occupies the site. Parts of the red-brick wall and the gateway to the stables may be seen in Gate Road, off Weybridge High Street. The site was excavated in the 1960s. A picture of Oatlands may be seen in the background of a portrait of Anne of Denmark, wife of James I, by Paul van Somer (Royal Collection).
21   In the Royal Collection and at Petworth House, Sussex.
22   Known as the Chatsworth Cartoon, it is now in the National Portrait Gallery.
23   Karel van Mander
24   *L&P*
25   Ibid.; *Lisle Letters*
26   *L&P*
27   Ibid.
28   Ibid.; *Lisle Letters*

29 Ibid.
30 *L&P*
31 *Crónica del rey Enrico*
32 *L&P*
33 PRO
34 The ceiling remains today, the most splendid example of its kind in England, but the rest of the chapel was refitted by Wren in the late 17th century. The gallery was remodelled, but the holyday closets survive, as does a fragment of the original floor. The ceiling of the King's holyday closet is still in good condition. The gold stars on the chapel ceiling were added on the advice of Augustus Pugin in the 19th century, when the ceiling was restored and the windows replaced in the positions they had occupied in Henry's day. The Tudor glass, however, was all destroyed under the Commonwealth.
35 For the christening, see B.L. Cotton MSS. Julius; Edward Hall; *L&P*; Charles Wriothesley; John Leland: *Collectanea*
36 Charles Wriothesley
37 Holbein's painting was probably lost in the fire which destroyed Cowdray House in 1793. A copy is in the Fitzwilliam Museum, Cambridge. Holbein's original portrait sketch is in the Royal Collection.
38 *L&P*
39 cited by Fraser
40 *L&P*
41 Ibid.; Edward Hall
42 B.L. Additional MSS.; John Leland: *Collectanea*
43 *L&P*
44 Ibid.
45 Anne Basset transferred to the household of the Countess of Sussex.
46 Edward Hall
47 *L&P*

51. 'THE VERY PEARL OF THE REALM'

1 Katherine was a connection of the Boleyns. She later married John Ashley, or Astley. Both remained in Elizabeth's service until their deaths.
2 cited by Neville Williams: *Henry VIII and his Court*. Lady Margaret and her husband Sir Thomas Bryan received grants of monastic lands in Buckinghamshire in recognition of her good service to the King's three children.
3 Bodleian Library MSS.; Thurley: *Royal Palaces*. The canopy was recorded during a visit to The More, but was probably a feature of all the Prince's cradles.
4 *Literary Remains of Edward VI*. Edward's lodgings were largely rebuilt after a fire in 1886, which destroyed 40 rooms in Chapel Court.
5 *Collection of Ordinances*
6 *L&P*
7 B.L. Additional MSS.; Rawlinson MSS.; Bodleian Library; *L&P*
8 PRO. James I may have been following the precedent set by Henry VIII when he gave St James's Palace to his son, Henry, Prince of Wales, as an official residence. (*History of the King's Works*; Strong; Thurley: *Royal Palaces*).
9 *L&P*
10 Still in the Royal Collection.
11 *CSP: Spanish*
12 Edward Hall
13 *Lisle Letters*; *L&P*
14 *L&P*
15 Ibid. Only the west range of Hatfield Palace survives; it contains the great hall (now used as a restaurant) with its original Tudor stained glass windows, a gatehouse with

traces of 16th century wall paintings, and various domestic chambers. The palace was granted to Robert Cecil, Earl of Salisbury, in 1607. He demolished most of it and used the materials to help build the present Hatfield House, which stands opposite.

16   It burned down in 1773.
17   *History of the King's Works.* It was granted to George Home, Earl of Dunbar in 1605.
18   Hatfield MSS.
19   cited by Neville Williams: *Henry VIII and his Court*
20   cited by Maurice Howard: *The Early Tudor Country House*
21   Various pictures of Nonsuch survive: a late 16th century drawing by Joris Hoefnagel (British Library) shows the elaborate south front, encompassing the inner court, while an anonymous early 17th century painting in the Fitzwilliam Museum, Cambridge, shows the more conventional entrance facade to the outer court.

Nonsuch became one of Elizabeth I's favourite residences, yet this astonishing palace lasted for only 140 years. The Stuarts did not like it, and it was confiscated by Oliver Cromwell. At the Restoration, Charles II gave it to his mother, Queen Henrietta Maria, who died in 1669. Samuel Pepys visited Nonsuch in 1663 and found the gardens in ruins; when John Evelyn dined in the palace two years later, it was still in good repair. Both diarists marvelled at the Renaissance reliefs on the outer walls. In 1670, however, Charles II gave Nonsuch to his mistress, Barbara Villiers, Duchess of Cleveland. Later, after he had discarded her, she had the palace demolished, divided up the park into farms, and sold off the lot. Most of the original park has now been built over; only a small part survives, the present Nonsuch Park at Cheam, Surrey. The Tudor banqueting houses, like the palace, have long since vanished. The palace site was excavated in 1959-60, when the layout of the house was discovered. The foundations then exposed are now underground in Nonsuch Park; the site is marked by a plaque. Some stonework and pottery uncovered during the dig are on display in the Tudor house known as Whitehall in Cheam, which has associations with the palace, and at Bourne Hall, Ewell. An inlaid wooden chest from the palace is also at Bourne Hall; its decoration is said to mimic the architecture of Nonsuch.

22   *History of the King's Works*
23   William Camden

52. 'A SORT OF KNAVES'

1   *L&P*
2   Ibid.
3   Ibid.; *CSP: Spanish*
4   *L&P*
5   Now in the National Gallery.
6   *L&P*; *CSP: Spanish*
7   *L&P*
8   John Foxe; *L&P*
9   *L&P*
10   Henry Pole died in the Tower in c1542. Edward Courtenay remained a prisoner there for nearly 15 years, only being released on the accession of Mary I in 1553.
11   *L&P*
12   cited by Starkey: *Henry VIII*
13   A copy of Holbein's lost original, by one of his followers, is in the possession of the Courtauld Institute, London.
14   Thomas Fuller
15   *CSP: Spanish*
16   Michell. Beddington was granted to Thomas, Lord Darcy in 1552 by Edward VI.
17   Examples of the Great Bible are in the British Library and the Royal Collection at Windsor.
18   *L&P*

19 Now in the Victoria and Albert Museum.
20 *L&P*
21 Charles Wriothesley
22 *Acts of the Privy Council*
23 Rawlinson MSS, Bodleian Library; Nottingham University Library MSS.; *L&P*; PRO
24 *L&P; PPE*. Ashridge, which was alienated in 1575 to Thomas, Lord Ellesmere, was in ruins by the late 18th century. What was left of it was cleared in 1808-14, when a neo-gothic mansion, designed by James Wyatt, was built on the site. This is now a college.
25 Elsynge, which stood near to the surviving Jacobean mansion Forty Hall, has disappeared. It was decaying by the late 16th century and was demolished under the Commonwealth. Trent Park is all that remains of its grounds. The foundations of one range of the Tudor house were excavated in the 1960s.
26 Rawlinson MSS., Bodleian Library. Edward VI demolished the manor house, which was located opposite the church on the present High Street, and built Enfield Palace in its place, which he granted to his sister Elizabeth in 1550. Much of Edward's palace was pulled down in the early 17th century, but parts survived until the 1920s.
27 It was extensively altered in the 17th century.

53. 'NOURISHING LOVE'

1 *Collection of Ordinances*. Mary I abolished the office of Lord Great Master and restored that of Lord Steward. Two of the Masterships of the Household lapsed on Henry VIII's death because they had been allocated to the Queen's side, and Edward VI never married.
2 cited by Erickson: *Great Harry*
3 Edward Hall
4 Palmer's portrait is in a private collection; Parr's is in the Royal Collection.
5 PRO; B.L. Royal MSS.
6 Henry's psalter is now in the British Library.
7 After Henry's death, Somers remained at court, acting in masques and interludes for Edward VI, Mary I and Elizabeth I. After he retired, Queen Elizabeth did not employ any more fools, preferring more sophisticated entertainment. Somers was therefore the last court jester.
8 *L&P*
9 Ibid.
10 *Collection of Ordinances*
11 *State Papers*
12 *Lisle Letters*
13 Ibid.
14 *L&P*
15 Ibid.
16 *Chronicle of Calais*
17 Edward Hall
18 *L&P*
19 Ibid.
20 Ibid.
21 Ibid.
22 Now in the National Gallery of Art, Washington

54. 'DISPLEASANT AIRS'

1 *L&P*
2 Ibid. There is no surviving contemporary evidence that Henry ever referred to Anne of Cleves as 'the Flanders mare'. This story dates from the late 17th century, when it was first written by Bishop Burnet, who quotes no source for it.

3   *L&P*; *CP*, ed. Kaulek
4   *L&P*
5   Edward Hall. Hall is the chief source for the reception of Anne of Cleves.
6   Ibid.
7   Ibid.
8   *L&P*
9   Edward Hall
10   Ibid.; *L&P*
11   Ibid.
12   Now in the Burrell Collection, Glasgow Museums.
13   *L&P*
14   Ibid.; Strype
15   Ibid.
16   Under Mary I, Anne was to become a Roman Catholic. She died in 1557.
17   Now in the Folger Shakespeare Library, Washington, D.C.
18   Holbein's designs for nine such jewels are in the British Museum.
19   *L&P*
20   Charles Wriothesley
21   *History of the King's Works*. The Tudor ceiling survives, although the chapel was enlarged, panelled and redecorated in 1836-40, when the box pews were installed and the royal closet reduced in size. The chapel was damaged by enemy action during the Second World War, but is now fully restored.
       St James's Palace became a favourite royal residence in the 17th century, when Sir Christopher Wren enlarged it and added the great staircase. After Whitehall burned down in 1687, St James's became the sovereign's chief London residence, remaining so until it was superseded by Buckingham Palace in the late 18th century; ambassadors are still accredited to the Court of St James's today. Much of St James's Palace was destroyed by a fire in 1809. The present St James's Park was designed by John Nash in 1827.
22   *Lisle Letters*
23   *L&P*. The gabled west wall and the great rose window of the 14th century Bishop's Hall are all that survives of this once vast mediaeval palace.
24   *Narratives of the Reformation*, ed. Nichols.
25   *CP*, ed. Kaulek; *L&P*
26   The original miniature is in the Royal Collection, while Holbein's copy is in the collection of the Duke of Buccleuch.
27   *CP*, ed. Kaulek; *L&P*
28   Roberts; *Princely Magnificence* catalogue
29   *CSP: Spanish*
30   *L&P*
31   Ibid.
32   cited Loades: *Tudor Court*
33   *Lisle Letters*; *L&P*
34   *CP*, ed. Kaulek; *L&P*
35   *Lisle Letters*
36   *Original Letters*, ed. Ellis; *L&P*
37   *L&P*
38   cited Neville Williams: *Henry VIII and his Court*
39   *L&P*
40   Ibid.

55. 'I HAVE BEEN YOUNG, AND NOW AM OLD'

1   *L&P*
2   Ibid.
3   Ibid.; *CP*, ed. Kaulek

4 Ibid.
5 Ibid.
6 Now at the Tower of London and Windsor Castle. The foot armour in the Tower has decorative borders designed by Holbein.
7 *L&P*
8 Ibid.; *CP*, ed. Kaulek; *English Historical Documents*
9 *CP*, ed. Kaulek; *L&P*
10 *L&P*
11 Ibid.
12 Ibid.
13 The reformer Philip Melanchthon, quoted in *L&P*.
14 *L&P*
15 Ibid.
16 Stephen Gardiner: *Letters*
17 *L&P*
18 *State Papers*
19 *L&P*
20 Ibid.
21 Ibid.; *CP*, ed. Kaulek
22 Ibid.
23 Nicholas Sander
24 *Statutes of the Realm*
25 *L&P*
26 B.L. Royal MSS.
27 *L&P*
28 Ibid.; *CP*, ed. Kaulek
29 When the book was reprinted in 1545, after Katherine Howard's execution, the dedication to her was omitted.
30 *L&P*; *CP*, ed. Kaulek
31 *L&P*
32 Ibid.; *CP*, ed. Kaulek
33 Seymour Papers; *State Papers*
34 *CP*, ed. Kaulek; *L&P*
35 *L&P*
36 *State Papers*
37 *CSP: Spanish*; *L&P*
38 *L&P*; PRO; *Literary Remains of Edward VI*; Seymour Papers; *State Papers*; B.L. Cotton MSS. Vespasian
39 *State Papers*; PRO
40 *CP*, ed. Kaulek; *L&P*
41 *L&P*
42 *State Papers*
43 *Collection of Ordinances*
44 *L&P*; Weir: 'Margaret Douglas'

56. 'IS NOT THE QUEEN ABED YET?'

1 *CP*, ed. Kaulek; *L&P*
2 *Acts of the Privy Council*
3 PRO; B.L. Harleian MSS.
4 *Acts of the Privy Council*
5 *L&P*
6 Now in the British Museum.
7 B.L. Royal MSS.; *State Papers*; B.L. Additional MSS.
8 In 1698, Whitehall Palace was destroyed by a fire accidentally started by a laundry

maid who left washing to dry over an open fire. The Holbein Gate survived the fire, but was demolished in 1749-50 when the thoroughfare now known as Whitehall was widened. The palace was never rebuilt, and government offices now occupy much of the site. The only surviving Tudor building is the underground wine cellar.

9   The only part of the original clock to survive today is the face. The mechanism has been repaired and replaced several times over the centuries, and the clock still works. During the 1830s, William IV had the face replaced with one taken from a clock at St James's Palace, but the original was later restored under Queen Victoria.

10   cited by C.R.N. Routh

11   Westenhanger was alienated from the Crown in 1585 and is still in private hands. The extensive ruins of the castle incorporate an 18th century house.

12   *L&P*

13   Ibid.

14   *CP*, ed. Kaulek; Raphael Holinshed

15   *Statutes of the Realm*

16   *L&P*; *CP*, ed. Kaulek; *CSP: Spanish*

17   *CP*, ed. Kaulek; *L&P*

18   *CSP: Spanish*

19   *L&P*

20   *CP*, ed. Kaulek; *L&P*

21   Ibid.

22   cited by J. Scarisbrick: *Henry VIII*

23   *L&P*

24   *CP*, ed. Kaulek; *L&P*

25   *L&P*

26   It is unclear from the few surviving records exactly what works were carried out. Most of the monastic buildings had disappeared by 1562, and the King's Manor was largely rebuilt before 1600.

27   *L&P*

28   Ibid.; *State Papers*

29   B.L. Cotton MSS. Augustus

30   *L&P*

31   Ibid.

32   Ibid.

33   Ibid.

57. 'LITTLE, SWEET FOOL'

1   *L&P*

2   *Acts of the Privy Council*

3   *L&P*

4   Ibid.; *Acts of the Privy Council*

5   *L&P*

6   Thurley: *Royal Palaces*

7   *CP*, ed. Kaulek; *L&P*

8   *L&P*

9   Ibid.

10   Ibid.; Edward Hall

11   Now in the Public Record Office; *State Papers*

12   *L&P*

13   Ibid.

14   Ibid.; *CP*, ed. Kaulek

15   *L&P*

16   Ibid.

17   Edward Hall

18 *State Papers*
19 *L&P*; Edward Hall
20 Edward Hall
21 *CSP: Spanish*
22 Ibid.
23 Nicander Nucius
24 *L&P*
25 Ibid.; *CP*, ed. Kaulek
26 Ibid.
27 *CSP: Spanish*
28 *L&P*; *CP*, ed. Kaulek
29 *Crónica del rey Enrico*
30 *L&P*
31 *Statutes of the Realm*
32 *CSP: Spanish*
33 *L&P*; *CP*, ed. Kaulek
34 *CSP: Spanish*
35 *L&P*

58. 'A NEST OF HERETICS'

1   *L&P*; *CSP: Spanish*
2   *L&P*
3   Wyatt's poem, and Surrey's, were first published in 1557 in Tottel's *Miscellany*.
4   *L&P*
5   After Browne's death, she married, in c1552, Edward, Lord Clinton, future Earl of Lincoln (d.1585), who had previously been married to Elizabeth Blount. Elizabeth died in 1590, and was buried alongside Clinton in St George's Chapel, Windsor.
6   Cowdray was destroyed by fire in 1793; extensive ruins remain.
7   *L&P*
8   Edward Hall
9   *L&P*; *Acts of the Privy Council*; B.L. Harleian MSS.
10 B. L. Sloane MSS.
11 PRO
12 *CSP: Spanish*
13 *L&P*
14 *CSP: Spanish*
15 A lock of her hair, taken from her coffin in the 18th century, is preserved at Sudeley Castle.
16 *L&P*
17 Marbeck later wrote the musical setting for Edward VI's first *Book of Common Prayer*. He died in c1585. The 15th century house where he lived survives at Windsor, and is still lived in by the organist of St George's Chapel.
18 Edward Hall
19 *Narratives of the Reformation*, ed. Nichols
20 Ibid.
21 For the heresy purge of 1543, see *L&P*; John Foxe, Edward Hall and *Acts of the Privy Council*.
22 cited by Starkey: *Henry VIII*
23 *State Papers*; *L&P*
24 *L&P*; only the gatehouse survives today.
25 cited by Starkey: *Henry VIII*
26 Ibid.
27 Ibid.
28 John Foxe

29   B.L. Cotton MSS. Cleopatra
30   *L&P*
31   *Statutes of the Realm*

59. 'THE GOOD EXPECTATIONS OF THE KING'S MAJESTY'

1   *L&P*
2   Ibid.
3   Anne was later granted a pension by Edward VI for her good services to Katherine Parr. She served Mary I as a lady in waiting, and in 1554 married Walter Hungerford, a Gentleman Pensioner. She died before 1557.
4   *Crónica del rey Enrico*
5   *L&P*
6   Ibid.
7   Ashdown. The Duchess fled England in 1554 to escape the Marian persecution. She returned on the accession of Elizabeth I in 1558, and died in 1580.
8   *L&P*
9   John Foxe
10   *L&P*
11   PRO
12   B.L. Cotton MSS. Vespasian
13   *Tudor Royal Proclamations*
14   PRO
15   This is the only one of Henry's many hunting lodges to survive today.
16   The King sat to Holbein in 1542. The painting was finished by less competent artists after Holbein's death, with the result that Henry's figure is disproportionately large, making the overall design look mediaeval. The picture is still in the possession of the Royal College of Surgeons of England.
17   PRO
18   *Privy Purse Expenses of the Princess Mary.* Both portraits are in the National Portrait Gallery. That of Katherine Parr was formerly incorrectly identified as Lady Jane Grey, although it had been known as Katherine Parr since at least the 18th century (B.L. Additional MSS.). The incorrect identification was made on the assumption that the coronet jewel on the sitter's breast is identical to that in a well attested engraving of Lady Jane Grey, but the pendant at her neck is the same as that in the National Portrait Gallery portrait of Katherine Parr. As Katherine was the wife of Lady Jane's guardian, she probably gave or bequeathed to Jane the coronet brooch. The sitter in the portrait attributed to Master John is a mature woman, and cannot have been Lady Jane, who was under ten, and notoriously undersized for her age, when it was painted.
19   Now in the National Portrait Gallery. The landscape background was probably added in the 17th century.
20   PRO. See the *Unknown Man* (c1545) in the National Portrait Gallery and *Sir William Cavendish* (also c1545) at Hardwick Hall. Bettes also painted William, the eldest son of Sir William Butts, in 1543. Bettes' son, John Bettes the Younger (d.1616), was a pupil of Nicholas Hilliard and one of the foremost artists of the Elizabethan/Jacobean period. His son, Edward Bettes (d.1661), was also a painter.
21   She later served as gentlewoman to both Mary I and Elizabeth I, for whom she painted several miniatures. She died in 1576.
22   Now in the National Portrait Gallery.
23   *CSP: Spanish*
24   B.L. Additional MSS.; Rawlinson MSS., Bodleian Library
25   *Literary Remains of Edward VI*
26   Ibid.
27   Ibid.

28   Ibid.
29   Now in the Public Record Office.
30   B.L. Additional MSS.
31   *L&P*
32   The clock salt no longer exists, but Holbein's design for it is in the British Museum.
33   Now in the Bodleian Library, Oxford
34   cited by Neville Williams: *Henry VIII and his Court*

60. 'THE ENTERPRISE OF BOULOGNE'

1   *Statutes of the Realm*
2   *L&P*
3   PRO; Fraser
4   *CSP: Spanish*
5   Ibid.; *Archaeologia*
6   Ibid.
7   Ibid.
8   *L&P*
9   John Foxe
10   This was Lord Darnley, who would later become the second husband of Mary, Queen of Scots, and the father of James VI and I.
11   *L&P*; Katherine would spend much time at Chelsea and Hanworth during her widowhood. Chelsea, which was now surrounded by 29 gardens, was demolished c1700.
12   *L&P*
13   Ibid.; *CSP: Spanish*
14   Ibid.
15   *Rutland Papers*
16   *Acts of the Privy Council*
17   *L&P*
18   PRO. Leeds was alienated from the Crown in 1552. It was restored in 1822, and more extensively in the 20th century by Lady Baillie, its late owner.

61. 'THE WORST LEGS IN THE WORLD'

1   The picture is still in the Royal Collection, but now hangs at Hampton Court.
2   Copies are in the Royal Collection, Windsor, the British Museum and the Bibliothèque Nationale, Paris.
3   Now in the collection of Lord Weidenfeld.
4   *L&P*
5   Ibid.
6   Stephen Gardiner: *Letters*
7   *CSP: Spanish*; *L&P*
8   Henry VIII: *Letters*
9   John Foxe
10   *CSP: Spanish*; *L&P*
11   PRO; *L&P*
12   *CP*, ed. Kaulek
13   *CSP: Spanish*
14   John Foxe
15   *CSP: Spanish*. Chapuys died in 1546.
16   *L&P*
17   Ibid.
18   *CSP: Spanish*
19   The house was greatly enlarged in the reign of James I.

20 *L&P*
21 It was badly vandalised, and perhaps totally destroyed, during Robert Kett's rebellion of 1549. No trace remains of it today.
22 *L&P*
23 Ibid.; *Acts of the Privy Council*
24 see Warnicke: *Women of the English Renaissance*
25 *CSP: Spanish*
26 Edward Hall
27 *L&P*
28 The dry stamp is now in the Public Record Office
29 *L&P*

62. 'PAINFUL SERVICE'

1 'A New Year's Gift' was edited by John Bale and published in 1549 under the title *The Laborious Journey and Search of John Leland for England's Antiquities* (now in the British Library). Leland's notes were collected and edited by Thomas Hearne in the early 18th century, and published at Oxford in 1710-15.
2 Thomas Cranmer: *Miscellaneous Writings and Letters*; John Foxe
3 cited by Neville Williams: *Henry VIII and his Court*
4 *L&P*; *Mémoires de Martin et Guillaume du Bellay*; *State Papers*
5 *L&P*
6 Ibid.; *CSP: Spanish*
7 *Acts of the Privy Council*
8 John Foxe
9 *CSP: Spanish*
10 *L&P*
11 John Foxe
12 cited by Neville Williams: *Henry VIII and his Court*
13 *CSP: Spanish*
14 *L&P*
15 Edward Hall
16 John Foxe
17 PRO; Inventory
18 *L&P*
19 *CSP: Spanish*
20 Ibid.
21 *State Papers*; *L&P*; Gilbert Burnet
22 *L&P*
23 *CSP: Spanish*
24 *Correspondence politique de Odet de Selve*
25 *CSP: Spanish*
26 Ibid.
27 *Chronicle and Political Papers of Edward VI*
28 John Foxe
29 For the Admiral's visit, see *CSP: Spanish*; Charles Wriothesley; Edward Hall
30 B.L. Additional MSS.; Rawlinson MSS., Bodleian Library
31 *L&P*
32 Rawlinson MSS., Bodleian Library
33 Loseley MSS.
34 *CSP: Spanish*; *L&P*
35 *L&P*
36 Ibid.
37 *Acts of the Privy Council*
38 *CSP: Spanish*

39   *L&P*
40   Stephen Gardiner; *Letters*
41   *L&P*
42   *L&P*

63. 'THE RAREST MAN THAT LIVED IN HIS TIME'

1   *L&P*
2   Ibid.; *CSP: Spanish*
3   *State Papers*; *L&P*
4   *CSP: Spanish*
5   *L&P*; *State Papers*
6   *L&P*; *Crónica del rey Enrico*
7   *L&P*
8   Ibid.; B.L. Stowe MSS.; B.L. Harleian MSS.; *CSP: Spanish*
9   *CSP: Spanish*; *Crónica del rey Enrico*
10   *L&P*
11   *CSP: Spanish*
12   PRO
13   *L&P*
14   Ibid.
15   Ibid.
16   Ibid.
17   Ibid.; *CSP: Spanish*
18   *CSP: Spanish*
19   Edward Hall; John Foxe
20   The original Will is in the Public Record Office, and is printed in Rymer's *Foedera*. See *CSP: Spanish*; John Foxe; B.L. Harleian MSS; B.L. Additional MSS.; Gilbert Burnet.
21   *L&P*
22   cf Starkey: *Henry VIII*; Elton; Scarisbrick: *Henry VIII*; Lacey Baldwin Smith: *Henry VIII: The Mask of Royalty*
23   *L&P*
24   Ibid.
25   *Correspondence politique de Odet de Selve*
26   *CSP: Spanish*
27   Henry VIII's Will
28   *State Papers*
29   *Crónica del rey Enrico*; Charles Wriothesley; *Chronicles of the Grey Friars*
30   *L&P*
31   Ibid.
32   *Correspondence politique de Odet de Selve*; *Chronicle and Political Papers of Edward VI*
33   *Acts of the Privy Council*; *CSP: Spanish*
34   *Crónica del rey Enrico*
35   He was buried in Framlingham Church, where his remains were found in 1835.
36   *CSP: Spanish*
37   *CSP: Spanish*
38   William Thomas: *Cronica del rey Enrico*
39   *CSP: Spanish*
40   *Journals of the House of Lords*
41   William Thomas; *Crónica del rey Enrico*; *Correspondence politique de Odet de Selve*. Norfolk remained in the Tower throughout the six years of Edward VI's reign, and was released and restored in blood on the accession of Mary I in 1553. He died in 1554.
42   John Foxe

43 Ibid.
44 B.L. Cotton MSS. Titus
45 *CSP: Spanish*
46 Tytler
47 Strype; Tighe; Henry VIII's Will; Charles Wriothesley
48 Henry VIII's Will
49 William Thomas
50 John Stow claims that 72,000 persons were executed in Henry VIII's reign, but this is a gross exaggeration.

House of York (Plantagenet)

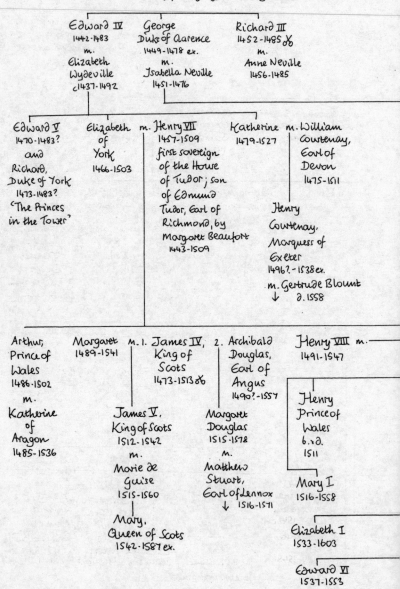

Edward IV
1442-1483
m.
Elizabeth
Wydeville
c1437-1492

George
Duke of Clarence
1449-1478 ex.
m.
Isabella Neville
1451-1476

Richard III
1452-1485 ⚔
m.
Anne Neville
1456-1485

Edward V
1470-1483?
and
Richard,
Duke of York
1473-1483?
'The Princes
in the Tower'

Elizabeth
of
York
1466-1503

m. Henry VII
1457-1509
first sovereign
of the House
of Tudor; son
of Edmund
Tudor, Earl of
Richmond, by
Margaret Beaufort
1443-1509

Katherine
1479-1527

m. William
Courtenay,
Earl of
Devon
1475-1511

Henry
Courtenay,
Marquess of
Exeter
1496?-1538 ex.
m. Gertrude Blount
↓ d.1558

Arthur,
Prince of
Wales
1486-1502
m.
Katherine
of
Aragon
1485-1536

Margaret
1489-1541

m. 1. James IV,
King of
Scots
1473-1513 ⚔

2. Archibald
Douglas,
Earl of
Angus
1490?-1557

Henry VIII m.
1491-1547

James V,
King of Scots
1512-1542
m.
Marie de
Guise
1515-1560

Margaret
Douglas
1515-1578
m.
Matthew
Stuart,
Earl of Lennox
↓ 1516-1571

Henry
Prince of
Wales
b. & d.
1511

Mary,
Queen of Scots
1542-1587 ex.

Mary I
1516-1558

Elizabeth I
1533-1603

Edward VI
1537-1553

The Tudors and their Rivals

ex. = executed
%6 = killed in battle
↓ = line continues

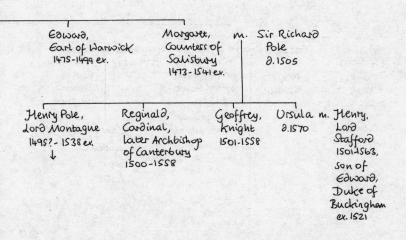

| Edward, Earl of Warwick 1475-1499 ex. | Margaret, Countess of Salisbury 1473-1541 ex. | m. Sir Richard Pole d. 1505 | | |

| Henry Pole, Lord Montague 1495?-1538 ex. ↓ | Reginald, Cardinal, later Archbishop of Canterbury 1500-1558 | Geoffrey, knight 1501-1558 | Ursula m. Henry, Lord Stafford 1501-1563, son of Edward, Duke of Buckingham ex. 1521 | d.1570 |

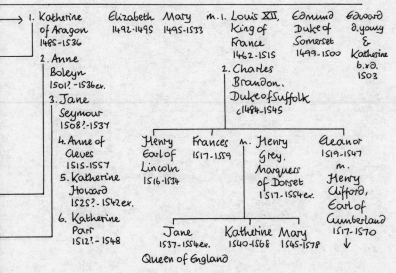

| 1. Katherine of Aragon 1485-1536 2. Anne Boleyn 1501?-1536 ex. 3. Jane Seymour 1508?-1537 4. Anne of Cleves 1515-1557 5. Katherine Howard 1525?-1542 ex. 6. Katherine Parr 1512?-1548 | Elizabeth 1492-1495 | Mary 1495-1533 m. 1. Louis XII, King of France 1462-1515 2. Charles Brandon, Duke of Suffolk c1484-1545 | Edmund Duke of Somerset 1499-1500 | Edward d. young & Katherine b. & d. 1503 |

| | Henry Earl of Lincoln 1516-1534 | Frances 1517-1559 m. Henry Grey, Marquess of Dorset 1517-1554 ex. | Eleanor 1519-1547 m. Henry Clifford, Earl of Cumberland 1517-1570 ↓ | |

Jane 1537-1554 ex. Queen of England   Katherine 1540-1568   Mary 1545-1578

Bibliography

Primary Sources

An Account of the Materials furnished for the use of Queen Anne Boleyn (Miscellanies of the Philobiblion Society, Vol. VII, 1862–3)

Accounts of the Chamber and the Great Wardrobe (Public Record Office)

Acts of the Privy Council of England (for the period 1542–58; 46 vols, ed. John Roche Dasent et al., HMSO, London, 1890–1964)

Additional MSS. (British Library)

Ambassades en Angleterre de Jean du Bellay, 1527–29 (ed. V.L. Bourilly and P. de Vassière, Paris, 1905)

André, Bernard: *Historia Regis Henrici Sept.* (in *Memorials of King Henry VIII*, ed. J. Gairdner, Rolls Series, London, 1858)

The Antiquarian Repertory: A Miscellany, intended to Preserve and Illustrate Several Valuable Remains of Old Times (4 vols, London, 1775–84; ed. F. Grose and T. Astle, London, 1808)

Archaeologia, or Miscellaneous Tracts relating to Antiquity (102 vols, Society of Antiquaries of London, London, 1773–1969)

Arundel MSS. (British Library)

Ascham, Roger: *The Whole Works* (3 vols, ed. J.A. Giles, London, 1864–5)

Ashmole, Elias: *The Institutions, Laws and Ceremonies of the Most Noble Order of the Garter* (London, 1672)

Ashmole MSS. (Bodleian Library, Oxford)

The Babees' Book: Mediaeval Manners for the Young. Done into Modern English from Dr. Furnivall's Texts (ed. Edith Rickett, London, 1923)

Ballads from Manuscripts: Ballads on the Condition of England in Henry VIII's and Edward VI's Reign (extracted from the Royal MSS. in the British Library; 2 vols, ed. F.J. Furnivall, Ballad Society, London, 1868–72)

Barclay, Alexander: *The Citizen and Uplandishman* (c1524; ed. F.W. Fairholt, Percy Society, 31, 1848)

Barclay, Alexander: *The Eclogues of Alexander Barclay* (ed. Beatrice White, Early English Texts Society, London, 1928)

Barclay, Alexander: *The Ship of Fools* (1509; 2 vols, ed. T.H. Jameson, London, 1874)

'The Birth of Mankind' (ed. J.W. Ballantyne, *Journal of Obstetrics and Gynaecology of the British Empire*, 10, 1906)

Blundeville, Thomas: *The Four Chiefest Offices belonging to Horsemanship. Part II: The Art of Riding* (London, 1565)

Bodleian Library MSS.

Boorde, Andrew: *A Compendious Regiment, or A Dietary of Health* (1542; ed. F.J. Furnivall, Early English Texts Society, Extra Series, 10, London, 1870)

Boorde, Andrew: *The Wisdom of Andrew Boorde* (ed. H.E. Poole, Leicester, 1936)

Bourbon, Nicholas, writing as Borbonius: *Nugarum Libri Octo* (Lyons, 1538)

Brantôme, Pierre de Bourdeille, Seigneur de: *Oeuvres complètes* (12 vols, ed. Ludovic Lalanne, Librairie de la Société de l'Histoire de France, Paris, 1864–96)

Burnet, Gilbert, D.D.: *The History of the Reformation of the Church of England* (4 vols, ed. E. Nares, London, 1839; 7 vols, ed. Nicholas Pocoke, Oxford, 1865)

Calendar of Letters, Dispatches and State Papers relating to the Negotiations between England and Spain, preserved in the Archives at Vienna, Simancas, Besançon and Brussels (13 vols, 2 supplements, ed. G.A. Bergenroth, Pascual de Gayangos, Garrett Mattingly, Martin A.S. Hume and Royall Tyler, HMSO, London, 1862–1954)

Calendar of the Manuscripts of the Most Hon. the Marquess of Salisbury preserved at Hatfield House, Hertfordshire (24 vols, Historical Manuscripts Commission, London, 1883)

Calendar of State Papers, Foreign Series, of the Reign of Edward VI, 1547–53. Preserved in the State Papers Department of Her Majesty's Public Record Office (ed. William B. Turnbull, London, 1861)

Calendar of State Papers, Foreign Series, of the Reign of Elizabeth Vol. I: 1558–9 (23 vols, ed. J. Stevenson and A.J. Crosby et al., London, 1863–1950)

Calendar of State Papers and Manuscripts existing in the Archives and Collection of Milan, Vol. I, 1485–1618 (ed. Allen B. Hinds, HMSO, London, 1912)

Calendar of State Papers and Manuscripts relating to English Affairs existing in the Archives and Collections of Venice and in other Libraries of Northern Italy (38 vols, ed. L. Rawdon Brown, G. Cavendish-Bentinck, H.F. Brown and Allen B. Hinds, London, 1864–1947)

Camden, William: *Annales rerum Anglicarum et Hibernicarum regnante Elizabetha* (London, 1615)

Carles, Lancelot de, Marot, Clément, and Milherve, Crispin, Lord of: *Epistre contenant le Procès Criminel Faict a l'encontre de la Royne Anne Boullant d'Angleterre* (Lyons, 1545; in *Lettres de Henri VIII*, ed. G.A. Crapelet, Paris, 1826; and in *La Grande Bretagne devant l'Opinion Française dupuis la guerre de cent ans jusqu' à la fin du XVIe siècle: Poème sur la mort d'Anne Boleyn*, ed Georges Ascoli, Paris, 1927)

Castiglione, Baldassare: *Il libro del cortegiano* (Venice, 1528; tr. Thomas Hoby as *The Courtier*, London, 1561; tr. W. Raleigh, London, 1900; ed. D. Henderson, New York, 1946; tr. George Bull, London, 1967)

A Catalogue of the Royal and Noble Authors of England, Scotland and Ireland (5 vols, ed. T. Park, London, 1806)

Cavendish, George: *The Life and Death of Cardinal Wolsey* (London, 1557; London, 1641; 2 vols, ed. S.W. Singer, London, 1827; ed. Richard S. Sylvester, Early English Texts Society, 243, London, 1959; ed. Richard S. Sylvester and Davis P. Harding in *Two Early Tudor Lives*, New Haven, Conn., 1962, ed. Roger Lockyer as *Thomas Wolsey, late Cardinal, his Life and Death, written by George Cavendish, his gentleman-usher*, Folio Society, London, 1962)

Cavendish, George: *Metrical Visions* (in *The Life of Cardinal Wolsey by George Cavenidsh*, 2 vols, ed. S.W. Singer, London, 1827; ed. A.S.G. Edwards, New York, 1980)

The Chronicle of Calais in the Reigns of Henry VII and Henry VIII to the Year 1540 (ed. John Gough Nichols, Camden Society, Old Series, 35, London, 1846)

Chronicle of the Grey Friars of London (ed. John Gough Nichols, Camden Society, 53, London, 1852)

The Chronicle and Political Papers of King Edward VI (ed. W.K. Jordan, London, 1966)

Clifford, Henry: *The Life of Jane Dormer, Duchess of Feria* (London, 1643; tr. E.E. Estcourt and ed. Rev J. Stevenson, London, 1887)

A Collection of Ordinances and Regulations for the Government of the Royal Household, made in Divers Reigns from King Edward III to King William and Queen Mary (ed. John Gough Nichols, Society of Antiquaries of London, London, 1790)

Constantine, George: 'Transcript of an Original Manuscript containing a Memorial from George Constantine to Thomas, Lord Cromwell' (ed. Thomas Amyot, *Archaeologia*, 22, 1831)

Correspondance du Cardinal Jean du Bellay (ed. R. Scheurer, Paris, 1969)

Correspondance politique de MM. De Castillon et de Marillac, ambassadeurs de France en Angleterre, 1537–42 (ed. Jean Kaulek, Paris, 1885)

Correspondance politique de Odet de Selve, ambassadeur de France en Angleterre, 1546–9 (ed. G. Lefèvre-Pontalis, Paris, 1888)

Correspondence of the Emperor Charles V and His Ambassadors at the Courts of England and France (ed. W. Bradford, London, 1850)

Correspondencia de Gutierre Gómez de Fuensalida, Embajador en Alemania, Flandes e Inglaterra (ed. El Duque de Berwick y de Alba, Madrid, 1907)

Cotton MSS: Augustus, Caligula, Cleopatra, Galba, Julius, Nero, Otho, Tiberius Titus, Vespasian, Vitellius (British Library)

Cranmer, Thomas: *Miscellaneous Writings and Letters of Thomas Cranmer* (ed. J.E. Cox, Parker Society, Cambridge, 1846)

Crónica del rey Enrico Ottavo de Inglaterra (*The Spanish Chronicle*) (sometimes attributed to Antonio de Guaras; written before 1552; ed. Marquis de Molins, Madrid, 1874; tr. Martin A.S. Hume as *The Chronicle of King Henry VIII of England, being a contemporary record of some of the principal events of the reigns of Henry VIII and Edward VI, written in Spanish by an unknown hand*, London, 1889)

Dialogus de Scaccario (ed. C. Johnson, London, 1950)

The Divorce Tracts of Henry VIII (ed. J. Sturtz and V. Murphy, Angers, 1988)

Documents relating to the Office of the Revels (2 vols, ed. A. Feuillerat, Louvain, 1908–14)

Dunbar, William: *The Poems of William Dunbar* (ed. W. Mackay Mackenzie, London, 1932)

The Earliest English Life of John Fisher (ed. Philip Hughes, London 1935)

Early English Meals and Manners (ed. F.J. Furnivall, Early English Texts Society, Old Series, 32, London, 1868; repr. London, 1931)

Early English Poems and Treatises on Manners and Meals in Olden Times (ed. F.J. Furnivall, Early English Texts Society, 32, Oxford, 1868, repr. 1931)

Early English Poetry, Ballads and Popular Literature of the Middle Ages (ed. P. Bliss, Percy Society, 11, 1844)

Egerton MSS. (British Library)

Elyot, Sir Thomas: *The Book named The Governor* (London, 1531; 2 vols, ed. H.H.S. Croft, London, 1883; Everyman's Library, London, 1907)

Elyot, Sir Thomas: *The Castle of Health* (London, 1541)

An English Garner (8 vols, ed. Edward Arber, London, 1877–82)

English Historical Documents, Vol. V, 1485–1558 (ed. C.H. Williams and D.C. Douglas, London, 1967)

English History in Contemporary Poetry, III: The Tudor Monarchy (ed. N.L. Frazer, London, 1930)

Erasmus, Desiderius: *The Complete Works of Erasmus* (tr. R.B. Mynors and D.F.S. Thomson, Toronto, 1974)

Erasmus, Desiderius: *The Epistles of Erasmus* (3 vols, tr. and ed. F. Morgan Nichols, London, 1901–18, repr. New York, 1962)

Erasmus, Desiderius: *Institutio Principis Christiani: The Education of a Christian Prince* (tr. L.K. Born, New York, 1936

Erasmus, Desiderius: *Opera* (10 vols, ed. J. Le Clerc, Leyden, 1703–6)

Erasmus, Desiderius: *Opus Epistolarum Desiderii Erasmi Roterdami* (12 vols, ed. P.S. and H.M. Allen and H.W. Garrod, Oxford, 1906–58)

Excerpta Historica (ed. S. Bentley and Sir Nicholas Harris Nicolas, London, 1831)

Excerpts from the Manuscript of William Dunche (ed. A.G.W. Murray and Eustace F. Bosanquet, *The Genealogist*, New Series, 30, 1914)

Fish, Simon: *A Supplication for the Beggars* (ed. Edward Arber, London, 1880)
Fisher, John: *The English Works of John Fisher* (ed. J.E.B. Mayor, Early English Texts Society, 27, London, 1876)
Fleuranges, Robert de la Marck, Seigneur de: *Histoire des choses mémorables advenues aux règnes de Louis XII et de François I* (ed. l'Abbé Lambert, Paris, 1753)
Fleuranges, Robert de la Marck, Seigneur de: Mémoires (in *Choix des chroniques et mémoires relatifs à l'histoire de France*, ed. Jean-Alexandre C. Buchon, Orléans, 1875, Paris, 1913)
Forrest, William: *The History of Grisild the Second: A Narrative in Verse of the Divorce of Queen Katherine of Aragon* (ed. M.D. Macray, Roxburghe Club, London, 1875)
Four Years at the Court of Henry VIII: Selections from Despatches written by Sebastian Giustiniano, January 12, 1515 to July 26, 1519 (2 vols, tr. and ed. L. Rawdon Brown, London, 1854)
Foxe, John: *History of the Acts and Monuments of the Church* (London, 1563; 8 vols, ed. S.R. Cattley and George Townsend, London, 1837–41, 1843–9, repr. New York, 1975)
Foxe, Richard: *The Letters of Richard Foxe, 1486–1527* (ed. P.S. and H.M. Allen, Oxford, 1929)
Francisca, Jacobus Sylvius: *Francorum Regis et Henrici Anglorum Colloquim* (tr. and ed. Stephen Bamforth and Jean Dupèbe, Renaissance Studies, 5, 1991)
Fuller, Thomas: *The Church History of Britain from the Birth of Jesus Christ until the year MDCXLVIII* (1655; London, 1968)

Gardiner, Stephen: *De Vera Obedientia Oratio* (1535; ed. P. Jones in *Obedience in Church and State*, Cambridge, 1930)
Gardiner, Stephen: *The Letters of Stephen Gardiner* (ed. James Arthur Muller, Cambridge, 1933)
Godwin, Francis: *Annals of England containing the Reigns of Henry the Eighth, Edward the Sixt, Queen Mary* (London, 1630)
Gough, John: *The Manner of the Triumph at Calais and Boulogne* (London, 1532)
The Great Chronicle of London (ed. A.H. Thomas and I.D. Thornley, London, 1938)
The Great Tournament Roll of Westminster: A Collotype Reproduction of the Manuscript (2 vols, ed. Sir Anthony Wagner and Sidney Anglo, Oxford, 1968)

Hall, Edward: *Hall's Chronicle: The Union of the Two Noble and Illustre Families of York and Lancaster* (London, 1542; ed. Richard Grafton, London, 1548; ed. Sir Henry Ellis, London, 1809)
Hall, Edward: *The Triumphant Reign of King Henry the Eighth* (London, 1547; 2 vols, ed. Charles Whibley and T.C. Jack, London, 1904)
Hall, Richard: *The Life of Fisher* (ed. Rev. Ronald Bayne, Early English Texts Society, Extra Series, 117, London and Oxford, 1921)
Hargrave MSS. (British Library)
The Harleian Miscellany (7 vols, ed. W. Oldys and T. Park, New York, 1965)
Harleian MSS. (British Library)
Harpsfield, Nicholas: *The Life and Death of Thomas More, Knight* (London, c1557; ed. E.V. Hitchcock and R.W. Chambers, Early English Texts Society, 197, London, 1935)
Harpsfield, Nicholas: *A Treatise on the Pretended Divorce between Henry VIII and Katherine of Aragon* (London, 1556; ed. Nicholas Pococke, Camden Society, New Series, 21, London, 1878; repr. New York, 1965)
Harrison, William: *A Description of England* (ed. F.J. Furnivall, London, 1877)
Hatfield MSS. (Hatfield House, Herts.)
Henry VIII: *Assertio Septem Sacramentorum* (ed. L. O'Donovan, New York, 1908)
Henry VIII: *The Letters of King Henry VIII* (ed. Muriel St Clair Byrne, London, 1936)
Henry VIII: *Lettres de Henri VIII à Anne Boleyn* (ed. G.A. Crapelet, Paris, 1826)
Henry VIII: *The Love Letters of Henry VIII* (ed. Jasper Ridley, London, 1988)
Henry VIII: *The Love Letters of Henry VIII* (ed. Henry Savage, London, 1949)
Henry VIII: *The Love Letters of Henry VIII to Anne Boleyn* (ed. J. Halliwell-Phillips, London, 1907)

Hentzner, Paul: *Travels in England in the Reign of Queen Elizabeth* (1598; tr. and ed. Horace Walpole, London, 1797)

Herbert of Cherbury, Edward, Lord: *The Life and Reign of King Henry the Eighth* (London, 1649; ed. White Kennett as *The History of England under Henry VIII*, London, 1870)

Hilliard, Nicholas: *The Art of Limning* (ed. R.K.R. Thornton and T.G.S. Cain, Manchester, 1992)

Histoire de la Royne Anne de Boullant (MS. before 1550; Bibliothèque Nationale, Paris)

The History of the King's Works, Vols III and IV, 1485–1660 (6 vols, ed. R. Allen Brown, H.M. Colvin, D.R. Ransome, J. Summerson and A.J. Taylor, London, 1959–82)

Holinshed, Raphael: *The Chronicles of England, Scotland and Ireland* (London, 1577; 6 vols, ed. Sir Henry Ellis, London, 1807–8)

Illustration of the Manners and Expenses of Ancient Times in England in the 15th, 16th and 17th Centuries (ed. John Gough Nichols, Society of Antiquaries of London, London, 1797)

Intimate Letters of England's Queens (ed. Margaret Sanders, London, 1957)

Inventories of the Wardrobes, Plate, Chapel Stuff, etc. of Henry Fitzroy, Duke of Richmond and Somerset, and of the Wardrobe Stuff at Baynard's Castle of Katherine, Princess Dowager (ed. John Gough Nichols, Camden Society, Old Series, 61, London, 1854)

Journals of the House of Lords, Vol. I: Beginning with the First Year of Henry VIII (London, 1771)

King Henry VIII's Jewel Book (ed. Rt. Rev. Edward, Bishop Suffragan of Nottingham, Lincoln Diocesan Architectural Society, 17, 1883–4)

The King's Book, or a Necessary Doctrine and Erudition for any Christian Man (London, 1543; ed. T.A. Lacey, London, 1932)

King's MSS. (British Library)

Lambarde, William: *A Perambulation of Kent* (ed. R. Church, Bath, 1970)

Lansdowne MSS. (British Library)

Les Lamentations de Mathéolus et le Livre de Leesce de Jehan Fevre, de Resson (ed. A.G. Van Hammel, Paris, 1892)

The Late King's Goods (ed. A. MacGregor, Oxford, 1989)

Latimer, William: *A Brief Treatise or Chronicle of the most virtuous Lady Anne Boleyn, late Queen of England* (MS. Don. C.42, Bodleian Library, Oxford; ed. Maria Dowling as *William Latimer's Chronickille of Anne Bulleyne*, Camden Miscellany, 4th Series, 39, 1990)

Leland, John: *Antiquarii de Rebus Britannicis Collectanea* (London, 1612; 6 vols, ed. Thomas Hearne, Chetham Society, Oxford, 1715, London, 1770)

Leland, John: *Leland's Itinerary of England and Wales: The Itinerary of John Leland in about 1535–1543* (9 vols, ed. Thomas Hearne, Oxford, 1710–12, 1745–7; 5 vols, ed. Lucy Toulmin Smith, London, 1906–10, repr. London, 1964)

Letters and Accounts of William Brereton (ed. Eric W. Ives, Record Society of Lancashire and Cheshire, 116, 1976)

Letters to Cromwell and Others on the Suppression of the Monasteries (London, 1965)

Letters of Denization and Acts of Naturalisation for Aliens in England, 1509–1603 (ed. W. Page, Huguenot Society, 8, 1893)

Letters and Papers, Foreign and Domestic, of the Reign of Henry VIII, 1509–47 (21 vols in 33 parts, ed. J.S. Brewer, James Gairdner and R.H. Brodie, HMSO, London, 1862–1932)

Letters and Papers illustrative of the Reigns of Richard III and Henry VII (2 vols, ed. James Gairdner, Rolls Series, London, 1861–3)

Letters of the Queens of England, 1100–1547 (ed. Anne Crawford, Stroud, Glos., 1994)

Letters of Royal and Illustrious Ladies of Great Britain (3 vols, ed. Mary Anne Everett Wood, London, 1846)

Lettres des Rois, Reines et Autres Personnages des Cours de France et d'Angleterre (2 vols, ed. J.J. Champolléon-Figeac, Paris, 1845–7)

'The Liber Niger of Edward IV: A New Version' (ed. Kate Mertes, *Bulletin of the Institute of*

Historical Research, 54, 1981)

The Lisle Letters (6 vols, ed. Muriel St Clair Byrne, London and Chicago, 1981)

The Literary Remains of King Edward VI (2 vols, ed. John Gough Nichols, Roxburghe Club, London, 1857)

Loke, W.: *An Account of Materials Furnished for the Use of Queen Anne Boleyn and the Princess Elizabeth* (ed. J.B. Heath, London, 1862–3)

Longleat MSS., Bath (Historical Manuscripts Commission)

Loseley MSS. (Guildford Muniment Room)

The Lumley Inventories (ed. Lionel Cust, Walpole Society, Vol. VI, 1917–18)

Lupset, Thomas: *The Life and Works of Thomas Lupset* (ed. John Archer Gee, New Haven, Conn., 1928)

Lyly, John: *Complete Works* (ed. R. Warwick Bond, Oxford, 1902)

Mander, Karel van: *Lives of the Netherlandish and German Painters* (extracted from the first edition of the *Schilderboek* of 1603–4; ed. Hessel Miedema, Doornspijk, 1994)

The Manner of the Triumph at Calais and Boulogne (Wynkyn de Worde, London, 1532; in *Tudor Tracts*, ed. A.F. Pollard, London, 1903)

Maps and Plans from Mediaeval England (ed. P.D.A. Harvey and R.A. Skelton, Oxford, 1986)

The Maps and Text of the 'Book of Idrography' presented by Jean Rotz to Henry VIII (ed. Helen Wallis, Roxburghe Club, Oxford, 1981)

Materials for a History of the Reign of Henry VII (2 vols, ed. William Campbell, Rolls Series, London, 1873)

Memoir of Henry Fitzroy, Duke of Richmond (ed. John Gough Nichols, Camden Miscellany, 3, Camden Society, 61, 1855)

Mémories de Martin et Guillaume du Bellay de plusieurs choses avenues au royaume de France depuis MDXIII jusques au trépas du roy François premier (Paris, 1569; 4 vols, ed. V.L. Bourilly and F. Vindry, Société d l'Histoire de France, Paris, 1908–19)

Les Mémoires de Martin et Guillaume du Bellay avec les mémoires du Maréchal de Fleuranges et le journal de Louise de Savoye (7 vols, Paris, 1753)

Memoirs of Henry the Eighth of England (ed. H. Herbert, New York, 1860)

Memoirs of Several Ladies of Great Britain who have been Celebrated for their Writings (Oxford, 1775)

Memorials of Archbishop Cranmer (3 vols, ed. John Strype, Oxford, 1854)

Memorials of King Henry VII (2 vols, ed. James Gairdner, Rolls Series, London, 1858)

Milles, T.: *Catalogue of Honour* (London, 1610)

Miscellaneous Antiquities, or a Collection of Curious Papers (ed. Horace Walpole, Strawberry Hill, 1772)

Monarchs and the Muse (ed. Sally Purcell, Oxford, 1972)

More, Sir Thomas: *The Correspondence of Sir Thomas More* (ed. Elizabeth Frances Rogers, Princeton, 1947)

More, Sir Thomas: *English Works* (London, 1557; 2 vols, ed. W.E. Campbell and A.W. Reed, London, 1931)

More, Sir Thomas: *Utopia* (Louvain, 1516; Oxford, 1551; tr. Ralph Robinson, London, 1556; ed. Edward Arber, London, 1869)

'Narrative of the Visit of the Duke of Najera to England in the Year 1543–4,written by his Secretary, Pedro de Gante' (*Archaeologia*, 23, 1831)

Narratives of the Days of the Reformation, chiefly from the Manuscripts of John Foxe, the Martyrologist (ed. John Gough Nichols, Camden Society, 77, London, 1859)

Newcastle MSS. (Nottingham University Library)

The Noble Triumphant Coronation of the Queen Anne, wife upon the Most Noble King Henry the VIII (Wynkyn de Worde, London, 1533; ed. A.F. Pollard in *Tudor Tracts*, London, 1903)

Nottingham University Library MSS.

Nucius, Nicander: *The Second Book of the Travels* (ed. J.A. Cramer, Camden Society, London, 1841)

'Original documents relating to Queen Katherine of Aragon' (*The Gentleman's Magazine*, New Series, 42, 1854)

Original Letters illustrative of English History (11 vols in 3 series, ed. Sir Henry Ellis, London: 1824 (1st Series, 3 vols), 1827 (2nd Series, 4 vols) and 1846 (3rd Series, 3 vols))

Original Letters relative to the English Reformation, written during the reigns of King Henry VIII, King Edward VI and Queen Mary: chiefly from the Archives at Zürich (2 vols, ed. Rev. Hastings Robinson, Parker Society, Cambridge, 1846–7, London, 1856)

The Paget Letters (Northampton Record Society)

Palsgrave, John: *L'Éclaircissement de la langue Francoyse* (London, 1530)

Parker, Matthew: *Correspondence of Matthew Parker, DD, 1535–75* (ed. John Bruce and Thomas T. Perowne, Parker Society, Cambridge, 1853)

Parr, Katherine: *The Lamentation, or Complaint, of a Sinner, made by the most virtuous and right gracious Lady, Queen Katherine, bewailing the Ignorance of her blind life, led in Superstition; very profitable to the Amendment of our Lives* (Harleian Miscellany, 5, 1810)

Platter, Thomas: *Travels of England* (London, 1599)

The Private Lives of the Tudor Monarchs (ed. Christopher Falkus, Follio Society, London, 1974)

The Privy Purse Expenses of Elizabeth of York, Queen of Henry VII, with a Memoir of Elizabeth of York and Notes; The Wardrobe Accounts of Edward the Fourth (ed. Sir Nicholas Harris Nicolas, London, 1830)

The Privy Purse Expenses of King Henry the Eighth from November MDXIX to December MDXXXII (ed. Sir Nicholas Harris Nicolas, London, 1827)

The Privy Purse Expenses of the Princess Mary, daughter of King Henry the Eighth, afterwards Queen Mary, with a Memoir of the Princess and Notes (ed. Frederick E. Madden, London, 1831)

Proceedings and Ordinances of the Privy Council of England, 1386–1542 (7 vols, ed. Sir Nicholas Harris Nicolas, London, 1834–7)

Puttenham, George: *The Art of English Poesie* (London, 1589; ed. G.D. Willcock and Alice Walker, London, 1936)

Rastell, William: *Life of Sir Thomas More* (fragment in the Arundel MSS., British Library)

Rawlinson MSS. (Bodleian Library, Oxford)

The Receipt of the Lady Katherine (1501; ed. G. Kipling, Early English Texts Society, London, 1990)

Records of the Reformation: The Divorce, 1527–1533 (2 vols, ed. Nicholas Pococke, Oxford, 1870)

The Register of the Most Noble Order of the Garter (2 vols, ed. J. Anstis, London, 1724)

The Reign of Henry VII from Contemporary Sources (3 vols, ed. Albert Frederick Pollard, London, 1913–14)

A Relation, or rather a True Account of the Island of England; with sundry particulars of the customs of these people . . . about the year 1500 (tr. Charlotte Augusta Sneyd, Camden Society, Old Series, 37, London, 1847)

'Religion and politics in mid-Tudor England through the eyes of an English Protestant Woman: the Recollections of Rose Hickman' (ed. Maria Dowling and Joy Shakespeare, *Bulletin of the Institute of Historical Research*, 54,1980; 55, 1982)

Reliques of English Poetry (3 vols, ed. Thomas Percy, London, 1885)

The Reports of Sir John Spelman (ed. J.A. Baker, Seldon Society, 93, 94, 1977–8)

Rhodes, Hugh: *The Book of Nurture for Men, Servants and Children* (London, 1545)

Roper, William: *The Life of Sir Thomas More, Knight* (ed. E.V. Hitchcock, Early English Texts Society, London, 1935; ed. Richard S. Sylvester and Davis P. Harding, London, 1962)

Rotuli Parliamentorum (6 vols, 1771–83; index 1832)

Rowley, Samuel: *When You See Me, You Know Me* (1605; Old English Drama Facsimile Edition, 1912)

Royal MSS. (British Library)

Royal Wills (Public Record Office)

Rutland MSS. (Historical Manuscripts Commission, 1888)

The Rutland Papers: Original Documents illustrating the Courts and Times of Henry VII and Henry VIII, selected from the private archives of His Grace the Duke of Rutland (ed. William Jordan, Camden Society, Old Series, 21, London, 1842)

Rymer, Thomas (ed.): *Foedera, Conventiones, Litterae et Cujuscunque Generis Acta Publica, inter Reges Angliae, etc.* (20 vols, London, 1727–35; 10 vols, The Hague, 1739–45; ed. T. Hardy, Records Commissioners, London, 1816–69)

Sadler, Sir Ralph: *The State Papers and Letters* (2 vols, ed. A. Clifford, Edinburgh, 1809)

Sander, Nicholas: *De Origine ac Progressu Schismatis Anglicani: The Rise and Growth of the Anglican Schism* (Rome, 1585; tr. and ed. David Lewis, London, 1877)

Sanuto, Marino: *Diarii* (59 vols, ed. R. Fullin, F. Stefani et al., Venice 1879–1903)

Scaino, Antonio: *Trattato del Giuoco Della Palla di Messer* (1553; ed. W.W. Kershaw, London, 1951)

The Seymour Papers, 1532–1686: Report on the Manuscripts of the Most Honourable the Marquess of Bath preserved at Longleat, IV (ed. M. Blatcher, Historical Manuscripts Commission, London, 1968)

A Short Title Catalogue of Books printed in England, Scotland and Ireland, and of English Books printed Abroad, 1475–1640 (ed. A.W. Pollard and G.R. Redgrave, rev. edn. W.A. Jackson and F.S. Ferguson, London, 1976)

Signature by Stamp Documents (Public Record Office)

Silver Poets of the Sixteenth Century (ed. Gerald Bullett, London, 1966)

Skelton, John: *The Complete Poems of John Skelton, Laureate* (ed. Philip Henderson, London, 1931, rev. edn. London, 1948)

Skelton, John: *Magnificence* (ed. P. Neuss, Manchester, 1980; also in *Four Morality Plays*, ed P. Happe, London, 1987)

Skelton, John: *The Poetical Works of John Skelton* (2 vols, ed. Alexander Dyce, London, 1843)

Skelton, John: *Skelton's Speculum Principis* (ed. F.M. Salter, *Speculum*, 9, 1934)

Sloane MSS. (British Library)

Songs, Ballads and Instrumental Pieces composed by King Henry the Eighth etc. (reproduced from British Museum MS 31922 for the Roxburghe Club; collated, ed. and arranged by Lady Mary Trefusis, Oxford, 1912)

Stapleton, Thomas: *Vita Thomas Mori: The Life and Illustrious Martyrdom of Sir Thomas More* (1588; tr. P.E. Hallett, London, 1928)

Starkey, Thomas: *England in the Reign of Henry VIII, Part I: Starkey's Life and Letters* (ed. Sidney J. Herrtage, Early English Texts Society, Extra Series, 32, London, 1878)

State Papers of Henry VIII (Public Record Office)

State Papers of the Reign of Henry VIII (11 vols, Records Commissioners, London, 1830–52)

Statues of the Realm (11 vols, ed. A. Luders et al., Records Commissioners, London, 1810–28)

Stow, John: *The Annals of England, or A General Chronicle of England* (London, 1592; ed. E. Howes, London, 1631)

Stow, John: *The Survey of London* (London, 1598; 2 vols, ed. C.L. Kingsford, Oxford, 1908)

Stowe MSS (British Library)

Strype, John (ed.): *Ecclesiastical Memorials . . . of the Church of England under King Henry VIII* (3 vols, London, 1721–33, and in his *Works*, 6 vols, Oxford, 1820–40)

Taylor, John: *The Praise of the Needle* (London, 1634)

Thomas, William: *The Pilgrim: A Dialogue on the Life and Actions of King Henry the Eighth* (c1546–7; ed. James Anthony Froude, London, 1861)

Three Inventories of the Years 1542, 1547 and 1549–50 of Pictures in the Collections of Henry VIII and Edward VI (ed. W.A. Shaw, London, 1937)

Tottel, Richard (ed.): *Tottel's Miscellany: Songs and Sonnnets by Henry Howard, Earl of Surrey, Sir Thomas Wyatt the Elder, Nicholas Grimald and Uncertain Authors* (London, 1557; ed. Edward Arber, English Reprints, 1870, Westminster, 1903; ed. Hyder E. Rollins, Cambridge, Mass., 1965)

Tradescant's Rareties: A Catalogue of the Early Collection in the Ashmolean Museum (ed. A. MacGregor, Oxford, 1983)

Trinity College, Dublin MS. 518

Tudor Royal Proclamations, Vol. I: The Early Tudors, 1485–1553 (3 vols, ed. Paul L. Hughes and James F. Larkin, London, 1964–9)

Tudor and Stuart Proclamations, 1485–1714 (2 vols, ed. R.R. Steele, London, 1910)

Tudor Tracts (ed. A.F. Pollard, London, 1903)

'Two Papers relating to the Interview between Henry the Eighth of England and Francis the First of France: Communicated by John Caley in a letter to Henry Ellis' (*Archaeologia*, 21, 1827)

Tyndale, William: *The Obedience of a Christian Man* (1528; ed. H. Walker, Parker Society, 1848)

Tyndale, William: *Works* (3 vols, ed. H. Walker, Parker Society, London, 1848–50)

Udall, Nicholas: *Nicholas Udall's Roister Doister* (ed. G. Scheurweghs, Louvain, 1939)

Udall, Nicholas: *Ralph Roister Doister* (ed. W.D. Cooper, London, 1847)

Vergil, Polydore: *Anglicae Hisoriae, AD 1485–1537* (Basel, 1534, 1546, 1570; Leyden, 1651; ed. Henry Ellis, London, 1846; tr. and ed. Denys Hay, Camden Society, 3rd Series, 74, Royal Historical Society, London, 1950)

Vives, Juan Luis: *Joannis Ludovici Vivis Valentini: De Institutione Foeminae Christianae, ad Inclytam d. Catherinam Hispanum, Angliae Libri Tres* (Basel, 1538; tr. Richard Hyrd as *A Very Fruitful and Pleasant Book called The Instruction of a Christian Woman*, London, 1540)

Vives, Juan Luis: *On Education (De Tradendis Disciplinis)* (1531; tr. Foster Watson, London, 1913)

Vives and the Renaissance Education of Women (ed. Foster Watson, London, 1912)

Westminster Abbey Muniments

The Works of Henry Howard, Earl of Surrey and of Sir Thomas Wyatt the Elder (2 vols, ed. G.F. Nott, London, 1815–16)

Wriothesley, Charles, Windsor Herald: *A Chronicle of England during the Reigns of the Tudors from AD 1485 to 1559* (London, 1581; 2 vols, ed. William Douglas Hamilton, Camden Society, New Series, 11, 20, 1875, 1877)

Wyatt, George: *Extracts from the Life of the Virtuous, Christian and Renowned Queen Anne Boleyn* (ed. R. Triphook, London, 1817; and as 'Some Particulars of the Life of Queen Anne Boleyn' in *The Life of Cardinal Wolsey by George Cavendish*, ed. S.W. Singer, London, 1827)

Wyatt, George: *The Papers of George Wyatt, Esquire, of Boxley Abbey in the County of Kent* (ed. David M. Loades, Camden Society, 4th Series, 5, 1968)

Wyatt, Sir Thomas: *Collected Poems* (ed. J. Daalder, Oxford, 1975)

Wyatt, Sir Thomas: *Collected Poems of Sir Thomas Wyatt* (ed. Kenneth Muir and Patricia Thomson, Liverpool, 1969)

Wyatt, Sir Thomas: *The Complete Poems* (ed. R.A. Rebholz, New Have, Conn.,1981)

Wyatt, Sir Thomas: *The Poems of Sir Thomas Wyatt* (2 vols, ed. A.K. Foxwell, London, 1913)

Wyatt, Sir Thomas: *The Poetry of Thomas Wyatt* (ed. E.M.W. Tillyard, London, 1929)

The Youth of Henry VIII: A Narrative in Contemporary Letters (ed. Frank Arthur Mumby, London, 1913)

Secondary Sources

Ainsworth, M.: '"Paternes for phisioneamyes": Holbein's portraiture reconsidered' (*Burlington Magazine*, 132, 1990)

Alberge, Dalya: 'A Head of her Time' (*Independent*, 23 April 1991)

Ancient Monuments and their Interpretation: Essays presented to A.J. Taylor (ed. M.R. Apted, R. Gilyard-Beer and A.D. Saunders, London, 1977)

Anderson Black, J., Garland, Madge, and Kennett, Frances: _A History of Fashion_ (London, 1982)

Anglo, Sidney: 'Archives of the English Tournament: Score Checks and Lists' (_Journal of the Society of Archivists_, 2, 1961)

Anglo, Sidney: 'The British History in Early Tudor Propaganda' (_Bulletin of the John Rylands Library_, 44, 1961)

Anglo, Sidney: 'Le Camp du Drap d'Or et les Éntrevues d'Henri VIII et de Charles Quint' (in _Fêtes et Cérémonies au Temps de Charles Quint_, Paris, 1959)

Anglo, Sidney: 'The Court Festivals of Henry VIII' (_Bulletin of the John Rylands Library_, 43, 1960–1)

Anglo, Sidney: 'An early Tudor programme for plays and other demonstrations against the Pope' (_Journal of the Warburg and Courtauld Institutes_, 20, 1957)

Anglo, Sidney: 'The Hampton Court Painting of the Field of Cloth of Gold Considered as an Historical Document' (_Antiquaries Journal_, 46, 1986)

Anglo, Sidney: _Images of Tudor Kingship_ (London, 1992)

Anglo, Sidney: _Spectacle, Pageantry and Early Tudor Policy_ (Oxford, 1969)

The Appetite and the Eye (ed. C. Anne Wilson, Edinburgh, 1991)

Armstrong, C.A.J.: _England, France and Burgundy in the Fifteenth Century_ (London, 1983)

Armstrong, Elizabeth: 'English Purchases of Printed Books from the Continent, 1465–1526' (_English Historical Review_, 1979)

Arnold, Janet: 'Fashions in Miniature' (_Journal of the Costume Society_, 11, 1977)

Ashdown, Dulcie M.: _Ladies in Waiting_ (London, 1976)

Ashley, Mike: _British Monarchs_ (London, 1998)

Aslet, Clive: _The Story of Greenwich_ (London, 1999)

Aston, Margaret: _The King's Bedpost_ (London, 1993)

Auerbach, Erna: 'The Black Book of the Garter' (_Report of the Society of the Friends of St George's_, 5, 1972–3)

Auerbach, Erna: 'Holbein's Followers in England' (_Burlington Magazine_, 93, 1951)

Auerbach, Erna: 'Notes on Flemish Miniaturists in England' (_Burlington Magazine_, 96, 1954)

Auerbach, Erna: _Tudor Artists: A Study of Painters in the Royal Service and of Portraiture on Illuminated Documents from the Accession of Henry VIII to the Death of Elizabeth I_ (London, 1954)

Auerbach, Erna: 'Vincent Volpe: King's Painter' (_Burlington Magazine_, 92, 1950)

Aungier, G.J.: _The History and Antiquities of Syon Monastery_ (London, 1840)

Bagenal, Alison, and Bagenal, Michael: _Music from the Past: Tudor England_ (Harlow, 1987)

Bagley, J.J.: _Henry VIII and his Times_ (London, 1962)

Bagrow, L., and Skelton, R.A.: _The History of Cartography_ (London, 1964)

Baldi, Sergio: _Sir Thomas Wyatt_ (tr. T. Prince, London, 1961)

Baldwin, David: _The Chapel Royal, Ancient and Modern_ (London, 1990)

Banqueting Stuffe (ed. C. Anne Wilson, Edinburgh, 1991)

Bapst, Edmond: _Deux gentilshommes-poètes de la cour de Henri VIII_ (concerning Rochford and Surrey; Paris, 1891)

Barber, Richard, and Barker, Juliet: _Tournaments: Jousts, Chivalry and Pageants in the Middle Ages_ (Woodbridge, 1989)

Baumer, Franklin le van: _The Early Tudor Theory of Kingship_ (London, 1940)

Bayles, Howard: 'Notes on Accounts paid to the Royal Apothecaries in 1546 and 1547' (_Chemist and Druggist_, 114, 1931)

Bayley, J.: _The History and Antiquities of the Tower_ (London, 1921)

Bayne-Powell, R.: _Catalogue of the Portrait Miniatures in the Fitzwilliam Museum, Cambridge_ (Cambridge, 1985)

Beard, C.R.: 'Dog Collars' (_Connoisseur_, March 1940)

Beckingsale, B.W.: _Thomas Cromwell, Tudor Minister_ (London, 1978)

Beer, B.L.: 'The Rise of John Dudley, Duke of Northumberland' (*History Today*, 15, 1965)

Benesch, O.: *The Art of the Renaissance in Northern Europe* (London, 1965)

Benger, I.O.: *Memoirs of the Life of Anne Boleyn, Queen of Henry VIII* (London, 1821; Philadelphia, 1850)

Bennett, H.S.: *English Books and Readers, 1475–1557* (Cambridge, 1952)

Bentley-Cranch, Dana: *Royal Faces* (HMSO, London, 1990)

Bernard, G.W.: 'The Fall of Anne Boleyn' (*English Historical Review*, 106, 1991)

Bernard, G.W.: 'The Rise of Sir William Compton, Tudor Courtier' (*English Historical Review*, 96, 1981)

Bernard, G.W.: *The Power of the Early Tudor Nobility: A Study of the Fourth and Fifth Earls of Shrewsbury* (London, 1984)

Bernstein, Jane A.: 'Philip van Wilder and the Netherlandish Chanson in England' (*Musica Disciplina*, 33, 1979)

Bevington, D.M.: *From Mankind to Marlowe: Growth and Structure in the Popular Drama of Tudor England* (Cambridge, Mass., 1962)

Biddle, M.: 'Excavation of the Manor of The More, Rickmansworth' (*Archaeological Journal*, 116, 1959)

Biddle, M.: 'Nicholas Bellin de Modena: An Italian Artificer at the Courts of Francis I and Henry VIII' (*Journal of the British Archaeological Association*, 3rd Series, 29, 1966)

Biddle, M.: 'Nonsuch Palace, 1959–60' (*Surrey Archaeological Collections*, 58, 1961)

Biddle, M.: 'The Stuccoes of Nonsuch' (*Burlington Magazine*, 1984)

Biddle, M.: 'The Vanished Gardens of Nonsuch' (*Country Life*, 26 October, 1961)

Bindoff, S.T.: *Tudor England* (London, 1950)

Binski, B.: *The Painted Chamber at Westminster* (Society of Antiquaries of London, London, 1986)

Birrell, T.A.: *English Monarchs and their Books from Henry VIII to Charles II* (London, 1987)

Blair, Claude: 'The Emperor Maximilian's Gift of Armour to King Henry VIII and the Silvered and Engraved Armour at the Tower of London' (*Archaeologia*, 99, 1965)

Blair, Claude: *King Henry VIII's Tonlet Armour* (Burlington House Fair catalogue, 1983)

Blair, Claude: 'The Most Superb of all Royal Locks' (*Apollo*, December 1966)

Blair, Claude: 'A Royal Swordsmith and Damascener: Diego de Çayas' (*Metropolitan Museum Journal*, 3, 1970)

Blezzard, Judith: 'A New Source of Tudor Music' (*Musical Times*, 122, 1981)

Blomefield, Sir Reginald: *The History of Renaissance Architecture in England* (2 vols, London, 1897)

Boas, Frederick S.: *An Introduction to Tudor Drama* (Oxford, 1933)

Bonney, R.: *The European Dynastic States, 1494–1660* (Oxford, 1991)

Boureaunu, Radu: *Holbein* (London, 1977)

Bouterwek, A.W.: 'Anna von Cleve, Gemahlin Heinrich VIII, König von England' (*Zeitschrift des Bergischen Geschichtsvereins*, 4, 1867, and 6, 1869)

Bowle, John: *Henry VIII* (London, 1965)

Bowles, Edmund: 'Haut et Bas: the Grouping of Musical Instruments in the Middle Ages' (*Musica Disciplina*), 8, 1954)

Braddock, R.C.: 'The Rewards of Office-Holding in Tudor England' (*Journal of British Studies*, 14, 1975)

Bray, A.: *Homosexuality in Renaissance England* (London, 1982)

Brayley, E.W., and Britton, J.: *The History of the Ancient Palace and Late Houses of Parliament at Westminster* (London, 1836)

Brears, Peter: *All the King's Cooks: The Tudor Kitchens of King Henry VIII at Hampton Court Palace* (London, 1999)

Brett, Philip: *Thomas Tallis* (London, 1965)

Brewer, J.S.: *The Reign of Henry VIII from his Accession to the Death of Wolsey, Reviewed and Illustrated from Original Documents* (2 vols, ed. James Gairdner, London, 1884)

Brinch, Ove: 'The Medical Problems of Henry VIII' (*Centaurus*, 5, 1958)

Brindle, Steve, and Kerr, Brian: *Windsor Revealed: New Light on the History of the Castle*

(English Heritage, London, 1997)

Brook, Roy: *The Story of Eltham Palace* (London, 1960)

Brooke, C.N.L.: *The Mediaeval Idea of Marriage* (Oxford, 1989)

Brown, A.L.: 'The Authorisation of Letters under the Great Seal' (*Bulletin of the Institute of Historical Research*, 37, 1964)

Brown, D.: *Raphael and America* (Washington, 1983)

Bruce, F.F.: *History of the Bible in English* (New York, 1978)

Bruce, Marie-Louise: *Anne Boleyn* (London, 1972)

Bruce, Marie-Louise: *The Making of Henry VIII* (London, 1977)

Brysson-Morrison, N.: *The Private Life of Henry VIII* (London, 1964)

Buch, M.L.: 'The Tudors and the Royal Race' (*History*, 12, 1970)

Buck, P.C. et al.: *Tudor Church Music* (10 vols, London, 1925–30)

Burke, Maurice: 'Charles Brandon, Gentleman Adventurer' (*Contemporary Review*, 179, 1951)

Burke, S.H.: *Historical Portraits of the Tudor Dynasty and the Reformation Period* (4 vols, London, 1879–83)

Burton, Elizabeth: *The Early Tudors at Home* (London, 1976)

Burton, Elizabeth: *The Pageant of Early Tudor England, 1485–1558* (New York, 1976)

Bush, Douglas: *The Renaissance and English Humanism* (Toronto, 1939)

Bush, M.L.: 'The Lisle–Seymour Land Disputes: A Study in Power and Influence in the 1530s' (*Historical Journal* 9, no. 3, 1966)

Byrne, Janet S.: *Renaissance Ornament, Prints and Drawings* (New York, 1981)

The Cambridge History of English Literature, Vol. III: Renascence and Reformation (15 vols, ed. Sir A.W. Ward and A.R. Waller, Cambridge, 1907–32)

Campbell, Lorne: *The Early Flemish Pictures in the Collection of HM the Queen* (Cambridge, 1985)

Campbell, Lorne: *Renaissance Portraits: European Portrait Painting in the 14th, 15th and 16th Centuries* (London, 1990)

Campbell, Lorne, and Foister, Susan: 'Gerard, Lucas and Susanna Horenbout' (*Burlington Magazine*, 128, 1986)

Campbell, W.E.: 'Erasmus in England' (*Dutch Review*, 211, 1942)

Cantor, L.M., and Hatherly, J.: 'The Mediaeval Parks of England' (*Geography*, 64, 1979)

Cardinal Wolsey: Church, State and Art (ed. S.J. Gunn and P.J. Lindley, Cambridge, 1990)

Carley, James: 'John Leland and the Foundations of the Royal Library: The Westminster Inventory of 1542' (*Bulletin of the Society for Renaissance Studies*, 7, 1989)

Carnicelli, D.: *Lord Morley's Tryumphs of Fraunces Petrarcke* (Cambridge, Mass., 1971)

Cart de Lafontaine, Henry: *The King's Musick* (London, 1909; rev. edn. 1973)

Cartellieri, O.: *The Court of Burgundy* (tr. M. Letts, London, 1929)

Caspari, F.: *Humanism and the Social Order in Tudor England* (Chicago, 1954)

Catalogue of the Principal Works of Art at Chequers (HMSO, London, 1923)

Cathcart King, D.J.: *The Castle in England and Wales* (London, 1988)

Ceremonial Masks (ed. V. Turner, Washington, 1982)

Chamberlain, Arthur B.: *Hans Holbein the Younger* (2 vols, London, 1913)

Chamberlin, Frederick: *The Private Character of Henry VIII* (London, 1932)

Chambers, Sir Edward K.: *English Literature at the Close of the Middle Ages* (Oxford, 1947)

Chambers, Sir Edward K.: *The Mediaeval Stage* (2 vols, London, 1903)

Chambers, Sir Edward K.: *Notes on the History of the Revels Office under the Tudors* (London, 1906)

Chambers, R.W.: *Thomas More* (London, 1935)

Chapman, Hester W.: *Anne Boleyn* (London, 1974)

Chapman, Hester W.: *The Last Tudor King: A Study of Edward VI* (London, 1958)

Chapman, Hester W.: *The Sisters of Henry VIII* (London, 1969)

Chapman, Hester W.: *Two Tudor Portraits* (concerning Henry Howard, Earl of Surrey, and Lady Katherine Grey; London, 1960)

Chappell, W.: *Popular Music of Olden Time* (2 vols, London, 1855–9)

Charlton, K.: *Education in Renaissance England* (London, 1965)

Chester, A.G.: *Hugh Latimer, Apostle to the English* (Philadelphia, 1954)

Chettle, G.H., Charlton, J., and Allan, J.: *Hampton Court Palace, Greater London* (HMSO, London, 1982)

Childe-Pemberton, William S.: *Elizabeth Blount and Henry VIII* (London, 1913)

Chinnery, V.: *Oak Furniture: The British Tradition* (Woodbridge, 1990)

Chrimes, S.B.: *Henry VII* (London, 1972)

Chronicles of the Tudor Kings (ed. David M. Loades, London, 1990)

Claremont, Francesca: *Catherine of Aragon* (London, 1939)

Clebsch, William A.: *England's Earliest Protestants, 1520–1535* (London, 1964)

Clepham, Robert Coltman: *The Tournament* (London, 1919)

Clough, R.H.: 'Relations between England and the Court of Urbino, 1474 to 1508' (*Studies in the Renaissance*, 14, 1967)

Colding, T.H.: *Aspects of Miniature Painting* (Copenhagen, 1953)

Collins, A.J.: *Jewels and Plate of Queen Elizabeth: The Inventory of 1574* (London, 1955)

Collins Baker, C.H., and Constable, W.G.: *English Painting of the Sixteenth and Seventeenth Centuries* (New York, 1930)

Colvin, H.M.: 'Castles and Government in Tudor England' (*English Historical Review*, 83, 1968)

The Complete Peerage (13 vols, ed. G.E. Cockayne, V.Gibbs, H.A. Doubleday, D. Warrand, Thomas, Lord Howard de Walden and G. White, London, 1910–59)

Conway, Martin: 'A Portrait of King Henry VIII' (*Burlington Magazine*, 45, 1924)

Cook, A.: 'Oatlands Palace: An Interim Report' (*Surrey Archaeological Collections*, 66, 1969)

Cook, Petronelle: *Queen Consorts of England* (New York, 1993)

Cook, T.A.: 'The Bronze Medallion in Henry VII's chapel at Westminster' (*Monthly Review*, August 1903)

Coope, R.: 'The Long Gallery: Its Origins, Development and Use of Decoration' (*Architectural History*, 9, 1986)

Cooper, C.H.: *Memoir of Margaret, Countess of Richmond and Derby* (ed. J.E.B. Mayer, Cambridge, 1874)

Copeman, W.S.C.: *Dcotors and Disease in Tudor Times* (London, 1960)

The Courts of Europe, 1440–1800 (ed. A.G. Dickens, London, 1977)

Cressy, D.: *Literacy and the Social Order: Reading and Writing in Tudor and Stuart England* (Cambridge, 1980)

Cripps-Day, Francis Henry: *The History of the Tournament in England and France* (London, 1918)

Croft-Murray, E.: *Decorative Painting in England, 1537–1837, Vol I: Early Tudor to Sir James Thornhill* (London, 1962)

Cruickshank, Charles Grieg: *Army Royal: Henry VIII's Invasion of France, 1513* (Oxford, 1969)

Cruickshank, M.: *Henry VIII and the Invasion of France* (London, 1990)

Crumpler, Alan, McGowan, Keith, and Pope, Martin: *Music from the Reign of Henry VIII* (London, 1995)

Cumming, Valerie: *Exploring Costume History, 1550–1900* (London, 1981)

Cummings, Anthony M.: 'The Transmission of some Josquin Motets' (*Journal of the Royal Musical Association*, 115/1 1990)

Cunningham, C.W., and Cunningham, Phyllis: *English Costume in the Sixteenth Century* (London, 1954)

Currie, A.S.: 'Notes on the Obstetric Histories of Catherine of Aragon and Anne Boleyn' (*Edinburgh Medical Journal*, 1, 1888)

Currie, Christopher K.: 'Fishponds as Garden Features, c1550–1750' (*Garden History*, 18, 1990)

Cust, Lionel: 'A Portrait of Queen Catherine Howard by Hans Holbein the Younger' (*Burlington Magazine*, 17, 1910)

Darr, A.P.: 'The Sculptures of Torrigiano: The Westminster Abbey Tombs' (Connoisseur, 200, 1979)

Davenport, Mila: The Book of Costume (New York, 1948)

Davey, Henry: A History of English Music (London, 1895, repr. 1921)

Deer, B.: 'Carnivore King and the Main Course of History' (Sunday Times, 3 September 1989)

De-la-Noy, Michael: Windsor Castle, Past and Present (London, 1990)

Denny, Roz: The Tudor Kitchens Cookery Book, Hampton Court Palace (London, 1991)

Dent, John: The Quest for Nonsuch (London, 1962)

Derrett, J., and Duncan, M.: 'Henry Fitzroy and Henry VIII's Scruple of Conscience' (Renaissance News, 16, 1963)

Destombes, M.: 'Nautical Clocks attributed to Verrazano (1525–1528)' (Imago Mundi, 11, 1954)

Dewhurst, Sir John: 'The Alleged Miscarriages of Katherine of Aragon and Anne Boleyn' (Medical History, 28, 1984)

Dewhurst, Sir John (as Jack Dewhurst): Royal Confinements (London, 1980)

Dickens, Arthur Geoffrey: The English Reformation (London, 1964)

Dickens, Arthur Geoffrey: Thomas Cromwell and the English Reformation (Cambridge, 1959)

Dickinson, J.C.: The Shrine of Our Lady of Walsingham (Cambridge 1956)

The Dictionary of National Biography (63 vols, ed. Sir Leslie Stephen and Sir Sidney Lee, London, 1885–1900)

Digby Wyatt, Sir Matthew: On the Foreign Artists Employed in England in the Sixteenth Century (London, 1868)

Dillon, Viscount: 'Barriers and Foot Combats' (Archaeological Journal, 61, 1904)

Dillon, Viscount: 'Tilting in Tudor Times' (Archaeological Journal, 55, 1898)

Dixon, P.W.: Excavations at Greenwich Palace, 1970-71 (London, 1972)

Dixon, W.H.: 'Anne Boleyn' (Gentleman's Magazine, New Series, 16, 1876)

Dodds, Madeleine Hope, and Dodds, Ruth: The Pilgrimage of Grace, 1536–7, and the Exeter Conspiracy, 1538 (2 vols, Cambridge, 1915)

Dodgson, C.: 'Woodcuts designed by Holbein for English Printers' (Walpole Society, 27, 1938–9)

Doernberg, Erwin: Henry VIII and Luther: An Account of their Personal Relations (Stanford, Calif., 1961)

Dolmetsch, Mabel: Dances of England and France from 1450 to 1600 (London, 1949)

Doran, John: Court Fools (London, 1858)

Dow, H.G.: 'Two Italian Portrait Busts of Henry VIII' (Art Bulletin, 42, 1960)

Dowling, Maria: 'Anne Boleyn and Reform' (Journal of Ecclesiastical History, 35, 1984)

Dowling, Maria: Humanism in the Age of Henry VIII (London, 1986)

Dowling, Maria: 'Humanist Support for Katherine of Aragon' (Bulletin of the Institute of Historical Research, 56, 1982)

Dowling, Maria: '"A Woman's Place": Learning and the Wives of Henry VIII' (History Today, 41, 1991)

Dowsing, James: Forgotten Tudor Palaces in the London Area (London, no date)

Drummond, J.C., and Wilbraham, Anne: The Englishman's Food: A History of Five Centuries of English Diet (London, 1957)

Du Boys, Albert: Catherine of Aragon and the Sources of the English Reformation (2 vols, tr. and ed. Charlotte M. Yonge, London, 1881, repr. New York, 1968)

Dunbar, Janet: A Prospect of Richmond (London, 1966)

Dunlop, Ian: Palaces and Progresses of Elizabeth I (London, 1962)

Dutton, Ralph: English Court Life from Henry VII to George II (London, 1963)

Dyer, C.: Standards of Living in the Later Middle Ages (Cambridge, 1989)

Dynasties: Painting in Tudor and Jacobean England, 1530–1630 (exhibition catalogue, Tate Gallery, ed. Karen Hearn, London, 1995)

Early Tudor England: Proceedings of the 1987 Harlaxton Symposium (ed. Daniel Williams,

Woodbridge, 1989)

Eccles, A.: *Obstetrics and Gynaecology in Tudor and Stuart England* (Kent, Ohio, 1982)

Edmond, M.: 'Limners and Picturemakers: New Light on the Lives of Miniaturists and Large-scale Portrait Painters working in London in the 16th and 17th centuries' (*Walpole Society*, 47, 1978–80)

Edwards, H.L.R.: *Skelton: The Life and Times of a Tudor Poet* (London, 1949)

Einstein, Lewis: *The Italian Renaissance in England* (New York, 1902)

Elias, N.: *The Court Society* (tr. E. Jephcott, London, 1983)

Elton, G.R.: *England under the Tudors* (London, 1955, rev. edn 1969)

Elton, G.R.: *Henry VIII: An Essay in Revision* (London, 1962)

Elton, G.R.: 'King or Minister? The Man behind the Henrician Reformation' (*History*, 39, 1954)

Elton, G.R.: 'Persecution and Toleration in the English Reformation' (*Studies in Church History*, 21, Oxford, 1984)

Elton, G.R.: *Policy and Police: The Enforcement of the Reformation in the Age of Thomas Cromwell* (Cambridge, 1972)

Elton, G.R.: *Reform and Reformation: England, 1509–1558* (Cambridge, Mass., 1977)

Elton, G.R.: 'Sir Thomas More and the Opposition to Henry VIII' (*Bulletin of the Institute of Historical Research*, 41, 1968)

Elton, G.R.: *Studies in Tudor and Stuart Politics and Government* (3 vols, Cambridge, 1974, 1983)

Elton, G.R.: 'Tudor Government: The Points of Contact: III: The Court' (*Transactions of the Royal Historical Society*, 5th series, 26, 1976)

Elton, G.R.: *The Tudor Revolution in Government: A Study of Administrative Changes in the Reign of Henry VIII* (Cambridge, 1953)

Emmison, F.G.: *Tudor Food and Pastimes* (London, 1964)

Emmison, F.G.: *Tudor Secretary: Sir William Petre at Court and Home* (London, 1961)

The English Court, from the Wars of the Roses to the Civil War (ed. David R. Starkey et al., London, 1987)

English Map-Making, 1500–1650 (ed., S. Tyacke, London, 1983)

Erickson, Carolly: *Great Harry* (London, 1980)

Erickson, Carolly: *Mistress Anne* (New York, 1984)

Essays for G.R. Elton from His American Friends (ed. J. Guth and John W. McKenna, Cambridge, 1982)

Evans, Maurice: *English Poetry in the Sixteenth Century* (London, 1967)

Evett, D.: *Literature and the Visual Arts in Tudor England* (London, 1990)

Ferguson, Arthur B.: *The Indian Summer of English Chivalry* (Cambridge, 1960)

Ferguson, Charles W.: *Naked to Mine Enemies: The Life of Cardinal Wolsey* (London, 1958)

Ffoulkes, C.J.: *The Armourer and His Craft* (London, 1912)

Ffoulkes, C.J.: *European Arms and Armour in the University of Oxford* (Oxford, 1912)

Ffoulkes, C.J.: *Inventory and Survey of the Armouries of the Tower of London* (London, 1926)

Fiddes, Richard: *The Life of Cardinal Wolsey* (London, 1724)

Fine Bindings from Oxford Libraries (exhibition catalogue, Oxford, 1968)

Firth, Charles H.: 'The Ballad History of the Reigns of Henry VII and Henry VIII' (*Transactions of the Royal Historical Society*, 3rd Series, 2, 1908)

Fisher, F.J.: 'The Development of London as a Centre of Conspicuous Consumption in the Sixteenth and Seventeenth Centuries' (*Transactions of the Royal Historical Society*, 4th Series, 30, 1948)

Fletcher, Benton: *Royal Homes Near London* (London, 1930)

Fletcher, C.R.L., and Halker, Emery: *Historical Portraits, 1400–1600* (Oxford, 1909)

Fletcher, John: 'A Group of English Royal Portraits painted soon after 1513' (*Studies in Conservation*, 21, 1976)

Fletcher, John: 'A Portrait of William Carey and Lord Hunsdon's Long Gallery' (*Burlington Magazine*, 123, 1981)

Fletcher, John: 'Tree Ring Dates for some Panel Paintings in England' (*Burlington Magazine*, 116, 1974)

Fletcher, John, and Trapper, M.C.: 'Hans Holbein the Younger at Antwerp and in England' (*Apollo*, February 1983)

Flood, A.G.H.: *Early English Composers* (London, 1925)

Flügel, J.C.: 'The Character and Married Life of Henry VIII' (in *Psychoanalysis and History*, ed. Bruce Mazlish, New York, 1963)

Foister, Susan: *Drawings by Holbein from the Royal Library, Windsor Castle* (London, 1983)

Foister, Susan: 'Tudor Miniaturists at the V & A' (*Burlington Magazine*, 125, 1983)

Ford, E.: *A History of Enfield in the County of Middlesex* (Enfield, 1873)

Forman, Benno, M.: 'Continental Furniture Craftsmen in London, 1511–1625' (*Furniture History*, 1, 1971)

Foskett, Daphne: *British Portrait Miniatures* (London, 1963)

Foster, R., and Tudor-Craig, Pamela: *The Secret Life of Paintings* (London, 1986)

Foucault, M.: *The History of Sexuality* (3 vols, tr. R. Hurley, London, 1980)

Fox-Davis, A.C.: *A Complete Guide to Heraldry* (London, 1950)

Franklyn, C.: *The Genealogy of Anne the Queen* (Brighton, 1977)

Fraser, Lady Antonia: *The Six Wives of Henry VIII* (London, 1993)

Friedlander, M.J.: *Early Netherlandish Painting* (Leyden and Brussels, 1975)

Friedman, Paul: *Anne Boleyn: A Chapter of English History, 1527–1536* (2 vols, London, 1884)

Froude, James Anthony: *The History of England from the Fall of Wolsey to the Death of Elizabeth* (4 vols, New York, 1881)

Froude, James Anthony: *The Life and Letters of Erasmus* (London, 1894)

Funck-Brentano, F.: *Luther* (London, 1936)

Gaimster, D.: 'London's Tudor Palaces Revisited: A User's Guide to the Backlog' (*London Archaeologist*, 8, 5, 1997)

Gaimster, D., and Redknapp, M.: *Everyday and Exotic Poetry from Europe c650–1900* (Oxford, 1992)

Gairdner, James.: 'The Age of Anne Boleyn' (*English Historical Review*, 10, 1895)

Gairdner, James: 'Mary and Anne Boleyn' (*English Historical Review*, 8, 1893)

Gairdner, James: 'New Lights on the Divorce of Henry VIII' (*English Historical Review*, 11, 1896)

Galvin, C., and Lindley, P.: 'Pietro Torrigiano's Portrait Bust of King Henry VIII' (*Burlington Magazine*, 130, 1988)

Gameson, R., and Coates, A.: *The Old Library, Trinity College, Oxford* (Oxford, 1988)

Gamon, S.R.: *Statesman and Schemer: William, First Lord Paget* (Newton Abbot, 1973)

Ganz, Paul: 'The Castle Howard Portrait of Henry VIII' (*Burlington Magazine*, 64, 1934)

Ganz, Paul: *Die Hanzeichnungen Hans Holbein des Jungeren* (Berlin, 1911)

Ganz, Paul: *Holbein* (London, 1950)

Ganz, Paul: 'Holbein and Henry VIII' (*Burlington Magazine*, 73, 1943)

Ganz, Paul: *The Paintings of Hans Holbein* (London, 1956)

Gardiner, D.: *The Story of Lambeth Palace* (London, 1930)

Garner, T., and Stratton, A.: *The Domestic Architecture of England during the Tudor Period* (2 vols, 1929)

Gask, Norman: *Old Silver Spoons of England* (London, 1926)

Gaunt, William: *Court Painting in England from Tudor to Victorian Times* (London, 1980)

Gee, E.: 'Heating in the Late Middle Ages' (*Transactions of the Ancient Monuments Society*, New Series, 31, 1987)

Gilbert, Creighton: *When Did Renaissance Man Grow Old?* (Studies in the Renaissance, Vol. XIV, 1967)

Gilpin, W.: *The Life of Hugh Latimer, Bishop of Worcester* (London, 1755)

Gingerich, O.: 'Apianus's Astronomicum Caesareum' (*Journal of the History of Astronomy*, 2, 1971)

Girouard, M.: *Life in the English Country House: A Social and Architectural History* (London, 1978)

Given-Wilson, C.: *The Royal Household and the King's Affinity: Service, Politics and Finance in England, 1300–1413* (London, 1986)

Glanville, P.: 'Robert Amadas, Court Goldsmith to Henry VIII' (*Proceedings of the Silver Society*, 3, 1986)

Glanville, P.: *Silver in Tudor and Early Stuart England* (London, 1990)

Glasheen, Joan: *St James's, London* (London, 1987)

Glasheen, Joan: *The Secret People of the Palaces: The Royal Household from the Plantagenets to Queen Victoria* (London, 1998)

Glück, G.: 'The Henry VII in the National Portrait Gallery' (*Burlington Magazine*, 63, 1993)

Goff, Cecilie: *A Woman of the Tudor Age* (concerning Katherine Willoughby, Duchess of Suffolk; London, 1930)

Gordon, M.A.: *The Life of Queen Katherine Parr* (Kendal, 1952)

Gotch, J.A.: *Early Renaissance Architecture in England* (London, 1901)

Graeme, Bruce: *The Story of St James's Palace* (London, 1929)

Greaves, M.: *The Blazon of Honour* (London, 1964)

Green, H.J.M., and Thurley, Simon J.: 'Excavations on the West Side of Whitehall, 1960–62. Part I: From the Building of the Tudor Palace to the Construction of the Modern Offices of State' (*Transactions of the London and Middlesex Archaeological Society*, 1987, 1990)

Green, Mary Anne Everett: *The Lives of the Princesses of England* (6 vols, London, 1849–55)

Green, R.F.: *Poets and Princepleasers* (Toronto, 1980)'

Greene, R.L.: 'A Carol of Anne Boleyn by Wyatt' (*Review of English Studies*, New Series, 25, 1974)

Greenslade, S.L.: 'The Morean Renaissance' (*Journal of Ecclesiastical History*, 24, 1973)

Griffiths, R.A., and Thomas, R.S.: *The Making of the Tudor Dynasty* (London, 1985)

Grossman, F.: 'Holbein, Torrigiano, and the Portraits of Dean Colet' (*Journal of the Warburg and Courtauld Institutes*, 13, 1950)

Gunn, Steven J.: *Charles Brandon, Duke of Suffolk, c1484–1545* (Oxford, 1988)

Guy, John A.: *Tudor England* (Oxford, 1988)

Guy, John A., and Fox, A.: *Reassessing the Henrician Age* (Oxford, 1986)

Gwyn, Peter: *The King's Cardinal: The Rise and Fall of Thomas Wolsey* (London, 1990)

Hackenbroch, Y.: *Renaissance Jewellery* (London, 1979)

Hacker, Peter, and Kuhl, Candy: 'A Portrait of Anne of Cleves' (*Burlington Magazine*, March 1992)

Hackett, Francis: *Henry the Eighth* (London, 1929, repr. Bath, 1973)

Hale, John: *Renaissance Europe: Individual and Society, 1480–1520* (New York, 1971)

Halliday, F.E.: *An Illustrated Cultural History of Britain* (London, 1967)

Halsted, C.A.: *Life of Margaret Beaufort* (London, 1839)

Hammond, Peter: *Her Majesty's Royal Palace and Fortress of the Tower of London* (London, 1984)

Hammond, Peter: *Royal Fortress: The Tower of London through Nine Centuries* (London, 1978)

Hampton Court Palace: Guidebook (London, 1993)

Hamy, P.A.: *Entrevue de François Ier ave Henry VIII à Boulogne-sur-Mer en 1532. Intervention de la France dans l'Affaire du Divorce* (Paris, 1898)

Harrier, R.C.: *The Canon of Sir Thomas Wyatt's Poetry* (Cambridge, Mass., 1975)

Harrier, R.C.: 'Notes on Wyatt and Anne Boleyn' (*Journal of English and Germanic Philology*, 53, 1954)

Harris, Barbara J.: *Edward Stafford, Third Duke of Buckingham, 1478–1521* (Stanford, Calif., 1986)

Harris, Barbara, J.: 'Marriage Sixteenth-Century Style: Elizabeth Stafford and the Third Duke of Norfolk' (*Journal of Social History*, 15, 1982)

Harris, Barbara J.: 'Property, Power and Personal Relations: Elite Mothers and Sons in

Yorkist and Early Tudor England' (*Signs*, 15, 1990)

Harris, Barbara J.: 'Women and Politics in Early Tudor England' (*Historical Journal*, 33, 1990)

Harris, J.: 'John Bale' (*Illinois Studies in Language and Literature*, 23, 1939)

Harrison, David: *Tudor England* (2 vols, London, 1953)

Hartnell, Norman: *Royal Courts of Fashion* (London, 1971)

Harvey, J.: 'The Building Works and Architects of Cardinal Wolsey' (*Journal of the British Archaeological Association*, 3rd Series, 8, 1943)

Hattaway, Michael: 'Marginalia by Henry VIII in his Copy of the Books of Salamon' (*Transactions of the Cambridge Bibliographical Society*, 4, 1965)

Haugaard, William P.: 'Katherine Parr: The Religious Convictions of a Renaissance Queen' (*Renaissance Quarterly*, 22, 1969)

Hawkins, E., Franks, A.W., and Grubber, H.A.: *Medallic Illustrations of Great Britain and Ireland* (London, 1885)

Hay, Denys: 'The Life of Polydore Vergil of Urbino' (*Journal of the Warburg and Courtauld Institutes*, 1949)

Hay, Denys: *Polydore Vergil, Renaissance Historian and Man of Letters* (London, 1952)

Hayward, J.: 'The Restoration of the Tudor Clock Salt' (*Goldsmiths Review*, 1, 1969–70)

Hayward, J.: *Virtuoso Goldsmiths and the Triumph of Mannerism, 1540–1620* (London, 1976)

Head, D.: ' "Being Led and Seduced by the Devil": The Attainder of Lord Thomas Howard and the Tudor Law of Treason' (*Sixteenth-Century Journal*, 13, 1982)

Heal, F.: *Hospitality in Early Modern England* (Oxford, 1990)

Hearsey, John E.N.: *The Tower* (London, 1960)

Hedley, Olwen: *Royal Palaces* (London, 1972)

Hellyer, B., and Hellyer, H.: *The Astronomical Clock, Hampton Court Palace* (London, 1973)

Hennell, R.: *The History of the King's Body Guard and the Yeomen of the Guard* (London, 1904)

Henry VIII: A European Court in England (exhibition catalogue, National Maritime Museum, ed. David R. Starkey, London, 1991)

Hepburn, E.: 'The Portraiture of Arthur, Prince of Wales' (*Journal of the British Archaeological Assocation*, 148, 1995)

Hepburn, Frederick: *Portraits of the Later Plantagenets* (Woodbridge, 1986)

Hervey, M.F.S.: 'Notes on a Tudor Painter: Gerlach Flicke' (*Burlington Magazine*, 17, 1910)

Hesketh, C.: 'The Manor House and Great Park of the Archbishops of Canterbury at Otford' (*Archaeologia Cantiana*, 31, 1915)

Hexter, J.H.: 'The Education of the Aristocracy in the Renaissance' (*Journal of Modern History*, 22, 1950)

Hibbert, Christopher: *The Court at Windsor* (London, 1964)

Hibbert, Christopher: *The Tower of London* (London, 1971)

Higgins, A.: 'On the Work of Florentine Sculptors in England in the Early Parts of the Sixteenth Century, with Special Reference to the Tombs of Cardinal Wolsey and King Henry VIII' (*Archaeological Journal*, 56, 1894)

Hill, G.F.: 'A Medal of Henry VIII as Supreme Head of the Church' (*Numismatic Chronicle*, 1916)

Hill, G.F.: *Medals of the Renaissance* (rev. edn. by J.G. Pollard, London, 1978)

Hillerbrand, H.M.: 'The Early History of the Chapel Royal' (*Modern Philology*, 18, 1920)

The Historical Association Book of the Tudors (ed. Joel Hurstfield, London, 1973)

Hobson, G.D.: *Bindings in Cambridge Libraries* (Cambridge, 1929)

Hoffman, Anne: *Lives of the Tudor Age* (New York, 1977)

Hogrefe, Pearl: *Tudor Women, Commoners and Queens* (Iowa, 1975)

Hogrefe, Pearl: *Women of Action in Tudor England: Nine Biographical Sketches* (Iowa, 1977)

Holbein and the Court of Henry VIII (exhibition catalogue, The Queen's Gallery, Buckingham Palace, London, 1978–9)

Holman, Peter: 'The English Royal Violin Consort in the Sixteenth Century' (*Proceedings of the Royal Musical Association*, 109, 1982–3)

Holmes, M.R.: 'The Crown of England' (*Archaeologia*, 86, 1937)

The House of Commons, 1509–1559 (3 vols, ed. S.T. Bindoff, History of Parliament Trust, London, 1982)

Howard, Maurice: *The Domestic Building Patronage of the Courtiers of Henry VIII* (London, 1985)

Howard, Maurice: *The Early Tudor Country House: Architecture and Politics, 1490–1550* (London, 1987)

Howard, Maurice: *The Tudor Image* (London, 1995)

Howard, Phillip: *The Royal Palaces* (London, 1960)

Hughes, A., and Abraham, F.: '*Ars Nova* and the Renaissance' (in *The New Oxford History of Music*, Vol. III, Oxford, 1960)

Hughes, Philip: *The Reformation in England, Vol. I: The King's Proceedings* (3 vols, London, 1951–4)

Huizinga, J.: *Erasmus and the Age of Reformation* (New York, 1957)

Huizinga, J.: *Erasmus of Rotterdam* (London, 1952)

Humphreys, David: 'Philip van Wilder: A Study of his Work and his Sources' (*Soundings*, 9, 1979–80)

Huray, P. le: *Music and the Reformation in England* (Oxford, 1967)

Hurst, J.G., Neal, D.S., and Van Beuningen, H.J.E.: *Pottery Produced and Traded in North-West Europe, 1350–1650* (Rotterdam, 1987)

Hurt, Nicholas: *Sudeley Castle and Gardens: Guidebook* (Wimborne, 1994)

Incontri, Maria Luisa: *Il Piccolo Levriero Italiano* (Florence, 1956)

Innes, Arthur: *Ten Tudor Statesmen* (London, 1934)

Ives, Eric W.: *Anne Boleyn* (Oxford, 1986)

Ives, Eric W.: 'Faction at the Court of Henry VIII: The Fall of Anne Boleyn' (*History*, 57, 1972)

Ives, Eric W.: *Faction in Tudor England* (London, 1979; rev. edn, London, 1986)

Ives, Eric W.: 'The Queen and the Painters: Anne Boleyn, Holbein and the Tudor Royal Portraits' (*Apollo*, July, 1994)

Jackson, J.E.: 'Wulfhall and the Seymours' (*Wiltshire Archaeological and Natural History Magazine*, 15, 1875)

Jacquot, J.: *Notice sur Nicolas Bourbon de Vandoeuvre* (Paris, 1857)

Jaffé, Deborah: *What's Left of Henry VIII* (Shepperton, 1995)

Jagger, Cedric: *Royal Clocks* (London, 1983)

James, M.E.: 'English Politics and the Concept of Honour, 1485–1642' (*Past and Present*, Suppl. 3, 1978)

James, Susan: 'The Devotional Writings of Queen Katherine Parr' (*Transactions of the Cumberland and Westmorland Antiquarian and Archaeological Society*, 82, 1982)

James, Susan: *Kateryn Parr: The Making of a Queen* (Bangor, 1999)

James, Susan: 'Queen Kateryn Parr, 1512–1548' (*Transactions of the Cumberland and Westmorland Antiquarian and Archaeological Society*, 88, 1988)

James, T.B.: *The Palaces of Mediaeval England* (London, 1990)

Jenner, Heather: *Royal Wives* (London, 1967)

Jesse, G.R.: *History of the British Dog* (2 vols, London, 1856)

Johnson, Hugh: *The Story of Wine* (London, 1989)

Jones, Michael K., and Underwood, Malcolm G.: *The King's Mother: Lady Margaret Beaufort, Countess of Richmond and Derby* (Cambridge, 1992)

Jones, Paul van Brunt: *The Household of a Tudor Nobleman* (Illinois, 1917)

Jones, W.: *Crowns and Coronations: A History of Regalia* (London, 1898)

Jordan, W.K.: *Edward VI: The Threshold of Power* (London, 1970)

Keen, Maurice H.: *Chivalry* (London, 1984)

Kelly, Henry A.: *The Matrimonial Trials of Henry VIII* (Stanford, Calif., 1976)

Kelso, Ruth: *The Doctrine of the English Gentleman in the Sixteenth Century* (Illinois, 1929)

592   *Henry VIII: King and Court*

Kennedy, H.A.: *Early English Portrait Miniatures in the Collection of the Duke of Buccleuch* (ed. C. Holmes, London, 1917)

King, D.: 'The Inventories of the Carpets of Henry VIII' (*Hali*, 5, 1983)

King, John N.: *English Reformation Literature: The Tudor Origins of the Protestant Tradition* (Princeton, 1982)

King, John N.: *Tudor Royal Iconography: Art in an Age of Religious Crisis* (Princeton, 1989)

King, Margaret L.: *Women of the Renaissance* (Chicago, 1991)

Kingsford, C.L.: 'Historical Notes on Mediaeval London Houses' (*London Topographical Record*, 10, 1916, and 12, 1920)

Kipling, G.: *The Triumph of Honour: Burgundian Origins of the Elizabethan Renaissance* (Leyden, 1977)

Kirby, J.W.: 'Building Works at Placentia, 1532–3 and 1543–4' (*Transactions of the Greenwich and Lewisham Antiquarian Society*, 5 and 6, 1954–61)

Kirkwood, Jean: *The Windsor Martyrs* (no date or provenance)

Kittredge, George Lyman: *Withcraft in Old and New England* (Harvard, 1929)

Knecht, R.J.: *Francis I* (Cambridge, 1982)

Knole: Guidebook (National Trust, 1989)

Koebner, R.: '"The Imperial Crown of this Realm": Henry VIII, Constantine the Great and Polydore Vergil' (*Bulletin of the Institute of Historical Research*, 26, 1953)

Kybett, Susan M.: 'Henry VIII, a Malnourished King?' (*History Today*, 39, 1989)

Lacey, Robert: *The Life and Times of Henry VIII* (London, 1972)

Laking, G.F.: *A Record of European Arms and Armour through Seven Centuries* (London, 1926)

Langdon, Helen: *Holbein* (Oxford, 1976)

Langsam, G.G.: *Martial Books and Tudor Verse* (New York, 1951)

Larson, J.: 'A Polychrome Terracotta Bust of a Laughing Child at Windsor Castle' (*Burlington Magazine*, 131, 1989)

Lasocki, David: 'The Anglo-Venetian Bassano Family as Instrument Makers and Repairers' (*Galpin Society Journal*, 38, 1985)

Lasocki, David: 'The Bassanos: Anglo-Venetian and Venetian' (*Early Music*, 14, 1986)

Lasocki, David: 'Professional Recorder Playing in England, 1500–1740' (*Early Music*, 10, 1982)

The Later Middle Ages (ed. S. Medcalf, London, 1981)

Laver, James: *A Concise History of Costume* (London, 1969)

Law, Ernest: *England's First Great War Minister* (London, 1916)

Law, Ernest: *Hampton Court Gardens* (London, 1926)

Law, Ernest: *The Royal Gallery of Hampton Court* (London, 1898)

Law, Ernest: *A Short History of Hampton Court Palace in Tudor and Stuart Times* (London, 1924)

Lebel, Gustave: 'British-French Artistic Relations in the Sixteenth Century' (*Gazette des Beaux-Arts*, 33, Paris, 1948)

Leeds Castle: Guidebook (London, 1994)

Leeds Castle: Illustrated History and Guide to the Rooms (London, 1985)

Lees-Milne, J.: *Tudor Renaissance* (London, 1951)

Lehmberg, S.E.: *The Later Parliaments of Henry VIII* (Cambridge, 1977)

Lehmberg, S.E.: *The Reformation Parliament, 1529–36* (Cambridge, 1970)

Lehmberg, S.E.: *Sir Thomas Elyot, Tudor Humanist* (Austin, Tex. 1960)

Levey, M.: *Painting at Court* (New York, 1971)

Levine, Mortimer: 'The Last Will and Testament of Henry VIII: A Reappraisal Reappraised' (*Historian*, 26 1964)

Lewis, C.S.: *English Literature in the Sixteenth Century excluding Drama* (Oxford, 1954)

Le Lieu Théâtral à la Renaissance (ed. J. Jacquot, Paris, 1964)

Lindsay, Philip: *The Secret of Henry VIII* (London, 1953)

Lingard, J.: *The History of England* (6 vols, London, 1855)

Lloyd, Christopher, and Remington, Vanessa: *Masterpieces in Little: Portrait Miniatures from the*

Collection of HM Queen Elizabeth II (London, 1996)

Lloyd, Christopher, and Thurley, Simon J.: *Henry VIII: Images of a Tudor King* (Oxford, 1990)

Lloyd, Stephan: *Portrait Miniatures from the Collection of the Duke of Buccleuch* (Scottish National Portrait Gallery, Edinburgh, 1996)

Loades, David M.: *Mary Tudor: A Life* (Oxford, 1989)

Loades, David M.: *The Politics of Marriage: Henry VIII and His Queens* (Stroud, 1994)

Loades, David M.: *The Tudor Court* (London, 1986)

Long, Basil, C.: *British Miniaturists, 1520–1860* (London, 1929)

Longman, C.J., and Walrond, H.: *Archery* (London, 1984)

Loseley Park: Guide (English Life Publications, 1993)

Lowinsky, Edward: 'MS 1070 of the Royal College of Music in London' (*Proceedings of the Royal Musical Assocation*, 96, 1969–70)

Lowinsky, Edward E.: 'A Music Book for Anne Boleyn' (in *Florilegium Historiale: Essays Presented to Wallace K. Ferguson*, ed. J.G. Rowe and W.H. Stockdale, Toronto, 1971)

Luke, Mary M.: *Catherine the Queen* (London, 1968)

de Lute, A.: *La Magnifique Histoire du Jeu de Paume* (tr. and ed. R. Hamilton, London, 1979)

MacDonagh, Katherine: *Reigning Cats and Dogs* (London, 1999)

Mackerness, E.D.: *A Social History of English Music* (London, 1964)

Mackie, John Duncan: *The Earlier Tudors, 1485–1558* (Oxford, 1952)

MacLean, I.: *The Renaissance Notion of Women* (Cambridge, 1980)

MacLean, John: *The Life of Thomas Seymour, Kt., Baron Seymour of Sudeley, Lord High Admiral of England and Master of the Ordnance* (London, 1869)

Maclennan, Hector: 'A Gynaecologist looks at the Tudors' (*Medical History*, 11, 1967)

MacMichael, J.H.: 'Baynard's Castle and Excavations on its Site' (*Journal of the British Archaeological Association*, 46, 1890)

MacNalty, Sir Arthur S.: *Henry VIII – A Difficult Patient* (London, 1952)

Mainwaring-Brown, J.: 'Henry VIII's Book and the Royal Title of Defender of the Faith' (*Transactions of the Royal Historical Society*, 1st Series, 8, 1880)

Maritime Greenwich: Guidebook (Andover, 1974)

Marius, Richard: *Thomas More: A Biography* (London, 1984)

Marks, R., and Payne, A.: *British Heraldry* (London, 1978)

Marlier, C.: *Ambrosius Benson et la peinture à Bruges au temps de Charles Quint* (Damme, 1957)

Marsden, P.: 'Baynard's Castle' (*Mediaeval Archaeology*, 17, 1973)

Marshall, J.: *The Annals of Tennis* (London, 1878)

Marsham, Robert: 'On a Manuscript Book of Prayers in a Binding of Gold Enamelled, said to have given by Queen Anne Boleyn to a Lady of the Wyatt Family' (*Archaeologia*, 44, 1873)

Mason, H.A.: *Humanism and Poetry in the Early Tudor Period* (London, 1959)

Mathew, David: *The Courtiers of Henry VIII* (London, 1970)

Matthews, Leslie G.: 'Royal Apothecaries of the Tudor Period' (*Medical History*, 8, 1964)

Mattingly, Garrett: *Catherine of Aragon* (London, 1942)

Mattingly, Garrett: 'A Humanist Ambassador' (concerning Eustace Chapuys; *Journal of Modern History*, 4, 1932)

Mattingly, Garrett: *Renaissance Diplomacy* (London, 1955)

Maynard-Smith, H.: *Henry VIII and the Reformation* (London, 1962)

McConica, James Kelsey: *English Humanist and Reformation Politics under Henry VIII and Edward VI* (Oxford, 1965)

McCoy, R.: *The Rites of Knighthood* (Berkeley, Calif., 1989)

McFarlane, K.B.: *The Nobility of Later Mediaeval England* (Oxford, 1973)

McKendrick, S.: 'Edward IV: an English Royal Collector of Netherlandish Tapestry' (*Burlington Magazine*, 129, 1987)

McKisack, M.: *Mediaeval History in the Tudor Age* (Oxford, 1971)

Mead, William Edward: *The English Mediaeval Feast* (London, 1931)

Merriman, Roger B.: *The Life and Letters of Thomas Cromwell* (2 vols, Oxford, 1902; repr. 1968)

Mertes, K.: *The English Noble Household, 1250–1600* (Oxford, 1988)

Michell, Ronald: *The Carews of Beddington* (London, 1981)

Millar, Oliver: *The Tudor, Stuart and Early Georgian Pictures in the Collection of HM The Queen* (London, 1963)

Miller, H.: 'The Early Tudor Peerage, 1485–1547' (*Bulletin of the Institute of Historical Research*, 24, 1951)

Miller, Helen: *Henry VIII and the English Nobility* (Oxford, 1986)

Millican, C.B.: *Spenser and the Round Table* (Cambridge, Mass., 1932)

Mitchell, Margaret: 'Works of Art from Rome for Henry VIII' (*Journal of the Warburg and Courtauld Institutes*, 39, 1971)

Monsarrat, Ann: *And the Bride Wore* (London, 1973)

Moore, Sir Norman: 'The death of Catherine of Aragon' (*Athenaeum*, London, 31 Jan. and 28 Feb., 1885)

Morris, Christopher: *The Tudors* (London, 1955)

Morshead, Sir Owen: *Windsor Castle* (London, 1957)

Morton, Bradley, M.: *Elizabeth Blount of Kinlet* (Kidderminster, 1991)

Mueller, Janet: 'Katherine Parr's prayers and meditations' (*Huntingdon Library Quarterly*, 53, 1990)

Muir, Kenneth: *The Life and Letters of Sir Thomas Wyatt* (Liverpool, 1963)

Muller, James Arthur: *Stephen Gardiner and the Tudor Reaction* (London, 1926)

Munrow, David: *Two Renaissance Dance Bands* (London, 1971)

Murdoch, J., et al.: *The English Portrait Miniature* (London, 1981)

Murray Baillie, H.: 'Etiquette and the Planning of State Apartments in Baroque Palaces' (*Archaeologia*, 101, 1967)

Murray, P.: *The Architecture of the Italian Renaissance* (London, 1969)

Murrell, V.J.: *The Way to Lymne: Tudor Miniatures Observed* (London, 1983)

Music at the Court of Henry VIII (ed. John Stevens, Musica Britannica, Vol. XVIII, London, 1969)

Music in Mediaeval and Early Modern Europe: Patronage, Sources and Text (ed. Iain Fenlon, Cambridge, 1981)

Myers, A.R.: *The Household of Edward IV: The Black Book and Ordinance of 1478* (Manchester, 1959)

Napier, H.A.: *Historical Notices of the Parishes of Swyncombe and Ewelme* (Oxford, 1858)

Nelson, William: *John Skelton, Laureate* (New York, 1939; rev. edn. 1964)

Newton, A.P.: 'Tudor Reforms in the Royal Household' (in *Tudor Studies presented by the Board of Students in History at the University of London to Albert Frederick Pollard*, ed. R.W. Seton-Watson, London, 1924)

Nichols, John Gough: 'Notices of the Contemporaries and Successors of Holbein' (*Archaeologia*, 39)

Nickel, H., Pyhrr, S.W., and Tarassuk, L.: *The Art of Chivalry* (New York, 1982)

Nicolson, A.: *Restoration: The Rebuilding of Windsor Castle* (London, 1997)

Nixon, H.M.: *Five Centuries of English Bookbinding* (London, 1978)

Noreña, Carlos G.: 'Juan Luis Vives and Henry VIII' (*Renaissance and Reformation*, 12, 1976)

Norman, A.V.B.: *Treasures from the Tower of London* (exhibition catalogue, London, 1982)

Norris, Herbert: *Costume and Fashion, Vol. II: Senlac to Bosworth, 1066–1485* (London, 1927)

Norris, Herbert: *Tudor Costume and Fashion* (London, 1938, repr. New York, 1997)

North, J.D.: 'Nicolaus Kratzer – "The King's Astronomer"; Science and History' (in *Studies in Honour of Edward Rosen*, Studia Copernica, Vol. XVI, 1978)

Nugent, Elizabeth M.: *The Thought and Culture of the English Renaissance* (Cambridge, 1956)

O'Day, R: *Education and Society, 1500–1800: The Social Foundations of Education in Early Modern Britain* (London, 1982)

O'Donoghue, E.G.: *Bridewell Hospital: Palace, Prison, Schools* (London, 1923)

Oman, C.: *British Rings* (London, 1974)

Oman, Charles W.C.: *A History of the Art of War in the Sixteenth Century* (New York, 1937)

Oman, Charles W.C.: 'The Personality of Henry VIII' (*Quarterly Review*, 269, 1937)

Omont, Henri: 'Les manuscrits français des rois de'Angleterre au château de Richmond (in *Études romanes dédiées à Gaston Paris*, Paris, 1891)

Orme, N.: *From Childhood to Chivalry: The Educating of the English Kings and Aristocracy, 1055–1530* (London, 1984)

Ormond, Richard: *The Face of Monarchy: British Royalty Portrayed* (Oxford, 1977)

The Oxford Book of Royal Anecdotes (ed. Elizabeth Longford, Oxford, 1989)

The Oxford Companion to English Literature (ed. Margaret Drabble, Oxford, 1995)

The Oxford Illustrated History of Tudor and Stuart Britain (ed. John Merrill, Oxford, 1996)

Paget, Hugh: 'Gerard and Lucas Hornebolte in England' (*Burlington Magazine*, 101, 1959)

Paget, Hugh: 'The Youth of Anne Boleyn' (*Bulletin of the Institute of Historical Research*, 55, 1981)

Palmer, Alan, and Palmer, Veronica: *Royal England: A Historical Gazetteer* (London, 1983)

Palmer, J.A.: *A Biographical Dictionary of Old English Music* (London, 1927)

Pardoe, Julia: *The Court and Reign of Francis the First, King of France* (2 vols, London, 1849)

Parker, K.T.: *The Drawings of Hans Holbein in the Collection of His Majesty the King at Windsor Castle* (Oxford and London, 1945; repr. London and New York, 1983)

Parmiter, Geoffrey de C.: *The King's Great Matter: A Study of Anglo-Papal Relations, 1527–1534* (London, 1967)

Parnell, G.: *The Tower of London* (London, 1993)

Paston-Williams, Sarah: *The Art of Dining: A History of Cooking and Eating* (National Trust, 1993)

Patronage in the Renaissance (ed. G.F. Lytle and S. Orgel, Princeton, 1981)

Pattenden, P.: *Sundials at an Oxford College* (Oxford, 1979)

Pattison, B.: *Music and Poetry of the English Renaissance* (London, 1970)

Paul, John E.: *Catherine of Aragon and her Friends* (London, 1966)

Penshurst Place and Gardens: Guidebook (Tonbridge, 1993)

Perry, Maria: *Sisters to the King* (London, 1998)

Pickthorn, K.: *Early Tudor Government: Henry VIII* (2 vols, Cambridge, 1934)

Pinches, J.H.: *The Royal Heraldry of England* (London, 1974)

Piper, David: *The English Face* (London, 1957)

Plowden, Alison: *The House of Tudor* (Stroud, 1976, repr. 1998)

Plowden, Alison: *Tudor Women: Queens and Commoners* (London, 1979)

Plumb, J.H.: *Royal Heritage* (London, 1977)

Polk, Keith: 'The Trombone, the Slide Trumpet and the Ensemble Tradition of the Early Renaissance' (*Early Music*, 17, 1989)

Pollard, Albert Frederick: 'Council, Star Chamber and Privy Council under the Tudors' (*English Historical Review*, 37, 1922)

Pollard, Albert Frederick: *Henry VIII* (London, 1902)

Pollard, Albert Frederick: 'The Privy Council under the Tudors' (*English Historical Review*, 38, 1923)

Pollard, Albert Frederick: *Thomas Cranmer and the English Reformation, 1489–1556* (London, 1904, repr. London, 1965)

Pollard, Albert Frederick: *Wolsey: Church and State in Sixteenth-Century England* (London, 1929, repr. 1953)

Pollard, Michael, Bingham, Caroline, and Parker, Josephine: *On Stage* (Chippenham, 1993)

Pollet, Maurice: *John Skelton, Poet of Tudor England* (London, 1971)

Pope-Hennessy, James: *The Portrait in the Renaissance* (New York, 1966)

Popham, A.E.: 'Hans Holbein's Italian contemporaries in England' (*Burlington Magazine*, 84, 1944)

Pouncey, R.: 'Girolamo da Treviso in the Service of Henry VIII' (*Burlington Magazine*, 95, 1953)

Powicke, Sir F. Maurice: *The Reformation in England* (Oxford, 1951)

Prescott, H.F.M.: *Mary Tudor* (London, 1940; rev. edn London, 1952)

Princely Magnificence: Court Jewels of the Renaissance, 1500–1630 (exhibition catalogue, Victoria and Albert Museum, ed. A. Somers-Cocks, London, 1980)

Princes, Patronage and the Nobility: The Court at the Beginning of the Modern Age, c1450–1650 (ed. R.G. Asch and A.M. Birke, Oxford, 1991)

Prior, Roger: 'Jewish Musicians at the Tudor Court' (*Musical Quarterly*, 69, 1983)

Protestantism and the National Church in the Sixteenth Century (ed. Maria Dowling and P. Lake, London, 1987)

Pyne, William Henry: *The History of the Royal Residences of Windsor Castle, St James's Palace, Carlton House, Kensington Place, Hampton Court, Buckingham House and Frogmore* (London, 1819)

Rady, J., Tatton Brown, T., and Bowen, J.: 'The Archbishop's Palace, Canterbury' (*Journal of the British Archaeological Association*, 1991)

Ransome, D.R.: 'Artisan Dynasties in London and Westminster in the Sixteenth Century' (*Guildhall Miscellany*, 2, 1964)

Rawcliffe, Caroline: *The Staffords, Earls of Stafford and Dukes of Buckingham, 1394–1521* (Cambridge, 1978)

Read, Conyers: *The Bibliography of English History, Tudor Period, 1485–1603* (Oxford, 1933)

Read, Conyers: *The Tudors: Personalities and Politics in Sixteenth-Century England* (Oxford, 1936)

Read, Evelyn: *Catherine Duchess of Suffolk* (London, 1962; pub. as *My Lady of Suffolk*, New York, 1963)

Reassessing the Henrician Age (ed. A.Fox and John Guy, Oxford, 1986)

Reath, N.A.: 'Velvets of the Renaissance, from Europe and Asia Minor' (*Burlington Magazine*, 50, 1927)

Redworth, Glyn: *In Defence of the Church Catholic: The Life of Stephen Gardiner* (Oxford, 1990)

Reed, A.W.: *Early Tudor Drama* (London, 1926)

Reese, Gustave: *Music in the Renaissance* (London, 1954)

Reform and Reformation: England and the Continent, c1500–c1700 (ed. D. Baker, Oxford, 1979)

Reid, J.W.: *The Lore of Arms* (London, 1976)

Reid, Rachel R.: *The King's Council in the North* (London, 1921)

Reid, William: 'A Royal Crossbow in the Scott Collection' (*Scottish Art Review*, 7, 1959)

Reilly, E.: *Historical Anecdotes of the Families of the Boleyns, Careys, Mordaunts, Hamiltons and Jocelyns, arranged as an Elucidation of the Genealogical Chart at Tollymore Park* (London, 1839)

The Renaissance in England (ed. J.V. Cunningham, New York, 1966)

Renaissance Painting in Manuscripts: Treasures from the British Library (ed. Thomas Kren, New York, 1984)

Reynolds, E.E.: *The Field Is Won* (London, 1968)

Reynolds, E.E.: *St John Fisher* (London, 1955)

Reynolds, E.E.: *Thomas More and Erasmus* (London, 1965)

Reynolds, G.: *English Portrait Miniatures* (Cambridge, 1988)

Richardson, Walter C.: *Mary Tudor, the White Queen* (London, 1970)

Richardson, Walter C.: *Tudor Chamber Administration* (Baton Rouge, 1952)

Richmond, C.H.: *Anglo-French Literary Relations in the Reformation* (Berkeley, Calif., 1981)

Ridley, Jasper: *Henry VIII* (London, 1984)

Ridley, Jasper: *The Statesman and the Fanatic: Thomas Wolsey and Thomas More* (London, 1982)

Ridley, Jasper: *Thomas Cranmer* (Oxford, 1962)

Rivals in Power: Lives and Letters of the Great Tudor Dynasties (ed. David R. Starkey, London, 1990)

Roach, E.A.: *Cultivated Fruits of Britain* (Oxford, 1985)

Roberts, Jane: *Holbein and the Court of Henry VIII* (exhibition catalogue, National Galleries of Scotland, Edinburgh, 1993)

Robinson, Brian: *Silver Pennies and Linen Towels* (London, 1992)

Robinson, John Martin: *The Dukes of Norfolk: A Quincentennial History* (Oxford, 1982)

Ross, Josephine: *The Tudors* (London, 1979)

Rosser, Gervase: *Mediaeval Westminster* (Oxford, 1989)

Rosser, Gervase, and Thurley, Simon J.: 'Whitehall Palace and King Street, Westminster: The Urban Cost of Princely Magnificence' (*London Topographical Record*, 26, 1990)

Roulstone, Michael: *The Royal House of Tudor* (St Ives, 1974)

Routh, C.R.N.: *Who's Who in Tudor England* (London, 1990)

Routh, E.M.G.: *Lady Margaret: A Memoir of Lady Margaret Beaufort, Mother of Henry VII* (London, 1924)

Rowlands, John: *The Age of Dürer and Holbein* (exhibition catalogue, British Museum, London, 1988)

Rowlands, John: *Holbein: The Paintings of Hans Holbein the Younger* (Oxford, 1985)

Rowlands, John: 'A Portrait Drawing by Hans Holbein the Younger' (in the *British Museum Yearbook*, 2, 1977)

Rowlands, John, and Starkey, Dávid R.: 'An Old Tradition Reassessed: Holbein's Portrait of Queen Anne Boleyn' (*Burlington Magazine*, 125, 1983)

Rowse, A.L.: 'Eminent Henrician: Thomas Wriothesley' (*History Today*, 15, 1965)

Rowse, A.L: *The Tower of London in the History of the Nation* (London, 1972)

Rowse, A.L.: *Windsor Castle in the History of the Nation* (London, 1974)

The Royal Encyclopaedia (ed. Ronald Allison and Sarah Riddell, London, 1991)

Royal River: A Guide to the River Thames (Andover, 1982)

Rupp, E.G.: *Six Makers of English Religion, 1550–1700* (New York, 1959)

Rupp, E.G.: *Studies in the Making of the English Protestant Tradition* (Cambridge, 1966)

Russell, Joycelyne Gledhill: *The Field of Cloth of Gold: Men and Manners in 1520* (London, 1969)

Rye, W.B.: *England as Seen by Foreigners* (London, 1865)

St George's Chapel, Windsor Castle: *Guidebook* (Norwich, 1993)

St John Hope, W.: *Windsor Castle: An Architectural History* (London, 1913)

St Maur, H.: *Annals of the Seymours* (London, 1902)

Salet, Francis:; *David et Bethsabée* (Éditions de la Réunion des Musées Nationaux, Paris, 1980)

Salter, Emma Gurney: *Tudor England through Venetian Eyes* (London, 1930)

Salzman, L.F.: *Building in England down to 1540* (Oxford, 1952)

Saunders, Beatrice: *Henry the Eighth* (London, 1963)

Scarisbrick, Diana: *Jewellery in Britain, 1066–1837* (Norwich, 1994)

Scarisbrick, Diana: *Tudor and Jacobean Jewellery* (London, 1995)

Scarisbrick, John J.: *Henry VIII* (London, 1968)

Scharf, George: 'Additional Observations on Some of the Painters Contemporary with Holbein' (*Archaeologia*, 39, 1862)

Schenk, W.: *Reginald Pole, Cardinal of England* (London, 1950)

Schofield, John, and Dyson, Tony: *Archaeology of the City of London* (London, 1980)

Scholes, Percy A.: *The Oxford Companion to Music* (Oxford, 1970)

Schott, H.: *Victoria and Albert Museum: Catalogue of Musical Instruments, Vol. I: Keyboard Instruments* (London, 1985)

Schroder, Timothy: *The National Trust Book of English Domestic Silver 1550–1900* (London, 1988)

Schulz, J.: 'Pinturicchio and the Revival of the Antique' (*Journal of the Warburg and Courtauld Institutes*, 1962)

Scott, R. Forsyth: 'On the Contracts for the Tomb of the Lady Margaret Beaufort, Countess of Richmond and Derby' (*Archaeologia*, 66, 1915)

Scott-Giles, C.Wilfrid: *The Romance of Heraldry* (London, 1929)

Seebohm, F.: *The Oxford Reformers: John Colet, Erasmus and Thomas More* (London, 1869)

Sergeant, Philip Walsingham: *The Life of Anne Boleyn: A Study* (London, 1923)

Seward, Desmond: *Prince of the Renaissance: The Life of François I* (London, 1973)

Seymour, William: *Ordeal by Ambition: An English Family in the Shadow of the Tudors* (London, 1972)

Shakespeare, Joy, and Dowling, Maria: 'Religion and Politics in mid-Tudor England' (*Bulletin of the Institute of Historical Research*, 55, 1982)

Shaw, W.A.: 'An early English Pre-Holbein School of Portraiture' (*Connoisseur*, 31, 1911)

Shaw, W.A.: *The Knights of England* (London, 1906)

The Shell Guide to England (ed. John Hadfield, London, 1975)

Shirley, Rodney: *The Mapping of the World, 1472–1700* (London, 1984)

Shrewsbury, J.F.D.: 'Henry VIII, a Medical Study' (*Journal of the History of Medicine and Allied Sciences*, 8, 1952)

Siegel, Paul N.: 'English Humanism and the New Tudor Aristocracy' (*Journal of the History of Ideas*, 13, 1952)

Sim, Alison: *Food and Feast in Tudor England* (Stroud, 1997)

Simon, André L.: *The History of the Wine Trade in England* (London, 1906)

Simon, Joan: *Education and Poetry in Tudor England* (Cambridge, 1966)

600 Years of British Painting: The Berger Collection at the Denver Art Museum (exhibition catalogue, Denver Art Museum, 1998)

Skeel, Caroline A.J.: *The Council in the Marches of Wales* (London, 1904)

Slavin, A.J.: *Politics and Profit: A Study of Sir Ralph Sadler, 1507–47* (Cambridge, 1966)

Smirke, S.: 'Notices of the Palace of Whitehall' (*Archaeologia* 30, 1834)

Smith, H, Clifford: 'Jewellery in Tudor Times' (*Illustrated London News*, 1949)

Smith, Lacey Baldwin: 'English Treason Trials and Confessions in the Sixteenth Century' (*Journal of the History of Ideas*, 15, 1954)

Smith, Lacey Baldwin: *Henry VIII: The Mask of Royalty* (London, 1971)

Smith, Lacey Baldwin: 'Henry VIII and the Protestant Triumph' (*American Historical Review*, 71, 1966)

Smith, Lacey Baldwin: 'The Last Will and Testament of Henry VIII: A Question of Perspective' (*Journal of British Studies*, 2, 1962)

Smith, Lacey Baldwin: *Tudor Prelates and Politics, 1536–1558* (Princeton, 1953)

Smith, Lacey Baldwin: *A Tudor Tragedy: The Life and Times of Catherine Howard* (London, 1961)

Softly, Barbara: *The Queens of Britain* (London, 1976)

Somerset, Anne: *Ladies in Waiting: From the Tudors to the Present Day* (London, 1984)

Somerset Fry, Plantagenet: *Chequers: The Country Home of Britain's Prime Ministers* (London, 1977)

Sotheby's Concise Encyclopaedia of Glass (ed. D. Battle and Simon Cottle, London, 1991)

Source Reading in Music History (ed. Oliver Strunk, London, 1952, repr. 1981)

Southall, R.: *The Courtly Maker: An Essay on the Poetry of Wyatt and his Contemporaries* (Oxford, 1964)

Southcott, John, and Grubb, Francis: *The Music of Henry VIII* (sleeve notes, Peerless Record Company, 1971)

Starkey, David R.: 'The Court: Castiglione's Ideal and Tudor Reality, being a discussion of Sir Thomas Wyatt's satire addressed to Sir Francis Bryan' (*Journal of the Warburg and Courtauld Institutes*, 45, 1982)

Starkey, David R: 'From Feud to Faction' (*History Today*, 32, 1982)

Starkey, David R.: 'Holbein's Irish sitter' (*Burlington Magazine*, 123, 1981)

Starkey, David R.: *The Reign of Henry VIII: Personalities and Politics* (London, 1985)

Steane, John: *The Archaeology of the Mediaeval English Monarchy, 1066–1547* (London, 1993)

Stevens, John: *Music and Poetry in the Early Tudor Court* (Cambridge, 1961, repr. 1978)

Strickland, Agnes: *Lives of the Queens of England* (11 vols, London, 1842)

Strickland, Agnes: *Lives of the Tudor Princesses* (London, 1868)

Strong, D.E.: *Eltham Palace, London* (HMSO, London, 1978)

Strong, Sir Roy C.: *Art and Power: Renaissance Festivals, 1450–1650* (Woodbridge, 1984)

Strong, Sir Roy C.: *Artists of the Tudor Court* (exhibition catalogue, Victoria and Albert Museum, London, 1983)

Strong, Sir Roy C: *The English Icon* (London, 1969)

Strong, Sir Roy C.:*The English Miniature* (London, 1981)

Strong, Sir Roy C.: *The English Renaissance Miniature* (London, 1983)

Strong, Sir Roy C.: *Hans Eworth: A Tudor Artist and His Circle* (Leicester, 1965)

Strong, Sir Roy C.: *Holbein and Henry VIII* (London, 1967)

Strong, Sir Roy C.: *Lost Treasures of Britain* (London, 1990)

Strong, Sir Roy C.: *The Renaissance Garden in England* (London, 1979)

Strong, Sir Roy C.: *Splendour at Court: Renaissance Spectacle and the Theatre of Power* (London, 1973)

Strong, Sir Roy C.: *Tudor and Jacobean Portraits* (2 vols, London, 1969)

Strutt, John, and Horn, W.: *Sports and Pastimes in England* (London, 1830)

Strutt, Joseph: *A Complete View of the Manners, Customs and Habits of the Inhabitants of England* (3 vols, London, 1775–6)

Stubbs, Blaxland: 'Royal Recipes for Plasters, Ointments and other Medicaments' (*Chemist and Druggist*, 114, 1931)

Sturgis, Matthew: *Hampton Court Palace* (London, 1998)

Summerson, J.: *Architecture in Britain, 1530–1830* (London, 1958, repr. 1983)

Symbols and Sentiments: Cross-Cultural Studies in Symbolism (ed. Ioan Lewis, London, 1977)

Syon House: Guidebook (English Life Publications, 1992)

Tait, H.: 'The girdle prayer book or "tablett": an important class of Renaissance jewellery at the court of Henry VIII' (*Jewellery Studies*, 2, 1985)

Tait, H.: *The Golden Age of Venetian Glass* (London, 1979)

Tanner, Lawrence: *The History of the Coronation* (London, 1952)

Tapp, W.H.: *Anne Boleyn and Elizabeth at the Royal Manor of Hanworth* (London, 1953)

Taylor, Eva Germaine Rimington: *The Mathematical Practitioners of Tudor and Stuart England* (Cambridge, 1954, repr. 1967)

Thomas, K.: *Man and the Natural World: Changing Attitudes in England, 1500–1800* (London, 1983)

Thomas, K.: *Religion and the Decline of Magic: Studies in Popular Belief in Sixteenth- and Seventeenth-Century England* (London, 1971)

Thompson, G.S.: 'Ampthill: Honour, Manor, Park, 1542–1800' (*Journal of the British Archaeological Association*, 13, 1950)

Thompson, W.G.: *A History of Tapestry from the Earliest Times until the Present Day* (London, 1973)

Thomson, Mrs A.T.: *Memoirs of the Court of Henry the Eighth* (2 vols, London, 1826)

Thomson, Patricia: *Sir Thomas Wyatt and his Background* (London, 1964)

Thorold, Peter: *The London Rich* (London, 1999)

The Thought and Culture of the English Renaissance, 1481–1555 (ed. Elizabeth M. Nugent, Cambridge, 1956)

Thurley, Simon J.: 'Henry VIII and the Building of Hampton Court: A Reconstruction of the Tudor Palace' (*Architectural History*, 31, 1988)

Thurley, Simon J.: *The Royal Palaces of Tudor England: Architecture and Court Life, 1460–1547* (London, 1993)

Thurley, Simon J.: 'The Sixteenth-Century Kitchens at Hampton Court' (*Journal of the British Archaeological Association*, 143, 1990)

Thurley, Simon J.: *The Tudor Kitchens at Hampton Court Palace* (London, 1991)

Tighe, Robert Richard, and Davis, James Edward: *Annals of Windsor* (2 vols, 1958)

Tjernagel, N.S.: *Henry VIII and the Lutherans* (St Louis, 1965)

Toesca, J.: 'The Royal Clock Salt' (*Apollo*, October 1969)

La Toison d'Or: Exposition du Musée Communal des Beaux Arts, Musée Groeninge (Bruges, 1962)

The Tower of London: Its Buildings and Institutions (ed. J. Charlton, HMSO, London, 1978)

Trapp, J.B., and Herbrüggen, Hubertus Schulte: *The King's Good Servant: Sir Thomas More, 1477/8–1535* (exhibition catalogue, National Portrait Gallery, London, 1977)

Treasures of the British Library (ed. N. Barker et al., London, 1988)

Trevor-Roper, Hugh: *Historical Essays* (London, 1957)

Tucker, Melvin J.: *The Life of Thomas Howard, Earl of Surrey and Second Duke of Norfolk, 1443–1524* (London, 1964)

Tudor-Craig, Pamela: *Richard III* (exhibition catalogue, National Portrait Gallery, London, 1973)

Tudor Men and Institutions (ed. A.J. Salvin, Baton Rouge, 1972)

The Tudor Nobility (ed. G. Bernard, Manchester, 1992)

Tudor and Stuart Portraits, 1530–1660 (exhibition catalogue, Weiss Gallery, London, 1995)

Turner, E.S.: *The Court of St James's* (London, 1959)

Turner, S.: *The History of the Reign of Henry the Eighth* (2 vols, London, 1826)

Turton, Godfrey, E.: *The Dragon's Breed* (London, 1969)

Tytler, P.: *England under the Reigns of Edward VI and Mary* (2 vols, London, 1839)

Ullman, W.: 'This Realm of England is an Empire' (*Journal of Ecclesiastical History*, 30, 1979)

Underwood, M.: 'The Lady Margaret and her Cambridge Connections' (*Sixteenth-Century Journal*, 13, 1982)

Vaughan, R.: *Charles the Bold* (London, 1973)

Vaughan, R.: *Philip the Good* (London, 1962)

Vaughan, R.: *Valois Burgundy* (London, 1975)

Wagner, Bernard M.: 'New Songs of the Reign of Henry VIII' (*Modern Language Notes*, 50, 1935)

Wainwright, J.P: *The Cardinall's Musick: Thomas Tallis* (York, 2000)

Walder, John: *Henry VIII* (London, 1973)

Walker, E.: *A History of Music in England* (Oxford, 1952)

Walker, G.: *John Skelton and the Politics of the 1520s* (Cambridge, 1988)

Walker, G.: *Plays of Persuasion: Drama and Politics at the Court of Henry VIII* (Cambridge, 1991)

Walker, Greg: 'The Expulsion of the Minions of 1519 reconsidered' (*Historical Journal*, 32, 1989)

Wallis, Helen: 'The Royal Map Collections of England' (*Revista da Universidade de Coimbra*, 28, 1980)

Walpole, Horace: *Anecdotes of Painting in England (1762–71)* (3 vols, ed. J. Dallaway and R.N. Wornum, London, 1826–88)

Walpole, Horace: *Horace Walpole's Correspondence with the Rev. William Cole* (ed. W.S. Lewis and A.D. Wallace, New Haven, Conn., 1937)

Warnicke, Retha M.: 'Anne Boleyn's Childhood and Adolescence' (*Historical Journal*, 28, 1985)

Warnicke, Retha M.: 'The Eternal Triangle and Court Politics: Henry VIII, Anne Boleyn and Thomas Wyatt' (*Albion*, 18/4, 1986)

Warnicke, Retha M.: 'The Fall of Anne Boleyn: A Reassessment' (*History*, 70, 1985)

Warnicke, Retha M.: 'The Lady Margaret, Countess of Richmond' (*Fifteenth-Century Studies*, 9, 1984)

Warnicke, Retha: *The Rise and Fall of Anne Boleyn: Family Politics at the Court of Henry VIII* (Cambridge, 1989)

Warnicke, Retha M.: 'Sexual Heresy at the Court of Henry VIII' (*Historical Journal*, 30–32, 1987)

Warnicke, Retha M.: *Women of the English Renaissance and Reformation* (Westport, Conn., 1983)

Warwick Castle: Guidebook (Birmingham, 1994)

Waterhouse, E.K.: *Painting in Britain, 1530–1790* (London, 1953)

Watkins, Susan: *In Public and in Private: Elizabeth I and Her World* (London, 1998)

Watson, Foster: *Luis Vives, El Gran Valenciano, 1492–1540* (Oxford, 1922)

Wayment, Hilary C.: 'The East Window of St Margaret's, Westminster' (*Antiquaries Journal*, 61, 1981)

Wayment, Hilary C.: *King's College Chapel, Cambridge: The Great Windows* (Cambridge, 1982)

Wayment, Hilary C.: *The Stained Glass in the Chapel of The Vyne* (National Trust Studies 1980, London, 1979)

Wealth and Power in Tudor England: Essays Presented to S.T. Bindoff (ed. Eric W. Ives, John J. Scarisbrick and R.J. Knecht, London, 1978)

Wegg, Jarvis: *Richard Pace, Tudor Diplomat* (London, 1932)

Weir, Alison: 'Margaret Douglas, Countess of Lennox' (unpublished research, 1974)

Weir, Alison: *The Six Wives of Henry VIII* (London, 1991)

Weiss, D.R.: *Humanism in England in the Fifteenth Century* (Oxford, 1941, 1957)

Westfall, Suzanne R.: *Patrons and Performance: Early Tudor Household Revels* (Oxford, 1990)

White, Beatrice: *Mary Tudor* (London, 1935)

White, H.: *Tudor Books of Private Devotion* (Madison, Wis., 1951)

Wickham, G.: *English Moral Interludes* (London, 1976)

Wickham-Legg, L.G.: *English Coronation Records* (London, 1883)

Wiley, D.: *The Gentleman of Renaissance France* (Harvard, 1954)

Willen, D.: *John Russell, First Earl of Bedford: One of the King's Men* (London, 1981)

Williams, J.: *Accounts of the Domestic Treasures Confiscated at the Dissolution* (ed. W.B. Turnbull, Abbotsford Club, 1836)

Williams, Neville: *The Cardinal and the Secretary: Thomas Wolsey and Thomas Cromwell* (London, 1975)

Williams, Neville: *Henry VIII and His Court* (London, 1971)

Williams, Neville: *The Royal Residences of Great Britain: A Social History* (London, 1960)

Williams, Penry: *Life in Tudor England* (London, 1964)

Williams, Penry: *The Tudor Regime* (Oxford, 1979)

Williamson, David: *Brewer's British Royalty* (London, 1996)

Wilson, Derek: *Hans Holbein: Portrait of an Unknown Man* (London, 1996)

Wilson, Derek: *A Tudor Tapestry: Men, Women and Society in Reformation England* (Pittsburgh, 1972)

Winchester, Barabara: *Tudor Family Portrait* (London, 1955)

Windsor Castle: The Official Guide (Royal Collection Enterprises, 1997)

Winter, Carl: *The British School of Miniature Portrait Painters* (London, 1948)

Winter, Carl: 'Holbein's Miniatures' (*Burlington Magazine*, 33, 1943)

Withington, Robert: *English Pageantry: A Historical Outline* (2 vols, London, 1918, repr. New York, 1973)

Wood, Anthony: *History and Antiquities of the Colleges and Halls in the University of Oxford* (ed. J. Gutch, London, 1796)

Wood, M.: *The English Mediaeval House* (London, 1981)

Woodfield, Ian: *The Early History of the Viol* (Cambridge, 1984)

Woods, H.: 'Excavations at Eltham Palace' (*London and Middlesex Archaeological Society*, 33, 1982)

Woodward, G.W.O.: *King Henry VIII* (Andover, 1993)

Woodward, John: *Tudor and Stuart Drawings* (ed. K.T. Parker, London, 1951)

Wyatt: The Critical Heritage (ed. Patricia Thomson, London, 1974)

Yarwood, Doreen: *Outline of English Costume* (London, 1967)

Young, A.: *Tudor and Jacobean Tournaments* (London, 1987)

Younghusband, Major General Sir George: *The Tower of London from Within* (London, 1919)

Index

Larder (Household department) 69, 71

Lark, Joan 198, 531

Lassels, John 453, 490, 491

Lassels, Mary 453

Latimer, Hugh, Bishop of Worcester 355, 404, 463, 468

Latimer, William 334, 335, 336, 539, 551

Laughton, Charles xiii

Laundry (Wardrobe department) 56, 60, 72, 514

Leconfield, Humberside 366

Leeds Castle, Maidstone, Kent 8, 35, 143–4, 226, 286, 300, 331, 481, 565

Lee, Edward, Archbishop of York 451

Leemput, Remigius van 402

Lee, Sir Richard 7

Lee, Roland, Bishop of Coventry and Lichfield 332, 547

Leez Priory, Essex 394

Lefèvre d'Étaples, Jacques 265, 324, 325, 337

Legh, Mr 531

Leicester Abbey, Leics. (see St Mary's Abbey, Leicester)

Leigh Hill, Surrey 110

Leigh, Sir John 459

Leland, John 11, 311, 340, 362, 488, 566

Leo X, Pope 45, 164, 171, 172, 195, 205, 208, 215, 227, 237, 238

Lewes, William 135

Leze, Zuan de 131

Lille, Burgundy 163

Lily, William 149, 240

Linacre, Dr Thomas 41, 145, 147, 150, 209, 210, 244

Lincoln, Cathedral and City of 451, 452

Lincoln's Inn, London 148

Lisle, Lady (see Honor Greville)

Little Sodbury, Gloucs. 367

Livio da Forli, Tito 153

Loke, William 372

London, City of 14–15, 34, 35, 51, 53, 56, 90, 115, 138, 143, 171, 195, 206, 208, 209, 212, 213, 242, 285, 287, 291, 292, 317, 319, 324, 331, 339–40, 346, 363, 365 , 389, 394, 396, 399, 403, 410, 411, 429, 440, 443, 445, 447, 456, 461, 462, 470, 488, 490, 496, 498, 555

London, Dr John 464

Longland, John, Bishop of Lincoln 132, 247, 254

Longueville, Duc de (see Louis d'Orléans)

Lord's Side Kitchen 68

Lorraine, Duke of (see Anthony of Vaudemont)

Loseley House, Guildford, Surrey 413

Louise de Guise 415

Louise of Savoy 219

Louis VII, King of France 393

Louis XI, King of France 66, 280

Louis XII, King of France 22, 138, 141, 158, 160, 161, 164, 169, 172, 173, 174, 175, 176, 177

Louis XIV, King of France 20

Louis d'Orléans, Duc de Longueville 165, 168, 174, 176, 347

Louvain, University of 4

Louvre, Paris 419, 537, 539, 540

Lovell, Sir Thomas 60, 157, 420

Lowe, Mother 425, 432

Ludgershall Castle, Wilts. 36

Ludlow Castle, Salop. 36, 256, 257, 258

Luke, Anne 28

THE POWER OF READING

Visit the Random House website and get connected with information on all our books and authors

EXTRACTS from our recently published books and selected backlist titles

COMPETITIONS AND PRIZE DRAWS Win signed books, audiobooks and more

AUTHOR EVENTS Find out which of our authors are on tour and where you can meet them

LATEST NEWS on bestsellers, awards and new publications

MINISITES with exclusive special features dedicated to our authors and their titles

READING GROUPS Reading guides, special features and all the information you need for your reading group

LISTEN to extracts from the latest audiobook publications

WATCH video clips of interviews and readings with our authors

RANDOM HOUSE INFORMATION including advice for writers, job vacancies and all your general queries answered

Come home to Random House
www.rbooks.co.uk